D1001655

WATER SUPPLY

ECONOMICS, TECHNOLOGY, AND POLICY

JACK HIRSHLEIFER
JAMES C. DE HAVEN
JEROME W. MILLIMAN

WATER SUPPLY

ECONOMICS, TECHNOLOGY, AND POLICY

THE UNIVERSITY OF CHICAGO PRESS
CHICAGO & LONDON

International Standard Book Number: 0-226-34281-6

Library of Congress Catalog Card Number: 60-14355

The University of Chicago Press, Chicago 60637
The University of Chicago Press, Ltd., London

Published 1960. Fifth Impression with new postscript 1970
Printed in the United States of America

TABLE OF CONTENTS

LIST OF ILLUSTRATIONS

FIG.

PUBLISHER'S NOTE

Since the first publication of this work in 1960, important developments have occurred in New York and southern California, which were the two main case-study areas. These developments have been studied by the authors, and their findings are included in this new printing in the form of a "Postscript on New York and Southern California."

PREFACE

The goals of this book are to inform the general citizen about water supply and to provide instruction for the administrator and professional in the field as to the application of economic and technological knowledge to the solution of practical problems. Many of the conclusions of the book are likely to be controversial. This is so because these conclusions are often at variance with present practice governing the use of existing water supplies and the development of new supplies. Also, they indicate that certain "reforms" now in process (e.g., changes taking place in water law) directed to an improvement in the decision-making practice will actually make things worse. In other words, this book tries to effect a major change, rather than merely a marginal modification, in the trend of current practice and thought on water-supply problems.

Perhaps our critical attitude will be more controversial than our substantive conclusions. In particular, we believe that this book should have the effect of pricking the bubble of complacency in which many water-supply professionals now live. We should say at once, perhaps, that we do not believe that specialists in the field of water supply are any worse than the general run of mortals—but neither are they living saints, to be sheltered against all criticism. There is a certain temptation for water-supply leaders to cast themselves in heroic mold as mighty battlers for the cause of pure and adequate water. To maintain the romance of this role, great projects are continually being conceived, planned, and executed, some of these schemes being sound, others unsound, and some bordering on the manic. As compared with such dreams and schemes, the possibility of improving the efficiency of water use by such unromantic devices as elimination of waste or rationalization of pricing procedures may seem drab indeed—the more so as the large gains achievable by merely making better use of supplies in hand may indicate postponement indefinitely of vast new engineering wonders.

We are speaking here, it must be remembered, only of temptations. Many of those in the field show a wholesome respect for the principles of economy and rationality. But no one has ever won contemporary acclaim as a hero for wise economy and rationality, nor is his name celebrated in history books or attached to magnificent dams—our modern equivalent of pyramids. Our book, it is hoped, will therefore provide a measure of vindication and support for those in the profession who—against all pressures—have resisted these temptations. In water supply as in all other fields, of course, there is a place for the "men of vision" and the great projectors, but in our opinion the current need is to correct a system which has given these men too much of their own way and has awarded too small a share of the praises to those who have been careful and prudent in the use of the resources intrusted to them by society.

The study of water supply resulting in this book was supported by The RAND Corporation as a part of its research program. In addition to its work for government and other agencies, the corporation regularly sponsors with its own funds research in areas of importance to national security and public welfare. This research is considered to be fundamentally the responsibility of the individuals involved, and the conclusions of the work are not necessarily indorsed by the corporation. The authors are deeply grateful to RAND both for the support of this study and for the freedom granted to them as individuals to arrive at conclusions which may be "different" and not always popular.

Among our many colleagues within RAND, we especially wish to acknowledge the assistance of Russell T. Nichols for his patient, detailed review of the manuscript at various stages and for his discriminating suggestions for improvement. We have also greatly benefited from a review by Richard R. Nelson and comments by Roland N. McKean of the RAND research staff. Of course, only the authors are responsible for the opinions expressed or for the errors of fact or of analysis remaining in the text.

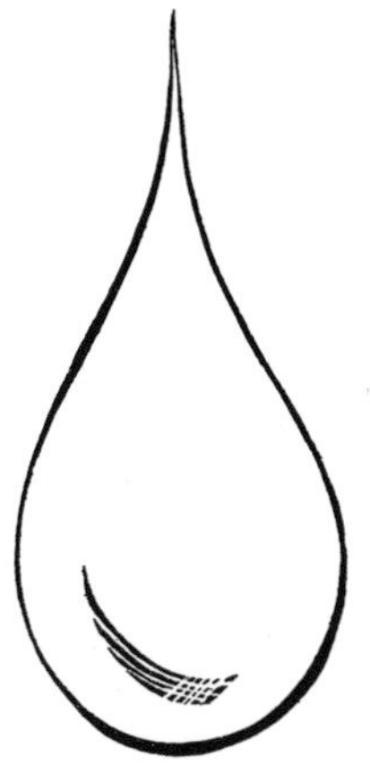

CHAPTER I

THE WATER PROBLEM

It is a commonplace to hear today that the supply of water for households, agriculture, and industry in the United States is a real and growing problem. In one area or another, even in the relatively humid East, it has become periodically necessary to place restrictions upon the use of water. In dry years reservoirs of some of our largest cities have fallen to dangerously low levels, and over large areas of the nation declining ground-water levels are threatening the structure of local economies based upon water from underground sources. To avert or remedy such conditions, enormously expensive projects have been built or are under consideration for the near future.

Evidently, then, water is a problem which should concern all intelligent citizens. Or should it? Consider a famous example often cited in economic textbooks: the problem of supplying food to the people of New York City. At first glance it would appear that here is a problem of truly appalling difficulty. Months if not years in advance of consumption, arrangements must be made to place under cultivation a myriad of items, including potatoes in Idaho, watermelons in California, and bananas in Panama, and to transport the harvested products at the right time and in the right carriers to the city, where the actual inventories of food supplies might not last a week if replenishment were not forthcoming. And yet, amazingly when one thinks of it, here is a problem which is solved without anyone's devoting any particular thought to it! It is solved, that is, by the decisions of thousands of private individuals typically pursuing each his own private advantage, though subject to a variety of general laws and specific regulations of government.

Food is no less essential than water. Why, then, does New York City have a recurrent water problem but no particular food problem? Or is the water problem simply an illusion, a creation of alarmist publicity? Since the first step to knowledge is to know what the question is, we shall devote this introductory chapter to an exploration of the nature of the "water problem." We shall show, indeed, that in some respects it is a false problem—a confusion of thought. Once this confusion is eliminated, we shall see that an important question concerning the wise utilization of water resources does remain. This remaining problem cannot be examined in its true light, however, until we have exorcised the specter, sometimes raised, of our civilization's collapsing for lack of water unless this or that grandiose scheme is adopted.

A. More Water Available—at a Price

During the last forty years, precipitation over the United States has averaged 30 inches, or a total of 1,564,800 billion gallons per year. According to a recent estimate, water utilization (as of 1955) in the United States for irrigation, industrial, public, and other supplies was at the rate of 87,600 billion gallons per year, a gross utilization of about 5.6 per cent of annual precipitation.[1] In addition, of course, a large quantity of water has been stored up by nature and, to some extent, by man in surface and underground reservoirs. The gross quantity available is, however, not ideally distributed in time and space, and, in addition, much is unavoidably lost. After deducting the loss of water through evapotranspiration from beneficial and nonbeneficial vegetation and from the soil, present gross utilization comprises 20 per cent of the recurring precipitation. For regions less endowed with water, the ratio is substantially higher.

Since, evidently, the gross rate of use of water is steadily rising while precipitation is not, it might appear that we do have, at least on the long view, cause here for real concern. Thus, improperly applying a type of reasoning often employed in engineering problems, one might think: "100 per cent efficiency is not attainable. In fact, frequently one is doing very well to get as high as 50 per cent efficiency, and here we are already at 20 per cent efficiency of utilization nation wide, even higher in some regions. How, then, are we going to meet the increasing demand?" The first point in answer to this chain of argument is that, since the figures in question refer to gross utilization of precipitation, there is no reason why "efficiency" in this sense cannot rise to 110, 200, or 10,000 per cent, even without drawing on the stored water from past ages. Today, even before gross utilization is anywhere near 100 per cent of precipitation, it is already economical to engage in multiple reuse of water supplies. This takes many forms: water in a river may rush through a turbine at a dam, then be diverted to a factory for cooling purposes, returning to the river somewhat warmer than before; it may then enter a public water supply, be used domestically, be returned to the ground via septic tank, and be pumped up hundreds of miles away for irrigation purposes, at which point it might end the ground phase of the hydrologic cycle by evaporating into the atmosphere from a growing plant. Clearly, this process may be expanded, if required, so that every bit of water is made to serve a multiplicity of purposes in the available ground phase of the cycle. The 20 per cent gross utilization figure implies an upper limit upon possible use of existing supplies where no such limit exists.

This point alone suffices to answer many of the arguments often heard about the urgency of the water problem. It is still not the most fundamental point, however. Suppose that, in fact, there were some absolute limit on the total use of water. Even then the "efficiency" of utilization of water supplies could always be increased as demand rises, since more highly valued uses could bid away some of the water from less highly valued uses. Under such circumstances, as pressure of demand upon water supplies increased, the price of water would rise. Water uses which cannot bear the burden of the higher costs would be forced to give up their supplies to those more intensely demanded uses which can. Thus, even should the amount of water available to society as a whole be fixed, the

[1] Kenneth A. MacKichan, *Estimated Use of Water in the United States, 1955* (U.S. Department of the Interior, Geological Survey Circular 398 [Washington, D.C., 1957]), p. 13.

amount available to any given use or user could be increased—at a price. For some commodities whose use is intrinsically destructive (e.g., coal, which is destroyed in serving its function of providing fuel), multiple reuse is not possible, and the available supply mined each year must be allocated to final users, each such use leaving a permanently diminished supply. Only the amount withdrawn from nature's stock in each unit of time can be varied, until the total stock is exhausted. Naturally, as coal becomes scarcer, it will pay to take more precautions to avoid waste and uneconomical use. For water, as for coal, we may state as the basic principle of supply that there is always more available to any user whose demand is sufficiently highly valued to permit him to bid an existing supply away from a current user. And, for a reusable resource like water, there is more available to society as a whole whenever people become willing to pay the costs of reclamation.[2]

B. Water Shortages

What, then, is a water shortage? Certainly, the people of New York City did suffer in the fall of 1949, when lawn-sprinkling and car-washing were forbidden and bathless days gained social acceptance. And, in some smaller communities throughout the country, local interruptions of supply occur which cause inconvenience or even harm. In ordinary parlance the word "shortage" is sometimes used to indicate absolute stringency of supply ("Water is short in the Sahara Desert") or sometimes any reduction of the supply to which people have been accustomed ("Rainfall is unusually light this year, so water will be short"). For our purposes, however, it will be instructive to use the term somewhat differently.

The reader is invited to cast his mind back to the great "meat shortage" of 1946. Here was a case where the current rate of meat consumption was by all previous standards quite high, yet for the individual housewife meat was always hard to find in the shops. The reason was that a larger quantity of meat was demanded by consumers than producers cared to supply at the then-effective controlled OPA prices. After the removal of controls meat prices rose sharply, inducing or compelling housewives to shift part of their effective demand to other commodities or to save their money instead, so the quantity of meat demanded in the markets fell until it balanced the supply. On the supply side the high prices made it unprofitable to hold back cattle from the market and also encouraged an expansion of production which improved the supply situation in following years. This type of "shortage" is neither absolute stringency nor a fall in supply but rather a situation in which more of a commodity is demanded in the market than is being supplied *at the going price.*

This definition brings to mind an obvious remedy for such shortages—raise the price! And, indeed, it will be shown that this is a solution which will frequently be the most advantageous possible. There are other possibly desirable solutions, however. The limited quantity available may be rationed by coupon or by informal arrangement of the seller, or the supply available may be increased by various government devices, including subsidies to producers. The demand may also be reduced by voluntary co-operation or by legal restrictions on

[2] We shall find, in later chapters, that to some extent existing law and custom prevent such reallocation of supplies among competing users either by fixing such use once and for all or by favoring certain users over others. In some cases such rules may be rationalized as instruments whereby certain values not expressible in market demands are still enabled to influence allocation of water supplies; frequently, however, these rules are due solely to certain patterns of political influence whereby some citizens gain at the expense of others for no justifiable reason. Or, sometimes, they may simply represent mistakes which harm everybody concerned.

quantities or types of permissible use. This will be discussed in detail later; our main point here is to indicate that this type of "economic water shortage" has a relatively simple cause and cure. When we say that the cure is simple, we mean that, from the economic point of view, it is easy to understand and that it could be carried out without great expenditure; from the political point of view, however, there may be most serious difficulties.

By way of contrast, absolute stringency is much harder to overcome. If water is very scarce in a region and cannot even be transported there without enormous cost, the region will simply not support much human habitation unless, indeed, the product yielded there by human effort is sufficiently valuable to yield a surplus over the cost of transporting water there. (It is also possible, of course, that on some extra-economic ground human habitation in such a region will be subsidized by an outside group.) As for a "shortage" in the sense of a fall in supplies as compared with past historical periods, if there is a real permanent decrease in supply (as when overdraft on an underground aquifer gradually reduces the quantity available to draw upon), the community must adjust to higher water costs or to reduced utilization—unless technological advance lowers costs or a source of subsidy can be found. Or, if it is a temporary or cyclical reduction in supply, the community must decide if it wishes to bear the burden of the reduction or, alternatively, to pay the cost of providing enough storage to even out such supply fluctuations.

C. The Alleged "Unique Importance" of Water

Much nonsense has been written on the unique importance of water supply to the nation or to particular regions. Granted that the nation, or any individual thereof, could not survive without water, that does not show uniqueness. No human can survive without food, without oxygen, and without a variety of other supporting environmental conditions, many not even fully known today. Nor could an individual survive very well, at least in the northern part of our country, without clothing, yet somehow we do not have frequent conferences and symposiums of public-spirited bodies on "the clothing problem." The reason seems to be that we have adjusted to the idea that clothing must be produced by employing human and material resources, and so the purchaser must be prepared to pay the going price to satisfy his wants. No one seems to call for special subsidies on parkas and mukluks to promote the development of Alaska or for subsidies on hip boots to ease the difficulties of agriculture on marshy soils.

Actually, this last rather odd idea brings us closer to the explanation as to why water is considered uniquely important. If development of Alaska could be affected significantly by the price of mukluks, no doubt there would be political forces at work supporting such a subsidy. It happens to be the case that the provision of water can make "the desert bloom even as the rose," a conception with dramatic and romantic appeal for all citizens, quite aside from the pecuniary appeal to those directly benefited. And, in urban areas, availability of water supplies may be a determining factor in the decision of an industry to move to one locality or another. But, still, analyzing the matter more closely, this situation is not due to any uniqueness of water as a commodity. There are extractive operations which could extend human habitation to the barren frigid regions if only a sufficiently cheap supply of fuel were provided. And the locational decisions of industry may be decisively affected by the availability of other productive essentials aside from water supply—power, transportation, raw materials, labor force, etc. This is not to deny that, as a commodity, water has its special features; for example, its supply is provided by nature partly as a store and partly as a flow, and it is available without cost in some locations but rather expensive to transport to others. Whatever reason we cite, however, the alleged unique *importance* of water disappears upon analysis.

D. Public Concern in Water Problems

Is there, then, any real water problem at all? Perhaps, if left alone, it might solve itself, like the food problem for New York City, without any need for the average citizen to worry about it. Unfortunately, this is not the case. The first reason is that private enterprise has in the past and will presumably in the future have only a limited role to play in water supply. The public agencies dominating the water-supply field are therefore not subjected to those checks of competition which we ordinarily count on to penalize inefficiency and restrain uneconomic practices in the production and supply of most commodities. The citizen should therefore be concerned as to the functioning of the process of supply and distribution of water by public agencies. In fact, even where water supply is provided privately, the nature of the industry is such that a "natural monopoly" usually exists—it is as inefficient to have competing water-supply systems as to have competing telephone systems. In the presence of these natural monopolies, competition cannot provide protection for the consumer under unrestricted private enterprise, and for this reason private firms supplying commodities under these conditions are generally publicly regulated.

Another fundamental reason for public concern in the field of water resources is the fact that the pervasive interdependence of water uses makes it impracticable or undesirable—or at least such has been the traditional thought—to extend conventional property rights to this field. Thus, if I own land, I can generally use it as I see fit. But, if a river flows across my land, I cannot generally use the stream without consideration for the rights of downstream property-owners. Similarly, since the beginning of our nation, navigable streams have been under the control of the federal government and could not become private property. Furthermore, where unrestricted use is permitted (in some jurisdictions, underground "percolating waters" may be captured by wells without consideration of the rights of others), the consequence has often been glaring waste of a valuable resource, leading to pressures to impose public controls of one sort or another. The functioning of our existing systems of water law, as well as possible modifications thereof, will be discussed in a later chapter, but it is evident that, from the first, water has been to a large extent considered to be a common resource in law and therefore a proper field for government action.

We may conclude by mentioning briefly two other commonly cited reasons for public interest in water problems. The first is that the best use of the nation's water resources seems, at times, to require projects of such enormous cost that only governments can amass the huge quantities of capital required. There may be something in this, but we do not believe it deserves much emphasis; the business corporation is a very efficient device for amassing large quantities of private capital wherever the returns seem sufficiently promising. Of rather more weight is the consideration that it may be impracticable to charge the beneficiaries of the development of water resources in any adequate way; to the extent that this is the case, private enterprise might require government subsidy in any event.

Finally, another justification frequently given for government intervention in this field is the need to develop resources in one particular region, where the reason given for doing so is outside the scope of market calculations—for example, to mitigate poverty in the Tennessee Valley or to populate the West. Generally speaking, these are more or less disguised pleas for special subsidies, which must be examined individually on their merits. We need only point out here that the process of development is not costless, and subsidized development of one region will (in the absence of general depression) absorb resources which could have been used to maintain or develop, without subsidy, the productivity of another.

For all these reasons, right or wrong, the various levels of government in our nation have been engaged in the development and utilization of our water resources. The subject would be, therefore, of *de facto* public interest even if all such public policies were mistaken, which they are not. Neither are they all correct, by any means, as we believe our analysis will show.

E. Our Approach to the Problem

In the analysis which follows, we attempt to spell out the substantive problems which face our community, and so the citizen and government, in connection with water resources. We divide the discussion into two stages: (1) an examination of the allocation of our *existing* supplies to see whether the use of what we now have meets an acceptable standard of efficiency and (2) an examination of alternative possible lines of development of *additional* supplies. We shall show, and we believe that this will be the part of our analysis likely to surprise the reader the most, that our existing water supplies, especially in the arid regions of the West, are grossly misallocated as a result of unwise water policies and laws of the past and present. (There is, furthermore, some reason to believe that these policies will be continued and even expanded in the future.) Our results on possible lines of future development, while highly controversial, will not be really new here, many others having pointed to the unwise course water-resource development has taken and is continuing to take.

For each stage of the analysis we first develop economic criteria demonstrating the principles upon which, we argue and believe, the use of existing supplies and the development of future supplies should be based. After developing the criteria, we examine past, current, and proposed practices to see how the more or less theoretical solutions previously derived can best be squared with the hard facts of the real world.

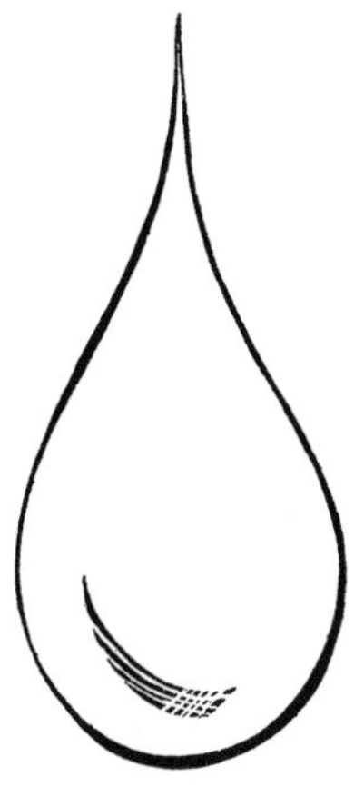

CHAPTER II

OUR WATER RESOURCES
THE PRESENT PICTURE

We shall attempt, first, to sketch briefly the salient physical features of the present water-resource and water-use picture. For each of these features—among them the hydrological cycle, the present use pattern, regional variations in supply, and water quality—there exists a tremendous volume of literature. We can hope here only to review the most important aspects of each to serve as background for the subsequent economic analysis of water as a commodity, which is the primary interest of this study.

Quantities, flow rates, and costs for water are stated in a number of different ways. Quantities may be given in gallons, in acre-feet, in tons, or in cubic feet. Flow rates may be stated as gallons, acre-feet, or cubic feet per second, per minute, per day, or per year, or as miner's inches. Costs may be related to any of these quantities. Costs or prices may appear disarmingly low when quoted in some of these terms. Thus, 10 cents a ton seems extremely cheap for any commodity, but it is more than the average current retail price of water for residential withdrawal in the United States. Table 1 has been prepared to assist the reader in relating these various water-measurement terms.

A. The Hydrologic Cycle

Water seldom stays put for very long in nature. Evaporated from the oceans, lakes, streams, or soil by solar energy, or transpired by plants, water in a vapor state may be transported long distances in the earth's atmosphere. Varying conditions of atmosphere flow rates and differences of energy inputs from above the atmosphere and from the surfaces below cause concentrations of water vapor to increase or decrease in the flowing atmosphere. Where these conditions are such that increased concentrations are obtained and temperatures are lowered, clouds of different configurations and at different altitudes are produced. Clouds are composed of condensed water or ice particles. When certain additional and incompletely known conditions of temperature, degree of saturation, and concentration of nuclei are reached, the cloud particles may grow in size and drop to the surface of the earth as rain, hail, or snow. Under other conditions the cloud particles may re-evaporate into the atmosphere, and the clouds disappear.

A number of things may happen to the water which falls to the earth:

1. It may almost immediately re-evaporate into the atmosphere.
2. It may soak into the earth or else fall or collect into ponds, lakes, or streams and later be directly evaporated, or it may go through the life-cycle of plants and pass back to the atmosphere from the foliage.
3. It may fall as snow on cold mountains to be stored on the surface until a thaw causes it to enter land portions of the hydrologic cycle.
4. It may percolate through surface soil to enter underground porous beds or strata which serve as underground reservoirs (aquifers).

TABLE 1

WATER-MEASUREMENT TERMS*

QUANTITY	
1 acre-foot	= 325,851 gallons
	= 43,560 cubic feet
1,000,000 gallons	= 3.07 acre-feet
1 cubic foot	= 7.48 gallons
	= 62.5 pounds
1 gallon	= 8.33 pounds
	= 231 cubic inches
	= 0.134 cubic foot
1 ton	= 240 gallons
FLOW	
1,000,000 gallons per day	= 694.4 gallons per minute
	= 1.55 cubic feet per second
	= 1,120 acre-feet per year
1,000 gallons per minute	= 2.23 cubic feet per second
	= 4.42 acre-feet per day
1 miner's inch	= 0.02–0.028 cubic foot per second (depending upon state definition)
1 cubic foot per second	= 1.98 acre-feet per day
1 acre-foot	= water supply for five people for one year at 180 gallons per person per day
COST	
10¢ per 1,000 gallons	= $32.59 per acre-foot
	= 7.48¢ per 100 cubic feet
10¢ per 100 cubic feet	= $43.56 per acre-foot
10¢ per ton	= $136 per acre-foot

* Some of the terms in this tabulation were taken from a list of hydraulic equivalents prepared by William P. Weiss, of Ford, Bacon & Davis, Inc.

5. It may run off the soil surface to enter streams and rivers.
6. It may be entrapped as ice in polar icecaps or in glaciers.

In the first two instances, commonly grouped together under the heading "evapotranspiration," the water re-enters the flowing atmosphere and becomes unavailable for withdrawal. In the other instances, the water enters phases of the dynamic hydrologic cycle in which it becomes, in varying degree, available for man's use in the liquid state before returning again to the atmosphere or to the oceans. Knowledge of many of the important features of this entire cycle is incomplete. However, some understanding of the important relationships which appear to exist within this cycle may be gained by a brief review of the present knowledge of the subject.

1. From Ocean to Atmosphere

The oceans cover more than 70 per cent of the earth's surface. Therefore, they receive the major portion of the energy radiated by the sun on the earth. The atmosphere does attenuate and absorb some energy directly as radiation passes through it to the earth's surface. The amount of energy absorbed varies with the amount of water vapor present and with the scattering effect of dust particles. Of the total solar energy absorbed at the sea surface during a year, approximately 50 per cent is used for evaporating sea water. Therefore, this energy is made available to the atmosphere in the form of latent heat of vaporization of water. This constitutes the most important component of the atmospheric heat budget.

There are certain areas on the ocean's surface where the amount of evaporation is high, some where it is low, and, at certain times of the year, some areas where it is negative. The areas of high and low evaporation seem to coincide with permanent high and low atmospheric pressure areas;

this may be important in determining weather patterns.

Variation, over time, in the energy radiated from the sun has not been precisely measured throughout a wide frequency range. There is evidence to indicate that large variations occur in radiation in the ultraviolet and far-ultraviolet regions. These variations appear to be related to sunspot maxima and minima. One of the working hypotheses regarding long-term and short-term variations in the earth's climate relates these changes to changes in solar radiation in this portion of the spectrum. Other hypotheses attempt to relate climatic changes to variations in atmospheric carbon dioxide concentration, to continental shifts, or to differences in atmospheric dust content as originating from terrestrial or cosmic sources. Perhaps each of these factors has its effect on climate.

However caused, the pattern of circulation of the earth's atmosphere, which determines our weather, is constantly changing. The fluctuations appear to occur in an almost continuous spectrum of periods varying in frequency from time measured in geological epochs to time measured in hours.

It has been estimated that for each square centimeter of the earth's total surface there are 273 liters of water,[1] distributed as follows:

Sea water.....	268.45 liters (98.33 per cent)
Fresh water...	0.1 liter (0.036 per cent)
Continental ice	4.5 liters (1.64 per cent)
Water vapor..	0.003 liter (0.0011 per cent)

These must be thought of not as static quantities but as representative of concentrations in the dynamic hydrologic cycle. The amounts in each category will vary slightly with seasons and to a more marked degree with the major climatic fluctuations. The amount of water present as vapor in the atmosphere at any one time seems small compared with the amounts distributed elsewhere. However, this water can be considered as being in transit. When it is decreased by precipitation, more will be evaporated to take its place. Also, when it is recalled that each gram of water in the vapor state represents a heat content 540 calories larger than 1 gram of liquid water at the same temperature, the greater import of the water vapor in the heat budget of the atmosphere can be appreciated. The vital importance of water acting as a thermal buffer against changes in energy received on the earth's surface cannot be overemphasized. Without this buffer action —provided by different phases of the hydrologic cycle—life as we know it would not exist. The temperature extremes even between day and night would be too great for present plants and animals to survive. By providing long-term large heat sources and heat sinks, the oceans and continental ice also damp the large climatic fluctuations.

2. *Water in the Land Portions of the Hydrologic Cycle*

We have already seen that water after precipitation may follow any of a half-dozen courses. An attempt will be made here to summarize the import of the different land phases of the hydrologic cycle. It is from this portion of the cycle that we obtain our present natural fresh water.

Surprisingly enough, water that is present at any moment of time in springs, streams, rivers, and lakes is a small portion of the water available on the land masses. Generally speaking, in areas having over 20 inches of annual rainfall, such as the eastern half of the United States, the water that percolates to the porous underground strata, called "aquifers," represents the major amount of available fresh water. Surface water is either the overflow from

[1] H. U. Sverdrup, M. V. Johnson, and R. H. Fleming, *The Oceans, Their Physics, Chemistry, and General Biology* (New York: Prentice-Hall, Inc., 1949), p. 215.

aquifers or water that has failed to reach them. In the western portions of the United States, where annual average precipitation is generally less than 20 inches, the snow pack on mountains represents the most important source of fresh water; the western ground-water basins are generally charged not directly by percolated precipitation but indirectly by water from the melting mountain snow. A great deal remains to be learned about these important underground aquifers. Only in a few localized areas are their total capacity and extent accurately known.

Water does not usually remain stationary in the aquifers[2] but flows from the charging areas either to areas of natural discharge, such as springs, swamps, ponds, and lakes, or to wells. (Charging areas are those specific land areas whose characteristics permit water to percolate down to an aquifer.) Water has been known to move 300 miles or more in these underground strata, although the usual distances range from 5 to 100 miles. The lowering of the water level in an aquifer through well-pumping does not necessarily mean that the water supply is being permanently reduced, in the sense that less remains available for future generations. On the contrary, a local lowering of the water level often causes increased flow through the strata and decreased waste in the charging and discharging areas. However, if the local lowering reduces the hydraulic level much below sea level in coastal areas, there may be danger of contaminating fresh water with saline water. This is especially true if impenetrable strata covering the aquifer have been pierced near the sea by artificial harbors or abandoned wells. Even without such penetration, contamination may occur because in coastal areas there may be hydraulic continuity of fresh-water bodies and marine water without barriers between them.

In some areas the natural aquifers are being recharged synthetically through spreading beds in porous recharge areas or through wells. The water used for recharging may be flood water, imported water (e.g., in the Los Angeles area, from the Colorado River), drainage from irrigation, suitable industrial discharge water, or the discharge from sewage-disposal plants.

Artificial recharge in this manner has many advantages. Aquifers are natural reservoirs, available without construction cost or operating cost. They provide large storage capacity, so that excessive supplies of water in moist years may be stored to extend supplies in dry years. Water so stored is not subject to the high evaporative loss rates of aboveground reservoirs. Aquifers may also be natural "pipelines" through which water can be transported from moist charging areas to drier areas for only the low cost of pumping. Of course, care must be taken in recharging to avoid contamination of the aquifer with too much high-salinity irrigation discharge water or with unhealthful industrial or sewage discharges. Care must also be taken that charging areas are not blocked by construction over them or by washed-in non-porous material.

The hydrologic cycle is completed when the water precipitated on the ground returns to the sea in rivers or from sewage outlets. Before this occurs, it may be economic to use and reuse the water any number of times.

B. Aspects of Natural Water Supply

1. Precipitation

Although on the average the United States receives about 30 inches of precipitation each year, the pattern of this supply varies widely from region to region and from season to season. Figure 1 shows that the average annual precipitation in the

[2] The so-called connate waters are an exception. These underground waters, usually too saline for use, were trapped and sealed by geologic processes.

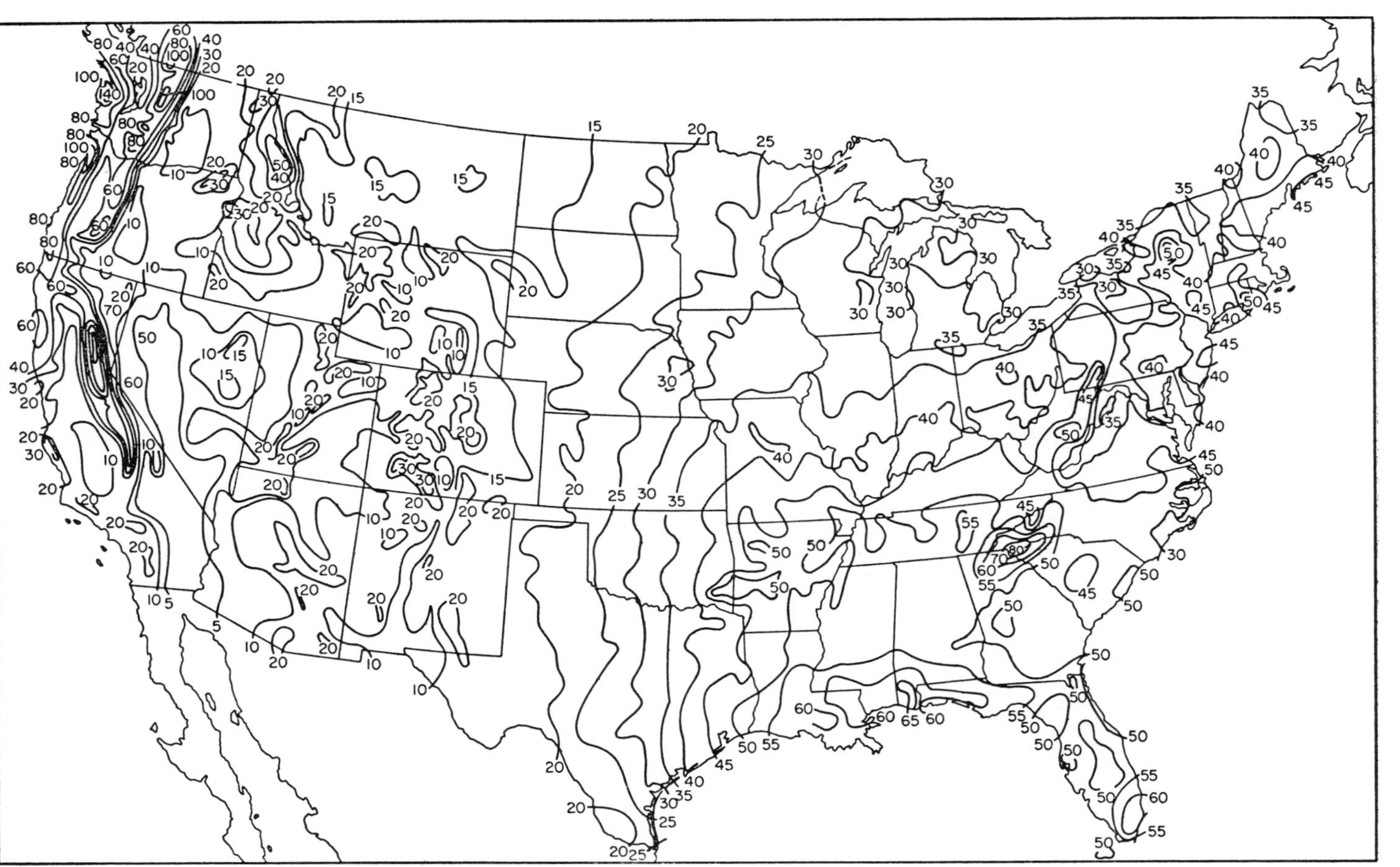

Fig. 1.—Average annual precipitation (inches) in the United States for the period 1899–1938. (From Interior and Insular Affairs Committee, House of Representatives, *The Physical and Economic Foundations of Natural Resources*, Vol. II: *The Physical Basis of Water Supply and Its Principal Uses* [Washington, D.C., 1952], p. 17.)

United States varies from 5 inches in the Mojave Desert to over 140 inches in the Far Northwest. Not only is there this wide variation in average annual precipitation but there is wide difference in the *seasonal* pattern of precipitation by region. West Coast areas typically receive most of their precipitation during the winter months. In contrast, the Deep South receives more of its precipitation during the summer months. Precipitation along the eastern seaboard is fairly uniform from month to month throughout the year.

Figure 2 illustrates this difference in seasonal distribution of precipitation for four cities in these regions—Portland, Oregon; San Diego, California; New Orleans, Louisiana; and Boston, Massachusetts. In the South, as represented by the New Orleans pattern, the precipitation received is closely in phase with the plant-growing season. In sharp contrast, precipitation is out of phase with the growing season in the Far West, and agriculture there must largely depend on irrigation. Municipal and industrial demands for water also tend to peak in the West during the summer because of air-conditioning and lawn-watering loads. As a consequence, western water systems must be designed with these unfavorable supply-and-demand characteristics in mind.

Even in regions with uniform distribution of precipitation over all seasons, which is typical of much of the northeastern and midwestern United States, the amount re-

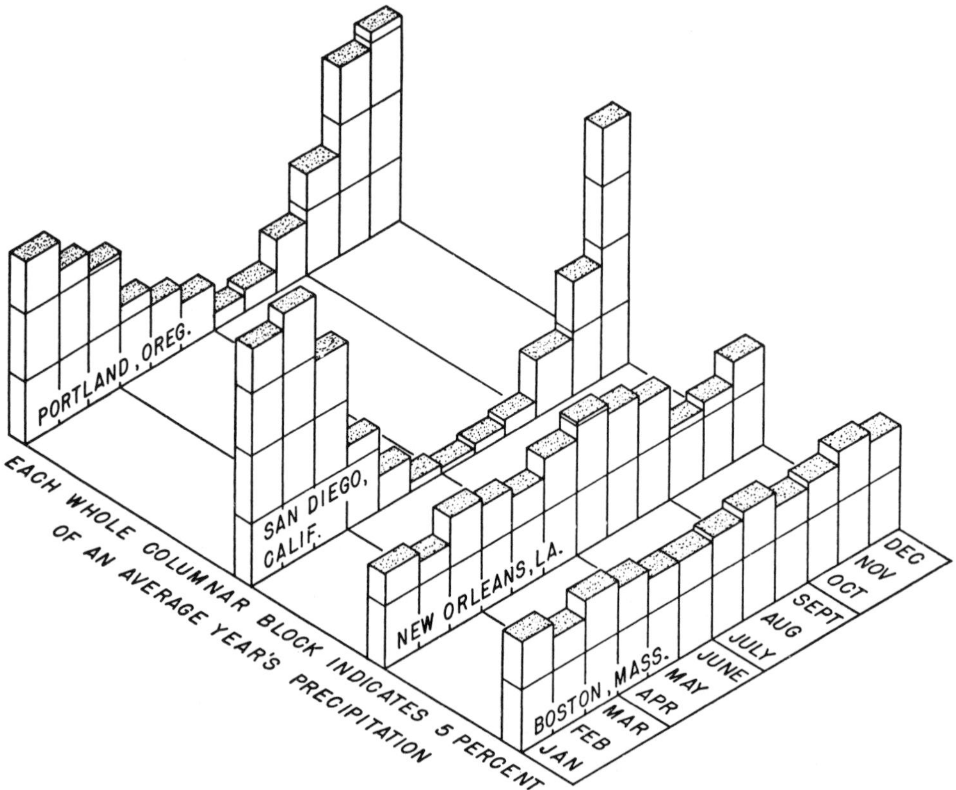

Fig. 2.—Typical seasonal pattern of precipitation in four regions of the United States. (From Interior and Insular Affairs Committee, *op. cit.*, Vol. IV: *Subsurface Facilities of Water Management and Patterns of Supply—Type Area Studies* [1953], p. 10.)

ceived during the growing season is often deficient in respect to the plant-growth potential (evapotranspiration potential).[3] This factor (plus the development of sprinkler irrigation systems) explains the rapid growth of supplemental irrigation in the East and Middle West.

In addition to these variations in precipitation by region, there are variations in the amount of precipitation through time in any one region. Figure 3, while distorting the original data, is useful in showing the variation in average precipitation in one region (Oklahoma) over a period of sixty-five years, by wet and dry periods each lasting about ten years.

More specifically for the three cities of San Diego, New Orleans, and Boston, Figure 4 shows both the variation in annual precipitation and the longer-term oscillations for a period starting as early as 1820 for Boston and extending through 1950. The longer-term swings can be distinguished in each of these areas even though the cities represent distinctly different climatic regions.

Unfortunately, the state of meteorological science at present is such that predic-

[3] Evapotranspiration potential is a measure of the plant-growth possibilities of a region when water is not a limiting factor. This important concept is described more fully in chap. viii.

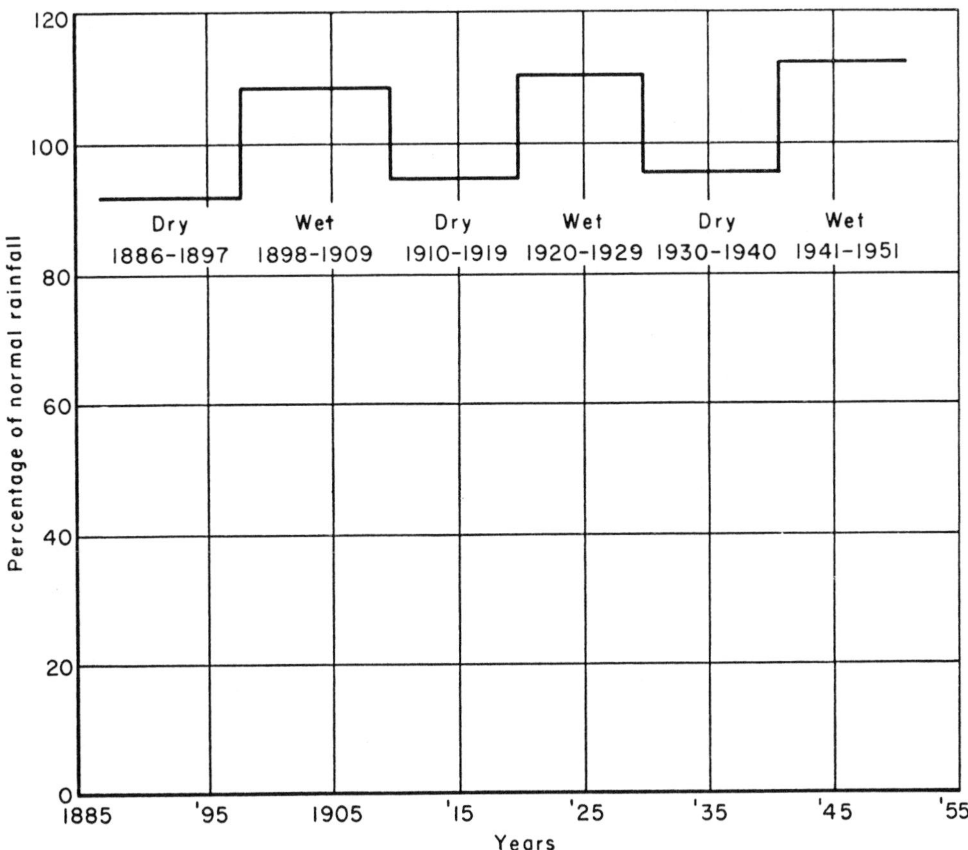

FIG. 3.—Cycles of dry and wet years in Oklahoma, 1886–1951, showing averages for dry and wet phases. (Redrawn from U.S. Department of Agriculture, *Water: The Yearbook of Agriculture, 1955* [Washington, D.C.: Government Printing Office], p. 88.)

tions of longer-term future precipitation do not command widespread assent within the meteorological profession. One of those who believe that such forecasts can be made with some reliability is Willett, who declared in 1951:

> The rainfall in lower middle latitudes, south of 50° N, will be substantially higher during the next twenty years, particularly in those regions which were driest between 1920–1940. There is no real probability of an extreme dust bowl decade in the western U.S. within the next century. Rainfall will be somewhat less during the next 20 years in the higher latitudes, particularly poleward of 60° N.[4]

[4] H. C. Willett, "Extrapolation of Sunspot-Climate Relationships," *Journal of Meteorology,* VIII, No. 1 (February, 1951), 1–6.

Historical records of precipitation suggest that both the annual variations and the longer-term swings will continue in the future. There will be some years with much less and others with much greater precipitation than the average. Averages for periods of years will show variations about the longer-time average precipitation. As total human withdrawal and consumption of water increase in comparison with the supply of water received, the value of water will increase, and it will become economic to apply more of the techniques for capturing and storing the greater supply provided by wet years and periods for use during the drier years and periods.

Climatic factors, then, generally determine the amount of water which an area

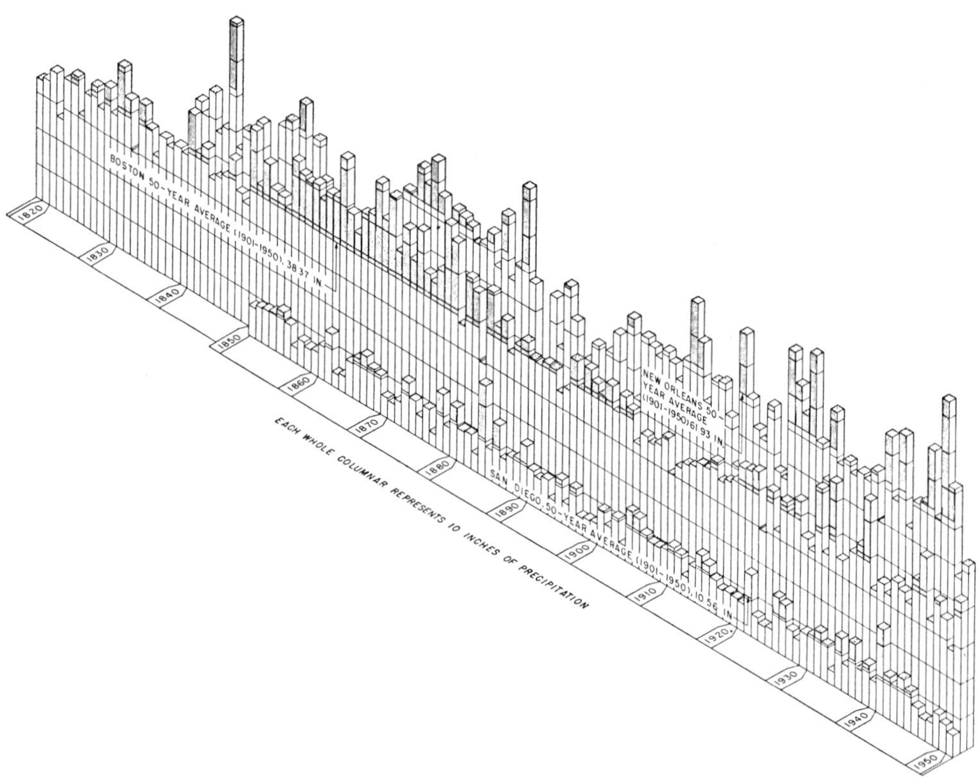

FIG. 4.—Variation over time in annual precipitation for three major United States cities. (From Interior and Insular Affairs Committee, *op. cit.,* IV, 11.)

may receive as precipitation. Additional factors, however, are important in determining how much of this gross supply received in any one location can actually be usefully applied for man's purposes. Intense precipitation during any one period may quickly saturate soil or exceed the recharge rate of local underground aquifers, resulting in large discharges to streams and eventually to the ocean. Measures can be taken, such as the construction of entrapment dams and reservoirs, to store this water for future use. In certain regions, however, the lack of suitable terrain features and the high cost of land and construction discourage the use of this technique at present.

2. Evapotranspiration

For the United States as a whole, around 72 per cent of precipitation is returned to the atmosphere by evapotranspiration. It will be recalled that evapotranspiration is a kind of short circuit of the hydrologic cycle wherein water returns to the atmosphere either by direct evaporation or through the life-process of vegetation. The national average of evapotranspiration hides a wide variation which exists from region to region. In the cooler, more humid areas the combination of evaporation and transpiration may be less than 40 per cent of precipitation. In contrast, evapotranspiration in many of the dry western areas averages 90 per cent of the precipitation. In some very arid regions 100 per cent of the water received passes to the atmosphere by evaporation and transpiration.

Some transpiration occurs in the growth of plants beneficial to man (crops, forests). However, a large amount of water is transpired by undesirable vegetation. Plants such as salt pine grow in profusion along watercourses in otherwise sparsely vegetated regions. These and similar plants, called "phreatophytes," send roots deep into aquifers along watercourses and essentially waste large quantities of water. In some areas quantities of this undesirable growth are being removed to the advantage of beneficial plant growth. These plants, growing in the seventeen western states, consume around 20–25 million acre-feet of water annually. This is about half again as great as the annual flow of the Colorado River. Native vegetation other than phreatophytes consume many times again this amount of water, which therefore never reaches the valley aquifers.[5]

The popular concept of the relationship of native vegetation to water supply, especially in the mountainous portions of drainage basins, is largely erroneous. The native perennial vegetation of the arid and semiarid areas has adjusted itself to the mean precipitation of these areas. The plants are deep rooted and draw their water from a large volume of the soil. The common belief is that, if the brush is removed from the watershed, the drainage-basin water supply will be reduced because of soil erosion and rapid discharge. Actually, when accompanied by the proper soil-conservation practices, the removal of non-beneficial plants will result in a net increase in water supply through reduced transpiration loss.

A similar error exists regarding larger trees and forests. It was once a popular belief that trees and forests in themselves caused an increase in the amount of precipitation as compared with other ground covers like grass. Although this error has been corrected, it is still commonly thought that trees and forests do contribute significantly to the amount of precipitation which percolates through the soil to underground aquifers by making the soil more permeable through their root systems. Again, however, it has been fairly well demonstrated that, although forests do reduce excessive

[5] C. L. McGuinness, *The Water Situation in the United States, with Special Reference to Ground Water* (U.S. Department of the Interior, Geological Survey Circular 114 [Washington, D.C., June, 1951]), p. 66.

surface flow, they accomplish this, among other ways, by actually using large quantities of precipitation which is subsequently transpired rather than by allowing the additional amount of water to reach the underground aquifers. If forests and trees are removed while proper measures are taken to prevent soil erosion, a net increase in underground supply can result. (Depending on circumstances, however, the cheap protection from soil erosion provided by forests, together with other possible benefits of tree growth, may outweigh in economic significance the water lost.)

Direct evaporative losses from storage lakes, reservoirs, and other parts of a water-supply system may under certain circumstances equal the amount of water being produced by the system. Recently, the combined efforts of several government agencies resulted in fairly precise measurements of the evaporative losses from two large storage reservoirs, Lake Hefner in Oklahoma and Lake Mead in Nevada. In Lake Hefner the loss averaged about 90 per cent of the outflow of the reservior. The evaporative loss at Lake Mead was found to be about 800,000 acre-feet per year,[6] equivalent to previous estimates of the evaporative loss for the whole lower basin system of the Colorado River.

In the past several years more attention has been given to the development of methods for reducing the evaporative loss from such bodies of water. It can be postulated that losses increase with the surface area of the water exposed, with high radiant energy absorption by the water, with higher air and water temperatures, with higher air velocity and water-surface roughness, and with lower relative humidity. This suggests that methods which favorably change any of these parameters will reduce evaporative losses. Such measures as the use of monomolecular films, roofs and floating covers, windbreaks, dredging to reduce surface area, and elimination of plant growth are being studied to determine their effectiveness and cost in reducing evaporation from lakes and reservoirs. These techniques are described more fully in chapter viii.

[6] *Water Loss Investigations: Lake Hefner Studies* (Geological Survey Professional Paper No. 269 [Washington, D.C., 1954]) and *Water Loss Investigations: Lake Mead Studies* (Geological Survey Paper No. 269 [Washington, D.C., 1958]).

3. *Inflow and Discharge*

In a specific hydrographic region the supply of water may be greater than that received as precipitation by the amount which enters the region naturally in surface or subsurface flow from other regions or as purposefully imported by constructed works. The boundaries of major hydrographic regions or drainage basins are usually defined by natural divides which separate areas having different directions of natural drainage into the oceans (or into other water sinks). Thus, by definition, these major regions will receive little water not originating there except for that which is imported by man. Most practical problems of water supply, however, involve subregions, subbasins, or metropolitan areas not in themselves integrated hydrographic systems. In such cases the natural flow into the region in streams or through aquifers may constitute an important element of supply.

The liquid discharge from major hydrographic regions is usually to the oceans or, in some arid regions, to landlocked saline lakes or playas, where the water evaporates. In subregions the discharge may constitute an important element in the supply of another adjoining area. Depending upon the intensity of withdrawal in the area of origin, the discharge water may have been used not at all, just once, or many times before discharge. The discharge may occur as a fairly uniformly flowing stream, surface or underground, as infrequent flood flow, or through sanitary- and storm-sewer outfalls.

In most regions it is a combination of all these.

Discharge of water from a region should by no means be construed as necessarily a "waste" of water. The carrying-away of effluents by flowing streams in a service of the water in the stream which should be valued by the costs of alternative methods for disposing of the effluents. Maintaining a minimum stream flow to provide for navigation is also a service of water which can be valued by the costs for alternative means of transportation.

4. The Hydrologic Balance

The measure commonly employed in totaling water uses is "withdrawal" from a natural supply source. This is not an ideal measure, since some beneficial uses (navigation, for example) do not require physical withdrawal but may still prevent use of water for other purposes. Use of water for hydropower is not usually considered a withdrawal. However, the total of withdrawals remains a useful indicator of the amount of water employed for industrial, agricultural, and domestic purposes. It is possible to combine withdrawals for any region with inflows and outflows into an identity which we may call the "hydrologic balance equation." Let us distinguish, first of all, between consumptive and non-consumptive withdrawals, the former representing those uses in which water withdrawn leaves the available phase of the hydrologic cycle by evaporation into the atmosphere, by chemical recombination, or in other minor ways. Quantitatively, of course, consumptive withdrawals necessarily equal total withdrawals less effluent from withdrawals.

Using the symbols defined below, consumptive withdrawals, $W_t - E_t$, in any period t and for any region, must be consistent with the equation

$$\underbrace{W_t - E_t}_{\text{Consumptive withdrawals}} = \underbrace{N_t}_{\text{New water}} - \underbrace{T_t}_{\text{Evapotranspiration}} - \underbrace{D_t}_{\text{Discharge}} - \underbrace{r_t}_{\text{Increase in storage}} .$$

The corresponding equation for total withdrawals, W_t, follows immediately by shifting E_t to the right-hand member above:

$$W_t = N_t - T_t - D_t - r_t + E_t ,$$

where W_t is liquid water withdrawn in the region; N_t is liquid water received in the region as precipitation and as inflow, natural or constructed, in surface streams or underground; T_t is the sum of losses of liquid water as vapor from transpiration and evaporation other than those associated with withdrawal uses; D_t is liquid discharge from the region in surface streams, underground, or in sanitary or storm sewers; r_t is the net change of liquid water storage on the surface or underground, natural or artificial (the value of r may be positive or negative); E_t is the amount of effluent from withdrawals within the region; and t is the time period of measurement, usually a water-year.

The first equation says that the new water entering a region in any period must exactly equal the sum of the differing possible ways of disposing of the water: consumptive withdrawals, evapotranspiration, discharge, and increase in storage. The second equation is helpful for interpreting the necessary consequences of changes in water supplies. Thus an addition of new water used for consumptive purposes only will be reflected in equal increases in W_t on the left and in N_t on the right; an addition of new water used exclusively for non-consumptive purposes will be reflected in equal increases in W_t on the left and in N_t, in E_t, and in the total of $(T_t + D_t + r_t)$ on the right (i.e., recycling of effluent if consumptively used must be at the expense of one of the other modes of disposition of the water supply). A recycling of effluent for non-consumptive purposes will be reflected in an increase in W_t on the left and in E_t on the right (the recycled water will simply become effluent again). Note that we speak of recycling of *effluent*, that is, of reuse of water discharged back by the previous user into a natural or constructed watercourse. A single user may also engage in multiple recycling of water within his premises, but this would still count as only a single withdrawal.

The considerations governing and limiting recycling as defined above are the difficulty of capturing effluent, the loss of some water at each stage due to consumptive uses, and quality problems. Setting aside the quality problems, it is possible under simplifying assumptions to derive an interesting expression for the quantum of water available through recycling. Assume that a certain fraction k of effluent can be recaptured at each stage; that of this a fraction, b, goes to withdrawals that are non-consumptive; and that the recycle period is short relative to the measurement period so that we can effectively assume an infinite sequence of recycles. Denoting non-consumptive withdrawals in a given period as W^n and consumptive withdrawals as W^c, we can derive the following expressions, where $E_0 = W_0^n$ is the effluent from the first use before any recycling and W_0^c is the consumptive use from non-recycled water:

$$W^n = E = E_0(1 + kb + k^2b^2 + k^3b^3 + \ldots)$$

$$= \frac{E_0}{1 - kb}.$$

But $E_0 = bW_0$, and $W_0^c = (1-b)W_0$. Therefore,

$$W^n = \frac{bW_0}{1 - kb},$$

$$W^c = W_0^c + k(1 - b)E_0 + k^2b(1 - b)E_0 + k^3b^2(1 - b)E_0 + \ldots$$

$$= W_0^c + \frac{k(1 - b)E_0}{1 - kb},$$

$$W^c = \frac{(1 - b)W_0}{1 - kb},$$

$$W = W^n + W^c = \frac{bW_0}{1 - kb} + \frac{(1 - b)W_0}{1 - kb},$$

$$W = \frac{W_0}{1 - kb}.$$

The use of non-recycled water, W_0, is of course equal to $W_0^c + E_0$. This may represent the use of new water or, if drawdown of storage is taking place, of water accumulated in a previous period. The use of recycled water, which we may denote C, is equal to $W - W_0$, which simplifies into

$$C = \frac{W_0}{1 - kb} - W_0 = W_0\left(\frac{1}{1 - kb} - 1\right),$$

$$C = \frac{kbW_0}{1 - kb}.$$

While these particular formulas apply only for the special assumptions made, they illustrate the logical process which has to be gone through to determine, in terms of the hydrologic balance, the amount of water used from recycle as opposed to use from new sources or from storage. To the extent that the formulas are valid, they also illustrate the nature of the change in withdrawals which would be made possible by modifying k or b. In particular, the "elasticity" of C with respect to k—that is, the proportionate change in C consequent upon a proportionate change in k[7]—is $1/(1 - kb)$, and the elasticity with respect to b is the same. This indicates that recycle availability is equally sensitive to changes in k (the recapture fraction) and to changes in b (the non-consumptive use fraction). If both b and k are in the neighborhood of 0.5, the elasticity of recycle availability with respect to each will be 4/3. The elasticity of total water use with respect to either k or b is $kb/(1 - kb)$, or, numerically, 1/3 if k and b are each equal to 0.5.

a) Runoff.—Often the term "runoff" is used to characterize the net supply of liquid water available for withdrawal. Runoff is sometimes defined as that portion of precipitation which drains from the land through surface channels. That is, it is the sum of all water flows *into* surface streams or standing bodies of water. In terms of

[7] Formally, the elasticity with respect to k is $(\delta C/\delta k) \cdot k/C$, and the elasticity with respect to b is $(\delta C/\delta b) \cdot b/C$.

the hydrologic balance, this corresponds roughly to the sum of discharge, consumptive withdrawals, and evaporative losses through or from surface channels, plus seepage from surface waters into the ground. It has been stated that the amount of runoff constitutes that portion of the water resources which is available for control, regulation, and distribution.[8] The amount of runoff is usually determined by gauging stream flow; it is usually stated as inches of water per year over the drainage area of the stream so as to provide figures comparable to precipitation over the area, which is also usually quoted as inches per year.

There is some confusion in the understanding and use of the concept of runoff. Sometimes underground flow as well as surface flow is included in determining runoff. Large amounts of water can and do flow underground, and this amount should be included, thus making runoff closer to our concept of "discharge." This underground flow is estimated to be 33–40 per cent of total runoff on a nation-wide basis and much more in certain localities.[9] Overlooking the underground flow can cause underestimates of certain specific regional supplies.

Often the statement is made that runoff is equivalent to discharge to the oceans. For the humid eastern United States, stream flows to the oceans are approximately equal to the runoff from their drainage areas.[10] Even when totals for the whole nation are considered, little difference between runoff and estimated discharge to the oceans is apparent. Thus, with an estimated average total precipitation of 30 inches, runoff is estimated as 8.6 inches and discharge to the oceans as 8.1 inches. However, the overriding influence of the humid areas in determining these averages hides the large difference between runoff and discharge to the oceans in the dry regions of the nation.

Another source of confusion in equating runoff with discharge to the oceans may arise from the procedure sometimes adopted of calculating an "estimated mean seasonal *natural* runoff" for a hydrographic area and assigning this flow to streams. Values for this parameter are determined by establishing what the flow in streams would have been in the absence of withdrawals and consumption, that is, without human activity, or in the natural state. Thus the total "estimated seasonal natural runoff" listed at the mouth for all the streams discharging into the Pacific Ocean in the South Coastal Area of California is given as 1,227,000 acre-feet.[11] Very much less than this amount (only about 200,000 acre-feet, not counting sewage) actually discharges to the ocean from this area.

Runoff does not correctly indicate the net *potential* supply of liquid water. Runoff, at best and in humid areas, just approximates net supply under the currently existing cultural, technological, and economic conditions in the region. As water increases in value, or as technology improves, it becomes economic to institute practices that increase net supply to a region through decreasing evapotranspiration losses, capturing formerly wasted discharges, multiplying reuse and exchanges between watersheds—all measures that can increase net supply in a region without altering runoff correspondingly.

b) Overdraft and "safe" yield.—The terms "overdraft" and "safe yield" are often encountered in discussions of net supply of water in a region. Their meaning

[8] California Department of Water Resources, *The California Water Plan* (Bull. 3 [Sacramento, 1957]), p. 11.

[9] McGuinness, *op. cit.*, p. 34.

[10] This is so because in the long run in the humid regions the total precipitation and its distribution are such that surface and underground storage remain near their natural equilibrium levels in spite of consumptive withdrawals.

[11] California State Water Resources Board, *Water Resources of California* (Bull. 1 [Sacramento, 1951]), p. 39.

can vary, depending upon the context in which they are used and the viewpoint of the individuals affected. The terms are usually applied in referring to the amount of water withdrawn from natural underground storage in aquifers, although in some cases the terms refer to the over-all supply to a region—integrating the elements entering into the hydrologic balance presented earlier. In general, an "overdraft" is said to be that portion of the utilization of water in a region which exceeds the long-term net supply (i.e., requires a drawdown of storage), with all other factors (cultural, technological, economic, new supply) remaining unchanged. In this same sense, "safe yield" is defined as that total water draft or demand in a region which equals the long-term net supply, other factors remaining unchanged.

Water-users who get their supply from wells often complain of an overdraft when the water levels in their wells drop below that of the recent past. This drop may or may not reflect an overdraft as defined above. The drop may be the result of new wells pumping in the neighborhood whose cones of depression influence the older wells. The lower levels may also reflect only a temporarily reduced supply in the region as the result of the natural variability of precipitation. Even a long-term, widespread lowering of well levels may not necessarily indicate an overdraft in the sense used above. Under such conditions it may be possible to maintain permanently the increased use responsible for the lower water levels, because the reduction in water levels may lead to greater natural recharge of the aquifers and to decreased natural discharge.

When the term "safe yield" is used in referring to the draft on underground basins, it is determined as the draft that equals the long-term natural recharge of the basin. In some instances safe yields of basins have been established in the courts and pumping rationed accordingly. A rather different concept of safe yield is sometimes used in connection with either surface or ground supplies that are highly variable in quantity from year to year because of fluctuations in annual precipitation. Here "safe yield" refers to that rate of utilization (again with cultural, technological, and economic factors governing recycling, losses through evapotranspiration, etc., held constant) which is low enough so as not to require a drawdown of storage *even in a dry year*. The commonly used one-hundred-year safe yield is that level so low as only to be experienced once in a hundred years of normal weather variation. The safe-yield concept suffers from the same faults as "runoff" in not properly characterizing the net water supply of a region (i.e., understating the potential influence of technological improvements, cultural change, reuse, and economic exchanges). Thus there may be nothing "unsafe" about the practice of gradually drawing down a stock accumulated over geologic time if, as is reasonable to believe, anticipated improvements in technology may make it as cheap in the future to pump up from 100 feet as it is today to pump up from 50 feet. Even if no such progress could be anticipated, furthermore, there is no difference in economic principle between "mining" water and mining coal or iron ore, as will be shown in the chapters that follow.

Exceeding the safe yield and consequent dewatering may, however, cause compaction in aquifers so as to reduce their subsequent storage capacity. We have not found studies in which any actual measurements of this compaction and storage reduction have been attempted. Based on the physical picture of the manner in which water is contained in aquifers of different types, it appears to us that water-storage capacity would not be significantly reduced over long periods of time by compaction in important water-bearing strata. If this judgment is wrong, the costs of permanent loss of storage capacity should be considered against the present benefit from use of overdraft water.

The intrusion of sea water or other contaminated water, as has been mentioned, can occur when underground water levels are reduced through pumping. If it were not for this intrusion problem, and possibly subsidence, we would be less concerned about overdraft or exceeding the safe yield. As water levels decrease, eventually an economic equilibrium would be reached. This would, of course, be lower in general than the "natural" equilibrium in which the water level, in the absence of pumping draft, would rise until inflow became balanced by discharge. At the economic equilibrium the cost of pumping will have risen so high that many marginal users have been displaced or at least induced to lessen their drafts. Thus the water inflow would eventually balance drafts. Economic equilibrium would also tend to be brought about by a shift to less water-intensive uses of the land or a shift to a source of water other than the underground aquifer. It is true, however, that in these "common-pool" cases the economic equilibrium will, in general, tend to stabilize at a level representing excessive use of the resource from the point of view of the community as a whole. The causes of and possible remedies for this overpumping problem are discussed in detail in Appendix B to chapter iii.

c) Net supply including recycle.—For the reasons brought out in the preceding discussion and in chapter i, it appears to be much more appropriate, when considering the water resources of the nation as a whole or in evaluating increments of water for a small region, to characterize the supply factors in the forms shown in our hydrologic identity rather than in the more usual classifications as "runoff," or "overdraft," or "safe yield." We will later on make use of the distinction between *existing* supply and *potential* supply. By "existing supply" we will mean ordinarily the present total of withdrawals, though this measure is somewhat imperfect in failing to count non-withdrawal uses (e.g., navigation may require that a limit be placed on withdrawals, so that a non-withdrawal use of water will thus be competing with the withdrawal uses). Once we begin thinking of potential supply, we see that, aside from additional import of new water, an increased total of withdrawal uses can be obtained by reducing evapotranspiration or discharge, by drawing on storage, or by increased recycling. And an augmentation of supply from recycling may be achieved by increasing the recapture fraction k or by increasing the fraction b going to non-consumptive uses. The crucial thing to remember about potential increased supply is that it is not a single quantity, as is existing supply, but a schedule or function showing the quantity of increased withdrawals made possible at different, increasing levels of cost. Furthermore, all possible sources of augmentation of supply, whether increased import of new water, reduction of discharge or evaporative loss, increased recycling, etc., should be considered in this potential supply function.

The definition of regional water supply proposed here also allows for a more rigorous and meaningful definition of "surplus" and "shortage" in respect to the demand for water. Thus a shortage of water exists when the current net supply (current withdrawal as defined by our equation) falls short of the quantity desired at the going price. A surplus may be said to exist when the quantity demanded by all users falls short of the supply which could be made available to users without the cost of incremental units exceeding the going price for water.

C. Water Quality

We have described briefly so far how the gross amount of water in a region may vary by location and through time and how the net supply available to man may vary from this gross amount as determined by many factors, some within the control of man. Another parameter which establishes the usefulness of the net supply of water available is the quality of water in the supply which man may tap. Ordinarily, raindrops contain very pure water. However, by the time this water has penetrated soil and the various minerals and rocks which may be contained in the underground aquifers and basins, and passed through streams contaminated by different effluents from sewage plants and industry, the quality of the water as determined by its content of bacteria, organic matter, and dissolved salts and acids may be such as to render it unfit for consumption. The usual standards for mineral content are to have the dissolved solids content below 1,000 parts per million (ppm) for human consumption[12] and below about 700 ppm for agricultural uses, plants being more sensitive than human beings to certain elements.[13] However, these allowable concentrations may vary up or down depending upon the elements present, the type of soil, and the specific tolerance of the crop. Sodium and boron, for example, are especially undesirable in water for agricultural use.

TABLE 2*

STANDARDS FOR DRINKING WATER

Constituent	Parts per Million
Mandatory maximum	
Lead	0.10
Fluoride	1.50
Arsenic	0.05
Selenium	0.05
Hexavalent chromium	0.05
Recommended maximum	
Phenolic compounds (in terms of phenol)	0.001
Iron and manganese	0.30
Copper	3.00
Zinc	15
Magnesium	125
Chloride	250
Sulfate	250
Total solids	
Desirable limit	500
Permitted limit	1,000

*Source: United States Public Health Service, "Drinking Water Standards," *Public Health Reports*, Vol. LXI, No. 11 (1946).

The movement of water through about 6 feet of soil appears to reduce the presence of most harmful enteric organisms below a tolerable level. Such a movement through soil, however, as occurs in natural percolation or in irrigation use of water, may significantly increase amounts of dissolved salts. Thus areas downstream from intensely irrigated areas may find that the water they are receiving is too saline to produce good crops. A city drawing its water supply from a river or stream may find upstream users discharging so much untreated sewage and toxic chemicals as to make the stream completely unsuitable or too costly to treat for use as a water supply. The effluents discharged by cities and industry can be controlled at their source. Salts picked up during natural percolation or during intensive irrigation, however, can be removed only by costly special treatments.

Table 2 lists the mineral standards for drinking water as established by the Public Health Service for public supplies in the United States. Table 3 shows criteria for classifying irrigation water by mineral content as suggested by the California State Water Resources Board in 1951. The relationships of ion or mineral species in irrigation water to each other and to the particular soil, plant, and climatic conditions are quite complex. However, the information in Table 3 gives some indication of the relative harmfulness of the different species.

For many industrial uses the quality of the water supply as determined by its combined physical, chemical, and biological characteristics is of utmost importance. The temperature of the water is of great

[12] See Table 2.

[13] See Table 3.

significance for the large industrial uses of water for cooling and air conditioning. Increased costs for larger heat-transfer devices or less efficient utilization of energy will result from higher cooling water temperatures. For some industrial uses (e.g., pharmaceuticals, boiler-feed water) even the highest quality naturally occurring water must normally be given further treatment before use. In other industrial applications, water of good quality may be used directly, but special treatment must be applied as the quality deteriorates or for sources of lower quality. Inasmuch as these treatments to reduce color, odor, or mineral content can be costly, a source of high-quality water may be an important factor in the geographical location of certain industries. Table 4 illustrates some of these special quality requirements for a variety of industries.

That the direct man-contributed pollutants can be controlled is attested by the success which has been achieved along these lines in some eastern watersheds. The Delaware and Susquehanna rivers have been largely cleaned up during recent years by control methods. As mentioned, the saline contaminates contributed by nature (a problem primarily in the western parts of the country) are more difficult to control because methods of removing these dissolved salts are expensive. A possible way out is to dilute with waters of lower salt concentration, so that the average water of the area, produced by mixing more and less saline waters, will be usable. In the planning for the development of future water resources in California, for example, the Department of Water Resources is now giving consideration to the average salt concentrations of water in determining the optimum water distribution within the state.[14] This matter of salt concentration, in fact, has been one of the primary reasons why California has objected so strenuously to the Upper Colorado River Project. Not only may the total quantity of water received from the Colorado River by California be reduced as a result of the project but, more importantly, the use of the head-source water of the Colorado for irrigation will impair its present function of diluting and reducing the saline concentration of the Colorado River and even add to the already high concentration which exists in this important source of water for California.

Although radioactive wastes from nuclear

TABLE 3*

CRITERIA FOR CLASSIFICATION OF IRRIGATION WATERS

Classification of Water for Irrigation	Per Cent Sodium of Total Na+K +Mg+Ca Present	Total Salts (Parts per Million)	Boron (Semi-tolerant Plants) (Parts per Million)	Chloride (Parts per Million)	Sulfate (Parts per Million)
Class I, excellent to good, or suitable for most plants under most conditions...	0–60	0–700	0–0.5	0–177	0–960
Class II, good to injurious, harmful to some plants under certain conditions of soil, climate, and practices.......	60–75	700–2,100	0.5–2.0	177–355	960–1,920
Class III, injurious to unsatisfactory, unsuitable under most conditions....	>75	>2,100	>2.0	>355	>1,920

* Source: Adapted from California State Water Resources Board, *Water Resources of California* (Bull. 1 [Sacramento, 1951]).

[14] California State Water Resources Board, *Water Utilization and Requirements of California* (Bull. 2 [Sacramento, 1955]), II, 341–58.

TABLE 4*

Water-Quality Tolerances for Certain Industrial Applications

(Parts per Million, except as Indicated)

Industry	Turbidity	Color	Color +O_2 Consumed	D.O.† (Milliliters per Liter)	Odor	Hardness	Alkalinity	pH	Total Solids	Ca	Fe	Mn	Fe+Mn	Al_2O_3	SiO_2	Cu	F	CO_3	HCO_3	OH	$CaSO_4$	Na_2SO_4 to Na_2SO_3 (Ratio)	General‡
Air conditioning§											0.5	0.5	0.5										A, B
Baking	10	10				‖					0.2	0.2	0.2										C
Boiler feed (pounds per square inch):																							
0–150	20	80	100	2		75		8.0+	3,000–1,000					5	40			200	50	50		1 to 1	
150–250	10	40	50	0.2		40		8.5+	2,500–500					0.5	20			100	30	40		2 to 1	
250 and over	5	5	10			8		9.0+	1,500–100					0.05	5			40	5	30		3 to 1	
Brewing:#																							
Light	10				Low		75	6.5–7.0	500	100–200	0.1	0.1	0.1				1				100–200		C, D
Dark	10				Low		150	7.0+	1,000	200–500	0.1	0.1	0.1				1				200–500		C, D
Canning:																							
Legumes	10				Low	25–75					0.2	0.2	0.2										C
General	10				Low						0.2	0.2	0.2										C
Carbonated beverages**	2	10	10			250	50		850		0.2	0.2	0.3				1						C
Confectionery					Low			††	100		0.2	0.2	0.2				0.2						
Cooling‡‡	50					50					0.5	0.5	0.5										A, B
Food, general	10				Low						0.2	0.2	0.2										C
Ice (raw water)§§	1–5	5					30–50		300		0.2	0.2	0.2		10								C
Laundering						50					0.2	0.2	0.2										
Plastics, clear, uncolored	2	2							200		0.02	0.02	0.02										
Paper and pulp:‖‖																							
Groundwood	50	20				180					1.0	0.5	1.0										A
Kraft pulp	25	15				100			300		0.2	0.1	0.2										
Soda and sulfite	15	10				100			200		0.1	0.05	0.1										
Light paper, HL-grade	5	5				50			200		0.1	0.05	0.1										B
Rayon (viscose) pulp:																							
Production	5	5				8	50		100		0.05	0.03	0.05	<8.0	<25	<5							
Manufacture	0.3					55		7.8–8.3															
Tanning##	20	10–100				50–135	135	8.0			0.2	0.2	0.2										
Textiles:																							
General	5	20				20					0.25	0.25											
Dyeing***	5	5–20				20					0.25	0.25	0.25										
Wool scouring†††		70				20					1.0	1.0	1.0										
Cotton bandage†††	5	5			Low	20					0.2	0.2	0.2										

* Source: American Water Works Association, *Water Quality and Treatment* (2d ed.; New York, 1950). (Reproduced by permission.)

† D.O. = dissolved oxygen.

‡ A, no corrosiveness; B, no slime formation; C, conformity with federal drinking water standards necessary; D, NaCl, 275 ppm.

§ Water with algae and hydrogen sulfide odors is most unsuitable for air conditioning.

‖ Some hardness desirable.

Water for distilling must meet the same general requirements as for brewing (gin and spirits mashing water of light-beer quality; whiskey mashing water of dark-beer quality).

** Clear, odorless, sterile water for syrup and carbonization. Water consistent in character. Most high-quality filtered municipal water not satisfactory for beverages.

†† Hard candy requires pH of 7.0 or greater, as low value favors inversion of sucrose, causing sticky product.

‡‡ Control of corrosiveness is necessary, as is also control of organisms, such as sulfur and iron bacteria, which tend to form slimes.

§§ $Ca(HCO_3)_2$ particularly troublesome. $Mg(HCO_3)_2$ tends to greenish color. CO_2 assists in preventing cracking. Sulfates and chlorides of Ca, Mg, and Na should be each less than 300 ppm (white butts).

‖‖ Uniformity of composition and temperature desirable. Iron objectionable, since cellulose absorbs iron from dilute solutions. Manganese very objectionable, clogs pipelines and is oxidized to permanganates by chlorine, causing reddish color.

Excessive iron, manganese, or turbidity creates spots and discoloration in tanning of hides and leather goods.

*** Constant composition; residual alumina <0.5 ppm.

††† Calcium, magnesium, iron, manganese, suspended matter, and soluble organic matter may be objectionable.

power plants or nuclear processes in general are not yet a major problem in the United States, the day may come when nuclear processes are common enough to make radioactivity a major source of concern in pollution. Already many major cities are monitoring their water supplies and the watersheds from which they obtain their supplies to be sure that radioactive contamination does not exceed a safe or tolerable level. Only very small amounts of radioactive wastes can be discharged into surface or subsurface water without creating a health hazard. All the earth's waters are simply inadequate to receive the bulk of the wastes of this industry. It is estimated, for example, that the nuclear generation of power to light a 100-watt bulb continuously would require the services of 5,500 acre-feet of water a year properly to dilute and dispose of the resulting radioactive wastes.[15]

D. The Present Distribution of Water Withdrawal

Table 5 shows the estimated gross distribution of water withdrawals by user category for the entire United States in 1955. It can be seen that agricultural, steam-power generation, and industrial-commercial withdrawals of water are by far the largest aside from water-power generation. Domestic (urban and rural) and municipal uses are only a small percentage of the total.

1. Withdrawals by User Categories and by Regions

The data for withdrawals are not usually reported by user category, nor can the reported total withdrawals be considered better than rough approximations because of the difficulty in obtaining the information. Table 5 was developed by drawing on all the referenced studies. For example, both Picton and MacKichan report 17 billion gallons per day (bgd) withdrawn for public water supplies. Based on the sampling of the deliveries of waterworks as reported by Seidel and Baumann, this 17 bgd may be assigned to user categories approximately as follows:

	Per Cent
Domestic	45
Commercial	18
Municipal	5
Industrial	32
Total	100

The commercial and industrial withdrawals from public supplies, about 8.5 bgd, must be added to the self-supplied industrial and commercial withdrawals esti-

TABLE 5*

ESTIMATED UNITED STATES WATER WITHDRAWALS, 1955

Use Category	Withdrawals (Billion Gallons per Day)	Percentage of Total
Domestic residential	8.7	3.6
Industrial and commercial	47.2†	19.6
Steam-electric power	72.2‡	30.0
Public municipal (fire, parks, etc.)	0.9	0.4
Agriculture	111.5	46.4
Total	240.5	100
Water power§	1,500	....

* Compiled from the following sources: Kenneth A. MacKichan, *Estimated Use of Water in the United States, 1955* (U.S. Department of the Interior, Geological Survey Circular 398 [Washington, D.C., 1957]); Walter L. Picton, *Water Use in the United States, 1900–1975* (Washington, D.C.: Water and Sewerage Industry and Utilities Division, BDSA, Department of Commerce, January, 1956); D. R. Woodward, *Availability of Water in the United States, with Special Reference to Industrial Needs by 1980* (Washington, D.C.: Industrial College of the Armed Forces, 1956–57); and Harris F. Seidel and E. Robert Baumann, "A Statistical Analysis of Water Works Data for 1955," *Journal American Water Works Association*, XLIX, No. 12 (December, 1957), 1531–66.

† Includes 6.9 bgd of saline water.

‡ Includes 12.0 bgd of saline water.

§ Not ordinarily considered a withdrawal use.

15 Warren J. Kaufman, "The Nuclear Energy Industry and Water Reclamation," *Proceedings [of the] Conference on Water Reclamation, Berkeley, California, January 26–27, 1956* (Berkeley, Calif.: Sanitary Engineering Research Laboratory, University of California, March, 1956), p. 40.

mated by MacKichan as 38.7 bgd. This total excludes water for steam-electric generation, which is almost wholly self-supplied.

Domestic withdrawal shown in Table 5 includes both urban withdrawals from public supplies and estimated rural self-withdrawal for domestic use. Agricultural withdrawals include an estimate of 110 bgd for irrigation and 1.5 bgd for stock-watering.

TABLE 6

HOW THE EAST AND WEST DREW THEIR WATER, 1950

(Per Cent)

	East	West
Withdrawn by domestic users....	16	5
Withdrawn by private industries.	81	3
Withdrawn by irrigators.........	3	92
Total.....................	100	100

* Source: Jack R. Barnes, "Water for United States Industry," in Report of the President's Materials Policy Commission, *Resources for Freedom*, Vol. V: *Selected Reports to the Commission* (Washington, D.C.: Government Printing Office, 1952), Report No. 9.

The use of water head for generating electric power is not conventionally considered a withdrawal for use. However, as we shall see, the use of water in hydroelectric generation may make that water unavailable for other purposes. Other non-withdrawal uses, the most important being navigation, waste disposal, recreation, and conservation of fish and wildlife, also have both costs and benefits associated with their use which will be discussed later.

Of the some 240 bgd non-hydroelectric withdrawals of water in 1955, about 194 bgd were from surface sources and 46 bgd from ground-water sources.

Gross national average figures, however, cover up many variations in water withdrawal and use patterns from region to region within the United States. For example, Table 6 shows the major differences in water-withdrawal patterns for the eastern and western portions of the United States. In the more arid West, irrigation accounts for approximately 92 per cent of the total of the water drawn. Domestic users and private industries draw only 5 and 3 per cent, respectively, while, in the East, 81 per cent of the total water drawn is by private industry, with domestic users taking 16 per cent and irrigators only 3 per cent of the total. Other portions of the United States will show use patterns ranging between these extremes.

The physiological minimum for human survival is about 1 quart of water per capita per day. United States troops in austere maneuvers in arid regions have used as little as 1 gallon per day over an extended period. Depending largely upon plumbing facilities, per capita domestic water draft may vary from a few gallons per day where water must be transported from a well or spring to the range of 30–60 gallons per day in typical American cities. The higher figures generally represent situations where supplementary irrigation of yards and lawns is required.

TABLE 7*

PER CAPITA PRODUCTION OF WATER BY UNITED STATES WATERWORKS, 1955

Population of City Served (1,000's)	No. of Cities	Production (Gallons per Capita per Day)		
		Minimum	Mean	Maximum
10–25......	178	53	132	333
25–50......	111	47	143	397
50–100.....	73	46	123	392
100–250.....	65	46	147	392
250–500.....	20	94	142	213
Over 500....	30	78	146	234
Total....	477	46	137	397

* Source: Seidel and Baumann, *op. cit.*, p. 1536.

Table 7 shows the average per capita production of water for a large sample of public and private waterworks in the United States, classified by size of city. The figures in this table are much higher than those we have just cited, because production by municipal water systems is not only for domestic use but also for industrial, commercial, and, in some cases, agricultural uses.

The actual amounts of water distributed are less by around 10–15 per cent than the amounts produced. This difference is attributed to line losses and other unaccounted disappearance of the water. The mean value for per capita distribution of water is 119 gallons per capita per day (gpcd) compared with 137 gpcd shown in Table 7 for production.

higher will be likely to show a smaller consumption of water per ton of steel produced. It pays the steel plant in the higher-priced region to apply measures to conserve and reuse water that would not be economical where water prices are low. For example, the Fontana Division of Kaiser Steel in California draws 1,500 gallons of water per ton of steel. In other areas, steel plants may draw as much as 65,000 gallons per ton of steel.[16]

For other industries as well, water withdrawn per unit of output may vary considerably, in part at least in response to differences in the price or availability of water. Table 8 lists maximum, typical, and minimum withdrawals of water by different industries per unit of product produced.

Withdrawals for irrigation can also vary widely, depending upon the evapotranspiration potential as determined by climate, the amount and distribution over time of precipitation, the type of crop, the kind of irrigation employed (sprinkler versus furrow), production of crops per acre, the

TABLE 8*

VARIANCE IN INDUSTRIAL UNIT WATER WITHDRAWAL

Product or User and Unit	Draft (in Gallons)		
	Maximum	Typical	Minimum
Steam-electric power (kw-h.)	170	80	1.32
Petroleum refining (gallon of crude oil)	44.5	18.3	1.73
Steel (finished ton)	65,000	40,000	1,400
Soaps, edible oils (pound)	7.5	....	1.57
Carbon black (pound)	14	4	0.25
Natural rubber (pound)	6	....	2.54
Butadiene (pound)	305	160	13
Glass containers (ton)	667	....	118
Automobiles (per car)	16,000	....	12,000
Trucks, busses (per unit)	20,000	....	15,000

* Source: H. E. Hudson and Janet Abu-Lughod, "Water Requirements," in Jack B. Graham and Meredith F. Burrill (eds.), *Water for Industry* (Publication No. 45 [Washington, D.C.: American Association for the Advancement of Science, 1956]), pp. 19-21.

Although these average per capita figures are of some interest in describing the present water-utilization pattern in metropolitan areas, they must not be taken as stable for predictive purposes. As will become more apparent in later chapters, the use pattern for water is a consequence of the price of the water and its value in different uses in different regions. As the price of water changes or as its value in use between one or another type of use changes, the pattern of water consumption may be expected to change as well. For example, a steel plant in one city may be a large net consumer of water per ton of steel produced, whereas a steel plant in another region where the price of water is much

[16] H. I. Riegel, "Water Problems in Manufacture of Steel," *Proceedings* [*of the*] *Conference on Industrial Uses of Water, Los Angeles, California, December 10–11, 1956* (Berkeley, Calif.: Committee on Research in Water Resources, University of California, 1957), p. 85.

efficiency of water use including distribution losses, and, of course, the price of the water. The average amount of water withdrawn for irrigation in the United States is 3.3 feet per acre irrigated.[17] Actual withdrawals vary from about 0.5 foot per acre to 8 feet per acre, depending upon the combination of conditions described above.

In short, there are few fixed requirements for water. Users can and will adjust their demands in view of the price of the water, the costs of their other inputs, and the values of their products.

2. *The Consumption of Water*

The original use to which water is put can in varying degrees alter its value in subsequent use. We have noted already that about 72 per cent of the water which falls in the United States passes directly as vapor from the surface or through the life-process of one sort of plant or another to be transpired to the atmosphere in vapor form. This vapor may or may not subsequently be reprecipitated in a form and at a time which will make the liquid water available for man. The formation of clouds and their release of water to the ground depend on factors other than just the moisture content of the atmosphere. Aerodynamic effects, such as flow over mountains and mixing of cold, dry air with warm, wet air masses, are usually necessary to provide precipitation. If these influences are not present, water vapor which may have been transpired from plant leaves or evaporated from reservoir surfaces may be carried hundreds or thousands of miles to be dumped, perhaps in the ocean, or even to contribute to floods in other areas of the country. Thus the original liquid water which has a certain value in its original position may be displaced in vapor form to a place where it has zero or even negative value. We do not know yet how to remove water from the atmosphere at the time and place we need it, as we can from streams and underground aquifers.[18] It would be fortuitous indeed if nature released the vapor in liquid form again in a location where its value was greater than where it was evaporated from the land. Thus any of nature's or man's processes that change liquid water into the vapor form may be considered to all intents and purposes as destroying the water for short-run future reuse. This loss occurs, for example, in evaporative air conditioning, where water is evaporated and advantage is taken of its latent heat of vaporization to cool the air. The same applies to various evaporative processes which are used generally for industrial cooling and, most importantly, for most of the water used for irrigation.

There are uses for water which cause relatively little loss or damage to the economic value of the water. The passage of water, for example, through hydroelectric turbines to generate electric power does no damage to the water for any subsequent use, aside from the change of elevation and location involved. Even here, however, we must consider that dams and reservoirs are required for adequate hydroelectric generation. The reservoir surfaces so provided usually cause an increase in the evaporative loss of the water stored behind the dam. Thus, even in a relatively harmless use for water, we must consider that some losses, such as the evaporative loss in this case, may occur. More important, a discharge for power purposes may preclude the use of that water for another purpose like irrigation.

In areas where most sewage is discharged through septic tanks, a large portion of the water may be recovered in the local un-

[17] Bureau of the Census, "Irrigation of Agricultural Lands," *1950 Census of Agriculture* (Washington, D.C.: Government Printing Office, 1952), III, 17.

[18] A partial exception to the general statements made here may exist in special situations where artificial nucleation of clouds is carried out. The present state of this art and some of the results and costs of its application are discussed in chap. viii.

derground supply by percolation from the septic-tank discharge through soil and back into the initial water supply. Under the proper conditions and aside from a slight increase in organic content and some dissolved salts, this water may be largely recouped with relatively little degradation in its value. In more heavily populated regions where the area is largely sewered, water may be recovered for further use in the same region by sewage reclaiming plants, but at a cost. Municipalities and industries that discharge either untreated sewage or chemical contaminates into flowing streams may in effect consume much more water than they actually carry through their systems if the effluents make the water unsuitable for downstream users. We shall discuss in later chapters and in more detail various economic and technical measures which can be used both to assess the relative consumptive use of water and to provide techniques to control and minimize losses which may occur through such consumptive uses.

The understanding and control of consumptive use are not trivial matters. A difference in the understanding of the meaning of "beneficial consumptive use" is one of the important aspects of a serious controversy between several western states. Arizona, for example, maintains that the term when applied to the Colorado River means net depletion of stream flow caused by a diversionary activity. California, on the other hand, maintains that the term means the actual measured flow diverted from the stream less credit for the water returned downstream. Although both states apparently agree on allowing credit for water returned, the difference in the definition of consumptive use alone amounts to over 1,000,000 acre-feet a year in the allocation of water from the Colorado to the state of California. This difference is largely due to the evaporative and other losses from the stream and its tributaries which, Arizona says, should be allowed for in the net accounting of the stream use. The fact that the water which is returned to the original stream may have such high dissolved salt content as to be literally valueless has not received the attention it warrants.

We can see, therefore, that the pattern for utilizing water is unlike that for coal, or oil, or natural gas as used for fuel. Water is not always completely destroyed by each of its uses but may be more or less degraded in value by such use and the disposal made of it after the use. This fact should be borne in mind in interpreting data such as those given in Table 5. This table and others like it give values for total water supplied to or withdrawn by different using categories (domestic, industrial, etc). Much of this water may be reused several times, and a separate counting for use is made each time it is recycled, just as if it were new water being drawn. Thus totals for water withdrawn by all categories during any period of time can conceivably exceed the quantity of new water received during this time without causing concern about "shortages" in supply. A similar situation occurs in the supply-and-use pattern for many metals. For example, the annual use of copper, lead, iron, or aluminum exceeds the annual supply of new metal, the difference being made up by secondary, reclaimed metal which is recycled through the market.

We have attempted, throughout this discussion, to suggest that supplies and demands for water are not absolutely determined by natural forces and engineering requirements but rather are to be measured in terms of the economic balance of all the needs and resources of the community. Where water is cheap and other resources are scarce, water can be liberally applied to industrial, domestic, and agricultural uses; recycling may be minimal; and consumptive uses need not be severely penalized. Where water is scarce and expensive (in terms of other resources that must be sacrificed to make more water available), it becomes justifiable to construct elaborate facilities to minimize intake, to recirculate quantities withdrawn, and to avoid uses that are consumptive.

All this has a bearing upon what may seem to be an omission in our survey of our water resources. We have presented data upon current or recent supplies and uses and have not attempted, as others have done, to predict what the supplies and uses will or should be in 1980, 2000, or 2200. We regard such forecasts, commonly based upon crude extrapolations of recent aggregate trends, as usually mistaken and even dangerous. The forecasts are typically mistaken because they ignore the factor of water costs; the growing scarcity of water in relation to the needs and desires of the community will, we believe, bring into being in the not-too-distant future a shift toward techniques and processes that are conserving rather than extravagant with respect to water inputs.[19] The recent trend toward ever more profligate use of water is in our opinion a response to special circumstances as well as to erroneous public policies that will not be easy to maintain in the face of growing real cost of water. In consequence, we regard forecasts of future "shortages" as dangerous in an alarmist sense; water will and should be "short" for wasteful or uneconomic uses. The implication that there are absolute and growing needs or "requirements" for water which are independent of water costs, and so can be predicted by mechanical extension of historic trends, lends seeming justification to premature and excessive construction to meet indicated shortages. But, in fact, required water inputs are highly variable in response to water availability and cost, and the cost of new construction should be measured against the value of the water produced thereby. We will see later, in both our New York and our California case studies, that crude demand projections of the type criticized here have been partially responsible for serious waste through overbuilding of water supplies in those regions.[20]

[19] Gilbert F. White has expressed a view similar to ours in his "Industrial Water Use—a Review," *Geographical Review,* L (July, 1960), 412–30.

E. Problems in the Utilization of Water Resources

In this chapter we have briefly surveyed the technological and economic facts forming the context for problems arising in the employment of our water resources. These problems may, in the last analysis, be reduced to conflicts in the use of society's resources. First, there are conflicts among present uses of water—conflicts among different types of use (for irrigation, indus-

[20] After completion of this chapter, a Senate committee report made public two studies of future water "requirements" which, in terms of thoroughness and attention to detail, represent a great improvement upon previous attempts in this direction. The two studies—by Resources for the Future, Inc. (RFF), and by the Business and Defense Services Administration (BDSA) of the Department of Commerce—covered six major manufacturing industries responsible for over half of the total industrial use of water. Methodologically, the studies incorporate a logical advance in attempting to allow for future reduction in water intake due to increased recirculation. However, no other possible sources of reduction in fresh water intake per unit of output (such as adoption of water-economizing process designs or use of saline or brackish water) appear to have received consideration. Despite the merits of these studies, the unreliability of the projections is indicated by the wide divergence between the two forecasts:

INDEXES OF WATER USE
(1954 = 100)

	1959	1980	2000
BDSA	128	282	523
RFF (median)	128	345	800

We believe that experience will prove that both of these forecasts err on the high side by a wide margin (see U.S. Senate Select Committee on National Water Resources, *Water Resources Activities in the United States: Future Water Requirements of Principal Water-using Industries* [86th Cong., 2d sess. (Washington, D.C.: Government Printing Office, 1960)], pp. 1–9).

try, municipal supply, salinity control, etc.), among geographical regions, and among specific users even within any type of use in a given area. Some such conflicts are direct and obvious. Water claimed by Arizona for irrigation purposes cannot be used in California for irrigation and municipal supply. Others are more subtle or complex. Desire to maintain a high head behind a dam for efficient power generation may conflict with demands of irrigators for release of water. Development of the Upper Colorado Basin will impair the quality of Colorado River water consumed in southern California. Diversion of upland water of the Delaware Basin to New York City creates salinity problems for the oyster industry in Chesapeake Bay.

Second, there are conflicts between present and future uses. If an underground aquifer is drawn on at a rate exceeding the average annual recharge, future use of water will take place under more adverse lift conditions, at the very least, and the aquifer may be permanently damaged by compaction. Another example of conflict between present and future is the reservation of dam sites for future use, when some interests are willing or anxious to develop the sites currently.

Finally, there are conflicts between the uses of water resources which could be made available by development and the alternative uses of all other types of resources (labor, land, machinery, etc.) which are foregone when these resources are invested in or destroyed by the process of water development. In extreme cases this is obvious. It would be the height of foolishness to spend a billion dollars to develop a water supply of 1 acre-foot (worth perhaps $50) per year. Even though the water might otherwise run to waste, it is clear that we are sacrificing alternative uses of a billion dollars' worth of resources —labor, land, and materials—to prevent this trivial loss. Nevertheless, the principle of the wise use of all resources is frequently lost sight of in the enthusiasm to develop one particular type—water resources. It is only natural to expect some loss of proportion in the thinking of groups with a parochial interest in water development, and so we encounter plans of federal or local agencies for "full" or "complete" development of the water resources of a region. Private enterprise tends (in its limited sphere) to balance the economic value of water against non-water resources sacrificed for water-development efforts by its calculation of profit and loss. Public enterprise, more important in the water-development field, should, and to some extent does, recognize that the goal is the best use of *all* resources rather than development of water resources at the sacrifice of all other interests.

In the chapters which follow we shall discuss the theory behind and the application of the principle of wise use of all society's resources—in short, the economic principle. We shall discuss the usual objections offered against the principle, which raise questions of some difficulty. Nevertheless, we vindicate the principle and then attempt to apply it—first, to certain types of problems which recur frequently in the resource development field (e.g., how to prevent wasteful use of "fugitive" resources in common pools underlying divided surface holdings) and, second, to the over-all water-resource problems of certain important regions of our country.

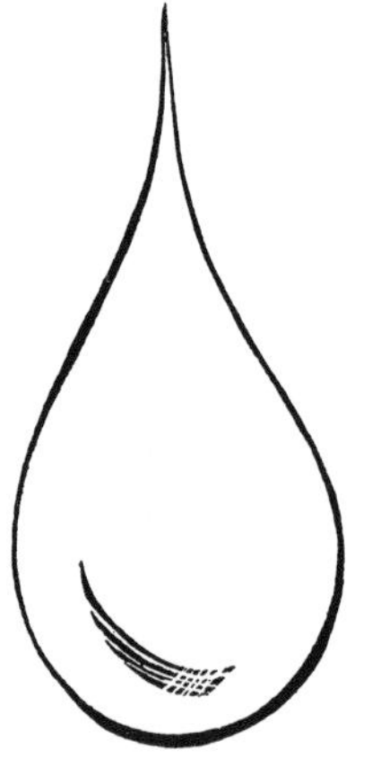

CHAPTER III

THE ECONOMICS OF UTILIZATION OF EXISTING WATER SUPPLIES

The present chapter contains, in a sense, the heart of the message of this book. Essentially all the limited analytical attention devoted in the past by other authors to the technology and economics of water supply has been directed to the question of when and how to develop *additional* water supplies and not to the question of whether *existing* supplies are being well utilized. Perhaps this has been due to the romantic appeal of solutions to water problems through construction of great dams and aqueducts as compared with the undramatic nature of solutions through better utilization or reallocation of existing supplies. While we will later have much to say on the development of additional supplies, our elaboration here of the principles that should govern the allocation of existing supplies between competing uses and competing users will have the advantage of novelty for students of water-supply problems. Furthermore, it so happens that the haphazard growth of water-allocation systems has created major departures from a satisfactory pattern of water utilization. The adoption of unromantic corrections to price systems, for example, may enable the postponement into the indefinite future of huge engineering projects for developing additional supplies.

After some introductory material setting forth the problem, we will assert two main economic principles which should govern the allocation of existing supplies; we will give some plausible supporting argument for these principles; and then we will discuss situations illustrating both correct applications and violations of these principles. In Appendix A we will attempt a somewhat more formal development of these principles, essentially at the level of an intermediate college economics course; this might be skipped with minimal loss of continuity by readers, although the theoretical solutions to certain important problems (e.g., choices involving large indivisibilities of supply) will then be missed. Appendix B will cover certain special problems arising from interdependencies of withdrawals and of use sometimes encountered in water-supply situations.

A. The Concept of Existing Supplies

The sources of water supply are, first, the recurring annual flow provided by nature through the hydrologic cycle and, second, the accumulated storage or stock from past ages available to man through operations analogous to mining. Use of the flow source without drawing down storage does not impair the supplies available in the future, but depletion of the stock ordinarily does. In addition, the waste or disposal water after completion of one use may still be available for additional uses before leaving the land phase of the hydrologic cycle. Man has developed utilization systems for providing water from these three types of sources. We may for our present purposes think of existing or developed supplies as those presently provided, at an annual rate, into such man-made utilization systems. The total of existing supplies is thus substantially the same (as of 1955) as the withdrawal totals shown in Table 5 (chap. ii).[1] Depending upon the purpose at hand, we may include or exclude the water-power use listed in that table, as well as certain other non-withdrawal uses (navigation, salinity control, recreation, etc.) not tabulated.

There are a number of difficulties in the interpretation of the concept of existing supplies which should be at least briefly alluded to. (1) Annual and seasonal fluctuations in rainfall will affect the quantities available over time to the nation as a whole and, to a still greater extent, to any particular locality. (2) Part of the uses tabulated involve drawing down water levels in underground aquifers, and so this portion cannot be considered permanently available as a recurring annual supply for the future. (3) "Water" is far from a perfectly interchangeable commodity, the annual amount available being more or less specific as to locality, seasonality, quality, etc.—the water now being withdrawn for a particular use in a given area with a given time pattern of utilization may or may not be capable of diversion at reasonable cost to some different use. (4) The water falling as precipitation or percolating underground in such a way as to be used directly to benefit growing plants without human diversion is not included in Table 5, though for some purposes it should be counted in existing supplies. (5) The withdrawal tabulations in chapter ii include a good deal of multiple use of water, that is, repeated withdrawals of the "same" water so as to serve successively several human purposes before being "consumed."

We may conclude the discussion of the nature of "existing supplies" in our sense by a comparison of their magnitude with the total possible supplies. The latter include, on a flow basis, the annual precipitation falling on the United States, all of which could conceivably be captured for beneficial use. This precipitation averages about 1,564,800 billion gallons per year, or 30 inches over the nation's land area. Aside from the annual flow, there is an enormous stock of fresh water stored in surface or underground reservoirs. It has been estimated that the part of the Great Lakes within the United States holds enough water to cover the national land area to a depth of more than 6 feet. While other surface storage is relatively minor, underground storage is believed to exceed storage in the Great Lakes.[2] The sources from precipitation and storage, while large, are still limited. When it is realized, however, that water can be reused, we see that in any absolute sense the total possible supply is unlimited.

B. Competition for the Use of Water

One of the obvious facts of life is that there is competition for the use of nature's

[1] The major differences are losses in transmission or distribution systems before reaching the withdrawing consumer.

[2] C. L. McGuinness, *The Water Situation in the United States, with Special Reference to Ground Water* (U.S. Department of the Interior, Geological Survey Circular 114 [Washington, D.C., 1951]), p. 11.

resources, and the water resource is no exception. Generally speaking, the more taken out of existing supplies for any one use or user, the less there will remain for the others. Of course, additional water could then be developed for the remaining uses, but this will not end competition for shares of the new enlarged total made available. As one example of competition, diversion of water from a stream for purposes of irrigation or municipal supply may impair navigation and power uses downstream by decreased stream level and flow and may create pollution problems affecting fish, wildlife, and recreational use. In the case of underground pumping, any individual's water withdrawals tend to reduce the quantity available at a given cost level for all his neighbors. Storage of flood waters, while achieving substantial benefits through regularization of the flow, will tend to increase evaporative losses and may also interfere with fisheries.

An interesting illustration of competitive demands for water arises in operation of a dam. Here navigation requirements dictate releases of water so as to maintain a minimum stream level; irrigation requirements indicate building up storage in the off-season to meet heavy demands in the growing season; for purposes of flood protection, on the other hand, the reservoir should be kept empty if possible, especially at the expected flood season; while the provision of power is best achieved with a high head of water.

Another obvious type of competition is regional. New York City would like a larger allocation from the flow of the Delaware River than other claimants are inclined to allow. In regard to the flow of the Colorado River, bitter disputes have raged especially between Arizona and California, but there is also competition between the Upper Basin states as a group and the Lower Basin states, and certain rights are also claimed by Mexico and by Indian tribes. A clear geographical conflict has taken place recently on diversions of water from Lake Michigan to the Mississippi River system; increased diversion was required to prevent a paralysis of navigation on inland waterways, but Canada and some lake-side cities objected to withdrawals threatening to reduce water levels in the Great Lakes.

A somewhat less obvious form of competition, to which we shall devote considerable attention later, is between the interests of the present and the future. Any drawing-down of the accumulated stock of water through withdrawals from underground or surface reservoirs, whether natural or man made, can be looked upon as a sacrifice of future uses for present uses.

The existence of all-pervasive competition[3] would seem to be too obvious to warrant such detailed elaboration on our part.[4] The recognition of this fact of life leads to asking correct questions about the use of water. Do existing processes for dividing the water available among competing claimants lead to results that can be considered satisfactory? If not, what courses of action are possible which might correct the situation? These are the questions we will attempt to take up in this and succeeding

[3] It is not true that all uses are competing in every respect. Thus, in dam management, navigation and waste-dilution requirements for water downstream are allied in demanding maintenance of a certain minimum flow. Allied, or *complementary,* uses of a given amount or flow of water do not compete with one another, but each group of complementary uses is still in competition with other groups. For example, water near the Continental Divide can be sent down the east slope, serving a number of complementary uses on the way to the Atlantic Ocean—or the water can be diverted to the west slope to serve a different set of complementary uses on the way to the Pacific.

[4] For more examples and discussion of competition for water use see W. G. Hoyt, "Competition for the Use of Water," in Task Force on Water Resources and Power for the Commission on Organization of the Executive Branch of the Government ("Hoover Commission"), *Report on Water Resources and Power* (Washington, D.C., 1955), III, 1095–1106.

chapters, which develop and apply the principles of economic choice relevant for water problems.

It is a reflection, however, on the level of public debate in this field that the obvious fact of competition is frequently denied. The implication of the California State Water Plan, for example, is that there is no competition among the regions of California: all the water needed in "deficit" areas is available in the form of water excess to all needs in "surplus" areas (assuming a favorable outcome of the Colorado River lawsuit with Arizona).[5] It is not surprising that conflicts within California have arisen over the plan's intent to meet the "deficits" of the south with the "surpluses" of the north; the north has objected to the determination that the water originating there exceeds its own "needs."

The idea of "needs" or "requirements" for water has an appealing ring of calculable definiteness about it, as compared with the connotation of words like "demands," "claims," or "desires." But, in fact, the former mean nothing more than the latter. A man has a certain physiological need of water to survive. Beyond this more water will improve his health and well-being, still more permits him to wash and cook, and so on down the line through the use of water for irrigation and industry, gardening and air conditioning, etc. Furthermore, for most or all of these purposes varying amounts of water may be applied: irrigation may provide the maximum the crops can use beneficially or any fraction of that amount, water-conserving measures can drastically reduce the water input per unit of industrial output, etc. Finally, even if any sense could be made of the idea that men "need" water in certain calculable amounts, it could not be inferred that regions "need" water, since men will choose what regions they desire to live in on the basis of water availability combined with all other considerations. Thus the water available per square mile in the Sahara Desert is much less than in the urban area of New York, but we do not hear much of the "needs" of the former region. The reason is that man has adapted to the fact that water is an extremely scarce commodity in the Sahara, and consequently only those limited human activities capable of coping with this fact can be carried on there. In the latter case, when all the shouting is over, the increasing cost of delivering water to New York as its population grows will be reflected in higher costs of all types of economic activity and thus act as one of the negative forces hindering the city's continued growth. If, however, the other advantages inhering in location in New York are sufficiently great, growth will continue despite this hindrance—at a rate determined by the net balance of all considerations, favorable and unfavorable.

Since "needs" for water are indefinitely expandable, there will always be competition for the use of existing supplies. Politicians interested in garnering wide political support will of course always be inclined to gloss over these conflicts of interest by promising all things to all men. And administrators may be inclined to say that competition for water can be ended if decisions on water allocation are only turned over to some bureaucratic agency under their direction. Instead of the ugly picture of competing efforts in the market place to buy up water rights and thus deprive others, a more pleasant image is painted of a committee of experts calmly and rationally dividing up the limited supplies to best meet the needs of all. Now there are indeed problems, which we will discuss later, arising out of market-place competition for water supplies—and, of course, there are also problems arising out of political or bureaucratic allocations of water. The point we wish to make here is

[5] California State Water Resources Board, *Water Utilization and Requirements of California* (Bull. 2 [Sacramento, 1955]), I, 227.

that the latter procedures cannot eliminate competition for water; the conflict of interest remains whatever the process for making the decision. The only effect is that competition is shifted from the market arena to the political arena, as each contestant attempts to influence the outcome through control of votes and political influence instead of dollars and economic influence.

C. Economic Principles of Resource Allocation

Granted that competition for the use of existing supplies of a resource like water exists, what principles or criteria are available to enable us to conclude that a given proposed division or allocation of the supplies is desirable or undesirable? And, second, what institutions or processes of decision will tend to lead to good allocations and so should be favored as against possible procedures or practices that tend to lead to defective allocations? One branch of human study has been devoted to the exploration of these questions—the science or field of learning known as economics. It is evidently not immediately clear to all, however, just how economic principles are to be applied to water-resource problems. In fact, perusal of the public press reveals that this ignorance is not limited to any special or backward group but is prevalent among legislators, government executives, scientists, engineers, businessmen, and public-spirited citizens when they come to deal with water-resource problems. Among the criteria bandied about in public discussions on the allocation of water supplies are such phrases as "fair shares," "reasonable requirements," "needs," "beneficial uses," etc.; in some cases these can only be regarded as noises with emotive content used as substitutes for rational analysis.

1. Efficiency Effects and Distribution Effects

The economic effects of any proposed policy can be divided under two headings: the effects on *efficiency* and the effects on *distribution*. Efficiency questions relate to the size of the pie available; distribution questions, to who gets what share. More formally, we can think of the pie as representing the national income or community income. Someone may propose reducing income taxes in the upper brackets on the ground that the high rates now effective there seriously deter initiative and enterprise and so reduce national income; he is making an efficiency argument that the present taxes reduce the size of the national pie. Someone else may point out that such a change will help large taxpayers as against small—a distributional consideration. In the field of water supply it is possible to find examples in the West where a certain amount of water could produce goods and services more highly valued in the market place if it were shifted from agricultural to industrial uses—this is an efficiency argument. On the other hand, this shift may hurt the interests of farmers or of their customers, employees, or suppliers while helping industrial interests—all distributional considerations.

Now economics can say something of the distributional consequences of alternative possible policies, but what it says stops short of any assertion that any man's interests or well-being can be preferred to another's. The fact that economics has nothing to say on such matters does not mean, of course, that nothing important can be said. Ethics as a branch of philosophy and the entire structure of law (which to some extent embodies or applies ethical thought) are devoted to the consideration of the rights and duties of man against man, and many propositions arising out of such thought may well command almost unanimous consent in our society. Ethics may say that no one should be permitted to starve, and law that no one should be deprived of property without due process, but these are propositions outside economics.

Most of what the existing body of economic thought has to say concerns the *efficiency* effects—the effects on size of the pie—of alternative possible policies or institutional arrangements. There is, of course, a sense in which enlarging the size of the pie may be said to be good for the eaters as a group irrespective of the distribution of shares. This sense turns upon the *possibility* of dividing the enlarged pie in such a way that everybody benefits. If such a distribution of the gain is not adopted, there may or may not be good reason for the failure to do so, but the reason is presumed to be legal or ethical and so outside the sphere of economic analysis. Economics alone cannot give us answers to policy problems; it can show us how to attain efficiency and what the distributional consequences are of attaining efficiency in alternative possible ways, but it does not tell us how to distribute the gain from increased efficiency.

It is true that it is often the case that the efficiency and distributional consequences of a proposed change cannot be so neatly separated. Any particular change in the direction of efficiency will involve a certain intrinsic distribution of gains and losses, and in practice it may be unfeasible to effect a redistribution such that everyone gains. Nevertheless, we feel that a presumption in favor of changes increasing the national income is justified, while conceding that this presumption can be defeated if there are irreparable distributive consequences that are sufficiently offensive on ethical or legal grounds.

Nothing is more common in public discussions of economic affairs, however, than a consideration of distributive effects of any change to the utter exclusion of the efficiency question. The agricultural price-support policy, for example, is usually and fruitlessly discussed pro and con in terms of the interests of farmers versus the interests of consumers and taxpayers. But a policy of expensive storage of perishing commodities to hold them out of human consumption is, obviously, inefficient. Concentration upon the efficiency question might readily suggest solutions that would increase the national income and would help consumers and taxpayers a great deal while hurting farmers relatively little or not at all.

2. The Principle of Equimarginal Value in Use

Suppose for simplicity we first assume that the stock or the annual flow of a resource like water becomes available without cost, the only problem being to allocate the supply among the competing uses and users who desire it. Economic theory asserts one almost universal[6] principle which characterizes a good or efficient allocation —the principle we shall here call "equimarginal value in use." The *value in use* of any unit of water, whether purchased by an ultimate or an intermediate consumer, is essentially measured by the *maximum* amount of resources (dollars) which the consumer would be willing to pay for that unit.[7] *Marginal* value in use is the

6 Aside from the distributional question, there are certain technical qualifications concerning complementary uses (see n. 3) to be discussed below.

7 "Value in use" is not currently part of technical economic jargon. The term has intuitive appeal, however, while corresponding technically to the demand price along the individual's demand curve, a concept we will introduce in Appendix A. Our use of the term follows Adam Smith, *Wealth of Nations* (Book I, chap. iv): "The word VALUE, it is to be observed, has two different meanings, and sometimes expresses the utility of some particular object, and sometimes the power of purchasing other goods which the possession of that object conveys. The one may be called 'value in use'; the other, 'value in exchange.' " Note, how-

value in use of the last unit consumed, and for any consumer marginal value in use will ordinarily decline as the quantity of water consumed in any period increases. The principle, then, is that the resource should be so allocated that all consumers or users derive equal value in use from the marginal unit consumed or used.

An example of the process of equating marginal values in use may be more illuminating than an abstract proof that this principle characterizes efficient allocations. Suppose that my neighbor and I are both given rights (ration coupons, perhaps) to certain volumes of water, and we wish to consider whether it might be in our mutual interest to trade these water rights between us for other resources—we might as well say for dollars, which we can think of as a generalized claim on other resources like clam chowders, baby-sitting services, acres of land, or yachts. My neighbor might be a farmer and I an industrialist, or we might both be just retired homeowners; to make the quantities interesting, we will assume that both individuals are rather big operators. Now suppose that the last acre-foot of my periodic entitlement is worth $10 at most to me, but my neighbor would be willing to pay anything up to $50 for that right—a disparity of $40 between our marginal values in use. Evidently, if I transfer the right to him for any compensation between $10 and $50, we will both be better off in terms of our own preferences; in other words, the size of the pie measured in terms of the satisfactions yielded to both of us has increased. (Note, however, that the question of whether the compensation should be $11 or $49 is purely distributional.)

But this is not yet the end. Having given up 1 acre-foot, I will not be inclined to give up another on such easy terms—water has become scarcer for me, so that an additional amount given up means foregoing a somewhat more urgent use. Conversely, my neighbor is no longer quite so anxious to buy as he was before, since his most urgent need for one more acre-foot has been satisfied, and an additional unit must be applied to less urgent uses. That is, for both of us marginal values in use decline with increases of consumption (or, equivalently, marginal value in use rises if consumption is cut back). Suppose he is now willing to pay up to $45, while I am willing to sell for anything over $15. Evidently, we should trade again. Obviously, the stopping point is where the last (or marginal) unit of water is valued equally (in terms of the greatest amount of dollars we would be willing to pay) by the two of us, based on the use we can make of or the benefit we can derive from the last or marginal unit. At this point no more mutually advantageous trades are available—efficiency has been attained.

Generalizing from the illustration just given, we may say that the principle of equimarginal value in use asserts that an efficient allocation of water has been attained when no mutually advantageous exchanges are possible between any pair of claimants, which can only mean that each claimant values his last or marginal unit of water equally with the others, measured in terms of the quantity of other resources (or dollars) that he is willing to trade for an additional unit of water.

What institutional arrangements are available for achieving water allocations that meet the principle of equimarginal value in use? Our example suggests that rationing out rights to the available supply will tend to lead to an efficient result if trading of the ration coupons is freely permitted; this is true so long as it can be assumed that third parties are unaffected by the trades. More generally, any such vesting of property rights, whether origi-

---

ever, that we give "value in use" a monetary rather than a "utility" dimension for comparison with market value or "value in exchange" by defining it as the maximum the consumer would *pay* for a unit of the commodity.

nally administrative, inherited, or purchased, will tend to an efficient solution if trading is permitted. (The question of the basis underlying the original vesting of rights is a serious and important one, but it is a distributional question.) A rather important practical result is derived from this conclusion if we put the argument another way: however rights are vested, we are effectively *preventing* efficiency from being attained if the law forbids free trading of those rights. Thus, if our ration coupons are not transferable, efficiency can be achieved only if the original distribution of rights was so nicely calculated that equimarginal value in use prevailed to begin with and that thenceforth no forces operated to change these values in use. As a practical matter, these conditions could never be satisfied. Nevertheless, legal limitations on the owner's ability to sell or otherwise transfer vested water rights are very common. While at times valid justification at least in part may exist for such limitations (one example is where third parties are injured by such transfers), it seems often to be the case that these prohibitions simply inflict a loss upon all for no justifiable reason. We shall examine some instances of limitations on freedom of transfer in a later section.

It is important to note here that the market price of water rights or ration coupons, if these can be freely traded, will tend to settle at (and so to measure) the marginal value in use of the consumers in the market. Any consumer who found himself with so many coupons that the marginal value in use to him was less than market price would be trying to sell some of his rights, while anyone with marginal value in use greater than market price would be seeking to buy. The process of trading equates marginal value in use to all, and the going market price measures this value. This proposition is of very broad validity, being in no way restricted to the commodity water. It is true, technical qualifications aside, that market price measures marginal value in use to its consumers for any commodity in which free trading is permitted and perfect rights can be conveyed.

Another possible institutional device for allocating water supplies of a community would be to establish, say, a municipal water-supply enterprise which would sell water, the customers being free to take any amount desired at the price set. The principle of equimarginal value in use then, setting aside possible complications, indicates a certain pattern of pricing: the price should be equal for all and at such a level that the customers in the aggregate use up all the supply. The reason for this pattern being the best is the same as that discussed earlier: if one individual had the privilege of buying units of water for $10 when another had to pay $50, mutually advantageous trading could take place if the water (or rights to it) could be transferred. If trading possibilities are ruled out, the marginal value in use would be $10 for the favored customer and $50 for the other—the former is taking so much in terms of his needs or desires that he is employing the marginal unit of water for very low-value purposes, while high-value uses are being deprived because water is so scarce to the other customer. The efficiency effects of trading can be achieved simply by setting the price to the two customers equal at such a level that the combined demands will take the supply in hand. Since the customer is permitted to purchase any desired amount, he will continue to buy additional units so long as the marginal value in use to him exceeds the price he must pay, marginal value in use being defined in terms of the price he is willing to pay for an additional unit. Evidently, he will stop purchasing where marginal value in use equals the price—and so, if the price is equal to all customers, marginal value in use will be equal to all. Then no mutually advantageous trading will be possible, so that we have achieved an efficient allocation of the water resource.

Note that there will be a distributional consequence of the removal of a privilege to buy water at a preferential price—the former holder of the privilege will lose as compared with all others. The attainment of efficiency in the new situation means that it is *possible* to insure that everyone is better off.[8] But whether it is or is not desirable to provide the compensation required to balance the loss of the formerly preferred customers is a distributional question.[9]

Our discussion of the principle of equimarginal value in use has led to two rules of behavior necessary if efficiency is to be achieved in different institutional contexts: (1) If rights to water are vested as property, there should be no restrictions on the purchase and sale of such rights, so long as third parties are unaffected. (2) If water is being sold, the price should be equal to all customers. This second rule was derived, however, under a special assumption that the water became available without cost. More generally, there will be costs incurred in the acquisition and transport of water supplies to customers; taking costs into account requires a second principle for pricing of water in addition to the principle of equimarginal value in use.

3. The Principle of Marginal-Cost Pricing

In our previous discussion we assumed that a certain volume or flow of water became available without cost, the problem being to distribute just that amount among the potential customers. Normally, there will not be such a definite fixed amount but rather a situation in which another unit could always be made available by expending more resources to acquire and transport it, that is, at a certain additional or marginal cost. The question of where to stop in increasing the supplies made available is then added to the question just discussed of how to arrange for the allocation of the supplies in hand at any moment of time.

From the argument developed earlier about the allocation of a certain given supply, we can infer that, whatever the price may be, it should be equal to all users (since otherwise employments with higher marginal values in use are being foregone in favor of employments with lower values). Suppose that at a certain moment of time this price is $30 per unit. Then, if the community as a whole can acquire and transport another unit of water for, say, $20, it would clearly be desirable to do so; in fact, any of the individual customers to whom the unit of water is worth $30 would be happy to pay the $20 cost, and none of the other members of the community is made worse off thereby. We may say that, on efficiency grounds, additional units should be made available so long as any members of the community are willing to pay the additional or marginal costs incurred. To meet the criterion of equimarginal value in use, however, the price should be made equal for all customers. So the combined rule is to make the price equal

[8] Following up the example above, suppose that the common price is set at $30. Then every unit no longer purchased by the preference customer had a marginal value in use to him less than $30 (but more than the price he was previously paying, $10). That same unit must have a marginal value in use to its new purchaser of more than $30. Evidently, for each such unit there is an increase in the marginal value in use as a result of the transfer, and this increase can be divided among the preference customer, the non-preference customer, and the water-supply enterprise so that all gain.

[9] From the distributional point of view, the sale of vested rights automatically insures that no one loses (since otherwise he would not participate in a voluntary exchange) in the process of attaining efficiency. The elimination of special purchase privileges, on the other hand, does necessarily involve redistribution. Even in the former case, though, the question naturally arises as to the fairness of the original vesting of rights.

to the marginal cost and equal for all customers.

One important practical consideration is that, because of differing locations, use patterns, types of service, etc., the marginal costs of serving different customers will vary. We will discuss these matters in detail in a later chapter, but at this point it is of some interest to know in principle how this problem should be handled. The correct solution is to arrange matters so that for each class of customers (where the classes are so grouped that all customers *within* any single class can be served under identical cost conditions) the prices should be the same and equal to marginal cost. *Between* classes, however, prices should differ, and the difference should be precisely the difference in marginal costs involved in serving the two.

Consider, for example, a situation in which there are two customers, identical in all respects except that one can be served at a marginal cost of $10 per unit and the other at $40—perhaps because the latter has a hilltop location and requires pumped rather than gravity service. If they are both charged $10, the community will be expending $40 in resources to supply a marginal unit which the latter customer values at $10; if they both are charged $40, the former customer would be happy to lay out the $10 it costs to bring him another unit. The principle of equimarginal value in use which dictates equal prices was based on the assumption that costless transfers could take place between customers, but in this case any transfer from the gravity to the pumped customer involves a cost of $30. Another way to look at the matter is to say that the commodity provided is not the same: the customer who requires pumped water is demanding a more costly commodity than the gravity customer.

Where water is sold to customers, therefore, the principles we have developed indicate that customers served under identical cost conditions should be charged equal prices and that the commodity should be supplied and priced in such a way that the price for each class of service should equal the marginal cost of serving that class. Where marginal costs differ, therefore, prices should differ similarly.

4. Allocation with Complementary Uses

The analysis above was based entirely upon the assumption that demands for water are competitive. While the competition of different uses for water is the most important fact of life which needs to be appreciated, it is true (as mentioned in n. 3 above) that certain uses are complementary rather than competitive. For example, suppose that a certain quantum of water may be diverted from a river for irrigation, after which we may assume that it is lost to ocean or atmosphere—or, alternatively, the water may be allowed to flow in the riverbed so as to be of value first for hydropower and then for industrial uses downstream. Here the power and industrial demands are complementary to each other, but jointly they are in competition with the use of the water for irrigation.

Our simple rules of equimarginal value in use and marginal-cost pricing are valid among uses that are competitive. Where demands are complementary instead, it is necessary to *add* the marginal values in use of the members of the complementary group to determine a joint marginal value in use for comparison with the marginal values in use of other, competitive, demands or with marginal cost. Thus in our example above water should be divided between the agricultural and the allied hydropower and industrial uses in such a way that the marginal value in use for irrigation equals the *sum* of the marginal values in the power and industrial uses. Or, if we are considering procurement of new water for, or sale of water to, the power-industrial combination, the principle is to equate marginal cost to the sum of the marginal values in use of the two allied uses.[10]

D. Comments on Some Existing Water-Allocation Practices

1. Limitations on Voluntary Exchange of Water Rights

In our theoretical discussion we saw that, given any particular vesting of water rights, an efficient allocation will tend to come about if free exchange of these rights between users is permitted. There is in practice, however, a wide variety of limitations upon the free exchange of water rights. Water rights are sometimes attached to particular tracts of land (i.e., the water cannot be transferred except as a package deal with the land), especially under the "riparian" principle; transfers of water rights or of uses within water rights also often must in a number of jurisdictions meet approval of some administrative agency. Some legal codes grant certain "higher" users priority or preference over other, "lower" users, transfers from "higher" to "lower" uses being hindered thereby. As a related point, "higher" uses sometimes have a right of seizure.[11] While voluntary transfers can usually be presumed to make both parties better off, and so be in the direction of increased efficiency, no such presumption applies for compelled transfers through seizure.

The above are all instances of violation of a general proposition about property rights.[12] If property is to be put to its most efficient use, there should be no uncertainty of tenure and no restrictions upon the use to which it may be put. When this is the case, voluntary exchange tends to make the property find the use where it is valued the highest, since this use can outbid all others on the market. Uncertainty of tenure interferes with this process, because people will be unwilling to pay much for property, however valuable, if a perfect right cannot be conveyed, and the existing holder will be wary about making those investments necessary to exploit the full value of the property if there is a risk of seizure. All restrictions upon free choice of use, whether the restriction is upon place, purpose, or transfers to other persons, obviously interfere with the market processes which tend to shift the resource to its most productive use.

The reasons underlying adoption of restrictions like those mentioned above are probably mixed, but at least one of them may have some validity: changes in water use may conceivably affect adversely the interests of third parties, such as complementary users downstream, for whom some protection seems needed.[13] This protection should not, as it usually does, go beyond what is necessary to insure preservation of the rights of the third parties. Under California law, for example, a riparian user might attempt to sell water to a non-riparian user who can use the water more pro-

[10] For an excellent analysis of a situation with important aspects of complementarity see George S. Tolley and V. S. Hastings, "Optimal Water Allocation: The North Platte River," *Quarterly Journal of Economics,* LXXIV (May, 1960), 279–95. We treat complementarity more fully, as an example of interdependency of use, in Appendix B below.

[11] Such a right was claimed for irrigation in a report of the National Reclamation Association (cited in McGuinness, *op. cit.,* p. 12). In the famous California case of *Chow* v. *Santa Barbara,* municipal seizure of Chow's agricultural water rights was permitted. By "seizure" we mean deprivation of rights with inadequate or no compensation. The laws of some states (e.g., Colorado) permit enforced transfers to "higher" uses only if full compensation is paid—a much sounder principle.

[12] This topic is described more fully in chap. ix.

[13] This situation is not, of course, unique to water. When my excellent neighbor sells his house to a most objectionable one, I certainly lose thereby. It is probably the case, however, that the technological interdependence of water usages is so unusual and important as to dictate protection for third parties which may be impracticable to provide in other contexts.

ductively, none of the other riparian users being harmed thereby. However, the non-riparian purchaser gains no rights against the other riparian users, who can simply increase their diversions, leaving none for the would-be purchaser. Again, a holder of certain appropriative rights might attempt to sell his rights to another. This transfer in some cases requires approval of an administrative board which protects the rights of third parties but whose latitude goes beyond this and permits disapproval on essentially arbitrary grounds as well.[14]

We may comment here that the growing trend to limitation of water rights to "reasonable use" is by no means a wholly obvious or desirable restriction. We might reflect on the desirability of legislation depriving people of their automobiles or their houses when it is determined in some administrative or judicial process that their use was "unreasonable." The purpose of such legislation is the prevention of certain wastes which, if only free voluntary exchange of water rights without unnecessary restrictions were permitted, would tend naturally to be eliminated by market processes (since efficient users can afford to pay more for water than it is worth to wasteful users).

The question of "higher" and "lower" uses has an interesting history. The California Water Code declares that the use of water for domestic purposes is the highest use of water and that the next highest use is for irrigation.[15] Essentially the same statement has been attributed to the emperor Hammurabi (2250 B.C.), a remarkable demonstration of the persistence of error.[16]

[14] See W. A. Hutchins, *Irrigation Water Rights in California* (California Agricultural Experiment Station Extension Service Circular 452 [April, 1956]), pp. 22, 33.

[15] *Ibid.*, pp. 25–26.

[16] A. R. Golzé, *Reclamation in the United States* (New York: McGraw-Hill Book Co., 1952), p. ix. Current authors, like Golzé, usually cite Hammurabi with approval on this point.

The correct idea underlying this thought seems to be that, if we had to do almost entirely without water, we would use the first little bit available for human consumption directly, and then, as more became available, the next use we would want to consider is providing food through irrigation. Where this argument goes wrong is in failing to appreciate that what we want to achieve is to make the *marginal* values in use (the values of the last units applied to any purpose) equal. It would obviously be mistaken to starve to death for lack of irrigation water applied to crops while using water domestically for elaborate baths and air conditioning; the domestic marginal value in use in such a case would be lower. Similar imbalances can make the marginal value in use in industry higher than it is in either domestic or irrigation uses. Actually, the principle of higher and lower uses is so defective that no one would for a moment consider using it consistently (first saturating domestic uses before using any water for other uses, then saturating irrigation uses, etc.). Rather, the principle enters erratically or capriciously in limiting the perfection of property rights in water applied to "lower" uses, however productive such uses may be.

2. Existing Pricing Practices in Water Supply

Our analysis of the principles of efficient allocation among competitive users led to the conclusion that prices should be equal for all customers served under equivalent cost conditions and that the price should be set at the marginal cost or the cost of delivering the last unit. Alternatively, we may say that the amount supplied should be such that the marginal cost equals the amount the customer is willing to pay for the marginal unit. There are considerable theoretical and practical complications in this connection which we are reserving for discussion in later chapters, but a general survey of the existing situation will be useful here for contrasting practice with the theoretical principles.

Examination of the allocation arrangements of local systems for domestic, commercial, and industrial water supply (primarily municipally owned) reveals that the great majority allocate water by charging a price for its use. The leading exceptions are in unmetered municipalities where, since water bills are not a function of consumption, water *deliveries* may be considered free to the consumer. While a certain amount is ordinarily charged as a water bill in such cities, this is a fixed sum (or "flat rate") and does not operate as a price does in leading consumers to balance the value of use against the cost of use. According to a report published by the *American City Magazine,* a survey made in 1949 of seventy-two cities discovered that 97.7 per cent of the services in those cities were metered. The survey excluded, however, several of the largest cities which were partially under flat rates—New York, Chicago, Philadelphia, Buffalo, and others. Since that time, according to the report, Philadelphia has abandoned the fixed-bill system, and generally it may be said that in the United States a condition of universal metering has been approached. As of 1954, the report estimates that metering covered from 90 to 95 per cent of all services.[17] Since unmetered services usually represent the smaller domestic users, the proportion of *use* that is metered is even greater than the proportion of *services*.[18]

In those cases, such as New York City, where some users (primarily domestic) are unmetered while other users are charged a price per unit of water used, our rule of prices equal to marginal cost is violated. An unmetered consumer will proceed to use water until its marginal value in use to him is nil to correspond to its zero price to him. This is of course wasteful, because the water system cannot provide the commodity costlessly, and hence society will lose (setting distributional considerations aside) by the excess of the cost of delivery over the value in use for such units of consumption.

It might be thought that the domestic consumers, who are the unmetered customers almost always (the only other substantial classes of use frequently unmetered are public agencies, such as park, sanitation, and especially fire departments), somehow deserve a priority or preference as compared with "intermediate" economic customers like industrial or commercial services. But an intermediate consumer is essentially a final consumer once removed. If consumers are required to pay more for water used in the production of food, clothing, and other items of value than they pay for water for direct consumption, an inefficient disparity in marginal values in use between the different uses will be created. Conversely, on efficiency grounds consumers should not be required to pay *more* for domestic water and for water used in industry than for water used to grow crops, such being the effect of existing policies which commonly grant the irrigation use of water a subsidy over all other uses.

A situation in which different prices are charged to different users, or to the same user for varying quantities of the same commodity, is called one of "price discrimination." While discrimination may under certain con-

[17] *Modern Water Rates,* published by the *American City Magazine* (New York, 1955[?]), pp. 1–2.

[18] Even for metered consumers, however, it is usual practice to have a certain periodic charge independent of the amount of water consumed—often in the form of a minimum bill, varying with the size of the service connection. This procedure is sometimes justified as covering the marginal "customer cost" of connecting the consumer to the system, reading his meter, processing his bill, etc. Alternatively, it may be considered a "demand charge" in the sense used in public utility pricing—a charge based on the fact that the utility system must reserve a certain amount of capacity against the possibility that the consumer may demand service at a system-wide peak period. These points will be discussed more thoroughly in chap. v.

ditions be justified on one ground or another,[19] it has the defect of preventing the marginal values in use from being made equal between the favored and the penalized uses or users. The only exception to this statement is where discrimination is applied within the purchases of a single individual —by, for example, a declining block rate. If there are no restrictions on use, the individual concerned will continue to equate all his marginal values in the various uses to the *marginal* price (the price for the last unit or for an additional unit) he must pay for the commodity purchased. So far as his own purchases are concerned, therefore, he will still equalize his marginal values in use for all his different uses. If such a block system is used for a number of individuals, however, marginal values in use will not in general be equated between individuals; some will tend to consume an amount such that they end up in the higher-priced block, and others will end up in the lower.

All price differences for the "same" commodity are not, however, evidence of price discrimination. In fact, there should be some difference of price where an extra delivery cost or processing cost must be incurred in serving certain users. These users can be considered as buying two commodities together—the basic commodity and the special delivery or processing. If the basic commodity is to be equally priced to all users, uses requiring such additional services must be charged more.[20]

Turning to the practical side, we should mention at once that our earlier metering discussion neglected one important consideration: the cost of metering and the associated increase in billing costs. It is clear that the additional cost of meters (especially for a great many small users) may well exceed the possible gains from the rationalization of use which would follow metering. (There would, in general, be an aggregate reduction of use as well.) While this question bears further investigation, the dominant opinion in the field of municipal water supply seems to be that universal metering produces gains that are worth the cost.[21] By way of contrast, it appears that in Great Britain domestic use is never metered.[22]

Even if we turn, however, to a consideration of that part of water supply that is metered, or to systems that are completely metered, we find that some non-uniform pattern of prices typically exists. There are some exceptions. In Chicago, for example, all metered users pay the same price per unit of water delivered. A more typical rate system is that of Los Angeles, where rates vary by type of use and also by amount of use (a declining or "promotional" block rate), with a service charge independent of use but based on size of connection. A rate distinction is also made in Los Angeles between firm service and service that the water department may at its convenience provide or refuse, and in some cases between gravity and pumped services.

Some of these rate differences may not be inconsistent with our theoretical discussion. The rate differential may reflect an extra cost or difficulty of delivering to the

19 In particular, we will later discuss a sophisticated defense of discrimination based on the idea that marginal-cost pricing may fail to recover the total costs of conducting a utility enterprise.

20 The extra charge should equal the marginal processing or delivery cost.

21 See *Modern Water Rates*, pp. 1–2. The main arguments employed there are that flat rates lead to wasteful use and also to inequities in distributing the cost of water supply. It is the wasteful-use argument which is the vital one for our purposes.

22 J. F. Sleeman, "The Economics of Water Supply," *Scottish Journal of Political Economy*, II (1955), 231–45, esp. pp. 244–45. Aside from the argument about the increased cost of metering and billing, a justification for not metering is also presented there in terms of public health. This either implies that consumers are irrational or that people will choose unsanitary conditions because the cost thereof may be largely borne by other members of society. In the present context the argument seems dubious.

customer (or customer class, where it is not worthwhile distinguishing between individual customers) charged the higher price.

Where customers' demands vary in the degree to which they impose a peak load on the system, some differential service or demand charge can be justified. In a sense, the commodity delivered off-peak is not the same as that delivered on-peak. The common system of basing a fixed-sum demand charge on the size of service connection is, however, very crude; it provides no deterrent to the customer's contributing to the peak load. Charging a lower rate for interruptible service is somewhat more reasonable. Ideally, the situation might be handled by having differing on-peak and off-peak prices.[23] In water enterprises storage in the distribution system usually smoothes out diurnal and weekly peaks. The seasonal peak in the summer is important, however. The Metropolitan Water District of Southern California has at times charged a premium price for summer deliveries.

Other differentiations can be justified by increased delivery costs necessary to reach certain classes of customers. A difference in rate between pumped and gravity service, for example, is eminently reasonable.[24] We have not gone into the question of just how great the differences should be, but for the present we shall not consider such differences as violations of the principle of a common per-unit price to all.

Certain frequently encountered differences, which we may now properly call "price discrimination," are not based on any special cost of providing the service in question. In Los Angeles, for example, there is an exceptionally low rate for irrigation use.[25] Domestic, commercial, and industrial services are not distinguished as such, but they are differentially affected by the promotional volume rates. More serious, because much more common,[26] is the system of block rates, with reductions for larger quantities used. There is typically some saving in piping costs to large customers, since a main can be run directly to the service connection, whereas the same volume sold to many small customers would require a distribution network of pipes. Ideally, the cost of laying down the pipes to connect customers to the system should be assessed as one-time charge against the outlet served—or the lump sum could be converted into an annual charge independent of the amount of water consumed, to represent the interest and depreciation on the capital invested by the water system to serve the customer. The point is that, once the pipes are in, the unit marginal cost of serving customers is almost independent of the volume taken. A lower block rate leads therefore to wasteful use of water by large users, since small users would value the same marginal unit of water more highly if delivered to them. We may say that the promotional or block-rate system in the case of water leads to a discrimination in favor of uses of water that happen to find it convenient to use a great deal of the commodity and against uses that do not need as much water. The customer paying the lower price will on the margin be utilizing water for less valuable purposes than it could serve if transferred to the customer paying the higher price.

Because of the enormous fraction of water being used for irrigational purposes

[23] See H. S. Houthakker, "Electricity Tariffs in Theory and Practice," *Economic Journal,* LXI (March, 1951), 1–25.

[24] Such rates should, ideally, be an increasing function of height.

[25] Such service can be refused by the department, a condition which justifies a somewhat lower rate, but hardly the extreme differential existing. There is reason to believe that the differential is based on Los Angeles' desire in the past to annex agricultural areas.

[26] A survey of sixty systems shows that only five have two rate blocks or fewer (*Modern Water Rates,* p. 34). Both Chicago and New York are exceptional in having only one rate, to the extent that service is metered in those cities.

(see Table 5), unusual interest attaches to the method by which water supplies of such projects are allocated to individual users. Not all irrigation water, of course, is distributed through an irrigation district or enterprise, a great deal being simply pumped or diverted by individual users. Such individual users can be considered to pay a price for water in the form of the costs actually incurred in its acquisition for irrigation purposes.

Reliable information is not available on the cost of water to irrigators, partly because of the differing methods of charging for water. The 1950 Census presented an over-all national average of $1.66 per acre-foot in 1949.[27] This figure is not very meaningful, since it is the result of dividing water charges *per acre* by an estimate of average deliveries of water per acre. But the water charges per acre depend, for farmers served by an irrigation district or other supply enterprise, upon the terms of the "payment complex," which may include taxes and assessments,[28] acreage charge, and service fees in addition to the water price.

Unfortunately, there do not seem to be any nationally compiled data on the methods used by irrigation enterprises to charge for water supplied. A tabulation by the Irrigation Districts Association of California[29] indicates considerable variation in practice: some districts make no charge except by assessment of property; others charge a flat rate, either (1) a fixed amount per acre or (2), depending upon the crop, a variable amount per acre; still others charge a price per unit of water, either on a fixed or on a declining block (promotional) basis; still others have a mixture of pricing methods. Where no charge or only a flat-rate charge is made for water, the marginal price of water to the user would be zero if in fact the user can take unlimited quantities as a domestic consumer normally can (subject only to the limited size of his connection). But it seems to be fairly common practice in irrigation districts that the water is more or less rationed to the user; any "price" set is a fiscal measure to cover the operating and maintenance costs of the district and not a market price in the ordinary sense.[30] We have seen that, with rationing of rights, efficiency can be achieved when trading is permitted. Purchase of water rights in irrigation districts normally takes place through purchase of land, which is usually freely possible (except for the so-called 160-acre limitation in Bureau of Reclamation projects), or through purchase of stock in mutual water companies. It may be remarked that a flat rate per acre varying by the type of crop grown is a kind of crude price, the higher flat rate generally corresponding to the more water-intensive crop. Irrigation districts may achieve reasonably efficient water allocations, but perhaps more often through the purchase of rights rather than the correct pricing of water itself. Where the water right cannot be detached from the land, this limitation on sale will create some inefficiency.

[27] *1950 Census of Agriculture*, III, 18.

[28] In this connection a hidden form of subsidy to agricultural users may consist of the inclusion of non-agricultural areas in the tax base of an irrigation district and subject to property taxes imposed by the latter. For example, the city of Santa Maria, California, constitutes a large percentage of the assessed valuation of the Santa Maria Irrigation District, although the city's water supply was ample and secure prior to formation of the district.

[29] Personal communication from Mr. Bert Smith, executive secretary, Water Economics Committee of the Irrigation Districts Association of California, September 12, 1955.

[30] The important Palo Verde Irrigation District on the Colorado River in California, which has no acre-foot charge for water, rations use by the device of denying the farmer the privilege of pumping excess water into district drains. His use of water is therefore limited by the natural drainage of the soil.

E. Potentialities of Major Water Reallocations

It appears that even less attention has been devoted to the optimal allocation of water *between* systems serving municipal or agricultural consumers than has been given to allocation of supplies among the customers of a given system. It is true that transfers of use within a given distribution network will almost always be much cheaper to effect than between such systems, so that the costs of transfer weigh more heavily against the exchanges considered in the present section. It is also true that some such transfers of use have taken place: the purchase of Owens River Valley water rights by the city of Los Angeles is a well-known example (though in some respects an unhappy one). More recently, the East Bay Municipal Water District (including the city of Oakland, California) purchased a water right from an irrigation district, and many other instances could be cited. Nevertheless, it seems that, by and large, water planners will go to considerable lengths to develop presently unutilized supplies rather than to consider shifts of use between already-developed sources.

So far as pure theory goes, there is no special difficulty about transfers between systems as opposed to transfers within systems. The ideal solution (so far as efficiency is concerned) is to make the marginal values in use everywhere equal—or, when we take transfer costs into consideration, transfers should take place so long as the disparity in marginal values in use exceeds the transfer cost. If perfect markets for water existed, this result would be brought about automatically, since the higher-valued uses could always buy out the lower-valued uses at some mutually advantageous price.

One rather important practical possibility of such an exchange exists in southern California. Here growing urbanization has led to large-scale schemes for importing water from great distances. It is proposed through the Feather River Project to carry "surplus" water all the way from north-central California to meet urban requirements in the south. But an alternative and cheaper way out might be for the urban interests to acquire a substantial additional quantity by purchasing the rights to existing supplies of relatively nearby irrigators.

What creates the possibility of mutually advantageous exchange between uses and distribution systems is the fact that water has been allocated defectively in the past. Various considerations—not the least of which may be the Hammurabist principles of the water codes[31]—have tended to prevent realization of an optimum solution. As a result, scope is left for human intelligence to improve the existing allocation. Prima facie evidence that room for improvement exists is provided when the costs incurred by distribution systems in procuring water differ by more than can reasonably be ascribed to the costs of transporting water between the areas under comparison. Apparent disparities are only a suggestive indication, however. Pricing of water, in particular, is irrational to such a widespread degree that mere differences of price cannot automatically be taken to indicate differences of marginal value in use. In some systems, for example, water may have a price of zero and yet be rationed among users, so that the marginal value in use will, for at least some users (those who desire to take more than their assigned ration), be greater than zero. We cannot then assume that a mutually satisfactory exchange can be made between such a system and a system charging its customers a positive price for water.

Two objections—one is fallacious, but the second is not—are commonly made to the exchange of water supplies between

31 We do not want to give these "principles" undue importance, since they have not been and could not be applied consistently. The major consideration impeding efficient allocation of water resources is undoubtedly the imperfection of property rights in water—most conspicuously, the limited transferability of water rights.

systems. To take the erroneous argument first: it is frequently stated that the price paid for water is no indication of its true value in use (even assuming no rationing), because the water makes the production of additional wealth possible. Thus an Imperial Valley farmer may pay his irrigation district $8.00 ($2.00 per acre-foot for 4 acre-feet of water) per acre,[32] but the value per acre of crops produced might be in the neighborhood of $175.[33]

This objection is fallacious in two respects. The less important error is in failing to take into account the costs of other factors of production. Thus the production of crops valued at $175 in the Imperial Valley requires not only an input of water but of labor, seed, machinery services, etc. If the water were taken away, these other inputs could be made available to assist in production elsewhere. Even allowing for this factor, the net productivity of water per acre might, on the average, still be considerably above $8.00—let us say it would be $50 after subtracting the cost of other co-operating inputs. The second and more important point is that this $50 is the *average* productivity[34] of water, not the *marginal* productivity—the productivity of the last unit. So long as the marginal productivity is above the price paid for water, it pays to increase the amount employed. If water is not rationed, we can then assume that this process has been carried to its limit so that the price per unit of water measures its *marginal* productivity, however great the average productivity may be.

Now it is true that, if it were proposed to deprive an area entirely of water, it would be the average productivity of the water which would be lost and which should, therefore, be taken into account in the comparison. That is to say, we would have to compare the aggregate value in use (essentially the sum of the marginal values in use) of the entire lump of water in the one use with the other.[35] In this case, the water should be taken for urban use only if the urban water system could afford to pay a price higher than $50 per unit, which is the minimum the agricultural users would accept for loss of their entire supply.

What would be more reasonable, however, would be a purchase of a fraction of the water supply—let us say one-eighth, so that the average agricultural use in our Imperial Valley example declines from 4 acre-feet per acre to 3.5 acre-feet. This change is sufficiently small so that the marginal productivity ($2.00 per acre-foot) essentially measures the loss suffered thereby. What this implies is that, with a loss of water available for application to crops, the farmer will modify his cropping practices[36] so that his net revenue falls practically *at the rate of* $2.00 per unit of water lost. Since one-half of an acre-foot would be withdrawn from each acre, the loss per

32 The $2.00 per acre-foot price was in effect as of April 1, 1959. Deliveries to users in 1958 were 3.9 acre-feet per acre, the bulk of this water being provided on an acre-foot charge basis (information from communication of G. E. Tank, general manager, Imperial Irrigation District, April 1, 1959).

33 Calculated from data in *1954 Census of Agriculture,* assuming that 90 per cent of Imperial County crop value is attributable to the Imperial Irrigation District.

34 For an intermediate purchaser of water (a purchaser for productive purposes rather than for personal use), the value in use of a unit of water is its contribution to the value of production—its productivity.

35 Technically, this is an example of a discontinuity of use, the theory of which is discussed in Appendix A.

36 While it is common to speak of irrigation "requirements" for crops, it is definitely not the case that a crop will survive only if given just so much water. A cutback in average water applied will not eliminate the crop but rather reduce the expected yield. (Even if each crop did "require" just so much water, the amounts per crop would vary, so that it would be possible to shift to other crops—or else plant fewer acres.) The rational farmer, given the fact that there will be a reduction in the amount of water applied, will reconsider his entire situation to find the best solution for a drier type of culture.

acre-foot of $2.00 would correspond to a loss per acre of little more than $1.00. The agricultural user should therefore be willing to sell a relatively small fraction of his supply at a price which need exceed only the marginal productivity, not the average productivity. As the fraction sold increases, however, the price required to find a willing seller will approach the average net productivity. Thus, increasing urban demands can probably be more economically served by the purchase of fractional shares of supplies in a number of agricultural areas than by purchase in their entirety of water allocations in just a few locations.[37]

The reader at this point is, of course, too sophisticated to be misled by arguments to the effect that, dollar considerations aside, we "need" in some absolute sense the food grown as a result of the use of water for agriculture. The food would no doubt be of value, but the fact that the water has a higher marginal value in use elsewhere means that our consumers value more highly what the increment of water in question can produce in industrial uses (or what it is worth to them in direct consumption for household purposes) than they value the additional food produced. A second line of defense for the irrigation-preference argument is that in the future the world will face greater needs for food. This is probably true, but, on the other hand, agricultural productivity is also making rapid strides. If, nevertheless, the demand for food grows so rapidly that consumers value the marginal use of water for food production more than its use for other purposes, irrigation will be able to outbid these other uses and recapture the water when the need arises. In neither case is any particular intervention in favor of irrigation necessary or desirable.[38]

The second and more correct objection to transfer of water rights between areas is based on the fact that such a transfer may adversely affect third parties. The buyer and seller may come to a mutually satisfactory agreement, but, if the costs imposed on others are sufficiently great, it may be wise to prevent its execution. It was the impact upon third parties which caused the difficulty in the famous Owens River Valley controversy. Despite wild statements which have occasionally been seen in print, no Owens Valley water rights were confiscated by the city of Los Angeles, nor was any farmer forced to sell at a price not satisfactory to himself.[39] The adversely affected interests fell into two major classes: (1) farmers who did not sell to the city were forced to bear an increased share of the costs of irrigation works when other farmers along the ditch sold out and (2) businessmen, employees of business establishments, and farm laborers suffered losses with the general decline of economic activity in the valley. The first of these classes was eliminated when practically all the

[37] Transportation cost, however, would have to be taken into account, and the cost of constructing many small aqueducts will exert pressure toward concentration of purchases.

[38] Irrigation-preference proponents will often cite not only "needs" for water but the value of crops produced, the provision of employment in crop-using industries or in communities serving farmers, the taxes paid by farmers, and the incidental benefits of irrigation projects in the way of power, navigation, and flood-control. For a typical list see L. N. McClellan, "Water Resources," in G. F. White (ed.), *The Future of Arid Lands* (Washington, D.C.: American Association for the Advancement of Science, 1956), pp. 193–94. All these considerations, whatever their true weight may be, are fallacious as justification for special preference to irrigation; it is clear that a corresponding list could be made up for the use of water in any sector. Our assertion is that the value in use for the increment of water in question is the relevant criterion. The next chapter considers to what extent other considerations, such as those just listed, may also validly enter into the decision.

[39] This is not to say that the city's policy was entirely above criticism. There is, for example, some reason to believe that the city's agents may have brought influence to bear against a proposed Reclamation Bureau project for the valley. A full discussion may be found in R. A. Nadeau, *The Water Seekers* (New York: Doubleday & Co., 1950), pp. 21–32.

farm land in the valley was purchased, and the second partially eliminated when the city purchased the bulk of the town properties at prices that compensated the owners for the loss of value suffered. Adverse effects suffered through impairment of business relations were not compensated, however; claims demanding reparation for such losses lapsed for failure of prosecution.[40]

If a project is definitely desirable, it is clear that it should be possible to compensate, in principle, all adversely affected parties. Whether or not compensation actually takes place we regard as a distributional question and not one of efficient allocation, though difficulty of such compensation might be a valid distributional argument for opposing such a project. The question of the effects of transactions upon third parties is one aspect of what is known as the "spillover" problem, that is to say, the effect of private actions of any kind upon outside parties. In this connection it is vital to distinguish "technological" and "pecuniary" spillovers.[41] A technological spillover represents a real loss or gain to society; for example, the flooding of agricultural lands consequent upon creating a reservoir behind a dam is a technological spillover loss. A contractual arrangement transferring water rights from a downstream to an upstream user might reduce the quality of water to users located between the two—also a technological spillover loss. If technological spillovers only are considered, it is clear that, if an allocational change is desirable, there must be enough increase of production of goods and services to compensate for the losses in production that take place. The question of efficiency concerns technological spillovers only.

A merely pecuniary spillover occurs when there is no change in real productive possibilities, but gains or losses are suffered because of changes in prices of inputs or outputs of affected third parties, the price changes being due to increased or decreased supplies of certain commodities brought about by the change under consideration. Thus, in the exchange of water between an upstream and a downstream use, the supply of coal might be increased and the supply of shoes decreased without any other changes in inputs. This is all technological. But the increase in the supply of coal will tend to drive down its price, and this will have a spillover effect hurting every coal supplier and helping every coal consumer in a wide region. The reverse argument applies to shoe suppliers and consumers. All these latter spillovers are pecuniary or distributional, since there has been no change in the technological possibilities for the other coal or shoe producers. If we limited ourselves to efficiency considerations, we could ignore pecuniary spillovers.

Whether or not we ignore them, if a proposed change is desirable, the "technological" beneficiaries in the aggregate should be capable of compensating those suffering technological spillover losses, and all beneficiaries together should be capable of compensating all those suffering losses. In the Owens River case such compensation evidently was possible and was in fact largely carried out. In New York, state law has required New York City to compensate interests adversely affected by the city's reservoir and aqueduct projects, under a very broad interpretation of damages (covering all technological spillover losses and possibly some pecuniary losses).[42]

Whether compensation should always be carried out is beyond the scope of our present interest. We may comment, however, that our system of law is such that certain types of "ordinary business risks" are not

[40] The discussion above is based upon V. Ostrom, *Water and Politics* (Los Angeles: Haynes Foundation, 1953), pp. 116–33.

[41] For a full discussion see Roland McKean, *Efficiency in Government* (New York: John Wiley & Sons, 1958), pp. 134–50. We treat the matter further in chap. vi.

[42] *New York Times,* July 28, 1957, p. 1.

considered compensable. The owner of a home or a factory may lose, for example, because a reduction in construction costs of new buildings reduces the value of his present one (a pecuniary effect) or because an increase in air pollution requires him to spend more on cleaning (a technological effect). Both, however, are considered uncompensable ordinary business risks. On grounds of economic efficiency, new inventions reducing construction cost should not be penalized in any way for the reduction imposed on the value of old houses (the effect being pecuniary), while new processes increasing air pollution should ideally be required to show that the increase in production exceeds the addition to cleaning costs and other such costs borne by other people; but neither innovation necessarily justifies a claim for compensation on the part of those affected. Whether or not compensation should be paid (or whether benefits should be charged for) is really connected not with the type of spillover effects involved but with the conception of legal rights and risks attaching to the property and so presumably taken into account in making decisions.

APPENDIX A

JUSTIFICATION AND EXTENSION OF ECONOMIC PRINCIPLES

In this chapter certain principles of the economic theory of choice—the principle of equimarginal value in use and the rule of marginal-cost pricing—were derived on the basis of common-sense considerations for application to the problem of best use of existing water supplies. Applying these principles, we pointed out deficiencies in existing practices relating to tenure of property rights in water, to pricing of water by public enterprises, and to exchanges of supplies between major water systems. In this appendix we intend to go somewhat more rigorously into the justification for these principles, in the process extending them so as to be able to cover certain decision problems beyond the scope of the principles as originally developed and stated.

1. The Demand Curve and Aggregate Value in Use

The principle of equimarginal value in use, it will be remembered, is a rule governing the division of a given quantum of a commodity among individuals. In the chapter we pointed out that, whenever marginal values in use are unequal, opportunities exist for mutually advantageous exchanges between individuals, these opportunities persisting until the marginal values everywhere are brought into equality.

In Figure 5 we show, for two different uses of water *of a particular individual,* entire schedules relating the marginal values to him of water in each use to the quantity used. Thus we might be comparing water for drinking and water for washing or else water for all personal consumption versus water for irrigation of crops. (As discussed above, if some uses are complementary, it is the sum of their marginal values in use, for each amount of water, which we want to compare with marginal values in other, competitive, uses.) The marginal value in each use (or set of complementary uses) declines as quantity increases, since the first units of water becoming available will naturally be applied to the most urgent needs, the next units to somewhat less intense needs, etc. Eventually, marginal value in any use may become zero (the schedule intersecting the horizontal axis), reflecting a situation of a saturated demand for water—no more will be desired for that use even at a zero price (i.e., even if it could be obtained with no sacrifice).[43]

[43] To bring out the essential idea of balancing marginal values in use, we have assumed no interaction between the uses—that the individual's

In the particular situation illustrated, the schedule for the first use is initially higher than that for the second use. Consequently, if only a very small supply of water is available (less than *OB* in the illustration), it should all be devoted to the first use. The marginal values in this use up to the quantity *OB* are all in excess of the magnitude *OU*, whereas the most intense marginal value, for the first unit consumed, in the second use is *O′U′*, equal to value in use in observing that, when the marginal values in one of the uses are sufficiently high, *all* the supply available should be directed to that use until its marginal value is brought down to equal the marginal value in use of the *first* unit in the next best use. In fact, what we have been doing is following a more general principle of optimal allocation, which we will call *maximization of aggregate value in use*. Aggregate value in use may simply

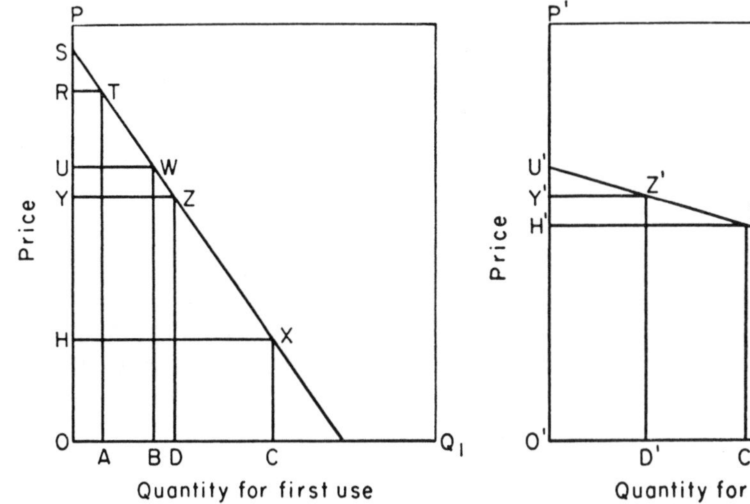

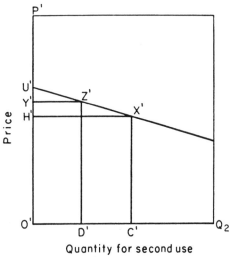

FIG. 5.—Two uses of water

OU. If, however, a quantum of supply greater than *OB* is available, a division between the two uses is indicated. For example, there is a certain quantity represented in the diagram by the allocation of *OD* to the first use and *O′D′* to the second, the marginal value in use being *OY* (= *O′Y′*).

In this short discussion we have already gone beyond our principle of equimarginal

schedule of marginal value in use for each use is independent of the other. For a single individual, such interdependence might be important. Our real interest, however, is in balancing marginal values in use between individuals (see below), and there we can assume that the schedules are independent.

be thought of as the sum of the successive marginal values in use. Geometrically (if we assume that the unit of supply is essentially infinitesimal), the marginal value in use at any point is the height of the schedule in Figure 5, while the aggregate value in use to that point is the area contained between the axes and below the curve. Thus, for the quantity *OA* in the first use, the marginal value in use is *OR* (= *AT*). But the aggregate value in use, being conceived as the sum of successive small units of quantity, the first having marginal value in use equal to *OS* and the last having marginal value in use equal to *AT*, is then measured by the area *OSTA*.

We next turn to the problem of discontinuities in supply, which can only be analyzed using the more general principle of maximization of aggregate value in use. Suppose, in Figure 5, that for some technological reason all the water available had to be devoted to the first use or else all to the second, no division of the supply among uses being possible. If the quantity so available is *OD*, the *marginal* values at that level of use (*O′D′* having been set equal to *OD*, by construction) are equal for the two uses considered (*OY* and *O′Y′*). But it is obvious that the water should be applied to the first use rather than the second, the aggregate value in use being higher in the former case, that is, the area *OSZD* is larger than the area *O′U′Z′D′*.

The relationship between the value-in-use concept and market values is of importance. For any given quantity the marginal value in use is essentially equal to that price at which the consumer would voluntarily purchase the quantity in question, assuming that he can freely choose to buy any quantity he pleases. Another way of putting this is to say that the schedule of marginal value in use is essentially equivalent to the "demand curve"[44] of economic theory, which relates quantities demanded to price. The reason for the equivalence, of course, is that a rational consumer will continue to purchase units of a commodity so long as his marginal value in use exceeds price, terminating his purchases when the two come into equality. The *aggregate* value in use, in contrast, represents the maximum lump-sum payment which could be extracted from the consumer for a certain indivisible amount of the commodity offered on a take-it-or-leave-it basis. Finally, the excess of aggregate value in use over cost of purchase, for a given level of consumption, is called the "consumers' surplus" for that amount of consumption. For example, if in Figure 5 the price of water is *OR*, the total quantity taken will be *OA*, the marginal value in use then being reduced to *AT* (=*OR*). The aggregate value in use is *OSTA*. The total cost of purchases is (*OR* × *OA*) or the rectangle *ORTA*, whence the consumer's surplus is the area *RST*.

So far we have been concerned with an individual consumer allocating water to different uses. The real problem is that of a society allocating water to *its* different uses, which directly or indirectly means to different individuals. The analysis in some respects remains similar, though a new element—interpersonal comparisons—unavoidably intrudes. We might say by analogy that an increment of supply should, if it is a small unit, go to that consumer whose marginal value in use is greatest (or group of complementary consumers whose joint marginal value in use is greatest)—or, if it is an indivisible large amount, to that consumer or group of consumers whose aggregate value in use for the increment is greatest. In each case, this simply means that the unit or units should go to those who are willing to pay the most. Where no discontinuity problems exist, supplying each unit successively to the individual with highest marginal value in use will equate marginal values in use for all those actually consuming the commodity (those not consuming at all must then have a marginal value in use for the first unit lower than the going rate for individuals actually consuming).

[44] One technical qualification is that, since marginal value in use (the maximum amount that the consumer will pay for another unit) depends upon the income available to the consumer, the schedule of marginal value in use will depend upon the price which the consumer has had to lay out for the earlier units purchased. If he has been paying a high price, we would expect his marginal value in use to fall more rapidly than if he has been paying a low price. In contrast, since the demand curve is ordinarily defined as representing quantities that would be purchased at hypothetical different fixed prices, each different price considered will give us only a new point on the same demand curve rather than an entirely different schedule. This divergence will be unimportant so long as purchases of the commodity in question represent a small fraction of total income, and we will henceforth neglect it.

Unfortunately, the problem of interpersonal comparisons—the choice between A's satisfactions and B's—cannot be entirely avoided. Our argument indicates that, if A's marginal value in use is $10.00 when B's is $4.00, another unit of supply should go to A. But how can we justify preferring A's $10.00 to B's $4.00? The explanation is that we could in principle force A to disgorge $4.00 of his $10.00 to B, leaving the latter no worse off than if he received the unit of commodity, while A is still the equivalent of $6.00 to the good. An obvious counterpart to this argument applies to the case of the discontinuous increment.

It is true that such compensation is not always paid. Sometimes there are practical difficulties preventing it. We have argued that at least a presumption in favor of a proposed change is justified if an improvement in efficiency is involved. Society should choose, among discrete employments of an increment of resources, that employment which creates the greatest aggregate value in use—failure to set up a system of compensations so that all interested parties benefit should ordinarily be considered a distributive choice. If an intrinsic distribution effect is both undesirable and irreparable, however, it may justify rejection of a proposal increasing efficiency.

The measurement of aggregate value in use or of consumers' surplus (the difference between aggregate value in use and market value) may be difficult, but the concept itself is by no means a mystical one. If two potential users of the resource simply had to bid against each other in an auction, each one's absolute top limit offer would represent his aggregate value in use, and, in fact, an auctioning process would assure that the resource would go to the user with the higher aggregate value in use. It is where auctioning is impracticable that the measurement problem exists. Where, however, no large discontinuities require an increment of water to be allocated exclusively to one use or to the other, the simpler criterion of equating marginal value in use applies; and this can be achieved simply by setting a fixed per-unit price, equal for all potential users. With some exceptions, allocation of existing supplies does not in practice require consideration of anything more difficult than marginal values in use, which are sufficiently indicated by market prices. The problems that do necessarily involve consumers' surplus calculations are generally those associated with the development of additional water supplies, since such development frequently seems to require choice among alternative large-scale projects.

2. *Cost Functions and the Theoretical Solution*

All the above referred to choice situations with costless supply. Since, ordinarily, more of any resource cannot be provided without cost (i.e., without sacrifice of something else that is also valued by consumers), the decision on how much of a certain good or resource to provide cannot be made without consideration of cost.

Figure 6 illustrates the cost function (i.e., the cost per unit as a function of output) of a productive enterprise as usually presented in economic analysis. Figure 6*a* shows marginal cost (the cost of producing an additional unit of output) as a function of output. There are normally also fixed costs (the costs that would be incurred even with zero output and remain the same regardless of output). From these two it is possible to derive the curve of average cost[45] shown in Figure 6*b*. The marginal and average costs can be either rising or falling throughout their range, though it is usual

45 For any level of output the sum of the fixed cost and of the cumulated marginal costs incurred on behalf of all the successive units produced equals the total cost. The total cost divided by the number of units produced is the average cost. It is sometimes useful to take the average of the total costs incurred exclusive of the fixed cost; this is called the "average variable cost."

to assume on the basis of what is known as "the law of diminishing returns" that the marginal cost curve will eventually slope upward. (In other words, the cost of producing an additional unit will eventually rise if we try to produce more and more from a given amount of capital invested, represented by the constant fixed costs.) The relation shown between the average- and marginal-cost curves is a standard result of economic theory. The main idea is that the average-cost curve must be falling whenever marginal cost is less than average cost (the marginal unit is pulling the average down); correspondingly, average cost must be rising whenever marginal cost is above it. From this it follows that, if average cost is neither rising nor falling, marginal cost must equal average cost.

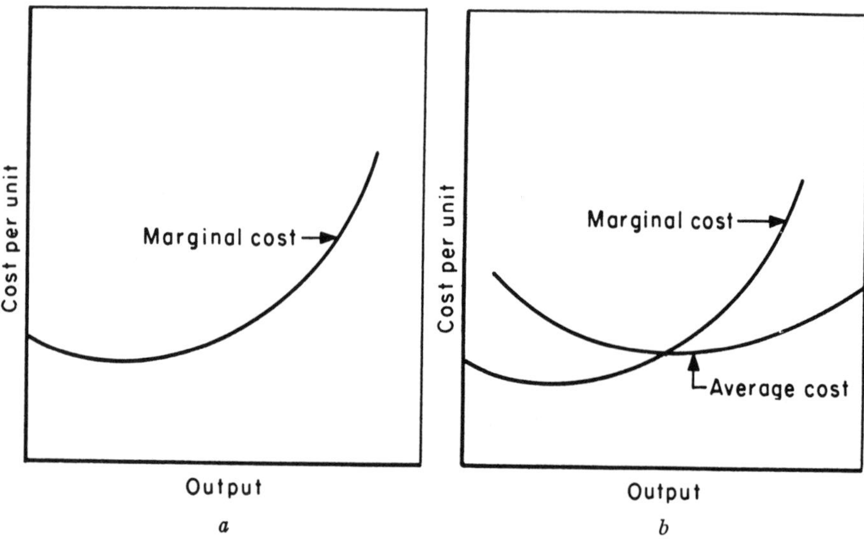

FIG. 6.—The cost function

In Figure 7 we juxtapose the demand curve and the marginal-cost curve for a particular enterprise, without concerning ourselves as to whether the enterprise is private or public in nature. How much should this enterprise sell and at what price? The theoretical solution is that the price and the quantity should be jointly determined at the intersection of the marginal cost curve and the demand curve. In Figure 7 the price should be OP and the quantity OK. This, of course, is our rule for marginal-cost pricing. The reason is that, if the price were above P (as, e.g., if a price of P' were set, the quantity Q' then being demanded on the market) the marginal value in use $Q'V$ $(=OP')$ of the consumers for the last or an additional unit exceeds the marginal cost $Q'T$ for an additional unit. If the price were below P, the marginal value in use would be less than the marginal cost. Marginal value in use for the products of this enterprise should be set equal to the marginal cost because the costs represent the value consumers and producers place on the resources used up, or the goods sacrificed elsewhere, in producing one more unit of output in this enterprise.[46]

[46] A technical objection has been raised against this conclusion. It has been argued that, if somewhere in the economy marginal cost is not set equal to price—and this will certainly always be the case—the justification for applying the rule to the industry under investigation collapses. In fact, no general statement can be made about whether production should stop short of the point where

Where complementary uses are involved, the demand curve will represent the schedule of joint marginal value in use (vertical sum of the separate marginal values in use). In such a case the intersection of the marginal-cost curve and the demand curve will indicate the *joint* price, which can be divided among the complementary uses according to their separate marginal values in use at the optimal output taken jointly by all. We should comment that, as always in this discussion, the statement that more should be produced here and less elsewhere is based on efficiency considerations, and the distributive consequences might also have to be considered in certain circumstances.

The above (or marginal) condition for the best outcome must in a fuller analysis be supplemented with what is called a "total condition." The enterprise, if it is operating, will produce its best output at *OK*, but should it be in business at all? The total condition is simply that the aggregate value in use associated with the enterprise should exceed the aggregate cost. Earlier we iden-

marginal cost equals price or should be pushed beyond this point. For a full discussion see R. G. Lipsey and R. K. Lancaster, "The General Theory of Second Best," *Review of Economic Studies,* XXIV (1956–57), 11–32. We will take this up in the next chapter in our consideration of objections to market valuations.

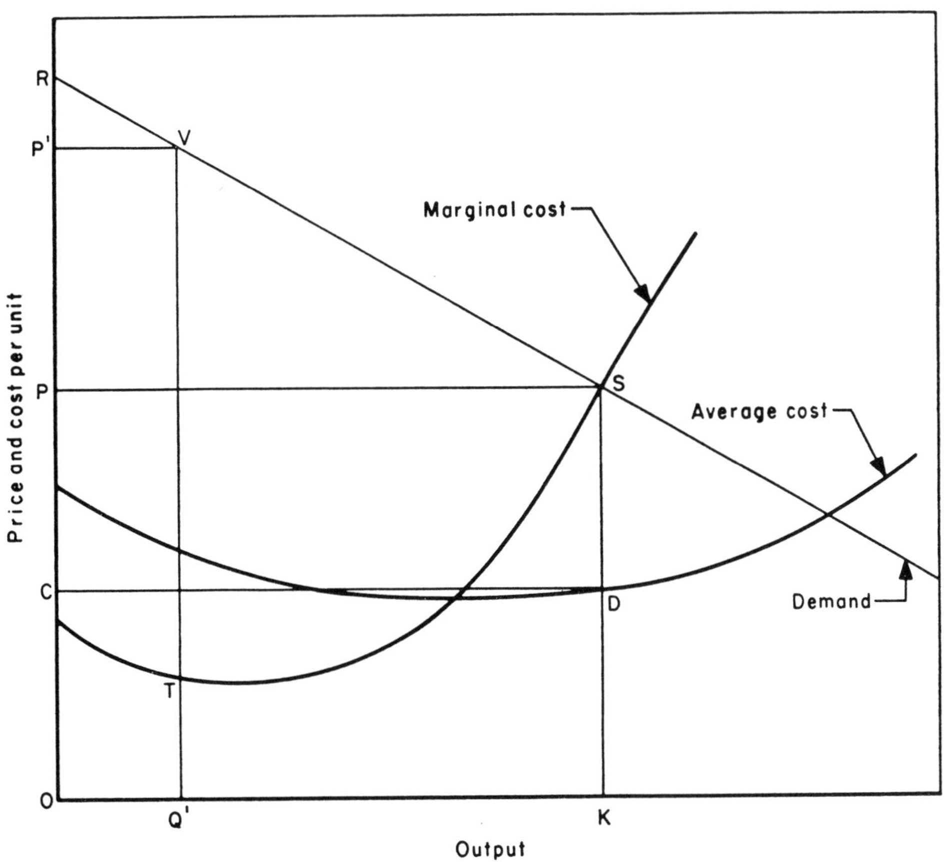

FIG. 7.—Best price and output—marginal conditions

tified the aggregate value in use with the area under the demand curve (*ORSK* for the output *OK* in Fig. 7). The total cost is *OCDK* (average cost times the number of units), and in the case illustrated in Figure 7 the total condition is met by the enterprise staying in existence.[47]

3. *Market Processes and Efficient Allocation*

How do market processes square with the outcome indicated as best by the economic theory of choice? That is, can we simply assume for any commodity that it will be ideally allocated by an unregulated market, assuming vesting of property rights and no technological spillovers? The crucial requirement here is the existence of competition in the economic sense. Indeed, it would be simple to show that for a pure monopoly situation the marginal condition will not be met if the monopolist is seeking maximum profit. In Figure 7 it is in his self-interest to set a somewhat higher price than *OP,* selling fewer units than *OK*. Competition is characterized by the existence of a considerable number of entrepreneurs in or able and willing to enter any industry. If a monopoly should temporarily exist in a given industry raising prices sufficiently to create extra-normal profits, new firms will crowd into the industry, lowering the product price. In consequence, no producer in a competitive industry can do better than accept the going price as a datum beyond his control, and entry and exit of firms will establish this price at a level just covering all the costs of operation of the firms, including normal return on the owners' capital investment and personal efforts. In these circumstances it is in the interest of each firm to produce that level of output which sets marginal cost equal to market price. If it is producing less, it can increase profit by expanding production (since the increment to revenue *OP* exceeds the marginal cost on an additional unit or units); conversely, if it were producing more, it could increase profit by reducing output. But, since consumers will set their marginal values in use equal to market price, we have the desired result that marginal cost equals marginal value in use—a result brought about by competitive market forces combined with rational pursuit of self-interest by consumers and by owners of firms. The total condition will also be obviously met, since no firm will stay in business unless its total revenue (price times number of units sold) is at least equal to its total cost, and aggregate value in use (the area under the demand curve) is always at least as great as the amount consumers will pay in as revenues to the firms supplying them.

Competition in the economic sense is by no means universal throughout the economy. Even where it does not exist, however, it is possible in principle at least to determine the price and quantity to be produced on the basis of the rule that price should equal marginal cost. In particular, for the class of enterprises known as public utilities, of which water supply is one, a condition of "natural monopoly" may exist; the size of plant necessary to achieve efficiency may be so large relative to the market that a competitive situation with many firms could not persist. In the case of water supply, for example, an element of local monopoly is generally deemed to be inevitable, because the cost of several competing water mains running down the same streets is so much in excess of the cost of a single large main.

Where natural monopolies exist, public regulation or public ownership has been commonly adopted to correct certain obvious departures from desirable economic practices which might tend to come about if the monopoly were left without restrictions in private hands. Public regulation or

[47] In certain interesting cases the total and marginal conditions for an optimum seem to conflict. We will discuss this problem in our detailed discussion of municipal water-rate policies in a later chapter.

public ownership has also been resorted to for reasons, good or bad, other than the existence of natural monopoly, but we do not need to examine here what these other reasons might be. It suffices to say that, whether an enterprise is private and unregulated, private and regulated, or public, the condition that marginal cost should be set equal to price is the desirable solution from the point of view of economic efficiency considerations if the total conditions for an optimum are also met. Where free competition in the economic sense exists, market processes tend automatically to bring about the optimum. Where competition does not rule, no such automatic result ensues, and we shall consider this problem in our discussion of objections to the market system in the next chapter. Where government policies dominate price-quantity determination because of public ownership or regulation, political processes replace market processes. Political processes have rarely been analyzed from the point of view of economic efficiency, and we will devote some attention to this problem too in the next chapter.

APPENDIX B

INTERDEPENDENCIES OF WITHDRAWAL AND USE

In this chapter our basic analysis was derived from general principles of the economic theory of resource allocation, with little particular or special reference to water as such. As in the case of most theories of a high level of generality, the application of results to particular problems requires some adaptation of theoretical constructs to make them fit, at least roughly, the hard facts of reality. This appendix is devoted to one special feature of water as a resource: the interconnected nature of its withdrawal and use. For a resource like coal, for example, we ordinarily think that its extraction from a particular mine does not affect the availability of coal in other sites—and its use certainly does not affect the availability of coal to others aside from the direct consumption of the amount used. Water supplies, however, typically overlie or underlie or are transported across large areas, which are or become hydrologically interconnected. Thus one individual's withdrawals will very commonly affect the availability of the water not withdrawn by him. The clearest instance of this type of interdependency is the "common-pool problem" in the case of ground water, and we will first discuss the adaptation of general economic principles called for by this type of interdependence of withdrawals. The second type of interconnection we will consider is interdependence of use. Here, since the *use* of water does not necessarily result in its being *used up*, everyone hydrologically downstream of any given user has an interest in the amount and character of the water discharged by that user. This is usually spoken of as the problem of "consumptive" or "non-consumptive" use. Our second subject will be the refinement of this concept and distinction and an examination of its implications for allocation of water resources, especially via the market mechanism. We should note here that interdependencies of withdrawal and use of water lead almost inevitably to what we have called "technological spillover" effects of private decisions upon other water-users. Since we deal here with physical (hydrological) effects of decisions, merely "pecuniary" spillovers do not enter in.

1. Common-Pool Problems

The common-pool problem in the exploitation of water resources, in the narrow sense, occurs when a number of overlying property-owners are engaged in competitive pumping of water from a common underlying aquifer. In the wider sense, all cases where users draw competitively on a "fugitive" supply—that is, where the commodity is no one's property until and unless captured for use, wildlife being the classical example—are common-pool problems. Since rights in percolating ground water can normally be obtained only by actual "capture" of the water,[48] pumpers are induced to withdraw at a rate greater than would otherwise be rational for fear that the withdrawals of others will lower water levels in the wells. Or, to look at the matter in another way, each individual considers in his decisions only the effect of his pumping upon the water level in his well—which may be negligible if there are many pumpers, since all are drawing upon a common pool—and does not consider the fact that his pumping will adversely affect all those interested in the pool.

It is evident from this discussion that this problem is not unique to water resources. A close analogy is the case of common oil pools, though, since the quantity of oil in an oil pool is fixed, all withdrawals will necessarily lower the oil level. In a ground-water pool, replenishment does take place,[49] though at a rate largely beyond the control of those exploiting the resource.[50] In fact, natural replenishment may bring about stationary or even rising water levels in spite of pumping. Nevertheless, the considerations adduced above remain correct (that each owner's private decisions fail to take account of the losses imposed on others), though the situation is most serious when natural replenishment is insufficient to maintain water levels. When water levels are falling, the loss imposed by pumping is a positive one; if they are stable or rising, the loss takes the form of failure of others to receive a benefit in the form of a raised (or a more rapidly raised) water level which would have come about in the absence of pumping. An exception to this generalization exists if the rise in water levels is itself harmful (creating drainage problems), in which case our argument is reversed; it is a benefit incurred by others, rather than a loss imposed on others, which fails of being taken into account in private pumping decisions.

A suggestive related example is a "pool" of fish in the ocean, which is "common" in that the law of capture applies in the absence of legal controls; no single fisherman takes into consideration the fact that his activities impose losses on other fishermen. That is to say, a fraction of the catch of any fisherman consists of additional fish which would not have been caught had he not been active—this part creates no difficulty—but another fraction consists of fish which would have been caught by others who would otherwise have benefited by an increased average yield. In the case of the common pool of fish, the rate of replenishment is partially under the control of man, so that another dimension is added to the problem of optimal exploitation of the resource.[51]

It is important to note that the common-pool problem is a manifestation of the "fugitive" nature of water resources. The span of property rights in such resources fails to include all the significant consequences of the private exploitation decisions. Ordinarily, the inducements are such as to encourage excessive exploitation, since a decision to conserve for future use does not provide a property right in the preserved resource still subjected to the law of capture. Occasionally, however, the in-

48 To some extent, recent developments in western water law have modified this principle.

49 The very lowering of a ground-water pool tends automatically to decrease runoff and to increase replenishment, since water sources formerly flowing elsewhere will now drain into the pool.

50 This is not entirely true, because of such possibilities as weather control and artificial replenishment.

51 See H. Scott Gordon, "The Economic Theory of a Common-Property Resource," *Journal of Political Economy*, XLIV (April, 1954), 124–42.

ducement is toward insufficient utilization, as in the case mentioned above where rising water levels were actually doing damage. Another instance of underutilization occurs sometimes in fishing when a "thinning-out," reducing the number of fish, would actually increase the later value of the catch. We mention these points to distinguish our position from that of certain doctrinaire "conservationists," the essence of whose position seems to be that resource preservation is desirable as such or that somehow future uses are more to be prized than present ones.[52] Our position, to be elaborated later, is that, given an appropriate system of property rights, the market mechanism provides a way of measuring and comparing future and present uses. Defects in the span of property rights can—indeed, usually do—lead to excessive exploitation and insufficient consideration of future uses, but the reverse can also occur at times.

Three solutions—that is, methods for assuring that the decisions made will meet the criteria of allocative efficiency—have been proposed for common-pool problems. They are (1) centralized decision-making; (2) assignment of pro rata production rights or quotas; and (3) imposition of "use" taxes.[53]

Centralized decision-making can be achieved by various devices, the most obvious being either sole ownership of the pool (public or private) or detailed public regulation. "Unitization" refers to the proposal in connection with oil pools that individual owners surrender competitive withdrawal rights in exchange for a fractional share in the whole pool, the latter to be managed by a committee or agent. It may be noted that there should be a certain tendency for private sole ownership or unitization to come about through market processes; since the value of the pool under centralized management is greater than the sum of the private values under competitive withdrawal arrangements, we might expect large individual users or co-operative groups to buy out minority rights, to the advantage of all concerned.

One deterrent to this development has been the shadow of antimonopoly statutes. It is clear that, if the pool is large enough, it may, when placed under centralized control, introduce an element of monopoly power. Another hindrance to unitization as a market process has been the fact that, if all merge save one or a few holdouts, the latter may expect to reap a large unearned gain in extractive efficiency if the unitized management adopts a more rational rate of exploitation; the holdouts thus may impose the loss of their own wasteful extraction upon the conserving group. In short, while it is in the interest of all to agree, it is in the interest of each to hold out so long as others agree. In the absence of legal powers of condemnation, a satisfactory measure of agreement (absolute unanimity is not really necessary) may not come about.

There are several difficulties in the application of the solution via centralized management to water-resource problems. In the first place, the very concept of a

[52] For an excellent analysis see A. Scott, *Natural Resources: The Economics of Conservation* (Toronto: University of Toronto Press, 1955), pp. 16–22.

[53] Scott (*ibid.*, pp. 119–21), in connection with petroleum, lists as three solutions quotas, sole ownership, and "unitization," the latter two falling under our heading of "centralized decision-making." The use-tax method, though ignored by Scott, might be called the "classical" economic solution for divergences between social and private costs (see A. C. Pigou, *The Economics of Welfare* [4th ed.; London: Macmillan & Co., 1932], p. 192). It was proposed as a solution for the problem of declining ground-water levels in James C. DeHaven, Linn A. Gore, and Jack Hirshleifer, *A Brief Survey of the Technology and Economics of Water Supply* (RAND Report R-258-RC [Santa Monica, 1953]), p. 40. An extensive comparison of the quota and use-tax methods may be found in J. W. Milliman, "Commonality, the Price System, and Use of Water Supplies," *Southern Economic Journal*, XXII (April, 1956), 426–37.

"pool" in the sense of a quantum of a resource effectively localized applies only roughly to water. There will be ground, surface, and atmospheric interconnection between "pools," and only in certain circumstances can the problems of a single area be isolated from others—unless, indeed, the area is made very large, in which case we face both the administrative and political difficulties involved in centralized administration of a resource subject to highly variable local conditions. In California, for example, the natural water supplies of the southern regions largely originate in the snow pack of the Sierras; centralized management of the pool of resources would require a bureaucratic determination of the optimal pattern of consumptive and non-consumptive uses among all the competing ends in widely separated geographical areas which could be served by the use of the resource.[54] Even in limited geographical areas, a highly varied pattern of use may exist which is hardly amenable to centralized government of the resource. Some users may pump water for irrigation, others may impound and divert for municipal supply, while still others may want sufficient river flow for navigation or saline-water repulsion. The course of action to be followed by a centralized management of the water resources of the area is far from clear and obvious. In contrast, for the oil-pool situation maximization of the monetary profit provides a comparatively simple criterion to guide solution of the problem of how, where, and when to extract the oil resource. Despite all the above, however, there are undoubtedly instances sufficiently similar to the oil-pool situation to permit a reasonable solution through centralization, most notably where a number of pumpers overlie a well-defined common underground basin. Even in this case, however, the simple profit criterion will not be available, since water is not ordinarily produced for sale on a market but for direct use by the producer. If the pumped water is used for irrigation, deciding how best to pump may also require deciding which lands to farm, a rather more complex problem than would exist if the water produced were merely to be sold on the market.

For the reasons indicated, sole ownership has rarely been the solution arrived at for common-pool problems arising in the exploitation of water resources. The solution by means of pro rata assignment of quotas (normally on some basis of historical use) is much more popular. The Colorado River Compact, for example, purported to assign the different consuming states quotas in the "common pool" (in the wider sense of the term) of the Colorado.[55] In the Delaware River cases, New York State was assigned a definite quota of the waters of the basin for use within its borders. For ground waters the famous judgment in *Pasadena* v. *Alhambra* (1949) set a precedent in apportioning property rights in a common pool.[56]

[54] We shall see that water authorities of the state of California have to some extent attempted to perform this function in the California Water Plan, with results which should not encourage emulation.

[55] We say "purported to assign" because the remarkable verbiage of the Colorado River Compact (it has been said that no two sentences in the compact are mutually consistent) seems capable of any number of equally valid or invalid divergent interpretations.

[56] A kind of apportionment had been recognized earlier in western states to the extent that prior appropriators of a common pool had rights as against subsequent appropriators (see H. E. Thomas, *The Conservation of Ground Water* [New York: McGraw-Hill Book Co., 1951], p. 256). In the Owens Valley the city of Los Angeles was enjoined from engaging in pumping operations which lowered water levels under lands owned by other interests (Ostrom, *op. cit.*, pp. 132–33). On the other hand, there has been, apparently, a growing body of thought, and at least one court decision (in Utah), denying redress to prior users (Thomas, *op. cit.*, pp. 256–57). The arguments for the latter position are based on the idea that necessity to pay damages would curtail fullest or best utilization of water supplies. This view seems to

The advantages of such an assignment include its simplicity and directness. A point of great practical importance is that the goal of the assignment is not the difficult and subtle matter of optimal use but an "equitable" apportionment of rights among claimants (some may, indeed, question that the latter is much easier than the former, but in many cases no doubt it is). Under such an apportionment the complicated questions of best use are left up to the successful claimants themselves, though perhaps with some restrictions. Another advantage is that in a certain sense the assignment of quotas does get really to the heart of the problem—the common nature of the resource—by replacing commonality of rights with specificity of shares.

There are, however, difficulties as well. First, there is the matter of "equitable" apportionment. Assignment of quotas has not prevented waste in the case of petroleum because apportionment has typically been based on "well potential," so that an incentive to drill unnecessary wells remains.[57] Where historical use is the basis, an incentive is created to initiate use excessively early in order to establish a history of use before final apportionment takes place.[58] Ideally speaking, rights to all water should be assigned once and for all, but this rarely occurs.

A second difficulty turns on the question of efficiency. A single user might, for example, concentrate all his withdrawals on a few wells near the more productive lands, whereas an "equitable" apportionment might give a distribution of quotas whose exploitation through a great many wells leads to some social waste. It might be argued that, in such circumstances, quotas will be bought and sold until they end up in the most efficient distribution. Aside from the fact that certain limitations on transfer of such rights may exist,[59] the process may not work perfectly. Thus there may be a gain in efficiency if both B and C sell their quotas to A, but it may be in the separate interest of each to hold out until the other sells, because, if C ceases pumping, B may be able to capture part of the gain in the form of locally increased water pressure or level, and vice versa. This is analogous to, if not so serious as, the problem of achieving rationality along a river, where intervening users may be in a position to reap a similar unearned benefit. The difficulty rests ultimately on the fact that the quotas really are not perfectly exchangeable between any two uses; the pool, while indeed common, has stream- or serial-use aspects.

The third and most serious difficulty turns upon the question of how to achieve rationality in the use of the resource over time. Quotas are normally thought of as being assigned to exhaust the "safe yield" of the common water pool, that is to say, the amount which on the average equals the recharge rate so as to keep water levels constant. But why should water levels be kept constant? To take a ridiculous case, suppose petroleum quotas were similarly based on safe yield—which is, of course,

---

be a reaction against the erroneous "conservationist" idea that no action should be ever taken to lower water levels, but it goes too far in implying that the loss in lowered water levels must be less than the gain from the fuller or earlier use of water. This may or may not be the case; what is necessary is some system for permitting overdraft when the loss is less than the gain but not where the reverse is the case.

57 Scott, *op. cit.*, p. 120.

58 This may have been one of the motives in the premature development of Colorado River supplies for the Metropolitan Water District of Southern California.

59 In California, for example, transfers for use outside the watershed of the basin or outside the county of origin stand in a somewhat dubious legal position, there being in each case some question of a possible superior reserved right inhering in the original location of the water. It is, of course, quite possible that some of the pumpers from a common pool might choose to adopt uses of the water that take it outside the original basin or county.

zero. To use more than the safe yield means the water supplied in past years is being "mined," but this is sometimes undoubtedly rational and may even be in the normal case. In the high plains of Texas an extreme instance of this situation exists wherein the accumulation of water over past ages has been immense, but the annual recharge is very small indeed. One other consideration is that steady improvement in the technology of pumping has taken place in the past and may be reasonably projected to the future, so that larger and larger pumping lifts may not always represent increased economic cost of pumping.

The engineering datum of the "safe yield" is not, then, the optimal rate of extraction of a water resource. Presumably, the optimal rate of extraction as a base on which to assign fractional quotas could be estimated by some centralized body acting as the agent of the owners of the pro rata rights. This optimal rate of extraction will vary with present and prospective costs and prices in the processes employing the water in question as well as with the rate of interest and pumping technology.

The third or "use-tax" solution to the common-pool problem is in some ways logically the neatest, but it has been applied in practice in only one case to the authors' knowledge—in Orange County, California. The economic theory of the solution is based on the following considerations. Each pumper, in deciding how much to withdraw, compares the marginal cost of pumping with the marginal value in use to him of the water. This will usually be the value of the marginal product, the water being normally used as an intermediate good in the production of goods and services for the market. But his withdrawals will tend to lower the water levels for everyone using the common pool—a consideration which he will ignore or at least not consider fully, because the impact on himself will be partial and may be negligible. (In certain cases, "spillover" costs of pumping may show themselves most conspicuously in the form of salt-water intrusion under someone else's lands.) The use-tax solution would require a payment which would be added to the cost of pumping so that, ideally, the individual would consider the marginal *social* cost in his decision on how much to pump rather than merely the marginal private cost. The payment, of course, would represent the loss of productivity on lands owned by others.

Figure 8 illustrates this solution. The curve labeled *vmp* represents the value of the marginal product of the water pumped for a typical individual pumper. After a certain point the curve turns downward because of diminishing returns as more and more water is applied to the productive process in question. The curve *mpc* represents the marginal private cost of securing water, that is, the cost of pumping plus the cost due to lowering of the water level under the individual's own land. The curve *msc,* or marginal social cost, differs from *mpc* in including the costs due to lowering of levels under others' lands which are a consequence of an additional unit withdrawal by this pumper. The ideal use tax would be a sliding scale equaling, for any quantity withdrawn, the vertical difference between the *mpc* and *msc* curves. Given this tax pattern, each individual would then be effectively operating along the *msc* curve; he would have to pay the cost of pumping and also the tax. In the absence of such a tax, the individual would tend to operate at the point *P,* where output is *OB* (since, to the left of *P,* he can increase output and incur an *mpc* which is less than the *vmp* gained, while, to the right of *P,* the opposite is the case). However, from the social point of view all the output between *OA* and *OB* involves a loss, because *msc* is greater than *vmp* in that range. With the tax, the rational individual will pump only to the point *Q* (output *OA*), where *msc* equals *vmp.*

In the case of Orange County, a constant per unit tax (currently $3.90 per acre-foot) on withdrawals, as well as a general property tax, has been imposed. The revenues are used to buy water from the Metropolitan Water District of Southern California and to cover the expenses of using that water to replenish the underground basin. Actually, there is no logical connection between collection of the tax and the utilization of revenues for replenishment. The primary function of the tax is to deter overdraft, and setting the tax at the appropriate level can achieve this. Purchase of outside water is only logical if the purchased water has lower marginal social cost than a corresponding drawdown of the underground supply, and use of the purchased water for replenishment rather than directly on the surface makes sense only if the underground aquifer provides a convenient distribution network. We may note that there is an element of subsidy to water-users to the extent that the general property tax levied on all, regardless of water use, is relied on for funds to benefit only those pumping water.

Turning once more to the theoretical illustration in Figure 8, we can see that, if a quota were to be set for this typical pumper, it should be equal to *OA*. A quota system would of course generate no revenue with which to repair the losses suffered.[60] Just as the aggregate of quotas

[60] Of course, the quotas might be set at such a level that no losses were suffered. It might generally be rational, however, to permit some overdraft, in which case there would be losses due to decline of water levels.

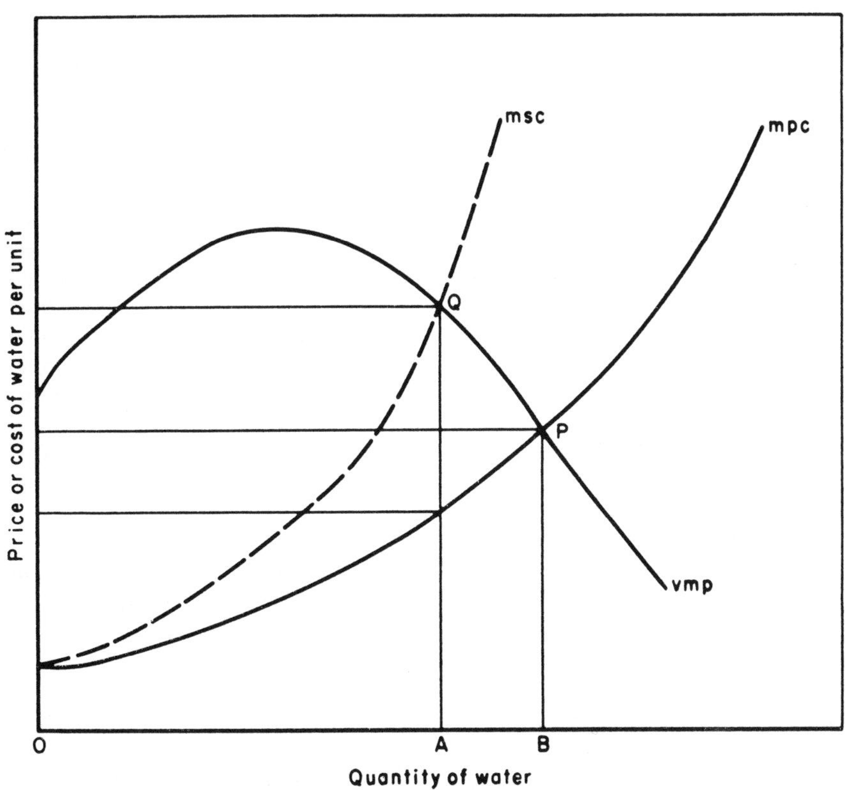

FIG. 8.—Social and private optimum in common-pool situation

would have to be decided centrally, so would the tax schedules and the use of the revenues. Both the optimum tax and the optimum quota would vary with changing prices; for example, a rise in the price of product would tend to raise *vmp,* while a reduction in the cost of electric power would tend to reduce *mpc* and *msc.* On grounds of administrative convenience, therefore, there is no clear advantage of one over the other. With regard to the difficulties adduced above in connection with the quota system, the apportionment problem is avoided by the use-tax system, and the question of efficiency in extraction probably applies equally to the two,[61] as does the difficulty in achieving rationality over time. The latter reveals itself in the use-tax solution in the problem of how to determine the marginal social cost, since the increased cost of pumping in the future imposed on others is the major element in the divergence between social cost and private cost.

Among the various possibilities, the solution to the common-pool problem that we find most attractive is the principle of establishing quota rights. The strongest arguments in favor are the simplicity and comprehensibility of the solution and the fact that the quotas come closest to remedying the logical essence of the common-pool difficulty—the non-specificity of property rights.

2. Consumptive and Non-consumptive Use

In our general discussion of resource allocation in the chapter, we did not systematically distinguish between resources being *used* and being *used up,* although this distinction really entered when we introduced the concept of complementary uses. The implicit assumption underlying the theory is that the residual value of a resource after use can be considered to be negligible or else that any residual worth can be treated as a deduction from the cost of procuring the resource. Where, as frequently occurs, the residual value is negative (i.e., where a waste product with disposal cost is what is left after use), the disposal cost is to be added to the procurement cost. In the case of water the situation is unusual in that after use the residual product, of perhaps impaired but still positive economic value, is generally passed on to some other user.

a) Technological and economic definitions of consumptive use.—The ordinary conception of consumptive use refers, as has been mentioned earlier, to phases of the hydrologic cycle. When water leaves the land phase by evaporation to the air or by runoff or percolation to the sea, it is said to be used consumptively—and otherwise not. This conception of consumptive use is clearly only a crude approximation to the underlying idea, which is that the resource has become unavailable for future use by man. To the extent that irrigation water percolates into underground reservoirs or runs off to surface streams, the use is considered non-consumptive—and yet the water may be so impaired in quality or diverted into such inconvenient channels that additional employment of the water is seriously hindered. Similarly for municipal water supplies in relation to sewage flow, the mere existence of sewage flow does not mean that something of economic value has not been consumed in the course of use of the inflowing water. Logically speaking, consumptive use of water should be thought of as a matter of degree. To the extent that subsequent uses of the water once it has gone through the process in question are impaired by the loss of one or more of the qualities that water may be considered to contain in its initial state, the process has been consumptive. The measure of consumption is not a physical but an economic one; it is the loss

[61] In theory, an ideal tax would vary for each individual in such a way as to reflect all the social costs properly, but in practice it would undoubtedly be necessary to make the tax uniform among individuals.

imposed upon society by the inability to carry on some desirable uses of the water in question or, alternatively, the extra costs in the way of purifying processes and so forth made necessary if the subsequent uses are not abandoned.

In fact, the question of consumptive versus non-consumptive use is obviously related to the existence of what we have previously called "complementary uses" of water (e.g., utilization of the water in a stream for navigation and waste-disposal simultaneously or sequential employment of water first for hydropower and then for irrigation or industry downstream). Any use of water is always and necessarily consumptive with respect to other uses that are competitive with it; a given use can be non-consumptive only to the extent that potentially complementary other uses exist. Along a river, therefore, upstream irrigation may be non-consumptive insofar as return flow contributes to downstream uses. But a downstream irrigator's use will be entirely consumptive, irrespective of return flows, if there are no users farther downstream.

With this economic definition, it is interesting to re-examine the usual technological definition of consumption in terms of hydrologic phases. Since it can be said that a marginal unit of water in the ocean is of negligible value to anyone, runoff to the ocean is wholly consumptive. But note that, in the strictest technological sense, the only consumptive use of water would be some sort of chemical recombination that actually reduced the amount of water available on the globe. (Such changes are, of course, negligible in magnitude compared with the recurring flow of water in the hydrologic cycle.) By considering runoff to the oceans consumptive, an economic rather than a strictly technological criterion is already being implicitly used.

Turning now to water in the atmosphere, it has already been remarked that, while only a very small fraction of the water is at any moment of time locked up in this form, nevertheless atmospheric water is critical in representing a kind of distribution pipeline between the ocean reservoir and man's utilization facilities. It seems reasonable to believe, then, that the loss of water in the land phase to the atmosphere is less consumptive than loss to the oceans. Qualitatively, this statement is undoubtedly true, and yet an increment to atmospheric water might still be of negligible economic value. In looking into the question of the marginal value of atmospheric water, we face considerable uncertainty about the underlying meteorological processes. If we assumed that, for example, the atmosphere simply absorbed an increment of water gained through evaporation, evaporative losses would be totally consumptive. As an alternative assumption, the atmospheric water might be considered substantially constant, so that an increase of evaporation entailed as a consequence a corresponding increase in precipitation somewhere else. Even under the latter assumption, the distribution of the increase in precipitation (which would be influenced by the initial temperature and humidity of the air, winds, topography, etc.) might be such as to produce little of economic value. Setting aside the possibility of the rainfall in question occurring outside the nation's land area, the current aggregate use patterns of precipitation provides some guide as to incremental economic value. Since current gross utilization constitutes about 6 per cent of precipitation (plus some undetermined fraction of the 72 per cent consumed via evapotranspirative loss, part of which is beneficial), it may well be that in terms of a calculation of probabilities an increase in atmospheric water due to evaporation does on the margin have a small expected economic value. In considering this residual value of evaporative loss, we must remember that the uncertainty of the benefit in time and place reduces it substantially (a firm water supply is more valuable than an occasional and variable one). The marginal value may be small enough to neglect as a practical matter, but this has not really been proved. All we really know is that no one in his *private* calculations takes account of it, but that may be due only to the fact that the benefit is a fugitive one. In any case, atmospheric water will definitely rise in value if and when control of precipitation becomes a practical matter. This atmospheric water will then constitute a "common-pool" problem of the type considered earlier.

If we examine the supposedly "non-consumptive uses," we shall see that almost in every case there is in the course of use some impairment of one or more of the qualities of water which give it economic value. The use of falling water to generate power is universally considered non-consumptive; actually, what is being consumed here is the potential energy, which is, evidently, of enormous value. Another apparently non-consumptive use is cooling, but here the temperature of the water is its valuable property and will be impaired by use. Navigation is normally non-consumptive in and of itself, but the provision of water for navigation may involve diversions affecting other uses (e.g., maintenance of stream flows for navigation may preclude use of water for irrigation). Water percolating underground after irrigational or domestic use may be impaired in quality or may flow to areas or depths where further use by man is costly.

b) *Economic implications of consumptive use.*—As implied in the above, water may contain a number of qualities of economic significance; among them are location in time and space, temperature, and purity in the chemical or bacteriological sense. The utilization of any of these qualities may impair the water for similar or dissimilar subsequent uses. What creates a social problem is the fact that the degraded water flows out of the influence and control of the user, so that in many cases he has no incentive to consider measures which might mitigate the impairment. To some extent, indeed, the impairment may be intrinsic to the use. Water power cannot be generated without loss of potential energy of water. In other cases, however, the impairment is capable of modification or correction. An industrial plant at some cost could adjust its processes so as to cease venting noxious chemicals into streams, or a municipality could treat its sewage before disposal. In various uses, losses to ocean or through evaporation can be reduced.

In all these cases it is not immediately clear or obvious that the steps necessary to reduce or prevent degradation in the economic quality of water in use should be adopted. The costs to society of the corrective measures may exceed those imposed by the loss of the value of water for some purposes. Nevertheless, under existing institutions there may be no way at all for the latter costs to be taken into consideration. Thus downstream users might in the aggregate be able to more than compensate an upstream industrial plant responsible for chemical pollution (this constitutes evidence that the loss through pollution is greater than the cost of correcting it by purification or by shutting down), but there may be no device for making the collective decision involved. Or there may be no way to control establishment of new sources of pollution. Finally, those forms of state control devised to cope with this problem tend to be highly arbitrary. For example, regulations that water to downstream users be passed on unimpaired in quantity and quality would prohibit even extremely valuable uses which, if undertaken, would allow of full compensation of downstream users for their losses through pollution or reduced deliveries. Actually, the problem involved may be one which calls not for prohibitions but for an economic solution to provide the correct incentives under a permissive system of private initiative.

c) Theoretical and practical solutions for problems of consumptive use.—Imagine a situation in which there are a number of landholders surrounding a surface body of water like a lake or overlying a common underground aquifer, and where the different landholders, while possibly all withdrawing the same gross amount of water, vary in the amounts they return to the common pool. A withdrawal that is returned, of course, is non-consumptive in that it makes possible reuse of the water; only withdrawals that are not returned represent water demands competitive with other possible uses. Since our basic principle is equimarginal value in use as among competitive demands, it follows in this simple case (neglecting possible complications involving water levels as discussed in Appendix A, or water quality) that the appropriate measure of water is consumptive use. If the water in question is sold to the landholders, there should be a common price to all in terms of units of water consumptively used. Or rights to a certain rate of consumptive use per year or per season could be vested as property, in which case a free market in such rights would tend to make the water find its most valuable use. It is normal, of course, to specify water prices or property rights in terms of gross use; this could be reconciled with our analysis by a system providing some form of credit for return flows.

A more complex and interesting set of problems arises when we consider use of water from a flowing river or stream. In this case exchanges between upstream and downstream users may affect uses at intermediate locations; instead of a simple common pool we have a situation of sequential use. Here each possible alternative upstream use is likely to be associated with a train of downstream uses complementary with it. Our basic principle where groups of complementary uses exist, it will be remembered, is that water should be so divided among competing groups as to equalize the joint marginal product of each such set. We also indicated that the joint marginal product of a group of complementary uses is to be found by adding the separate marginal products of each member of the group, so that the height of the joint demand curve is the vertical sum of the separate demand curves.[62]

However, this rule is rather too simple in failing to recognize that allied uses along a stream are likely to be only partially complementary, because upstream uses are usually consumptive to some extent and also because there are transport losses to consider. Limiting ourselves to the least complicated case for illustration of the principle involved, we will ignore losses in transport and will, in addition, suppose that the stream under consideration has but a single source or else that all users are downstream of a point beyond which the river receives no further accretions of supply. Then the joint marginal product of a group of complementary users can be evaluated at such an upstream point, for comparison with other, competing groups of complementary users, according to the following formula, in which there are assumed to be r separate users, and where JMP represents joint marginal product, MP_i the specific marginal product in the ith sequential use, f_i the fraction of water withdrawn by the group (at the upstream point of measurement) that is employed in the ith use, and c_i the proportionate consumption of water employed in that use:

$$JMP = f_1 MP_1 + f_2 MP_2 + \ldots + f_r MP_r .$$

The joint marginal product will only equal the simple sum of the separate marginal products if each successive use takes the full original flow (all the $f_i = 1$), which can occur only if all uses before the last are fully non-consumptive. In general, the sum of the f_i will exceed 1, since

$$1 = f_1 c_1 + f_2 c_2 + \ldots + f_r c_r ,$$

62 This principle was stated in Tolley and Hastings, *op. cit.*, p. 283.

and each of the $c_i \leq 1$, except that c_r necessarily equals 1—the absence of any uses further downstream makes the rth use wholly consumptive.

It is *JMP* as defined here which is to be equalized among the competing groups of complementary users. However, we have not yet explained the crucial step of how the f_i are determined. Clearly, the basic principle must be to establish the f_i so that *marginal products per unit of consumptive use are equalized:*

$$\frac{MP_1}{c_1} = \frac{MP_2}{c_2} = \ldots = \frac{MP_r}{c_r}.$$

Optimal allocation within a (partially) complementary group, therefore, is determined by equating marginal products per unit of consumptive use—and among groups by equating joint marginal products.

Turning now to market processes, there is a possible source of difficulty if water is sold as a commodity by a public or private utility, because of the necessity for complementary users to join together in presenting a unified demand for water in competition with other groups. Nevertheless, this does commonly occur when, for example, a private or mutual company or irrigation district is set up to divert water from a stream and serve it to all users along a given ditch. Within the complementary group the price of water delivered to downstream users should tend to be higher than for upstream users, because of the factor of losses in transport which we have omitted in our simplified analysis.[63] That is, equal prices for water *reserved* upstream will amount to differentially higher prices for water *delivered* to locations subject to greater loss from evaporation and seepage en route. If, instead of sale of water as a commodity, vesting of rights as property is adopted, water will tend to find its most efficient use if purchase and sale of rights among and within complementary groups are permitted. Vesting as between competing groups should be in terms of diversions from the stream (if the groups are strictly competing, there should be no return flows from one group to another); within a partially complementary group, vesting should, as in the simpler non-sequential pool case analyzed earlier, be in terms of consumptive use.[64]

When we turn to the consumptive use of qualities of water, the problem becomes more difficult. In principle, for example, rights to waste pollutants into a body of standing water could be held and sold. However, there is here an unavoidable "technological spillover" not ordinarily present in the case where it is only the quantity which is of concern. If one consumer wished to upgrade the quality of his water by buying up some of the pollutant rights, an unearned benefit will be reaped by all other users of the water in the form of enhanced quality of input water. Therefore, although all users may be in a position to gain by a reduction of pollution, it may be impossible to get them to club together voluntarily and use the market mechanism to buy up pollutant rights; each may hope the others will go ahead and confer the unearned benefit upon him. Here it is the addition to purity of the water which becomes a "fugitive" resource so that market incentives do not work properly.

The same spillover problem exists, in a somewhat modified context, where waters of a flowing stream are involved. Here any exchanges in consumptive use of quality between upstream and downstream users will obviously affect, for good or ill, all intervening users. And the complexity of

[63] A method of allowing for losses in transport in finding the optimal pattern of sequential water use is demonstrated by Tolley and Hastings (*ibid.*, pp. 284–86).

[64] One clear case is the Colorado River Compact which explicitly allocates or "apportions" consumptive use; one of the quarrels among the signatories of the compact concerns just how the return flows are to be credited in determining the "beneficial consumptive use" allowed each state.

the problem is far greater than we have indicated in view of the tremendous number of dimensions of quality which may or may not be of significance in particular situations—temperature, color, dissolved salts, bacteriological contamination, radioactivity, etc.

In such circumstances an efficient allocation is not impossible of achievement, even if we set aside the possibility of state dictation of the solution. The difficulty inheres in the fact of intervening users (or their counterparts when waters other than those of a stream are in question) who are necessarily affected in any attempt to change the pattern of utilization. What is required is some sort of institution for permitting changes to take place while assuring that the value of rights of intervening users will be preserved, without impairment or accretion. Where intervening users are harmed, some estimate of damage must be provided so that they may be compensated; where the change is for some important public purpose, under present law the exercise of eminent domain makes provision for such compensation. The problem of preventing intervening users from appropriating gains paid for by others may require some kind of legal device for coming to an arrangement equitable to all interests. What is involved here is a kind of adjudication not wholly unrelated to the apportionment of original rights in water, for which provision is presently made in the water laws of at least the arid states. While the institutions are not yet developed, the underlying principle is reasonably clear: all two-party agreements should be permitted and given legal effect, while affected third parties should be granted full compensation for damages but prevented from capturing unearned benefits. To some extent the role of the watermaster in adjusting water rights to variations in stream flow and the like provides a precedent here.

A legal solution of the type discussed will, unfortunately, sometimes involve compulsion for some of the affected third parties. The latter may refuse to accept, for example, the valuation placed on their impaired rights by a compensation board or by a judicial reviewing authority. This problem already exists, of course, where eminent domain is exercised. In such cases there is a conflict between the requirements for economic efficiency and the general desire for a free society, including in the latter concept the freedom to enjoy one's property as legally acquired and used. In view of the strong appeal of the latter idea, it is quite possible that the institutions necessary to achieve economic efficiency in the cases described may never develop beyond those exercises of the law of eminent domain reluctantly accepted today; and, of course, the loss of economic efficiency in such cases may not be too high a price to pay for such freedom.

There are, fortunately, wide classes of cases in which the market will lead to efficient solutions because third parties are not substantially affected or because voluntary agreement can be arrived at such that all share in the benefit of the change (if the change is actually desirable, there must be a net benefit capable of being shared). We may comment here that the trend to state regulation of market exchanges of water, to be discussed in chapter ix, in our opinion can be justified only by the existence of spillover problems like those discussed. It appears, however, that the water commissions set up under the new state water codes will be used to bar perfectly good transfers of use rather than, as we recommend, to provide compensation for adversely affected third parties (or to prevent unearned gains to favorably affected ones).

d) Charges for consumptive and nonconsumptive use.—We may now turn to a consideration of the possibility of instituting a set of charges for water use which would somehow reflect not gross use (as all present rate systems do) but rather net or consumptive use. A city reclaiming water from sewage, for example, might want to encourage uses of water that make sewage available as opposed to other uses that lead to evaporation or underground percolation. More frequently, it is return of water through underground percolation which is desirable, since the increase in ground-water levels will make pumping easier. In each case, of course, there would be qualitative as well as quantitative considerations to be taken into account.

To some extent, systems of regulation have grown up which do distinguish between gross and consumptive use, usually by barring "excessively" consumptive uses. In many areas, for example, restrictions are placed on lawn or irrigation sprinkling[65] and on pollution of streams by factories. But, it follows from our argument earlier, there is no sound reason for discriminating against such uses once the extra consumption is allowed for; if someone valued his lawn very highly and was willing to pay for the full consumption of water in intensive sprinkling, he should not be arbitrarily barred from doing so. The problem, rather, is to find a method of charging which would reflect the consumptive use.

Actually, an ideal method of charging should take some account of both gross use and consumptive use rather than depend on the latter entirely. Thus to take 100 units of water and return 0 may not be the same as to take 200 and return 100. The ideal solution would recognize that there are two commodities, input water and output water; it would charge for the first and give a credit for the second.

The practical difficulty here is measuring the water returned, especially where variations in quality are also involved. That is to say, the problem is akin to the metering question in municipal water supply: Are the avoidable losses due to inefficient allocation greater than the increased costs of measurement? While this problem has rarely been explicitly faced, it does seem to be the case that the practical difficulties of return metering of sewage are great. Even if the degree of contamination were not in itself a problem, it would make upkeep of meters more difficult, and there are other troublesome technical factors as well. Furthermore, where it is ground return which is valued, difficulties of measurement are generally even greater.

There are, nevertheless, some instances in which a credit for return water would not be impractical. In the case of users along a stream or ditch, the diversion net of returns can be measured simply by differences in flow upstream and downstream of the use in question. If only the consumptive use were important, this net diversion would be the relevant unit of water for pricing purposes. In the general case when both gross and net diversions are of significance, the former could be measured by an ordinary input meter and the latter by difference in net flows, with perhaps some adjustment for quality.

Another case of some significance exists when there are two interconnected basins, the lower one benefiting by ground return from upper-basin uses. It is conceivable that the lower basin could, as a collective unit, offer the upper basin some form of bounty to encourage such ground return, the benefit being measured by changes in ground-water levels in the lower basin. This leaves open the question of just how the upper basin as a collective acts to encourage such ground return by its members.

Finally, some closer approximation of an

[65] We are speaking of restrictions on sprinkling imposed because of the high degree of consumptive use rather than merely as a way of rationing a limited gross supply in a period of "shortage." To the extent that the latter is the case, the price being charged for water is too low, and it is inefficient to correct this error by arbitrarily penalizing one among the great many classes of water-users. The restriction will make the marginal value in use for sprinkling higher than for unrestricted uses paying only the low established price.

efficient allocation can come about by charging special license fees for water-consumptive uses of various kinds rather than simply barring or arbitrarily restricting such uses. Thus sprinkler irrigators might have to pay a license fee of $\$x$ per acre per year, the amount x being calculated as the difference between the value of return water from normal irrigation (percolation which replenishes ground water for others pumping from the same pool) and that from sprinkler irrigation. This solution is not ideal because, once the license fee is paid, there is no incentive to conserve, but there will be some partial deterrent effect of the fee itself. An absolute prohibition, by comparison, would bar the use of sprinklers even where the gain from their use exceeded the loss incurred by reduction of return flow.

As a concluding generalization, it seems safe to say that the distinction between gross and net, or consumptive and non-consumptive, uses is one which still has not been properly appreciated. At least, those in responsible positions have not yet understood that what is involved is an economic problem rather than a moral problem of "waste" or of "failing to consider the rights of others." As the rate of gross utilization of the nation's water supplies steadily rises, the problem of efficient *reuse* of water will increase in importance—and, of course, this problem is simply the problem of consumptive versus non-consumptive use seen from a different aspect.

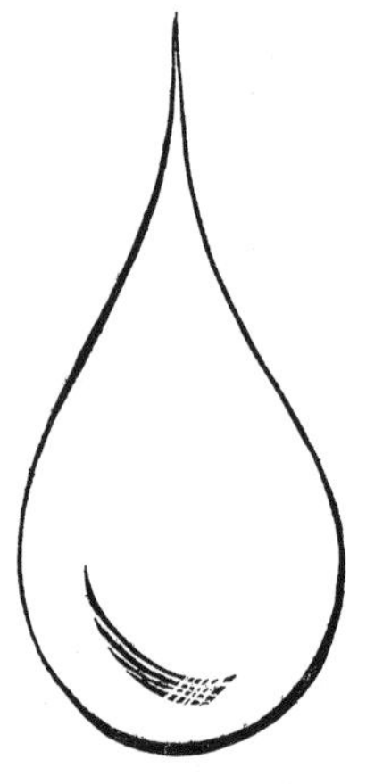

CHAPTER IV

CRITICISMS OF MARKET ALLOCATIONS
THE POLITICAL ALLOCATION PROCESS

In this chapter we plan to take up certain more or less philosophical questions turning upon objections which can be or have been made against the line of argument of our chapter iii. We shall attempt to evaluate the significance of a number of the more important or more familiar criticisms commonly raised against economic analyses of resource allocation alternatives or against the central idea of achieving an economic optimum using market values as the criterion of the marginal desirability of the goods produced and the resources consumed.

Individuals who make such criticisms usually go on to infer that the valid demonstration of defects in market solutions calls for or justifies government intervention to correct them. This, however, is a *non sequitur;* it seems to imply that the government decision process is free from error or at least can be relied on to correct in the right direction—which might well be debated. Accordingly, the second major topic of this chapter will be a consideration of the political decision process as a method of performing the economic function of allocating a commodity like water.

A. Some Objections to the Theory of Choice and to Market Allocations

In the discussion which follows, we shall for the sake of convenience classify the objections considered[1] into two categories: (1) those that, while possibly conceding that market values are correct in terms of what they purport to measure (the relative scarcity of goods and resources and consumers' valuations of them), maintain that there are certain *extra-economic values* which should be considered as well, and (2) those that maintain that market processes lead to *incorrect* valuations even in their own terms. To some extent this discussion parallels our treatment in chapter vi of "intangibles" in water-resource investment decisions.

1. Extra-economic Values

a) *"Valued ideals."*—It is clear that society, or rather the individuals composing society, value other things aside from com-

[1] A rather different list of objections is considered, on a more abstract level, in R. A. Dahl and C. E. Lindblom, *Politics, Economics, and Welfare* (New York: Harper & Bros., 1953), pp. 385–93.

modities (goods and services). "Liberty, equality, fraternity" comprises one such set of valued ideals, not reducible in any obvious way to economic measurement. While some such set of ideals (the French Revolutionary formulation may not really be perfectly apt for present-day America) is almost unanimously held, it is hard to show what bearing these ideals have on the allocation of resources. If, for example, a change in the direction of our nation's producing more water and fewer shoes definitely increased our liberty, other things being equal, many of us might favor the change even if it was not indicated by market valuations, but it seems unlikely that any such effect would be ascertainable.[2] On the other hand, consideration of the costs of producing the two commodities—the goods and services the resources in question might produce in alternative employments—or of how much consumers are willing to pay for them is, while mundane, unquestionably relevant.

b) *"Higher" and "lower" tastes.*—Economic values place all desires (or, rather, all desires expressed in the form of monetary demands) on a par. The desire to provide one's children with milk is given no special weight or preference in the market as compared with the desire for entertainment. In part this question touches upon the matter of the distribution of wealth (to be discussed later), but for the present we may assume that we are comparing the desires of people at a given income level. It seems plausible to assert that there are higher and lower tastes and that economic values fail to indicate this distinction, though society does recognize it in extreme cases. For example, society prohibits satisfaction of the taste for consumption of narcotics, taxes heavily such tastes as those for cigarettes and alcoholic liquor, and largely disregards the preferences of certain of its members (e.g., infants, mental defectives, and convicts).

This problem raises difficult philosophical questions. If we regarded individual preferences as ultimate and so as the only criterion of value in our society, then such government interventions could be justified only on the grounds that the individual was somehow incompetent to judge or act on his own preferences or that satisfaction of the tastes in question harmed other individuals. While the interventions we are speaking of can be defended along such lines, it may be that a full explanation is not provided thereby. Consideration of this question will, however, lead us far astray. As a practical matter, it is not unreasonable under normal conditions to assume that at any moment of time the existing pattern of prohibitions, penalties, and taxes, on the one hand, and commandments, bounties, and subsidies, on the other—together with corresponding extralegal social pressures—reflects the degree to which society on balance would have the preferences in question encouraged or discouraged in their attempt to seek satisfaction through the market place. So, while tastes may be higher or lower, law and custom presumably allow for this. (We are on somewhat difficult ground here because, on the one hand, we are subjecting laws and policies to critical analysis and making recommendations with a view to their improvement, but, on the other hand, we at times accept results of the political process as data reflecting social preferences and so outside the sphere of criticism. We attempt to explain this paradox in the next section.)

It is worth pointing out, however, that

[2] That is, we can scarcely ever assert that "liberty" is tied up with producing one commodity rather than another. Valued ideals may, however, be closely associated with the *process of decision.* For example, a strong concern for liberty would imply minimal use of the coercive state power—a leaning in the direction of laissez faire. Our own evaluation of the market and the political *processes* does take into account these valued ideals in addition to the question of comparative economic efficiency.

usually a crude error is committed in arguing about higher and lower tastes. The example of children's milk versus entertainment is really in this class of argument. The confusion here consists of failing to take account of the fact that all tastes are balanced on the margin. Thus, if one had to choose between the combination of entertainment but no milk for children and milk for children but no entertainment, undoubtedly milk for children should be chosen. But this is not the relevant choice, and there is no call for intervention on this score. Surely, there is nothing wrong with purchasing entertainment (which is, after all, a valid human need) with a dollar when the increment to satisfaction of an extra dollar on milk falls sufficiently low as a consequence of having spent a reasonable amount already for that purpose. Since all rational consumers are behaving in this way, we can say that *on the margin* the taste for milk is no "higher" or more worthy of satisfaction than the taste for entertainment. Of course, if society felt that there was a systematic pattern at least among some classes to choose too much entertainment and too little milk, it could tax the former and subsidize the latter. Presumably, this is not the dominant opinion except, possibly, as such an undesired pattern of consumption is brought about through inequalities in the distribution of wealth, to which we now turn.

c) Economic values and the distribution of wealth.—There are two main questions which come up under this heading. First, it might be maintained that the desire for a more equal distribution of wealth is an extra-economic value which ought to be taken into consideration in resource allocation problems. Second, and more radically, some would argue that, since the existing distribution of wealth and talents clearly affects the conditions of demand and of supply which determine prices and values in use, and since this distribution is generally agreed not to be ideal, it follows that the entire structure of economic values is a highly defective guide for resource allocation.

There is no doubt that "equality" is a widely shared ideal in American life, but the concept itself is a somewhat vague blend of equality before the law, equality of opportunity, and equality of status (status being primarily due to wealth and income). These "equalities" are not only not identical but hardly even mutually consistent; equality of opportunity, for example, conflicts with equality of wealth and income. Furthermore, it might even be argued that there is some public preference for inequality. Finally, there is difficulty even defining equality of wealth and income where some jobs require more time, trouble, and expense invested in education than others or have a different set of nonpecuniary advantages or disadvantages.

When all is said and done, some degree of preference probably exists, on balance,[3] for equality of status. Presumably, our population would be willing to accept a somewhat smaller real income in exchange for a somewhat more equal division. Our progressive income tax and death duties constitute evidence for this proposition. But this equalitarian sentiment has its limitations. While the dominating opinion is that the rich should share disproportionately in bearing the general cost of government, we do not have a "redistribution budget" which clearly and purposively transfers wealth from the rich to the poor.

So far as resource allocation is concerned, a "redistribution budget" would simplify matters; then the most efficient allocation could always be adopted, with any undesired redistributive consequences corrected through the redistribution budg-

[3] The phrase "on balance" here is to be taken to mean "as preferences are balanced through our existing political and economic processes."

et.[4] The absence of such an institution, on the one hand, generates some doubt about the genuineness of the sentiment for equality of status and, on the other, requires that redistribution be achieved largely through inefficient economic allocations. In general, our presumption will be that the existing pattern of redistributive legislation is a deliberate social choice establishing a generally accepted balance between aggregate income and equality of status. This balance implies that additional redistribution one way or the other within a given total would be of dubious general acceptability; but improvements in efficiency increasing total wealth without drastically affecting distribution can be presumed to be desirable.

We turn now to the more radical question involving economic values and the distribution of wealth—the allegation that, since the determination of economic values is dependent upon the pre-existing ownership of resources, the arbitrariness or inequity of the latter (and presumably of the distribution of native talent as well as wealth) carries over to cast great doubt upon the social significance of economic values and economic efficiency. Here again we can conclude that, from its mere existence which can in part be regarded as a social choice, the existing distribution of wealth (or, more properly, the existing socioeconomic system which generates wealth and its distribution) can claim considerable social sanction. Even if, on balance, society might prefer a different distribution (setting aside the question of how this might be determined), it seems hardly probable that any politically conceivable redistribution would change the structure of market values very much. An equalitarian redistribution, for example, would very likely lower the prices of yachts and of lard (commodities primarily consumed at the ends of the wealth spectrum) and raise the prices of goods appealing to the middle-income groups, but it does not seem likely that the effect would be governing for water-resource allocation decisions.

[4] This implies the possibility of redistribution at zero or at low cost. If only moderate redistribution were desired, it could very likely be achieved at little cost through capital levies and grants. Sufficiently drastic redistributions become very costly, primarily because of the impact on incentives.

2. *Incorrectness of the Market Values*

Economists think of market values as serving a number of functions in our economic system. Prices by their fluctuations register and signal the continually changing relative intensities of demand and supply of commodities and resources; they ration the limited supplies available at any moment of time to the potential consumers or users whose effective demands are the greatest; and they guide production, through the profit motive of producers, into those lines where the demand is the strongest relative to the goods available and the costs of production.

In contrast, there is a rather widespread, if naïve, belief held by many that market prices are arbitrary measurements imposed in a capricious manner on goods and services. *The Report of the President's Water Resources Policy Commission* (1950) perhaps illustrates this belief, as indicated by the following:

> There are many types of public objectives and gains which defy analysis in commercial terms. For example, market price valuation can give quite misleading results when applied to public measures designed to stop resources deterioration and to strengthen the resources base of the country. Market prices reflect scarcity values; thus, if half our forests were burned, the remainder would be worth more money than the existing forests because of the very sharp rise in prices of forest products that would take place.
>
> A commercial property has *dollar* value according to scarcity; a Nation's resources have *security* value if they are so plentiful as to be

cheap. Thus, a successful irrigation or drainage program might lead to a great reduction in the dollar value of some particular crop; the more that is planted and protected, the less it is worth; and *the stronger is the Nation.* This basic conflict between private values based on scarcity and public values based on plenty lies at the very heart of the conservation problem.[5]

This puzzling quotation is an attempt to justify public construction of uneconomic projects—projects whose outputs are of lower market value than the required resource inputs—on the ground that scarcity values in the market represent merely commercial considerations. The technical error is the inference from the sound premise that abundance is undoubtedly good and scarcity bad to the unsound conclusion that abundance should be sought by ignoring scarcity. Unfortunately, scarcity is a fact of life, and it is not difficult to show that abundance is more effectively sought by taking account of this fact. Thus, if a given resource input could produce a barrel of petroleum or a barrel of water, we would be wise to adopt the former project under present conditions in this country, though we could imagine situations in the Sahara Desert where the reverse would be true. This is, of course, equivalent to saying that we should decide so as to produce the higher-valued product.[6] And if a choice between a barrel of oil or a barrel of water as an input in producing some commodity had to be made, each being equally productive, again it is clear that scarcity relative to demand is the governing consideration, the relative market price correctly telling us to consume the less scarce (cheaper) resource.

Despite the fact that dissatisfaction with market values may often reflect confused thinking, or at times deliberate obfuscation on the part of those seeking to derive some benefit thereby, there are a number of arguments with substance which can be made on this score. We will discuss here market imperfections (whether a result of private or government actions), divergences between social and private costs, collective consumption goods, and the problem of depression and unemployment.

a) Market imperfections.—The theoretical and empirical consequences of a number of market imperfections—monopoly and oligopoly, rigidities and frictional elements hindering the response of price to changing conditions, irrational behavior,[7] and the lack of full information—have been studied in considerable detail in technical economic literature. The traditional analysis of monopoly leads to the conclusion that a monopolized good is made artificially scarce, in the sense that the price of the good is raised by the monopolist over the cost to society of producing more of the good (the marginal cost). In this

[5] *The Report of the President's Water Resources Policy Commission,* Vol. I: *A Water Policy for the American People* (Washington, D.C.: Government Printing Office, 1950), pp. 60–61.

[6] The forest illustration used in the quotation may seem to contradict this. Burning down half the nation's forests would obviously not be a good "project" even if the remaining half, because of the sharp consequent rise in price, had a higher market value than the original forests. (The price rise might or might not be great enough to make this so.) The basic error here is that the rise in market value of the undestroyed forests is a "pecuniary spillover effect" in terms of our analysis in chapter iii. The price rise represents no real increase in the productive capabilities of the economy but rather an improvement in the competitive market position of the fortunate owners of the remaining forests—and actually their gain is exactly balanced by a corresponding additional cost imposed on their customers. The owners and customers for the products of the destroyed forests suffer a real loss, not balanced by gains elsewhere. So this example, which purports to show the incorrectness of market values, really demonstrates the error involved in counting certain pecuniary spillovers as "secondary" or "indirect" benefits or costs of a project. This error will be discussed in some detail in chapter vi.

[7] By "irrational behavior" we mean behavior not consistent with the preferences of the economic unit making the decision. Such behavior presumably tends to be eliminated by the learning process and so may be regarded as associated with disequilibrium situations.

country there is a variety of regulatory and market checks on private monopoly power, and it is difficult to make any general statement about how wide the divergence between marginal cost and price actually is. While in principle allocation decisions for any commodity should take these divergences into account, we would regard the attempt to do so as requiring analyses more refined than the current state of economic science permits.

Perhaps the strongest case for taking market imperfections into account can be made for those commodities whose prices are inflated by government action—most conspicuously, supported agricultural commodities, though a number of mineral products are also price supported, and the argument could be extended to tariff-protected industries as well. Consider a supported commodity in excess supply at the going market price—cotton, for example. The true value to the society of additional excess cotton may be zero (if the cotton will just be uselessly stored, it is of no use to anyone) rather than its market price. In principle, then for any other commodity like water, an argument can be made for using water allocations to encourage the consumption of cotton (e.g., by a favorable water price to cotton-consuming industries) and to discourage the production of cotton (by, e.g., an unfavorable water price to irrigators on farms producing cotton). For a variety of reasons we regard this idea as impractical and believe that the water industry should leave the cure for market imperfections to others. Analysts might reasonably go so far as to point out to Congress or to the executive agencies that, for instance, a new cotton irrigation proposal is based on an inflated estimate of benefits to the extent that it credits the prospective cotton yield of the project at artificial scarcity values when the true value of additional cotton may be much lower or even zero. But the place to correct the error is in the decisions of Congress and the executive agencies rather than in water pricing or allocation. Similarly, for private monopolies, perhaps they should be regulated or broken up; but the pricing of water is a rather poor instrument for correcting the failure to do so. And again the same argument applies against attempting in water-allocation decisions to correct for rigidities, irrational behavior, imperfect information, or disequilibrium conditions in general elsewhere in the economy.

b) *Divergences between private and social costs.*—In resource allocation decisions in general, and in water allocations specifically, divergences between social and private cost are not uncommon; they represent possible "spillover" effects of private decisions upon other members of society. What we have called "technological" rather than merely "pecuniary" spillovers are those which should be taken into account (from an economic efficiency point of view). Conspicuous instances of such divergences exist in the case of "fugitive" resources—resources that are not definitely owned by any individual but are subject to the law of capture. Wildlife is a particularly clear example, becoming property only if captured. The case of a common pool of water or petroleum underlying divided surface holdings, where each owner may pump up the resource without restriction, is logically parallel (it has been discussed in detail in Appendix B to chap. iii). In each of these cases, private incentives work so as to give insufficient weight to society's need for the resource in the future. The reason is that anyone who sacrifices a current use (e.g., by refraining from shooting buffalo) cannot be assured that he will reap the benefit of his abstinence by increased availability of buffalo to him in the future, since other individuals might and generally would come along and exercise the rule of capture on the privately preserved resource. This situation represents the strongest argument of and justification for the "conservation movement." Still other divergences between private and social cost affect current resource allocations. A well-known example is water or air pollution—a part of the real cost to society of waste from certain industrial or extractive processes does not affect the private calculations of those responsible for the polluting uses.

How should these divergences between private and social costs (and benefits) of alternative actions be taken into account in resource allocation decisions? The most common solution is state intervention to prohibit certain actions imposing conspicuous or very large costs on others, while other types of action go completely unregulated. Several solutions suggested by economic theory have been discussed in detail in Appendix B to chapter iii for the case of common exploitation of ground-water resources. We may point out here, however, that the essential difficulty is improper or incomplete delimitation of property rights. If one could gain property rights in a buffalo by not killing it today, there *would* be a motive rationally to compare present and future uses of that animal. If one were not permitted to pump up all the oil in a common pool but instead had a pro rata share in the over-all exploitation of that pool, there would be no incentive to drill offset wells simply to prevent loss of oil to neighbors.

c) *Collective consumption goods.*—One interesting class of goods and services which a laissez faire market tends to undervalue are those which are intrinsically consumed collectively—by the entire community rather than by particular individuals. The classical illustration is national defense. The argument here goes that, if, for example, the armed services determined their expenditure levels on the basis of individual payments in return for enhanced national defense, too low a level of defense would be provided. The reason is not any lack of individual appreciation for the benefits of defense but rather the fact that each individual's payment would redound to the advantage of all, with little or no observable increment of protection for himself. In these circumstances the temptation is for each individual in isolation to pay little or nothing, despite the fact that he might be willing to pay a large amount on condition that others did also. In a way, the problem of collective consumption goods can be regarded as an instance of a divergence between social and private benefits and thus analogous to the topic considered just above.

Now, while it is true that the market under laissez faire undervalues these collective consumption goods (other examples are lighthouse services, non-toll highways, and flood protection), we can regard the communal and governmental institutions as being established primarily to provide agencies for expressing these group demands. Governments will therefore bid in the market against individuals for the resources necessary to provide defense, police services, lighthouses, etc., and we cannot readily conclude that the structure of existing market values is incorrect unless we maintain that there is some systematic source of error here—for example, that government is doing generally too much or too little or perhaps too much in some areas and too little in others. In the absence of any such demonstration, we see no reason to object to existing market values on the score of undervaluing collective needs.

Benefits to national defense are often claimed on behalf of particular water-resource projects. It should be remembered that we are here speaking not of the general gain to the nation's economy and welfare from the adoption of efficient projects but rather of some special national defense advantage justifying the adoption of what would otherwise be an inefficient project. In principle, there may be such a "spill-over" benefit, in which case it should be credited to the project at the best estimate of its economic worth in terms of military expenses avoided or improvement in protection obtained (see our discussion of benefit-cost analysis in chap. vi). As a practical matter, however, we must recognize that national defense considerations are usually dragged into resource allocation problems as a rationalization by parties at interest. One way of separating valid from invalid defense arguments would be to require, where an economically inefficient allocation is to be made on the basis of defense considerations, that the proposal come from the military departments of government and that the extra costs involved be borne by the military budget. In this way, the military authorities will be led to balance the costs and gains from economically inefficient dispersal, for example, against the costs and gains of ships, tanks, and planes.

We cannot pretend, however, that this suggestion solves the problem. For administrative reasons, it might be quite impractical to expect the armed forces to support certain economic measures, however important they may be to national defense. Still, it remains reasonable to demand some serious demonstration that a proposed project would, in fact, substantially contribute to defense in a way not already shown by the economic calculations which measure its contribution to economic wealth. As an example of the misuse of defense considerations, the Upper Colorado River Storage Project was supported before Congress by the federal Civil Defense administrator on the ground that the project would induce a dispersal of resources which would reduce the nation's vulnerability to bombing.[8] It would be difficult indeed to see the Civil Defense administrator giving up any substantial fraction of his minuscule budget to help support the project, nor would his entire budget be even noticeable in the accounts of that vast enterprise. The small size of the Civil Defense budget is presumably a sign of the low importance our authorities assign, rightly or wrongly, to federal participation in this type of defense.

d) Depression and unemployment.—Quite a different problem relating to the significance of economic values comes to the fore under conditions of general unemployment.[9] In such conditions, resources, from the point of view of the consumer, can be secured only at a cost; but, from the point of view of society, it can be argued that the unemployed resources are really free. If, then, an increment of presently unemployed resources currently valued in the market at $100 could be used in a certain project to produce goods and services currently valued at $50 (with no adverse effects on employment elsewhere), the project would be socially desirable, not undesirable as implied by the earlier discussion. Such a project would not, of course, be undertaken by private enterprise. Similarly, it might be contended that the prices paid by consumers for goods and services producible by such unemployed resources are too high. In the authors' view, these contentions are essentially correct (though as a practical matter it should be mentioned that the attempt to increase employment in some areas may create adverse effects elsewhere). Economic reasoning in the ordinary sense becomes largely inapplicable under the topsy-turvy conditions of general unemployment, when even sheer make-work may be socially beneficial. While we reserve fuller treatment of this topic for chapter vi (where we examine employment effects as "secondary benefits" of government projects), we may say here that the monetary and fiscal measures necessary to cure general unemployment will generally be assumed by us to be effective, since otherwise there is little point in a wise economy of use of the resources available to society.

[8] *New York Times,* March 3, 1955, p. 15.

[9] We need not concern ourselves here with the technical definition of this concept, which involves some difficulties.

3. *Concluding Comment*

The balancing of all the considerations pro and con raised in this section is evidently a matter of the greatest difficulty. The position of the authors, and on such a fundamental matter all positions must be recognized to contain an element of sheer faith, is that the system of market values—as regulated and modified by the existing pattern of legal interventions—can be considered to be a generally satisfactory guide to resource allocation decisions. The important qualifications to this statement which the authors would make refer to (1) conditions of unemployment, in which case the economic problem of resource allocation can hardly be said to exist, and (2) divergences between private and social cost and benefit which, properly speaking, are due to defects in the system of property tenure rather than to defects in the price mechanism. Subject to these qualifications, existing supplies of a resource like water should be allocated so as to equalize the marginal value in use and marginal cost everywhere, providing no essential discontinuities in use exist, or to maximize aggregate value in use where discontinuities do exist. This conclusion assumes that the distributive implications of resource allocation decisions, where significant, will be given explicit and separate consideration and not confounded with the determination of economic efficiency.

B. The Political Allocation Process

Critics of the market allocation process often tabulate its defects, after which they proceed to assert or more often assume that government intervention either should or does already correct for these defects. We have used such arguments ourselves—in arguing, for example, that law and analogous social pressures tend to correct market forces on the matter of "higher" versus "lower" tastes. There is a paradox here alluded to earlier. If government intervention is consistently viewed as expressing deliberate social preferences, there is relatively little we can say in criticism of existing policies and procedures. We could not then object to the subsidies given to irrigation, since what is presumably involved is a correction of the market process which must be failing to take into account certain extramarket values attached to irrigation, or which possibly has an imperfection prejudicing its unregulated result against irrigation enterprises. Obviously, we cannot here regard the political process as automatically insuring socially optimal results. On the other hand, we cannot regard the political process as utterly devoid of rationality either. Since our own discussion leads to recommendations for government action or restraint, the implication is that the political process is one which can respond to rational analysis. The truth, of course, is somewhere in between. We will at times assert that certain policies are mistaken, that is, that they incorrectly represent what we believe the correct social preferences are. In such cases the political process will be regarded by us as having failed, though it remains possibly amenable to correction. The subsidy to irrigation, for example, will be regarded in this light, because it ultimately can be justified only on the basis of a preference to particular interests which we cannot believe others would generally concede once the fallacies and obfuscations surrounding the policy were stripped away. The progressive income tax, on the other hand, we regard as a deliberate policy signifying a certain social preference for equality of income. Obviously, there is an important element of judgment involved here, and we shall try as consistently as possible to separate judgments of social preferences from analysis.

To believe in or to look toward government for correction of errors in market allocation processes is not, of course, to assume that the political process is perfect, or even generally better than the market process;[10] rather, the assumption need only be that an improvement is yielded by the type of intervention under discussion. Even this limited assumption, however, has hardly been vindicated by careful analysis on the theoretical or empirical levels.

Theoretically speaking, there are many grave disadvantages of political processes for allocating resources; we have pointed and shall point to a number of defects ourselves, and political and economic theorists have also discussed the matter to some extent. There is, however, what strikes most people as one overwhelmingly important advantage of the political process—the equalitarian distribution of the franchise. Most informed people are willing to concede that market processes allocate goods and services reasonably well in terms of individuals' preferences—but subject to the principle of "one dollar, one vote." In the political sphere, of course, the principle is "one man, one vote." Many would be willing to exchange an efficient process based upon an arbitrary distribution of wealth and talents for an inefficient one with a more equalitarian distribution of power. Not that the equality in the political sphere is perfect, of course. The possessor of wealth can derive political power therefrom, through command over the means of influencing votes (conversely, the possessor of political power may find the acquisition of wealth relatively easy). This fact still leaves the equality greater in the political sphere, however, since the formal principle of "one man, one vote" still carries some weight. A rather more troublesome consideration for those favoring political processes on grounds of equality is the complete dependence of this desirable condition upon the distribution of the franchise. Obviously, in a total dictatorship equality would fail utterly. Even in the United States, it is almost certainly the case that southern Negroes have relatively more economic than political weight. Despite this consideration, however, in our present society an informed preference for political over market processes may be based upon the equalitarian principle.

[10] Socialists, of course, are more or less dedicated to the view that the political process is a better one generally. In this connection it is interesting that one of the central topics in the economic theory of socialism has been the use of or the simulation of market processes. Similarly, practical experience in the Soviet Union and the nations under its domination has seen conflict and compromise between the ideologically purer concept of total state dictation and the use of the market process in the interests of economic efficiency.

We should mention, however, that another stream of feeling which tends to support political decision-making is the urge to be dominated or to have decisions made for one by others—a revolt from freedom, so to speak. While this concept is rather foreign to official political philosophy in America, it must be an important phenomenon, since it is difficult otherwise to account historically for the popular appeal of a number of highly authoritarian political systems. It seems reasonable to believe that the same psychic urge, in at least a submerged way, enters into the political popularity of extensions of the political process into new spheres of activity in democratic countries.

It will not serve our purposes here to go into any very extensive criticism of political processes in general. Instead we will mention some of the defects of political processes for allocation of goods and resources, that is, of political processes that overlap or preclude functioning of the market mechanism. Even this is a very general topic, which we will discuss on a rather abstract level in this chapter; the relation between private and public decision-making with more specific reference to water supply will be studied in chapter ix.

The different levels of government in our country engage in such a bewildering variety of activities relating to the allocation of resources that even classification of them poses a considerable challenge. First of all there is the basic bedrock of government activity: establishment and enforcement of law governing relations among individuals (in the economic sphere, the law of property and exchange) and protection of citizens against internal and external violence and threats. Second is the provision for other group wants: collective consumption goods. Third is the regulatory function designed to prevent certain abuses of economic power or position: pure food and drug legislation, antitrust prosecutions, the activities of the Interstate Commerce Commission and Securities and Exchange Commission, etc. More closely related to our present discussion is the wide range of commodities and services provided, on at least a semicommercial basis, to customers. These operations are sometimes in competition with private firms (federal and state lending agencies), sometimes in cooperation with them (federal mortgage insurance), and sometimes are protected by law against private competition (the federal post office, state liquor monopolies, TVA). Finally, we may mention the procedures whereby the allocation of resources is affected by the granting of subsidies and bounties to some private undertakings and the imposition of punitive taxes, regulations, or prohibitions on others.

Government activities can also be classified by the type of agency involved: judicial, independent (e.g., the Interstate Commerce Commission), legislative, or executive. It is also possible to distinguish in a number of different ways the types of interventions involved; thus an administrative agency may be charged only with impartially applying and enforcing existing law, or else it may have essentially discretionary power to promote some individuals and interests over others.

Obviously, it is difficult in brief compass to analyze the possible defects of activities the range of which was only quite inadequately suggested above. We will mention first the danger of misuse of power for corrupt or dictatorial ends. In the private sphere the same human propensities exist but are checked by the existence of competitive opportunities for the suppliers, customers, and employees who might be adversely affected thereby. The forces of competition work to some extent even in the government sphere—a corruptly managed city may tend to lose residents and industry, a well-managed government program may find it easier to secure further funds than a badly managed one—but, at best, only in an attenuated way. The danger of misuse of power will be greater the wider the discretionary authority given the agency, and the broader the scope of its activities. The recent indications of corruption in the Federal Communications Commission were clearly related to the power unwisely placed in that agency to make a free gift of valuable properties (radio and television channels) at its discretion, within very broad limits, to commercial interests. Corruption would have been much less likely to develop if arrangements had been made for award of the properties by an objective rather than discretionary process; for example, the channels might have been sold to the high bidder in an auction open to all or to anyone willing to meet certain objective requirements. This problem is of some significance for water-resource decisions, because of the growing trend in state legislation (see chap. ix) toward placing all water use under the jurisdiction of a water commission generally given only some vague high-sounding phrase[11] on the basis of which to decide who should be granted the use of the water resource and who should be refused.

The temptation to dictatorial use of powers is also present though more difficult to document because an element of opinion

[11] "Greatest beneficial use" (Iowa); "Comprehensive development of the state's water resources" (Model Water Use Act of the National Conference of Commissioners on Uniform State Laws).

intrudes in determining when an agency is being "dictatorial." As a possible example, one state water official at a public meeting argued for wide discretion to his agency so that water allocations could be used to achieve a more "balanced" population distribution in his state—that is, he asked for power to subsidize small cities at the expense of large, and sparsely populated regions at the expense of the densely populated. It is of some historical interest that Wittfogel's monumental study of oriental despotism assigns a crucial if not all-determining role to centralized control of water resources in the historical formation and maintenance of that characteristically bureaucratic form of government.[12]

A familiar set of problems for political allocation processes are the traditional defects of bureaucracies: agency aggrandizement, empire-building, and inefficiency, the classic reference in the field being Parkinson's Law.[13] Here again it is the lack of competition which is crucial. Private agencies may not be any more efficient intrinsically than public agencies or any less inclined to administrative elephantiasis—but, if they go too far in those directions, they will be destroyed by their competitors.

Up to this point we have been considering political processes as primarily bureaucratic; that is, an agency is formed to handle some problem and is granted powers with which to achieve its end. In fact, most of the ordinary work of government is conducted in this way, and in a non-democratic polity bureaucracy and government might be identical. But ordinarily we think of political processes, in a democracy, as being fundamentally *representative* in nature—decisions are made "by the people" through their agents the Congress, the President, etc. On the federal level the Congress and the President between them organize the bureaus and select their heads and can abolish them for unsatisfactory performance. If, therefore, what we may call the representative-political process functioned perfectly, it would cure the ills of the bureaucratic-political process, just as competition tends to cure the corresponding defects of the market process.

In fact, most of us do have faith that the process of democratic representation does at least mitigate the evil of unchecked bureaucracy. Nevertheless, representation in practice is insufficient to work a complete cure. We cannot go at all deeply here into the reasons but shall instead mention briefly some imperfections of the representative process.[14] One of the most apparent is the relatively harsh treatment of minority preferences. In the market there is a kind of proportional representation giving each dollar "voted" equal weight, whereas democratic political systems necessarily work on the majority-decision principle. For example, a large majority usually support the principle of free public schools, but the minority are also taxed to support public schools even if they send their children elsewhere. Where the market principle governs, this situation would ordinarily not occur—parents of Yale students need not pay to educate Harvard students, and those not receiving private-college education do not pay for either.

Turning to other points, the demonstration of preferences through the political franchise is infrequent as compared with the continual day-to-day "voting" in the market place. Perhaps even more important

[12] Karl A. Wittfogel, *Oriental Despotism* (New Haven, Conn.: Yale University Press, 1957).

[13] C. Northcote Parkinson, *Parkinson's Law* (Boston: Houghton Mifflin Co., 1957). Dahl and Lindblom also analyze shortcomings of bureaucratic procedures, but their emphasis is on the technical problems of calculation, securing information, and the like (*op. cit.*, pp. 372–84), though elsewhere they concern themselves about conditions which lead to dictatorship in political systems (pp. 272–323).

[14] For a somewhat parallel discussion see J. M. Buchanan, "Individual Choice in Voting and the Market," *Journal of Political Economy,* LXII (August, 1954), 334–43.

is that, when elections do take place, the issues are inextricably tied together—so that, if the voter is to support a candidate he favors on most or the most important of the issues, he must vote against his true preferences on others. Free competition does not prevail in the competition of votes, there being essentially only two parties in our country effectively sharing a monopoly of power, as compared with the multitude of competing firms seeking customers in the market.[15] A multiparty system would be superior on this score, but then it becomes necessary usually to carry on government by a coalition of minorities, which leads to other difficulties mentioned below. As a somewhat more subtle point, it does not pay the voter to study political issues or to go to great trouble in the expression of his political preferences, since his own effect on the outcome of the voting is negligible. In the market, on the other hand, each decision has a direct observable effect on the individual's well-being, so it pays the consumer or the producer to exercise considerable care about the disposition of his dollar "votes" or his real resources in the market. Most important of all the defects is that the individuals acting in the capacity of representatives cannot in the nature of the case be expected to be merely disinterested agents of the voters. Inevitably, they develop interests in conflict with those of the people they serve. Again, so do firms in the market, even to a greater degree; in fact, firms scarcely even pretend to act in the interests of any but their owners. It is the relative weakness of the check of competition in the political sphere which makes improper representation so important and persistent.

Turning to the practical side, phrases like "logrolling," "pork barrel," and "patronage" denote various observed imperfections of our democratic political apparatus. The latter two we may classify as instances of improper representation—the agent succumbs to temptation to further his own or his friends' interests against those whom he supposedly serves. Logrolling is the product of a coalition of minorities against the majority interest, as when congressmen trade a wasteful reclamation program in the West for an inefficient flood-control project in the East. This is possible because a minority to whom an issue is vital can afford to invest more in the way of threats and promises to congressmen than the majority for whom the issue is only one of many, even though the loss to the majority in the aggregate exceeds the gains reaped by the minority. In the illustration above, the eastern interests involved hardly care that their pro rata burden of national taxes is increased by an inefficient reclamation project, so long as their particular gain on flood control is large enough; and, of course, the western interests reason correspondingly. An exchange of support between such minorities then achieves the desired result.

The frequent success of demogogues, the constant revelations of corruption, and the low level of public debate all support the inference that perfection is no more achieved in the political than in the market process. We obviously cannot attempt here to assess the performance of one process against the other, either in general or in particular sectors. Rather, our purpose is to establish somewhat convincingly that one cannot readily assume that perfect or even reasonably satisfactory political processes are available to correct market imperfections. Instead, it is necessary to consider the prospects for useful corrective intervention case by case.

[15] For an excellent discussion of the role of competition in the political sphere as a condition for optimality of the representative process see Gary S. Becker, "Competition and Democracy," *Journal of Law and Economics*, I (October, 1958), 105–9. The concept of political parties as teams competing for the support of voters to win power and office is also developed in A. Downs, "An Economic Theory of Political Action in a Democracy," *Journal of Political Economy*, LXV (April, 1957), 135–50.

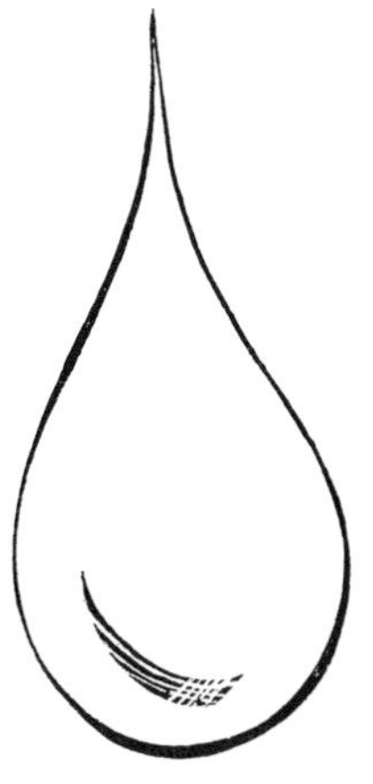

CHAPTER V

MUNICIPAL WATER RATES

In chapter iii municipal water rates were examined in a limited context. The question there emphasized was whether existing systems of rates equate marginal values in use for all consumers served under identical cost conditions. Equalization of marginal values in use can be achieved most simply by non-discriminatory sale of water (charging a common price to all, except for taking into account any differences in the marginal cost of serving the various categories of demand). Our previous examination also indicated that marginal-cost pricing was the appropriate principle for determining the general level of rates as well as the procedure indicated by economic theory for differentiation of rates where cost differences of service do exist. We propose in this chapter to look into municipal water pricing in somewhat more detail, evaluating existing and recommended practices of the industry in the light of the principles developed earlier.

The optimal allocation of municipal water supplies is of considerable economic importance. Actually, municipal water systems provide only about 7 per cent of current gross supplies, defined in terms of withdrawals. But municipal water is generally the most highly valuable, from both the cost and the demand points of view. Crowded urban areas present the most intense demand for water, and, in serving this demand, relatively heavy costs are incurred in transporting, purifying, and distributing water supplies possibly gathered at great distances from points of consumption. As of 1955 the replacement value of capital investment in public water supplies was estimated as about $23 billion in 1954 dollars.[1] Annual revenues are perhaps around 5 per cent of this figure.[2]

These figures, while large, are not overwhelmingly so when compared with investment figures for, say, electric utilities. No valid purpose is served by exaggerating the significance of the water industry. We may, however, say that, while it is an overstatement to hold, as many do, that water resources are in some special or unique sense the basis for civilization, it is probably the

[1] U.S. Department of Commerce, Business and Defense Services Administration, *Public Water Supplies, Capital Investment Values* (Business Service Bull. 146 [Washington, D.C., April, 1956]).

[2] As we will see later, this is an extraordinarily low return to cover not only interest and depreciation but all operating expenses as well.

case that almost nowhere else is the total *value in exchange* of the resource so low relative to the aggregate *value in use*. This argument does not imply that the low market price for water is in some sense incorrect but rather that the importance of water-allocation decisions may be far greater than is suggested by the relatively small market value involved.

Turning now to water rates, we shall concentrate our analysis upon what may be considered to be the standard viewpoint of the industry. In May, 1953, at the annual conference of the American Water Works Association, a committee under the chairmanship of L. E. Ayres presented a report on water rates[3] which was reprinted, with some supplementary material, as the *Water Rates Manual*[4] of the American Water Works Association. We assume that this report represents the current best thinking of the industry on the matter of water rates, and, in fact, while we will criticize the report from the standpoint of economic analysis, it is on the whole an intellectually impressive document.

The central idea or principle underlying the report is that prices should be set so as to cover the cost "distributed" to each class of user. In the words of the report: "An attempt is made to present definite rules for the formulation of rates which will distribute normal expense among *all* customers, as nearly as possible in proportion to the cost of supplying the commodity."[5] From the theoretical point of view, this principle is defective on several counts. First, it certainly implies prices based on average cost rather than marginal cost. Second, where several classes of customers exist, certain joint expenses will typically be incurred on behalf of all which cannot be properly assigned to any class separately, but the principle embodied in the report evidently would require division of such costs among the separate customer classes. Third, the report assigns historical or sunk costs which are not those relevant for current decisions. We will here concentrate first on applying theoretical principles of correct pricing in the practical context of municipal water enterprises and will then turn to the committee's report in more detail.

[3] "Determination of Water Rate Schedules," *Journal American Water Works Association,* XLIV (March, 1954), 187–219.

[4] American Water Works Association, *Water Rates Manual* (New York, 1957).

[5] "Determination of Water Rate Schedules," *op. cit.*, p. 188.

A. Average-Cost versus Marginal-Cost Pricing

To consider the first point above, let us suppose that no difficulty arises with regard to classes of consumers of the utility under investigation. All the customers may for present purposes be regarded as falling into one common class, on behalf of whom all the costs are incurred. In order to derive the solution of economic theory for the best price to charge under these circumstances, it will be necessary to make use of the methods of diagrammatic analysis introduced in Appendix A to chapter iii. In Figure 9, *DD* is the demand curve of the consumers for the product of the utility. Since only one class of customers exists, we may define a unique average cost as a function of the quantity supplied, and this is the curve labeled *AC*. The curve showing *marginal cost* as a function of output is labeled *MC*. The marginal cost is necessarily less than average cost where the latter is declining and greater than average cost where the latter is rising, whence it follows that the *MC* curve cuts through the low point of the *AC* curve. If a single price is charged so as to "cover" cost, while clearing the market, that price can only be equal to *OT*,[6] since at a price of *OT* the quantity *OA* would be demanded, the production of which involves an average cost of $AR = OT$.

[6] We rule out, as obviously an inferior solution, charging a price of *OW* and producing *OC*.

At this solution, zero profits are being earned in the economic sense; price equals unit cost, including a normal interest return on capital invested as part of cost. But this is not the solution that corresponds to the best use of society's resources. To see this, consider the units of output between *OB* and *OA*. For each of these units the marginal cost—the additional cost of supplying the unit considered—is greater than the amount anyone is willing to pay for the extra unit supplied—the consumers' marginal value in use. The quantity *OB* is demanded at the price *OU* = *BS*, and, if any larger quantity is to be taken by consumers, the price will have to be reduced below *BS*. But the marginal cost is higher than *BS* throughout the range being considered, which means that there are alternative uses of the resources entering into this marginal cost which consumers value more highly than they value what those resources can produce in the use here considered. The solution for best use of resources is to produce just up to the point where the marginal cost begins to exceed the price that consumers are willing to pay for the additional unit produced; that is to say, the correct output is *OB* at the marginal-cost price *BS*.

We may also note that the price *BS* is greater than the average cost *BV* corresponding to the output *OB*, so that there is a profit to the private or public enterprise here considered. Just what becomes of that profit is a distributional question and will not be further considered by us. It is worth noting, however, that the existence of the positive discrepancy between revenues and costs suggests that, on the basis of long-run calculations, some further expansion of this enterprise may be desirable.

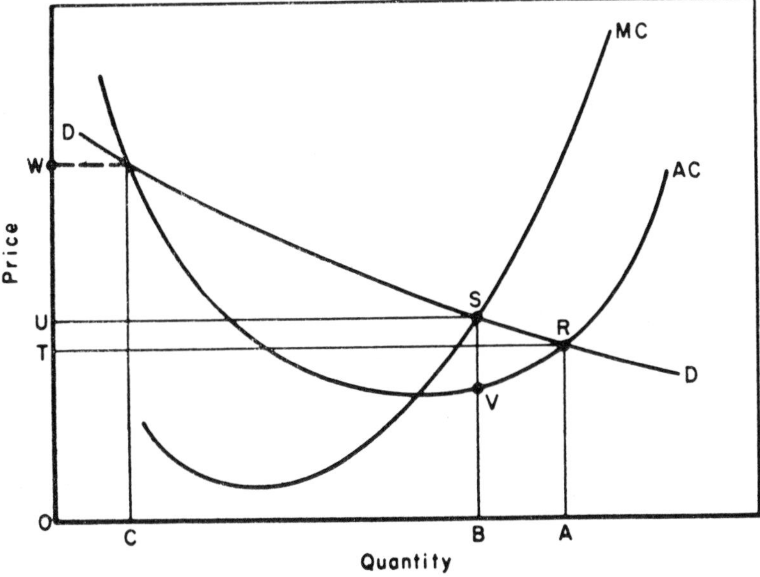

FIG. 9.—Solution in range of rising average cost

A vexing problem does arise for marginal-cost pricing, however, in the case illustrated in Figure 10. Here the demand curve *DD* intersects the average-cost curve *AC* in the range where the latter is still *declining*. Some analysts have alleged that such a situation is typical for public utilities in general. The average-cost output and price are *OA* and *AR*, respectively, and the marginal-cost output and price are *OB* and *BS*, respectively. But note that in this case the marginal-cost output is greater than *OA*, whereas in the previous case considered it was smaller—and, correspondingly, the marginal-cost price is here lower, whereas before it was higher. In consequence, whereas in the previous case the enterprise earned a profit at the marginal-cost output and price, here it will incur a loss. The loss (the shaded area in the figure) will be equal to the difference between average cost and price, *SV*, multiplied by the number of units produced (*OB*).[7]

We might say, as before, that just how the loss is to be made up is merely a distributional question and that the same argument for the superiority of the marginal-cost price and output over the zero-profit price and output applies. A privately owned utility could not simply operate at a loss, however, and there might be good reasons (on grounds of incentives) to prefer even public enterprises to have at least a chance to avoid losses, so that it may be worth our while analyzing how the loss might be covered. Let us first point out that it is clear that the enterprise or the operation illustrated in Figure 10 should not be simply abandoned. Evidently, at outputs less than *OA* the price consumers are willing to pay exceeds the average cost, so that a profit *can* be made. At such outputs consumers prefer resources to be invested in this industry rather than elsewhere, so the enterprise should certainly produce up to *OA*. But, along the lines of the argument made earlier, the output *OB* is clearly the best on efficiency grounds and so still better than the outputs less than *OA* which we know to be already desirable. Should the demand curve *DD* lie *entirely* below the average-cost curve, then there would be no point at which a profit would be possible so long as a single price was charged. In such circumstances the enterprise may or may not be desirable on efficiency grounds; the fundamental criterion is whether or not the *aggregate* value in use exceeds the aggregate cost at any output. If there is such an excess, it will be greatest at the marginal-cost solution. (The aggregate value in use, it will be remembered, is equal to the largest amount the consumers would be willing to pay for the output on an all-or-nothing basis.)

In either case, whether or not a profit is possible, a loss is incurred at the optimal output if a single price is charged. There are several possible ways out of this difficulty.

1. The most obvious way of covering the loss is through a government contribution (subsidy). Aside from the argument that such a guaranty might promote inefficiency and that the collection of public funds is itself not costless, there is the objection that the procedure does not distinguish between projects or operations

[7] While we cannot here devote the space to discuss the topic adequately, we should perhaps say explicitly that an *economic* loss, which is what we are discussing, is not necessarily the same as an *accounting* loss. The differences between the two are generally discussed in elementary economics textbooks. For our present purposes the most important difference is that accounting profit deducts from net operating revenues a figure for capital consumption based on historical cost and one or another conventional depreciation formula, whereas the economic estimate of capital consumption would be based upon the actual loss in value of the equipment to the enterprise. "Replacement cost" valuation of equipment is less incorrect than historical cost but still imperfect, since in many cases the economic value of equipment will have been degraded below replacement cost by the development of cheaper or more efficient machines. In any case the conventional depreciation formulas will be incorrect, since in economic principle what is desired is to recognize loss of value only as and if it occurs over time. As a secondary difference between economic and accounting profit statements, the former would exclude from profit a normal return on the owned equity in the business, while accounting profit deducts only the capital return paid out on borrowed funds.

that should be abandoned and those that should not. We may note, however, that a somewhat analogous government contribution takes place, in effect, when costs are allocated to "non-reimbursable" purposes (e.g., flood control) in a multipurpose water-resource project. Government contributions are in fact by no means uncommon in public water-supply enterprises. The Metropolitan Water District of Southern California, for example, has typically run an enormous loss on water sales, the balance being levied as a property tax on the member communities. The typical low over-all level of water rates in publicly owned systems, to be discussed later, can in fact only be maintained with a government contribution—direct or hidden.

2. The other modes of procedure we will discuss all attempt to capture as revenue part of what would otherwise be "consumers' surplus." A theoretical possibility is to operate at the optimal output but to announce that the enterprise will be abandoned unless sufficient voluntary contributions from customers are received to cover the total cost incurred. In this case, so long as there is a threat of the utility going out of business, each customer will have an incentive to contribute any amount that still leaves him with some positive excess of aggregate value in use over the total of cost plus voluntary contributions. If this method worked ideally, it would distinguish between the desirable and the undesirable operations, since the latter could not accumulate the necessary contributions. Unfortunately, the former may not either, because it is in the interest of each customer to hold out and contribute nothing so long as the total contribution of others may cover the bill, or at least to contribute less than the full amount he would in the last analysis be willing to give. Another objection is that the procedure seems impractical; we would have to add to the annual polio drive and Heart Fund campaign a water-supply drive, a gas-pipeline drive, etc.

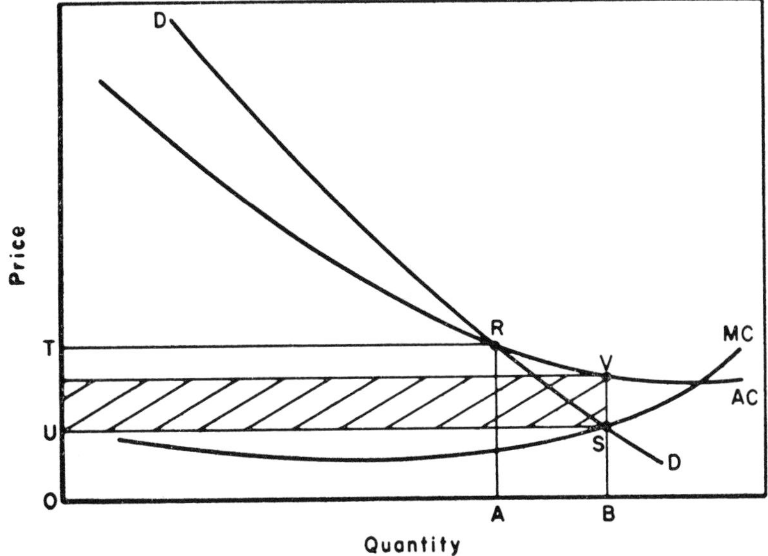

Fig. 10.—Solution in range of falling average cost

3. Another solution would have the utility discriminate by setting up a descending

scale of prices as a function of quantity taken, but subject to the guiding rule that each customer must end up paying the same *marginal* price (i.e., price for the last unit consumed) and that this marginal price equal marginal cost. This could conceivably be achieved by a process of trial and error. The customers would be segregated into various groups, each with a separate declining price scale. On the first trial some individuals would end up on too high a rate block and others on too low a block as compared with marginal cost. And the aggregate revenue might or might not suffice. A second trial would then possibly be made, reclassifying some of the customers and possibly shifting some of the scales. Ideally speaking, this process could go on until either the optimum was achieved at a satisfactory revenue or it was determined that the project should be abandoned. The practical difficulty, of course, consists in the probable unacceptability of the trial-and-error process. Nevertheless, there is an important idea here which should be more widely appreciated: if a scheme of discrimination is to be adopted, the goal on efficiency grounds should be a common *marginal* price to all customers equal to marginal cost.

4. A fourth possible solution is the two-part tariff: each customer could be charged a single price per unit of output purchased, but, in addition, he could be required to pay a lump-sum amount for the privilege of being permitted to buy at all. This method would work ideally only if the lump sums were differentiated according to the intensities of demand of the different consumers (but still not varying, for any single consumer, with the quantity taken). While perfect differentiation could not be achieved, in cases where the revenue deficit from optimal operation is not too great, the lump-sum contributions based on convenient customer classifications could provide the required supplementary income. This solution does have an imperfection in terms of efficiency. Some customers who might otherwise have taken only one or just a few units of product may now decide to dispense with it entirely, even though they are willing to pay for the output more than the marginal cost of producing it. The difficulty is in the practice rather than in the theory; ideally, customers in such a situation should be charged no lump sum at all, or only a very small amount, so that their total payments do not exceed their aggregate value in use. Evidently, however, many customers will claim to be in this situation and threaten to eliminate purchases entirely if not so classified, so the process of individual differentiation is impractical; nevertheless, some approximation of this goal may be achievable. As we will see later, two-part tariffs are quite common in public utility rate systems.

5. Finally, we turn to the solution most similar to practices and procedures actually in effect—ordinary price discrimination not satisfying our conditions in 3 above. Such discrimination consists in classifying customers so as to separate the market into two or more sectors, with prices varying from submarket to submarket. This is neither marginal-cost nor average-cost pricing, but it is a way of coping with the problem of deficits at a single price. It would take us too far afield to discuss the details of price-discrimination theory here, so we will only repeat that optimal efficiency conditions are not satisfied when marginal prices differ from consumer to consumer, because in such cases marginal values in use cannot be equated everywhere.[8]

[8] There seems to be some misunderstanding of this point on the part of textbook authors in the field of public utility economics. Troxel, for example, views the objections to discrimination as based on a sentiment for "democratic" equality and opposition to the "acquisitive" motives of the private companies and, indeed, the whole problem as one of "distributive justice" (see E. Troxel, *Economics of Public Utilities* [New York: Rinehart & Co., 1947], pp. 589–90). Clemens also fails to bring out the correct objection on efficiency grounds, though it is implicit in his requirement that mar-

To summarize briefly at this point, average-cost pricing is inefficient; it is marginal-cost pricing which leads to the best use of resources. No special problem arises where the marginal-cost price is higher than average cost at the output determined by that price. Where the marginal-cost price is lower than average cost, however, a loss will be incurred at the optimal price. Various solutions are available in theory for coping with the problem thus created without sacrificing economic efficiency, but each of these faces more or less serious objections in practice. Nevertheless, we feel that the goal of marginal-cost pricing even in this difficult case can be approximately achieved. Our preference is for method 3—discrimination with equal *marginal* prices for all. Our second choice is method 4—the two-part tariff, involving a common price for all units purchased plus possibly differentiated lump-sum charges.

These various devices for coping with the problem of losses at marginal-cost pricing are, it should be borne in mind, outside the main stream of our argument. We will indicate shortly that, at least in the large, average-cost functions of water-supply enterprises are typically rising so that marginal-cost pricing will generally yield a surplus over average costs. Since there may be disagreement with our factual generalization here, and since in any case there will be some exceptional situations which do not fall under it, we thought that a discussion of how to cope with losses if and when they occur might serve a useful purpose. Henceforth, however, unless otherwise stated, we will be speaking of the implications of the simple marginal-cost pricing principle, which is our basic recommendation.

ginal cost equal demand price (see E. W. Clemens, *Economics and Public Utilities* [New York: Appleton-Century-Crofts Co., 1950], pp. 256–61). Clemens' discussion does at times appear to be groping toward our solution 3 above.

B. The Problem of Joint Costs

Where, as is the case for water utilities, different classes of service exist for which some costs are separable and some are common or joint, the average-cost concept runs into additional difficulty. The relevant classes of service involving cost differentials may be defined by geographical location, by quantity demanded, by time pattern of demand, and, on occasion, by other features (distinctions between gravity and pumped service, firm and intermittent service, and qualities of water delivered are among the possibilities here). In each of these cases some costs will clearly be *separable* in the sense that they are incurred solely for the benefit of a single user or a single defined class of users; for example, the cost of an irrigation ditch is separable to irrigation users. Such costs may be fixed or variable (i.e., incurred independently of the level of output delivered or as a function of output). Other costs may represent investment or current outlays on behalf of facilities that serve several users or several classes of users in common, for example, the cost of a main aqueduct bringing water to a variety of users.[9]

In order to determine separately the average costs for a number of different uses or users, the total of the joint or common costs would have to be "allocated" among these classes of use and then added to the respective separable costs. This leads to a difficulty often expressed by some phrase like "the allocation of joint costs is arbi-

[9] As a technical point, there has been some confusion due to differing theoretical definitions of *joint* and *common* costs. Some analysts would restrict the use of the term "*joint* costs" to the costs of producing "joint products"—products which are necessarily generated in fixed proportions, such as hydrogen and oxygen in the electrolysis of water. We will however, treat "joint" and "common" costs as synonymous terms representing the total of those costs not incurred exclusively on behalf of a single class of use—the residue after assignment of all separable costs to their respective use classes.

trary."[10] This may be somewhat misleading because, for any economic decision, there *is* a unique incremental cost "allocation" which is the relevant one. If the decision involved, for example, is whether to add power features to a dam, no part of the common dam cost should be weighed as an offset against the power benefits in making the decision. For this decision, there is a correct unique "allocation" to power—precisely zero. On the other hand, if the question at issue is whether to build the dam in the first place, the aggregate of benefits (value in use) should be compared with the aggregate of costs, so there is no need to "allocate" costs at all. In any problem the question to ask is: What costs are incremental to this possible choice or decision as compared with the alternative?

The crucial point, however, is that these allocations of total cost are of relevance only for certain investment decision problems and not for the *pricing* problem we are investigating here. Only under the false average-cost pricing principle is it necessary to divide somehow the total of common or joint costs among the different classes of use. For pricing decisions all that is economically relevant is the *marginal* cost, and in principle there will be no difficulty in finding the increase in the total of the common costs due to a unit increase in output of one product or for one category of use.[11] To this increment in common cost must be added, of course, the increment in the appropriate separable cost for the product or use involved, the sum being the correct marginal cost.

If, nevertheless, average-cost pricing is practiced when there are common costs, the consequence will be most clearly visible if we consider a simple case of only two classes of use, with no separable costs, and such that the marginal cost of delivery to either class is always identical. Here, certainly, each class of use should be charged the same price. But that can come about only under average-cost pricing if the allocation of the common costs is in proportion to the quantities taken. While it would be tedious to prove this algebraically, it is not hard to see that, even if this (rather unusual) principle for allocating joint costs were adopted, the common price arrived at must in general diverge from marginal cost. (While it does not concern us immediately here, it is worth mentioning that allocation in proportion to use is only meaningful and possible if the same product is provided to the different classes of service. If two different products, like water and power, are produced under conditions of common cost, the incommensurability of power output and water output makes it impossible to distribute the common cost between the two "in proportion to output.")

Where joint-cost problems exist, an average-cost solution must then be objectionable in one of the following ways. First, if differing prices are charged because of cost allocations not proportional to use, the principle of equimarginal value in use is violated (the last unit has more value in the high-priced than in the low-priced use). If this result is avoided by using proportionate cost allocations and, consequently, a common price, the marginal-cost principle will in general be violated.

C. Costs as a Function of Scale of Output

With the help of these concepts, we now turn to a consideration of the cost structure of municipal water-supply enterprises. The

[10] See, e.g., Troxel, *op. cit.,* 538; Otto Eckstein, *Water-Resource Development* (Cambridge, Mass.: Harvard University Press, 1958), p. 262.

[11] The only case where difficulty arises is when products are produced in strictly fixed proportions. As this never occurs, for all practical purposes, we will ignore this qualification henceforth.

first question (considering, for the moment, all classes of service together) is whether water is supplied under conditions of diminishing or increasing average cost. The latter creates no problems, but, if the former is the case, the marginal-cost price will fail to generate enough revenue to cover total cost. One consideration definitely points to rising average costs—in the large. A city like Los Angeles or New York will first exploit readily available local sources and then gradually reach out to more and more distant and expensive supplementary supplies. On the other hand, once an aqueduct or other major fixed installation is in existence, there may be little extra expense required to increase its output from zero up to designed capacity. In this case the average cost will clearly be declining until capacity is reached. These considerations appear to define a jagged average-cost curve like that labeled *AC* in Figure 11, the general upward trend taking effect through a series of discrete jumps, separated by regions of declining average cost.[12] This picture is somewhat more extreme than actual situations, where average costs may well rise even before a technical capacity limitation is encountered, because such costs as power for pumping may begin to increase sharply when on-peak rather than off-peak electricity becomes required for the additional output.

With regard to the situation illustrated in Figure 11, suppose that fixed capacity is such that we are operating on the notch labeled *IV*. The average-cost curve reaches its lowest point at "designed capacity" (A_4), where a jump to notch *V* takes place. Corresponding to the declining average cost in this range is the short-run (i.e., relevant for this notch of fixed investment only) marginal-cost curve $SRMC_4$ (*dashed lines*). This curve may be rising or falling, but it must be below *AC* throughout notch *IV* because *AC* is falling, and it must equal *AC* where the latter reaches its local minimum at A_4. We show it as first horizontal, then vertical.[13] Turning to Figure 12, if the demand curve is D_1, pricing at the intersection with *SRMC* will produce a loss.[14] If the demand curve is D_2, it will intersect the $SRMC_4$ curve in its vertical branch at A_4, so revenues will equal costs. And, for D_3, marginal-cost pricing will yield a profit.

In this picture the discontinuities are probably much sharper than in the real world. The ordinary analysis of this situation in economic theory, illustrated in Figure 13, assumes complete continuity. There are supposed to be an indefinite number of short-run average-cost curves like those numbered in the diagram. The *LRAC*, or long-run average-cost curve, is the "envelope" of the short-run average-cost curves; it connects those points on the short-run curves that represent the lowest cost of producing any given output. There will also be long-run and short-run *marginal*-cost curves. Given a demand curve like *D*, the intersection of *LRMC* and *D* at the point *M* determines the best output to produce in the long run. At the optimal scale of

[12] We should mention that this generally rising cost function is supposed to represent the alternatives available at a moment of time. The rising trend of the *AC* curve is not therefore related in any way to the historical rise in water-procurement costs due to inflation or to changes in relative prices. Rather it expresses the fact that at a particular moment of time expansions of supply can be achieved only by turning to increasingly less advantageous sources or sites.

[13] The vertical curve indicates that additional output cannot be obtained because of technical capacity limitations, which we interpret to mean that the short-run marginal cost rises sharply to an extremely high level.

[14] A loss will be incurred because short-run average cost in notch *IV* (along *AC*) is greater than short-run marginal cost, price being set equal to the latter.

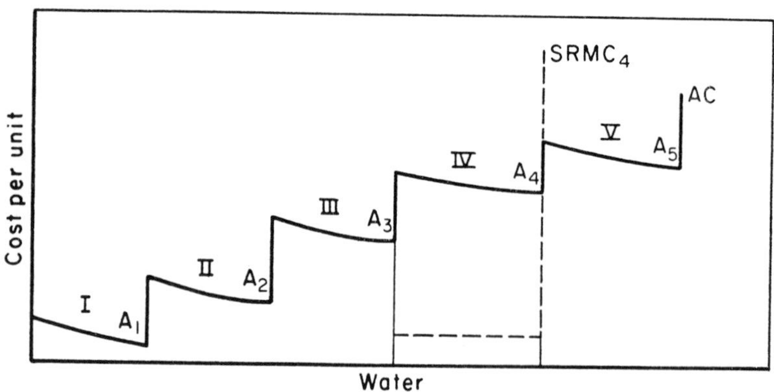

FIG. 11.—Short-run average costs of water supply

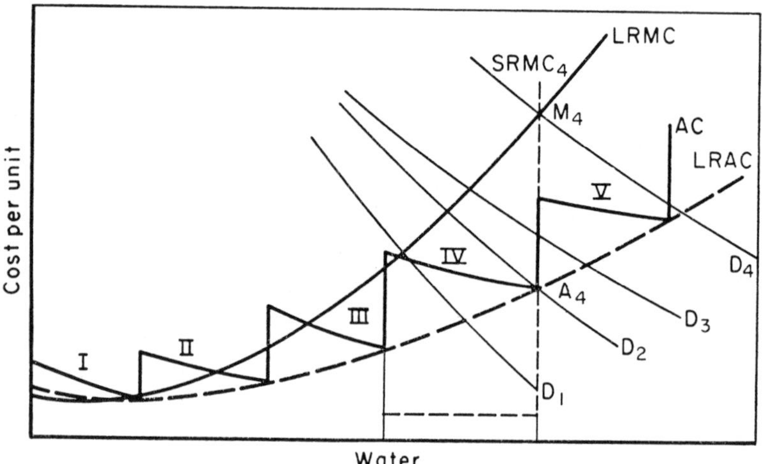

FIG. 12.—Long-run and short-run average costs of water supply

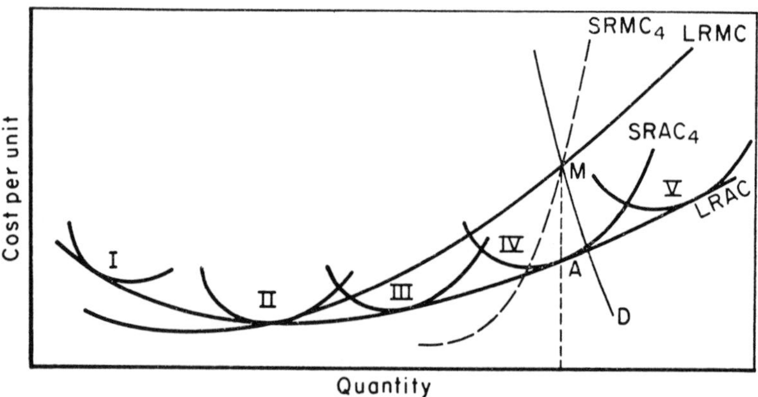

FIG. 13—Long-run and short-run average costs—theoretical

plant, the short-run marginal-cost $SRMC_4$ will also intersect D at the point M (this follows necessarily from the tangency of $SRAC_4$ and $LRAC$ at the point A). In general, the best short-run solution is to have short-run marginal cost equal price, and the best long-run solution (the optimal scale of plant) is achieved when long-run marginal cost and short-run marginal cost both equal price.[15]

Turning back to Figure 11, we can see that it is essentially a discontinuous representation of Figure 13. Instead of an indefinitely large number of short-run average-cost curves there are just a few, and each turns sharply upward instead of gradually upward at the points A_1, A_2, etc. These points may be regarded as on an envelope or $LRAC$ curve, and a hypothetical $LRAC$ curve is actually sketched in Figure 12. Similarly, a long-run marginal-cost curve $LRMC$ is there shown. In drawing these curves, we assume that the nature of the world is such that levels of plant investment intermediate between those illustrated *could actually be constructed*, which assumption we believe to be practically always true. The remaining peculiar property of Figure 11—the vertical jumps in the short-run marginal-cost curves after the points of contact with the $LRAC$ curve at A_1, A_2, etc.—we may accept as a property of the cost functions of water utilities, though in our view this discontinuity is softened in the real world by a tendency to increasing cost as designed "capacity" is approached and by possibilities of operating beyond "capacity" at high but not infinite cost.

One problem sometimes raised is whether efficient pricing should be at short-run or long-run marginal cost. In principle, it should be at short-run marginal cost, for the reason that the normal sale of water is in the nature of a short-run agreement; a purchase of water at this minute does not bind the customer to take more water at any later date. At each moment of time, therefore, the enterprise is faced with the short-run problem of selling its output given its current capacity. Pricing at long-run marginal cost would be appropriate if water sales normally took the form of long-run contracts, in which case the water company would never face any problem of disposing of its current output, already arranged for by contract. For such a company the problem would be to adjust its capacity to handle any additional contract it takes on, so that the long-run marginal cost would be relevant. This discussion considerably oversimplifies the real-world problem, because there will be various "runs"—one corresponding to the life of an aqueduct, another to the life of a pump, etc.—and a decision that is short run with respect to one part of the facilities may be long run with respect to another part. This does not affect the principle, however, or the fact that practically all water sales are in the nature of extremely short-run agreements.[16]

We may conclude that it is not possible to state generally whether marginal-cost pricing will generate a surplus or a deficit in water utilities. Typically, just after a

[15] We emphasize this point because it is a fairly common error to reason in the following fashion. The distinction between long run and short run is that the scale of plant investment is considered fixed in the short run, variable in the long run. Since marginal costs obviously depend only on the variable costs and not at all on the fixed costs, and since more costs are variable in the long run, it might be thought that the long-run marginal costs must be greater than the short-run marginal costs. Short-run marginal costs refer only to operating costs, but in the long run some of the capital costs enter into marginal costs. All these statements are correct except the conclusion that long-run marginal costs are necessarily higher—the correct relation between the two is illustrated in Figures 11–13.

[16] See J. Hirshleifer, "Peak Loads and Efficient Pricing: Comment," *Quarterly Journal of Economics,* LXXII (August, 1958), 460–61.

major increment is made to capacity, a range of decreasing average cost will be entered where pricing at marginal cost will produce a deficit. As increasing demand over time approaches utilization of the full capacity of the new increment, marginal cost will begin to rise sharply. As prices are raised to "clear the market," a profitable range will be entered until, ultimately, an addition to capacity becomes justified. To continue our previous illustration with capacity at notch *IV* in Figure 12, when demand is D_1, losses are incurred under marginal-cost pricing. But, as demand rises over time to D_2, a profit will begin to be earned. The upper branch of the $SRMC_4$ curve may be regarded as vertical indefinitely. At a certain point this branch becomes higher than the point M_4 on the long-run marginal-cost curve, and, when the demand grows above D_4 (which intersects $SRMC_4$ at M_4), an increase in capacity is called for. It does not follow in general that an increase as large as that shown in notch *V* is required; the *LRMC* curve is based on the assumption of continuity. If the jump must be a discrete one to notch *V*, it should ideally be made when demand grows just enough so that the increased aggregate value in use (area under the demand curve within notch *V*) just exceeds the aggregate increase in cost due to notch *V* deliveries. Such deliveries will, of course, be calculated as those taken by the market on the assumption of short-run marginal-cost pricing.

One possible difficulty with this solution is that it requires a changing pattern of prices: low just after a new increment of capacity, rising high as that capacity is fully utilized, and then falling once again when new capacity is constructed. While a popular prejudice against such changing prices may be a real difficulty, we would emphasize that it is just that—a prejudice. No buyer has any good reason to expect that prices will remain fixed while conditions of demand and supply change, unless indeed he is willing to bind himself to a long-range contract.[17] So, while recognizing the prejudice to the extent that it exists, water authorities should not tamely submit to it but rather attempt to educate the public as to the wastes and social costs thereby imposed on all.[18]

D. Classification of Costs: Customer, Capacity, and Commodity

It has become common to classify the costs of utilities into capacity (or demand), customer, and commodity costs. These are usually defined as the costs that are proportional, respectively, to the size of plant, the number of separate services, and the volume of the commodity delivered.[19] While this "Hopkinson" classification is in some respects instructive, it should be clear from our earlier discussion of joint costs that there is no correct way to segregate total costs into one component due to customers, another due to capacity to serve, and another due to actual deliveries. This is

[17] In principle, we see no reason why the water-supply agency should not, for those customers with a strong aversion to price fluctuations, enter into such a long-term supply contract at a prefixed price. For a demand pattern guaranteed by a long-term contract, the price can essentially be set at the relatively stable long-run marginal cost of service rather than at the fluctuating short-run marginal cost, since the water enterprise will be in a position to construct immediately whatever incremental facilities are necessary to serve that guaranteed demand in an optimal manner.

[18] While some jurisdictions (e.g., New York City) have kept prices constant to an amazing degree over the years, others (e.g., the Metropolitan Water District of Southern California) have changed water prices frequently.

[19] See "Determination of Water Rate Schedules," *op. cit.*, pp. 193–95. See also I. R. Barnes, *The Economics of Public Utility Regulation* (New York: Appleton-Century-Crofts Co., 1942), pp. 324–32. Some economic analysts have accepted this classification (mistakenly, we believe). See, e.g., H. Houthakker, "Electricity Tariffs in Theory and Practice," *Economic Journal*, LXI (March, 1951), 1–25 (at pp. 2–3).

logically equivalent to the impossible task of correctly dividing sheep costs into wool costs, mutton costs, and hide costs. A new reservoir, for example, may at one stroke increase system capacity, permit connection of a new class of consumers, and lower unit costs of delivering the commodity.

Nevertheless, there is something behind the Hopkinson cost classification, once it is dismissed as a device for segregating and allocating cost. Rather, its true meaning is that water costs may be regarded as varying in three dimensions: the number of customers, the total ability to serve or delivery capacity, and the actual deliveries. (Each of these is really a simplification; it is not the simple number of customers which is relevant but the number in each of several service classes, not the simple delivery capacity but capacity to serve various areas at varying times, etc.) While total cost cannot be divided among the dimensions, the *marginal* cost for each is determinable: the cost of adding another customer, with capacity and deliveries constant; the cost of adding a unit of capacity, with customers and deliveries constant; and the cost of increasing delivery by a unit, with customers and capacity constant. These costs are measurable and relevant for pricing.

As has already been mentioned, the Water Rates Committee of the American Water Works Association, following conventional practice in public utility pricing, attempted to establish correct rates on the principle of recovering costs assigned to different classes of users. Their analysis led to a recommendation in favor of what is already common practice in the industry: a multipart tariff, consisting of a fixed charge[20] plus a schedule of declining block prices for actual deliveries.

Following the Hopkinson classification, appropriate parts of the annual costs, including both fixed and operating costs, were assigned by the committee to special uses (see below), to customers, and to meters and services. The remaining fixed costs were initially assigned to the "capacity" component and the remaining operating or running costs to the "commodity" component of cost. However, the nature of water-enterprise technology is such that the fixed costs are relatively large (from one-half to perhaps two-thirds of all costs), requiring under this allocation-of-cost principle a very high "capacity" or "demand" charge independent of the actual quantity of the commodity consumed.[21] The committee was sufficiently disturbed by this as to be led to quote with approval a suggestion that "theory should not be carried to extremes" and that "consumption [commodity] charges should, in all cases, carry the major part of the entire cost of service."[22] Later, the report says: "Capital costs are as much a part of the cost of production as labor, fuel, electricity, and other operation and maintenance expense. No business produces goods without capital costs. Therefore, some part of depreciation, taxes, and interest should be included in the cost of the commodity." An allocation of 50 per cent of capital costs to capacity and 50 per cent to the commodity was recommended;[23] this division was justified in the report by the observation that the average-day water delivery is commonly about half that of the maximum day.

We believe that this argument is not well founded. The basic difficulty, as we have indicated earlier, is that the capital costs of water service cannot be correctly divided between the different dimensions of service, represented by capacity and by deliveries, any more than the purchase price

[20] In practice the fixed charge often takes the form of a minimum bill, within which a small water allowance may be consumed without additional charge.

[21] "Determination of Water Rate Schedules," *op. cit.*, pp. 193–94.

[22] *Ibid.*, p. 194.

[23] *Ibid.*, pp. 207–8.

of a sheep can be separated into amounts paid out for wool and for mutton. It seems likely to us that the custom of the industry has dictated a certain proportion between a fixed service charge and the amount paid for water as a function of deliveries, and the committee was forced to bend a defective theory to accord with this usage.

Turning to the customer costs, the report assigns certain elements like billing equally to all customers. Other customer costs, listed in the report under the heading of "meters and services," are a function of the size of connection.[24] These costs are probably separable to a satisfactory extent.

Our view has already been sketched out in our analysis above. With respect to customers, the additional expenses incurred in connecting another customer to the system —installation of a service connection and meter, adding a name to the accounts, etc. —is the marginal cost which should be assessed, as a once-and-for-all payment, to the customer.[25] Other customer costs are of a continuing nature (e.g., the cost of reading meters and billing), and all customers should periodically pay the current marginal cost of this service.

The most interesting question—and, possibly, the error of most serious practical importance—in the committee report relates to the commodity charges. The committee, following the procedure adopted as standard by the American Water Works Association in 1923, recommends the principle of declining block rates. These are used to recover the total costs remaining after assignment of appropriate parts of the annual costs (including both capital costs and operation and maintenance costs) to special uses, to customers, and to meters and services and allocation of 50 per cent of the remaining capital costs to the fixed service (demand) charge. The remaining costs are divided into two categories: production and distribution (there are both fixed capital costs and operation and maintenance costs in these categories). The production costs alone are then divided by the annual output[26] to get the "wholesale rate," while the distribution costs are allocated primarily to domestic users and secondarily to "intermediate users." The typical rate structure derived in this way is 4.3 cents per 1,000 gallons for wholesale consumers, 5.8 for intermediate, and 8.2 for domestic.[27]

This analysis would, if it could be assumed that the figures above showed the marginal costs to the various classes of users, justify the different rates arrived at for the different classes of users. For some unexplained reason, however, a *single* rate schedule is then applied in the report to *all* customers on a block basis: the first 75,000 gallons even to wholesale users are charged at the domestic rate, the next 675,000 at the intermediate, and all over 750,000 gallons at the wholesale rate.[28] It should be pointed out that the committee report is relatively conservative on the matter of rate steps. In the tabulation by the *American City* referred to earlier, only fifteen of sixty cities studied had as few as the three steps recommended by the committee.[29]

Our view, again, is that the rates derived above can be justified only if they show the marginal costs to the various classes of users. On the principle that we recommend, a single rate corresponding to the marginal cost should be applied to each class. Obviously, if a wholesale user gets a lower rate because no distribution system ex-

[24] *Ibid.*, p. 210.

[25] Such a lump-sum payment can, equally well, be converted into an annual fixed charge representing depreciation and interest on the investment involved.

[26] Note the implicit (and untrue) assumption that the output is independent of the rate charged.

[27] "Determination of Water Rate Schedules," *op. cit.*, pp. 211–13.

[28] *Ibid.*, p. 216.

[29] *Modern Water Rates* (New York: American City Magazine, 1955[?]), p. 34.

penses are incurred on the margin for such service, he should not have to pay even for his first 75,000 gallons a domestic rate based on the existence of such expenses. Conversely, an intermediate user who must be served through a distribution system should not get the benefit of the wholesale rate just because he happens to consume unusually large quantities. (Declining block rates for a single user can be justified, we argued earlier, as a means of capturing as revenue part of what would otherwise be consumers' surplus under conditions where the utility would otherwise operate at a loss—but, if this is the motive, no cost justification can or need be given for the high prices charged on the first units consumed.)

On the basis of our brief discussion of the attempt in the committee report to produce a rational system of charges based upon an allocation of costs to capacity, to consumers, and to commodity deliveries, the conclusion is inescapable that the standard rate systems now recommended by the American Water Works Association are not only defective in theory but inconsistent in application.[30]

E. Capacity Charge or Peak-Load Pricing?

The question of capacity charges raises some subtle questions. One might be tempted to contend on the basis of the theoretical discussion earlier that there is no need to charge for capacity or "ability to serve" as opposed to actual deliveries. More capacity is built when rising demand for the commodity drives the marginal-cost price sufficiently high as to make an increased supply economically desirable. There is then no need to charge explicitly for the cost of increasing or maintaining capacity.

We believe that this view is theoretically correct in the case of water or utility service generally. The capacity charges would not be required in an ideally operating price system. We will, however, present below what we believe is a sensible argument for a two-part tariff with fixed capacity charge. This argument is entirely apart from the justification, discussed earlier, of the two-part tariff as a device to capture some of the consumers' surplus or aggregate value in use (area under the demand curve) while still charging a price equal to marginal cost, the purpose being to obtain more revenue for an enterprise that would otherwise incur a loss. The present justification is based on the marginal cost of increasing system capacity to meet random fluctuations of demand.

One of the conditions of utility service is that the company stands ready to deliver at any time—that is to say, it stands ready to enter instantly into a contract for delivery at the option of the buyer. In order to meet this requirement with a given level of statistical confidence, the company must provide some excess capacity over the actual average demand it can anticipate. A buyer who has a large connection can then reasonably be expected to pay more in total than a buyer with a small connection, even though both may in a given period actually purchase the same amount. Both have what is in the nature of an option on the water company, but the former has an option for a larger amount than the individual with a small-capacity connection. From the company's point of view the long-run cost of these options is the reserve capacity it holds in readiness to serve. The appropriate charge for this option or for the reserva-

[30] In this discussion we have ignored the "functional cost basis" for rates, which the committee report apparently considers an equally desirable alternative to the "demand basis" discussed above. The functional cost basis has all the failings of the demand basis, with the additional objectionable feature that there is neither a service charge for capacity costs nor a peak-load charge, all costs being recovered through commodity charges independent of the load on the system ("Determination of Water Rate Schedules," *op. cit.*, pp. 213 ff.).

tion of this capacity is the cost of providing a fractional marginal unit of capacity, the fraction being based on the system's reserve factor. For example, if the company's practice is to hold in readiness system capacity equal to 50 per cent of the extreme limit of possible maximum demand (all taps wide open), then the appropriate charge for each unit of maximum potential demand (the fixed "demand charge") is the marginal cost of one-half a unit of system capacity. The cost is evidently one that is proportional to time and should reasonably be charged as a fixed item in the monthly bill.[31] The additional capacity may, of course, be provided either by better maintenance or by new construction.

This idea is too simple because in fact much more is known about the pattern of actual demands than that they follow a random law. In the first place, for given maximum connected capacity different classes of users may consistently place differing maximum actual demands on the system. This is the so-called diversity factor.[32] The company can then, with a given level of statistical confidence, hold a smaller fraction of reserve capacity against certain potential demands than against others, adjusting the demand charges accordingly. What this amounts to is that the cost of the option on the system represented by the maximum connected capacity is lower for those classes of demand that either exercise their options rarely or do not exercise them simultaneously.[33]

Another predictable element in the maximum demand is the systematic pattern of daily and seasonal variation. In the case of water, the maximum delivery will tend to take place during hot dry spells in summer. Within the twenty-four hours of the day there will also be a well-marked pattern.[34] We might consider, as a simplification, that the utility holds a single level of capacity in readiness the day and the year round to meet the expected maximum peak. Under this assumption the company must hold more capacity on behalf of classes of customers whose high demands occur at system-wide peaks than for those whose class peaks do not coincide with system peaks. The principle for determining the demand charge remains the same, however: for each customer or class of customer, the marginal cost of the fraction of a capacity unit that the company holds in readiness for his demand is to be charged.

In public utility pricing this principle corresponds generally to what is known as the "peak-responsibility method" of capacity-cost allocation, except that it is the marginal cost of capacity which is relevant rather than the conventional "allocated cost."[35] However, as we will see, the peak-

31 We mean "fixed" in the sense of "independent of the volume delivered." The charge should vary over time as the cost of reserving the marginal unit of capacity changes.

32 Technically, the diversity factor is measured by the ratio of the sum of the highest individual *experienced* demands to the group highest experienced demand, whereas our analysis above runs in terms of the ratio of individual *potential* maximum demands to group experienced demand. No issue of principle is involved, but our usage lends itself more neatly to the interpretation of the demand charge as the price of an option (see Barnes, *op. cit.*, pp. 329–30).

33 Actually, it is not the class maximum which is relevant but rather the class demand at the system peak (see below).

34 An interesting mystery in this connection has recently been solved. In the postwar years a new demand pattern had been noticed: a tendency for small evening peaks in water demand to recur at fifteen-minute or thirty-minute intervals. This pattern was eventually traced to a tendency to concentrate use of bathroom fixtures during commercials and program breaks on television.

35 Barnes, in line with conventional thinking which we have refuted above, speaks of demand charges based on "allocating" the *total* of costs listed under the heading of "demand" or "capacity" expenses among the classes of customers, where we would assign the *marginal* cost of the fractional unit of capacity held for each unit demand. Barnes approves of use of the "diversity factor" but rather inconsistently disapproves of allocating the capacity cost on the basis of contribution to peak demand. The logic underlying the two is of course the same

responsibility method even at best has its weaknesses.

With regard to the structure of the demand charges in water supply, the committee report brings out the interesting fact that these frequently lie heavily on domestic users. In the city (unidentified) used in the report for illustration, the smallest-sized meters accounting for 37 per cent of the output bore about 75 per cent of the demand charges.[36] This may not be unreasonable, however. The report states that the maximum simultaneous demand in a residential area "could" be about six times average use, while in an industrial area the maximum will be "nearer" twice the average use.[37] From our point of view, we would say that the system must hold in readiness more capacity for a residential area than for an industrial area with the same aggregate consumption.

The importance of the peak-load problem is suggested by the following percentages of average water demand in 206 cities: peak month, 140; peak day, 162; and peak hour, 257.[38] Furthermore, the relative importance of the peak day and the peak hour have been sharply increasing in recent years. Wolff forecasts an annual 1 per cent increase in the peak-day-to-average ratio. Peak hourly demands (primarily due to lawn-sprinkling and air conditioning) have risen so drastically as to require widespread imposition of restrictions on water use,[39] including special charges for air-conditioning uses.

A third and most important non-random element influencing water demand is price. Fourt has shown that, for domestic users (the class of use generally considered least responsive to price) the elasticity of demand for water is around —0.4 (a 1 per cent increase in water price will bring about a 0.4 per cent decrease in quantity taken).[40] The Seidel-Baumann study indicates slightly greater elasticity.[41] These findings are also consistent with the well-known inverse association of water metering and water use.[42] This consideration permits an alternative approach to the problem of on-peak and off-peak demands. The capacity-charge method regards the consumer as purchasing an option to take the commodity at a prefixed price, the cost of the option being related to the peak load imposed on the system. The other approach, called "peak-load pricing," is to regard on-peak and off-peak service as really two different commodities or, with greater generality, to regard the commodity delivered as different according to the heaviness of the load on the system. This consideration would dispense with the

—that it is not the maximum possible demand which is significant but the maximum likely to be imposed on the system. The "improved" conventional practice Barnes recommends bases the demand charge on the contribution to the sum of the non-coincident maximum demands, an utterly irrelevant and pointless measure (*op. cit.*, pp. 325–31). Davidson, in an extensive discussion of alternative modes of allocating capacity cost, defends the peak-responsibility method, correctly converting it into a charge for the *marginal* cost of the system capacity required to meet the peak (see R. K. Davidson, *Price Discrimination in Selling Gas and Electricity* [Baltimore: Johns Hopkins Press, 1955], pp. 111–47).

36 "Determination of Water Rate Schedules," *op. cit.*, p. 208.

37 *Ibid.*, pp. 209–10. Again this argument refers to the class maximum, when it is the contribution to system peak which is relevant.

38 J. B. Wolff and J. F. Loos, "Analysis of Peak Water Demands," *Public Works*, LXXXVII (September, 1956), 111.

39 J. B. Wolff, "Forecasting Residential Requirements," *Journal American Water Works Association*, XLIX (March, 1957), 225–35.

40 Louis Fourt, "Forecasting the Urban Residential Demand for Water" (University of Chicago Agricultural Economics Seminar Paper, February 14, 1958) (unpublished).

41 Harris F. Seidel and E. Robert Baumann, "A Statistical Analysis of Water Works Data for 1955," *Journal American Water Works Association*, XLIX (December, 1957), 1531–66 (at p. 1541).

42 Ralph Porges, "Factors Affecting Per Capita Water Consumption," *Water and Sewage Works*, May, 1957, pp. 199–204.

need for a two-part tariff to distinguish between commodity and capacity charges. The customer would simply pay the relevant marginal cost for each type of service actually received by him. This necessitates, of course, a commodity price varying by time of day and season.[43] In the case of electric utilities a distinction is frequently made between off-peak and on-peak prices, and occasionally even more detailed differentiation of rates will be made.[44]

Actually, a capacity charge based on the peak-responsibility method differs conceptually only a little from peak-load pricing, since, in the former case, the consumer is also being charged a premium as a function of the quantity taken in the peak period. The peak-responsibility method does have two difficulties, however. First, it is generally incorrect to load all the weight of the marginal cost of capacity upon the peak; Steiner has shown that, in general, some of the marginal cost of capacity is ascribable to demands of the non-peak periods.[45] More fundamentally, basing the capacity charge on the marginal capacity cost is logically equivalent to *long-run* marginal-cost pricing, when it is short-run marginal-cost pricing which is relevant.[46] With a given capacity in existence, the long-run marginal cost is a constant; it is the short-run marginal cost of service which varies on-peak and off-peak. In electricity supply short-run marginal cost will ordinarily be higher on-peak because less efficient equipment will be on line to supplement the more efficient equipment used to carry the basic load. Indeed, if a capacity limitation is actually hit, the short-run marginal-cost curve may be on a steeply rising branch, as in Figure 11. In water supply the major cost of an increment in peak service is probably the reduction in quality of service imposed on others through loss of pressure. In either of these circumstances a higher on-peak price is required to deter on-peak use to the point where marginal cost equals the marginal value of the service. Since the demand on-peak is not a random factor, as assumed in the capacity-charge approach, but rather a consequence of human decisions capable of adjustment to the price charged, variation of the latter to accord with changing marginal cost would produce a more efficient use of society's resources.

Another way to meet the problem of peak loads is to charge for "special uses" such as lawn-sprinkling and air conditioning. This is a procedure recommended in the committee report.[47] One defect of this approach is that all special-use consumers are assessed the special charge, whether in fact they contribute to the peak or not. In other words, consumers are not required to meet a price actually deterring them from on-peak consumption.

With the exception of fire protection (as

[43] See Houthakker, *op. cit.* Probably the best analysis available is M. Boiteux, "La Tarification des demandes en pointe: application de la théorie de la vente au coût marginal," *Revue générale de l'électricité,* LVIII (August, 1949), 321–40. A translation of this article, with some revisions and additions, has been published under the title, "Peak-Load Pricing," *Journal of Business,* XXXIII (April, 1960), 157–79. It is worth noting that Boiteux, a vice-president of the Électricité de France (the French nationalized power industry), has been able to achieve adoption of a sophisticated rate structure with a very considerable element of peak-load differentiation.

[44] Barnes, *op. cit.,* pp. 344–46.

[45] P. O. Steiner, "Peak Loads and Efficient Pricing," *Quarterly Journal of Economics,* LXXI (November, 1957), 585–610.

[46] Hirshleifer, *op. cit.,* pp. 460–61.

[47] "Determination of Water Rate Schedules," *op. cit.,* pp. 204–7. The report distinguishes between normal and special uses, the latter being those with an unusually large ratio between maximum demand and average demand—and so requiring more reserved capacity than their aggregate actual use alone would call for. The largest such use is fire protection; other special categories are air conditioning and refrigeration, lawn-sprinkling, irrigation supplies, and certain commercial and industrial uses (*ibid.,* p. 199). We will discuss fire protection separately below.

we shall argue), there would be no need to distinguish among uses at all if higher rates could be charged for the more scarce and expensive on-peak commodity than for the plentiful and cheap off-peak commodity. The varying rates would tend to equalize use (complete equalization, however, would not be achieved) by leveling the peaks and filling in the valleys, and so a considerable increment to reserve capacity could be provided without cost. In practice, a small demand charge might still be required to cover the excess capacity presently carried for the predictable seasonal and hourly peaks.[48]

Turning now to some practical considerations in water-supply peaking problems, brief peaks like those due to lawn-sprinkling can ordinarily be handled by local storage, although, as we have seen, a degradation in quality of service (loss of pressure) usually occurs as well. Air conditioning tends to create longer-lived peaks in hot spells, for which additional distribution and possibly even production capacity must be provided.[49] Finally, there is the seasonal summer-long peak, which will ordinarily require either very large reservoir storage or an increment to production capacity.

While we have not investigated the matter in detail, we are inclined to believe that for water supply the ideal solution, involving a sophisticated system of peak-load pricing, is impracticable because of the high cost of special metering. A seasonal premium price for water (in the summer, ordinarily) would not require any special metering, however, and we strongly believe that it would have a most beneficial effect in a wide variety of situations. In the absence of peak-load pricing, or to supplement a limited introduction of it, we favor capacity or demand charges based on the contributions that the different classes of service concerned make to the system peak. Still less satisfactorily, the peak-responsibility penalties by customer classes could be loaded onto their respective commodity charges, so that each class of service would pay a single compromise price representing a kind of weighted average of the low-cost and high-cost water provided it off-peak and on-peak.

F. Fire Protection

Certain special uses, and in particular the need to provide a large excess of capacity for the purpose of fire protection, are of the greatest importance in water rate structures. Fire-protection service is one area where a demand or capacity charge can be justified with little or no qualification. We have seen that the essential idea justifying a demand charge is that the amount taken, while in the aggregate responsive to price, varies over time in a random fashion not responsive to price. This is close to the true situation for fire protection. Fire service is desired at unpredictable moments, and to stint on the amount of water used at such times would seldom be rational.

The capacity required for fire protection is, of course, by no means an absolute. A convenient guide exists, however, in the form of standards set up by the National Board of Fire Underwriters. The committee report favors a charge on the basis of the cost of the incremental capacity required by these standards over the capacity for

48 If rates could fluctuate freely, no demand charge would ever be required. On exceptionally heavy-use days the rates would naturally rise to the level which equated marginal cost and the marginal value in use. In practice, it does not pay in the utility business to have such continuously fluctuating rates; the commodity is simply not expensive enough to justify the costs of disseminating the information and making the required decisions. This holds particularly in the case of water.

49 The extraordinary importance of the air-conditioning uses in the peak load is brought out in W. Victor Weir, "Surcharge for Nonconserved Air Conditioning in St. Louis County," *Journal American Water Works Association,* XLVII (November, 1955), 1091–1100.

normal uses (or, alternatively, the charge is to be based on extra storage provided in lieu of capacity), plus the clearly separable costs ascribable to fire protection.[50] This is the correct cost, if interpreted as the current cost of providing and maintaining the capacity in operation, rather than the sunk historical cost incurred in originally acquiring it. Quantitatively, the committee estimated that, for a city of 100,000, the fire-protection charges should come to about 14 per cent of total cost; the fraction is generally a declining function of size of city.[51] For a city of 10,000 the comparable figure appears to be perhaps around 20 per cent, while for a city of 1,000,000 it might be 10 per cent of total cost.

Several secondary points also require comment. The report considers that there is "some justification" for offsetting property taxes upon the water system against the fire charge levied on the municipality, as these magnitudes are often similar.[52] This procedure, though frequently adopted, is most unwise; it has the consequence of obscuring the amount actually paid for fire protection, thus making more difficult rational decisions as to the scale of investment in this direction. If the water authority, whether private or public, cannot show on its books any credit for fire-protection investments, there will be a tendency to spend no more than the minimum possible. And the municipal authorities are not clearly given information that might assist them in, for example, balancing expenditures for additional firemen against expenditures for additional water capacity.

Where the water supply falls short of the standard adopted by the National Board of Fire Underwriters, the report argues that the amount of capacity allocable to fire remains unchanged (i.e., the portion of capacity ascribable to fire is thereby *increased*), basing this contention on the assumption that as a matter of fact sufficient water for fire will in emergencies be obtained, although normal users may suffer.[53] This amounts to saying that the capacity provided for fire protection is, except possibly in extreme cases, always up to standard. The deficiency will be in that provided for normal service, though this will not become apparent unless the unusual fire demand materializes. Under these assumptions it does seem plausible to hold that the full standard requirement is always being reserved for fire protection, though of course a considerable arbitrary element enters into the determination of the standard.[54]

In discussing the incidence of the fire charges, the report correctly suggests that these should be related to the applicable fire insurance rates of the different properties.[55] The report does not criticize strongly enough the pernicious practice of collecting the fire charges by increasing either the commodity rates or the demand charges.[56] Actually, the public fire charges

[50] "Determination of Water Rate Schedules," *op. cit.*, pp. 200–202. The report violates this principle, for unexplained reasons, in stating that, "where the source of supply is a large reservoir, no part of the cost of such storage would be chargeable to fire" (p. 201). Perhaps what is assumed here is that sufficient excess capacity is already available in the reservoir. Certainly, in building a reservoir, there would be extra costs in scaling it up to meet fire-protection requirements.

[51] *Ibid.*, p. 202.

[52] *Ibid.*, p. 203.

[53] *Ibid.*

[54] Ideally, the standard should be determined as the optimum balance between the expected value of fire losses (possibly adjusted for a risk-aversion factor to recognize the fact that people value more heavily the risk of unusually high losses) and the cost of the capacity provided for protection.

[55] "Determination of Water Rate Schedules," *op. cit.*, pp. 203–4.

[56] *Ibid.*, p. 204. We refer here to spreading the fire charge in this way across the board to all customers. In principle, it might be a sensible practice to assess a fire-capacity charge differentially to customers in proportion to the fire risk presented.

should most sensibly be collected from the fire budget of the municipality, and the latter agency should take on the job of assessing property for fire protection.[57]

G. Underpricing and Overbuilding in Water Supply

The American Water Works Association conducts a quinquennial survey of public and private waterworks which generates a great deal of statistical information shedding light on current practices of American water-supply enterprises. In our analysis of water pricing, we will make use of the latest of these staff-report surveys, for the year 1955,[58] and the Seidel-Baumann analysis thereof.[59]

Table 9 illustrates the range of retail prices charged at the time of the 1955 survey by public water-supply systems as a function of differing monthly rates of water use. Figure 14 similarly illustrates the pattern of declining block rates[60] for a number of specific important cities. The prices charged by privately owned systems are systematically higher. As can be seen in Table 10, the reasons for the higher charges are, primarily, the enormously heavier taxes incurred by private systems and, secondarily, the somewhat higher operation and maintenance expenses. The privately owned sector of the industry has declined relatively in recent years (privately owned enterprises supplied 28 per cent of the total population served by water utilities in 1956),[61] perhaps less because of the tax disadvantage than as a result of the generally unremunerative level of rates imposed by regulatory commissions (see below).

In view of this comparison, one of the first questions which arises is whether water rates, and especially the rates charged by publicly owned enterprises, are too low. The question of underpricing is most fundamentally viewed as connected with the

[57] The discussion above refers to public fire-protection service. There is also private fire-protection service, for which similar principles apply.

[58] "A Survey of Operating Data for Water Works in 1955," *Journal American Water Works Association,* XLIX (May, 1957), 555–696.

[59] Seidel and Baumann, *op. cit.*

[60] Since the survey called for charges only at certain specific use rates, Table 9 and Figure 14 do not show the block break points correctly but only a smoothed-out picture of them.

[61] W. L. Picton, "Financial Requirements of Water Utilities," *Willing Water,* October, 1958, p. 9.

TABLE 9*

RETAIL PRICES OF WATER IN AMERICAN CITIES (PUBLICLY OWNED UTILITIES ONLY)

(Prices in Dollars per 1,000 Cubic Feet†)

No. of Cities	Minimum	Maximum	Unweighted Mean	Median
	Rate for Monthly use of 1,000 Cubic Feet			
432........	$0.68	$7.50	$2.62	$2.50
	Rate for Monthly Use of 10,000 Cubic Feet			
431........	$0.433	$4.450	$1.900	$1.845
	Rate for Monthly Use of 100,000 Cubic Feet			
425........	$0.3555	$3.274	$1.34	$1.26
	Rate for Monthly Use of 1,000,000 Cubic Feet			
383........	$0.161	$3.207	$1.060	$1.010

* Source: Harris F. Seidel and E. Robert Baumann, "A Statistical Analysis of Water Works Data for 1955," *Journal American Water Works Association,* XLIX (December, 1957), 1548.

† A price of $1.00 per 1,000 cubic feet equals $43.56 per acre-foot.

phenomenon of overbuilding of water supplies. We should first make clear, however, what the economic sense is in which rates can be said to be too low. We have argued earlier in this chapter that water rates should be based on short-run marginal cost but that in equilibrium a level of capacity should be established such that short-run marginal cost equals long-run marginal cost, both then equaling price (see the solution at point M in Fig. 13). If our idealizations of the cost functions of water enterprises in Figures 11–13 are correct in showing that long-run marginal cost is rising in the relevant range,[62] the correct equilibrium price represented by the vertical height of M in Figure 13 or M_4 in Figure 12 exceeds the unit cost represented by the height of A or A_4, correspondingly. In consequence, enterprises pricing correctly in equilibrium should typically show a profit over all costs (or, alternatively, a high earnings yield on the capital invested).

It is true, however—and especially so, since, we have seen, water-supply increments are typically constructed in discrete notches—that at any given time a great many or even the bulk of the different systems may be out of equilibrium with respect to capacity. But, if there were no systematic pattern of overbuilding, we would expect to see a fairly balanced distribution of errors. Systems that are underbuilt would have to ration water by charging a fairly high price (or, of course, they may impose non-price rationing to a greater or lesser extent). Systems that

[62] While there are certain economies of scale, these are overweighted (we argue) by the need to go to more distant, more expensive, and/or lower-quality sources to achieve greater system yield.

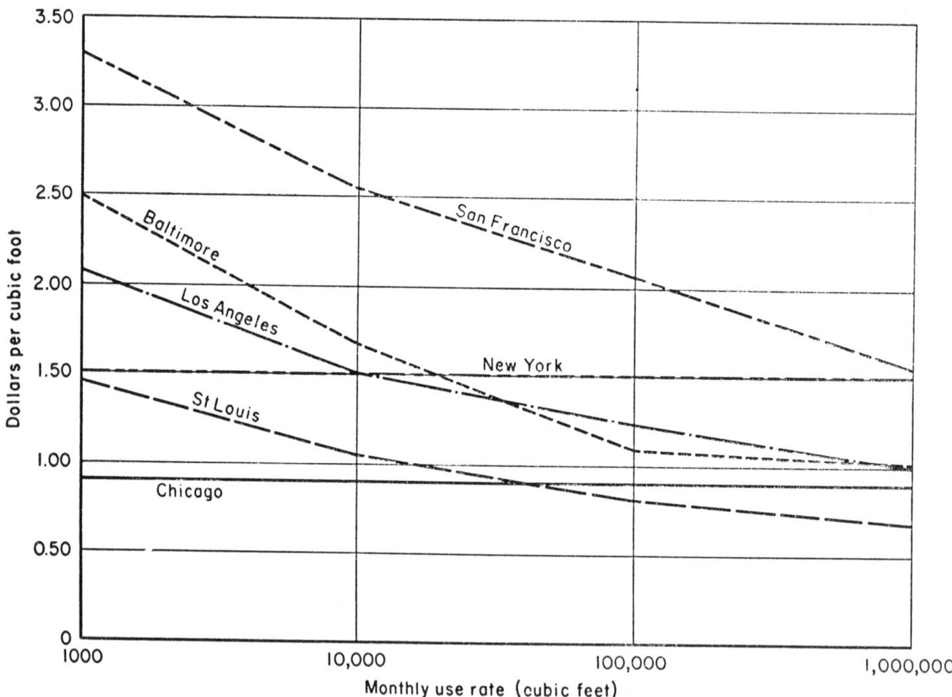

FIG. 14.—Water prices at differing monthly use rates. (From data in "A Survey of Operating Data for Water Works in 1955," *Journal American Water Works Association,* XLIX [May, 1957], 555–696.)

are overbuilt will tend to set very low prices on water to make some use of their idle capacity (and, we have seen, this will ordinarily be justified in terms of short-run marginal cost, given the fact that the overcapacity exists). On the average and in the aggregate, if errors tended to be balanced, we would still expect to see a reasonable return on capital earned in the water industry, even allowing for some sporadic instances of non-price rationing in underbuilt systems.

Even though overbuilding of supplies predominated in the industry, if the average extent of overbuilding were not too large we might still expect to find a normal or average return on capital invested (since equilibrium capacity with correct pricing should lead to a comfortable rate of return with profits being earned over all costs including interest). A subnormal return on capital invested in the water industry would therefore imply a strong degree of overbuilding. If this were so, we could say that rates are too low in a long-run sense (even though in the short run, given the overcapacity, setting low rates is making the best of a bad situation) because, as demand rises, an increase of price is an alternative to expansion of facilities. A low aggregate rate of return demonstrates that in such circumstances new capacity is usually built prematurely to provide for demand increases that should instead be handled by price adjustments.

Unfortunately, since the American Water Works Association study did not call for replacement values of capital investment, we cannot directly tell whether, on the average, a normal return on capital was being recovered in 1955. However, the Department of Commerce as of the end of 1954 estimated replacement value of public water supplies (including privately owned facilities apparently) at $22.8 billion, and the population served at 111,000,000, yielding a replacement value per capita of some $205.[63] In contrast, the AWWA study indicates a *gross* return on capital, including depreciation, of only $4.90 per capita for public enterprises and $3.94 per capita for private enterprises.[64] (Both figures are unweighted means for a large number of systems.) This return on capital is after taxes but, even so, is amazingly small, including, as it does, interest on debt, equity earnings (for privately owned facilities), and depreciation.

TABLE 10*

COMPARISON OF PUBLICLY AND PRIVATELY OWNED WATER SYSTEMS

(Unweighted Mean Values Throughout)

	Public	Private
Monthly rates ($/1,000 cu. ft.) at monthly use of:		
1,000 cu. ft.	$ 2.62	$ 3.70
10,000 cu. ft.	1.90	2.59
100,000 cu. ft.	1.34	1.66
1,000,000 cu. ft.	1.06	1.22
Revenue, $/mil. gal. produced†	228	330
Revenue, $/capita	10.65	12.16
Expense, $/mil. gal. produced:		
Operation and maintenance	118	136
Miscellaneous	3	3
Taxes	2	84
Total‡	$123	$223
Book value, $/capita	$ 82	$ 68
Earnings, $/mil. gal. produced§	105	107
Earnings, $/capita‖	4.90	3.94

* Source: Seidel and Baumann, *op. cit.*, p. 1563.

† $100 per million gallons is equivalent to $32.59 per acre-foot.

‡ Excluding all capital charges.

§ Earnings are revenue less expense as reported in the table and so are before any charges for capital.

‖ Calculated by us from other data in table.

In fact, this figure is so astonishingly low (roughly a 2 per cent or 2.5 per cent capital return gross of depreciation) as to be scarcely believable were it not consistent

63 U.S. Department of Commerce, Business and Defense Services Administration, *op. cit.*, p. 1.

64 The so-called earnings in Table 10 are before any deduction for capital charges.

with other evidence available. The Seidel-Baumann mean figure for gross revenue before *all* expenses, for example, is only $10.65 per capita (publicly owned systems), or around 5.2 per cent of investment replacement value per capita. The essential explanation for this phenomenon appears to be that, despite our recent price inflation, public rates are based on the idea of recovery of costs expended, which amounts to valuing the capital at historical or original cost. Private rates are not so exclusively based on original cost but, on the average, represent a compromise between original and replacement values,[65] probably weighted more heavily toward the former (even where commissions recognize reproduction cost in principle, the regulatory lag in a period of rapid inflation has led to a substantial departure in practice). Howson believes that the average incremental investment required currently for new public water service to handle increased population is "at least $250 per capita,"[66] which is roughly consistent with the Department of Commerce figure (since Howson's figure is in terms of 1959 dollars). As another check, the Seidel-Baumann "book value" (depreciated original cost) of water plants of $82 per capita for public enterprises can be inflated to 1955 replacement values by use of a construction-cost index. Assuming that the appropriate average age of existing investment in 1955 was ten years,[67] and applying the *Engineering News-Record* construction-cost index, a figure of $176 per capita is obtained,[68] again roughly consistent, given the inaccuracies of this crude calculation. The private book value shown by Seidel and Baumann is lower—$68 per capita. Despite this lower book value, the private rate of return on capital is about equally unfavorable because of the lower gross return. Applying the *Engineering News-Record* correction gives a per capita replacement value of $146, on which the $3.94 gross return inclusive of depreciation represents a rate of 2.7 per cent. It is also worth noting that the private $68 per capita book-value figure has risen just over 10 per cent since 1945, while the public figure has risen almost 60 per cent.[69] This apparently reflects the fact that private water utilities have found it extremely difficult to secure the capital required for expansion—a result again consistent with the exceptionally low rate of remuneration indicated by the data here reviewed.

The answer seems clear, therefore, that water rates are too low to cover replacement cost, because of failure to allow for price inflation in general as well as for what seems to be a relative price increase of construction costs as compared with price averages. As between publicly and privately owned systems, the former have the advantage of being able to finance exclusively by debt, whereas a private system cannot ordinarily secure capital except by a balance of debt and equity. Not only is the interest charge on debt characteristically lower than the earnings required to make equity acceptable to investors, especially as local governments can issue debt whose interest is exempt from federal income tax, but, even more importantly, returns to equity are taxed at the heavy 52 per cent corporate income-tax rate. Furthermore,

65 L. R. Howson, "Fifty Years' Experience with Water Works Costs and Revenues," *Journal American Water Works Association,* LI (June, 1959), 639–700.

66 *Ibid.,* p. 697.

67 Howson remarks that 75 per cent of waterworks expenditure has occurred since 1943 (*ibid.,* p. 698), but the ten-year average age seems still reasonable in view of the fact that the remaining 25 per cent is stretched out over quite a long period, and, of course, each earlier dollar counts for more real cost.

68 The *Engineering News-Record* cost index for 1955 on a 1945 base is 214, which, when multiplied by the $82 book value, gives the figure in the text (see *Engineering News-Record,* October 17, 1957, p. 84).

69 Seidel and Baumann, *op. cit.,* p. 1563.

the publicly owned systems generally escape property and other minor taxes.[70] In chapter vi we will argue that, because of the interacting risk and tax considerations, and in order to prevent the adoption of publicly owned projects inferior in efficiency to privately owned ones, an interest rate of around 10 per cent should be used for evaluating investments of public enterprises (corresponding to a 10 per cent before-tax or 5 per cent after-tax private discount rate). In practice, water rates of publicly owned systems are usually calculated to cover the 2–4 per cent interest charges at which local governments have been able to finance water-supply projects. The divergence between revenues and true economic costs revealed by a gross return to capital of around 2.5 per cent becomes very great when measured against such a high standard of investment yield.

It seems quite conclusively established, therefore, that water rates—especially those of publicly owned systems—are characteristically far too low to recover a correctly calculated average cost. If our argument above was sound that marginal cost for the expanding water-supply industry probably exceeds average cost, by and large, we may conclude a fortiori that current rates are far too low, primarily as a result of rate calculations based on the recovery of total historical cost without allowance for inflation or for the special low-interest advantages which apply to the publicly owned enterprises.[71]

[70] The tax figure of $84 per million gallons shown in our Table 10 for private systems was distributed as follows: 34 per cent for local taxes, 11 per cent for state taxes, and 55 per cent for federal taxes (*ibid.*, p. 1564).

[71] We may mention that, despite analytical differences between our approach and conventional thinking in the water industry, there appears to be a widespread, perhaps partly instinctive, feeling in the industry that rates really are too low (see Howson, *op. cit.*, pp. 699–700; J. H. Murdoch, Jr., "75 Years of Too Cheap Water," *Journal American Water Works Association,* XLVIII [August, 1956], 925–30; Picton, *op cit.*).

While the extraordinarily low level of rates in general is undoubtedly the outstanding feature of the existing situation, several other points are worthy of mention. The one of greatest importance is the crucial role of the peak-load demands discussed earlier in the underpricing-overbuilding picture. The over-all rate of return to water enterprises looks so bad because, in large part, new water facilities are constructed to serve a peak demand only, thus being condemned to idleness off-peak. It will usually be a highly desirable policy to attempt to cut down the peak by a premium price (or by a peak-responsibility capacity charge), thus postponing new construction until (ideally) an increment to supply is justified by the level of the *average* demand rather than required only for localized peaks.

Table 9 also reveals the significance of the declining block or "promotional" rate structures already questioned as possibly inefficient in discriminating in favor of large users (the marginal value in use of large users may be less than that of small users). For seventy-eight publicly owned utilities studied by Seidel and Baumann, residential customers took some 48 per cent of water sold but contributed 56 per cent of revenue, while industrial users, with 33 per cent of consumption, paid in only 17 per cent of revenue.[72] The same seventy-eight utilities showed only 3 per cent of revenue as public and private fire-service charges,[73] as compared with the committee report calculation discussed above indicating that fire service accounts for from 10 to 20 per cent of total cost, calculated incrementally. Evidently, a serious degree of relative underpricing applies for this category of service.

[72] Seidel and Baumann, *op. cit.*, pp. 1552 and 1539.

[73] *Ibid.*, p. 1552.

H. Conclusion

The committee report shows an excessive preoccupation with the amount of revenue in relation to cost. In this respect it is consistent with a general attitude which has dominated the thinking on rate problems of public utilities. Utility companies have demanded enough revenue at least to cover their costs, while regulatory bodies have viewed their role as that of preventing the revenues from exceeding costs—except for a normal return on the capital invested. In this concentration upon the distribution of wealth between stockholders and the consuming public, no one (save a few professional economists) seems to have paid any attention to the problem emphasized here of efficient use of resources.

Water appears to be a commodity whose supply is increased in discontinuous notches or steps; average costs will be rising in the large but may be falling on any given notch of capacity. The optimal marginal-cost price pattern, we have argued, will tend to generate losses along a given notch by indicating low prices until capacity is approached by the gradually growing demand—but then marginal-cost prices will tend to rise rather sharply, producing revenue surpluses until new capacity is constructed. This discussion considers water as a single commodity. Actually, because of the peak-load factor in water demand, in any period of time like a day or a year there will be some off-peak demand not pressing on capacity limitations and some on-peak demand which does. Instead of the growing demand over time (or, rather, in addition to it), there is a regular diurnal and seasonal variation of demand. The marginal-cost principle is still the same; the on-peak demand should generally be paying a higher price than the off-peak demand. The procedure in municipal water rates of attempting to recover the cost of extra capacity by a fixed demand charge on users is an inferior expedient, from the point of view of theory, to charging differential prices. This expedient will, however, be justified if the extra cost of pricing and of special metering exceeds the saving in more rational utilization of water supplies. Fire protection is a use clearly falling in this category, and more generally it will be impractical to vary prices by the hour or even by the day.

As a practical matter, it is probably most urgent to introduce *seasonal* peak-load pricing, and, as it happens, this particular mode of differential pricing will not involve special metering problems. To take a possible instance, suppose that there is a city which appears to require an expensive increment of supplies because its peak summer demand is pressing on system capacity, although during the rest of the year there is a wide margin of surplus over demands. Such a city should immediately introduce a summer peak-load differential. If the storage and distribution network of the system is such that the daily peak is crucial (the hourly peak being met by drawing down storage), if the daily peak is 160 per cent[74] of system average demand, and if this peak demand has a price elasticity of about —0.4,[75] then a 50 per cent summer premium in price would tend to reduce the daily peak to only about 128 per cent of system average demand. This crude example suggests the great possibilities offered by peak-load pricing as an alternative to expensive new construction. In addition, the prices people are willing to pay on-peak provide a way of valuing the additional water that would be supplied by such new construction. We may mention that, while seasonal differentials are not entirely unknown, their significance is so little appreciated that the last (1955) quinquennial survey of the American Water Works Association did not even call for any informa-

[74] Wolff and Loos, *op. cit.*

[75] Fourt, *op. cit.*

tion on this score. Seasonal price differentials are not uncommon, in contrast, in the rate schedules of gas utilities.

We may close with some comments on the cost to the economy of the various objectionable practices criticized here. In the past water has been so cheap that no very great rationality in its use was called for. For the future, however, it appears that water supply will increase in cost relative to goods in general; more and more inferior raw supplies and incovenient sites are being resorted to, while no great inventions seem to be impending that promise to reduce these costs. Accordingly, we may expect a higher degree of rationality to be required in the future. The costs of irrationality become most clear when designed capacity of existing installations is being approached: then communities are faced with a choice between an expensive increment to supply or a more rational use of present supplies. There have been many instances, of which the industry is quite aware, of reduction of use by 50 per cent or more when metering was introduced to replace a flat-rate system. The industry is not yet so aware of similar possibilities available in pricing according to marginal cost, in charging higher on-peak prices in place of the flat demand charge, and in eliminating discriminatory favoritism which provides some classes of users with water at a lower marginal price than others.

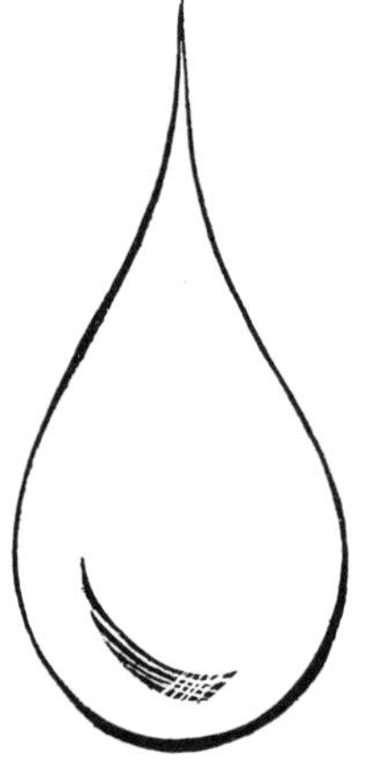

CHAPTER VI

INVESTMENT IN ADDITIONAL WATER SUPPLIES

This chapter is designed to explore the theoretical criteria for determining when expansions of water supplies should take place and which of the many technologically possible projects should be adopted. Discussion of the technological possibilities themselves is reserved for a later chapter. We here present and discuss the usual solution for the investment decision given by economic theory and then contrast theory with existing practice of public authorities, federal or local, responsible for undertaking water-supply development projects.[1] The following chapter is concerned with the problems of formulation and measurement involved in practical application of the theory presented here.

In chapter iii we initiated an analogous discussion of the theory and practice governing utilization of *existing* water supplies. In connection with the use of already-developed supplies, the economic theory is rather simpler than where it is necessary to compare the values of resources sacrificed in one time period with the value of the increased output gained thereby in a later period. It also happens to be the case that the possibilities available when one begins to think about the best use of existing supplies seem (at least to us) to be often more interesting, because less obvious, than those involving augmentation of supplies through investment. Thus the fact that more water can be provided for southern California by major dam-aqueduct projects or, more unconventionally, by desalinization of ocean water is so well known that our contribution to knowledge on that score can only be a quantitative one—a detailed consideration of the economic desirability of the alternatives available. But that 90 per cent of the existing

[1] The subject matter of this chapter largely coincides with that of a number of important recent works by economists designed primarily to evaluate past and present water-resource development programs of agencies of the federal government. The major studies which we will be citing are: Roland N. McKean, *Efficiency in Government through Systems Analysis* (New York: John Wiley & Sons, 1958); Otto Eckstein, *Water-Resource Development* (Cambridge, Mass.: Harvard University Press, 1958); and John V. Krutilla and Otto Eckstein, *Multiple Purpose River Development* (Baltimore: Johns Hopkins Press, 1958). The work of Edward F. Renshaw, *Toward Responsible Government* (Chicago: Idyia Press, 1957), should also be mentioned. As our space requirements necessitate a relatively cursory consideration of this range of topics, we will make extensive use of the analyses of these authors.

water supplies of California are being used for relatively low-value irrigation purposes is a much less well-known fact and one that strongly suggests the less conventional conclusion that, as population and industry grow in California, a large fraction of the water supply required could profitably be made available by cutting back on existing irrigation uses. We have seen that a free market in water rights would automatically provide a mechanism which would work in the direction of reallocating supplies toward the most highly valued uses. But, since for a number of reasons a free market in water rarely exists, or works imperfectly where it does exist, we devoted considerable time and space to a consideration of the forms and types of state regulation or intervention that might promote or might hinder achievement of the same results.

Similarly, in connection with the development of additional supplies, a free market in water rights would tend, under ideal conditions, to develop additional supplies of the right kind and at the right pace. Here, however, a comparatively well-established form of government intervention does exist governing the development of water supplies in place of the free market. Rather than starting with a relatively clean slate, therefore, we shall be able to criticize the principles and the historical record of existing decision-making agencies. Our conclusions, however radical, are not likely to be very new—every existing institution has its enemies who will probably have thought of all the criticisms that can fairly (or unfairly) be levied against it.

A. The Economic Theory of Choices over Time

1. Future Benefits and Costs Must Be Discounted

In our discussion of municipal water rates in chapter v, we spoke of those rates as allocating existing supplies among competing uses and users. With increasing population, wealth, and economic activity generally, these competing demands rise in intensity until, at a certain point, augmentation of the existing supplies becomes clearly desirable. The condition developed in our earlier chapter—that an increment to capacity is justified if marginal value in use (the value consumers would pay for an additional unit) exceeds long-run marginal cost (the cost incurred, per unit, on account of the incremental expansion)—did not explicitly treat the intertemporal aspect of the decision. Implicitly, however, the intertemporal aspect entered because one of the costs of expansion will be the interest paid for the use of "capital" (current resources set aside from current consumption for purposes of investment). Unless the future receipts that consumers would be willing to pay for the use of additional supplies are sufficient to cover these interest costs over and above the operating costs which will be incurred in utilizing these supplies, these supplies should not be developed, or so the theory maintains.

In this theory the competition between the demands of the future and of the present expresses itself by discounting future benefits and costs through the rate of interest. If no discounting took place (i.e., if the rate of interest were zero), the implication is that a dollar a year from now is valued as highly as a dollar today. Setting aside the possibility of relative price changes,[2] this means that the valuation placed now upon a loaf of bread, a bottle of milk, or a haircut a year from now would be the same as upon the equivalent goods or services today. If the rate of interest

[2] We speak in terms of dollars rather than real resources so that we can drop the proviso "setting aside relative price changes." We would have to repeat this phrase constantly if we pitched our main argument in terms of physical goods or services like haircuts or bushels of wheat.

were zero[3] into the indefinite future, the same statement could be made about the values of goods and services ten years from now, twenty years, or a thousand years. It would be worthwhile sacrificing a bushel of wheat today if thereby a net increase of resources of one bushel plus a fraction could be assured one thousand years from now. If, on the other hand, the rate of interest were infinitely high, future satisfactions would be discounted entirely; we would gobble up any resources yielding immediate satisfaction today without a thought for tomorrow.

In comparing nearer with more distant future periods, it is of course necessary to take account of the compounding of interest. A simple formula will illustrate this. If we denote the annual rate of interest by i, the successive annual terms (which may be positive or negative) of an income stream by the symbols s_0, s_1, s_2, etc., then the value V_0 of that income stream today, with annual compounding or discounting, is expressed by

$$V_0 = s_0 + \frac{s_1}{1+i} + \frac{s_2}{(1+i)^2} + \dots .$$

The income stream may in this formula either terminate or continue to infinity. If we decrease s_0 by 1, value V_0 remains unchanged if we compensate by increasing s_1 by the amount $1+i$, all the other terms s_2, s_3, etc., remaining unchanged. We may interpret this statement, equivalently, by saying that a dollar compounds into $1+i$ dollars in one year, i being the annual rate of interest, or that a dollar one year from now must be discounted (divided) by the factor $1+i$ to find its value in today's dollars.

Despite the rather obvious logical necessity for discounting future benefits and costs to compare them with present benefits and costs, we will see below that important water-supply projects have been proposed, authorized, and constructed without any such an analysis.

2. The Discount Rate Should Balance Time Preference and Productivity

The crucial question we must now turn to is how the free market determines the rate of interest,[4] and whether or to what extent the rate so determined can be said to be the appropriate guide for society (i.e., for both private and government decision-making agencies) to use in making choices involving intertemporal comparisons. The classical economic theory of the rate of interest views the latter as a rate of discount on future goods and services whose level is determined by a balance of considerations of *time preference* and *productivity*. On the one hand, it seems natural to argue that, other things being equal, a dollar today is preferred by consumers in general to a dollar one year from today (or, if that is not convincing, compare your preferences between a dollar today and a dollar a thousand years from now, even if the latter payment were quite certain). It is true that it may be possible to construct examples where a consumer might prefer future to present dollars or satisfactions; he might anticipate being poorer in the future than he is today and, consequently, be willing to conserve present assets for the future even if he had to pay storage charges. Nevertheless, a certain ultimate preference for present over future seems plausible.[5] Actually, however, sys-

[3] If the rate of interest were negative, we would actually value the future higher than the present; we would be willing to sacrifice a dollar today in exchange for something less than a dollar tomorrow.

[4] The concept of "the rate of interest" is a considerable abstraction, since we can observe on the market a number of different rates, varying primarily with the length of the loan and the type of security offered. The theoretical abstract rate of interest refers to riskless loans (perfect security) and may vary according to term.

[5] If the individual were sufficiently poor, present preferences would tend to dominate if only because survival in the present is a necessary con-

tematic preference for present over future is not a necessary condition for a positive rate of discount on future satisfactions; the influence of productivity alone would dictate a positive rate of interest even if time preferences were perfectly symmetrical between present and future. This would be true so long as opportunities anywhere in the society were available with positive net time productivity (see below).

The productivity explanation of interest is based upon the observed fact that it is possible to find situations in the economy where an input of resources today will generate a larger or more highly valued output of resources in the future. Examples are the growth of trees, the multiplication of rabbits, the aging of wine. These opportunities exist over the economy as a whole, for we observe almost everywhere that business firms are willing and able to pay more than a dollar in the future in exchange for a dollar today.[6] There are, of course, ways of investing that would not yield any net productivity over time (e.g., after a certain point aging wine ceases to improve and quality begins to fall off), but the existence of such unfavorable opportunities is not relevant, since they would never be exploited so long as opportunities remain with positive net productivity over time. (We can imagine societies with only such negative possibilities, for example, a group of sailors stranded on an utterly barren island and having in their possession as their only resource a stock of hardtack which deteriorates over time. Only for such a society would the rate of interest be negative.)

dition for enjoyment of future satisfactions. This argument would fail, however, if the individual valued his desires for his heirs as highly as his desires for himself.

[6] Some such loans are defaulted and not repaid, of course, but the statement in the text holds true even if we consider riskless investments or, alternatively, adjust the expected future returns of risky loans to take account of the probability of default.

3. *Implications of the Theory*

These brief notes are not intended to represent more than the rudiments of the classical economic theory of interest. A more detailed analysis would be necessary to handle certain complex problems, especially that of "capital rationing."[7] The rudiments of the theory suffice, however, to give at least a plausible justification for the use of the market rate of interest for intertemporal comparisons where investment decisions are involved. When such decisions are made under private auspices, the market rate of interest would tend to govern more or less automatically. From the point of view of the investor, a project would recommend itself only if the future returns it yielded were greater than the interest required to finance the project (even if the investment could be self-financed, it would not be undertaken unless this condition were met, since otherwise lending to others would be superior to undertaking the investment). This statement is subject to some qualifications we shall make later about the perfection of the market for capital funds, and the influence of risk and uncertainty must also be allowed for.

Accepting the rule, at least tentatively, as operative in the private sphere, the next step implied by this approach is to assert that, in those sectors of the economy where government decisions dominate, the same rule should be followed. That is, government should undertake those projects, and only those projects, that will yield more than the interest cost on the capital invested. In terms of our formula above, it should adopt those projects whose associated time streams have a net positive value when discounted at the market rate of interest. The reason is that such projects are more highly valued by consumers, taking into consideration the discounting of future benefits, than the alternative use of

[7] Discussed in our next chapter.

the capital in other investments or for consumption purposes. The market rate of interest measures the marginal rate of net time productivity of capital and also the marginal rate of time preference between future and present resources. If a higher rate is used by government in deciding on public projects, public projects will fail of adoption whose yield is more highly valued by consumers than the marginal private alternatives of investing or consuming. If a lower rate is used, public projects will be adopted where the capital could alternatively be used for purposes of private investment or consumption that are valued *more* highly by consumers.

B. Objections to This Solution

Most of the objections considered earlier in connection with the economic theory of choice in general—in particular, the existence of extra-economic values, the problem of "higher" and "lower" tastes, the dependence of the solution upon the existing distribution of wealth and talents, the existence of market imperfections, and divergences between private and social costs—are also relevant for the economic theory of intertemporal decision; but, since they do not involve the latter in any unique way, we shall not attempt to discuss them further here. There are, however, a number of more or less cogent objections to the classical theory that apply exclusively or with particular force when intertemporal decisions are considered. In the former category is the question of how to weigh the claims of posterity properly as against the claims of current generations. Another, somewhat technical, consideration is the argument that the interest rate is not an outcome of market forces but rather a datum arbitrarily under control of government. In the latter category we will discuss market imperfections peculiar to the capital market itself.

1. The Claims of Posterity

The allegation that market determinations of values as between present and future goods and services neglect the claims of future generations is at the heart of the more sophisticated expositions of "conservationist" philosophy. It is true that men do to some extent save for the benefit of their heirs and so do take the claims of future generations into account insofar as these make themselves indirectly felt through the affections of the present generation. But, conservationists may maintain, the market does not of itself provide any direct way for the needs and desires of unborn individuals to influence current choices between consumption for the benefit of the present and investment for the benefit of the future. Consequently, human selfishness being what it is, the decisions actually made through the market are almost bound to be one-sided. According to one view: "It is the clear duty of government, which is the trustee of unborn generations, as well as for its present citizens, to watch over, and if need be, by legislative enactment, to defend the exhaustible resources of the country from rash and reckless spoliation."[8] (We may, as an aside, reiterate the doubts we expressed earlier about such preaching of the "duties of government," with its implicit assumption that government is the repository and defender of social conscience on all economic questions rather than a complex institution composed of human beings with their own self-centered needs and desires.)

If, in fact, government seeks deliberately to act as the trustee of future generations, there is a variety of instrumentalities available. For preservation of fish and game resources there are license fees, season and

[8] A. C. Pigou, *Economics of Welfare* (4th ed.; London, 1932), p. 29. The views of Pigou and a number of other authors are described in A. Scott, *Natural Resources: The Economics of Conservation* (Toronto: University of Toronto Press, 1955), pp. 88–97.

bag limits, protected species, size limitations, and numerical quotas. Subsidies are granted farmers under a number of programs whose official purpose is to encourage them to undertake future-directed investments. Certificates of rapid tax amortization have had somewhat the same effect in the industrial sector, though the official purpose here is development of a mobilization base for national defense. In the case of oil and natural gas, monthly extraction quotas are established by a number of the major producing states. (In this and some other of the instances cited, the allegation has been made that the *official* purpose of conservation is rather less important than the actual purpose of holding down production for purposes of monopolistic gain.) In a few cases, regulation of one type or another has been applied to prevent drawing-down of underground water levels by pumping.

For the present, however, we want to restrict our consideration to the question of possible intervention through the interest rate to validate the claims of future generations.[9] There are two general ways by which the government could attempt to counteract the effect of an "excessively" high interest rate or discount of future costs and benefits. The first is to let the market rate govern in the private sphere but, in the government's own operations, to make decisions on the basis of a somewhat lower rate. This is actually done today, though as a more or less accidental consequence of tax legislation rather than as a deliberate policy. Thus, costs and benefits of federal projects are normally discounted at rates between 2.5 and 4 per cent, whereas even for conservative investments in the private sphere the future is likely to be discounted at a much steeper rate—6 per cent after taxes or 10 per cent before taxes may not be untypical.[10]

It is simple to show that the existence of differing rates of discount for public and private investments, after adjustment for risk, is undesirable on efficiency grounds. Assuming that the private and public spheres are divided on some principle which need not concern us here, the adoption, say, of a 3 per cent discount rate in the public sphere and a 6 per cent rate in the private sphere for investments of comparable risk means that there will be investments in the private sphere not undertaken because they will not be justified except for discount rates below, say, 5 per cent. Meanwhile, however, projects yielding only 3 per cent are being adopted in the public sphere. On efficiency grounds the disparity of interest rates will lead to the adoption of public projects that are less productive than private projects not being adopted. Note that the question of the claims of the future versus the present does not enter into this conclusion. The disparity of interest rates means that, given the aggregate amount of present sacrifice, less is provided for the future when less productive investments are undertaken.[11]

9 To the extent that the regulations cited above can be justified on economic grounds, they represent attempts to correct divergences between private and social costs. The magnitude of these divergences, granting that a correction is required, can still only be measured once a rate of discount for intertemporal comparisons is agreed on.

10 The operative rates in the public and private spheres are discussed in more detail in later sections of this chapter.

11 This argument implicitly assumes that the public investment is to be compared with the marginal private alternative, holding aggregate investment constant. Another possible approach would be to compare the public investment alternative with the private spending that would result if the tax moneys required for the public investment were left in private hands instead. This would lead to a somewhat different conclusion, since presumably part of the money left in private hands would then be spent for consumption purposes, thus quite possibly leaving less available for future generations despite the higher productivity of capital in the private sphere. Which comparison is the relevant one depends upon the purpose at hand. The inefficiency of differing discount rates between the private and public sectors is sufficiently shown by the fact that undertaking a public 3

The second broad alternative for the government, not subject to the same criticism on efficiency grounds, would be to increase the volume of real saving and investment, enforcing throughout the economy a rate of interest lower than that which would prevail otherwise in the market. Various monetary and fiscal measures are available to achieve this end. We cannot enter into a discussion of this branch of economic theory here, and so we will simply assert that the following policy would achieve the desired results: the government could make sufficient funds available on the loan market so as to drive the interest rate down to the desired level, while holding down the inflationary potential by a sufficiently high level of consumption taxes. The net effect is to squeeze consumption for the benefit of investment —the present for the benefit of the future— without introducing inefficiencies by creating disparities between the advantages of investment in the private and public spheres.[12]

The central question as to the desirability of additional sacrifice of the present on behalf of the future, assuming that the transfer mechanism is not subject to criticism on efficiency grounds, is one of distribution and as such not directly amenable to economic analysis. One extreme view is that the interests of the future should be weighted just as heavily as those of the present; that is, time preference should be neutral or symmetrical. An important point to realize is that, even accepting this argument, it does *not* follow that the correct discount rate is zero. Remember that interest is determined by the interaction of time preference and productivity. Even if the former were ruled out of court, so long as the net time productivity of the last investment undertaken is positive, some rate of discount on future goods is required to balance the demands of present and future.[13] The other extreme view is expressed in the slogan, "What has posterity done for us?" The legacy we have inherited from the past no doubt imposes a debt of gratitude, but what claim has the future to collect on that debt?

Most people would probably adopt an intermediate position between these two extremes. But, even if some obligation of the present to the future is recognized, it does not follow that any government intervention is required. First, as has been mentioned, the ties of family forethought and affection already dictate a certain amount of sacrifice on behalf of the future. Second, there are important motives for saving quite apart from the desire to provide for one's descendants or loved ones. Individuals who do not care to make any such provision at all may nevertheless save to accumulate funds for their own retirement

per cent investment prevents at least some private 5 per cent investments. The question of the optimum aggregate amount of current sacrifice is a distributional one between the present and the future.

[12] Note that the lower interest rate is not the *cause* but the *consequence* of the higher level of real investment (the larger amount of capital formed entails a lower marginal productivity of capital).

[13] Consider this example. Suppose that each pair of rabbits "invested" (not eaten) this year generate twice their number next year, assuming that we are clever enough in selecting sexes for our pair. For simplicity, assume that none dies naturally. If we were concerned with only two discrete time periods, now versus a year from now, and if initially the stock were 12 rabbits, a zero rate of discount would imply eating no rabbits (4 rabbits one year from now are valued more highly than eating 2 rabbits today). But this solution is obviously wrong (unfair to the present) if we value present and future equally; the consequence is eating no rabbits this year and 24 next year. The correct solution is to eat 8 currently and invest 4, the latter growing to 8 at the end of the year. This is equivalent to discounting the future at a rate of 100 per cent (the factor $1/[1+i]$ becomes $1/2$), equal to the time productivity of our original rabbit capital. If we wished to be able to continue our consumption at a level rate *in perpetuity,* we should eat only 6 of our original stock of 12—the remaining 6 will in turn become 12 at the end of the year.

years—or, more generally, because they would prefer having principal plus interest at some later date rather than consume the principal today. Finally, other individuals may accumulate funds to provide personal security against misfortune, to wield economic power, or for a variety of other reasons. Whatever the motive for saving may be, whenever an individual of positive net remaining wealth dies, future generations reap the reward of his abstinence. Whether provision for the future is on balance excessive or inadequate is one of those questions that are unanswerable within the framework of our analysis; that is, it is a question of taste or of ethics on which there is no social consensus we can use as a guide.[14] A rather important point in this connection is that, barring atomic holocaust, we can confidently expect our descendants to be wealthier than ourselves. Consequently, any deliberate redistribution in favor of the future may be a transfer from a poorer to a richer group.

On balance, therefore, we do not find any compelling reasons, arising out of failure to consider the interests of future generations, that justify "correction" of the results of the market discounting process. Even if we agreed that there is insufficient provision for the future, the way to remedy that is to squeeze current consumption (increase real saving), thus enforcing a lower interest rate throughout the society. The existence of a different (and lower) discount rate in the sphere of public as compared with private investment decisions is inefficient. That is, given any amount of real saving, use of an artificially low discount rate will lead to *less* provision for the future than might otherwise be attained; conversely, given the provision for the future, less will be retained for the present than could be made available were it not for the disparity of discount rates in the two spheres.

[14] Some might say that the public concern as expressed in the conservation "movement" is itself an indication of such a consensus. This is not entirely clear; for many of its proponents, being for conservation is undoubtedly like being for motherhood. If the issue were made explicit in terms of the desirability of sacrifice of current income on behalf of the future, in excess of that amount already being provided through the market mechanism, we do not feel any confidence as to how most people would stand.

2. *Does the Market Interest Rate Measure Correctly?*

The theory of the interest rate sketched above had interest determined by the interaction between the forces of productivity and time preference. This interaction was supposed to express itself in the market place where people bid for current dollars in exchange for future dollars—the capital market. Equilibrium in the capital market takes place when a sufficient premium is established on current dollars so that the quantities supplied and the quantities demanded are equal.

a) *Government intervention through fiscal and monetary policy.*—This theory, however, by implication assigned only a passive role to government in the determination of the interest rate. So long as the government acts in the capital market in a way which is the result of its own need for or generation of funds, this approach is not too difficult to maintain. The government might be looked upon as simply the agency through which certain collective consumption or investment decisions are made: provision for national defense, establishment of national parks, construction of roads, etc. To the extent that these expenses are not met by service charges or by general taxation (the "income" of government), the government turns to the capital market to provide the funds in much the same way as would individuals or firms attempting to make investments or to consume in excess of current income.

The difficulty with this approach is the fact that the federal government has the power to finance its expenses in a third way not available to private agencies or local government: it can either crudely print the money required or achieve much the same effect through more sophisticated measures (bonds are sold to the Federal Reserve banks, which then create credits upon which the government draws checks). Furthermore, the government has in the past (and very likely will in the future) deliberately made use of this power in an attempt to influence the rate of interest determined in the market. Thus, in time of depression, the government may attempt, by printing money or by subtler equivalents, to greatly increase the supply of current funds with the object of reducing the premium on them, thereby encouraging the undertaking of consumption or investment plans by those who need current funds and expect to have future funds with which to repay.

The market discount rate which in principle reflects a balance between time preferences and the productivity of current funds in terms of future funds is thus affected by a variety of government policies, even aside from the fact that government is the agency for certain collective spending and saving decisions. The policy used to stabilize the over-all level of the economy can affect the interest rate, and the policy discussed earlier of favoring the future over the present (forcing a rate of growth greater than that which would come about automatically) also would affect (lower) the rate of interest.

The problem created for optimal choices over time by such policies is not essentially different from the problems resulting from government interventions favoring some lines of activity (e.g., housing) and penalizing others (e.g., liquor) which we discussed in an earlier chapter. These interventions can be looked upon idealistically as attempts to realize in the interest of the entire society certain values not expressed properly through the automatic operation of the private sector of the economy—or they can be looked on more cynically as attempts to propitiate certain interests and penalize others under the guiding aim of maximizing the well-being of the groups wielding government power. In view of considerations like those raised here, it cannot be conclusively shown that the existing pattern of interest rates is either economically efficient or ethically ideal. Nevertheless, we can scarcely believe that those responsible for making water-investment decisions can do better than to accept the admittedly imperfect market rates of interest as their guide to relative intertemporal values of goods and services. A somewhat parallel problem, it will be remembered, arose earlier in connection with water-pricing decisions. We there considered arguments like the following: since agricultural price-support programs of government obviously raise the market prices of supported commodities above their true economic values, production of such commodities might be discouraged by charging their suppliers penalty prices for water. Quite aside from possible extramarket justifications for government policies relating either to agricultural price supports or to interest rates, we do not think it wise or appropriate for water planners in their pricing or investment choices to concern themselves with repairing the consequences of decisions obviously falling in the proper sphere of other agencies.

b) Imperfection of the capital market.—Like many other markets, the capital market is imperfect. Banking is a field where entry is severely restrained, and other types of financial institutions also work under highly complicated regulatory provisions. The regulation of the capital market and, in particular, the limitations on freedom of entry have sometimes been thought to lead to a type of monopoly return to those in the industry. The divergence between borrowing and lending rates and the strong preference of corporations for internal as opposed to external financing have been pointed to as evidence of such monopoly return. We cannot go into this question exhaustively here, but we believe that the evidence is by and large against the existence of such monopoly power, except possibly in isolated localities where only one or a few financial institutions may operate. The divergence between lending and borrowing rates is not too large to be explained, we believe, by the risk factor and the cost of doing business, while corporate preference for internal financing is in part a result of this divergence and in part due to the tax advantages of internal financing (if dividends are paid out, personal income taxes have to be paid before the funds become available for reinvestment). Consequently, we do not think it appropriate to correct the market interest rate to make any allowance for monopoly return in the capital market.

C. Current Practices Evaluated

In turning to an evaluation of current practices with regard to investment in additional water supplies, we find ourselves on territory that has been exhaustively worked over by others. In fact, an enormous literature already exists on the major topics we will discuss in this section: cost-benefit criteria, secondary benefits, and the correct discounting rate. In our discussion we will center upon the recommendations made in McKean's work,[15] while as the guide to best existing practices we will use the so-called *Green Book*.[16] As it happens, the latter tends to approach what we would regard as economic rationality much more closely than does actual practice, the report being itself an attempt to establish a norm for practice which has never been wholly adopted by the action agencies. On the recommendations side we shall at times mention the work of other analysts, particularly Eckstein, Krutilla and Eckstein, and Margolis. On the practical side we shall refer primarily to the Bureau of Reclamation in the Department of the Interior.[17]

1. Financial Feasibility versus Economic Feasibility

Most of the policy issues in connection with water-resource developments turn upon the distinction between financial feasibility and economic feasibility. Since these terms have not been entirely consistently used in either the official or the critical literature, we shall employ common-sense definitions of our own in order to expose the essential disagreements. By "financial feasibility" we mean what is sometimes known as the "self-liquidating" character of a project—a financially feasible project generates revenues that suffice to cover all costs, including interest on funds borrowed to finance the project.[18] Or, using our discounting formula above, for a financially feasible project V_0 must equal or exceed zero, counting capital outlays as costs and monetary receipts as incomes of the appropriate years, all being discounted

[15] *Op. cit.,* esp. Part III.

[16] Subcommittee on Benefits and Costs of the Federal Inter-Agency River Basin Committee, *Proposed Practices for Economic Analysis of River Basin Projects: Report to the Federal Inter-Agency River Basin Committee* (Washington, D.C.: Government Printing Office, May, 1950), pp. 8–9 (hereinafter cited as "*Green Book*"). A revised edition has since become available (dated May, 1958). Our analysis, based on the earlier edition, still largely applies, although the new version is improved at several points.

[17] We should mention that, since the practices of federal agencies are continuously subject to revision, our comments and criticisms do not necessarily relate to current actual practices but only to the procedures described in the published documents available to us and cited here.

[18] Our definition of "financial feasibility" more or less corresponds to the meaning of the term in the early reclamation acts. As the generosity, not to say laxity, of congressional standards for water-resource projects has increased over the years, the legal meaning of the term has been weakened. Currently, Bureau of Reclamation projects are considered "financially feasible" if the "reimbursable" costs are expected to be returned by the beneficiaries. Costs attributed to flood-control and navigation functions are non-reimbursable. Costs attributed to irrigation are reimbursable *without* interest. For a discussion see A. R. Golzé, *Reclamation in the United States* (New York: McGraw-Hill Book Co., 1952), pp. 123–30.

at that rate of interest at which the funds required are actually obtained. By "economic feasibility" we mean that the economic valuation of the "benefits," to whomever they accrue, exceeds the economic valuation of the "costs," to whomever they accrue. Here V_0 must again be non-negative, but the valuation placed on costs and benefits may diverge from actual monetary outlays and receipts, and the discount rate may diverge from the actual borrowing rate. Just how the economically relevant measures of benefits, costs, and discount rate may diverge from the monetary or market measures is a question we will take up in detail below.

As defined by us, a calculation of financial feasibility is essentially what every private investor makes in deciding whether to undertake a project with his own or with borrowed capital. Most of the criticisms that have been levied against the use of this criterion for public decisions have been based upon a showing that it is appropriate for government in its decisions to take into account certain real or alleged costs and benefits that would not enter into the calculations of private investors; for example, the fact that the product may be worth more to society than the monetary revenues received for it, that employment may be generated by the investment, or, on the other hand, that losses are imposed upon the owners of competing facilities, etc. As an illustration of this line of thinking:

> Financial feasiblity has been urged by some as the determining factor in evaluation, that is, they believe that all water resources projects should be self-liquidating. This view implies that Federal agencies should seek out sound business opportunities wherever they may be found in the water resources field.
>
> The basic fallacy in such reasoning is that it seeks to transfer to public investments the limitations common to private investments. The Federal Government seeks to conserve and develop the Nation's natural resources for the general welfare and not for profit. Hence, financial feasibility is not the same as economic feasibility. Financial costs and returns should be considered in analysis, but financial feasibility alone should not determine the desirability of a program or project. For this reason the Commission is recommending that Congress eliminate the requirement that irrigation projects show financial feasibility.[19]

This argument implies that financial feasibility is too narrow a criterion. There is at least one respect in which it might be considered too lax, however, as compared with economic feasibility. This turns upon the government's power to borrow more cheaply than private investors, which at least suggests the possibility that funds are being used for projects that are less productive than alternatives being foregone for lack of funds in the private sector. These questions will be discussed below.

2. Cost-Benefit Analysis and Extra-financial Considerations

The distinction usually made between financial feasibility and economic feasibility is that the former fails to take account of certain economic values which are not shown in the financial accounts of the agency responsible for the decision. We will consider in this section several possible divergences between the financial accounts and the real economic costs and benefits.

a) *Consumers' surplus*.—It will often be the case that construction of a water-supply project will necessarily be highly indivisible, meaning that, if any more water is to be provided at all, a large increment of supply must be constructed. As an example, an irrigation project will open to a humid type of cultivation a region not farmed at all before or else farmed only under extremely arid conditions. In such circumstances it might well be the case that the market revenues from water sales fall far short of

19 *The Report of the President's Water Resources Policy Commission*, Vol. I: *A Water Policy for the American People* (Washington, D.C.: Government Printing Office, 1950), p. 59.

the real value of the water. The reason, discussed in detail in Appendix A to chapter iii, is that, if water is sold freely on the market, consumers will take just so much as to bring their marginal value in use down to the market price. But the aggregate value in use to the consumers includes the value in use they derive from the earlier units, which will be at least as great and may well be considerably greater than the value of the last unit. Thus it has been estimated that the aggregate value of water to be provided by the Ainsworth Project in Nebraska is $679,550 annually, or something over $10 per acre-foot, while the marginal value of the last unit provided farmers is in the neighborhood of $3.00 per acre-foot.[20] Using a different example, water in a certain area may be freely available at $50 an acre-foot, which then is also the measure of its marginal value in use. If a certain project makes a large new supply available which is sold at $10 an acre-foot, the marginal value in use of the water will decline until the $10 level is reached, since it is now worthwhile for consumers to apply water less frugally and to less vital uses. The aggregate value of the increment of water is measured not by the quantity supplied times $10 but by the quantity times some average value which lies between $50 (the value of the first small increment) and $10 (the value of the last small increment).

The practical significance of this consideration is that private enterprise would be led to take too conservative a view of the benefits where important indivisibilities exist and that public enterprise (if rationally conducted) should count also the consumers' surplus—the aggregate value to consumers over and above the market value[21]—of the water received.[22] The limiting condition (indivisibility) is quite important and by no means applies in all contexts. Construction of a large dam and aqueduct, of course, could not be justified unless a rather substantial increment of water were to be provided. Increments of water provided through pumping or diversion, however, frequently are insufficient to drastically affect marginal values in use for water.

It must not be forgotten that an upper limit as well as a lower limit can be placed on the benefits; in no case are they greater on a per-unit basis than the previous price being paid for the water applied.[23] (If, as will normally be the case, construction for the future is involved, the "previous price" must be interpreted as the price that would have been effective if the additional supply were not provided.) We emphasize this because, in evaluating projects, quite commonly the market value of the water will be computed, after which there will be rather grand talk about "intangibles" or "development benefits." These supposed benefits may or may not exist, but, if the extrafinancial values of indivisible supplies from large water projects can at least be bracketed between certain limits,

[20] J. A. Dawson, "The Demand for Irrigation Water in the Ainsworth Area of Nebraska" (unpublished doctoral dissertation, University of Chicago, 1957), pp. 47–52.

[21] We should mention that, in principle at least, it makes little difference whether a public subsidy to cover such extrafinancial considerations is granted to a private or to a public enterprise. In fact, there are many precedents for grant of public subsidies to induce establishment of private enterprises. It should also be remembered in either case that the collection of public funds is not costless.

[22] An interesting question arises as to whether the costs might similarly fall short of their market price (i.e., whether there is a "producer's surplus" corresponding to the "consumer's surplus" we have just been describing). In principle there is, but in practice we usually neglect this consideration because the project is unlikely to involve major indivisibilities on the cost side corresponding to the large increment of water supply assumed. This gain is usually considered a "secondary benefit" and, as such, will be discussed below.

[23] Assuming that the water was freely available at the quoted price. If rationing existed at the previous price, that is a sign that the marginal value of the water was greater than that price.

this may suffice to answer the relevant questions of desirability. A more direct estimate of the aggregate value in use might be based upon a total monetary comparison of the consumers' well-being before the project and after, over and above the amount paid out to the water-supplying agency. This in fact is the procedure used by the Bureau of Reclamation in evaluating the benefits of irrigation projects (the benefit in question comes under the heading of direct farm benefits, not secondary benefits).[24] By way of contrast, the *Green Book* definition of benefits is too conservative, omitting the consumers' surplus factor from both primary and secondary benefits.[25]

b) *"Secondary benefits."*[26]—In current discussions it is usual to divide the benefits of projects into "primary" and "secondary," or sometimes "direct" and "indirect." We shall define primary benefits as the net value of the increase in production of outputs associated with the project.[27] If instead of the net value of the products we use the implied or derived value of the water, the corresponding quantity is the aggregate value in use of the water; the surplus of this aggregate value over the market value of the water is then a primary benefit, as argued in the section above.

We discussed at some length earlier the problem of spillover effects of private activities, an idea closely related to the concept of secondary benefits. Spillovers are the costs and benefits imposed upon or received by others as a consequence of private actions but not normally taken into consideration in private decisions. Sometimes they are spoken of as divergences between private and social costs (or benefits). For public projects there will similarly be spillover costs and benefits, and the question arises as to whether or not they should be considered in government investment decisions. Our conclusion earlier was that technological spillovers (those involving real increases or decreases in productivity outside the project) should be considered if we are concerned with maximizing the real national product. For example, the creation of drainage problems on land near a reservoir is a cost that should be considered, while the provision of flood control downstream of a dam is a benefit that should be considered even if the dam were constructed solely for the purpose of water supply. On the other hand, purely pecuniary spillovers (those involving increases or decreases in capital values or incomes solely because of the competitive effect of the facilities constructed) should not be considered on efficiency grounds, although they involve definite distribution effects.[28] This is not to say that such losses should *not* be compensated or that reimbursement should *not* be sought for such benefits but only that, whether they should or should not, the benefits or losses do not enter into the efficiency calculations. A pecuniary spillover benefit to labor occurs, for example, when the establishment of an irrigation project increases the price of labor in a nearby town; on the other hand, if the project produces watermelons in sufficient quantity to drive down their price, competing watermelon farmers suffer a pecuniary spillover loss.

Actual rules of practice are not entirely

[24] U.S. Department of the Interior, *Bureau of Reclamation Manual,* Vol. XIII: *Benefits and Costs* (March, 1952), par. 2.2.1 (hereinafter cited as *"Reclamation Manual"*). McKean (*op. cit.,* pp. 166–67) considers that the Bureau's formulation is too sweeping and allows some double-counting, although he approves the underlying principle.

[25] *Green Book,* pp. 8–9.

[26] The logic of the "secondary benefit" concept has been exhaustively analyzed elsewhere, especially by McKean (*op. cit.,* pp. 151–67) and by Eckstein (*op. cit.,* pp. 202–14).

[27] The *Green Book* (p. 8) defines primary benefits in a gross rather than net sense as the total value of the production of the project. The costs incurred in production (e.g., labor and seed in irrigation projects) are called there "associated costs." For our purposes it is more convenient to define primary benefits as net of the associated costs.

[28] For an excellent analysis see McKean, *op. cit.,* pp. 134–50.

clear on the matter of technological spillovers, which have not been emphasized much in the "secondary-benefit" discussion.[29] The *Green Book* does have a discussion indicating that technological "consequential damages" should be considered, but this is accompanied by remarks indicating that such damages can be offset by certain benefits that may be pecuniary in nature.[30] There is no discussion of technological spillover benefits, but, knowing the facts of life, we can perhaps be reasonably confident that the interests pushing projects will not fail to claim such benefits as "multipurpose" aspects of the project.

One type of spillover often emphasized involves a "secondary" surplus to processors or consumers of the product somewhat analogous to the "primary" surplus considered earlier of aggregate value in use over market value of the water itself. Consider the case where the increased wheat production associated with a project drives down the nation-wide price of wheat from \$2.10 to \$2.00 a bushel. The pecuniary spillover loss to competing wheat farmers because of the fall in price of wheat should not, we have argued, be considered as a real loss to the nation, and, in fact, it is not so considered in official practice. On the other hand, the *Green Book* lists the same fall in price as a *benefit* to secondary activities like the milling of flour.[31] Similarly, any project effect in driving up the wage rate in an area is considered not as a spillover cost to non-project employers but as a benefit to labor.[32] Clearly, these effects, while pecuniary in any case, cancel each other out. The fall in the price of wheat would not be of any lasting benefit to the milling industry if competition prevailed there, since flour prices would be forced down correspondingly. But it would be of benefit to the final consumer. The difference between the price of \$2.10 and the price of \$2.00 on the old amount of wheat products consumed is then only a pecuniary transfer between consumers and the non-project wheat farmers. On the increment of production due to the project, however (and there must be a net increment, since otherwise prices would not fall), the price of \$2.00 measures the marginal value in use (in this case, in consumption). The *aggregate* value in use, however, takes into consideration the fact that the first small increment had a marginal value in use of \$2.10. We may conclude, therefore, that where a project brings about a large indivisible increment of, say, wheat production, the market value after the increase (\$2.00 per unit) does somewhat understate the true social value. Note, however, that a correction of \$0.10 per bushel would be excessive; we should more reasonably, perhaps, split the difference and make the correction \$0.05 (but only on the increment of production). As a practical matter, we should add that the increment of production would rarely be large enough to make the effect worth worrying about—certainly not for wheat in this case.[33] We

29 A very elaborate analysis of such spillovers for river systems, however, is provided in Krutilla and Eckstein, *op. cit.*, pp. 52–68.

30 *Green Book,* pp. 32–33. One important instance in which "consequential damage" apparently was not taken into account is the construction of the Upper Colorado Storage Project despite the prospect of seriously adverse effects upon quality of water for municipal supply and irrigation in the lower Colorado.

31 *Green Book,* pp. 10–11.

32 According to McKean (*op. cit.*, p. 156), this benefit, though secondary in nature, is classified as primary in Bureau of Reclamation practice.

33 In the case of labor a similar argument applies as the project attracts workers from other employments (including leisure). The wage rise involves a "producers' surplus" analogous to the consumers' surplus considered above. In the old lines of production affected, the wage rise will be a pecuniary redistribution between employer and employee, but for the workers who shift there will be a gain not balanced by an offsetting loss. The rise in wage rates in the project area will typically overstate this gain, however, unless a condition of unemployment exists (a topic to be taken up shortly).

may remark that if, as is actually the case with wheat, the existence of a price-support program makes the addition really of no benefit to society (or of sharply reduced benefit if, for example, it will have to be dumped abroad at a loss), the market price grossly overstates the *primary* benefit.

A rather more important class of "benefit" officially taken into account, which is partially pecuniary and partially technological, is the increase in real estate values associated with the project.[34] Consider a town near a new project, where increased demand for all types of services has been brought about by the movement of people into the area and by the increase in income of those already there. As a result, land values rise. Is this a real benefit? To some extent the effect may be purely pecuniary, that is, the land may not be shifted to more productive uses but rather the same uses are more highly demanded, and so the scarcity value rises. The increase in value of residential land is essentially in this category. In part, however, the higher demand may involve an improvement in the real productivity of town sites, owing to the fact that customers have been brought into propinquity with the land. As an example, a restaurant in the town may now stay open for three meals a day instead of only two. While this effect is not merely pecuniary but real, it must be remembered that pecuniary effects still account for at least part of the increase in value of commercial land as well as essentially all the increase of residential land. Furthermore, the gains from bringing customers into propinquity with the sites in question must be balanced against the corresponding real loss to sites in other towns as customers move away from them. While it cannot be proved that the loss elsewhere will match the gain here, we feel that, as a practical matter, they can be assumed to balance off. Incidentally, much of the local political support for large projects comes essentially from real estate interests anxious to realize a gain in land values. The gain reaped here is typically much larger than that received by the primary beneficiaries.

The real heart of the "secondary-benefit" issue concerns the question of whether to count as a benefit the increased income or profit of those who process or deal with the products associated with the project or else provide services to those directly engaged in the project. The first three classes of the list below fall into this category:

> Indirect irrigation benefits are project effects which comprise the *increase* in:
>
> A. Profits of local wholesalers and retailers from handling the increase in sales of farm products consumed locally off the project without processing.
>
> B. Profits of all other enterprises between the farm and the final consumer, from handling, processing, and marketing the increase in sales of farm products locally and elsewhere.
>
> C. Profits of all enterprises from supplying goods and services for the increase in farm purchases for family living and production expenses.
>
> D. Land value of local residential property.[35]

The *Green Book* list includes the following:

> Where products of an irrigation project enter into secondary stages of production, such as processing and distribution, the increase in net income in such secondary activities under conditions with the project as compared with the net income expected in such activities without the project can be considered a secondary benefit. . . . Where secondary facilities are expected to be unused or underutilized, in the absence of the project, the increase in net income of such activities as a result of handling the project surplus of farm products may be a secondary benefit. . . .
>
> Where an irrigation project results in increased incomes to businesses supplying goods and services to the project area or results in increases in the value of property for nonresidential purposes, the difference between the

[34] *Reclamation Manual,* par. 2.2.4; *Green Book,* p. 40.

[35] *Reclamation Manual,* par. 2.2.4.

amount of such increased income or value expected as a result of the project and the increased income or value that may be expected in secondary activities stemming from the most likely alternative use of project resources in the absence of the project is a net secondary benefit [p. 40].[36]

By the analysis we went through earlier about the supposed gain from the lower price to the miller, we know that, if the processing and marketing industries are competitive, there will be no increased profit to them as a result of the project. If there is an observable increase of profits, it will be due to imperfections of competition, perhaps only as a temporary lag before competitive pressures force down prices. The case for this secondary benefit really rests upon the idea that the primary benefit is less than it would otherwise be because the "middleman" makes a profit on the margin between the price paid by the consumer and the price received by the farmer, this profit being over and above the cost of providing the services of processing, transporting, wholesaling, etc.

This argument has some logical validity and may even be of some local practical significance where, for example, a single processor in a region has considerable bargaining power facing a large number of competitive farmers.[37] As against this, it should be remembered, first, that it is only the *marginal* profit which is relevant (the increase in processor's profits due to the increment of production) and, second, that the value of the resources in their alternative employments might also have been understated because there, too, marginal profits were perhaps being reaped by processors, wholesalers, etc. Everything said here can also be applied to possible gains of noncompetitive *suppliers* discussed in the second paragraph of the quotation above. On balance, we feel confident that this class of secondary benefits should be considered as of negligible real importance. The practice of the Reclamation Bureau is to allow 5 per cent for indirect benefits *A* (marketing to local consumption) and for indirect benefits *B* (processing, marketing, etc.) to allow percentages varying from 83 of direct benefits (for cotton) to 6 (for poultry products).[38] These obviously can be an enormous factor in inflating cost-benefit ratios. In particular, an unpromising cotton project with a primary cost-benefit ratio of 0.6/1.0 would be built up by this procedure alone to show a ratio of 1.13/1.0.

When it comes to enterprises supplying goods and services to the farms assisted by the project, we have already recognized that, to the extent that labor or land moves from less productive to more productive employments as a result of the project, there is a real "secondary" gain. By analogous reasoning we could come to the same conclusion about possible increased return to capital and increased profits to enterprises whose services are used for the project. Now it is conceivable that these returns are relatively high compared to the primary benefits to the farmer, but in the absence of a general condition of unemployment (to be discussed shortly) there will be alternative uses foregone, at least by the more mobile resources, which should be little poorer than uses in connection with the project.

The Bureau uses a flat 18 per cent for this class of benefit.[39] While this figure is not necessarily unreasonable, it obviously will vary from project to project and should be made the subject of special investigation. In general, we are less confident that the real benefit here will be really

[36] Note that the *Green Book* refers broadly to *net income* (apparently including the cost of labor hired, for example) in secondary activities, while the *Reclamation Manual* speaks more narrowly of *profits* in such activities. The broader version is obviously incorrect; the resources employed are withdrawn from other occupations where their product is lost.

[37] Eckstein, *op. cit.*, p. 210.

[38] McKean, *op. cit.*, p. 155.

[39] *Reclamation Manual,* par. 2.2.4.

negligible in comparison with the primary benefit, but still some kind of showing is needed to demonstrate just how the project can tap sources of labor or capital and attract the services of enterprises whose alternatives are so poor that the project yields them a marked gain.[40]

c) Employment considerations.—Where general unemployment exists, of course, alternatives may well be quite poor, and secondary benefits to suppliers may become quite substantial. Secondary benefits in processing and marketing may also become large. In fact, the formulation in the official documents understates their potential magnitude, since in principle they could include not only the profits of processing and marketing firms but some of their expenses as well; these expenses become wages, interest, and profits to labor, capital, and to other enterprises whose services might have been entirely unemployed. What this really comes down to is the fact that economics, as the study of efficient use of scarce resources, has nothing really useful to say if resources are "free" in the real sense (i.e., if nothing has to be sacrificed elsewhere in order to employ the resources in activities associated with a project).

In fact, there is no need to turn to secondary benefits at all in justifying projects under conditions of general unemployment. If all resources are free, there will be no real costs of projects that bring resources into employment, and any project yielding any primary benefits could then be justified. This raises the possibility of projecting into the future an estimate of the proportion of years that will see some degree of general unemployment and of not charging any costs for the use of resources supposed to be "free" in such years. Actually, current practice as recommended by the Federal Inter-Agency River Basin Committee is to take projected future unemployment into account for secondary benefits,[41] the equally valid fact that unemployment negates much of the primary costs being omitted.

Any procedure of attempting to take unemployment into account in the analysis raises a number of problems. The first is the difficulty of prediction of both the timing and the extent of unemployment. Second, there is the matter of the interaction between the project under consideration and other economic activity in the private or public sphere. It may be, for example, that the project does have a favorable employment effect but that, in the absence of the project, other government measures like tax reduction would be adopted which would also tend to reduce unemployment. Or it is not inconceivable that either the direct or the indirect effects of the project may tend to reduce *private* investment. The Hells Canyon controversy is a possible instance of a public investment which, if approved, would have displaced a certain amount of private investment.

In any case, it is wrong to consider employment or antideflationary effects as a benefit without qualification. If the economy is operating properly, under neither depression nor inflationary conditions, the necessity to employ labor or capital on a project deprives us of the possibility of using those resources elsewhere and so represents a real cost. Under inflationary conditions, and this is a vital point, the supposed employment benefits can achieve no real gain and in addition will add to the losses that inflation imposes on the society. Only where generally depressed conditions can be anticipated to persist during the construction period is it reasonable to credit any such benefit. Under such conditions, and assuming that we can ignore

40 A penetrating analysis of Bureau of Reclamation practice on secondary benefits in the light of economic theory may be found in J. Margolis, "Secondary Benefits, External Economies, and the Justification of Public Investment," *Review of Economics and Statistics,* XXXIX (August, 1957), 284–91.

41 See discussion in McKean, *op. cit.,* p. 160.

possible unfavorable repercussions on public or private economic activity elsewhere, we not only should credit secondary employment benefits but should eliminate from primary costs those resources that are effectively free (have no alternative uses).

It is, in principle, more sensible to recompute the benefits and costs for depression conditions than simply to use a more relaxed criterion (e.g., dropping the requirement that benefits exceed costs) with the usual computations. The reason is that some resources might be closer to being "free" than others. On this point, our view differs from that of the Federal Inter-Agency River Basin Committee's subcommittee.[42] The judgment is made there that economic resources other than labor do not become "free" under depressed conditions. We do not see any fundamental difference between the phenomena of labor unemployment and high vacancy rates in office buildings.

Our conclusion, however, is that it is wrong to credit employment benefits to projects generally, since ignorance of the future is such that we cannot tell whether projects may involve losses through stimulation of inflation more or less often than gains through reduction of unemployment when depressed conditions hold. As a practical matter, it is worth noting that most of the costs of projects are incurred in the early years. Therefore, it might not be unreasonable for the agencies to work up a backlog of projects, so that, when and if a depression takes place, projects might be constructed with a justifiable expectation that much of the "costs" would involve the use of unemployed resources. In view of administrative lags, however, this policy might be helpful only in circumstances of a protracted depression. In ordinary circumstances, we therefore argue, only those projects should be adopted that are justified in terms of their use of scarce resources—charging for all resources utilized and without credit for any secondary employment benefits.

d) Conclusion on extrafinancial considerations.—To summarize the above, then, we regard the excess of aggregate value in use over market value (the consumers' surplus) as an element that should be considered where projects involve large increments of supply. Its quantitative significance, while not directly measurable, can be easily bracketed within upper and lower limits. Secondary costs and benefits should be considered insofar as they represent real technological spillovers; such spillover benefits would normally be counted as a multipurpose aspect of the project, but spillover costs are likely to be neglected. The great bulk of secondary benefits as usually counted (gains of individuals in economic association with primary beneficiaries) are illusory; only in exceptional circumstances may they be both real and of some importance. Employment considerations may be important in providing secondary benefits—or even in eliminating primary costs—to the extent that depression can be anticipated during the investment phase of the project. To the extent that inflationary conditions dominate, however, projects will involve the economy in additional real costs. While it might be wise to have a backlog of projects ready for execution if and when depression occurs, under present conditions it is possible that employment-generating benefits are less likely than inflation-generating costs as secondary project effects.

3. "Intangibles"

Another consideration that may be important in practice concerns the so-called intangible effects of water-supply projects. The *Green Book* lists effects on scenic or historic sites; "strengthening of national security and national economy; the substitution of power from replenishable water resources for power produced from limited and nonreplaceable fuel resources; the encouragement of a more widely dispersed

[42] *Green Book,* pp. 28–29.

industry; the provision of opportunities for new homes and new investment; and the provision of new avenues for the enjoyment of recreation and wildlife." Saving of human life is also mentioned.[43] These give the general idea, while by no means exhausting the list of possibilities. Some people, for example, place high value upon the preservation of private enterprise as an alternative to the extension of government powers.[44] Distribution effects of projects may also be an important "intangible."[45]

It may be helpful in thinking about such intangibles to classify them into those of a material or economic nature and those involving values beyond the economic. Thus the provision of recreation facilities is obviously economic in nature in that additional commodities or services are made available to the public; it is "intangible" solely because of difficulties of measurement which are not, as a matter of fact, completely intractable. The preservation of human life or of democratic processes, on the other hand, brings into account values beyond the economic. The distinction between the two is helpful because economic analysis can in fact expose certain fallacies about claimed intangible benefits of an economic nature. The supposed benefit cited above of replacing fuel power with water power is a fallacy, for example; these are competing market alternatives, and the alleged superiority of water power (its non-wasting nature) is already fully accounted for in the higher price the market charges for the use of the non-replenishable resource, fossil fuel. Similarly, irrigation projects will often be justified on "intangible" grounds because of the need for food here or abroad, now or in the future;[46] but these are already accounted for in the price of food products and the value of agricultural land.

The discussion of "intangibles" parallels, once we get beyond the purely material considerations like recreation values, the problem of "extramarket values" taken up in chapter iv. In general, while we can imagine circumstances in which some of these intangibles might become valid, by and large we feel that they seldom have any important weight and usually are dragged in to serve the purpose of obscuring the real magnitudes of the costs and benefits. Only rarely, for example, will an inefficient water-supply project importantly improve national defense or the national economy or democratic processes or public health or the mobility of resources or the degree of competition; and, in the exceptional cases, it may be possible to quantify the effect at least within broad limits. Other intangible effects, while possibly more visible, may not be obviously desirable, such as dispersal of industry, preservation of the family farm,[47] or benefits to particular regions at the expense of others.

One non-quantifiable "intangible" which raises some interesting questions is prevention of loss of life through floods. Here again it is easy to speak vaguely and grandly of benefits over and above the eco-

43 *Ibid.*, pp. 26–27.

44 See, especially, Ben Moreell, *Our Nation's Water Resources—Policies and Politics* (Chicago: The Law School, University of Chicago, 1956).

45 Among recent analysts, Margolis seems the most concerned about insufficient weighting of intangibles in the decision process (see his "The Economic Evaluation of Federal Water Resource Development," *American Economic Review*, XLIX [March, 1959], 96–111). At one point he mentions (p. 96) "lives saved in floods, municipal decentralization, regional growth, and recreational use," and at another (p. 97) "conservation, the family-sized farm, mobility of resources, effect upon degree and type of competition, implications for public health, income redistribution, or balanced regional development."

46 *Report of the President's Water Resources Policy Commission*, I, 172–73.

47 The reasons usually given for this goal—the life of sturdy independence led by the farmer, close to the soil and removed from the artificiality and corruption of city life—contrast rather oddly with the means adopted to achieve it, which make the farmer an economic dependent upon subsidy checks and a political client of the agencies and interests responsible for their continuation.

nomic property damage and loss of human services caused by flood. Actually, few realize how small the loss of life due to floods actually is. From 1946 through 1954 the average annual figure for deaths from floods was 52 (93 in the highest year, 1950), as compared with, for example, 38,000 deaths in 1953 from automobile accidents and 57,000 from other accidents.[48] Even 50 deaths per year are regrettable, of course, but it is fairly clear that the expected gain on this score from any single flood-control project will be very small, as compared with the expected gains from equivalent expenditures in cancer research, highway safety, hospital facilities, and the like. Actually, it seems very likely that the loss of life due to construction accidents on flood-control projects[49] exceeds the possible saving on this score from flood control. Also worth mentioning, perhaps, is that the risk of loss of life due to collapse or failure of dams is not utterly negligible. Failure of the St. Francis Dam near Los Angeles was responsible for 385 deaths in 1928.[50] (This was a water-supply dam, however, not a flood-control dam.) During the year 1959 two major dam failures led to deaths of 274 persons in France and 132 in Spain.

One supposed intangible benefit is so important as to deserve extended discussion—regional or local *development,* particularly of the West or South. We see no special reason to prefer, for example, development in the West to development in New England. Nevertheless, it is clear that the slogan of "developing the West" has high political appeal, even in the East. The following quotation from a midwestern congressman perhaps catches the flavor of the sentiment: "I have in mind, gentlemen, the Estancia Valley in New Mexico, a beautiful valley. All it needs is water, and you can raise anything. . . . It is a big valley, a beautiful valley. If we could afford it, that valley should have water on it by all means."[51]

There are a number of ways of interpreting such a statement. The first is the idea of "balanced development"—that, in principle, every state, every region, and presumably every acre has a right to equal development (i.e., equal numbers of houses, farms, factories, traffic jams, hot-dog stands, etc.). It is impossible to accept this as a goal, since economic activity is designed to serve mankind and not to serve real estate. The second possibility is that westerners are to be preferred to easterners. Development of the West in particular would then be good, since it redistributes wealth from the effete East to the vigorous West and also induces some easterners to become westerners. This is a rather odd idea when stated so baldly, but it perhaps has some currency in popular thought as indicated by folk-myth heroes like the frontiersman and cowboy. Both of these explanations are fairly obviously irrational.[52] We prefer to think that the

48 Eckstein, *op. cit.,* p. 142.

49 There is no direct information available on this point, but an old rule of thumb in the construction business was that there was one fatality per million dollars spent. Results today are probably superior because of increasing attention to safety—not to mention the inflation of dollar costs. New York City statistics indicate 371 fatalities in constructing the Catskill System (total cost $189,000,000, constructed between 1907 and 1917), or a fatality rate of 1.96 per million dollars. On the stages of the Delaware System constructed between 1936 and 1950, there were 84 fatalities (total cost $253,000,000), or a rate of 0.33 per million dollars (see *Origin and Achievements of the Board of Water Supply, City of New York* [New York, 1950], pp. 75, 89). To give some idea of magnitudes, the funds required to complete only the Corps of Engineers flood-control projects already under construction in 1952 amounted to $2,088,400,000 (see W. G. Hoyt and W. B. Langbein, *Floods* [Princeton, N.J.: Princeton University Press, 1955], p. 193). A fatality rate of as low as 0.1 per million dollars would imply 209 deaths in carrying these projects to completion.

50 R. A. Nadeau, *The Water Seekers* (Garden City, N.Y.: Doubleday & Co., 1950), pp. 116–22.

51 Quoted in McKean, *op. cit.,* p. 163.

52 Margolis is one of the few who explicitly recognize an areal preference function as a valid so-

congressman was simply expressing in sentimental language his belief (or, perhaps, hope) that the proposed investment would be a sound economic proposition, that is, that the value created by providing water to the valley, such value to be received by both residents and purchasers of the valley's products, would be more than the cost of bringing the water there.

There is a sophisticated economic argument for subsidized development of new or backward areas, at the expense of old or already developed ones, which turns on the contention that market forces alone do not lead to the optimum *speed* of development. Old areas, it is argued, are overdeveloped and new areas underdeveloped, the disparity exceeding what it should be in terms of the costs of moving and the like.[53] The reasoning underlying this view is that fundamental utilities of a region like power, water, transport, etc., can be developed for a while at decreasing cost until the most efficient scale is attained, after which further development can take place only at increasing cost. Consequently, on the margin the cost of servicing a potential migrant with utilities may be equal in overdeveloped New England and underdeveloped New Mexico, thus providing the individual with no incentive to move on this score. But each individual who leaves New England reduces the unit cost of utility service there (since average cost is assumed to be in the increasing range in that area), and in moving to New Mexico he will also reduce the unit cost of utility service in the latter region (where average cost is in the decreasing range). This very plausible argument is actually a fallacy; given the premises, the conclusion that subsidized movement from New England to New Mexico will reduce aggregate social cost of utility service is a *non sequitur.* While the averages in both areas fall, the individuals who transfer may be shifting from the low-average to the high-average area, and the result can go either way.[54]

Our view is that the political strength among non-westerners of the idea of "development of the West" is an illusory belief, fostered by the beneficiaries, that such development benefits the nation as a whole by increasing the real national product. The romantic aspects help the illusion to gain

cial judgment ("Secondary Benefits, External Economies, and the Justification of Public Investment," *op. cit.,* p. 290). We cannot believe that, if the issue were clearly put, easterners rich and poor would voluntarily tax themselves to benefit westerners rich and poor, or northerners benefit southerners.

[53] We believe that Margolis (*ibid.*) is in error in pointing to the existing *fact* of underdevelopment of the West relative to the East as justifying, on efficiency grounds, public investments transferring resources from the East to the West and so tending to eliminate the indicated disequilibrium. While a disequilibrium perhaps exists, the scarcity of capital in the light of the costs of movement indicate a certain optimum *rate* at which this disequilibrium should be corrected. Thus the gains from capital invested to correct this regional maldistribution of population and industry must be compared with the productivity of capital in other uses. This comparison of course is made automatically by the market process of bidding for capital. Consequently, deliberate regional redistribution of wealth cannot simply be assumed to have a favorable efficiency effect; as the text states, it would have to be shown that market processes lead to the wrong *speed* of redistribution.

[54] A numerical example may be helpful. Suppose that the marginal cost of utility service is $500 per individual per annum in both New England and New Mexico, average cost being $1,000 and in the declining range with respect to number of individuals served in the latter area while only $400 and in the rising range in the former area. Then a transfer of one individual from New England to New Mexico will reduce average costs in both areas, but the national aggregate cost of utility service is unchanged, because it costs $500 to serve him in either area. Even if we go beyond marginal effects in considering shifts of larger groups, there is no clear benefit. After the first individual is shifted, the marginal cost of serving a second migrant may be lower in New Mexico, but not necessarily (declining average cost does not necessarily imply declining marginal cost). Furthermore, marginal cost of utility service in New England will very likely have declined after departure of the first migrant.

currency, but the romance could not flourish in the absence of obfuscation about the real costs. The practical success of this idea in terms of legislation can be ascribed to the same reasons as the success of logrolling generally. When the benefits go to a well-defined interest group for whom it is worthwhile making the political investments necessary to assure passage of the legislation, while the costs are dispersed so widely as not to justify anyone's organizing political opposition, special-interest groups are all too likely to win out against the general public. Along this line, Golzé's discussion suggests rather strongly that political opposition to the reclamation program benefiting the seventeen western states evaporated when the grant of federal subsidies in the form of flood-control projects largely benefiting the East became an established policy between 1927 and 1936.[55] The logrolling implications are obvious, the flood-control projects representing "pork" which eastern legislators could bring home to their constituents, thus providing a more balanced distribution of the spoils.

Municipal or local "development" is also often a goal for expansion of the water supply of a city or region, that is, development is considered to be an end justifying investments over and above the merely economic matter of supplying a commodity to actual or potential consumers when its worth is more than the cost of providing it. Who has not read the paeans of praise sung out by historians or less scholarly publicists for the magnificent foresight of early municipal leaders in building water supply ahead of demand, thus laying the foundation for the development of cities like New York and Los Angeles?

Such lyricism is seldom subjected to critical analysis. If it were, interesting questions would begin to arise immediately. What kind of goal is "development" for the residents of a city? While some may object to this judgment, we think it reasonable to say that the increased crowding of the Los Angeles area, for example, has significantly reduced the net desirability of that city to its previous residents. (On the other hand, the new residents presumably gained, if their relocation decisions were correct from their point of view.) While real estate and other interests behind civic "boosting" have certainly profited, the over-all balance of advantage from growth is unclear. Even this does not get to the real point, however; the basic question is the desirability or feasibility of encouraging development, granting that it may be desirable to do so, in a particular way, through subsidizing water supply or through building ahead of demand. Each of these is worth some comments.

Building ahead of demand is sometimes economically justified, of course. Where construction must take place in large indivisible lumps, and when there is uncertainty about the growth of demand, at a certain point the economic risk of insufficient capacity and the economic risk of excessive capacity balance. This balance might be such, if the risk of being caught short were weighed heavily enough, as to justify building additional capacity even if it were fairly probable that the capacity would be excessive for a few years. We definitely do not want to imply, however, that building ahead of demand can always or even normally be justified on this ground; in fact, the specific question we want to investigate is the possible justification for building ahead of demand when the economics are unfavorable.

Few civic leaders have been so praised for their foresight as the "water-seekers" of the Los Angeles metropolitan area. Yet at least one vast water-supply project—the Colorado River Aqueduct—has involved a truly major economic loss to the region,[56]

[55] *Op. cit.*, pp. 82–90.

[56] J. W. Milliman, "Economic Problems of the Metropolitan Water District of Southern California," *Proceedings of the 32d Annual Conference of the Western Economic Association* (Salt Lake City, Utah, 1957), p. 44.

as we shall point out in chapter xi. This loss, paid for by the taxpayers of the region, certainly has deterred development of its resources and industries as a whole, despite the undoubted benefits reaped by some particular activities or localities.[57]

Despite the economic loss, however, the praise received by the "water-seekers" may possibly have been justified from the point of view of the areas or municipalities involved, because elements of the existing structure of water law make the construction of uneconomic projects almost a necessity if water is to be secured at all. These elements are the fact that water rights other than riparian are acquired and kept by actual use and the fact that transfers of use are hindered in a number of ways. If to get and hold a water right the water must be used, it obviously may become necessary to use the water earlier than economic rationality would dictate in order to prevent others from pre-empting the supply. If transfers posed no difficulty, this problem would be much less serious, since the city fathers could buy out existing rights held by others. The combination of the two—rights dependent on use and limitations on transfer—impose terrific pressure in the direction of early construction and wasteful use. (We will discuss these topics more fully in chap. ix.)

What about encouraging development through a subsidized price for water? Building ahead of demand (again, we are speaking of construction beyond that indicated by the relative balance of the costs of oversupply and undersupply) involves one kind of subsidy, but the issue can be posed more generally. Should water be deliberately provided at a loss in order to encourage development of a region? The arguments for such a course, as for any subsidy, usually point to specific benefits which could be attained by such a policy, without consideration of the costs. Thus it is undoubtedly the case that certain industries or plants that would not otherwise be attracted could be induced to locate in an area by a favorable water price. But somebody must still pay the cost, which is simply thrown onto the general tax burden—or, if it is a preferential rate which is granted, the non-preferential water-users will share the cost. Furthermore, what kinds of industries will be attracted by subsidized water prices? Logically, these would be industries with relatively heavy water usage but providing rather slight tax base to take full advantage of the subsidy. Thus, if water is scarce in an area and this constitutes a barrier to development, subsidizing the water will attract precisely the wrong kind of industries in view of the real natural advantages and disadvantages of the region. In terms of theory it is possible to show that the consequence must be a net loss because the artificially low price on water will enable users granted preferential rates to employ water where its marginal value in use is low and, in particular, lower than its real cost.

We conclude, therefore, that "development" is not an intangible worthy of consideration as a goal in water-supply projects over and above the economic consideration of costs and benefits. Rather, development in terms of exploitation of the real advantages of particular regions is best furthered by the construction of economic projects and by avoiding the waste of resources entailed by the construction of uneconomic ones. In general, the heading of "intangible" benefits usually covers certain considerations that are economic in nature; classifying them as intangibles permits proponents to make vague sweeping claims as an alternative to serious attempts at measurement or as a way of getting twice the mileage out of a real economic benefit already counted. Real "intangibles" certainly do exist, such as the preservation

[57] It should be mentioned, however, that the initial construction took place between 1933 and 1941—that is, in part during years of serious unemployment.

of human life or of democratic processes. But, in general, the concept has been overworked, and few if any projects in the water-supply field have major implications beyond the mundane sphere where economic analysis is appropriate.

4. The Criterion Problem and Cost-Benefit Ratios

Assume that all the benefits and all the costs associated with a project have been evaluated. How do we determine whether the project is good or bad? The traditional method has been to compute the *ratio* of benefits to costs, which we shall denote B/C. Here B and C are either discounted present or annual values (we will consider the discounting process in the next section). The *Green Book* states that "the ratio of benefits to costs reflects both benefit and cost values and is the recommended basis for comparison of projects."[58] This recommendation actually has two aspects: (1) for a project to be justified, the ratio must exceed unity, and (2) as between projects, the one with the higher ratio is the better.

The first of these conditions is generally admitted, although where intangible benefits and costs exist the ratio may not be capable of being measured. Some, indeed, have challenged this restriction, asserting that the job of the Bureau of Reclamation, for example, is to expend its budget on the best available projects even if there are none with a B/C ratio greater than 1. This idea really belongs to the intellectual underworld. Its implication of "my agency at all costs" is one which motivates much activity but will only rarely be openly professed. Clearly, the budget granted an agency should be the outcome of its demonstration that the funds can be spent on beneficial projects rather than it being the case that projects are merely the best available ratholes down which to dump the funds voted by Congress.

The second condition, that projects may be comparatively rated by the B/C ratio, sounds plausible but happens to be logically erroneous.[59] That this is so can be shown by a simple example. Suppose that we must choose between two mutually exclusive projects (with all risk and uncertainty being assumed away), one with a cost of \$1.00 and a benefit of \$5.00, the other with a cost of \$1,000 and a benefit of \$1,200. The former has a B/C ratio of 5, and the latter of only 1.2, but we would clearly be mistaken to forego a \$200 gain for a mere \$4.00 on the other project. The ratio does not, therefore, lead to the right answer in choosing among mutually exclusive projects. In choosing the scale of investment in a given project, an example in the *Green Book* itself shows that the B/C ratio leads to the wrong answer again. An illustration is there provided where, if costs of \$50 are incurred, the benefits will be \$70 (ratio is 1.4). Now suppose that, by expanding the scale of cost by \$1.00, it is possible to reap a benefit of \$1.30. Since the B/C ratio for the increment is only 1.3, it is going to pull the over-all ratio below 1.4—but clearly the increment yields more benefits than costs and is therefore desirable.[60] McKean has also pointed out a rather important ambiguity in the ratio itself. Sometimes all costs will be segregated in the denominator, but at other times it is convenient to count the benefits as net of certain associated costs. If the basic outlay is \$40 and benefits of \$170 will be yielded if \$50 of expenses are incurred, the one ratio is $(\$170 - \$50)/\$40 = 3$, while the other is $\$170/(\$40 + \$50) = 1.9$.[61] Neither of these ratios is

[58] *Green Book*, p. 14.

[59] This has been conclusively demonstrated in McKean, *op. cit.*, pp. 107–16.

[60] See *Green Book*, p. 12 (lower diagram). (A drafting error obscures this point in the upper diagram.)

[61] McKean, *op. cit.*, pp. 112–13.

better than the other; basically, the error is in the use of a ratio at all.

What is the right criterion? It is the *difference* between the benefits and costs (which we denote $B - C$) which should be maximized. To take the example just given, the $B - C$ criterion shows a wealth gain of \$170 — \$50 — \$40, or \$80, the same result being derived whether the accounting is on a net or a gross basis. As between the mutually exclusive projects we considered earlier, the project with a $B - C$ of \$1,200 — \$1,000, or \$200, is obviously a better alternative than the one with a $B - C$ of \$5.00 — \$1.00, or \$4.00. Similarly, any increment to the scale of a project that yields a greater increase of benefit than of cost is one that obviously makes the $B - C$ difference greater, and again the correct answer is achieved.

Those who argue against the use of the $B - C$ criterion cite comparisons like the following. Suppose there is one project with benefit of \$2.00 and cost of \$1.00, and another with benefit of \$1,000,002 and cost of \$1,000,001—is not the former preferable? The answer is really "No," *risk and uncertainty aside.* The latter investment seems dubious because we know that estimates of costs and benefits are unlikely to be accurate in the seventh figure, so as a practical matter we may doubt whether the supposed net $B - C$ of \$1.00 will be forthcoming. This, however, does not affect the logical correctness of $B - C$. Furthermore, we know that we are much less inclined to risk \$1,000,000 than to risk \$1.00 for the same net benefit, and this also makes us doubtful. However, allowance for risk should enter by discounting B or by adjusting C (we shall discuss this in the next section), so that the criterion $B - C$ already incorporates any risk aversion we may choose to assign.

The reader may be interested in the following conundrum which has also been used as an argument against the criterion of $B - C$. Suppose that, by spending our entire national wealth (say, \$1,000 billion), we could triple wealth next year, whereas, by spending only \$10 billion, we could double wealth. The criterion of $B - C$ says that the former is better, and so is it not in error? The idea of course is that we will starve to death before the returns of the former project come in. The difficulty here is that the market value involved in the national wealth figure of \$1,000 billion is less than the aggregate value in use of all our resources (the area under the demand curve). We can ignore this consideration in speaking of projects of relatively minor scale but not in the example cited. Obviously, the aggregate gain of a tripled national wealth next year will be valued less by us than its aggregate real cost, starving to death this year, for exactly the same reason that a man under certain circumstances in the Sahara Desert might be willing to give all his wealth for a gallon of water while normally he will not pay a dollar for 1,000 gallons. This conundrum is not completely devoid of practical implications, however. It suggests, correctly, that, as projects become large, we should take into account the fact that the resources sacrificed become more valuable to consumers.

In practice, however, the use of the logically incorrect B/C criterion is a relatively unimportant defect in project selection and evaluation. In fact, if benefits and costs are calculated correctly, it is obvious that every project with a B/C ratio greater than 1 should be adopted, since, if B/C is greater than unity, then $B - C$ must be positive (there is a net surplus of benefit over cost). The major practical difficulties lie in the tendency toward optimistic inflation of B and the underestimation of C, together with the use of an excessively low interest (discounting) rate, which we now turn to consider.

D. Risk, Taxes, and the Discount Rate

1. The Discount Rate and Financial Feasibility

In the calculation of both benefits and costs, the rate of discount is typically a critical element. Costs are incurred, predominantly, in the early years of a project, while benefits may be stretched out into the relatively distant future. The arithmetic of compound interest so works out that a benefit of $1.00 fifty years from now has a present value of $0.37 at a discount rate of 2 per cent, $0.14 at a rate of 4 per cent, and $0.03 at a rate of 7 per cent. High discount rates make projects look undesirable; low discount rates make them look desirable.

In the earlier portion of this chapter we distinguished between financial feasibility and economic feasibility. Conservative critics of government investment projects have typically been anxious to insist on a criterion of financial feasibility, that is to say, a showing that a project will lead to revenues sufficient to cover all costs including interest on the capital borrowed for the project.[62] Supporters of enlarged government programs, on the other hand, have typically attempted to justify projects by showing that there are economic benefits over and above the financial revenues which the project might bring in.

It is essential to the logic of the idea of "financial feasibility" that the discount rate be equal to the rate at which the government can borrow. If the government can borrow $1 million at 2.5 per cent, then a project yielding net revenues of $25,000 a year is financially feasible, because the government's interest cost is $25,000 a year. Any return over 2.5 per cent represents a good project, that is, one that yields a financial "profit" to the government, permitting a reduction in taxes or an increase in other government expenditures.

The school of thought that maintains that the financial feasibility requirement is too stringent tends to favor the use of a lower rate of interest than the government borrowing rate for evaluating public projects. All such low-interest schemes (compare the artificially low rates on loans to such groups as veterans) are typically defended by certain distributional arguments which we will not attempt to analyze. Abstracting from the distribution question, we argued above that such a procedure must lead to the construction of inefficient projects if in some sectors of the economy a standard of perhaps 5 per cent is insisted on while in others projects yielding only, say, 2.5 per cent are permitted. Even if the government uses a constant rate (lower than the market) for all its projects, the market rate will be the rate used as a standard by private interests, and so again there will be inefficiency.

2. Risk

In the opposite direction, an important argument to evaluate is the contention that what is financially feasible may *not* be economically desirable and, specifically, that a rate *higher* than the government borrowing rate should be used in discounting costs and benefits of government projects—primarily to allow for risk, though, as we shall see, taxes and certain other considerations may also enter in. In private and public investment decisions, considerations of risk must obviously play an important role. In fact, for wide classes of investments the risk premium insisted upon by lenders exceeds in magnitude the pure interest charge for the use of the capital. It is of great importance to recognize that there are *two different kinds* of risk premiums. Consider, for example, a debt instru-

[62] See, e.g., Task Force on Water Resources and Power for the Commission on Organization of the Executive Branch of the Government ("Hoover Commission"), *Report on Water Resources and Power* (Washington, D.C., 1955), I, 104–6.

ment of a given maturity for which the riskless rate would be 5 per cent but where there is a one-half chance of default of the interest (repayment of the principal is assumed to be certain). The quoted interest rate would then have to be 10 per cent to give the investor the same "expected" or average return as the 5 per cent rate on riskless instruments. If there were some risk of default of principal as well, a still higher quoted rate would be required to yield 5 per cent after allowance for average loss through default. This risk premium we shall call the "expected-value adjustment." The second factor to be considered is "risk aversion"—that the investor might dislike risk for its own sake and might be unwilling to lend in the case just discussed (a 50 per cent chance of default of interest) until the quoted rate reached, say, 12 per cent. That is, he is indifferent between a riskless return of 5 per cent and a one-half chance of getting 12 per cent. On the other hand, an investor who liked to take chances might be indifferent between a riskless rate of 5 per cent and a one-half chance of 8 per cent. The risk-aversion premium can thus be either positive or negative. Whether on balance investors demand a positive risk premium over and above the expected-value adjustment is a question on which evidence is conflicting.

The distinction between the two kinds of risk premiums is relevant for an argument often made about the comparative superiority of government when it comes to bearing the risk of large projects. Since the government is in a position to pool the risks of many such projects, the law of large numbers permits it (so it is argued) to act purely on the basis of the expected return, whereas private capital may insist on a risk-aversion premium in addition. We cannot evaluate this argument until we know something more about whether in fact investors do demand such premiums.[63] Even if they do, however, the corporate form permits investors to spread their risks by buying small shares in many different enterprises, so it is still by no means obvious that government has any such advantage in engaging in risky projects as that claimed. It is vital to remember, however, that this entire argument relates to the risk-aversion factor and not to the expected-value adjustment, though in fact the two are often confused.[64] If government is in a position to make an investment that will double with 50 per cent probability, or else be lost entirely, the expected gain is zero. The fact that government can pool many risks does not in any way permit it to ignore the effect of the risk of failure upon the expected return for this or any particular project or group of projects.

Let us suppose that a certain project might be built by the federal government or by a private corporation, the risks of failure of the project *being the same in either case*. (By "failure of the project" we mean that the actual outcome reveals either an overestimate of benefit or an underestimate of cost, or both, sufficient to make the net balance of economic considerations a negative one.) The federal government can at times borrow, say, at 3 per cent when the corporation would have to pay perhaps 5.5 per cent (assuming a balance between debt and equity capital). Because of its unlimited repayment ability,

[63] If they do, the expected rate of return (after expected-value adjustment) on capital invested in risky industries and enterprises should be greater than in relatively safe industries and enterprises. The existence of insurance is some evidence in favor of the existence of risk aversion, since insurance is not mathematically fair and involves a sacrifice of expected return for greater security of return. On the other hand, not all insurable risks are in fact insured, so the existence of insurance does not prove that the capital market as a whole insists on a positive risk-aversion premium. The existence of gambling provides some evidence in the opposite direction—that some people are willing to sacrifice expected return for *insecurity* of return.

[64] The discussion in Krutilla and Eckstein (*op. cit.*, pp. 122–24) does not clearly distinguish between the two concepts in making the "pooling of risks" argument.

the borrowing power of the federal government is essentially unaffected by the riskiness of the projects engaged in. Nevertheless, the government should use as its discount rate the one effective for private borrowers engaged in projects of comparable risk (in this case, 5.5 per cent, ignoring any tax adjustments) if the marginal productivity of capital is to be equated between the private and government sectors. The pooling-of-risks argument does not apply here unless the higher private borrowing rate incorporates an element of risk aversion (which we believe to be small at best).

If there were on balance positive risk aversion, there would in fact be a kind of natural advantage of large enterprises over small and, in particular, of federal enterprises as compared with any others, since the federal government could engage in more pooling of risks. In the case of states or local authorities, again there is generally some ability to borrow at favorable rates because the taxing power provides a protection to the investor over and above the prospective profits of the projects engaged in. (Even for private corporations there will typically be a fair amount of reserve ability in the corporation to pay debts over and above that based on the prospective success of particular projects.)

One interesting point here is the existence of the institution of the revenue bond, for which the repayment power is limited to the prospective revenues of the projects borrowed for. Revenue bonds, of course, typically must be sold at prices yielding higher interest rates than general obligations of the government unit involved. The market rates involve investors' estimates of the real riskiness of the projects. Our present argument really comes down to saying that ideally all projects should be evaluated as if they were to be financed by revenue bonds. Only if this were done would the principle of financial feasibility be appropriate, so far as the discounting rate is concerned.

3. *Taxation*

For state and local borrowings, an entirely different factor enters in—the fact that the interest on such bonds is exempt from federal income tax to their owners. To adjust for this discrepancy, state and local government projects should ideally be discounted by the rate at which a non-exempt revenue bond would have to be sold.

The most important discrepancy of all has still not been considered, however. That is the fact that the taxation of the alternative private and public projects differs, where we are speaking now of the taxation of the project assets and income rather than the taxation of the interest or dividends received by investors. The most important of these considerations is the federal corporate income tax, although in certain circumstances personal income taxes,[65] property taxes,[66] sales taxes,[67] and others may become relevant. We shall illustrate the operation of the differential tax treatment by an example, which assumes that only the federal corporate income tax is relevant, at a 52 per cent rate.[68]

Suppose that a corporation is considering a project requiring an outlay of $100,000, after which annual net returns of $10,000 will be forthcoming in perpetuity. This is a project with a real yield of 10 per cent. Assume that, to maintain a balance of debt and equity securities, it will secure half the funds required by selling bonds yielding 4 per cent and the other half by issuing stock with a desired earnings yield of 6

65 Relevant if the private alternative considered is a partnership or proprietorship.

66 State-owned enterprises are usually exempt from local property tax. Federal enterprises often make payments in lieu of local taxes, and sometimes municipal enterprises have similar internal accounting arrangements.

67 Some sales taxes are not assessed if the purchaser is a government agency.

68 The current rate is 52 per cent for income over $25,000.

per cent.[69] There will be $2,000 interest due on the bonds, which may be deducted from income before tax. The remaining $8,000 yield of the investment becomes $3,840 after payment of corporate income tax. This still leaves an excess over the $3,000 earnings at 6 per cent on the common stock, but the tax has reduced the aggregate yield to the investors as a group

TABLE 11*

AFTER-TAX EQUITY YIELDS†

Project Financed with Debt-Equity Proportions (Per Cent)	Project Yield (Per Cent)			
	10	8	6	4
Equity 100	4.80	3.84	2.88	1.92
Debt 25; equity 75	5.76	4.48	3.20	1.92
Debt 50; equity 50	7.68	5.76	3.84	1.92
Debt 75; equity 25	13.44	9.60	5.76	1.92

* Assumptions: Corporate income tax is at 52 per cent, and bonds issued at 4 per cent.

† Formula: Let d be proportion financed by debt, p be project yield, and e be after-tax equity yield. Then the project yield is in effect a weighted average of the payments to debt-owners, shareowners, and tax-collector, as follows:

$$p = 0.04d + (1 - d)e + (p - 0.04d)(0.52),$$

or

$$e = (0.48p - 0.0192d)/(1 - d) \text{ (for } d < 1) .$$

More generally, denoting the bond rate as b, the formula becomes $p = bd + [(1 - d)e]/(0.48)$, or $e = [0.48(p - bd)]/(1 - d)$.

from 10 per cent ($10,000/$100,000) to 5.84 per cent ($5,840/$100,000). For the equity investors alone, the yield is 7.68 per cent ($3,840/$50,000). Table 11 shows, for varying project yields, the after-tax yield to corporate equity investors as a function of the debt-equity ratio used to finance the investment. Table 12 shows the project yield necessary to permit the project just to "break even," that is, to yield 4 per cent to bondholders and 6 per cent to stockholders with no surplus remaining. For the example just considered (1:1 debt-equity ratio), the "break-even" project yield would have to be 8.25 per cent in order to pay the bond interest and maintain 6 per cent earnings.

[69] We assume that it is the earnings yield which is relevant to stockholders rather than dividend yield.

4. Price-Level Changes

One question which commonly arises is how to allow for the fact, if it be a fact, that inflation of monetary values can be expected to take place over time. It would, of course, be a crude error to inflate future revenues in proportion to the price levels expected to govern in those periods and then to weigh these inflated revenues against costs measured in today's dollars. The entire comparison of costs and revenues should be calculated using dollars of constant purchasing power of some convenient period, usually the present period. (That this is a crude error does not prevent some administrators in the water-supply field from congratulating themselves on their foresight in having built projects some time in the past when money costs were lower.)

TABLE 12*

BREAK-EVEN PROJECT YIELDS

Project Financed with Debt-Equity Proportions (Per Cent)	Break-Even Project Yields (Per Cent)
Equity 100	12.5
Debt 25; equity 75	10.375
Debt 50; equity 50	8.25
Debt 75; equity 25	6.125
Debt 100	4

* Assumptions: As in Table 11, and desired equity yield is 6 per cent.

However, a more sophisticated argument turning upon the discount rate can be applied here, though we are unaware of its having been employed in this context before. The interest rate, we have argued, measures the real marginal productivity of capital. Even if this be conceded when price levels are constant, suppose that the community confidently anticipates a steady increase in the price level over time. Since a rise in the price level is equivalent to a depreciation of the value of money, lenders in the capital market are going to insist upon an interest yield to cover this anticipated depreciation (the fact that repayment will be made in "cheaper" dollars) in addition to compensating them for giving up the real marginal productivity of the capital. Consequently, monetary interest rates on riskless investments (meaning investments free of default risk, not of this inflation risk) may perhaps incorporate an allowance for anticipated monetary depreciation, so that the real marginal productivity of capital is less then the monetary rate by the amount of this allowance.

We believe that this argument is essentially correct. It seems plausible to us that one of the reasons interest rates are historically high at present is precisely that people are reluctant to lend out money without some compensation for the inflation they have learned to anticipate from experience in the last two decades. If this be accepted, it then follows that, since costs and revenues will be stated in dollars of constant purchasing power, the discount rate should be adjusted to correspond to what would be the ruling rate if in fact people *were* confident that dollars would have constant purchasing power. That is, the market rate of interest should be marked down by a monetary depreciation adjustment, which we place in the neighborhood of 0.5 per cent per annum. (The particular figure arrived at represents a conjecture on our part about market sentiment concerning price levels over a considerable period into the future. For a variety of reasons, this figure is not inconsistent with the recent tendency of the Consumer Price Index to rise about 1 per cent per annum. The interest-rate structure incorporates a long-term prediction of price movements; popular expectations of inflation have historically been conservative; wholesale price rises have been smaller than 1 per cent per annum; and, finally, the Consumer Price Index probably has an upward bias.) Some analysts might nevertheless be inclined to maintain that the allowance should be somewhat greater—but 1 per cent per annum certainly represents a fairly high estimate of the monetary depreciation allowance incorporated in current market rates of interest.

As a related point it may be the case that, while an increase in the general price level is not anticipated, a relative price change in the form of a rise in project construction costs is expected to take place in the future. This consideration does represent an argument for early construction of projects, the assumption being that project revenues follow the general price level rather than the relative price of construction activities. However, no *special* attention need be given this argument, since its import is already taken account of in the standard procedure of adopting projects of positive present value V_0 (to be discussed more fully in chap. vii). If a project has positive present value this year, it should be adopted this year; the fact that V_0 may decline or even become negative because of rising construction costs if adoption is delayed is thus irrelevant. On the other hand, if present value V_0 is negative today, the fact that it will be still more negative next year is no argument for adopting a bad project this year.

Returning to the topic of general rises in the price level, it is well known that debtors gain and creditors lose from inflation. More strictly, we should say that debtors gain and creditors lose if the rate of inflation exceeds the monetary depreciation allowance already incorporated, at the insistence of creditors, into the market interest rate. If, as has apparently occurred in the last two decades, the rate of inflation does exceed the rate already allowed for in the interest rate, the effect is to import a favorable bias into project financial histories (interest and amortization payments can be made in "cheap" current dollars upon debts originally incurred in dollars representing greater real claims to resources). Clearly, projects have in recent years benefited from inflation as debtors. From the social point of view, however, this is not a net gain; there are real losses suffered by the bondholders which exactly offset the debtors' gains, unless we bring in some special distributional considerations to the effect that one group's interests are to be weighted more heavily than the other's.

5. Recommended Procedures on Discounting

Turning to recommended government procedure, there are at least three different lines of approach we regard as worth discussing. The logically purest method, in our opinion, is not to incorporate the risk allowance in the discount rate at all. Instead, the costs and benefits would be estimated in such a way as to have each annual figure represent at current price levels the expected value of its probability distribution, ignoring risk aversion. Or, if risk aversion is to be considered, the costs would be estimated on a conservatively high basis and the benefits on a conservatively low basis as compared with their respective mean values. These risk-adjusted costs and benefits could then be discounted at the "pure" or riskless rate of interest,[70] the latter including a downward correction for anticipated monetary depreciation. This method is logically superior to incorporating the risk adjustment in the discount rate because under the latter procedure the risk is assumed to be strictly a compounding function of time, like interest. In fact, the risk may be irregularly variable over time; a figure for a given year may be quite certain, and that for another year quite uncertain, following no particular pattern at all. Clearly, explicit risk adjustment for each annual cost and benefit figure is the indicated method for handling this situation.

The riskless rate of interest before monetary depreciation adjustment can with sufficient closeness be approximated by the federal borrowing rate for loans of the same order of maturity as the anticipated project life. The longest-term federal bonds would be ordinarily used, recent yields (April, 1960) being around 4.25 per cent. Allowing 0.5 per cent for monetary depreciation brings this down to the range of 3.5–4 per cent as the adjusted (real) riskless rate.

Unfortunately, the logically purest method has a fatal practical flaw. Who is to say when project benefits and costs have been estimated so conservatively as to be effectively riskless? Probably, all agencies if asked would assert that their own benefit-cost estimates are highly conservative. The trouble is that there is no outside check on the reliability of the estimates.

Each of the two other procedures suggested earlier in the text would provide something in the nature of an outside check. The first would be to finance each project by an issue of revenue bonds. In this case, the purchasers of the bonds would be staking their own money upon their knowledge of the true costs and risks, including monetary depreciation. Here the market, not the government agency, would determine which projects were adopted, since, for projects regarded as unpromising, the requisite funds could not be collected. This may be illustrated by some examples of different projects, each requiring $1 million of funds. For an excellent project yielding high benefits with little uncertainty, investors will compete among each other to bid for the bonds until the yield approaches the riskless rate, say, 4 per cent. For a good project with some degree of uncertainty, the market will insist on a higher rate. For example, consider a project regarded by investors as having one chance in five of failing to such a degree as to have zero yield (but returning principal unimpaired) but otherwise as having a relatively good yield of, say, 10 per cent. The investors will then insist on a nominal yield of perhaps 5 per cent before being willing to part with the $1 million of capital re-

[70] This technique is briefly discussed, though not recommended, in Krutilla and Eckstein, *op. cit.*, pp. 122–24. A good presentation may be found also in the *Green Book*, pp. 21–22.

quired to initiate the project; assuming no risk aversion, they equate a four-fifths chance of 5 per cent with the riskless rate of 4 per cent. Finally, consider a project regarded by investors as having a 50 per cent chance of failing in the same sense just discussed and a 50 per cent chance of yielding 6 per cent. Here the bonds could not be sold at all. Investors desiring a 4 per cent expected yield would insist upon a nominal yield of 8 per cent to allow for the 50 per cent risk of failure, but they also know that even under a favorable outcome they could not receive more than 6 per cent.[71]

This arrangement, like the previous one, suffers from practical difficulties. First, non-monetary benefits are not allowed for. As a second practical matter, it would be necessary to allow for income-tax exemption of interest on local government bonds where that factor applied to distort the market decision. The most important practical objection, however, is the unconventionality of having the market decide which project to adopt (though this has occurred to some extent in the case of turnpikes, where revenue-bond financing is common). Major changes in legislation and in administrative procedures would be required.[72] For this reason, we regard this method of approach as an impractical one.

The next thought that naturally occurs is that the agency itself might attempt to determine hypothetically for each project whether the market would provide the funds under the approach just outlined. For obvious reasons, this is not a very promising idea. Perhaps the closest approach to rationality it might be possible to achieve along this line would be to have each agency use in its analyses a uniform discount rate that somehow reflects its average record of overoptimism in cost-benefit determinations. It is of course no secret that federal agencies, at any rate, have had a notorious history of overoptimism even on factual matters relating to prospective costs and benefits,[73] quite aside from their conceptual errors which double-count or otherwise inflate[74] their optimistic estimates.

[71] This may perhaps seem paradoxical, as the bond price could always fall sufficiently to make the effective yield 4 per cent. Thus, in the circumstances described, the bonds might have a stated 6 per cent coupon on a face value of $1,000; but, if sold actually at $750, the real yield to investors will be 8 per cent if the outcome is favorable, or the required 4 per cent on the average. However, while it is true that individual bonds could be sold on that basis, it can be seen that in the aggregate the receipts from bond sales will be insufficient to finance the project. No tricky method of selling bonds can overcome the fact that, in terms of expected value, there is only $3.00 in real yield available for every $100 invested.

[72] Furthermore, the procedure raises the interesting question as to why the projects are conducted by government at all, if a market test of efficiency is to be determining. We regard this as a valid question which should in fact be raised from time to time, though we cannot discuss it here as we are accepting the existing division of the economy between the private and government sectors as a datum for our analysis.

[73] See, e.g., Task Force on Water Resources and Power, *op. cit.*, I, 130–39. We may mention here that the perennial overoptimism observed is not necessarily a sign of incompetence or dishonesty on the part of those making the estimates. In an interesting paper, two French statisticians have studied this apparently universal phenomenon (see R. Giguet and G. Morlat, "The Causes of Systematic Error in the Cost Estimates of Public Works," *Annales des ponts et chaussées*, No. 5 [September–October, 1952], pp. 543–62 [translation by W. W. Taylor, The RAND Corporation T-76, March 24, 1958]). They provide two major explanations: (1) Cost estimates are usually based on the most probable value of an uncertain outcome, but the *mean* value of the probability distribution exceeds the *most probable* value. The reason is that there are a large number of independent possibilities of things "going wrong," and, while each such may have low probability, some of them are bound to occur. (2) Because an accidental underestimate increases the likelihood of a project's being adopted, there tends to be a selection bias toward overoptimism. (Of course, everything said there about underestimate of costs applies equally well to overestimate of benefits.)

[74] As discussed earlier in this chapter.

Once we have gone this far, however, we might as well turn to the third approach—the one we recommend—to handling the problem of risk. This involves an attempt to determine the real *marginal opportunity rate* which the market insists upon in providing capital to *private* companies whose investment decisions are most comparable to those of public agencies in water supply, namely, to corporations in the public utility fields. The line of argument here is that any historical study will show that the real project risks faced by government agencies are at least as serious as those faced by privately owned concerns in this most closely comparable sphere; that the market, in combination with the working of the corporate income tax, restricts these private companies to projects that (subject to their average degree of risk) promise to return at least a certain rate; and that, consequently, the estimated costs and benefits of government projects should be discounted at least at that private marginal opportunity rate.[75]

To get an actual number (because of the many uncertainties, a crude approximation will suffice), we need only use the method discussed above in connection with Tables 11 and 12. To a fair approximation, market considerations and regulatory practices require that privately owned utilities finance projects with debt and equity in about equal proportions,[76] the debt yielding around 4.7 per cent and the equity around 5.7 per cent earnings yield (1959 averages).[77] (We ignore preferred stocks, whose role is becoming unimportant.) This indicates that the marginal opportunity rate, subject to the degree of risk associated by the market with such investments, must be about 8 or 9 per cent (the calculated figure is 8.29 per cent),[78] which should be adjusted downward slightly for monetary depreciation to obtain the real rate. We should also allow, however, for the effects of taxes other than the corporate income tax. Figuring property and other taxes at 1–2 per cent of project capital investment cost annually would raise the marginal opportunity rate to over 9 per cent. If in fact government risks are typically greater, 10 per cent would then be close to a minimum rate of discount to use for government projects as an across-the-board figure. We will generally use the 10 per cent figure in our analyses which follow. It must be emphasized that the 10 per cent figure is not the pure interest rate but rather an estimate of the implicit marginal opportunity rate in the private sphere including the allowance for risk insisted on by the capital market, the difference between 10 per cent and the pure rate of just above 4 per cent representing mainly the market evaluation of the risks encountered in private utility investments considering the interaction with equity financing requirements and the tax effect thereof.[79] Note that the market insists

[75] The capital market, of course, acts to equate the risk-adjusted returns on capital in the utility and the non-utility fields within the private sector.

[76] Since regulatory practice is to allow a rate of return to utilities that will cover cost of capital but still permit minimum prices for service to consumers, both regulatory commissions and the companies are anxious to minimize capital cost—there is no conflict of interest here. Troxel reports that state commissions and the Securities and Exchange Commission strongly prefer capital structures with not more than 50–60 per cent debt, however (E. Troxel, *Economics of Public Utilities* [New York: Rinehart & Co., 1947], p. 156). In the period 1947–57, for public utilities and communications, equity sources (stock issues plus depreciation plus retained profits) accounted for about 53 per cent of funds and debt sources 47 per cent (see *Survey of Current Business,* October, 1958, p. 20).

[77] These figures change rather rapidly with fluctuations in money-market conditions and stock-market values. The latest figures available at the time of writing were, for December, 1959, public utility bond yields, 4.86 per cent, and stock earnings yields, 5.82 per cent (see *Survey of Current Business,* March, 1960, p. S-20).

[78] Using the December, 1959, bond and earnings yields (see n. 77 above) leads to a calculated marginal opportunity rate of 8.49 per cent.

[79] A point of view rather similar to our own has

on a large fraction of equity capital despite the tax advantages of financing through debt. The crucial role of the tax effect is evidenced if we consider what the risk-adjusted discount rate would be in the absence of corporate taxes. The figure then would be only 5.2 per cent, assuming that corporate financing would still remain at 50 per cent debt yielding 4.7 per cent and 50 per cent equity yielding 5.7 per cent.

One major objection to this analysis concerns the significance of the corporate income tax. It might be argued with some plausibility that the corporate tax is not a mere distorting factor in the capital market but rather a charge society places upon the special legal advantages (especially limited liability) granted to the corporate form of organization, in view of the costs these advantages impose on the rest of the community. This is a rather deep philosophical question for which we have no ready answer. If the argument were accepted fully, it appears at first to make a substantial difference for the result; eliminating the corporate-tax effect, the opportunity rate for the private sphere would be only around 5 per cent rather than 9–10 per cent. This implies, however, that the market would be willing to supply debt and equity capital on the same terms as assumed before without protection of the corporate form, which is certainly untrue. The debt capital is supplied now almost on a riskless basis (as measured by the corresponding rate on United States obligations) despite limited liability under the corporate form, and so the charge on debt could hardly go much lower. Equity capital, however, would certainly insist on a much higher return if investors were to bear unlimited liability. How much higher we do not know, but the universality of the corporate form of organization for large business indicates that the corporate tax is a price willingly paid to avoid this cost. Ultimately, therefore, whatever the philosophical merit of this view of the corporate income tax, it does not affect the discount rate determination; in the absence of the corporate form, the market would undoubtedly insist on a still higher discount rate.

To summarize our viewpoint on discounting, the market provides two bench marks which can be used as a guide for practical procedure. The first is the pure rate of interest for long-term investments, which we believe to be currently just above 4 per cent. This rate is to be used in discounting if in fact the estimated stream of costs and benefits can be regarded as certainty-equivalents. Certainty-equivalents will be expected values of the associated probability distributions if risk aversion is absent; with risk aversion, the certainty-equivalents will be somewhere on the conservative side of the expected value (with risk preference, the certainty-equivalents would be on the optimistic side). The other bench mark is the opportunity rate of close to 10 per cent implicit in the market's evaluation of the

---

been maintained by J. A. Stockfisch in a recent study prepared for the Navy Department on the social cost of capital tied up in military inventories. Stockfisch argues that the government's cost of borrowing, being effectively a riskless rate, is too low an estimate of the productivity of alternative uses of capital in the private sphere. On the basis of estimates of the over-all rate of return from investment in the private sector, Stockfisch recommends a discount rate of 15 per cent. We would differ from Stockfisch on two analytical points: (1) it is the *marginal* rate of return on investment in the private sphere which is relevant, and the marginal should be lower than the average here, and (2) in deriving an over-all private rate of return by averaging figures for different industrial portions of the economy, Stockfisch should have allowed for the differing riskiness of investments in the various sectors. With such an allowance, his figure of 19.6 per cent for rate of return in manufacturing might not really be different from his 10.2 per cent yield for utilities. (Note the similarity between the Stockfisch figure for utilities and our own, derived by an entirely different approach.) See J. A. Stockfisch, *The Interest Cost of Holding Military Inventory* (Los Angeles: Planning Research Corporation, 1960), esp. p. 11.

riskiness of investments of privately owned taxed public utilities. If the riskiness of government projects may be regarded as comparable or only slightly worse, the 10 per cent rate may be used. Actually, we believe it fair to state that experience shows the real riskiness of projects engaged in by government agencies to be substantially greater than those in the private sphere,[80] a rate higher than 10 per cent thus being indicated. This result is, of course, subject to our fundamental proviso of neutrality between public and private projects; that is, we assume that (at least on the margin) there is no "social preference" favoring the adoption of government projects economically inferior to alternative private projects.

The consequence of neglecting to allow for risk of project failure in government choice is obvious enough: some projects will be lucky, but others unlucky, so that, on the average, the return on capital will be lower than the apparent rate applying "if all goes well." Rather more important, as our figures show, is the interaction of risk and taxes (risk considerations require some equity financing, the return on which is heavily taxed). If this interaction is ignored, and it is not widely appreciated, any shoestore or macaroni factory could be shown to be more "profitable" if government owned, since the enterprise could then be entirely debt-financed, escaping the corporate income tax. This has undoubtedly been a factor in the trend to public ownership of utilities.[81] The state of New Mexico has apparently tried to take advantage of this consideration by permitting municipalities to buy any of a variety of what would normally be private business concerns, the purchase to be financed with revenue bonds.[82] Of course, none of these tax-avoidance arrangements can improve real community income unless indeed there is some improvement in management efficiency in shifting from private to government ownership.

5. Official Discounting Procedures

The recommended practice of the *Green Book* is, after separate adjustment of costs and benefits for the calculable risks, to use a rate of 2.5 per cent of federal and non-federal government costs and a rate of not less than 4 per cent for private costs and for all benefits.[83] By way of contrast, the Bureau of Reclamation still seems to be using a rate of 2.5 per cent to discount project costs and benefits. The state of California has recently been using (in principle) a rate of 3.5 per cent, to correspond to the state's current long-term borrowing rate on general obligation bonds.

The basic principle used in the *Green Book* analysis is that the discount rate should equal the expected long-term borrowing rate of the agency, whether private or government, involved. At the time of writing of the *Green Book* (the publication date is May, 1950), interest rates were substantially lower than today, though the "expected" long-term rates might still be, in the opinion of some, as there specified. Most people would probably adopt the current rates as the best expectation for the future, in which case the *Green Book* suggestions might be converted into 4 or 4.5 per cent for government costs and perhaps 6 per cent for benefits and for private costs. We would argue that, for comparable project risks, the same rates should be used for private and for public costs and benefits. The lower borrowing rates of governments are due to the fact that the borrowing rates do not reflect the expected project risk but

80 The record of federal investments is surveyed briefly in chap. ix. Our case studies suggest that local governments are also adopting projects involving high risk of social loss.

81 See E. W. Clemens, *Economics and Public Utilities* (New York: Appleton-Century-Crofts Co., 1950), p. 568.

82 *Economist*, CXCII (July 4, 1959), 31–32.

83 *Green Book*, pp. 21–24.

only the negligible default risk, together with the tax discrimination against private as opposed to government enterprises. To prevent more productive projects in the private sphere from being foregone in favor of less productive investments in the government sphere, the rate used should equal the marginal opportunity rate in the private sphere.

6. *Other Views Evaluated*

It may be convenient to discuss here briefly the views on the rate of discount expressed by McKean, Eckstein, and Krutilla and Eckstein.

In McKean's theoretical discussion he argues for discounting at the "market rate of interest" if there is no "capital rationing"[84] or at the marginal internal rate of return under capital rationing.[85] The capital-rationing situation, where the investor has just so much funds to spend and cannot obtain more, he regards as the applicable case for government agencies, though not for private firms.[86] We will discuss this view in the following chapter and in the appendix to that chapter; we may say here that we regard the capital-rationing assumption as fundamentally inappropriate for the analysis of government investment decisions, as it implies that the funds are available or will be spent regardless of the projects under consideration. Such a procedure removes the question of the appropriate size of the agency budget from the sphere of economic analysis—a very damaging concession for those interested in economic efficiency. However that may be, this assumption permitted McKean to omit any attempt to study or employ the opportunity cost in the private sphere of funds invested in government projects. Since he assumes the funds will be invested regardless, the only question left is to select among the possible projects. McKean's treatment of risk is not very clear; he seems to regard uncertainty or variability of outcome as a kind of intangible which enters as a judgment factor in final decision but cannot be imported into the calculations except by showing alternative outcomes under a number of different assumptions about the uncertain elements in the picture.[87]

McKean's use of the discount rate in his practical case studies is consistent with this viewpoint. Results are shown under a range of discount rates (2.5, 5, and 8 per cent), evidently intended to represent different estimates of the marginal internal rate of return under the agency's rationed budget. An indication of the amount of likely variability of outcome (apparently calculated at a 5 per cent discount rate) is also provided.[88] At the time of decision, informed judgment is relied upon to select the appropriate rate.

In contrast with McKean's omission of the discount-rate question, Krutilla and Eckstein present a very elaborate analysis of the social cost of federal financing.[89] They examine alternative possible ways of securing federal funds and measure the differential impact of the alternatives considered upon the various investing and consuming sectors. In the case of the personal income tax, for example, a reduction of which is considered as an alternative to a water-resource project, the incidence of the reduction is traced through various income groups. The next step is to average on the basis of family-budget information the rate of interest yielded on investments (or saved by repayment of debt) for each such income group. The results (under 1955 market conditions) are an opportunity rate of 5–6 per cent for the social cost

[84] *Op. cit.*, pp. 76–81.

[85] *Ibid.*, pp. 82–87.

[86] *Ibid.*, pp. 85, 148.

[87] *Ibid.*, p. 98.

[88] *Ibid.*, pp. 206–7, 240–41.

[89] Krutilla and Eckstein, *op. cit.*, pp. 78–130.

of federal capital; the comparable figure would be slightly higher today (1960). This analysis is entirely vitiated (we would argue) by its failure to make any adjustments for risk. All quoted rates are averaged on an equivalent basis, despite the fact that some involve high risk (e.g., consumer credit in low-income brackets) and some low (secured mortgage debt). On an over-all basis, the average 5–6 per cent figure incorporates some unknown average degree of risk premium and thus is not inconsistent with our belief that a somewhat lower figure approximates the pure or riskless rate of interest.

Rather surprisingly, Eckstein's other work represents quite a different approach, more in line with our analysis.[90] He recognizes three methods of analyzing risk: shortening the period of analysis (i.e., requiring a quick "payout"), adding a risk premium to the pure interest rate, and employing safety allowances to make cost and benefit estimates more conservative. While he allows some role for each of these, he considers an interest premium of 0.5–1 per cent (no justification of the specific figures is provided) to be the "most useful adjustment."[91] Our analysis diverges from his in attempting to estimate directly what the risk premium should be to insure that public projects with lesser expected return than the most comparable private alternatives (private utility investments) are not adopted. This consideration leads to a strikingly larger adjustment than that proposed by Eckstein, based on the interaction among risk, equity financing, and the high corporate income tax (we do get a correction of around 1 per cent if all tax effects are ignored).

We may comment briefly here on a suggestion by Eckstein[92] that the same effect achieved by the use of the marginal opportunity rate in discounting could also be secured with the use of a lower rate, together with a B/C ratio somewhat greater than 1. Eckstein, in fact, argues in favor of such a procedure, urging a lower rate because of the problem discussed earlier about the votes of future generations not being considered in the market place today. But if in fact the B/C ratio is then made high enough with, say, a 2.5 per cent rate so that the same amount of aggregate investment is undertaken as would come about with a B/C ratio of unity and a marginal opportunity (say, 10 per cent) rate, it can be shown that his proposal is inefficient. That is, it is possible to achieve more wealth for the future from a given amount of present sacrifice with the use of the 10 per cent rate and a B/C ratio of unity.[93] (This argument is quite aside from the difficulties of working with B/C ratios alluded to earlier.) If it is desired to allow for a supposed bias against the future, the way to do so is to continue to adopt the most efficient projects while increasing the amount of current sacrifice.

E. Concluding Comments

Our long theoretical discussion and evaluation of existing practices in the light of that discussion inevitably give a somewhat misleading impression of the real-world problems in the water-resource develop-

90 Eckstein, *op. cit.*, pp. 81–90.

91 *Ibid.*, p. 90.

92 *Ibid.*, pp. 101–4. But cf. Eckstein and Krutilla, *op. cit.*, pp. 126–27.

93 To take a specific illustration, suppose that the amount of current sacrifice permitted is just $1.00 and that the choice lies between two projects. The first investment opportunity, *I*, involves a sacrifice of a current dollar in exchange for $1.10 after one year; the other opportunity, *II*, involves a sacrifice of a current dollar in exchange for $1.20 accruing after two years. At the market opportunity rate of 10 per cent, only the first project is desirable (marginally). But at a discount rate of 2.5 per cent, *I* has a B/C ratio of 1.074, smaller than the figure of 1.144 for *II*. Consequently, the Eckstein rule would adopt *II*, which is obviously inefficient if 10 per cent is the marginal opportunity rate for both one-year and two-year investments.

ment field. While we have been discussing questions of intricate theoretical detail, it is easy to forget that annual expenditures of hundreds of millions, or even billions, depend for their justification upon such details. For example, the cost of completing construction of the Bureau of Reclamation program after fiscal 1954 was estimated at $4 billion.[94] If our recommendations were adopted (discounting Bureau-estimated prospective costs and benefits at a rate of around 10 per cent, and eliminating the bulk of "secondary benefits"), there would be little left to the Bureau's program. A possible explanation is that irrigation projects that are sound economic propositions tend to be undertaken by private enterprise without government assistance; promoters of uneconomic proposals, on the other hand, turn to government, since they are not so foolish as to risk their own funds on such projects.

Another aspect of the real world which might be lost sight of in the theoretical discussion is that it is often the most elementary rather than the most advanced theory which is neglected in official or popular discussions. Thus, the view that there are certain objective "needs" or "requirements" for water which must be satisfied regardless of cost is a position that anyone with the slightest knowledge of economic theory or of the facts of life could demolish, but it has nevertheless been responsible for huge waste of our national resources.

In the hope of giving the reader some idea of how the theoretical and practical details interact in the evaluation of major investment projects, some later chapters are devoted to the detailed project analysis of several of the largest water-supply ventures executed or proposed in this nation. Our reason for concentrating on large projects, aside from their intrinsic interest, is the fact that government agencies might be expected to have some real advantages over private capital in large complex projects, primarily because the benefits of such projects tend to be diffused over so large a field that private interests would not be able to capture enough of them to make the investment look worthwhile. (This is an argument in terms of technological spillover benefits, examples of which are flood protection, improvement of hydropower efficiency downstream, and wildlife benefits.) We would like to note that the argument frequently given about large size itself being a deterrent to private enterprise depends upon the somewhat doubtful assumption of private risk aversion. Certainly, recent developments like the spread of gas pipelines and the introduction of television broadcasting show that it is possible to amass large private capital aggregates if the investments look promising. As a matter of actual fact, however, government agencies are engaged in a whole host of small-size, in addition to the more publicized large-size, developments, nor is there any reason to believe that a higher standard of wisdom has been in effect for the former.[95]

[94] Task Force on Water Resources and Power, *op. cit.*, I, 6.

[95] The relatively small Ainsworth Project examined by Dawson (*op. cit.*, p. 55) involved annual costs of about $1.6 million and annual benefits of about $0.5 million, or an annual wealth loss of some $1.1 million. This project was officially described by the reclamation commissioner as "one of the more favorable irrigation units of the Missouri River Basin Project" (quoted *ibid.*, p. 2).

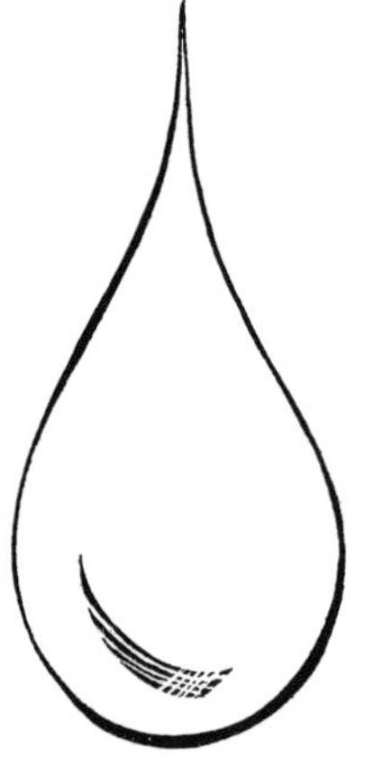

CHAPTER VII

THE PRACTICAL LOGIC OF INVESTMENT EFFICIENCY CALCULATIONS

In our chapter on investment in additional water supplies we discussed the principles underlying the economic solution for investment decisions, without going into the practical details of how to go about actually computing such a solution in a real problem. This question of application is, however, both important and by no means free of difficulties, and so we are devoting this chapter to an examination of such topics as the formula embodying the criterion of choice, the measurement of benefit and of cost, and the practical treatment of considerations like depreciation, interest, and risk. Actually, these topics are ordinarily discussed in textbooks of engineering economy; we will make particular use of Grant's important text.[1]

A. Decision Formulas

Three different techniques in common use propose logically plausible ways of integrating measurements of the costs and benefits associated with an investment project in a formula designed to indicate the correct investment decision. These three will be called here (1) the "present-value rule"; (2) the "annual-net-benefits (or annual-net-receipts) rule"; and (3) the "internal-rate-of-return rule."[2]

1. The Present-Value Rule

For reasons we will advance later, we regard the present-value rule as logically prior to the others, and we recommend its use. The rule may be stated as follows: Adopt any project for which the present value of the associated stream of net benefits or net receipts, discounted at the appropriate rate of interest, is greater than zero. (Just what rate of interest is "appropriate" we shall discuss later.) It is assumed that dollar figures are available for the benefits and costs.

Present value is defined by the formula

$$V_0 = \frac{s_1}{1+i} + \frac{s_2}{(1+i)^2} + \frac{s_3}{(1+i)^3} + \ldots + \frac{s_n}{(1+i)^n}, \qquad (1a)$$

where V_0 is present value, s_t $(= b_t - c_t)$ is

[1] E. L. Grant, *Principles of Engineering Economy* (3d ed.; New York: Ronald Press Co., 1950).

[2] *Ibid.*, p. 85. Grant emphasizes the formulas and does not explicitly state the *rule* for decision in each case, but his application of the formulas is consistently correct.

the value of the net benefit (benefit less cost) or net receipt attributable in the year t to the investment under consideration (calculated as of the end of the year), i is the discount or interest rate per annum, and n is the last year in which the investment has any effect.

In this analysis the costs represent actual sums expended on physical equipment, labor, material, taxes, etc.—but not charges for interest, depreciation, or amortization of debt. As will be explained below, debt amortization is unrelated to project efficiency, while interest and depreciation are implicitly allowed for in the formula itself.

Our statement implies that annual compounding is appropriate. If more frequent (e.g., quarterly) compounding is desired, the formula can still be used, but t should be numbered in terms of quarter-years, s_t should represent the quarterly rather than annual net benefits or receipts (calculated as of the end of the quarter), and i should become the quarterly discount or interest rate. Formulas are also available for continuous compounding or discounting, but we will not present them here; in general, we will employ annual compounding.

Formula (1a) also assumes that the first term in the net receipts sequence occurs in period or at time 1 (i.e., at the end of year 1 if the year is the period used). It will frequently be the case, however, that there is an immediate cost or outlay at time $t = 0$—that is, at the very inception of the project. We will denote such an immediate outlay as c_0, the subscript indicating its contemporaneity with V_0. Where such an initial outlay occurs (e.g., payment of the purchase price today of a capital asset with the future net receipt stream above), present value with allowance for this payment is expressed as

$$V_0 = -c_0 + \frac{s_1}{1+i} + \frac{s_2}{(1+i)^2} + \cdots + \frac{s_n}{(1+i)^n}. \quad (1b)$$

Equation (1b) may be regarded as our basic formula for discounting net receipts streams.

It is also possible to discount independently the stream of annual receipts or benefits—$b_1, b_2, \ldots, b_n$—in the same way to get a present value B_0 for the benefit stream alone; to discount independently the stream of annual costs—$c_0, c_1, c_2, \ldots, c_n$—to get a present value C_0 for the cost stream alone; and to find V_0 as simply the difference $B_0 - C_0$.

Some special cases are also of interest. If the stream to be discounted is constant and perpetual, beginning with time 1, so that $s_1 = s_2 = \ldots = s_t = \ldots$ to infinity, we may denote the constant annual value as s and write the present value as

$$V_0 = s\left[\frac{1}{1+i} + \frac{1}{(1+i)^2} + \cdots + \frac{1}{(1+i)^t} + \cdots\right] = \frac{s}{i}. \quad (1c)$$

EXAMPLE 1.—Suppose that a certain project yields a perpetual annual benefit stream, beginning with time 1, of 100. The only cost involved is an outlay of 1,000 incurred at time 0. The annual rate of interest is 5 per cent.

Then $b_1 = b_2 = \ldots = b_t = \ldots = b = 100$, and $c_0 = 1{,}000$.

The present value B_0 of the benefit stream equals b/i, or $100/0.05 = 2{,}000$.

The present value C_0 of the cost stream equals $c_0 = 1{,}000$.

The net present value $V_0 = B_0 - C_0 = 2{,}000 - 1{,}000 = 1{,}000$.

If the stream to be discounted is constant but *finite*, beginning at time 1 and terminating at time n, the formula is

$$V_0 = \frac{s}{i}\left[1 - \frac{1}{(1+i)^n}\right] = s\,\frac{(1+i)^n - 1}{i(1+i)^n}. \quad (1d)$$

EXAMPLE 2.—Using the data of Example 1, suppose now that the annual benefit stream is finite, persisting only through the twentieth year.

Then

$$B_0 = 100\,\frac{(1.05)^{20}-1}{0.05\,(1.05)^{20}}$$

$$= 100\,\frac{2.653-1}{0.05\,(2.653)} = 1{,}246.2\,.$$

The net present value $V_0 = B_0 - C_0 = 1{,}246.2 - 1{,}000 = 246.2$.

Interest tables are of course helpful in practical computations with these formulas, as well as with the formulas associated with the other decision rules here considered. The coefficient of s on the right of equation ($1d$) is sometimes known as the "present-worth factor" or, more strictly, as the "uniform annual series present-worth factor."[3]

2. *Internal-Rate-of-Return Rule*

Turning back to equation ($1b$), the internal rate of return (often called, less suggestively, the "rate of return") for any investment is the discount rate, which we may denote ρ, that makes the present value V_0 of the net benefit stream for that investment equal to zero. Explicitly, we may write

$$0 = -c_0 + \frac{s_1}{1+\rho} + \frac{s_2}{(1+\rho)^2} + \ldots + \frac{s_n}{(1+\rho)^n}. \tag{2}$$

Alternatively, ρ could be defined as the discount rate that makes the present value of the cost stream equal the present value of the receipts stream. This is equivalent to the other definition, for, if $C_0 = B_0$, $V_0 = 0$. The *rule* for decision is: Adopt any project for which the internal rate of return, ρ, is greater than the "appropriate" rate of interest, i. In practice, determining ρ for a project ordinarily requires a technique of successive approximations.

It is mistakenly thought by many analysts that these two rules are equivalent—that is, that, if the present-value rule indicates adoption of a project, the internal-rate-of-return rule must also, and vice versa. Only relatively recently has it been appreciated that the internal-rate-of-return rule may give ambiguous answers; for a general net receipt or net benefit stream, there may be no, one, two, or any number of "solving rates of interest" ρ in equation (2). Ambiguity of result does occur in practice but not too frequently, since it is usually the case that, if the costs are predominantly incurred in the early part of the sequence and the benefits are predominantly received in the later part, the solution for ρ will be unique—and, in fact, investment projects are ordinarily of this nature.[4] Nevertheless, the possibility of a non-unique result is a serious practical objection to the use of the internal-rate-of-return decision rule, especially as the technique of successive approximations necessary to attain a single solution cannot be counted on to give any clue as to whether other solutions exist. The logical priority of the present-value rule is evidenced by the fact that it gives correct results without difficulty whether the internal-rate-of-return calculation leads to a satisfactory solution or not, as illustrated by one of our examples in the last section of this chapter.

3. *Annual-Net-Benefits Rule*

The annual-net-benefits or annual-net-receipts rule does lead to identical answers with the present-value rule, provided that the correct formula is used. The rule may be stated as follows: Adopt any project for which the annual net benefit is greater than zero when computed at the "appropriate"

[3] *Ibid.*, p. 45.

[4] For a precise statement of the conditions under which multiple solutions occur, as well as a general discussion of investment criteria, see J. Hirshleifer, "On the Theory of Optimal Investment Decision," *Journal of Political Economy*, LXVI (August, 1958), 329–52.

rate of interest. The annual net benefit calculation is based upon the principle of finding the level net stream that corresponds to the actual stream of costs and benefits associated with the project.

Denoting the level annual net flow as s, it is desired to solve for s in the equation[5]

$$\frac{s}{1+i}+\frac{s}{(1+i)^2}+\ldots+\frac{s}{(1+i)^n} = -c_0+\frac{s_1}{1+i}+\frac{s_2}{(1+i)^2}+\ldots+\frac{s_n}{(1+i)^n}. \quad (3a)$$

Since the right-hand side of ($3a$) equals V_0 in formula ($1b$), we may use ($1d$) to write

$$s\frac{(1+i)^n-1}{i(1+i)^n}=V_0 = -c_0+\frac{s_1}{1+i}+\frac{s_2}{(1+i)^2}+\ldots+\frac{s_n}{(1+i)^n}. \quad (3b)$$

It will be observed in ($3b$) that, with i and n fixed, to each present value V_0 there will correspond a unique figure for s. Furthermore, if V_0 is greater than zero, s must also be positive, and vice versa, subject only to the condition that i exceeds zero (the interest rate is not negative or zero). Therefore, the annual-net-benefits rule is equivalent to the present-value rule. As in the case of the present-value calculation, it is possible to make the annual-net-benefits calculation separately for the benefits and the costs. That is to say, one can find an annual benefit b equivalent to the observed benefit stream $b_1, \ldots, b_n$; an annual cost c equivalent to the observed cost stream $c_0, c_1, \ldots, c_n$; and the annual *net* benefit s is then simply $b - c$. In making this calculation, of course, c and b must both be determined for the same number of years n.

EXAMPLE 3.—Using the data of Examples 1 and 2 above, and equation ($3b$), we can solve for the net annual benefit s:

$$s=\frac{V_0 i(1+i)^n}{(1+i)^n-1} = \frac{246.2(0.05)(2.653)}{1.653} = 19.76$$

Alternatively, we can separately find b and c.

$$c=\frac{1{,}000(0.05)(2.653)}{1.653}=80.24,$$

$$b=\frac{1{,}246.2(0.05)(2.653)}{1.653}=100.00.$$

Then $b - c = 19.76$ as before.

Incorrect formulas are often used in computing average annual costs. Capital costs (see below) are sometimes averaged out over the years of project life by simply adding an annual straight-line depreciation charge to annual interest. The latter is sometimes approximated on the basis of the "average amount invested"—halfway between the initial investment and the salvage value recoverable at the end of project life. More elaborately, a simple time average might be figured from the annual sums of depreciation and interest on the undepreciated balance; the result of this latter calculation will vary with the depreciation formula used. Both of these methods are relatively crude approximations of the cor-

[5] There is a minor algebraic complication here. Note that formula ($3a$) converts the series on the right with $n+1$ terms into a level series on the left with only n terms. While to some extent writing the formula in this way, rather than having $n+1$ terms on the left too (which would mean including an undiscounted initial s corresponding to time 0) is arbitrary, we believe that the convention adopted here most closely expresses the idea of an equivalent annual net flow. The reason for the disparity in the number of terms is that the series on the right has a payment in the present (time 0) in addition to the end-of-year net receipts for years 1 through n. Since the project life is really n years, and not $n+1$, the best annualizing formula has just n terms as shown, representing that level series of end-of-year net receipts s in years 1 through n that is equivalent to the series of net receipts under consideration.

rect average annual cost, which ordinarily can be exactly determined with little or no additional computational effort.

4. Comparison and Evaluation of the Rules

The present-value rule and the annual-net-benefits rule are equivalent and logically satisfactory for the cases we have considered, though before they can be used in practice the question of just what is the "appropriate" interest rate to employ in the calculation must be faced. The internal-rate-of-return rule will often, and even normally, also lead to the same correct conclusions. However, it is not logically equivalent, and the user may unknowingly find himself in one of the classes of cases in which this rule fails to give unique correct answers. On this ground, and also for another reason to be described shortly, we strongly urge that it never be used.

It is worthwhile, however, to step back and take a larger look at the subject of the decision criterion to see whether perhaps we have been omitting discussion of some classes of cases where the result might be different or else making certain implicit assumptions that condition the results obtained. For one thing, we have been implicitly assuming complete certainty about the prospective costs and benefits to be anticipated from an investment. As a practical matter, it is of the utmost importance to make allowance for risk and uncertainty, and we will discuss techniques for doing so below. We have also explicitly assumed the existence of an "appropriate" rate of interest for each of the three rules considered, and here again discussion of the matter is reserved until later.

One other implicit assumption of our analysis above was project independence—that any investment could be considered in isolation as having a stream of costs and benefits associated with it alone. Normally, investment possibilities will interact, and it is necessary to consider the effect of one upon another. In simple cases this would be done automatically, since, if a particular investment increases or decreases the net advantages of other activities also being undertaken, these effects would be counted in the benefits or costs. One troublesome case is that of mutually exclusive projects, where adoption of one project means that another will not be undertaken.[6] It so happens that, for mutually exclusive projects, the internal-rate-of-return rule may give answers that are actually wrong rather than merely ambiguous,[7] thus providing another strong reason for foregoing the use of that dangerous rule. The obvious adaptation of each of the other rules will lead to the correct result for mutually exclusive projects, however. For the present-value rule, the principle is to adopt whichever alternative has the positive present value, if either has; to adopt neither if both present values are negative; and, if both present values are positive, to adopt the one that is higher.[8] Similarly for the annual-net-benefits rule, the principle is to choose the project with the higher s so long as that figure is positive.

The opposite case from mutually exclusive investments occurs when one project makes profitable adoption of another that would not otherwise have been economic. This might be called the "tie-in" situation. Here it is obvious that the net benefit of the second project is also to be counted in evaluating the first, which can most simply be

6 It makes no difference whether the projects are mutually exclusive for purely technological reasons (e.g., two prospective building projects competing for the use of the same land) or for economic reasons (e.g., construction of building A on site A makes uneconomic the construction of building B on site B).

7 See A. A. Alchian, "The Rate of Interest, Fisher's Rate of Return over Cost, and Keynes' Internal Rate of Return," *American Economic Review*, XLV (December, 1955), 938–43.

8 While choosing the project with the higher present value is highly plausible, an explicit rationale for the procedure is provided in Hirshleifer, *op. cit.*, pp. 329–43.

done by considering the two as a joint package. The treatment of project interdependence is illustrated in one of the examples in the last section of this chapter. The basic principle, however, is simply to define uniquely each possible alternative project or set of projects as one of the choices available.

Another implicit assumption underlying our formulas and rules is that the appropriate rate of discount, whatever it may be, is a constant over time. Actually, while the importance of this point does not seem to have been recognized, the rate of interest may well be expected to vary over time in a known way, in which case it is obviously necessary to take the pattern of variation into account in making investment decisions. For example, a recession widely believed to be temporary will cause current interest rates to fall below those anticipated for the future (this will be evidenced by a widening of the ordinary excess of the long-term rate over the short-term rate). To take another case, a particular firm might anticipate opening new avenues of credit, at some definite date in the future, which will have the effect of reducing interest cost to it.

Generalizing formula (1*b*) to allow for varying rates of discount, we have

$$V_0 = -c_0 + \frac{s_1}{1+i_1} + \frac{s_2}{(1+i_2)(1+i_1)} + \ldots + \frac{s_n}{(1+i_n)(1+i_{n-1})\ldots(1+i_2)(1+i_1)} \,. \tag{4}$$

Here i_1 is the discount rate between time 1 and 0, i_2 is the rate between time 2 and time 1, etc. The most general formulation of the present-value rule is to adopt any project for which the value derived from equation (4) is positive, still leaving aside the question of just how to determine the appropriate rate or rates of discount. The annual-net-benefits rule may also be adapted to the case of changing discount rates by generalizing equation (3*a*); the computation becomes awkward, however, since the simpler form (3*b*) cannot be used. As for the internal-rate-of-return rule, note that the calculation of ρ in equation (2) is entirely unchanged, but there is no clear way of employing the rule which dictates comparing ρ with *the* rate of discount. Inability to cope with the problem of changes in the appropriate rate of discount over time is another unsatisfactory aspect of the internal-rate-of-return rule.

5. Present-Value Calculations for Water Costs

The principles adduced above apply for investments when a specified set of figures for annual benefits and costs, in dollar amounts, is available for calculation purposes. Sometimes this is exactly the form in which projects appear when efficiency calculations are to be made, in which case the principles above can be applied directly. However, problems of efficiency calculation in water-supply problems often or even typically appear in a rather indirect way as follows: the water yield and total costs of a water-supply project are known, but it is desired to calculate the unit or average cost of the water supplied to determine if this project is preferable to an alternative. This problem could be reduced to one involving the formulas above simply by placing a dollar value on the water, but the practical decision process often calls for a calculation of the average cost of water before any determination of water value is made.

The basic formula for determining the unit cost of an increment of water supply is:

$$x q_0 + \frac{x q_1}{1+i} + \ldots + \frac{x q_n}{(1+i)^n} = (c_0 - z_0) + \frac{c_1 - z_1}{1+i} + \ldots + \frac{c_n - z_n}{(1+i)^n},$$

or

$$x\left[q_0 + \frac{q_1}{1+i} + \ldots + \frac{q_n}{(1+i)^n}\right] = (c_0 - z_0) + \frac{c_1 - z_1}{1+i} + \ldots + \frac{c_n - z_n}{(1+i)^n}, \tag{5}$$

where x is the unknown unit cost of water, q_t represents the water deliveries in year t, c_t is the dollar cost in year t, z_t is the dollar value of offsets to cost associated with the project in year t, and i is a constant rate of discount. This formula is an adaptation of the present-value calculation; it can be solved for an average cost of water x such that the present value of the deliveries over time, costing each unit delivered at x, equals the present value of the known stream of dollar costs over time, allowing for any offsets to cost credited for benefits other than water supply associated with the project.[9] We will call this x the *present-worth* (or *present-value*) *average cost* of deliveries.

B. Capital Costs

1. Capital Costs and Discounting Formulas

We may define capital costs as expenses incurred more or less as a lump sum to achieve certain ends, where these latter accrue or are received over a considerable period of time. By way of contrast, current or operating costs are incurred to achieve certain immediate purposes, and the expenditure must be constantly renewed if it is desired to continue receiving the benefits. The distinction is obviously just a question of degree rather than a fundamental dichotomy, since practically all expenditures will have some continuing effects.

In equations (1) through (5), we made no distinction between capital and other costs; the formulas consider any cost incurred as simply a negative item in the stream of net benefits, as of the date the expenditure is made. Nor is there, in our opinion, any important reason in efficiency calculations to attempt to maintain the distinction between capital and non-capital costs. In practice, it sometimes happens that capital and non-capital expenses are funded separately, so that financial accountants do have to keep track of the categories for record-keeping purposes; but only under peculiar circumstances in which funds are available for one type of cost but not another is there any reason why the distinction should be of importance for decision-making.[10]

Still, it is perhaps worthwhile indicating explicitly how our formulas do handle the problem of capital expenses, since there may be some misunderstanding on this score. In every case the method is to record each project expense and benefit when actually incurred or received but to omit merely financial or accounting transactions (i.e., depreciation and "amortization"). This means that a capital expenditure at the beginning, say, of a project is to be recorded as a negative lump-sum receipt as of time 0; later capital expenditures will be correspondingly recorded as of the date they are actually incurred. If the benefits accrue over time, as will ordinarily be the case, they will be recorded as an annual stream (constant or fluctuating) of receipts.

The question may then arise: What of depreciation, interest, and amortization as recurrent capital costs? These, however, have already been fully allowed for by treating the amount of capital invested as a negative receipt when incurred. Since the full amount sacrificed has already been counted, any allowance for annual depreciation of investment would obviously be double counting. (It is of importance, however, to credit a *salvage value* as the equivalent of a receipt if, at the end of the analysis period, the capital surviving is still

[9] For an illustration of the use of this formula see J. C. DeHaven and J. Hirshleifer, "Feather River Water for Southern California," *Land Economics,* XXXIII (August, 1957), 198–209 (at p. 202).

[10] We are aware that there has been a certain amount of attention paid by theoretical economists to the problem of decision-making when capital funds are arbitrarily restricted, but in our opinion the belief that this situation is important in the real world is a mistaken one. This is the capital-rationing problem to be discussed below.

expected to be of some value for production or resale. The salvage value at the end of the period is an offset to the capital cost incurred earlier.) As for interest, since the project has been charged for the full capital sum, it would be double counting to charge for interest on that sum. "Amortization," using that term to denote periodic charges designed to provide a fund for extinguishing a debt, is often charged as a cost (usually as an alternative to a depreciation charge). But in reality amortization payments are involved only in project financing and do not belong in efficiency calculations. The method of handling capital costs, then, is extremely simple: simply charge for the full expenditure whenever incurred and then credit for salvage value surviving at the termination of the period of analysis.

This discussion and the conclusion that it is unnecessary and incorrect to charge for interest, depreciation, or amortization where the invested capital sums have been fully counted apply to calculations under the *present-value* rule which we recommend. Where an annual-net-benefits calculation is made instead, it is true that the capital expenses occurring in any year are spread over the entire project life. This is logically equivalent to counting depreciation and interest instead of the capital sums invested. Under our formulas (3*a*) and (3*b*), however, it is still unnecessary to make the interest and depreciation charges explicitly; they are accounted for in the formulas which determine the annual net benefit by dividing present value V_0 by a factor representing the interest rate and the project life.

Engineering economy studies sometimes make use of the so-called capital recovery factor,[11] the coefficient of the present value C_0 in the formula below for determining the annual cost c over a period of n years equivalent to a cost stream of present value C_0.

$$c = \frac{C_0 i (1+i)^n}{(1+i)^n - 1}.$$

Conceptually, the capital recovery factor, when multiplied by the present value of the capital costs, is the level end-of-year annual amount over the life of the project necessary to pay interest on and recover the capital costs in full. Computationally, this level annual amount is identical to the annual cost, c, equivalent to an actual cost stream $c_0, c_1, c_2, \ldots, c_n$, discussed above in connection with equation (3*b*)—but where the c's refer not to all costs but to capital costs alone. The capital recovery factor was used by us in Example 3 above to convert an initial capital cost of 1,000 into an annual cost of 80.24. If there is a terminal salvage value, that may simply be entered as a negative c_n for the terminal project year n in the calculation of C_0.

Use of the capital recovery factor involves the danger of treating capital costs as somehow different from other costs, and of course it adds nothing conceptually, since analysis can be conducted using annual costs and present values of cost streams. However, the capital recovery factor is a computationally handy concept, since the values it takes on for different i and n have been summarized in a number of interest tables.

2. Depreciation and Length of Life

In project efficiency calculations, depreciation is a forecast subject to a great deal of uncertainty. Even physical life of equipment is subject to great variation, but actually this may be only a minor part of the problem. The dominant cause of depreciation in the relevant sense—loss of value for productive purposes—often is economic change, which is far less predictable than physical life.

The source of change usually thought of in this connection is technological obsolescence—the result of the development of

[11] Grant, *op. cit.*, pp. 44–45.

improved equipment or processes which compete with the old for doing the same job. Other types of economic change may also causes a loss in economic value, however; markets may diminish or disappear, or required inputs may become scarce and expensive. In the case of water supply, there have been instances of abandonment of systems because of movement of population, increasing operating costs relative to alternative new developments, competing demands for land use, and pre-emption of supply for other uses or users, among a host of other reasons.

In the light of such possibilities, forecasts of service life are necessarily speculations. One redeeming feature is that the power of interest in discounting future returns gives the relatively far-off periods much less influence than the near future on the efficiency calculation. We will not attempt here to give any quantitative guide for estimating service lives; the subject is discussed to some extent in our chapter on the technology of water supply. We warn against the common practice, however, of accepting financial amortization arrangements—the length of term for which bonds can be sold—as in any way equivalent to economic service life.

3. *The Interest or Discount Rate*

It is not often realized how sensitive efficiency calculations are to the rate of interest or discount assumed. Since in water-supply projects the bulk of the expenses are normally incurred early in the history of the development, while benefits are stretched over a relatively long period, a low interest rate makes projects look good, while a high interest rate makes them appear bad. In the previous chapter we have seen that typical government procedure—on federal, state, and local levels—is to use in efficiency calculations the relatively low rates in the range of 2–4 per cent at which governments can borrow. Also, we have seen that, for private utility corporations, the influence of the corporate income tax requires a project to promise somewhere in the range of 10 per cent pretax yield before it can be considered profitable, implying the use of a discount rate in this higher range.

In recommending practice for public works, Grant urges the use of a "minimum attractive rate of return," which would normally be higher than the borrowing rate. For this he adduces two different types of considerations: (1) that, if there are projects that are economic but are not being adopted because of limited budgets, the discount rate should be the marginal opportunity rate (the prospective return from alternative investments), and this will be higher than the borrowing rate; (2) that there should be allowance for such factors as risk, tax exemption of state and local bonds, and the value of money to taxpayers.[12]

We regard these points as generally well taken[13] though requiring some discussion. The first consideration refers to the "capital-rationing" situation mentioned earlier. In this case the limited budget of an agency may require it to stop investing when it still has marginal projects capable of yielding, say, 10 per cent, despite the fact that the market rate of interest is lower, say, 3 per cent. Here discounting at the market rate may lead to the adoption of a project yielding barely 3 per cent, which would be a mistake if alternative investments yielding more are available as assumed. The natural solution to this problem, and the one urged by Grant (and others), is to use the marginal opportunity rate—in this case the internal rate of return on the marginal project—as the discount rate. Unfortun-

[12] *Ibid.*, pp. 505–8.

[13] We disagree, however, with one of Grant's points—that investments reducing government costs should be accepted with a lower required rate of return than investments reducing private costs. This departs from the fundamental principle of equating the productivity of capital on the margin in all employments.

ately, this solution is not a generally correct one, as will be shown in the appendix to this chapter. A preferable procedure, which will always lead to correct results so long as only funds of the current period are assumed to be rationed, is to compare projects on the basis of their present value as of time 1 (the value of the time stream for periods 1 through n, calculated back to time 1) *per dollar of current funds.* The formula to use is V_1/c_0, where

$$V_1 = s_1 + \frac{s_2}{1+i} + \ldots + \frac{s_n}{(1+i)^{n-1}}$$

(assuming a constant market rate of interest, i), and c_0 is the fund input for the current period. The formula is only applicable where a fund input for the current period is required (where no current input is required, the rationing of current funds is irrelevant). The rule is successively to adopt projects with the highest values of this ratio until the fixed budget is exhausted or until the alternative use of funds elsewhere becomes more desirable than further investments. Which of these conditions will apply depends upon whether the rationing *requires* exhaustion of the budget on investments or merely *limits* the total current funds so as not to exceed the budget made available, without ruling out shortfalls. A general treatment of the problem of investment decision under capital rationing appears in the appendix to this chapter.

We have relegated the technical discussion of optimizing under capital rationing to an appendix because we do not believe that this represents a practically important situation. The size of government budgets for water supply, or for other types of projects, should not be considered fixed but should be determined by the efficiency of the projects that might possibly be undertaken. For this reason, we believe that cases will only rarely arise requiring use of the rather complex efficiency calculations described in the appendix as strictly necessary under conditions of capital rationing.

With regard to the second type of consideration raised by Grant (allowance for risk, tax advantages of public projects, etc.), we indicated in our theoretical discussion of the previous chapter that risk should ideally be handled by expected-value estimation of costs and benefits, plus risk-aversion adjustment, if any, rather than through the interest rate. The discount rate to use would then be an estimate of the riskless marginal productivity of capital in the private sphere, which we estimated as currently near 5 per cent (including allowance for property taxes). It is vital to emphasize that so low a discount rate is appropriate only if the cost and benefit estimates have been made so conservatively as to be certainty-equivalents as far as decisions are concerned. Unfortunately, we know that a degree of overoptimism is almost inevitably involved in the selection and evaluation of investment projects. Even for utility investments in the private sphere, we have seen that the capital market will supply funds only for projects promising (with the average degree of riskiness experienced in that sector) to yield around 9 or 10 per cent. Unfortunately, public investment decision processes have on the whole a far worse record of overoptimism, so that the lowest discount rate for public projects we would recommend in practice, unless and until their record improves, is around 10 per cent.

C. Measurement of Costs and Benefits

1. The Incremental Principle

In making efficiency calculations, only those costs and benefits that are incremental to the decision are to be taken into account as relevant for the decision. This rule is so obvious as hardly to bear stating, except for the fact that violation of the principle is extremely common in practice. It is standard procedure, for example, in the case of a multiple-purpose project like a dam to "allocate" to each individual purpose like flood control, water supply, and navigation separately some of the costs incurred for all purposes in common. Similarly, in pricing water to users, conventional practice is to base prices on an "allocation" of costs to user classes. We regard standard "allocating" procedures as wholly erroneous.[14] In economic analysis costs are relevant only for decisions, and the relevant part of cost is that part incremental to the decision in question. If the decision involved is whether or not to build the dam, then the total of all the costs should be compared with the total of all the benefits; there is no need to determine a cost for each purpose separately. If the choice is whether or not to add water-supply features to a dam to be built for other purposes, then the entire increment of cost associated with the water-supply features, but no other costs, should enter into the determination. And, as we have seen, in water-pricing decisions it is the marginal cost that is relevant, the social decision involved being at any point whether to produce a little more or a little less of the commodity. Our New York and California case studies below will illustrate methods of estimating incremental costs of particular projects or for particular purposes.

Another instance of violation of the incremental principle is the so-called basin-account approach, most conspicuously used to justify inefficient irrigation aspects of the enormous Missouri River and Upper Colorado projects.[15] The idea here is that the accounts of all planned projects in a river basin should be pooled and that, if the benefit-cost calculations show the pooled result to be favorable, the entire basin plan is justified. The consequence, of course, will be the adoption of a number of bad projects just because their adverse balances of costs and benefits are submerged in the over-all account.[16] The only sensible excuse for this approach is that some projects may have spillover benefits (or costs) upon others; but, if so, these can be specifically considered and credited to the projects in question, as discussed in our treatment of spillovers in the previous chapter.

2. *Monetary and Non-monetary Costs and Benefits*

From a purely financial point of view, only the monetary costs and the monetary receipts associated with a decision will be relevant. In projects undertaken by public authorities, however, it is standard procedure to allow for benefits (and sometimes costs) that do not appear in the financial accounts. In the case of water-supply projects, these might include (1) non-reimbursable features like flood control; (2) value of water over and above price paid by recipients; (3) increase in private land values; (4) improvements in employment opportunities; (5) profits of businesses dealing with water recipients; and so on, including analogous effects on the cost side. This topic has been exhaustively discussed in the previous chapter and will not be repeated here, except for the comment that standard procedures of certain federal agencies permit and even require the grossest exaggeration and multiple counting of benefits.

To the extent that such related project effects are to be admitted in the calculation, an estimate of their monetary value

[14] A full treatment will be found in Otto Eckstein, *Water-Resource Development* (Cambridge, Mass.: Harvard University Press, 1958), pp. 259–72.

[15] See Edward F. Renshaw, *Toward Responsible Government* (Chicago: Idyia Press, 1957), pp. 111–17.

[16] The basin-account principle is criticized as a disguised subsidy to bad projects in Task Force on Water Resources and Power for the Commission on Organization of the Executive Branch of the Government ("Hoover Commission"), *Report on Water Resources and Power* (Washington, D.C., 1955), I, 145–47.

should be included in the cost and benefit streams of whichever of equations (1) through (4) is being used for the project efficiency determination. In the case of a water-cost calculation, these non-financial benefits (to the extent that they are real) should be counted as offsets to the stream of costs as shown in equation (5). Non-financial costs should similarly be included with the financial costs.

One question which arises about money costs and benefits concerns price-level changes. As indicated in the previous chapter, projects can best be evaluated by adjusting all annual monetary figures to an equivalent price-level basis (most conveniently, by making all future estimates in terms of current price levels). A monetary depreciation allowance can be incorporated in the discount rate if inflation is anticipated.

3. *Actual Yield, Safe Yield, or Available Capacity?*

A question which frequently arises in water-cost determinations is what measure of yield to use for the deliveries q_t in equation (5). The three possibilities ordinarily are: the capacity of the works (a maximum measure), the "safe yield" in an unusually dry year (a minimum measure), and the expected actual yield which presumably falls between the two. Our answer to this question is that the measure of output to set off against the anticipated expenses in determining cost of water is the expected actual deliveries, incorporating some prediction of demand-and-supply fluctuations. The effect of a given amount of capacity is fully measured by the above-average actual deliveries made possible in wet years, and the effect of a given amount of safe yield is measured by the minimum of deliveries which can be counted on with high assurance.

Nevertheless, there is some justification for the common use of the dry-year safe yield as a conservative measure of the output of water-supply projects. The underlying idea here is that, because of the law of diminishing returns, the marginal water actually delivered has a higher economic utility in a dry year than in a wet year. As a result, 1 acre-foot of fully certain yield is preferable to an uncertain yield that averages 1 acre-foot but actually yields zero half the time and 2 acre-feet otherwise. To the extent that such considerations are important, equation (5), which treats all deliveries as of equal value, is inappropriate. What really must be done, if it is desired to take account of this factor, is to assign separate values to at least safe-yield deliveries and excess-over-safe-yield deliveries and then to allow for the probabilities of excesses or deficiencies. (A more thoroughgoing technique would be to assign a complete declining scale of values to increments of supply.) A problem of this kind will turn up in our New York case study in a later chapter.

A point to remember in assessing yield is that, because a water-supply system may form an integrated network, it will sometimes be the case that the yield *of* a project (the water physically flowing through it) may exceed or fall short of the true incremental yield *due to* the project. Adoption of a project of a certain physical yield may require compensating water releases elsewhere in the system or, alternatively, may eliminate a bottleneck permitting fuller use of other system components. In each case it is the true increment of yield due to the project which should enter into the calculation.

D. Some Practical Formulas

1. *Cost of Perpetual Capacity*

Sometimes it is of importance to calculate the cost of providing an increment of capacity, with replacement of equipment as it wears out, into the indefinite future. This is the cost of a perpetual capacity and can be calculated by figuring the present value of the associated cost stream.

To take a simple case, suppose that a capital cost c is to be incurred in year 0 and also in year n (n being the life of the equipment), $2n$, $3n$, . . . , to infinity. Operating costs are at the level o throughout. Denoting the present value of the entire cost stream by C_0, and assuming a constant discount rate i, we have

$$C_0 = c + \frac{c}{(1+i)^n} + \frac{c}{(1+i)^{2n}} + \dots$$
$$+ \frac{o}{1+i} + \frac{o}{(1+i)^2} + \frac{o}{(1+i)^3} + \dots, \quad (6)$$
$$C_0 = \frac{o}{i} + c\,\frac{(1+i)^n}{(1+i)^n - 1}$$
$$= \frac{o}{i} + c + \frac{c}{(1+i)^n - 1}.\ ^{17}$$

2. Cost per Acre-Foot of Delivery

At times data on deliveries and capital and operating costs over the length of project life will be given, the question being to determine unit cost for deliveries over the project life. The general solution is to find the present-worth average cost of deliveries using formula (5). In the simplest case deliveries and annual operating costs will be constant beginning with year 1, and capital cost c_0 will be incurred only in the initial period at time 0. Using the same symbols as before, with x the unknown unit cost, we may under these conditions derive a short-cut formula

$$C_0 = c_0 + o\left[\frac{1}{1+i} + \frac{1}{(1+i)^2} + \dots + \frac{1}{(1+i)^n}\right]$$
$$= xq\left[\frac{1}{1+i} + \frac{1}{(1+i)^2} + \dots + \frac{1}{(1+i)^n}\right].$$

This formula gives the present value of the cost stream over the project life in two ways: a direct way in terms of the capital and operating expenses and an indirect way in terms of the deliveries multiplied by the unknown unit cost of deliveries. Solving this equation for x, we have

$$x = \frac{o}{q} + \frac{c_0}{q}\,\frac{i(1+i)^n}{(1+i)^n - 1}. \quad (7)$$

Here the coefficient of c_0/q is the capital recovery factor, which can conveniently be found in many interest tables.

It would also be of interest to have quick formulas which would allow for load-building—that is, which would show the average cost in such a way as to allow for the fact that deliveries will ordinarily not start immediately at full capacity but will gradually build up over time. Such formulas do not seem to reduce to very simple forms. We present, below, a formula based upon the following considerations: (i) the load builds up arithmetically over a load-building period starting with q^*/L in year 1 and reaching full-capacity deliveries q^* in year L; (ii) capital costs are incurred only in year 0 in the amount c_0; (iii) operating costs remain constant at the level o throughout; and (iv) n is the life of the investment. Then[18]

[17] The formula on the right is given in H. E. Babbitt and J. J. Doland, *Water Supply Engineering* (New York: McGraw-Hill Book Co., 1955), p. 9.

[18] The crucial step in the development of the formula is deriving the sum of a series, which we may denote V, of the form

$$V = \frac{1}{1+i} + \frac{2}{(1+i)^2} + \frac{3}{(1+i)^3} + \dots + \frac{L}{(1+i)^L}.$$

This can be found by the following device:

$$U = V(1+i) = 1 + \frac{2}{1+i} + \frac{3}{(1+i)^2} + \dots + \frac{L}{(1+i)^{L-1}}$$

[Footnote continued on following page]

$$x = \frac{c_0 + o\,\frac{(1+i)^n - 1}{i(1+i)^n}}{q^*\left\{\frac{1+i}{Li}\left[\frac{(1+i)^L - 1}{i(1+i)^L}\right] - \frac{1}{i(1+i)^n}\right\}}\,. \tag{8}$$

If, alternatively, operating costs are assumed to increase in proportion with deliveries, attaining a full capacity level o^*, the formula becomes

$$x = \frac{o^*}{q^*} + \frac{c_0}{q^*\left\{\frac{1+i}{Li}\left[\frac{(1+i)^L - 1}{i(1+i)^L}\right] - \frac{1}{i(1+i)^n}\right\}}\,. \tag{9}$$

EXAMPLE 4.—We are considering the cost, per acre-foot of water delivered, of a facility which at full capacity will provide an annual supply of 100,000 acre-feet. The capital expenditure involved is $20 million, all at time 0. The life of the facility is seventy years, and the load-building period twenty years. Operating costs are in proportion to actual deliveries, at the rate of $3.00 per acre-foot delivered. A 10 per cent discount rate is to be employed.

Without consideration of load-building, formula (7) can be used, with $c_0 = \$20{,}000{,}000$, $q = 100{,}000$, and $n = 70$. Then

$$x = \frac{20{,}000{,}000}{100{,}000}(0.10013) + \frac{300{,}000}{100{,}000}\,,$$

$$x = \$23.03\,.$$

If, instead, we allow for load-building, formula (9) is appropriate:

$$x = \frac{300{,}000}{100{,}000} + \frac{20{,}000{,}000}{100{,}000\left[\frac{1.1}{2}(8.514) - 0.013\right]}\,,$$

$$x = \$45.83\,.$$

Note that the cost per acre-foot has about doubled, a not untypical result of taking load-building into account.

E. Sensitivity Analyses

Anyone who has worked through practical efficiency calculations knows that at a great many points uncertainty enters in. Nevertheless, it is common to make a single best estimate of the uncertain element and then to use that figure in the remainder of the analysis. Ideally, what should be done is to set down a kind of probability or confidence distribution for values of the uncertain parameter and carry that distribution rather than just a single figure through the analysis. In this way, one would end up with a probability or confidence distribution for the over-all outcome of the project. Unfortunately, this procedure becomes impracticable with more than a very few uncertain elements.

As a practicable alternative—and it is vital to make at least this much allowance for uncertainty—the calculations should be repeated under a number of different assumptions about the unknown values of the most crucial elements of the problem. This is called "sensitivity testing," and wise procedure would be to check sensitivity of the calculations to construction-cost changes, weather variation, discount rate, etc. It is often useful to note differences in outcomes between optimistic assumptions all along the line, neutral assumptions, and pessimis-

---

[Note 18 continued]

Define

$$X = U - V = 1 + \frac{1}{1+i} + \frac{1}{(1+i)^2} + \ldots + \frac{1}{(1+i)^{L-1}} - \frac{L}{(1+i)^L}$$

$$= \frac{1+i}{i}\left[1 - \frac{1}{(1+i)^L}\right] - \frac{L}{(1+i)^L}\,.$$

But $X = U - V = V(1+i) - V = iV$. Therefore, $V = X/i$, or

$$V = \frac{1+i}{i^2}\left[1 - \frac{1}{(1+i)^L}\right] - \frac{L}{i(1+i)^L}\,.$$

tic assumptions. Even a few such calculations would provide much more information to decision-makers than they ordinarily get, though an element of judgment is irreducibly necessary in the weights to be attached to the different possible outcomes.

F. Illustrative Calculations and Discussion

1. Varying Length of Life

As an illustration of the influence of varying length of project life on efficiency calculations, we might compare two projects defined as follows. Project I has the net receipts pattern (—10, 6, 6),[19] while Project II has the pattern (—10, 5, 5, 5). Variation in the length of life does not place any obstacle in the way of efficiency calculations, which can formally be performed with any of the formulas set out above for any length of life assumed. The logical basis for this comparison is that discounting calculations in effect transfer income or expense in any time period to some common time where the adjusted quantities can be arithmetically compared. This procedure is economically sound if it is true that the periodic incomes or expenses can in fact be transferred—by borrowing or lending at the discount rate. (This justification does not apply to the internal-rate-of-return formula, which compares income in different periods at the solving rate rather than a market rate.)

TABLE 13

EVALUATION OF TWO PROJECTS OF DIFFERING LENGTH OF LIFE—THREE METHODS

Project	Present Value at 10 Per Cent	Annual Net Benefits at 10 Per Cent	Internal Rate of Return
I: (−10, 6, 6).....	0.413	0.166*	0.131
II: (−10, 5, 5, 5)..	2.434	0.979	0.234

* For ease of comparison with Project II, this calculation is on a three-year basis; that is, the project is evaluated as if the associated end-of-year receipts to be set against the initial outlay were (6, 6, 0). On a two-year basis the calculation would show an annual net benefit of 0.238.

The results are summarized in Table 13. We find that at a (constant) discount rate of 10 per cent Project I has a present value, determined by formula (1*b*), of 0.41, and Project II of 2.43, so that both are indicated as desirable. Using the annual-net-benefits formula (3*b*), with $n = 3$,[20] we get 0.166 for Project I and 0.979 for Project II, again indicating both as desirable. Also, reference to formula (3*b*) will show that the annual-net-benefits formula requires a tedious further calculation after the present-value figure (which already provides sufficient information) has been obtained. Finally, using formula (2), we find that ρ_{I} is 13.1 per cent, while ρ_{II} is 23.4 per cent, both projects being indicated as desirable when the interest rate is 10 per cent. Project I becomes undesirable under all three methods of calculation when the interest rate rises above 13.1 per cent (the value of ρ_{I}), and Project II when the interest rate rises above 23.4 per cent (the value of ρ_{II}). In this case the internal-rate-of-return rule does not lead to error.

2. Initial Cost versus Continuing Cost

Another illustrative calculation is to compare two projects, one of which involves heavy continuing cost while the other has heavy initial cost. We might as well assume that the benefits for each of the two are the same, so that the only question is how properly to weigh the costs. Letting Project I have the cost stream (6, 6, 6) at times 0, 1, and 2, respectively, and Project II the stream (12, 2, 2) at corresponding

[19] That is, an expense or net outlay of 10 is incurred in time 0, followed by a net receipt of 6 at (the end of) year 1 and another net receipt of 6 at (the end of) year 2.

[20] Project I has a life of two years (see n. 19), but the formula with $n = 3$ has been used to allow a synchronous comparison with Project II.

times, we may calculate present values of the cost streams using formula (1*b*). The results are summarized in Table 14. Note that, at a very low rate of interest (0 per cent, for example), Project I is more expensive (I has a present cost of 18, while II has a present cost of 16). At a rate of interest of 30 per cent, Project II is more costly, the reason being that a high discount rate places more emphasis on immediate costs and less on future costs.

TABLE 14

EVALUATION OF COSTS OF TWO PROJECTS AT DIFFERENT DISCOUNT RATES—HEAVY INITIAL COSTS VERSUS HEAVY CONTINUING COSTS

COST STREAM	PRESENT VALUES			
	0 Per Cent	10 Per Cent	20 Per Cent	30 Per Cent
I: (6, 6, 6)....	18	16.413	15.167	14.166
II: (12, 2, 2)...	16	15.571	15.056	14.722

3. Ambiguous Solutions with Internal-Rate-of-Return Rule

Table 15 illustrates a number of cases of projects where the internal rate of return fails to give an unambiguous answer for the acceptability of the project. For arithmetical convenience, all but Project III have solutions at high rates of discount (100 per cent, 200 per cent, etc.), but ambiguity can just as well occur between solutions at the more familiar lower discount rates. The table also indicates, for each project, whether present value is positive or negative over the range of discount rates. From this information it may simply and unambiguously be determined whether the project is desirable or undesirable at any given rate of interest. For Project I, for example, present value is positive only between the two solving rates at 100 and 200 per cent. Consequently, the project is desirable only if the rate of interest lies between those values. Project II has three solving rates, present value being negative between the first and second but positive between the second and third. Project V is interesting in having *no* internal rate of return—there is no solving rate of interest (algebraically, the solution is imaginary). Calculating present values, we find that the project is never desirable. (By reversing the signs of all the terms, however, we would get a project which is always desirable but still with no internal rate of return.) These ambiguities illustrate the superiority of the present-value method for evaluating investment projects.

4. Interdependent Projects

Table 16 illustrates six different patterns of project interdependence to show how

TABLE 15

AMBIGUOUS INTERNAL RATES OF RETURN AND UNAMBIGUOUS PRESENT VALUES

PROJECT	SIGNS OF PRESENT VALUES			
	0–100 Per Cent	100–200 Per Cent	200–300 Per Cent	Over 300 Per Cent
I: $(-1, 5, -6)$, $\rho=100\%$, 200%......	−	+	−	−
II: $(-1, 6, -11, 6)$, $\rho=0\%$, 100%, 200%	−	+	−	−
III: $(-1, 2.1, -1.1)$, $\rho=0\%$, 10%.....	+ below 10%; − above 10%	−	−	−
IV: $(-1, 2\frac{1}{2}, -1)$, $\rho=1$ (unambiguous) ..	+	−	−	−
V: $(-1, 3, -2\frac{1}{2})$, $\rho=$ no solution........	−	−	−	−

this factor enters into project evaluation. In each case it is assumed that the basic project under consideration is the same; it is not necessary to specify the net benefit stream for this project. Adoption of the basic project, however, is assumed to affect the net benefit stream for a related project. In the first three cases the related project has the net benefit pattern (—1, 3) *before* adoption of the project under consideration; at the assumed interest rate of 100 per cent (selected only because of arithmetical simplicity), the related project then has a positive present value and so would be adopted. The project under consideration in the first case would increase and in the second would decrease present value for the related project, but leaving the present value still in the positive range. In these cases the change in present value of the related project, which would still be adopted, is credited to or charged against, as the case may be, the project under consideration. In the third case the adoption of the project under consideration reduces the present value of the related project to a negative figure, so that the latter would no longer be adopted. In this case the entire foregone positive present value of the related project is to be charged against the project under consideration. In the remaining three cases the related project has a negative present value and would not have been adopted in the absence of the project under consideration. In the fourth and fifth cases the present value of the related project is changed but remains in the negative range; since the related project would then still not be adopted, no correction of any kind is indicated to the present value of the project under consideration. Finally, in the sixth case the improvement is so great that the related project would be adopted; in this case the entire positive present value of the latter is to be credited to the project under consideration.

The basic principle is simple, of course. In each case, variations in the present value of related projects are to be taken into account insofar as these variations lie within the positive range of present value, that is, insofar as the related projects remain in the adopted range. Variations of present value within the negative range are irrelevant because, once present value falls below zero, the project would not be adopted anyway. In each case, since only projects of positive value are adopted, only gains or losses of positive present value are relevant.

TABLE 16

SIX PATTERNS OF INTERDEPENDENCE

Pattern No.	Related Project (Before)	Present Value at 100 Per Cent	Adopted?	Related Project (After)	Present Value at 100 Per Cent	Adopted?	Addition to Present Value of Project Considered
1.	(−1,3)	0.5	Yes	(−1,4)	1.0	Yes	0.5
2.	(−1,3)	0.5	Yes	(−1, 2½)	0.25	Yes	−0.25
3.	(−1,3)	0.5	Yes	(−1,0)	−1.0	No	−0.5
4.	(−1,1)	−0.5	No	(−1, 1½)	−0.25	No	0
5.	(−1,1)	−0.5	No	(−1,0)	−1.0	No	0
6.	(−1,1)	−0.5	No	(−1,3)	0.5	Yes	0.5

5. *Varying Rates of Interest*

Table 17 illustrates the significance of allowing for varying rates of interest over time, it being assumed that the pattern of future variation is known in the present. A number of projects are compared at assumed constant and varying rates. Formula (4) is used for the varying rates, setting

$$V_0 = -c_0 + \frac{s_1}{1+i_1} + \frac{s_2}{(1+i_1)(1+i_2)},$$

for the two-year comparison. The rates $i_1 =$ 100 per cent and $i_2 =$ 200 per cent are used in these examples.

Table 17 reveals some interesting curiosities, especially about the projects analyzed earlier lacking an unambiguous internal rate of return. Project III, of zero present value at both constant discount rates, has a positive present value under the varying rate pattern assumed. This is not too surprising, perhaps, since III does have a positive present value at any constant discount rate between 100 and 200 per cent (see Table 15). What is really surprising is that Project IV, whose present value is negative at any positive constant rate of discount, can have a positive present value (and therefore be indicated as a desirable project) under the varying pattern used here. Evidently, then, allowing for variation of the discount rate may well affect the outcome of the analysis.

TABLE 17

EVALUATION OF PROJECTS COMPARING CONSTANT AND VARYING INTEREST RATES

PROJECT	PRESENT VALUES UNDER CONSTANT AND VARYING INTEREST RATES		
	Constant Rate (100 Per Cent)	Constant Rate (200 Per Cent)	Varying Rate ($i_1 =$ 100 Per Cent; $i_2 =$200 Per Cent)
I: $(-1, 5, 0)$	$1\frac{1}{2}$	$\frac{2}{3}$	$1\frac{1}{2}$
II: $(-1, 0, 12)$	2	$\frac{1}{3}$	1
III: $(-1, 5, -6)$	0	0	$\frac{1}{2}$
IV: $(-1, 3, -2\frac{1}{2})$	$-\frac{1}{8}$	$-\frac{5}{18}$	$\frac{1}{12}$

APPENDIX

EFFICIENCY CALCULATIONS UNDER CAPITAL RATIONING

1. Significance of Capital Rationing

By "capital rationing" is ordinarily meant a situation in which the decision-making agent, whether an individual, a firm, or an agency of government, is constrained in making investments to select those that fall within (or just exhaust) a certain "fixed capital (or investment) budget" determined by some higher or outside authority. The usual language is unclear as to the precise meaning of the words "capital" or "investment," on the one hand, and of the word "rationing," on the other. Much of the difficulty disappears when we clarify these terms. The ordinary "fixed capital budget" situation is one in which the decision-making agent is limited to working with a certain amount of current funds (funds of time 0) in making investment decisions (decisions sacrificing current for future funds). In principle we could imagine that there might be only a fixed amount of funds available for investment projects in periods other than the current one or that the constraint applied not to any single period but to some weighted total of the funds available in all periods. However, the case where the limitation applies exclusively to current funds is the only one that seems to be of any practical importance, the idea being that funds are fixed in the short run but that future budgets will be adjusted to the demands of the projects available. The fact that fixity of current funds is the only important situation is fortunate because that case is analytically by far the simplest.

Turning now to the word "rationing,"

there are at least two different ideas here. The first we might call "specific rationing"; in this case the decision-making agent has a certain amount of current funds which he must dispose of through investment in projects yielding future returns. In the other case, which we will call "maximum rationing," the decision-maker can invest any amount up to, but not in excess of, the maximum amount indicated. This implies that some other use for the current funds is recognized as having value. For individuals, the alternative to investment of current funds is consumption; for firms, the alternative might be distribution of funds to stockholders; for departments of corporations or agencies of government, the alternative would be return of funds to the general treasury. The maximum rationing situation is obviously more interesting, being the more rational (or less irrational) of the two limitations considered.

Before proceeding further, it is worthwhile to clear up a misconception about borrowing which has confused thought on the subject of capital rationing. The economic way of looking at borrowing is not to think of funds as coming into the decision-maker's control from "out of the blue." Rather, since funds borrowed must be repaid, the act of borrowing amounts simply to shifting the time distribution of the investor's funds, giving him more in the present in exchange for less in the future. In a sense, the investor ultimately can borrow only from himself (through the mediation of the market, of course). That is, he can transfer to the present, at some discount rate, only funds that he has an assurance of possessing in the future, since, in the absence of the availability of such future funds to repay borrowings, no one would lend to him. In this light we can interpret the usual capital-rationing situation as follows. The investor has available to him a productive investment opportunity (or set of opportunities) for converting current funds to future funds at a favorable rate, but the amount of current funds he would like to have for this purpose exceeds that initially available to him. Whereas ordinarily he would then be able to borrow on the security of these future prospects, under capital rationing some form of imperfection of the market constrains him to work only with the funds initially available to him.

As indicated in the body of the chapter, we do not believe that the capital-rationing situation is of much importance in the real world, despite the great deal of attention devoted to it in recent analytical literature. Investment budgets—whether of individuals, firms, or governments—are not fixed but are a function of (among other things) the productivity of the projects available and the cost of securing funds to finance these projects. It is true that, once a decision upon an allocation of current funds to investment (in either the specific or the maximum sense) is irretrievably determined, any remaining decision to select one or another project operates under conditions of either specific or maximum rationing, as the case may be. But to determine a fixed investment budget, independently of efficiency calculations as to the desirability of projects which might employ the funds made available under that budget, is a procedure so obviously unwise as to be relatively rare, though (it must be admitted) not absolutely unheard of.

2. *An Incorrect Rule*

However this may be, it is at least of intellectual interest to examine the solution to investment decision problems under capital rationing. The procedure mentioned in our text as recommended by both Grant and McKean is to use the marginal opportunity rate—the internal rate of return on the marginal project—as the discount rate in the present-value calculations. That is, in practice one would go down the list of projects, adopting one project after another, until the marginal internal rate of return fell so low that the total current fund requirements of projects adopted just exhausted the fixed budget in the case of a specific ration or until the marginal internal rate of return fell below the value of alternative use of the funds in the case of a maximum ration.[21]

This procedure, while regarded as a plausible approach to a rational selection of projects under capital rationing, is not in fact a strictly correct one. It amounts to determining the discount rate by the internal rate of return on the marginal project, but we have seen that the internal rate of return is an unsatisfactory guide for investment decisions. The marginal project may not have an unambiguous internal rate of return, or, if it does, use of that rate may lead to the wrong solution. While it is true that the procedure of selection by marginal internal rate of return will often (perhaps usually) lead to the correct choice of projects, there are strictly correct methods of evaluation available which are no more difficult to apply and so should always be used instead.

It is perhaps worthwhile to present a concrete instance of failure of the procedure we are criticizing. Remember that only the current budget is fixed (only current funds are rationed) and assume that funds may be transferred between future periods by borrowing or lending at some constant market rate, r. For arithmetical simplicity, we will make use of numerically high interest rates; specifically, let r equal 100 per cent per annum. Now suppose that we have two projects competing to be the marginally accepted one; both require inputs at time 0 of \$1.00, but the first yields \$3.00 in period 1, and the second \$9.00 in period 2. These opportunities may be symbolized as (—1, 3, 0) and (—1, 0, 9), respectively. Calculation shows that each has an internal rate of return of 200 per cent, and, of course, one or the other must be the marginal project. Under the rule here criticized there is no basis for choosing between them—either will do, since both present values are zero when discounted at 200 per cent, the internal rate on the marginal project, whichever is adopted. However, by assumption we can transfer funds between periods 1 and 2 at the market rate of 100 per cent (we cannot transfer funds to period 0 because of the fixed budget assumption), to convert the project symbolized by (—1, 0, 9) to (—1, $4\frac{1}{2}$, 0), at which point its superiority to (—1, 3, 0) becomes evident.[22]

The cause of the failure of this procedure is the same trouble as that encountered previously with the use of the internal rate of return. Even aside from possible ambiguity in its determination, the internal rate as usually defined takes no account of the market terms on which funds needed later in the project history can be obtained or of the market earning value of the cash proceeds thrown off by the project. To the

21 Grant (*op. cit.*, pp. 506–7) indicates that he has the more interesting maximum rationing case in mind. In discussing his instance of capital rationing —highway projects financed by road-user taxes— he states that, when the rate of return on such projects falls low enough, taxes should be reduced, since the value of funds left in the hands of the taxpayers is higher than if invested in highway projects. McKean seems to have specific rationing in mind (Roland McKean, *Efficiency in Government through System Analysis* [New York: John Wiley & Sons, 1958], p. 85). He does not entirely or unambiguously indorse the rule here discussed; his numerical illustration seems to depart from the verbal statement (*ibid.*, pp. 82–83, 98–99). It appears that McKean defines the internal rate of return in such a way as to incorporate in the calculation the external earnings of the cash throwoffs of the project; this method, while logically inconsistent with the concept of the *internal* rate of return of a project, will lead to correct analytical results under conditions to be explained below.

22 This analysis is rather similar to McKean's numerical illustration (*ibid.*, pp. 82–83), in which he argues that the prospective earnings from reinvestment of intermediate proceeds must be considered in choosing among projects. This amounts to converting the stream (—1, 3, 0) to (—1, 0, 6), in which case it is shown to be inferior to (—1, 0, 9).

extent that possible outside reinvestment opportunities for cash proceeds, or the cost of funds in the outside market for required cash inputs, are considered, the analyst will be departing from the purely "internal"-rate-of-return concept in the direction of correctly considering the relevant market alternatives.[23]

3. Present-Value-per-Current-Dollar Method

In our text we recommend a rule which leads to correct results in the simple case where only funds of the current period are rationed, the procedure differing importantly for specific and maximum rationing. The principle of the present-value-per-current-dollar method is to calculate for each project the ratio V_1/c_0, where the relevant market rate is used for the discounting between all periods other than the current period (since market transfers of funds through borrowing or lending between all other periods are permitted). It is not quite correct to call V_1 a *present* value; it is the discounted value as of time 1 of the time stream for periods 1 and after, expressed most generally by the formula:

$$V_1 = s_1 + \frac{s_2}{1+i_2} + \frac{s_3}{(1+i_3)(1+i_2)} + \cdots + \frac{s_n}{(1+i_n)(1+i_{n-1})\cdots(1+i_2)}. \quad \text{(A1)}$$

For a constant market rate r,

$$V_1 = s_1 + \frac{s_2}{1+r} + \frac{s_3}{(1+r)^2} + \cdots + \frac{s_n}{(1+r)^{n-1}}. \quad \text{(A2)}$$

The rule is to choose among projects in descending order on the basis of the V_1/c_0 ratio.[24] If the rationing in the current period requires a *specific* amount of current expenditures, rather than merely indicating a maximum, the decision-maker should go down the list until the specified amount is just expended. If the ration is only a maximum, however, it may be desirable to stop short of the point where the full budget is expended. An individual or firm should stop investing when the marginal time productivity on investments (the ratio V_1/c_0 on the marginal investment) falls to equality with the marginal time preference as between current and future funds. Thus a marginal investment with a V_1/c_0 ratio equal to 1.09 should not be adopted if on the margin time preference is equivalent to a 10 per cent discount on future funds. A branch of government, we would argue (following Grant), should stop investing even if some of its rationed current budget is not yet expended when the marginal V_1/c_0 ratio falls to equality with the rate measuring the marginal productivity of alternative investments in the private sphere.

4. Other Correct Methods

While we believe that the method just set forth is as simple as any, while involving the smallest departure from the present-value principle recommended for ordinary (no capital-rationing) investment situations, there are a number of other methods that will also lead consistently to correct results. We will briefly discuss here two of these alternative methods.

Instead of the present-value-per-current-

[23] We interpret McKean's discussion of his numerical illustration cited above in this light.

[24] Possible complications may arise because of discontinuities. For example, the best project according to this formula may use up 90 per cent of the budget, requiring adoption of another project rather low down on the list to just fit the remaining 10 per cent available. It might then be possible that two projects intermediate on the list, each requiring 50 per cent of the available budget, might in combination be superior to the other pair. Where discontinuities arise, it will be necessary to take account of such possibilities by examining the alternative combinations. The existence of discontinuities may make a solution impossible under specific rationing, as there may be no set of projects *exactly* meeting the constraints.

dollar of equations (A1) and (A2), we could use in the calculations the terminal-value-per-current-dollar method. That is, instead of discounting all the future terms back to time 1, we could compound them all to some terminal date, since either lending or borrowing at the market rate between all future periods is permitted under our assumption that only funds of the current period are rationed.[25] In comparing different projects, the compounding must be carried forward to a common terminal date, of course. Denoting the compounded value as V_n, and assuming a constant market interest rate r, the equation involved is:

$$\frac{V_n}{c_0} = \frac{s_1(1+r)^{n-1} + s_2(1+r)^{n-2} + \ldots + s_{n-1}(1+r) + s_n}{c_0}. \quad \text{(A3)}$$

As before, the rule for using this ratio differs as between specific and maximum rationing. Under specific rationing, projects would be adopted in descending order of this ratio until current funds were exactly exhausted. Under maximum rationing, it might be desirable to stop somewhere short of this point if uses of current funds alternative to investment become sufficiently valuable on the margin. It is perhaps worth noting that by trivial modifications of the formula we could use the discounted-compounded value at any time period whatsoever as an equally valid basis for comparison of projects.

The other method we will discuss here differs rather importantly from those previously considered. In fact, it points the way to a solution of the problem of generalized capital rationing (fixed capital budget for any number of periods). We will not attempt to pursue that development here, however, since we regard the situation as most unlikely ever to arise in practice. We will call this procedure the "shadow-price method."[26]

Under the variant of the shadow-price method we will describe, projects are evaluated on the basis of an adjusted present value, which we will denote V_0^*. This is the ordinary present value adjusted for the artificial scarcity of current funds by in effect charging a special price λ for their use. Specifically, we compute equations (A4) and (A5) (at the bottom of the page), where V_1 is defined as before. Under this method, in a specific rationing situation, we will successively try different values of λ until a level is found such that adoption of all the projects with positive present value V_0^* just exhausts the available current funds. Maximum rationing is handled by the same method, except that, if the value of λ falls below A, which represents the return on current funds in uses alternative to the range of investment projects under consideration, V_1 should be divided through by $1 + A$ instead of $1 + \lambda$. The effect is then to adopt a set of projects which do not in the aggregate exhaust the maximum of current funds made available.

$$V_0^* = -c_0 + \frac{s_1}{1+\lambda} + \frac{s_2}{(1+\lambda)(1+r)} + \frac{s_3}{(1+\lambda)(1+r)^2} + \ldots + \frac{s_n}{(1+\lambda)(1+r)^{n-1}}, \quad \text{(A4)}$$

$$V_0^* = -c_0 + \frac{V_1}{1+\lambda}, \quad \text{(A5)}$$

25 McKean's analysis (*op. cit.*, pp. 82–83) may be interpreted as essentially involving this method, although his verbal description of his method is not fully consistent with this interpretation.

26 This was first suggested for capital investment decisions in J. H. Lorie and L. J. Savage, "Three Problems in Capital Rationing," *Journal of Business*, XXVIII (October, 1955), 229–39.

5. Some Complications

For completeness, we should at least mention some possible complications, although they cannot be adequately discussed here. It has already been indicated that uncertainty and risk are ignored. We do not take account of discontinuities, which may be troublesome without involving any essential new principle.

McKean and others lay considerable stress on capital-rationing situations where "resale" is permitted.[27] The idea is that, while the investor is forbidden to borrow to augment current funds, he can sell the physical good embodying the investment project immediately after making the decision to undertake the investment (i.e., still in time 0), thus securing more current funds. We do not regard this as a capital-rationing situation, since to sell a title to future funds (which is what the physical object of investment represents) for current funds is logically indistinguishable from borrowing current funds in exchange for future funds.

The final complication we will consider is project interdependence. Really this involves no new principle, although too much interdependence may compound computational difficulties enormously. The general idea of interdependence is that each project's net benefit stream may depend upon which of the others are adopted. The common-sense way of handling the problem is to consider each interdependent set as one compound project. This is easier to express in an example than verbally. Suppose that there are three interdependent projects: A, B, C. Then the problem is to choose some *one* of the following simple or compound projects: A, B, C, AB, BC, AC, and ABC. If the nature of the interdependence is such that some of the projects are mutually exclusive (in the sense of its being physically impossible to undertake them jointly), then those particular combinations simply are ruled out. If two projects are not mutually exclusive on physical grounds but rather are economically competitive, their combination will fall out of the calculation without any special efforts (e.g., it will be found that it does not pay to build a second railroad alongside the first).

[27] Cf. McKean, *op. cit.*, pp. 81–82.

6. Concluding Comments

To sum up, we do not believe that the simple case of rationing of current funds poses any great intellectual difficulties, despite the confusion which seems to exist on the subject. We would suggest that the analyst might handle the problem by asking himself a series of questions:

1. Is this really a capital-rationing situation? (Most of the time the answer will be "No!")
2. Is it specific or maximum rationing that applies? (The answer should be the second, unless indeed there are no alternative uses of current funds.)
3. Am I sufficiently certain about the net benefit streams? (If not, results must be interpreted with caution.)
4. Are the projects interdependent? (If so, account must be taken of this complication, as indicated above.)
5. Under maximum rationing, what is the marginal alternative value of funds if not invested in the range of projects under consideration? (This is important because it may not be optimal to exhaust the fixed budget.)
6. Finally, which of the various correct analytical methods (present-value-per-current-dollar, terminal-value-per-current-dollar, or shadow-price method) is most convenient to apply here?

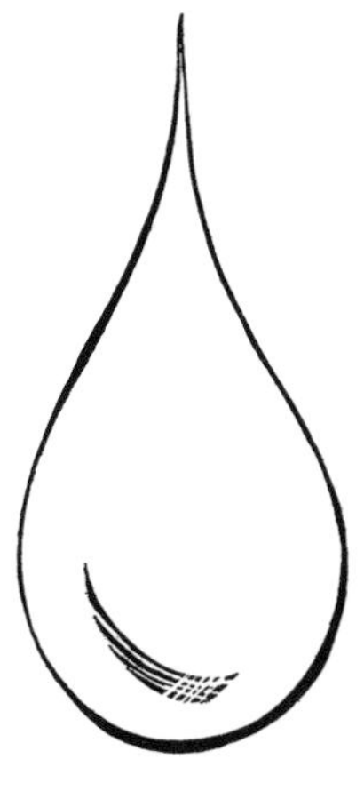

CHAPTER VIII

TECHNOLOGICAL FEATURES AND COSTS OF ALTERNATIVE SUPPLIES OF WATER

In chapter ii we described very generally the hydrologic cycle—where water comes from and where it goes. Subsequent sections dealt with the economics of utilizing our existing water supplies and of investing in additional supplies. In the present chapter we consider more specifically those portions of the hydrologic cycle from which our supplies of water are presently, or may be, obtained. We will examine the techological prospects and the costs of procuring, treating, and distributing water in a variety of ways, including all important present procedures as well as a selection of future possibilities not yet reduced to current practice.

The procedure followed in this chapter is first to examine the methods presently used to distribute, treat, and collect water from faucet back to dam or well. Next, the various sources of raw water, present and possible, are described in order to indicate their merits and limitations as actual or potential water supplies. We should say at once that, because of the wide range of the topics covered, each must be treated all too briefly (whole books have been written on several of the subheadings of this chapter). Nevertheless, as will be seen, there remain large gaps in our present information. Subject to these qualifications, we will attempt to present here the technological context within which economic choices as to alternative sources and treatments of water supplies must be made.

Throughout this chapter, unless otherwise indicated, costs of alternative sources or treatments on a per acre-foot basis will have been calculated using our short-cut equation (7) of chapter vii—involving the implicit assumption of level full-capacity deliveries over the life of the works.

A. Present Public or Municipal Water Supply

1. General Characteristics

Only about 7 per cent of the total water withdrawn in the United States in 1955 was taken by public water-supply systems, but this supply served almost 115,000,000 people.[1] While one-third of the public supply is sold for industrial and commercial use, this amount is a small fraction (12

[1] Kenneth A. MacKichan, *Estimated Use of Water in the United States, 1955* (U.S. Department of the Interior, Geological Survey Circular 398 [Washington, D.C., 1957]).

per cent) of total industrial and commercial withdrawal. (The remainder is self-supplied.) Public supply provides a small amount of water for irrigation.

Public water-supply systems consist of all or many of the following features: (1) sources of raw water—ground water tapped by wells (28 per cent of the total), surface water from streams, lakes, or reservoirs, or a combination of both sources; (2) a transmission system for bringing the raw water from its sources to the area where it is subsequently treated and distributed; (3) treatment facilities for filtering, disinfecting, and softening; (4) a network to distribute the treated water to the consumers, including fire protection and public services; (5) pumps and storage capacity associated with the collection, transmission, and distribution of the water; and (6) valves, hydrants, and meters to control and measure the flow.

From the scattered and inadequate data available, one gains the impression that the total cost of water supplied by municipal systems typically includes the following major elements: (1) production, transmission, and treatment costs; (2) distribution costs (including customer services); and (3) fire protection. The first two of these cost elements each account for from 40 to 45 per cent of the total, with the third element, fire protection, contributing the remainder.[2] One occasionally sees statements to the effect that distribution typically accounts for two-thirds to three-fourths of the cost of municipal water, with collection, transmission, and treatment making up the rest. It is possible that these statements are influenced by the relative capital investment costs alone without allowing for the larger operating costs associated with the non-distribution features. Also, such statements may include costs of fire protection within the distribution category. In any case, over-all or typical relative cost contributions are not too reliable a guide. Investment and operating costs will vary tremendously from city to city, depending upon the size of the city, the particular location and quality of the source water, the terrain, and the density and demand characteristics of the consumers.

2. *Distribution and Treatment*

Distribution-system piping may be laid out in a city in a series of circles or belts, in a gridiron pattern, or in a tree pattern. Where there is marked difference in elevation, the distribution system may be separated into a gravity-flow sector and a sector where pumping is required to maintain adequate pressures. Distribution reservoirs of various types, such as elevated steel tanks or earthen reservoirs at ground level, are usually installed to equalize rates of flow and pressures and to provide storage to carry supplies over to meet periodic peak demands. In addition, the capacity of the distribution system nearly always includes a reserve for possible fire demand.

The facilities required for the treatment of raw water before distribution may vary from none at all where the source water is suitable for direct consumption to an extensive plant in cases where the source water is of poor quality. A complete treatment may consist of the following steps: sedimentation, coagulation, filtration, softening, and disinfection. Where special taste, odor, color, hardness, or corrosion problems occur, additional treatments ranging from aeration to the use of ion-exchange resins may be required to produce a suitable water.

The most recent comprehensive study of water-treatment costs is that of Orlob and Lindorf,[3] who examined the construction and operating costs of some thirty-two

[2] "Determination of Water Rate Schedules" (committee report), *Journal American Water Works Association,* XLVI (March, 1954), 187–219.

[3] Gerald T. Orlob and Marvin R. Lindorf, "Cost of Water Treatment in California," *Journal American Water Works Association,* L (January, 1958), 45–55.

treatment plants in California. In terms of estimated 1956 construction costs for all plants, they found that unit construction costs decreased with increasing capacity between 1 and 300 acre-feet daily capacity. Operation and maintenance costs per unit processed decreased with increasing flow and flow capacity within the same range. They estimated construction costs (1956) for a plant of 30 acre-feet daily capacity at $1,220,000. The operation and maintenance costs for a plant of this size, operated at 70 per cent capacity, were estimated at $10.00 per acre-foot. With an expected plant life of twenty years and interest at 5 per cent, these figures yield a cost per acre-foot treated of about $21.50.

The total cost for complete treatment in a smaller plant, of 15 acre-feet daily capacity, was estimated at about $26.00 an acre-foot. Large plants of 150 and 300 acre-feet daily capacity were estimated to have total treatment cost of about $11.00 and $10.00, respectively. The cost of disinfection alone (by chlorine) was estimated to range between $0.30 and $0.65 per acre-foot treated. From the data in this study, the unit costs for complete treatment were calculated by us at both 5 per cent and 10 per cent interest rates for three sizes of plants operating at 70 per cent and 100 per cent capacity, with expected plant life of twenty and thirty years. These costs are given in Table 18.

3. *Transmission from Sources*

Water supply for public use may be obtained locally from wells or surface sources, so that no transmission facilities are required. The 1955 staff report survey of the American Water Works Association,[4] which

[4] "A Survey of Operating Data for Water Works in 1955," *Journal American Water Works Association,* XLIX (May, 1957), 555–696.

TABLE 18*

WATER-TREATMENT COSTS

Plant Capacity (Acre-Feet per Day)	Unit Costs (Dollars per Acre-Foot)†			
	Operating at 70 Per Cent Capacity		Operating at 100 Per Cent Capacity	
	5 Per Cent Interest	10 Per Cent Interest	5 Per Cent Interest	10 Per Cent Interest
	For Twenty-Year Expected Plant Life			
3.07‡	52.03	64.20	40.68	49.22
30.7	21.46	26.76	16.68	20.40
307	9.56	12.18	7.34	9.18
	For Thirty-Year Expected Plant Life			
3.07	47.06	60.48	37.20	46.61
30.7	19.30	25.14	15.17	19.26
307	8.49	11.38	6.59	8.61

* Source: Calculated from data in Gerald T. Orlob and Marvin R. Lindorf, "Cost of Water Treatment in California," *Journal American Water Works Association,* L (January, 1958), 45–55.

† Based on California construction and operating experience and 1956 costs.

‡ 3.07 acre-feet per day is equivalent to 1,000,000 gallons per day (1 mgd).

covered five hundred separate public systems, showed a wide range of transmission distances in use. These varied from a high of 388 miles for San Francisco (375 miles for New York and 338 miles for Los Angeles) to zero transmission distance for many systems. A large number of systems transported at least a portion of their water between 10 and 60 miles from the sources. Of course, many systems obtain part of their water locally and import the remainder.

The smaller conveyance systems are usually pipelines (steel, cast iron, concrete, or wood), mostly with associated pumping plants, although some rely on gravity feed. The larger systems may be more complex. They may have stretches of open canal, closed conduit, tunnels through mountains, siphons, aqueducts, and large pumping plants. These large systems may also have multipurpose aspects, generating electric power or providing flood protection in addition to transporting water. Systems generating power will probably include fore- and afterdams and storage reservoirs to equalize flow.

The choice of transport system is influenced by terrain features, total capacity, length of the system, and the relative costs of the alternative types of elements and of pumping. Although open lined canals are cheaper per unit of length than equivalent closed conduits, water can only be conveyed down a mild gradient in open canals. A canal must therefore snake around contour lines in descending a slope; the increased length may make cost of an open canal greater than the cost of closed pipes descending directly. Then, too, consideration must be given to the evaporation of water from open canals (and perhaps greater seepage loss) and to possible increased contamination as compared to a closed system.

In designing a large conveyance system over uneven terrain, it is customary to examine the comparative costs of accomplishing the conveyance by different means or by an optimum combination of several. Thus, in determining whether to pump over a mountain or to tunnel through, the incremental costs of increased pumping lift versus increased tunnel length are compared. A solution in terms of balanced marginal costs usually involves a combination of pump lift and tunneling in which the tunnel is located part way up the mountain and thus is shorter than if drilled through the base. Similar incremental cost comparisons are made with respect to closed conduits versus open canals, conduit size versus pumping costs, etc.

Possibly because of the specialized nature of very large water-transmission systems, no generalized cost information has been developed relating to their unit capacity costs. Generalized water conveyance costs have been determined by Louis Koenig for smaller systems, with capacities from 20 to around 100,000 acre-feet per year. The largest of these might supply a city of 500,000 population. With basic assumptions of flat terrain, level deliveries (at full capacity), forty-year average life, interest, taxes, and insurance at 6 per cent, electric power at $0.005 per kilowatt-hour (kw-h.), and 84 per cent pumping efficiency, Koenig develops the total unit costs shown in Table 19 for different capacities.

The lower of the two sets of costs shown in Table 19 is for a situation where no pumping is required because the terrain allows gravity flow. The economies of scale with increasing capacity are apparent from this table. There appear also to be some economies of scale relating to the length of the transmission system. These are most apparent in Koenig's study for systems less than 200 miles in length. Thus, while a system of 200 miles costs only about 10 per cent more per mile for the same capacity than one of 1,000 miles, one of 100 miles may be 20 per cent more; 50 miles, 25–35 per cent more; and one of 10 miles, 50–90 per cent more.

Occasionally, and usually only as a temporary expedient, water is transported by means other than conduit or canal. Tank trucks, railroad cars, and tanker vessels all have been used for this purpose. Because these transportation methods are emergency measures, they have not usually been properly designed or organized for the job, and their costs are high. In one study the Bureau of Reclamation examined the costs of large-scale transportation of water in tanker ships from the Klamath River in northern California to Los Angeles, a distance of about 640 miles.[5] Their system was designed for the purpose on a long-term basis, and the estimated costs include all the necessary loading and discharge pumping equipment, operation, maintenance, depreciation, etc. For the particular situation examined, the costs were calculated to be $115 per acre-foot. This figure seemed so promising that we consulted a company engaged in transport service, which informally quoted an estimate of between $1,000 and $1,200 per acre-foot—for a shorter haul and without consideration of storage and mooring costs. This disparity is startling and perhaps instructive.

Supply by tanker for areas near seacoasts seems to remain a dubious possibility, even as compared with expensive alternatives like sea-water conversion (see below). Tanker service might possibly be used until total demand builds up to the point where construction of a permanent facility is justified.

TABLE 19*

WATER-CONVEYANCE COST

	CAPACITY (ACRE-FEET PER YEAR)				
	22.4	224	1,120	2,240	112,000
Dollars per acre-foot per mile, with pumping..	$13.00	$5.88	$2.90	$2.10	$0.36
Dollars per acre-foot per mile, gravity flow..	10.40	3.50	1.30	0.95	....

* Source: Louis Koenig, "Disposal of Saline Water Conversion Brines: An Orientation Study" (Office of Saline Water, Department of the Interior, Research and Development Progress Report No. 20 [Washington, D.C., April, 1957]).

4. Consumptive Loss in Public Systems

The collection, transmission, distribution, and withdrawal of water from public systems all result in loss of water to varying degrees. Evaporation loss from impounding, storage, and distribution reservoirs will depend upon climatic conditions and the design and capacity of the reservoirs. Methods and costs of reducing these evaporative losses are discussed later in this chapter. Leaks and other unaccounted losses in distribution are estimated at about 12 per cent of the water produced in typical systems.[6] Since evaporation and leakage do not ordinarily result in a return of liquid water to the system,[7] they may be considered as 100 per cent consumptive loss.

Most of the water uses of a municipal system are fully consumptive within that system; evaporation losses in any of a variety of uses represent obvious examples.

[5] U.S. Department of the Interior, Bureau of Reclamation, *United Western Investigation—Interim Report on Reconnaissance of California Section* (Washington, D.C.: Department of Interior Duplicating Section, December, 1952), pp. 151–52.

[6] Harris F. Seidel and E. Robert Baumann, "A Statistical Analysis of Water Works Data for 1955," *Journal American Water Works Association,* XLIX (December, 1957), 1538–39.

[7] In certain cases leakage may re-enter a ground-water supply to become available again for withdrawal.

To some small degree, water after being used (for lawn-sprinkling, for example) may re-enter the ground-water supply to become available for reuse within the system. The large volumes of water discharged through sewage are also fully consumptive so far as the discharging system is concerned. However, while recycling of sewage within water systems is extremely rare (see below), it is very common for downstream systems to take in and reuse (after treatment, of course) the sewage effluent of upstream systems. Within a broader frame of reference, therefore, discharge to sewage is only partially consumptive if there are downstream users.

The use of water from public systems for air conditioning raises special problems. First, the demand for cooling water is seasonal, peaking drastically in the summer months. Whereas the ratio of the usual demand without air conditioning between summer and winter is about 1.5:1, the intrusion of air conditioning without cooling-water recycle raises the ratio to 4.5:1, or even higher. Aside from the usually high marginal costs of supplying the extra water to meet these high peak demands, sewage systems are often overloaded by the peak water discharges. The installation of cooling-water recycle devices can reduce the consumption of cooling water by about 95 per cent. The purchase and operating costs of the recycle equipment are usually less than the marginal costs of producing and supplying the peak water demanded from public systems by non-conserving air conditioners.[8] (But, as noted in chapter v, current price schedules lack peak-load premium charges and so may not induce users to instal recycle equipment even where well justified in terms of system economy.)

B. Self-supplied Commercial, Industrial, and Rural Systems

About 46 per cent of the water withdrawn in the United States in 1955 was self-supplied by industrial users, including use for generation of fuel-electric power. Fuel-electric power withdraws 30 per cent, and all other industry 16 per cent. Between 91 and 98 per cent of this amount is taken from surface sources, with small amounts taken from underground, saline, and reclaimed sewage sources. About 94 per cent of the water for fuel-electric power is used for condenser cooling. A lesser but still large percentage of the other industrial withdrawals is also used for various cooling purposes.[9]

For many cooling purposes no water treatment is required, the water being merely withdrawn from the local surface source and returned at a higher temperature. This use of water for cooling does involve evaporative loss, even where recycle and cooling towers are employed. It is estimated that about 50 per cent of the water presently used by industry for cooling is consumed by evaporation.[10] However, certain industrial process water and boiler-feed water require carefully controlled treatments before use. Especially where multiple in-plant recycling of water is employed, water-treatment plants similar to those used in public supply systems may be required. The variability in industrial unit water withdrawals is illustrated in Table 8 (chap. ii).

About 0.4 per cent of the water withdrawn in 1955 was self-supplied for rural domestic use. This water was largely withdrawn from wells. A substantial fraction of the rural population still lives in homes

[8] W. Victor Weir, "Surcharge for Nonconserved Air Conditioning in St. Louis County," *Journal American Water Works Association,* XLVII (November, 1955), 1091–99.

[9] MacKichan, *op. cit.*, pp. 6–7.

[10] *Proceedings* [*of the*] *Conference on Industrial Uses of Water in California, Los Angeles, December 10–11, 1956* (Committee on Research in Water Resources, University of California), p. 109.

without plumbing, using about 10 gpcd. The remainder, living in homes with running water, have a per capita withdrawal close to the national domestic average of 65 gpcd.[11]

Distribution costs may be very high for a low density of consumers such as occurs in rural and some suburban areas. Typical population densities for public water systems are 330–500 people per mile of distribution main. The prices that must be charged to cover the greater distribution costs in more sparsely settled areas are such as to make individual supply from wells an attractive substitute. As population increases in an area, however, a density may be reached where the ground water becomes contaminated with septic-tank or other individual sewage discharge. For public health reasons, therefore, a water-distribution system may be required, even with costs considerably higher than the cost of water from individual wells.

C. Water for Irrigation

Irrigation is widely employed in arid and semiarid regions where the plant-growth potential (evapotranspiration potential) is high but where the natural precipitation is insufficient to permit realization of this growth potential. Irrigation is also increasingly being used in humid regions where, although the total is sufficient, the seasonal pattern of precipitation does not match the plant-growth requirements for water. In these regions irrigation also serves as insurance against the loss of crops caused by variability of precipitation from year to year.

About 47 per cent of the water withdrawn in the United States in 1955 was for irrigation. This is by no means the full measure of agricultural use of water. Natural precipitation that falls directly on crop land and is subsequently transpired by plants as vapor is in a real sense part of the consumptive use of water by agriculture. A rough idea of the lower limit of this consumption may be obtained by assuming that the 30-inch average United States rainfall falls on the 320,000,000 cultivated farm acres, 72 per cent being lost by evapotranspiration. If beneficial transpiration contributes 80 per cent of this loss, then 17.3 inches are so transpired over this number of acres every year. This is around 400 bgd, or almost four times the amount usually credited to agriculture by irrigation withdrawals alone. Inclusion of transpiration by forests and range land used for pasture would probably at least double this figure.

1. Evapotranspiration Potential

A brief explanation of the important concept of "potential evapotranspiration" is in order.[12] Basically, where the amounts of water or of essential nutrients are not limiting, plant growth through photosynthesis is determined by the amount and distribution of energy received from the sun. This energy is transmitted to the plant by direct radiation and through contact with the warmed air. The plant-growth potential for any region is determined by parameters that describe the time the plant is exposed to the radiation during the growing season, as, for example, temperature-days above 32° F. Latitude is a good indicator for the hours of daylight of the region. Thus, if the temperature-days above 32° F. and latitude are known for any region, the plant-growth potential for the region can be established.

A convenient measure of this growth potential is in terms of inches of water. The statement that the potential evapotranspiration is 30 inches means that, if nutrients

[11] MacKichan, *op. cit.*, pp. 6, 13.

[12] For a more complete exposition of the concept see C. W. Thornthwaite, "An Approach toward a Rational Classification of Climate," *Geographical Review,* XXXVIII (1948), 55–94.

and water are not limiting, the climatic conditions are such that plants would grow to the extent of requiring 30 inches of water during the year. This inches-of-water measure serves as a convenient means of comparing the growth potential with the natural precipitation received or the amount of irrigation required. The values for potential evapotranspiration vary from a low of about 15 inches in the higher elevations of the western United States to highs of 60 inches in certain warm southwestern regions, such as the Imperial Valley of California. The average for the United States is about 30 inches.

2. *Irrigation Techniques and Consumptive Loss*

Water for irrigation may be obtained from wells on the land or from nearby streams or may be transported from a distance through pipelines or canals. In the latter cases, laterals from the main conveyance system serve to distribute the water to specific areas and individual farms. The water may be applied to the land by flooding, through furrows, or by overhead sprinkling. Irrigation may be used to supply essentially all the water required in arid regions, or it may be used to supplement natural precipitation in the more humid regions.

Surface irrigation is used for more acres than are overhead sprinklers, but the use of the latter is increasing, particularly for supplemental irrigation in the more humid eastern states. Sprinkler irrigation has cost advantages where the ground is not level or where the soil is shallow and where irrigation water is applied as a supplement or at less frequent intervals.

Essentially all the water applied by sprinklers is consumed and discharged as vapor through transpiration or evaporation. It is estimated that surface irrigation is consumptive of 70–90 per cent of the applied water. The remainder returns as liquid water to the underground basins or to surface streams.

The consumptive use of the water applied at the field is only a partial measure of the use of water for irrigation. Of the amount withdrawn from streams or storage reservoirs, it is not unusual for less than 60 per cent to be recorded at the farm.[13] The remainder is lost in conveyance through evaporation and seepage in the main canals and laterals, though we believe that the disparity represents in part underregistration by small meters. These losses do not include evaporation from the storage reservoirs constructed to provide the initial supply of water. Water supplied from wells on the land irrigated is not subject to these conveyance losses.

D. Sources of Raw Water

1. *Surface Water*

The most obvious and often cheapest supply of water is from surface sources. As might be expected, about 75 per cent of the water withdrawn for use in the United States in 1955 for all purposes was from streams and lakes.[14] The percentage of supply obtained from surface sources varies by region, being much greater in the humid East than in the more arid West.

Where the water supply is obtained from a stream with varying flow, it is the usual practice when demand becomes large enough to build storage reservoirs for an assured supply of water. The reservoirs may be provided by damming the stream itself or constructed in favorable locations distant from the stream. Particularly in the more arid West it is common to provide major reservoir storage capacity in sufficient amount to allow for cyclic variations in precipitation extending over a period of

13 Alfred R. Golzé, *Reclamation in the United States* (New York: McGraw-Hill Book Co., 1952), pp. 395–99.

14 MacKichan, *op. cit.*

years. This practice is usual when multipurpose dams and reservoirs for power and water supply are constructed. The larger amount of firm power which can be generated and sold under these conditions often warrants incurring greater costs for increased storage capacity than would be justified for water supply alone.

Reservoir capacity is expensive. In addition to the initial costs of construction and operation and to maintenance costs, note should be taken of the addition to evaporative loss due to the reservoir. The initial costs, of course, vary tremendously depending upon the size of the reservoir, topography, soil conditions, and the value of the land and appurtenances that are flooded. In the past, very large reservoirs (over 1,000,000 acre-feet capacity) have averaged about $5.00 an acre-foot of storage capacity, and smaller reservoirs have averaged about $20 an acre-foot of capacity.[15] However, as the more desirable locations have been used, and as land values and construction costs have increased, the trend has been definitely upward. The proposed Oroville Dam, a part of California's Feather River Project, is estimated to cost about $120 per acre-foot of storage capacity. Fore- and afterbays associated with this main reservoir may cost up to $500 per acre-foot of capacity. The capacity cost of San Luis Dam and reservoir in this proposed project is estimated at $50 per acre-foot for storage capacity of 2,100,000 acre-feet.[16] Some municipal supply reservoirs constructed in less favorable locations have cost over $1,000 per acre-foot of capacity.[17]

A recent study of the estimates for reservoirs proposed for construction in the Appalachian Mountain area shows that the costs there range from about $82 per acre-foot of capacity for total capacities of 40,000 acre-feet to $650 per acre-foot for smaller reservoirs of 3,000 acre-feet capacity.[18]

A study by Byron Bird, United States Army Engineer District, Washington, D.C., shows a range of reservoir costs (1957 dollars) from $54 to $567 per acre-foot of capacity in the Potomac River Basin area. There is no apparent relation between total capacity and cost per unit capacity among these reservoirs, which range in size from 550 to 1,450,000 acre-feet total capacity.[19]

Reservoirs do not create water, but in a very real sense they can provide increments of firm supply, the cost of which may be compared with alternative methods for accomplishing the same ends. In the real world the complexities of both the hydrologic factors and the costing techniques make the determination of the costs of water "produced" by reservoirs a complicated and difficult operation. However, the following greatly simplified examples will illustrate the principles involved.

Suppose that the time unit of measurement is the water-year, that we have a surface stream of variable flow as a source of supply during the year, and that our demand for water is uniform over the year. Table 20 represents an example of how storage regularizes usable supply.

We can see under these simplified conditions that the storage capacity required to meet all demands is 500 units and, be-

[15] Interior and Insular Affairs Committee, House of Representatives, *The Physical and Economic Foundations of Natural Resources,* Vol. II: *The Physical Basis of Water Supply and Its Principal Uses* (Washington, D.C.: Government Printing Office, 1952), p. 77.

[16] Bechtel Corporation, *Report on the Engineering, Economic, and Financial Aspects of the Feather River Project (San Francisco, December 31, 1955)* (Sacramento, 1956).

[17] Private communication, Los Angeles Department of Water and Power.

[18] Richard Hazen, "Economics of Stream Flow Regulation," *Journal American Water Works Association,* XLVIII (July, 1956), 767.

[19] Byron Bird, "Planning Water Supply Expansion for Washington Metropolitan Area," *Journal American Water Works Association,* L (July, 1958), 893.

cause the reservoir cycled once, that the water "produced" by the dam over the water-year is also 500 units; that is, 500 units in excess of the number normally obtainable from the naturally flowing stream can be utilized as a result of the reservoir. Suppose for simplicity that there are no operating costs for this dam and reservoir and that the construction cost, all incurred in the present, is $100 per unit of capacity. If the water "produced" is a level flow in perpetuity, its unit cost c is determined by the following formula, based on equation (1c) of chapter vii, where C_0 is the unit capacity cost and i is the rate of discount:

$$c = C_0 i\,.$$

If we accept 6 per cent as an appropriate rate of discount, then $c = \$100 \times 0.06 =$ $6.00 per unit of water produced.

A similar situation obtains if the stream flow is uniform, but the demand varies. These conditions may be as illustrated in Table 21.

In this latter case we can see that the storage capacity of the reservoir required to meet all demands is 250 units. Because the reservoir cycles twice within the measurement period, the water "produced" by this reservoir is 500 units. Looked at differently, an alternative supply with a capacity of 500 units for the year would be needed to meet these same demand conditions. With a similar unit storage-capacity cost as for the previous reservoir ($100), twice the amount of water is "produced" per unit stored; therefore, the cost per unit of water is one-half that for the first example, or $3.00 per unit—neglecting possible minor differences in operating costs.

If a reservoir is constructed to entrap

TABLE 20

HOW STORAGE REGULARIZES USABLE WATER SUPPLY: STREAM FLOW VARIABLE, DEMAND UNIFORM

	Period of Water-Year			
	1st Quarter	2d Quarter	3d Quarter	4th Quarter
Stream flow, units	750	750	250	250
Demand, units	500	500	500	500
Reservoir storage change, units	+250	+250	−250	−250
Condition of 500-unit reservoir, end of period	Half-full	Full	Half-full	Empty

TABLE 21

HOW STORAGE REGULARIZES USABLE WATER SUPPLY: STREAM FLOW UNIFORM, DEMAND VARIABLE

	Period of Water-Year			
	1st Quarter	2d Quarter	3d Quarter	4th Quarter
Stream flow, units	500	500	500	500
Demand, units	250	750	250	750
Reservoir storage change, units	+250	−250	+250	−250
Condition of 250-unit reservoir, end of period	Full	Empty	Full	Empty

and "produce" water over longer-term fluctuations in a situation where the average flow of the stream is sufficient to meet demand without the reservoir except in widely spaced dry years, the unit cost of the water "produced" by the reservoir may be very great. This is so because, on the average, only a fraction of the total capacity of the reservoir "produces" water when averaged over many years. Looking at it another way, the capacity of the reservoir must exist during the many normal years but only "produces" water during the infrequent dry years.

Future stream-flow conditions are customarily predicted from historical records. The practice is to project the past annual flows into the future to serve as a basis for predicting future conditions and thus for determining the proper reservoir capacity. Varying patterns of future demand may also be considered. Under these conditions of fluctuating flow and varying demand possibilities, determining the costs of water "produced" by reservoirs of different sizes requires tedious computations involving the most general cost equation (5) in chapter vii.

Unfortunately, the data are not available that would permit us to calculate and to present here the range of unit costs of water "produced" by existing reservoirs throughout the country. We can derive only a broad range of unit water costs, based on the reservoir capacity costs given earlier in this section and assuming one cycle per water-year for these reservoirs. At 6 per cent interest, the water costs with this recycle assumption range from $0.30 to $60 per acre-foot; at 10 per cent interest they range from $0.50 to $100 per acre-foot. This summary statement excludes the very expensive (per unit of storage capacity) municipal distribution reservoirs; these typically recycle a considerable number of times over the water-year.

2. Underground Supply

The hydrologic relationships between surface and underground waters have been described in chapter ii. The large capacity of underground aquifers and the other advantages of using them as a source of water supply were mentioned there. Underground water is tapped for domestic, industrial, irrigation, or municipal use by wells sunk into the water-bearing strata. The wells and associated equipment vary both in complexity and in cost depending on their capacity and the depth of the well. In determining the relative cost of water from wells in comparison with other sources, both fixed or capital costs and operating costs must be considered. The capital costs include those for drilling, casing, and "developing" the well and the costs of the pumps, motors (or engines) and associated valves, piping, and controls. The operating costs include those for fuel or electricity, maintenance, and operating labor. The capital costs will increase with increasing depth of the well and height of lift and with increasing diameter of the well and capacity of the pump. The operating costs will increase with increasing costs of power or fuel and with decreasing efficiency of the pumping system. Because these factors vary so widely from location to location and because reliable cost data are sparse, it is difficult to generalize on the unit costs of water from wells throughout the United States. At best, we can hope to indicate the general range of these costs based on the limited data available.

The cost for drilling alone varies in different localities but was estimated in 1951 as approximately $4.00 per foot for 16- to 20-inch-diameter holes. For smaller holes the per foot cost should be somewhat less.[20] Under more difficult conditions—medium or hard rock—the drilling costs may be as

[20] J. B. Brown, *Pumping Problems, Arithmetical and Graphical Computations* (Davis, Calif.: University of California, College of Agriculture, September, 1951).

high as $1.75 per inch of diameter per foot of depth.[21]

Casing costs vary with diameter and wall thickness. In addition, there are costs for developing and proving the well and for gravel packing to increase the yield.

A recent (1958) detailed study of representative water wells in Orange County, California, indicates that the well costs, including developing and casing as well as drilling, range from $10 per foot for 12-inch-diameter wells to $16 per foot for 16-inch-diameter wells.[22]

No similar generalization is apparent in the costs for pumping equipment and its installation. In the Orange County study the pumping equipment costs vary from 28 to 63 per cent of the total capital costs for the wells studied. The total capital costs for these wells range from $4,478 to $21,871 for depths of 165–1,315 feet and for annual deliveries of from 61 to 596 acre-feet. At 4 per cent interest, electric power at block rates from 0.57 cent to 1.3 cents, service charge of $6.00 to $6.50 per horsepower per year, and an average life of twenty years, the unit cost of water pumped ranges from $6.02 to $25.95 per acre-foot. At a 10 per cent interest rate, these unit costs are increased by about 22 per cent. The estimated long-term pumping efficiency for these wells is from 60 to 65 per cent.

The unit costs of water can be expected to decrease with increasing hours of well pumping during the year. In the western United States, where wells may be operated 1,000 hours a year for irrigation, or elsewhere for municipal or industrial use where demand is fairly continuous, water from wells will vary in cost from about $4.00 an acre-foot to about $30 an acre-foot, depending on the other factors mentioned above. In eastern and southeastern United States, cost of water from wells for irrigation use may be higher than these values even though the lifts may be quite modest. The higher unit costs are largely due to the short periods of use during the growing season.

Snyder has examined the effect of volume of pumpage as well as the effects of power or fuel costs, size of well and pumping equipment, and technological improvements on the cost of water pumped in the Antelope Valley, California.[23] Sortor has also shown the influence of technological improvement in well and pumping design on the costs of water obtained from wells over the period 1916–56.[24] These references demonstrate that until very recently the cost of pumping water from wells remained fairly uniform over time because, despite increasing lifts, the improving efficiency of pumps and better design of wells kept pace with these increasing lifts and cost of equipment. Since 1956, however, the costs per unit lift have been increasing. In both these studies the economies of scale of the larger units are also shown.

3. *Reclaimed Water*

The use of surface waters directly for domestic purposes without some prior treatment is fast disappearing. Especially in the more heavily populated areas of the country, surface waters are so frequently recycled and contaminated by domestic and industrial wastes that treatments prior to use involving at least disinfection and fre-

[21] Elwyn E. Seelye, *Data Book for Civil Engineers* (New York: John Wiley & Sons, 1957), II, 17–19.

[22] Orange County Water District, *Cost of Producing Ground Water* (Santa Ana, Calif., January 23, 1958).

[23] J. Herbert Snyder, *Ground Water in California: The Experience of Antelope Valley* ("Giannini Foundation Ground Water Studies," No. 2 [Berkeley: University of California, February, 1955]), pp. 98–112.

[24] Charles H. Sortor, "The Trend in Cost for Ground Water," *Proceedings [of the] Conference on the California Ground Water Situation, Berkeley, December 3–4, 1956* (Committee on Research in Water Resources, University of California).

quently settling, filtration, and aeration are required.

The natural self-purification action of a flowing stream is truly remarkable. However, streams may be so contaminated with organic and inorganic wastes which either overload the natural purification actions of the stream or poison the purifying mechanisms that the normal flow becomes unfit for use without treatment. Along many watercourses unified action is being taken to prevent the discharge of raw sewage and noxious industrial and mine wastes into the stream. Most organic contaminants can be removed or their effects minimized by treatments that are not costly. The soluble inorganic materials, however, are difficult to remove from the water source. The best practice in these cases may be to segregate and separately treat wastes that contain such materials and thus prevent their discharge into common surface-water supplies. In some instances it has been found that a recovery plant for removing these wastes will pay for itself from the value of the recovered materials.

In the case of municipal wastes, the technology of modern sewage treatment is such that a high-quality water can result. Often the effluent water may become comparable in quality to the initial source of the municipal supply. There have been relatively few instances of the intentional use of reclaimed water in the United States. There are cases of its application in irrigation, for decorative or wildlife lagoons, and for industrial purposes.[25] In municipalities that are sewered, a large portion of the water used for domestic and industrial purposes is available for reclaiming.

In those instances where such high-quality effluent is now discharged to the sea, its use for beneficial purposes will involve additional costs only of storage and transportation to the places of use. Responsible proposals for the large-scale use of reclaimed water usually include the construction and operation of reclaiming plants separate from the normal sewage-treatment plants. It is pointed out that the usual sewage-treatment system must be able to handle any and all wastes delivered to it regardless of quality and quantity. In contrast, a reclaiming plant, if separate, would not be forced to operate with input of such character as to render the process ineffective. Neither would such a plant be plagued by the necessity of disposing of the solids removed. They could be emptied back into the regular sewage system.[26]

The processes used in a water-reclaiming plant are essentially the same as those in sewage-treatment plants. Very generally these consist of (1) primary treatment, involving the removal of floating and suspended solid matter by screening, skimming, and sedimentation; (2) secondary treatment, a biological aerobic oxidation wherein suspended and dissolved organic materials are removed by the activity of living organisms in the presence of atmos-

[25] There is only one recorded example in the United States of the intentional reuse of reclaimed water in a public water-supply system. This is the case of the city of Chanute, Kansas, during the period October 14, 1956, to March 14, 1957, when the usual source of raw water failed at the end of a long drought. This city recycled the discharge of the sewage-treatment plant through the water-treatment plant and distributed the treated water through the municipal water system. Careful surveillance of water quality and public health was maintained during this period. It was estimated that the water was recycled an average of eight to fifteen times (depending upon the indicator of reuse). Except for a build-up of salts and organic substances, water quality met all health standards during the period of recycle. The water developed an unpleasant musty taste and odor, had a pale yellow color, and foamed when agitated. There was no apparent ill effect on public health (Dwight F. Metzler *et al.*, "Emergency Use of Reclaimed Water for Potable Supply at Chanute, Kansas," *Journal American Water Works Association,* L [August, 1958], 1021–57).

[26] C. E. Arnold, H. E. Hedger, and A. M. Rawn, *Report upon the Reclamation of Water from Sewage and Industrial Wastes in Los Angeles County, California* (Los Angeles: Board of Engineers, County Sanitation Districts of Los Angeles County, 1949).

pheric oxygen; (3) disinfection, usually by chlorine or chlorine compounds; and (4) disposal of the solids and sludges by a variety of processes.[27] Water-reclaiming plants would probably take their feed after primary treatment from a sewage plant and discharge the sludges back into the sewage system. They would then provide secondary treatment, disinfection, and perhaps a final "polishing" by filtration.

There is still some question for both "aesthetic" and health reasons as to whether reclaimed water should ever be introduced directly into a municipal system for human consumption. The treatments used appear conclusively to prevent the transmission of diseases caused by bacteria, fungi, or worms. Whether the treatments also can prevent transmission of viral infections, if indeed such infections are carried by public water supplies, is not really known. An interesting possibility now being explored is the use of reclaimed water for recharging underground supplies in the more arid regions, the passage through underground strata providing an additional margin of safety. Recharge may be accomplished by discharge in dry stream beds, in spreading grounds, or by use of injection wells.

The amount of water that may be potentially available and suitable for reclamation is very large. The quantity of water collected and discharged as sewage is usually at least as great and may even be greater than the amount of water supplied by the municipal water system, since evaporation and other losses of water may be more than compensated for by seepage of ground water into the sewer lines and by the admixture of storm runoff water. It has been estimated, for example, that presently (1956–57) about 950,000 acre-feet of sewage outfall discharges annually into the tidal waters of California, mostly from the San Francisco Bay area south to the Mexican border. About 60 per cent of this amount may be suitable for reclamation at reasonable costs.[28] As localized supplies are more fully developed in the future, the supply available for reclamation will increase further. In the South Coastal Area of California this amount may reach 1,200,000 acre-feet per year.[29]

The determination of the costs of reclaiming water and the price at which such water should be sold is complicated by the interdependence of sewage disposal and the production of reclaimed water. Effluent from a presently operating sewage plant that is "picked up" at the plant by irrigators or industrial users can be regarded as water produced at zero cost to the community. This is so because the community is required to treat and dispose of sewage in any event. The cost of supplying these customers may even be negative if the municipality is saved the costs of constructing and operating a discharge line to ocean, lake, or stream, so that in these situations it may be economic for the municipality to pay potential users to take delivery of this water.

In situations where a municipality may plan the construction of new sewage plants, the decision to include secondary treatment should be influenced by the possible market value of the superior water which results from secondary treatment. Estimated income from the sale of this water is an offset to costs of construction and operation of the plant in determining which alternative (primary alone, or complete treatment) is best.

If, as here assumed, the reclamation plant is to be constructed separately from the regular sewage system, two importantly different situations arise which influence costs. If the input to the reclamation plant

[27] *American Civil Engineering Practice,* ed. Robert W. Abbett (New York: John Wiley & Sons, 1956), II, 19-20 to 19-41.

[28] "Report of the Subcommittee on Water Reclamation," *Assembly Interim Committee Reports, 1957–1959,* XIII, No. 9 (Sacramento: Assembly, State of California, March, 1959), 10.

[29] C. C. Elder, personal communication.

is of such quality (as from domestic and commercial sewage) that the plant can always operate to take its capacity load off the regular sewage system, the incremental costs of the reclamation plant and of the water it produces may be essentially zero when the alternative is to build increased capacity in the regular sewage system to handle the same incremental load. (Of course, if no increase in sewage capacity is required, then a separate reclamation plant would involve substantial cost.) If, however, the quality of the feed varies and if the reclamation plant can operate only when the quality is at high levels, reliance must be placed on the regular system to carry and treat all the flow in periods when quality is unsatisfactory. In this case the full construction and operation costs of the reclamation plant are pertinent in determining the costs of the reclaimed water, though it may be possible to achieve offsetting savings in operating costs at the sewage-disposal plant because of the smaller aggregate throughput that can be anticipated.

This brief discussion indicates that a calculated unit cost of reclamation based on plant investment and operating costs may be misleadingly high. Even for the situation where a new plant is constructed for reclamation, the true incremental cost of the water may be zero or may range up to the full unit cost dictated by the cost of the plant and its operation. To illustrate this upper limit of possible costs, we have estimated the costs of complete reclamation plants as shown in Table 22. Based on these values, the unit costs of reclaimed water are calculated at three interest rates and are shown in Table 23.

The costs shown are for complete (primary and secondary) treatment and sludge handling. If the feed were obtained from an operating primary plant, the capital costs shown would be reduced by about one-third. If sludge were returned to the sewage system, the costs would also be somewhat less. However, the costs in our tables do not include feed pipelines or pumping from the sewage system or sludge-return lines. Our figures also do not reflect the costs of

TABLE 22

ESTIMATED COSTS OF WATER-RECLAMATION PLANTS

(Adjusted to 1957 Dollars)*

ITEM	CAPACITY		
	3.07 Acre-Feet per Day	30.7 Acre-Feet per Day	153.5 Acre-Feet per Day
Primary and secondary treatment plants	$538,010.00†	$2,800,600.00†	$ 8,844,000.00†
Land	25,000.00	50,000.00	100,000.00
Engineering and contingencies at 20 per cent	112,602.00	570,120.00	1,788,800.00
Total capital costs	$675,612.00	$3,420,720.00	$10,732,800.00
Operating costs per acre-foot	$ 13.00‡	$ 11.50‡	$ 9.50‡
Annual delivery in acre-feet	1,121	11,210	56,050

* Using *Engineering News-Record* construction index.

† Alex N. Diachishin, "New Guide to Sewage Plant Costs," *Engineering News-Record*, October 17, 1957, pp. 316–18.

‡ C. E. Arnold, H. E. Hedger, and A. M. Rawn, *Report upon the Reclamation of Water from Sewage and Industrial Wastes in Los Angeles County* (Los Angeles: County Sanitation Districts of Los Angeles County, April 14, 1949), pp. 14–15; Organization for European Economic Co-operation, United Nations Technical Assistance Mission No. 46, *Water Supply and Sewage Disposal* (May, 1953); and P. H. McGauhey, "Economic Worth of Reclaimed Water," *Proceedings [of the] Conference on Water Reclamation, Berkeley, January 26–27, 1956* (Sanitary Engineering Research Laboratory, University of California, March, 1956), pp. 72–75. The values for operation and maintenance given in these three references were averaged and increased to 1957 values by use of the Department of Labor index for earnings of utility workers.

delivering the water to industrial or irrigation users or the costs of spreading or injection to replenish underground sources. It has been estimated[30] that the costs of delivering and spreading for deep percolation may range from $1.50 to $9.00 an acre-foot, depending upon the location of the spreading grounds, cost of land, and percolation rates.

Before leaving the subject of reclaimed water, we should mention the entrapment of water from otherwise uncontrolled storm flows for recharge of underground basins. This practice is increasing in the more arid regions. The recharge may be provided by catchment basins in stream channels, by offstream spreading grounds or pits, or by injection wells. In the Los Angeles area there are plans to use this water by injection to build up fresh-water mounds as barriers to sea-water intrusion.

TABLE 23

ESTIMATED UNIT COSTS FOR RECLAIMED WATER, COMPLETE TREATMENT

(Adjusted to 1957 Dollars)*

CAPACITY (ACRE-FEET PER DAY)	DOLLARS PER ACRE-FOOT† AT:		
	3.5 Per Cent	6 Per Cent	10 Per Cent
3.07 (1 mgd)......	$38.70	$51.10	$73.75
30.7 (10 mgd)......	24.50	30.80	42.30
153.5 (50 mgd)......	17.65	21.60	28.80

* Using *Engineering News-Record* construction index.
† Fifty years' average life assumed.

In the Netherlands, sand dunes along the seacoast have been used as storage for fresh water. In the cases of the cities of Amsterdam and Leiden, water from the Rhine River has been diverted and spread on the dunes for storage and later withdrawn for use through shallow wells.[31] In a sense the dunes are used and operate as aquifers. An interesting feature is that the total fresh-water capacity in the dunes is quite large because each foot of head of fresh water above sea level results in a fresh-water "lens" within the dunes and below sea level of about 40 feet. There is the possibility that this technique may find application in the United States, especially in coastal arid regions near metropolitan areas where high land costs make the construction of inland entrapment reservoirs and spreading grounds very expensive. Artificial dunes or aquifers might be built up by dredging at the mouths of streams that have high seasonal discharge to collect water that would otherwise waste to the ocean.

Under the proper conditions, storage capacity might be obtained by this technique at costs that compare favorably with the cost of present-day surface-reservoir capacity. Of course, the stored water would have to be pumped from wells in the artificial dune-aquifer and transported, probably with pumping, to the water-distribution system.

4. Reduction of Evaporation, Transpiration, and Seepage Losses

As mentioned in chapter ii, evaporation from streams, lakes, and reservoirs can result in a major loss of water. Technological methods for reducing these losses are beginning to receive attention. The potentialities for reduction of evaporation through the use of monomolecular films on water surfaces seem particularly attractive. Figure 15 shows that evaporative losses from bodies of water in the United States range typically from 15 to 100 inches per year. In a few areas in the Southwest, losses as

[30] Arnold, Hedger, and Rawn, *op. cit.; Proceedings [of the] Conference on Water Spreading for Ground Water Recharge, Davis, California, March 19, 1957* (Committee on Research in Water Resources, University of California), p. 76.

[31] W. F. J. M. Krul and F. A. Liefrinck, *Recent Ground-Water Investigations in the Netherlands* (New York: Elsevier Publishing Co., 1946).

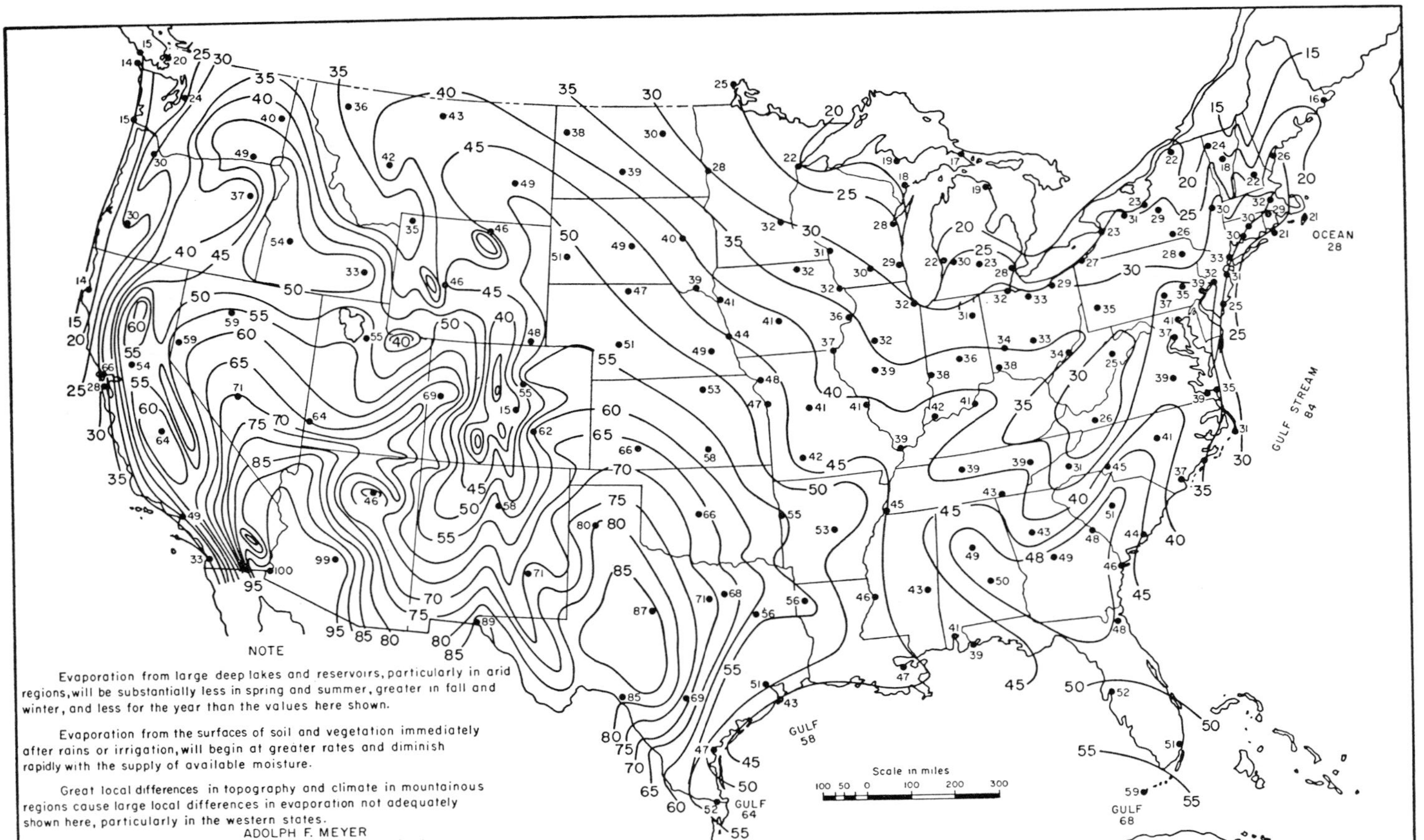

OCEAN 28
GULF STREAM 84
GULF 58
GULF 64
GULF 68
Scale in miles
100 50 0 100 200 300
NOTE
Evaporation from large deep lakes and reservoirs, particularly in arid regions, will be substantially less in spring and summer, greater in fall and winter, and less for the year than the values here shown.
Evaporation from the surfaces of soil and vegetation immediately after rains or irrigation, will begin at greater rates and diminish rapidly with the supply of available moisture.
Great local differences in topography and climate in mountainous regions cause large local differences in evaporation not adequately shown here, particularly in the western states.
ADOLPH F. MEYER
Director of Evaporation Study

Fig. 15.—Mean annual evaporation from shallow lakes and reservoirs. (From Adolph F. Meyer, *Evaporation from Lakes and Reservoirs* [St. Paul: Minnesota Resources Commission, 1942].)

great as 130 inches are encountered. The values shown for evaporation are estimates calculated by an empirical formula which relates evaporation to the vapor pressure at 25-foot altitudes, the maximum water-vapor pressure at the water surface (as determined by the temperature of the surface water), and a constant which depends upon the size and characteristics of the body of water.[32]

The fact that certain organic materials—such as long-chain aliphatic alcohols, acids, and esters—can, when present as monomolecular films on the surface of water, reduce the rate of evaporation was shown as early as 1925.[33] Only within the past several years, however, has there been any serious attempt to evaluate the practical utility and possible costs of such treatments. The work of W. W. Mansfield and others at the Commonwealth Scientific and Industrial Research Organization of Australia is probably the pioneer effort along these lines.[34]

Using primarily hexadecanol (cetyl alcohol), and working both in the laboratory and with reservoirs of small size but known characteristics, these investigators have shown that reduction of evaporation averaging about 50 per cent can be achieved in practice. In their studies the film was applied by dispersion of the material from floats anchored in the reservoir. They concluded:

> Assuming that a treatment of the present type lasts six weeks, we find that the cost of preparing floats, laying them, replacing them as written-off stock once a year, and providing the floats with appropriate replenishments of hexadecanol is about £11 [Australian] per yr. per acre [$24.74/yr/acre]. If the evaporation is 8 ft./yr., we may expect to save about 1.1×10^6 gal. of water/yr./acre, which gives the cost of the treatment as 2.4*d.*/1,000 gal. of water saved [$0.0225/1,000 gal. of water saved, $7.34/acre-foot]. In many parts of Australia, costs several times greater than this would be quite economical. At the present time, we are not recommending the process—not because it is considered uneconomical—but because the probability of vast improvement in technique in the near future is high and because we have not yet acquired sufficient knowledge of the many ramifications of the technique to be able to answer a reasonable proportion of the many questions which will arise from widespread application.[35]

The 8 feet of evaporation per year mentioned is high for this country; such rates occur only in limited areas in the Southwest. The same film costs will be encountered whatever the evaporation rate may be. Consequently, the treatment is most promising for high-evaporation areas. A saving of half the estimated 800,000 acre-foot loss from Lake Mead on the Colorado River, to cite one promising possibility, would provide 30 per cent more water than is supplied to the city of Los Angeles through the city's Owens River Aqueduct. It is about 20 per cent of the total of water now used by the whole South Coastal Area of California—a region containing over 50 per cent of the population living in the state.

The quoted cost of $7.34 per acre-foot for water saved through evaporation control is more costly water than that sometimes provided by the construction of dams and reservoirs. For example, if we capitalize $7.34 at 6 per cent, we find that any water "produced" by dams and reservoirs

[32] Adolph F. Meyer, *Evaporation from Lakes and Reservoirs* (St. Paul: Minnesota Resources Commission, June, 1942).

[33] E. K. Rideal, "The Influence of Thin Surface Films on the Evaporation of Water," *Journal of Physical Chemistry,* XXIX (1925), 1585.

[34] *Proceedings of the First International Conference on Reservoir Evaporation Control, Southwest Research Institute, San Antonio, Texas, April 14, 1956.*

[35] W. W. Mansfield, "The Use of Hexadecanol for Reservoir Evaporation Control," in *Proceedings of the First International Conference on Reservoir Evaporation Control, Southwest Research Institute, San Antonio, Texas, April 14, 1956.*

constructed at less than about $122 per acre-foot of storage capacity (assuming one reservoir cycle per year) will be cheaper than water saved by reduced evaporation with the present state of the art. The comparison will be even more favorable for dams in regions of lower evaporation rates. There are many regions, however, where reservoir storage capacity will be much more costly than this, where reservoir cycle conditions are unfavorable, or where additional water is not available for entrapment. In such cases incremental water produced by reduced evaporation may well prove to be the cheapest source.[36]

More recent work in the United States has shown that improved methods of film formation are possible using fine dispersions of hexadecanol in water pumped over the surface. In a situation where evaporation is 48 inches per year (70 per cent in the six summer months), for a reservoir 1 × 4 miles, a saving of 2,864 acre-feet was estimated at a cost of $4.57 per acre-foot. This was based on 40 per cent effectiveness of the film; cost for material, $11,340 per year; equipment and engineering, $4,100 (five years' life); labor, power, and maintenance, $880 per year (six months' operation); and interest at 6 per cent.[37] At 10 per cent interest the unit cost becomes $4.61 per acre-foot.

These films appear to create no problems involving toxicity to humans or to animal life.[38] It can be anticipated that their use will spread widely as the practical difficulties of application and control are solved. The widespread employment of evaporation-control films could eventually save and make available for use about 20 bgd now lost by evaporation from reservoirs, lakes, and ponds.[39] This compares with a grand total of 240 bgd for all withdrawal uses in 1955 (see Table 5 in chap. ii).

Evaporation may also be reduced in reservoirs by decreasing the surface area per unit volume of water stored and by eliminating parasitic plant growth in and surrounding the storage lake. The depth of reservoirs is often reduced by sedimentation. In fact, the life of dams and reservoirs is usually determined by the time required for useful capacity to be reduced by sediment. Dredging out sediment or improving the natural cross-section contour of a storage lake involves considerable costs. Until recently, the usual situation was that the value of the water saved by these procedures did not warrant incurring the cost involved. However, as the value of water increases, more operations of this kind may be economic in the future. The appropriate costs to consider for comparison are those of obtaining the equivalent amount of water from alternative sources—not the original cost of providing the initial storage capacity. The costs of dredging and plant removal per unit of water salvaged *plus* the costs for transporting the additional reclaimed water to the place of use are the pertinent values to compare with the alternative supply delivered to the same location.

A recent specific study of an operation of this type was conducted at Lake Worth near Fort Worth, Texas.[40] Here it was

[36] In these estimates no credit is given for the favorable influence of reduced evaporation on water quality. Evaporation removes only pure water, leaving the resulting body more concentrated in respect to objectionable dissolved material. In arid regions where the natural water may already contain so much material in solution as to reduce its value, high evaporation rates in storage may have serious adverse effects on quality. The increase in value due to control of evaporation should accrue to the credit of the treatment but is difficult to estimate except case by case.

[37] Russell G. Dressler and A. G. Johanson, "Water Reservoir Control," *Chemical Engineering Progress,* LIV (January, 1958), 66–69.

[38] Bernard B. Berger, "Use of Hexadecanol in Reservoir Evaporation Control," *Journal American Water Works Association,* L (July, 1958), 855–58.

[39] Dressler and Johanson, *op. cit.*

[40] S. W. Freese, "Reservoir Evaporation Control by Other Techniques," *Proceedings of the First International Conference on Reservoir Evaporation Control, Southwest Research Institute, San Antonio, Texas April 14, 1956,* pp. 47–49.

estimated that 112 acres of water surface could be eliminated and plant life eradicated or reduced over an additional 349 acres at a cost of $429,300. With an evaporation and transpiration rate of 4 feet a year, the cost was estimated to be $21,450 (on an annual basis, at 5 per cent interest), to increase the available water by 1,500,000 gallons per day (with a stated value of $27,200, or about $16 per acre-foot). At 10 per cent interest, however, the annual costs would be $42,930 (about $25 per acre-foot), an amount greater than the value of the water saved.

In this situation further sedimentation of the reservoir was not expected because of entrapment by a dam more recently constructed upstream. For reservoirs where continued sediment deposit is expected, the annual cost will be higher because of the shorter life-expectancy of the treatment. For regions with higher evaporation rates the amount of water saved at given costs will be greater.

The possibility of reducing seepage losses from reservoirs has apparently received little attention. Usually, reservoirs are not constructed where the soil is known to be very permeable. However, it is difficult to measure soil permeabilities, especially over large areas. Similarly, direct reliable seepage measurements are difficult, if not impossible, to make in operating reservoirs. Most investigations of seepage have been in connection with such loss in irrigation canals. In this work the effects of various lining materials and surface-sealing techniques have been investigated. The possible treatments considered include thin linings of more impervious soil, the creation of soil cements, and the use of Portland cement and asphaltic concrete linings and of thin organic membrane seals. The effectiveness and life of these various techniques seem to be correlated with their cost. Techniques costing from just under $1.00 per square yard (for thin membranes) to about $3.00 per square yard for concrete linings appear necessary to reduce seepage effectively for any long period. Extending this experience directly to reservoir seepage control would mean the expenditure of a minimum of about $4,800 per acre of wall or bottom to reduce seepage effectively. Such a high-cost treatment can be justified only where the value of the stored water is exceptionally high or where seepage losses are very large. For example, if the loss is 1 foot per acre per year, the water lost must be valued at least at $288 an acre-foot, calculating at 6 per cent on a perpetuity basis, or $480 per acre-foot at 10 per cent interest, to break even with treatments this costly.[41]

The flow conditions in a reservoir are not the same as for a canal, however. One reason for the high costs of canal linings is that they must resist the scouring action of water flowing fairly rapidly. In contrast, the water in reservoirs is usually not moving with a velocity sufficient to exert scouring action on the bottom and sides. Less costly techniques might therefore be evolved for reservoir treatment to reduce seepage.

Some leads along this line might be obtained from studies of techniques for treating soils for the opposite purpose of increasing their permeability. This work has been under way in the study of methods of spreading water in recharge areas to store water in aquifers. Here the intent has been to increase and maintain the permeability of large areas by chemical and mechanical methods to permit effective recharge of water through soils. To decrease permeability, we will wish to reduce the floccing of fine clay particles. We will want to reduce the influence of naturally occurring organic matter in increasing permeabil-

[41] This estimate ignores the possible negative value of the water that seeps out of reservoirs or canals. Sometimes seepage can so saturate nearby soils that crops are destroyed and the land becomes useless. In such cases the treatment may be justified on the combined basis of water-saving and land protection.

ity and encourage, perhaps by purposeful additions, a soil-particle-size distribution that minimizes permeability. As the value of water increases, it will become more important to determine the technical feasibility and costs of treatments to reduce seepage loss.

E. The Cost and Value of Water Quality

In chapter ii we described some physical, chemical, and biological standards established for water when used for public, industrial, and irrigation supply. We saw that, with a few important exceptions (e.g., certain toxic chemicals and enteric organisms), these standards are not maximum fixed values but rather are variables that are among the determinants of the economic value of the water. We shall find in our case studies in chapters x and xi that relatively small differences in some of these quality dimensions are important in determining the comparative values of alternative sources of new supply. Although quality characteristics are often used as arguments for or against one or another source of supply, these arguments are practically never quantified. We hope to show briefly in this section (and in our case studies) that quality considerations can be quantified in economic terms and, indeed, must be before a proper analysis can be made.

Probably the most important of the various quality variables are palatability (taste, odor, color), softness, corrosiveness, temperature, and total dissolved solids and their relative composition. Several general principles apply to the evaluation of any of these characteristics. First, when new increments of supply are being considered, the effects of each on the quality of the entire system is the pertinent phenomenon to evaluate, not the relative quality of the individual alternatives in isolation. Second, in making decisions about how far to go in improving quality either by selection of costlier sources or by treatment of inferior ones, the principle to use is to adopt any improvement for which the community's aggregate value in use (the amount consumers would in the last analysis be willing to pay for the improvement) exceeds the cost. If improvement of quality can be regarded as a continuum of possibilities (as, for example, is the case for softness where any degree desired may be obtained), this reduces to setting the marginal cost of another degree of enhancement of quality equal to the marginal value to consumers of that enhancement.

The principle of making comparisons in terms of entire-system effects is clear and should require no further explanation. It has, however, been overlooked in several studies of water-quality values that have come to the authors' attention. The second principle (marginal cost equal to marginal value in use) is an extension of an important economic criterion, which we presented in earlier chapters, to the factor of quality. It applies, of course, not only when new supplies are being considered but also when decisions are to be made regarding the construction of new water-treatment facilities with no change in supply source. When applied to the selection of a new softening-plant design, this principle says that a design should be selected so that the net marginal costs of a higher degree of softening will equal the net marginal value of the increased softness of water to all users. Note that we speak of *net* value to all users. Softer water may have a negative value for some users, and these negative values must be included in the summation.

In the following sections we shall attempt to present briefly what is known about some of these water-quality dimensions and in particular about the costs and values to different users of waters varying in these characteristics.

1. Palatability

Palatability is probably the most difficult quality characteristic to evaluate. Palatability is determined by a number of factors—taste, odor, color, turbidity, temperature, and the presence of dissolved gases and solids. The purest water is not the most palatable; in fact, distilled water is unattractive to the taste. Taste panels have been used to compare the palatability of different waters and the effects of different treatments.[42] While these panels can indicate preference for one water or treatment over others and signify the threshold taste or odor level for certain contaminants, they have not been used to qualify the economic value to consumers of one water over another in respect to palatability. While individuals on panels could perhaps be asked how much they would be willing to pay for superior waters, the responses might not be reliable. One objective indication of the economic value of palatability is the relative expenditures of consumers for bottled water in various cities where the public supplies differ in palatability.

Palatability of water is adversely affected by algae, by decaying vegetation, and by trade and sewage wastes.[43] Fortunately, the water-treatment art is such that many if not all of these problems can be solved.[44] An important source of difficulty here is upstream pollution by industrial or sewage wastes. Many states (and also the federal government in the case of navigable waters) have regulations that can be applied to require the treatment or elimination of noxious wastes by those discharging them.

[42] E. A. Sigworth, "Control of Odor and Taste in Water Supplies," *Journal American Water Works Association,* XLIX (December, 1957), 1515.

[43] *Ibid.,* p. 1518.

[44] F. M. Middleton, A. A. Rosen, and R. H. Burttschell, "Taste and Odor Research Tools for Water Utilities," *Journal American Water Works Association,* L (January, 1958), 21–28.

If the palatability problem must be handled within the water system itself, one or another of the following measures may be indicated: (1) the use of activated carbon; (2) applications of additional chlorine; (3) the use of chlorine dioxide; or (4) aeration.[45] The costs of these treatments will depend upon the amounts and types of the noxious materials present and the threshold residual amounts tolerable and will therefore vary with each local situation.

Taste, odor, color, and turbidity of water can also be important factors in certain commercial and industrial operations, as indicated in Table 4 (chap. ii). Although the undesirable characteristics of the water can be corrected by in-plant treatments, the relative costs of such treatments can be an important determinant in selecting plant locations for certain operations.

2. Softness or Hardness of Water

The hardness of water is frequently quantified by an empirical test that involves determining the amount of a standard soap solution required to allow foaming in a fixed volume of water. The more soap needed before foaming begins, the harder is the water. Hardness is produced by soluble salts of calcium and magnesium, usually carbonates, bicarbonates, chlorides, or sulfates. These salts react with soaps to produce insoluble curds until the reacting ions are reduced below the threshold precipitating concentrations. Soap must then actually soften the water before serving a useful function of cleansing, and the amount of soap used in softening is unavailable for cleansing purposes. The hardness value is often reported in terms of parts per million of calcium carbonate equivalent. The cleansing effectiveness of synthetic detergents, the so-called syndets, is also im-

[45] Sigworth, *op. cit.,* p. 1510.

paired by hardness but not quite to the same degree as in the case of soaps.[46]

An important measure of the value of water softness to users is therefore established by the cost of additional cleansing agents required as hardness increases. Figure 16 shows the variation in per capita costs for cleansing agents with changes in hardness observed in studies conducted in 1930 and 1955. The values shown are for both soap and syndets. Insofar as can be determined from the reference, the costs are given in terms of the dollar values of the years indicated.

There are, of course, alternatives to the use of cleansing agents for softening. The water may be softened in a central plant in the public system, and/or individual household softeners may be installed. The central plant may use one of several methods for softening, usually either the lime-soda process or a cation-exchange process.[47] Certain plant-design factors establish the usual minimum hardness of the output of central plants, which is about 85–100 ppm $CaCO_3$. The costs of softening in a central plant depend upon its capacity, the type and amount of hardness to be reduced, and whether filtration and coagulation would be required in the absence of softening. Within these limitations, softening costs in the United States appear to range from 3 to 7 cents per 1,000 gallons ($10–$23 per acre-foot). The higher cost figure is for a

[46] William H. Aultman, "Syndets and Water Softening," *Journal American Water Works Association,* L (October, 1958), 1355–57.

[47] Harold E. Babbitt and James J. Doland, *Water Supply Engineering* (New York: McGraw-Hill Book Co., 1955), pp. 488–507.

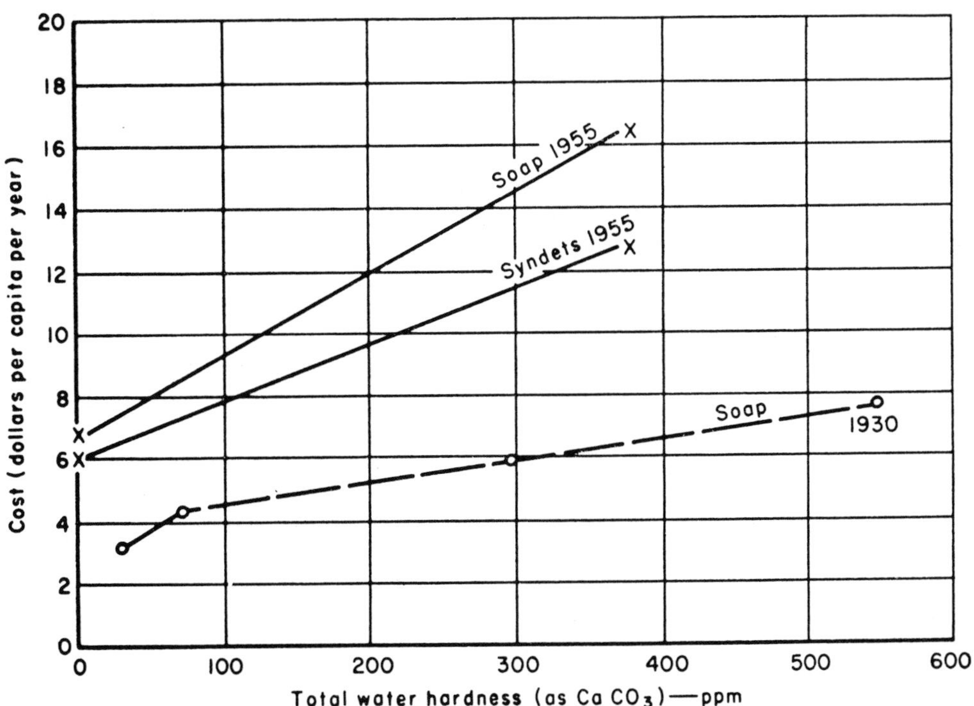

FIG. 16.—Cost of cleansing agents versus water hardness. (From T. E. Larson, "Syndets and Water Softening: Discussion," *Journal American Water Works Association,* L [October, 1958], 1364.)

30,000,000 gallons per day plant softening water from 380 ppm down to 100 ppm hardness. With the average use of domestic water, this amount of softening at 7 cents per 1,000 gallons in a municipal plant would mean a per capita saving of about $4.10 per year in terms of syndets, and $6.94 in terms of soap (1958 dollars).[48] There are additional benefits from softening, such as prevention of scale on hot-water heaters, avoidance of certain scale-caused plumbing repairs, reduction in wear on utensils and fabrics, and reduction in skin irritation.

Home-owned or rental-type softeners are usually installed on the hot-water lines only. These devices, mostly containing natural or synthetic ion-exchange materials, can reduce hardness down to essentially zero. In the referenced paper by Aultman, the costs of operating these units were reduced by previous central softening of water to 85 ppm. The marginal costs of central station softening to 85 ppm appear to be less than the marginal value of the softening to users, including those with home softeners.

Softening is not an unmixed blessing for all users, however, especially when taken to very low values. The usual softening processes do not reduce the total solids content; in fact, they increase it somewhat.[49] In addition, they substitute sodium ion for calcium ion. This substitution makes the water less desirable for drinking, especially for children and for adults with certain pathological conditions. The water also becomes less suitable for lawn-watering and for agricultural irrigation.

In addition, softer water has a tendency to be more corrosive (at least when reduced below about 85 ppm hardness). The scale formed by a moderate amount of hardness tends to reduce corrosion in pipes, meters, water heaters, etc. In fact, increased plumbing failures are sometimes experienced when central station softening is first introduced into a system or when a new source of water is introduced having different scaling characteristics.[50]

3. *Corrosiveness*

Even very pure water can be corrosive to many metallic materials under certain conditions. For example, small amounts of dissolved oxygen from the air can alter the reactions of distilled water with metals. Increased temperature usually increases the rates of reaction, and hot-water or steam systems are more subject to corrosion failures.

The chemistry of corrosion or the inhibition of corrosion by water containing various mixtures of impurities is quite complex. Although much is known about the mechanisms of these reactions, final determination of the corrosion effects of a new increment of supply or a change in treatment must usually be determined for each specific case by means of a series of empirical tests.[51] As a result of these tests and a knowledge of the techniques and costs of corrosion inhibition, estimates can be made of the cost of corrosion and the cost of possible inhibition treatments.

Much can be and is accomplished at central treatment plants to alter the corrosiveness of raw waters—in addition to the control of hardness and scaling effects already noted. Waters that are acidic ($pH < 7$) tend to be more corrosive than waters that are basic. The acidity of raw waters is often reduced during conventional treatment. Special treatments that can mitigate corrosiveness of waters are (1) deaeration; (2) addition of substances like sodium silicate that have desirable buffering and film-

[48] Aultman, *op. cit.,* p. 1361.

[49] A costly acid-and-base exchange process would be needed to reduce the total solids during softening. This is used for preparing some industrial process waters.

[50] Lee Streicher, "Effects of Water Quality on Various Metals," *Journal American Water Works Association,* XLVIII (March, 1956), 220.

[51] *Ibid.*, pp. 219–38.

forming characteristics; and (3) use of a fungicide (or bactericide) like copper sulfate to reduce the corrosive actions of certain micro-organisms.

In industrial and commercial uses of water, corrosiveness is a most important consideration for boilers, condensers, recirculating cooling systems, and for hot-water and steam systems for heating and processing. Corrosive water or its resulting steam can so drastically reduce the life of expensive equipment that careful treatment of water is almost universal for large users. The costs of treatment will vary widely depending upon the specific characteristics of the water involved. For these industrial uses, inhibiting treatments may be employed that are out of the question for a central station of a public system whose water output must also be potable. For example, chromate inhibitors may be used for industrial water treatment at a concentration that would be highly toxic for human consumption.

Recirculating cooling devices are often employed for industrial water where a cheap source of self-supplied water is not available. The corrosiveness, total solids content, and scale-forming tendencies of the water build up during recycling. In designing these devices, a balance is struck between the incremental treatment and other costs of an additional cycle and the expense of additional input water. Unfortunately, these costs are specific for each water source and for each industrial application. No generalized cost data are available in the literature. An illustration of such cost determinations for a particular situation is a recent study by Stanford Research Institute and the National Aluminate Corporation of two waters under consideration in California.[52]

[52] California Department of Water Resources, *Investigation of Alternative Aqueduct Systems To Serve Southern California* (Bull. 78), Appendix B: "Effects of Differences in Water Quality, Upper Santa Ana Valley and Coastal San Diego County" [January, 1959], pp. 153–58.

4. Temperature Effects

Increased temperature of raw water can have both beneficial and detrimental effects on central station water-treatment plants.[53] All in all, study of the literature indicates that the benefits from increased temperature would about balance the disadvantages for water-treatment plants.

Increased temperature does decrease the palatability of water for most consumers, and, it is claimed, consumers will waste more water as temperature increases by allowing taps to flow. This effect can be expected to be of any significance only where meters are not used (New York City, for example) and where, therefore, the marginal cost of the running water is zero to the consumer. For commercial and industrial establishments, the costs of installation and operation of cooled drinking fountains indicate the value of cooler water for this use.

For the case of once-through air conditioning, water temperature increases can be important. Once-through cooling is usually limited, either by the price of water or by local regulations or special charges, to less than 5-ton-capacity coolers. For New York City we calculated that an increase in average summer water temperature from 62° F. to 70° F. would increase the cost of once-through cooling of small units by about $2.13 per ton per year. This may not be a trivial magnitude over a whole city system.

Larger commercial or industrial users of public supply for any cooling purpose usually employ recycle cooling devices, in which case the temperature of the small amount of make-up water has an insignificant effect on cost. Other dimensions of water quality, equipment design, and atmospheric conditions overwhelm this small effect.

Higher temperature may also have cer-

[53] Charles E. Renn, "Warm-Water Effects on Municipal Supplies," *Journal American Water Works Association,* XLIX (April, 1957), 405–12.

tain advantages. About 30 per cent of the water used for domestic purposes is heated for bathing, dish- and clothes-washing, etc. An increase in average water temperature in the mains will then tend to decrease the cost for the operation of hot-water heaters. Industrial consumers must also heat a substantial proportion of the water they use. Each degree of temperature rise of the incoming water will reduce the fuel required for heating 1 gallon of water to the desired higher temperature by an amount greater than a fuel value of 8.33 BTU's, depending upon the efficiency of the heater. This saving to the consumers can be significant in large public systems, especially where fuel for heating is not cheap.

5. Dissolved or Suspended Materials

Dissolved or suspended materials that affect water quality constitute a wide variety of materials living and inert, including bacteria and esoteric chemicals. Standards for micro-organisms in water have been established[54] for a number of years both by the Public Health Service and by the individual states, not only for potable water but also for water used for other purposes where quality might have an effect on health (swimming pools, irrigation of leafy vegetables, etc.).

The Public Health standard specifies the maximum content for certain known harmful organisms and toxic chemicals. The levels of other less harmful chemicals are given as suggested maximums. Other studies have developed at least tentative threshold tolerable levels for a large variety of possible inorganic and organic contaminants.[55] Public supplies are almost always well within these limitations. Indeed, it is quite a remarkable accomplishment on the part of the water industry to have been able to furnish such large quantities of a product meeting rigorous standards, often in the face of considerable technical and economic obstacles. There are several quality problems which may not yet be completely in hand, however, and which may present growing difficulties as population and industrial densities increase in the future and as water is used and reused more intensively.

The first of these is the question of contamination by viruses—about which much less is known than about bacterial contamination. Viruses are difficult to isolate and identify. Relatively few laboratories (in the water business) are equipped or qualified to determine their presence, and many viruses and their relations to diseases are perhaps as yet unknown. A second quality problem is associated with the identification and control of the more esoteric chemicals which may become increasingly common contaminants because of growth in the manufacture and use of insecticides, herbicides, hormones, drugs, and generally more complex and unusual chemical products.

Dissolved materials in water used for irrigation present a somewhat different set of problems.[56] Some dissolved materials are plant nutrients and within limits are beneficial to growth (e.g., nitrogen compounds, calcium, magnesium, phosphorous, iron, potassium, and a long list of trace elements). In modern irrigation practice some of these nutrients, especially nitrogen compounds, are often purposefully added to the irrigation water. Dissolved materials in irrigation water may operate directly on the plants or indirectly through their effects on soils. As an example, the total content of dissolved materials, whether they are all nutrients or not, will affect the so-

[54] California State Water Pollution Control Board, *Water Quality Criteria* (Publication No. 3 [Sacramento, 1952]).

[55] Herbert E. Stokinger and Richard L. Woodward, "Toxicological Methods for Establishing Drinking Water Standards," *Journal American Water Works Association,* L (April, 1958), 515–29.

[56] For an excellent discussion see Milton Fireman and H. E. Hayward, "Irrigation Water and Saline and Alkali Soils," in *Water: The Yearbook of Agriculture, 1955* (Washington, D.C.: Department of Agriculture).

called water tension of the soil. This is a measure of how easily the plants can obtain water from the soil for growth and transpiration. To maintain the same growth rate, soil-moisture content must increase with rising salt concentration. A greater amount of irrigation water is therefore usually required for water of high salt concentration because of the increased evaporation and seepage losses. Also, where the dissolved materials are directly harmful to the plants or adversely affect the soil characteristics, additional water must be added to leach out the build-up of the undesirable consituents in the soil. In these circumstances the cost or value of water quality for irrigation can be stated in terms of the cost of the additional quantity of lower-quality water required.

In some cases the quantity and type of dissolved contaminants may be such that no amount of additional water for leaching can bring the growth conditions to the level obtained with purer water. Several possibilities are open to the irrigator in this circumstance. He may accept a lower crop yield or may switch to crops of a more salt-tolerant type, in which case the value of water quality is measured by the reduction in his crop return. He may treat the water or soil to correct the effect of the poorer water, in which case the quality value is measured by the cost of treatment.

One frequently encountered contaminant which has a deleterious effect both on the soil characteristics and on plants directly is sodium ion. Irrigation-water quality classifications (e.g., Table 3 [chap. ii]) usually list the effects of sodium ion in one or another empirical relation to the concentration of other cations, especially calcium and magnesium. An important reason for this type of categorization is that sodium ion can exchange with other cations (particularly calcium) normally contained in soil clays. Sodium clays do not floc or agglomerate within the desirable range of soil acidity, so that such soils tend to become dense, hard, and sometimes almost impenetrable by water. Fortunately, this condition can often be corrected at relatively low cost because the addition of calcium ion (as from gypsum) and leaching can force the ion exchange in the other direction so that the undesirable sodium drains away. Synthetically softened water is usually undesirable for irrigation use because of its higher sodium-ion concentration (or sodium-to-calcium ratio).

The amounts of dissolved salts and minerals in irrigation water are reported in different and sometimes confusing ways. They may be given as parts per million or tons per acre-foot of total dissolved solids or of specific ions or compounds; the figures are usually obtained by evaporating the water to dryness and weighing the residue. They are sometimes reported as ton-equivalents per acre-foot, values for which are obtained by electrical conductivity measurements. To be chemically and physiologically most meaningful, the values should be determined and reported as equivalents (chemical combining weights) per unit volume, or as mass per unit volume for the specific ions or compounds as they exist in the water.

Data are not available to permit generalized conclusions as to the cost and value of varying irrigation-water quality. It is possible, nevertheless, to make rather good estimates of the effects of irrigation-water quality in each specific, important situation where the question is raised. Very few such attempts have come to the authors' attention. The southern California water study previously mentioned[57] does accomplish this valuation in a technically skilful manner for two alternative irrigation waters (Feather River and Colorado River supplies) by establishing the costs of the extra leaching, drainage, and fertilizer requirement due to the use of the higher salt-content Colorado supply.

[57] California Department of Water Resources, *op. cit.*, Appendix B, pp. 81–121.

6. Fluoridation

Certainly, no treatise on water supply would be complete without mention of fluoridation of domestic water. The question of whether to fluoridate the public supply for the purpose of reducing dental caries has been a subject of much heated controversy in many cities during the past decade. It appears to be established that fluoridation has the effect of reducing the incidence of dental caries in children in many areas and that the presence of fluorides in the small amounts used does not ordinarily constitute a health hazard. However, there is some doubt whether children will consume enough water, at the low concentration utilized, to have the desired effect. On the other hand, it is possible that there will be adverse effects of fluoride intake for the elderly or for those with certain pathological conditions (e.g., individuals requiring much more water than normal). Opponents of fluoridation have argued that fluorides are poisonous in themselves and therefore constitute a hazard when added to water. However, many other chemicals (including chlorine gas) that are added to water during treatment or which occur naturally are also poisonous in sufficient concentrations.

On the other hand, it is not sheer nonsense if some individuals choose to take an extremely conservative position about possible still-unknown adverse effects of fluorides. Unfortunately, since public water is usually supplied by a monopoly, either the one group or the other (those favoring fluoridation or those opposed) must accept the less-desired water or else turn to bottled water at increased cost. An alternative worth considering is the production of fluoridated milk for voluntary purchase[58] to avoid the compulsion intrinsic in adding fluoride to the public water supply. Fluoride treatment by dentists or the use of fluoride pills under the direction of a physician are probably more effective than ingestion via water or milk.

Also worth mentioning is the usually unexpressed fear among the opponents that, if governments can add fluorine to the water for social purposes unrelated to the supply of water itself, they might in the future add other chemicals—perhaps tranquilizers, soporifics, aphrodisiacs, anaphrodisiacs, etc.—for various social purposes. While most of us would regard such fears as exaggerated, they are perhaps not utterly ridiculous.

Turning to the economics of the question, the fluoridation of public supplies is not so cheap as is suggested by quotations of the extremely low cost per gallon of water supply. Only a tiny fraction of the volume fluoridated will be used by those (children under twelve) who can derive any benefit therefrom. As a rough indication of this fraction, average United States water production is 137 *gallons* per capita per day, but only about 25 per cent of the population in under twelve, and their ingestion is certainly under 2 quarts per day (this last figure includes a generous allowance for water in cooking, soft drinks, etc.). The remainder of the water is consumed by adults, used for washing, flushing, irrigating lawns, or for industrial or commercial purposes.

Sodium silicofluoride is the chemical most commonly used to add fluoride to public supplies. It costs about $7.50 per 100 pounds F.O.B.[59] If pure, it would contain about 60.6 per cent fluoride. If 1 ppm of fluoride is added to the public supply, the cost is close to $1.00 per million gallons treated, or one ten-thousandth of a cent per gallon. This figure does not incorporate any charge for freight or for the capital equipment and labor costs required, but it is believed that these will be minor. On a

58 Personal communication, Jack N. McKee, Department of Sanitary Engineering, California Institute of Technology.

59 "Status of Fluoridation" (Task Group Report), *Journal American Water Works Association* XLIX (January, 1957), 45.

2-quart-per-day basis, this comes to 0.018 cent per individual per year. Allowing for the fact that the benefit is only to 25 per cent of the population increases this by a factor of 4, and allowing for the non-ingestion uses of water requires another factor of 274. The net result is a figure of 19.8 *cents* per year per individual benefited. This is probably substantially cheaper than any of the leading alternatives (application of fluoride by dentists, ingestion of pills, or bottled milk or fluoridated water) for those benefiting from fluoridation. Note, however, that no charge is assessed for the violation of the preferences of those rightly or wrongly opposing fluoridation. In fact, some individuals may switch to non-fluoridated bottled water at a cost of around $20 per year. Costs to the community would just about balance if there were one such individual for every hundred benefited, except for the likelihood that in the absence of fluoridation of the public supply there might be comparable purchases of bottled *fluoridated* water, so that this factor can perhaps be assumed to cancel out.

There are also the non-health aspects to consider. It seems reasonable to believe that the increase in solids content associated with fluoridation will accelerate corrosion. With only about 1 ppm, the effect will be small and hard to quantify, but a 1 per cent increase in corrosion losses might be a substantial cost to the community. So far as our knowledge goes, there has been no attempt to study such matters in advance of widespread adoption of fluoridation techniques.

All in all, it appears that fluoridation of the public supply is really quite cheap as compared with alternative modes of protection against caries but that doubts as to the wisdom of the policy cannot be definitely set to rest in view of possible adverse effects on health elsewhere and failure to quantify such effects as the cost of increased corrosion.

F. The Manufacture of Fresh Water from the Sea

Proposals are often made to short-circuit the natural hydrologic cycle by manufacturing fresh water directly from the sea. This procedure is completely feasible technically. For hundreds of years ships at sea have obtained fresh water by distillation of salt water. The major question to be examined is whether fresh water can be manufactured by any method that will compete economically with water from natural sources. Some forty-nine elements are known to exist in sea water. However, many of them are present in such small quantities that they may be tolerated in the majority of uses for fresh water. The largest concentrations are of chlorine, sodium, magnesium, sulfur, calcium, and potassium. These occur in ionic form and represent a total dissolved solids content of about 35,000 ppm of water. Of course, this concentration varies somewhat throughout the ocean areas, depending on rate of evaporation, local dilution by large fresh-water outlets, etc. There are certain inland sources of water having lower saline content. These waters are called "brackish" and may range from 1,500 to 10,000 ppm of dissolved salts. As indicated in Tables 2 and 3 of chapter ii, Public Health Service standards set a limit of 1,000 ppm for human consumption, with 500 ppm indicated as the "desirable limit," while plants are injured increasingly as solids content rises from 700 to 2,100 ppm—the latter being an outside limit. These allowable concentrations may vary somewhat depending on the elements present. Sodium and boron are especially undesirable for plants, the former being the major problem here because of its predominance in sea water.

It is perhaps unnecessary to point out that there are just two basic ways to manufacture fresh water from saline: either to remove the water from the salts or to remove the salts from the water. It will be shown in the next section that these two methods require the same theoretical minimum of energy per unit of water produced. These two procedures serve as convenient categories for classifying the numerous techniques used and proposed for producing fresh water from saline.

1. The Thermodynamics of Salt and Water Separation

Any process for producing pure water from sea water will consume power at a rate corresponding to the theoretical energy required to separate the salt from the water, plus the energy lost in friction, heat losses, etc. The frictional and heat losses depend on the method of purification used and on the design of the associated machinery. However, the theoretical minimum energy required to purify sea water can be calculated from well-known thermodynamic principles.

The average salinity of ocean water is about 35 grams of salts per kilogram of sea water. It can be shown that the minimum power required for separation is 2.6 kw-h. per 1,000 gallons yield of pure water.[60] This figure represents the power required to separate the first fraction of pure water from a given batch of sea water. If the separation is carried further, the power required will rise as the fraction of fresh water separated from the salt water is increased. To separate half of the water from sea water requires about 40 per cent more power for the same yield, or 3.6 kw-h. per 1,000 gallons, while to perform a complete separation into pure water and dry salt requires a theoretical minimum of about 9 kw-h. per 1,000 gallons. (This last value was estimated from the properties of pure sodium chloride solutions, since data on actual sea water could not be found.)

From energy considerations alone, it appears that the most efficient separation process would use many gallons of sea water for each gallon of fresh water produced, returning the slightly saltier residue brine to the ocean. Actually, however, a plant using such a process would have to be much larger physically than one with equal output that separated a larger fraction of the water from sea water. The extra pumping expenses, heat losses, and carrying costs of the larger capital investment could easily amount to many times the theoretical power savings, so some compromise must be struck. Modern conversion plants separate between 30 and 80 per cent of the water from sea water, depending upon their type and design.[61]

The distinction made between processes that remove the water from the brine and processes that remove the salt from the brine is not significant from a theoretical thermodynamic standpoint. Disregarding losses, the theoretical power required for separation is determined entirely by the amount and quality of the salt water processed and the fraction of pure water removed from it. However, as these heat and friction losses make up 90–99 per cent of the power costs of operating any presently designed water-purification system, the distinction between water removal and salt removal does have great practical significance.

In a distillation process, a large amount of heat (about 2,500 kw-h. per 1,000 gallons) must be supplied to evaporate the

[60] This value should be increased up to 5 per cent for equatorial ocean waters, decreased by 5 per cent for polar waters, and also increased about 1 per cent for each 5° F. temperature rise. In salt-water seas (as distinguished from larger oceans) the variation is considerably greater. For example, purification of water from the Mediterranean requires 10–15 per cent more power than the average value quoted above. The authors are indebted to Forrest R. Gilmore, of The RAND Corporation, for these theoretical calculations.

[61] Louis Koenig, "Disposal of Saline Water Conversion Brines: An Orientation Study" (Office of Saline Water, U.S. Department of the Interior, Progress Report No. 20 [Washington, D.C., April, 1957]), pp. 1–6.

water. Theoretically, all this heat—except the 2.6 kw-h. per 1,000 gallons separation energy—can be recovered when the pure water condenses and then is reused to heat the incoming salt water. Because of practical limitations on heat exchangers, an appreciable fraction of the 2,500 kw-h. per 1,000 gallons is lost, and thus the actual process requires many times the theoretical amount of power. It is to be noted, too, that the losses are almost independent of the salt concentration. Because of these losses, the purification *by distillation* of brackish water containing only one-tenth as much salt as sea water actually requires almost as much power as the purification of sea water. Costs of processes that remove salt from water are more sensitive to the salt concentration. Such processes, therefore, tend to have an advantage over distillation when brackish water is being used, distillation becoming relatively more desirable when sea water is being used.

2. Description and Costs of Fresh-Water Manufacturing Processes

a) *Distillation systems.*—Of those methods that remove water from salt, distillation in one form or another is the most advanced from the practical point of view. Figures 17 and 18 illustrate four different distillation systems which will be described. Almost every American naval vessel uses distillation to provide potable water at sea. During World War II, large distillation units were set up on arid islands to provide water for military use.

In 1958 there were nine large units of the *multiple-effect evaporator* type (greater than 100,000 gallons per day capacity) operating or being installed, mostly in isolated places where fresh water is not available or is very costly.[62] Two units in Kuwait (on the Persian Gulf) have a combined capacity of 5,000,000 gallons per day of fresh water. All these multiple-effect evaporators are designed to recoup a sizable portion of the latent heat of the water vapor. Steam is supplied to the first-effect evaporator, causing the salt water therein to be partially vaporized. The heated vapor from the first effect is allowed to pass through a second effect, where it condenses and heats more sea water, the vapor of which passes to a third effect, where it condenses and heats more sea water whose vapor passes to a final condenser from which much of the remaining heat is transmitted to the inflowing raw sea water. Units of this type having six or more effects have been built in attempts to gain high thermal efficiencies. All parts of the equipment contacted by sea water must be made of corrosion-resistant materials.

Vapor-compression evaporators are a more recent development and operate on the heat-pump principle. Vapor is withdrawn from an evaporator shell by a pump. It is then compressed to increase its condensation temperature a few degrees and returned to a heat exchanger within the evaporator shell, where its latent heat is given up to produce fresh water and evaporate more saline water. The energy economy of this system is better than that for multiple-effect evaporators, and it can be built more compactly. A number of relatively small units of this type have been built and operated. Several larger units (between 100,000 and 225,000 gallons per day capacity) have recently been constructed and installed, mostly at isolated military bases. There are also indications that developments in heat exchangers, pump efficiencies, and scale control may allow a considerable improvement of this type of evaporator in the future.

B. F. Dodge and others working at Yale University have shown that the application of forced circulation and dropwise condensation techniques to a vapor-compression cycle can substantially improve the

[62] U.S. Department of the Interior, *Saline Water Conversion Report for 1957* (Washington, D.C., January, 1958), p. 92.

operation. These techniques substantially increase over-all heat-transfer coefficients, retard the formation of scale, and reduce the energy requirements to the order of 13 BTU per pound of product.[63]

K. C. D. Hickman has developed a rotating evaporator-condenser for use with the vapor compression cycle that yields very high over-all heat-transfer coefficients, reduces scaling markedly, and promises to reduce the size of units, all in comparison with presently operating vapor-compression evaporators.[64] The estimated total power requirement for units of this type is about 42 kw-h. per 1,000 gallons or 17 BTU per pound (compare with 2.6 kw-h. per 1,000 gallons, the theoretical minimum).

In 1930 Claude proposed a *temperature-difference evaporator* to use the rather large temperature differences that occur between surface and deep ocean waters in certain parts of the world to produce both electric power and potable water. An attempt to construct a plant in Cuba failed when great difficulty was experienced with the deep-water pipeline. Rather greater temperature differences occur between inlet and outlet cooling-water temperatures in steam or diesel electric plants and industrial processing plants, and these might also be used for producing power or for converting salt water.

Scientists at the University of California are re-exploring the application of Claude's original idea. In their system the warm sea water is piped into an evaporator under reduced pressure. A small fraction of the water evaporates, gaining its latent heat through a 5° F. cooling of the remainder of the water. The vapor formed passes through a turbine (which turns a generator) and then into a condenser which is at a lower pressure than the original evaporator. The vapor is condensed by the colder sea water. A very small model currently in use requires 10 horsepower to generate 4.6 horsepower plus water. However, improvements in efficiency should result if the unit's size is increased. It is estimated that a unit producing 100,000 gallons of water per day would produce a little more power than that required to operate the various pumps. (The simplified diagram of this system shown in Figure 18 is a sketch of a small unit; therefore, the numbers shown do not reflect potential values.)

The French, through the activities of Énergie des Mers, a joint government-private enterprise, are continuing their investigation of the possibilities of constructing an ocean thermal difference plant on the island of Guadaloupe in the French West Indies.

Solar-energy evaporators were employed in one form of the life-raft water kits developed during World War II. The only large solar distillation land unit known to us was operated for about ten years in the 1880's to furnish water for mule trains hauling minerals in the mountains of Chile. This unit covered a ground area of about 1 acre and produced a maximum of 6,000 gallons of water per day. Solar evaporation has been examined as a method to provide additional potable water for the Virgin Islands.[65] The design studied is similar in many respects to the Chilean installation. The equipment consists of glass-covered wooden trays to hold the brine and a system of pipes and troughs to collect the fresh-water condensate after it has formed on the inside of the sloping glass covers. The solar energy passes through the glass, heats the bottom of the tray, and is re-emitted in the infrared range to be trapped in the still, thereby evaporating water which condenses on the glass.

[63] *Ibid.*, pp. 15–16.

[64] K. C. D. Hickman, "Centrifugal Boiler Compression Still," *Industrial and Engineering Chemistry,* XLIX (May, 1957), 786–800.

[65] George O. G. Löf, "Solar Distillation of Sea Water in the Virgin Islands" (Office of Saline Water, Department of the Interior, Saline Water Conversion Program, Research and Development Progress Report No. 5 [Washington, D.C., February, 1955]).

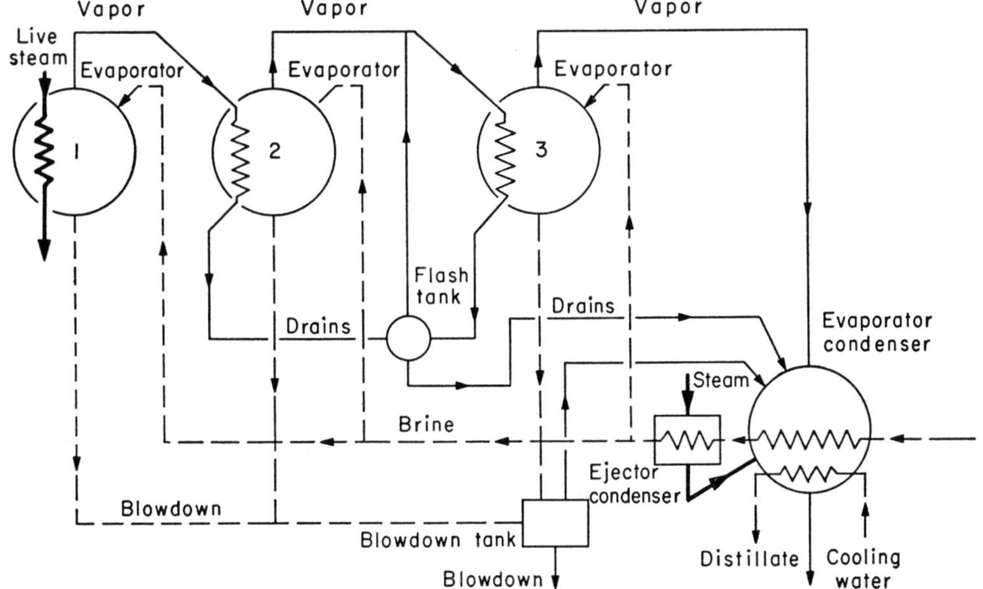

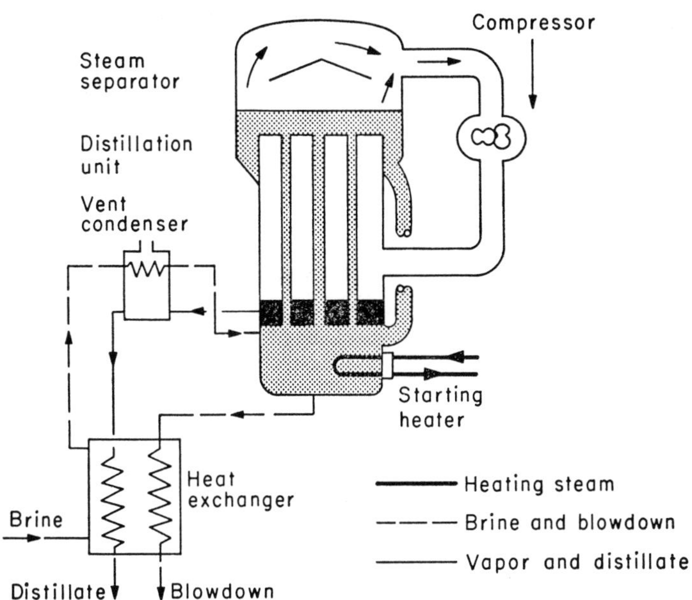

FIG. 17.—Distillation systems. (Adapted from Water: A Special Editorial Report," *Power,* September, 1952, p. 98. [Copyright McGraw-Hill Publishing Co., 1952.])

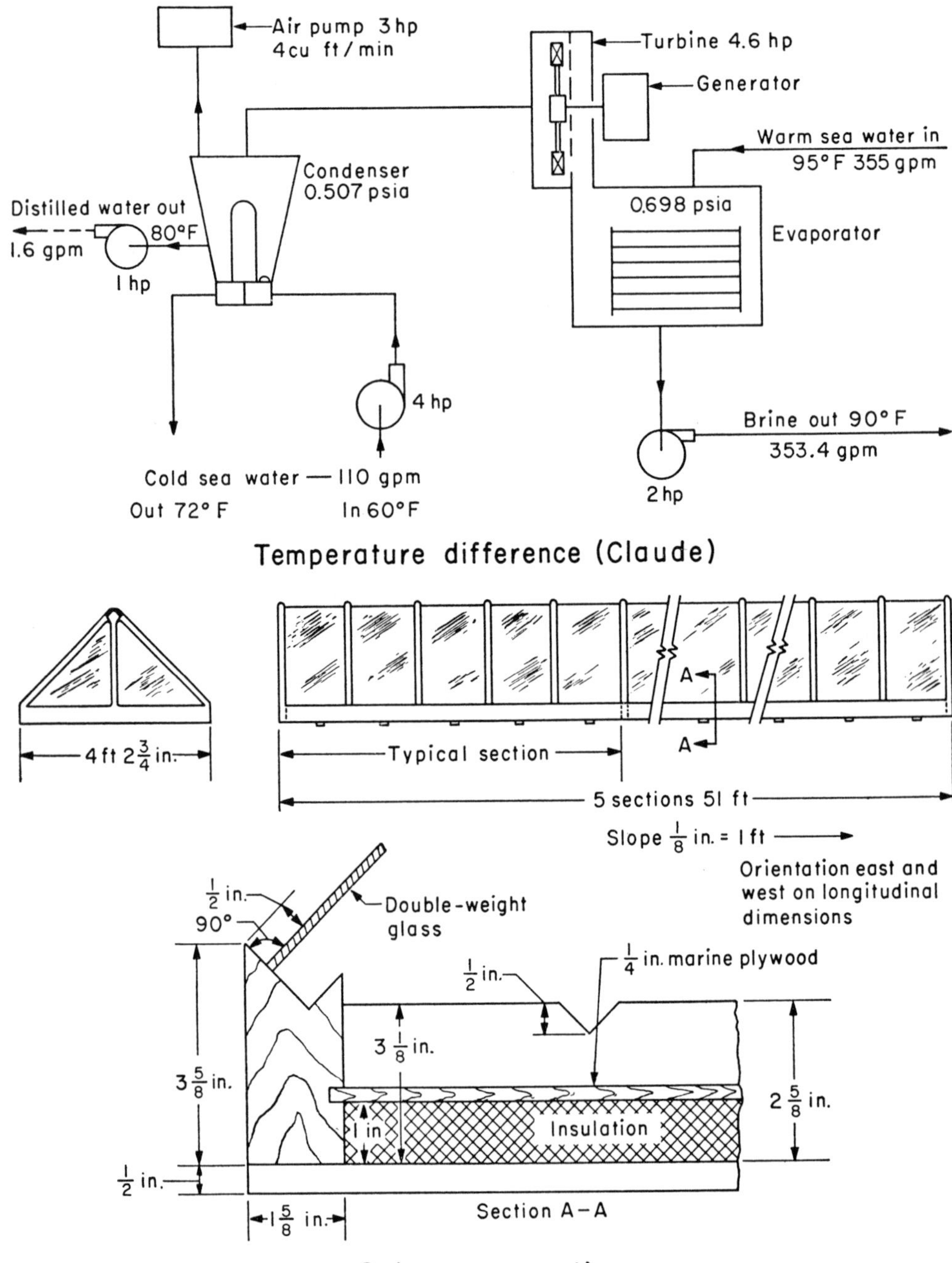

FIG. 18.—Distillation systems. (Adapted from E. D. Howe, "Sea Water as a Source of Fresh Water," *Journal American Water Works Association,* XLIV [August, 1952], 693–94.)

During the past few years considerable attention has been paid to the possibilities for improving solar-energy evaporators. The work in this country has largely been supported by the Office of Saline Water of the Department of the Interior and by the University of California. Additional investigations are under way in Israel, Australia, and North Africa. Generally, the efforts have been to develop cheaper construction materials and to improve thermal efficiency in order to increase the output per unit of area and thereby reduce the capital costs.

Although some improvement has been obtained in the design of evaporators and in adapting less costly construction materials, one gains the impression that the full potentialities of solar evaporators have not yet been reduced to practice. Efficiencies in collecting incident solar energy of the order of 35–50 per cent are reported, but the over-all thermal efficiences based on the actual fresh water produced and the minimum separation energy required are still very low—less than 1 per cent. The apparent reason for this low efficiency is the poor condensing characteristics of the present designs of solar evaporators. Some effort has been made to incorporate integral multiple-effect condensers, which show some promise. The possibilities of reducing costs through the use of external multiple-effect condensers do not appear to be too attractive. However, external condensing by means of a vapor-compression cycle may yield one of the lower-cost solar-evaporator systems.

A disadvantage associated with all solar-energy systems is the low over-all utilization factor imposed by the hours of darkness or overcast. Under the best conditions solar-energy systems might be expected to operate only about 25 per cent of the total hours in a day or year. This requires, for equal volumes produced, construction of a plant of about four times the capacity of a system that can operate around the clock.

Certain modifications in evaporation techniques have been proposed or applied to several of the distillation systems mentioned. One of these modifications is flash evaporation. Saline water at a given pressure and temperature is released into a chamber at lower pressure; the liquid flashes into vapor and is subsequently condensed. This technique is claimed to reduce the shutdown times required for descaling.

Another proposal involves distillation under conditions of pressure and temperature that are supercritical in respect to water. Improved heat transfer and higher thermal efficiencies were claimed for this process. However, laboratory investigations showed that some difficult operational problems exist. Expensive materials, perhaps titanium, are required to resist the corrosion and stress at the high temperatures and pressures involved, and scaling appears to be severe.

A suggestion has even been made that nuclear bombs might be used to convert sea water to fresh. The idea for the process arose during the examination of possible peaceful uses of nuclear explosives by the Livermore Laboratory of the University of California, supported by the Atomic Energy Commission. Briefly, this proposal involves detonating a thermonuclear bomb (energy yield perhaps 1,000,000 tons of TNT-equivalent, or 1 MT) at the bottom of a well 5,000–6,000 feet deep and reaching into a thick salt stratum. The well would be located offshore in the ocean, so that sea water could flow by gravity down one of two concentric pipes to the cavity formed by the explosion. The cavity would be surrounded or filled with molten salt, which would act as a heat reservoir. After conversion of sea water to water vapor at near-critical conditions, the vapor would rise in the other tube, condensing to liquid fresh water on the way to the surface and transferring its heat to the downward-flowing sea water in the concentric pipe. Many technical (not to mention political) questions must be answered before the feasibility of this process can be determined. It is possible that, if every aspect of this process works out favorably, it might convert water more cheaply than the other processes discussed. Among the favorable features are the apparent low cost of thermal energy from a bomb, avoidance of capital costs for constructing a reactor, and the low costs of the associated equipment—a well and piping. The support of the earth does away with the need for heavy, thick-walled pressure vessels and condensers. The depth of the salt deposit allows gravity to be used for pressurization and eliminates or greatly reduces the need for pumping and power recovery equipment. It should be re-emphasized, however, that many questions, including the possibility of radioactive contamination and the availability of suitable sites, remain yet unanswered.

b) *Systems other than distillation for removing water from salt.*—Several methods other than evaporation are proposed for removing the water from the salt. Most of these are newer ideas and have not as yet been studied as intensively; they are, therefore, more difficult to evaluate.

Some studies have been made of *fractional freezing* methods designed to separate fresh-water ice crystals from saline water. The latent heat of fusion of water is only one-seventh the latent heat of vaporization. While the difference is of no theoretical thermodynamic significance in a process where this heat is recovered, we have seen that the practical efficiency of heat recovery is severely limited. On the other hand, where freezing temperatures are involved, effective heat transfer to maintain thermal efficiency will be more difficult and perhaps more costly than for processes occurring at higher temperatures. Also, the frozen ice crystals entrap saline water on freezing, which makes separation difficult. Some early German investigators employed centrifuging to obtain good separation of fresh ice and brine. More recently, countercurrent washing of the frozen slurry has yielded a satisfactorily salt-free ice.

Direct freezing techniques using either water vapor or an immiscible recoverable vapor as a refrigerant are being explored and may offer promise. Several combinations of freezing and water-recovery cycles are being examined on a small scale.[66]

Several variants of *osmotic systems* are of some interest. When fresh water and saline water are separated in a cell by a semipermeable membrane, the fresh water will diffuse into the saline side and increase the pressure there until equilibrium is reached. This pressure is known as the osmotic pressure of the particular type and concentration of solute. It is possible in small-scale laboratory equipment to reverse the flow of water by imposing a greater pressure on the saline side than the equilibrium osmotic pressure. For sea water the minimum reversal pressure is about 350 pounds per square inch.

On a theoretical basis there should be no difference in the energy requirements per unit of water produced between a membrane osmotic system and a perfectly efficient thermal system. In practice, however, the latter process requires the circulation of a very large portion of the energy (the latent heat of vaporization), so even a small percentage loss of this circulating energy represents a relatively large portion of the energy required for conversion. An osmotic process would not involve the latent heat of vaporization of water; consequently, practical efficiencies might be higher if an osmotic process without membrane troubles could be discovered. A major problem is to develop a membrane having the necessary ion-retention, water-permeable char-

[66] One of these processes, called "cold distillation," is under investigation in Israel (see L. Shafer, S. F. Mulford, and E. D. Howe, *An Analysis of the Zarchin Scheme for Demineralizing Sea Water by Cold Distillation* [Berkeley: Institute of Engineering Research, University of California, August, 1954]).

acteristics combined with adequate strength and durability. Studies by Breton and Reid at the University of Florida show that films of cellulose acetate meet most of the requirements except durability;[67] they deteriorate and lose their screening properties after several days' use. Based on bench-scale tests and conservative estimates of pump and turbine efficiences (for recovery of work used in pressurization), an estimate of 12.8 kw-h. per 1,000 gallons of fresh water converted from sea water appears reasonable (compare 42 kw-h. per 1,000 gallons for an improved vapor-compression cycle).

Another practical difficulty associated with the pressure-osmotic membrane system is the possibility of plugging the membrane with finely suspended material in the sea water. All in all, and in spite of these present difficulties, the potentialities of osmosis appear to warrant continued investigation.

c) Systems that remove salts from water.—As has been mentioned, processes that remove salts from water have one basic difference from systems that remove the water from salt—their costs will usually vary significantly with the amount of dissolved solids present and the amount removed. In consequence, such processes are relatively more promising if the source water is brackish. Processes for removing salts are generally chemical in nature. The classic process is the silver-salt precipitation unit developed for life-raft use during the war. This and other chemical precipitation processes are suitable only for emergency use because of the very high cost of the chemical reactants. Two of the chemical processes of more practical significance are shown in Figure 19.

In recent years cation and anion exchange resins have been developed to a high degree of selectivity; *ion-exchange systems* for desalting water are based on their use. It is possible to pass saline water through a bed of cation exchanger where the cations of the salts are replaced by hydrogen ions from the resin. The resulting dilute acid solutions are then passed through a bed of anion-exchange resin where the anions are taken up by the resin in exchange for hydroxyl ions. This can result in a complete desalting of the saline water to yield a distilled-water equivalent. The resins, however, have only a certain capacity for exchange before they must be regenerated—the cation exchanger with an acid, and the anion exchanger with a base. In addition to the costs for these acids and bases, some of the desalted water must be used in the regeneration cycle. These factors limit the competitive position of this system to treatment of brackish waters of 2,000 ppm or less. An ion-exchange process pilot plant has been installed in Israel to study the removal of about 1,000 ppm of salts from brackish waters. This degree of desalting may make these waters potable and suitable for specialized irrigation.

Just recently, at the University of California, resins that can be regenerated with ammonium bicarbonate have been developed. In this process of regeneration, ammonia and carbon dioxide are subsequently evolved by heating and are then recycled and recombined to form new ammonium bicarbonate. Savings in the amounts of acids and bases and wash water for regeneration make this ion-exchange process a promising one, especially for use with brackish water.

Ion-exchange resins form the basis of a desalting process known as *electrolytic ion exchange* (or *electrodialysis*), which raised excessive hopes for a cheap fresh-water manufacturing system when first announced. The technical operation of this process may be understood by first imagining an insulated tank filled with saline

[67] E. J. Breton, Jr., "Water and Ion Flow through Imperfect Osmotic Membranes" (Office of Saline Water, Department of the Interior, Research and Development Progress Report No. 16 [Washington, D.C., April, 1957]).

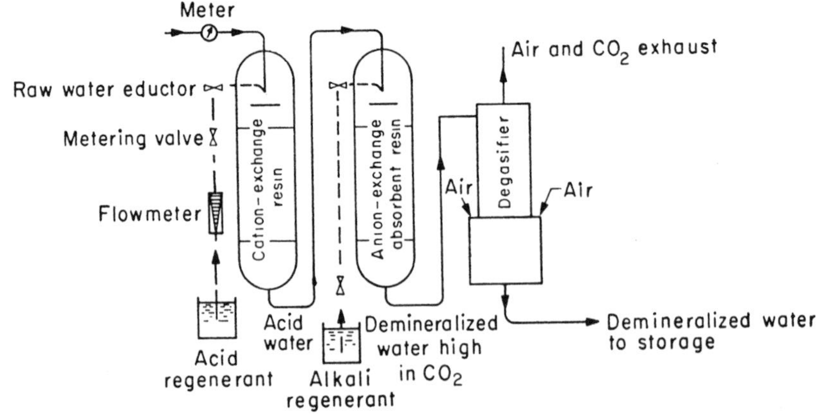

Ion exchange

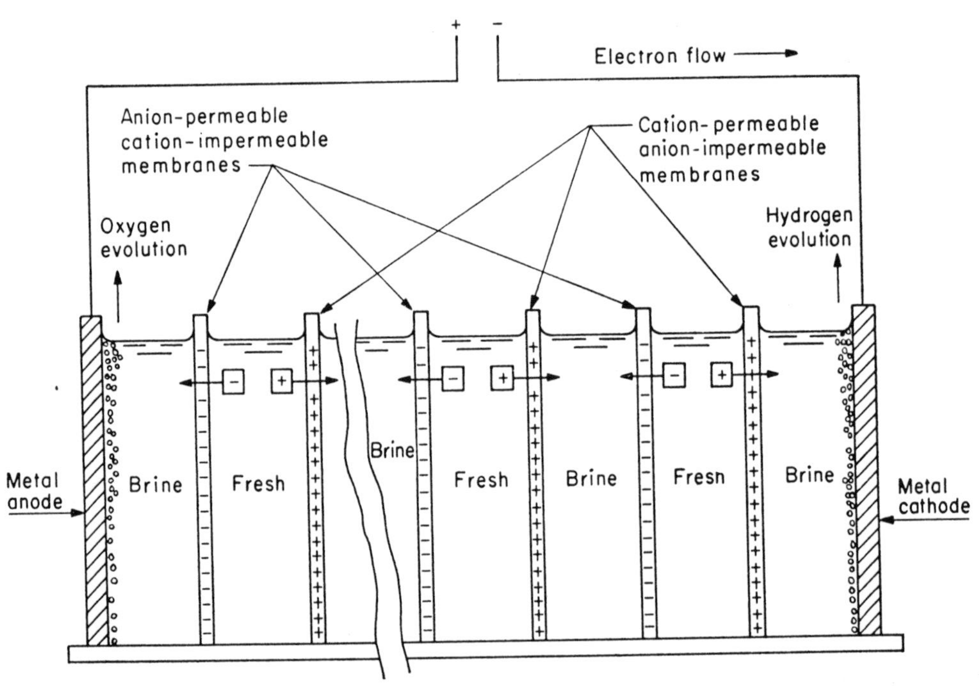

Electrolytic — ion exchange

FIG. 19.—Chemical systems. (Ion-exchange diagram from W. W. Aultman, "Desalting Sea Water for Domestic Use," *Journal American Water Works Association,* XLII [August, 1950], 791; electrolytic-ion-exchange diagram from W. F. Langelier, "The Electrochemical Desalting of Sea Water with Permiselective Membranes—a Hypothetical Process," *Journal American Water Works Association,* XLIV [September, 1952], 846.)

water and containing an inert electrode at each end. If direct current is caused to flow through the salt solution, electrolysis will take place. The reaction at the cathode can be represented as

$$2\,e^- + 2H_2O \rightarrow H_2 + 2OH^- \,.$$

The reaction at the anode will be

$$2H_2O \rightarrow O_2 + 4H^+ + 4\,e^- \,.$$

Within the solution the current is carried by the motion of the dissolved ions—the negative ions moving toward the anode, the positive ions toward the cathode. Under these conditions, of course, water is used up to form hydrogen and oxygen gas, and the solution becomes more concentrated. However, if two membranes are placed across the cell dividing it into three sections, and if one of the membranes is cation-permeable and the other anion-permeable, fresh water will eventually be formed by the electromigration of the ions out of the center portion. The cations will flow to the cathode through the cation-permeable membrane (the excess OH^- there cannot flow back through this membrane—it is anion-impenetrable), and the anions will flow to the anode through the anion-permeable membrane (the excess H^+ there cannot flow back through this membrane—it is cation-impenerable).

A simple two-membrane, three-cell system would be very inefficient because each coulomb of electrical energy would decompose 1 mole equivalent of water and transport only 1 mole equivalent of salt. However, if many sets of membranes forming many cells (alternately salt and fresh) are placed in the tank, each mole of water electrolyzed will cause the transport of 1 mole equivalent of salt in each of the cells in the tank. Thus the current efficiency theoretically increases proportionately as the number of cells is increased. In practice, the current efficiency is largely controlled by the amount of internal electrical resistance of a bank of cells, especially the resistance of the alternate cells containing fresh water. An actual operating unit would be constructed to allow a continuous flow of the salt water and deionized water through the alternate cells, made as thin as possible to reduce resistance.

Claims of electrical energy requirements as low as 20–30 kw-h. per 1,000 gallons of water reclaimed from sea water and total costs of 10–20 cents per 1,000 gallons ($32.50–$65.00 per acre-foot) of fresh water produced were originally made for this process. These early cost estimates were extremely optimistic. More recently, costs many times these amounts have been estimated for this process when operating on sea water.

The costs of fresh water produced by this system vary with the amount of dissolved salts to be removed from the water. First applications of the method, therefore, will be for the demineralization of brackish water where it may have cost advantages over the bed-type regenerative ion-exchange processes and over distillation processes. Pilot-scale units of this type have operated in the United States for several years using various brackish-water feeds. A number of larger units are being designed or constructed to operate in several locations in the United States, in Arabia, in Africa, and in the Netherlands.

Osmionisis is a newer process which is similar in many respects to electrodialysis except that the driving force is produced by the concentration difference between a brine and the feed water instead of by an imposed electrical current. To maintain the process, either salt must be added to the brine or some water evaporated to maintain the concentration difference. It is possible that this process may show some cost advantage over electrodialysis in areas near salt deposits or brine wells or where water may be evaporated favorably by solar energy and where electric-power costs are high.

3. *Estimated Costs for Manufacturing Fresh Water from Saline*

The costs of producing fresh water by the different systems described are much harder to estimate than are their technical feasibilities. Only a few plants of capacity large enough to supply water to a community have ever been built. Some of the processes mentioned have been operated only on a small laboratory scale. In addition, many of the costs quoted in the literature are suspect because no details are given as to whether depreciation, interest, operating expenses, and energy costs have all been taken into account. A few of the processes appear to have about reached the peak performance allowed by the present or estimated future states of the art. In other instances, considerable advancement can be anticipated with improved technology.

A major improvement in the reliability of cost estimates for conversion processes resulted after the development in 1956 of a standardized procedure for estimating costs by the Office of Saline Water.[68] All investigators of conversion processes sponsored by this agency are now required to report estimated costs in terms of this procedure. Included are:

1. All essential capital costs for plant, service facilities, and engineering.
2. Depreciation based on expected equipment and facility life, varying from seven to twenty years, depending upon their types.
3. Interest at 4 per cent.
4. Electric power at 7 or 5 mills per kilowatt-hour, depending upon demand.
5. Fuel at $0.25 per 1,000,000 BTU.
6. Land costs at $3.00 per 1,000 gallons per day capacity.
7. Storage for product water (ten days).
8. Steam at $0.55 per 1,000 pounds.
9. Supplies, maintenance, and operating labor based on percentages of plant costs.

Items not included are costs for disposal of concentrated brines (these will vary depending upon the location of the plant), transportation costs for the potable water, and distribution costs to the ultimate consumer. No treatment costs are included for the water produced, but it is quite likely that no conventional treatment, except possibly disinfection, will be required for water produced by any of the conversion processes.

The costs calculated by this procedure are appropriate for a conversion plant very near the sea or other source of saline water (costs allowed for raw water supply are modest) and adjacent to the city or other customer for the water (no costs for transportation are included). These costs are comparable to water supplied by conventional means at the main distribution reservoirs *before distribution to the ultimate customers.* Distribution costs must be added to these "wholesale" costs. Data given previously in this chapter show that these distribution costs are close to one-half of the total costs of municipal water obtained from present sources.

The technical problems and costs of disposing of waste brines are not insignificant. They are the subject of a study by Louis Koenig, who shows that waste brine disposal costs may range from about $0.07 to $1.92 per 1,000 gallons ($22.80–$630.73 per acre-foot) for a series of realistic plant situations.[69] The different conversion processes each operate most economically under different product-to-waste ratios, ranging from 0.5 to 4.0. Thus the problem and costs of waste disposal may have an important influence on the selection of a process and on the design of the unit for any given location.

On the basis of our discussion in chapter vi of appropriate interest rates, the 4 per cent figure quoted by the Office of Saline Water for use in estimating costs for conversion processes, while consistent with common practice in public water-supply enter-

[68] Office of Saline Water, Department of the Interior, *A Standardized Procedure for Estimating Cost of Saline Water Conversion* (Washington, D.C., March, 1956).

[69] Koenig, *op. cit.*

prises, represents too low a charge for interest, given the opportunity cost of capital in the economy. In view of the special uncertainties and risks involved in the construction and operation of novel installations like those here considered, our generally recommended 10 per cent would not be too high a rate of discount.

Subject to the limitations discussed above, the estimated costs for various conversion processes are listed in Table 24. The figures presented are based on the cost-estimating standards described and are obtained from reports of the Office of Saline Water unless otherwise indicated. The first cost figure in the table represents estimates based on the present state of the art for each type. The second figure is an extrapolation based on the future application of possible improvements now realized only in the laboratory. These costs will, of course, vary with the scale of operation, but, in almost every case, the range of uncertainty is so great as not to warrant expressing cost as a function of output. The capacities are, however, appropriate for community supply, 100,000–10,000,000 gallons of product water per stream day. The quality standard for the water is a maximum of 500 ppm dissolved solids.

Where data permitted, we estimated costs ourselves at 10 per cent interest, to show the effects of the higher interest rate. Another element having an important influence on cost is the expected useful life of the plant. Most of the components of the conversion processes have anticipated useful lives of twenty years or less. The expected lives of components of conventional water-supply systems (dams, aqueducts, pipelines) are usually much greater —fifty, seventy, even up to a hundred years in some cases. The costs given in Table 24 for the reinforced tubular plastic-film, solar-evaporation process illustrate the influence of short life on unit costs. Although the use of thin plastic film instead of glass and concrete decreases the original capital costs, the relatively short life of such plastic materials increases the charges for depreciation significantly.

Figures for costs of solar evaporation much lower than those given here are often quoted. These figures usually result from not including the cost for land, which is a significant factor in this process.

Changes in any of the standardized factors will alter the resulting cost figures and the relative positions of the different processes. For example, with land costing more than $100 an acre, the combined compression-distillation solar evaporator, which requires much less land per unit output, may show a relative advantage over the simple glass-covered pan. For small units the improved vapor-compression or freezing processes may have a comparative cost advantage over multiple-effect evaporation.

It should be mentioned that until the cost of electric power generated by nuclear reactions can approach the cost of power produced by conventional means, there is no reason to consider nuclear-electric power as a panacea for the cheap production of fresh water from the sea. If, in a specialized location lacking natural water, it proves cheaper to generate the power by nuclear reaction rather than to transport conventional fuels to the area, then some of the power, including waste heat, can also be used to produce potable water from the sea.

Recently, a cost estimate was prepared for the use of low-temperature thermal energy from a nuclear reactor to generate low-temperature steam ($\sim 250°$ F.) for one or another of the conversion processes.[70] It appears that this low-temperature steam may be generated in a reactor

[70] D. B. Brice, M. R. Dusbabek, and C. R. Townsend, "Study of the Applicability of Combining Nuclear Reactors with Saline Water Distillation Processes" (Office of Saline Water, Department of the Interior, Research and Development Progress Report No. 19 [Washington, D.C., 1958]).

TABLE 24

ESTIMATED PRESENT AND FUTURE LARGE-SCALE COSTS FOR SELECTED SALINE-WATER CONVERSION PROCESSES

TYPE OF PROCESS	ESTIMATED COSTS (DOLLARS PER ACRE-FOOT OF FRESH WATER PRODUCED FROM SEA WATER)	
	Present	Possible Future
Multiple-effect evaporation..........	$1,240*	$ 205†
Same at 10 per cent interest........	....	245
Vapor compression..................	550‡	355§
Same at 10 per cent interest........	....	452
Low-temperature difference–flash evaporation.........................	....	404‖
Same at 10 per cent interest........	....	525
Solar evaporation:		
Reinforced tubular plastic film.....	....	2,500#
Combined compression distillation..	....	1,290**
Simple glass-covered pan...........	....	1,070**
Freezing...........................	756††	326‡‡
Electrolytic ion exchange (electrodialysis) (treatment of brackish water only)	260§§	134‖‖

* T. K. Sherwood, "Fresh Water from the Sea," *Technology Review* (MIT), November, 1954, p. 17.

† Estimated for combined long-tube vertical-flash evaporators of 50,000,000 gallons per day capacity and steam costing 20 cents per million BTU's as bled from high-pressure steam-electric plant or as produced by a low-temperature nuclear-steam generator (D. B. Brice, M. R. Dusbabek, and C. R. Townsend, "Study of the Applicability of Combining Nuclear Reactors with Saline Distillation Processes" [Office of Saline Water, Department of the Interior, Research and Development Progress Report No. 19 (Washington, D.C., 1958)], p. 37).

‡ Sherwood, *op. cit.*

§ Brice *et al.*, *op. cit.*, for 1,000,000 gallons per day capacity.

‖ "Research on and Analysis of Single-Effect Low-Temperature Flash Evaporation Process" (Office of Saline Water, Department of the Interior, Research and Development Progress Report No. 18 [Washington, D.C., 1958]), p. 44.

\# Data for performance and cost of components from George O. G. Löf, "Demineralization of Saline Water with Solar Energy" (Office of Saline Water, Department of the Interior, Conversion Program Research and Development Progress Report No. 4 [Washington, D.C., August, 1954]), pp. 44–45, recalculated on the basis provided by Office of Saline Water, Department of the Interior, *A Standardized Procedure for Estimating Costs of Saline Water Conversion* (Washington, D.C., March, 1956), including charges for land and maximum useful life of films of five years.

** Data from above source recalculated according to standardized procedure with charges for land and estimated useful life at twenty years.

†† H. W. Hendrickson, "Saline Water Conversion by Freezing," *Refrigerating Engineering*, LXVI (August, 1958), 37.

‡‡ Office of Saline Water, Department of the Interior, *Saline Water Conversion Report for 1957* (Washington, D.C., January, 1958), p. 59.

§§ *Ibid.*, p. 41. Cost shown is for reduction of salinity of brackish water from 4,000 ppm to 350 ppm, estimated for plant of 1,500,000 gallons per day with present state of the art and membrane durability.

‖‖ "Design, Construction, Field Testing, and Cost Analysis of an Experimental Electrodialysis Demineralizer for Brackish Waters" (Office of Saline Water, Department of the Interior, Research and Development Progress Report No. 11 [Washington, D.C., December, 1956]). Cost is estimated for large-scale plant (10 acre-feet per hour) with greatly improved membrane durability, operating on brackish water as in n. §§ above.

using inexpensive aluminum-clad fuel elements at a cost on the order of 20 cents per million BTU's. This is comparable to the costs for obtaining low-temperature bleed steam from a conventional high-pressure steam-electric plant. Among the conversion processes, a combination long-tube multiple-effect flash evaporator appeared to be most suitable for use with the nuclear reactor. The cost given in Table 24 of $205 per acre-foot (63 cents per 1,000 gallons) is estimated for this combination.

It will be recalled that the cost per unit of water for processes that remove salt from the water is much lower when only small amounts of dissolved salts are removed. One of these processes, electrodialysis, has already been applied to the treatment of brackish waters for which removal of 1,000–4,000 ppm yields water suitable for human consumption. The conventional counterflow ion-exchange system may remove 1,000 ppm of solids for about $190 per acre-foot. Our estimate indicates that the electrolytic ion-exchange system might reduce 4,000 ppm dissolved salts to 350 ppm at a cost of about $260 an acre-foot of product water. It does not appear that these chemical processes can compete with other types for the treatment of more concentrated feeds like sea water.

Throughout this analysis no cost reduction has been credited for the possibility of producing salable by-products. It is technically feasible to extract many potentially valuable products from sea water —at least traces of perhaps half the elements are actually present. Apparently, however, only sodium and magnesium salts and bromine are presently at all economic to extract. The increased concentration of the waste brine flowing from a desalting process may confer a certain cost advantage over present salt-extraction plants which must begin with ordinary sea water. However, it appears that no substantial profits are attainable by presently known techniques, mostly because the value of the easily extracted salts is so low; a large increase in their production from a conversion plant might further reduce their value. A rigorous proof of this point would require an examination of the economics of each product that might be produced from sea water, and we have not undertaken such a study. However, our impression of the minor value of by-products in reducing conversion costs is confirmed by a detailed study made by the Conservation Foundation.[71]

From Table 24 it can be seen that the estimated costs of synthetically produced water are significantly higher than water presently available in most parts of the United States, when properly compared on the basis of costs before distribution. These costs for converted water are also higher than the estimated costs of obtaining additional increments of water by other methods like reclamation and evaporation control but possibly less than the cost of supply by tanker. There are areas in the world, and perhaps isolated locations in the United States, where natural water costs already approach the cost of water produced from the sea (or other saline source) and where demand for additional water might be generated by domestic needs or by desire abroad for the commodities exported by the region (e.g., petroleum products along the Persian Gulf). It is reasonable to expect that production of fresh water from the sea will be first applied in such areas.

G. Assisting Nature To Increase Present Natural Water Supplies

1. "Rain-making"

Since prehistoric time man has attempted to make rain. The Indian medicine man and the French cannoneer had their loyal

[71] Cecil B. Ellis, *Fresh Water from the Ocean* (New York: Ronald Press Co., 1954), p. 196.

adherents, but their efforts were of dubious value. Since World War II, we have learned a little more about what conditions are conducive to cloud formation and precipitation, but our general knowledge of the subject is still limited. The process of artificially nucleating clouds to produce precipitation is being widely used today with uncertain over-all results.

It is hopeless to attempt to explore all the legal, social, economic, technical, or metaphysical arguments that have been advanced to support or disprove the value of artificial nucleation for increasing precipitation. However, a review of the literature and discussions with meteorologists indicate the following conclusions about nucleating efforts to date:

1. There is some evidence, still not universally accepted, that suggests that artificial nucleation may slightly modify the precipitation pattern over a wide area downwind. Although this effect may represent a perturbation of the normal, it does not appear to be significant in changing the climate.

2. The primary effects of nucleation are in a localized region and last for a short time, so that precipitation may be encouraged to occur a little sooner than it would otherwise in a situation where rain is likely to occur naturally.

3. It is difficult to evaluate the degree of any localized increase in precipitation through nucleation because past rainfall figures have not been collected at a sufficient number of stations to determine natural fluctuations within a local region.

4. There are a few local areas where sharp terrain features combined with the short-range effects of nucleation have produced a significant increase in local precipitation.

5. The details of the processes of precipitation are still poorly understood, but there is evidence that artificial nucleation under some conditions serves to decrease rather than increase precipitation.

It appears that, while nucleation may have beneficial effects in increasing precipitation in certain specific local areas, it is not a general panacea for increasing precipitation and available water supplies.

In August, 1953, an Advisory Committee on Weather Control was created by act of Congress. This group was directed to make "a complete study and evaluation of public and private experiments in weather control for the purpose of determining the extent to which the United States should experiment with, engage in, or regulate activities designed to control weather conditions." The committee used statistical methods for evaluating increases in precipitation due to seeding projects.[72] They found, in five Pacific Coast projects studied, that statistically significant increases in precipitation did occur. Average increases in actual above-expected precipitation over the periods analyzed ranged from 9 to 17 per cent.[73]

These increases occurred under the favorable localized conditions mentioned earlier, that is, where cold, moisture-laden air in winter and spring is caused to rise by the presence of mountains. Additional study is necessary to determine the possible effectiveness of various types of "seeding" operations both in these favorable regions and in non-mountainous regions and with the so-called warm clouds which are present in large regions of the United States and the world for much of the year.

With the present knowledge, it is diffi-

72 *Final Report of the Advisory Committee on Weather Control* (Washington, D.C., December 31, 1957).

73 Frederic A. Berry, "Evaluation of Weather Modification Experiments," *Journal American Water Works Association,* XLVIII (August, 1956), 973–81. It should be mentioned, however, that the statistical techniques and conclusions of the Advisory Committee's *Report* have been criticized by K. Alexander Brownlee in "Statistical Evaluation of Cloud Seeding Operations," to be published in *Journal of the American Statistical Association,* Vol. LV (1960).

cult to assess the economics of artificial nucleation operations. One study estimates the benefit-to-cost ratio at about 100 to 1 for specific local operations in portions of the western United States. The estimate is based on increases in crop yields in otherwise near-normal rainfall years caused by localized increases in precipitation due to seeding.[74] Even granting the localized benefits from these operations, it may be that the seeding in one locality removes water from the atmosphere that might otherwise precipitate elsewhere, so that there are possible offsetting losses to consider.

In spite of the enthusiasm of some proponents of artificial nucleation and the pessimistic reaction of the opponents, there are indications that the present efforts to modify precipitation are but in their infancy and that, as greater knowledge of the atmosphere is obtained, techniques will improve and will be more widely applied—perhaps on a nation-wide or even a world-wide co-ordinated basis.

This prediction is based on bits and pieces of present evidence, particularly on some recent work by Bowen[75] in Australia and on discussion of the general subject by Schaefer.[76] Preliminary analysis by Bowen of long-time, world-wide precipitation indicates that there may be a relationship between periods of high precipitation and the passage of the earth's atmosphere through areas in solar or even cosmic space where higher than normal concentrations of dust particles occur. The presence of such particles appears to be related to meteor showers and their periodicity to the paths of meteors in relation to the path of the earth through space. Bowen concludes that these particles cause nucleation of clouds during these periods and thereby increase precipitation.

Sampling of the atmosphere shows that the number of natural nuclei present, whether from terrestrial or extraterrestrial sources, varies widely over time. It also appears that under certain conditions the atmosphere may be overseeded, with the result that clouds may not form, or may be dissipated if present. In other situations, none of the presently known types of nucleation influences precipitation one way or the other, factors other than nucleation being controlling. However, where insufficient nuclei are naturally present, the artificial seeding and control of nuclei may either (1) cause precipitation to occur when it is needed or (2) prevent the build-up of excessively severe storms with perhaps associated damaging precipitation in the form of hail or sleet. When natural nuclei are present in excessive amounts, precipitation that would otherwise occur may be prevented. In this circumstance it may be possible to develop and disperse antinuclei or seed "poisons" so as to reduce the effective number of nuclei. The measurement, addition, or reduction of nuclei may therefore become important operations in the future. At least, one might anticipate that such operations could have an important leveling influence on the peaks of precipitation intensity and the valleys of precipitation scarcity and that such effects could have significant economic value even if the total precipitation in a region remained unchanged.

The lack of adequate knowledge about the operation of the hydrologic cycle has already been mentioned. The comment is especially pertinent to that part of the cycle in which water is evaporated from the oceans and precipitated upon the land. In particular, more information is needed

[74] Irving P. Krick, "Increasing Water Resources through Weather Modification," *Journal American Water Works Association,* XLIV (November, 1952), 996–1020.

[75] E. G. Bowen, "The Relation between Rainfall and Meteor Showers," *Journal of Meteorology,* XIII (April, 1956), 142–51.

[76] Vincent Schaefer, Jr., "Snow and Its Relationship to Experimental Meteorology," in Thomas F. Malone (ed.), *Compendium of Meteorology* (Boston: American Meteorological Society, 1951), pp. 221–34.

about the physics and thermodynamics of cloud formation. Better knowledge is required of the internal mechanisms of cloud and precipitation formation and the relationships of clouds to their environment—the land surface beneath, the surrounding dynamic atmosphere, and the atmosphere above. Man's potential ability to exercise some control over weather, including precipitation, depends on a more complete understanding of the natural processes involved. What has been accomplished so far, including the practical application of synthetic nucleation of clouds, is but a first step in this direction.

Although it is presumptuous to speculate at this time on the techniques such control of weather may employ, some general factors may be noted:

1. Efforts to alter climate by attempting to feed in or remove energy will probably not be profitable except in a very small area. The total energy contained, even in small volumes of the atmosphere, is huge in absolute magnitude.

2. Any successful attempts to alter climatic conditions will probably employ a combination of techniques that "trigger" or encourage the weather desired by working through and with natural forces.

As an example of "triggering" effects, reference has been made to the success of a combination of synthetic cloud nucleation and favorable terrain features in inducing precipitation. Hills and mountain ranges trigger precipitation under certain conditions through their aerodynamic effects on the atmosphere. The use of artificial, portable, aerodynamic barriers combined with nucleation is another possibility for future research.

The *albedo* of a surface is the percentage of incident solar energy received by the surface that is reflected. For the earth's surface, this varies from 3 per cent for green fields or forests to 86 per cent for fresh snow. A desert reflects about 26 per cent of the energy. The stability of clouds is influenced by (among other factors) the amount of energy received from the earth's surface. If the albedo or the infrared emission of large areas can be reduced, more clouds may form above these surfaces, permitting opportunity for precipitation. Alternatively, if the temperature distribution of the surface could be formed into regular patterns, it might be possible to induce convective activity over the heated sections, thereby causing cumulus-type clouds and rain. The radiative balance of a desert might be changed artifically by (1) plowing, (2) spreading a layer of black material, or (3) inducing the growth of black molds or other vegetation requiring little water. These measures, plus artificial barriers, plus nucleation (if necessary) might induce nature to increase the amount of precipitation in desert areas. Another device which might be useful for favorably altering the relationships of clouds to their environment is the application of artificial thermal barriers (e.g., releasing water vapor in patterns underneath and above the clouds).

The specific suggestions made here are, of course, merely research possibilities, since little is known as yet regarding their practicability.

2. The Direct Use of Sea Water

For many purposes the direct use of saline water is almost as satisfactory as fresh water. Bathing, washing, sanitary uses, and fire protection could be satisfied by water too saline for human ingestion. Many industrial purposes could also be served by saline water. However, since some fresh water will always be required for residential and industrial use, an expensive dual piping and plumbing system for municipal areas would be required. Saline water cannot be used for irrigation.

As an alternative to desalting ocean water, more attention might, perhaps, be given to the possibilities of increasing the supply of food for arid regions near the sea (or near saline water equivalent to sea water) by what is known as "ocean farming." The artificial culture of oysters for pearls and food represents the most advanced development along these lines. However, the technical and economic possibilities of raising food fish synthetically in closed ocean areas near to the points of consumption have perhaps not been fully explored.

The same applies to vegetative crops grown purposefully in "farmed" ocean areas. While the varieties of plant life occurring in the oceans are much fewer and generally simpler than those that grow on land, they provide the basic food for all the extensive marine animal life. Some marine plants might be artificially cultivated for use as animal or human food. Or, possibly, land forms of vegetation—perhaps rice—might be adapted to marine growth by a process of selective breeding. Some of the highest forms of marine plants appear to have been land forms that have become self-adapted to marine growth.

Further study of ways such as those mentioned in which nature may be encouraged to increase the effective amount of fresh water available to man, either through increased precipitation or through direct use of the sea, may show many or all to be technically impossible or economically unsound. These possibilities are presented to indicate that there may be alternatives that have not received much attention as yet for meeting man's increasing future demands for water.

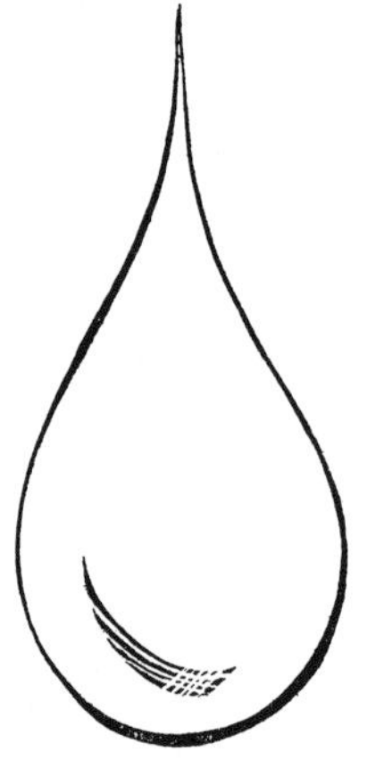

CHAPTER IX

WATER LAW: GOVERNMENT DISCRETION OR PROPERTY RIGHTS?

The purpose of this chapter is to analyze the legal and institutional bases for decisions concerning the allocation and development of water resources. How are decisions made? Who makes them? How can conflicts be resolved? What can be done to improve the decision-making processes?

A. General Considerations

As we have pointed out in earlier chapters, efficient use of water resources requires that the allocation and development of water supplies be in accordance with the same economic principles that govern the use of all other economic resources. The special physical factors that affect water supplies (e.g., the hydrologic cycle and the interdependencies of supply and use) must be taken into account in applying the economic theory of use, but they do not in any way invalidate it. The problem of economizing in the use of water is essentially one of allocating water supplies, and the resources devoted to water supply, to their most productive uses.

Broadly speaking, there are two methods of decision-making which can be used to achieve efficient use of resources. Under either method private individuals, firms, or public agencies will have desires for use of water; the crucial decisions are those that allocate the supplies among these competing uses. The first method, which we may call "centralized planning," co-ordinates the requests for and supplies of water through an ultimate authority—administrative or judicial. At the other extreme, the decisions of the separate individuals, firms, and agencies may be co-ordinated through the balance of supply and demand in an unregulated market, although a certain general "planning" still remains necessary to establish the legal framework of property rights within which the market operates. Centralized planning as a decision process is direct and obvious in its operation. The market mechanism, on the other hand, is more subtle in its workings. Each method has its potential advantages and difficulties, and each has some applicability to the problem of achieving efficient use of water resources.

In the United States it is regarded as normal for decisions about the employment of our economic resources to be made predominantly by private individuals and firms, interacting through the market mechanism. Individuals act as buyers and sellers, with the result that the price system allocates resources among competing ends and uses. We have argued that, in general, freedom of individual resource owners and buyers to contract for their best advantage tends to insure that resources will be used efficiently in accordance with individual preferences. By contrast, it is rather important to note the relatively limited roles which private decision-making and the market process are presently permitted to play in the development and use of water resources. With the possible exception of nuclear energy, no other basic resource is subject to more public and centralized control; no other resource is less subject to allocation through the market-price system.

To a considerable extent, centralized decision-making in allocating water resources is inevitable and necessary. There are certainly many problems in the use of water supplies that seem to require subjection of private property rights to unified development and control in order to deal with problems of interdependence and commonality of supply or of use. In addition, it will always be difficult to have some water-related services provided by private firms because of the impossibility of denying the service to any one potential customer without simultaneously denying it to all (the problem of "collective consumption goods" discussed in chapter iv). In the case of flood control, for example, a private firm providing the service could not deny the benefit of protection to those refusing to pay for it.[1]

Three basic points need to be stressed in regard to the question of governmental decision-making in the use of water supplies. First, even though centralized operation may be required to achieve efficiency in the use of water supplies, it does not follow that economic principles should be abandoned. On the contrary, the achievement of efficiency requires that the benefits of any action exceed in value the costs of the action. It is somewhat ironic that public intervention in the field of water resources, ostensibly to achieve efficient operation, has often shown a flagrant disregard for the requirement that benefits exceed costs. Second, the need for unified operation of a particular water resource does not necessarily require that the operation be public in nature. It is quite conceivable that efficient operation can be achieved through the co-operation of private firms and individuals. It is also possible that joint public-private action can be very effective in many cases. Third, the possibilities for the development of private property rights and the use of the market system in the allocation of water resources are much greater than is commonly recognized. As we shall argue in our subsequent discussion of water law, the failure to develop an adequate structure of property rights in water supplies and the restrictions placed upon utilization of these rights through the price system are important obstacles to the efficient use of water resources.

B. Public Decision-making

Public control over water resources is important at all levels of government—federal, state, and local. Generally, one can say that the federal government is dominant in the control and development of the major river basins of the country, while state laws govern the distribution and use of surface and ground waters at the local level. The federal government has characteristically been concerned with flood control, navigation, and reclamation in major river basins; in recent years the federal government has become increasingly involved in the production of hydroelectric power until it has become the largest single producer of electric power in the United States. Beginning in

[1] For an excellent discussion of the problems of private development of water resources see John V. Krutilla and Otto Eckstein, *Multiple Purpose River Development* (Baltimore: Johns Hopkins Press, 1958), chap. iii.

the twentieth century, the federal government has also increased the magnitude of its participation in water-resource development. Starting with small navigation and reclamation projects, federal activities have expanded to include development of entire river basins, for example, of the Tennessee, Columbia, Colorado, and Missouri rivers.

State governments are permitted to adopt whatever system of water law they choose for the disposition of waters within their boundaries. Even more important is the authority of a state under its police power to regulate water supplies in the interest of the safety and general welfare of the community. Local governments are important in the provision of water supplies to urban users—domestic, commercial, and industrial. Possibly because they are relatively simple to operate, water utility firms are well suited to public ownership. In any event, some 70 per cent of the cities (with a population of 5,000 or more) in the United States have municipally operated water systems.[2]

Although the extent and influence of federal action in the field of water resources have been recognized and extensively studied, the role of state control has received relatively little attention despite the fact that it is probably even more important in influencing water-allocation decisions than are the relatively well-publicized federal actions. As we shall see later, state systems of water law are tending to place primary reliance upon judicial and administrative allocation of water supplies as opposed to market allocation. This development has been largely a result, we believe, of the "water-is-different" philosophy rather than of any rational comparison of the alternative policies available.

1. Federal Legal Aspects

The legal basis for federal action in the field of water-resource development stems from a number of sources. It is interesting to note that there is no such thing as a federal law of water rights. All federal powers stem from the enabling authority of the Constitution and are inferred from more general powers rather than being enumerated explicitly. Water resources as such are not mentioned specifically in the Constitution. The two most important legal sources of federal prerogative are the commerce power and the proprietary power (control over the use of federal public lands).[3]

The commerce power has been interpreted as giving Congress jurisdiction over all navigable water in the United States, including tributary streams. Under this power the federal government builds navigation works and flood-control dams which may also provide for the generation and sale of hydroelectric power. The right of the federal government to engage in comprehensive river-basin development stems from this power.

> It is for Congress alone to decide whether a particular project, by itself or as a part of a more comprehensive scheme, will have such a beneficial affect on the arteries of interstate commerce as to warrant it. That determination is legislative in character.[4]

And, on the same basis, Congress has exclusive power to decide whether the benefits to commerce exceed the cost of the undertaking.

Apparently the authority of Congress to control the use of federal public lands is unlimited, under recent Supreme Court decisions. This proprietary power is derived from the clause of the Constitution that permits Congress to make "all needful rules and regulations" respecting the property of

[2] E. W. Clemens, *Economics and Public Utilities* (New York: Appleton-Century-Crofts Co., 1950), p. 549.

[3] For a detailed discussion of the legal basis of federal water activities see *Report of the President's Water Resources Policy Commission,* Vol. III: *Water Resources Law* (Washington, D.C.: Government Printing Office, 1950). The constitutional foundations are discussed on pp. 5–72.

[4] *Oklahoma* v. *Atkinson,* 313 U.S. 508, 527 (1941).

the United States. It is the legal foundation for the Reclamation Act of 1902, which is the original and basic reclamation law for irrigation development in the seventeen western states.

In addition to the commerce and proprietary powers, the federal government is able to exercise controls over the use of water resources on the basis of war and treaty-making powers, the power to legislate in the general welfare, the power of equitable apportionment to decide water controversies between states, and the power to approve interstate compacts.

2. *Federal Activities*

According to the Hoover Commission Task Force Report, there are twenty-five federal agencies involved in one phase or another of water-resource development. Of these agencies, the Corps of Engineers and the Bureau of Reclamation are by far the most influential and important. From 1824 through 1954 the federal government spent some $14.3 billion on water projects.[5] The Corps of Engineers was responsible for almost two-thirds and the Bureau of Reclamation for approximately 20 per cent of the total. The Tennessee Valley Authority was credited with expenditures of $1.6 billion, or 11 per cent of the total.

In recent years Congress has launched what appears to be a large-scale watershed and flood-control program under the administration of the Soil Conservation Service of the Department of Agriculture. Although the Department of Agriculture had previously been given some flood-control responsibility in the Flood Control Act of 1936, it was not until 1946 that Congress actually appropriated funds for watershed control. In 1954 Congress passed the ambitious Watershed and Flood Prevention Act, with funds to permit the construction of fifty small watershed projects in some thirty-four states. Although the program of the Soil Conservation Service has been comparatively small, its future plans are relatively large, so that in time its expenditures for water-resource development may rival those of the Bureau of Reclamation and the Corps of Engineers.

As an indication of the effective widening of the scope of federal action in water development in recent years, 92 per cent of federal expenditures on water-use projects has taken place since 1920, and over 68 per cent of the total amount has been spent since 1941. In recent years federal spending for such activities has averaged over $800 million a year. In 1954 it was estimated that the cost of completing authorized water projects would be a further $18.5 billion.[6] At current rates of construction this represented a twenty-two-year backlog of federal construction.

The major categories of federal expenditure to 1954 represented the following proportions of the total: power, 27 per cent; flood control, 23 per cent; navigation, 18 per cent; and irrigation, 12 per cent. It is somewhat surprising to find that irrigation expenditure ranks only fourth. Several factors influence this ranking. For one thing, the Corps of Engineers is concerned only with the first three functions. Second, the Bureau of Reclamation, which is the major agency dealing with federal aid for irrigation, has actually spent almost 50 per cent of its funds for power development and flood control. On this point it is important to note that flood-control expenditures are non-reimbursable by project beneficiaries and are paid for by federal taxpayers. This fact may have had some influence in reducing the incentive to "allocate" portions of project costs to irrigation. Since revenues from the sale of hydroelectric power are often used to repay costs allocated to irri-

[5] Task Force on Water Resources and Power for the Commission on the Organization of the Executive Branch of the Government ("Hoover Commission"), *Report on Water Resources and Power* (Washington, D.C., 1955), I, 5.

[6] *Ibid.*, p. 4.

gation, it is also important for the Bureau to select projects that have power production features.

The civil functions of the Corps of Engineers date back to 1824, when the Corps was authorized to clear a navigable channel on the Ohio and Mississippi rivers. Until 1917 the Corps confined itself to navigation improvements, although flood control was often a by-product of these activities. Following legislation in 1917 and in the Flood Control Act of 1936, the Corps began to expand its scope in flood control and into the related activities of power development and river-basin planning. The Corps has been highly successful in securing congressional approval for its projects, perhaps largely because of their pork-barrel aspects.[7]

With the passage of the Reclamation Act of 1902, Congress established the Bureau of Reclamation with the basic task of promoting the development of irrigation in the seventeen western states. In his message to Congress, President Theodore Roosevelt hopefully declared: "Our people as a whole will profit, for successful homemaking is but another name for upbuilding of the Nation."[8]

To further the objective of creating farm homes rather than farms as business ventures, the act limited entry of irrigation lands to a maximum of 160 acres. This limitation has been interpreted, however, to permit combined farming by members of a family or otherwise as long as each member of the group owns no more than 160 acres. In a recent Supreme Court decision the 160-acre limitation was upheld, and the California Supreme Court decision in the Ivanhoe cases,[9] which had declared the acreage limitation void in California, was reversed. The Supreme Court stated:[10]

> As to the claim of discrimination in the 160-acre limitation, we believe that it overlooks the purpose for which the project was designed. The project was designed to benefit people, not land. It is a reasonable classification to limit the amount of project water available to each individual in order that the benefits may be distributed in accordance with the greatest good to the greatest number of individuals.[11]

In comment upon the 160-acre limitation it may be pointed out that the restriction probably acts to reduce the economic efficiency of the farm units affected, in that it may prevent the use of large-scale methods of production which are often advantageous under western farming conditions. On the other hand, the view supporting the acreage limitation becomes more understandable when it is realized that the irrigation interests concerned are bearing but a small fraction of the cost of the irrigation-water facilities provided by federal funds.[12] The federal government may well be concerned with how a subsidy contributed by taxpayers is distributed among the beneficiaries. Second, the extent of the subsidy raises questions of the economic wisdom of the projects to begin with, so that pleas to abolish the 160-acre limitation on the grounds

[7] See Arthur Maass, *Muddy Waters: The Army Engineers and the Nation's Rivers* (Cambridge, Mass.: Harvard University Press, 1951).

[8] Quoted in *The Report of the President's Water Resources Policy Commission,* III, 183.

[9] *Ivanhoe Irrigation District* v. *All Parties,* 47 Calif., 2d 603, 306 Pac., 2d 824 (1957).

[10] Supreme Court opinion dated June 23, 1958, reprinted in *Western Water News* (California Irrigation Districts Association), X, No. 7 (July, 1958), 6.

[11] Perhaps it should be mentioned that "the greatest good to the greatest number" is a criterion that is impossible to apply because it involves a logical fallacy. A given amount of benefit or gain can be distributed in a number of ways, but it is clear that the more people who are to share the gain the less there will be for each to receive. The danger of such a criterion, assuming that it is intended to be more than an expression of good intentions, is that it may lead to the selection of divergent and inconsistent policies.

[12] This fact was explicitly recognized by the United States Supreme Court in regard to the Ivanhoe cases.

of promoting economic efficiency have a somewhat hollow ring.

The Reclamation Act of 1902 required that project irrigators repay the capital costs of the projects in ten years, *without* interest. The interest subsidy was presumably justified by the social concern for "development of the West." These repayment requirements proved too heavy, so in 1914 the standard period was extended to twenty years; in 1926 to forty years; and in 1939 to fifty years by the addition of a ten-year development period.[13] Furthermore, for particular projects even larger pay-out periods have been authorized.[14] One obvious effect of extending the pay-out period has been to increase the interest subsidy. In addition, under present interpretations of reclamation law, even the capital charges without interest need only be repaid by irrigation users if within their "ability to pay" or "repayment capacity." Costs in excess of repayment ability are covered in project accounts by revenues from sale of power or from other sources (e.g., sale of water to municipalities).[15]

3. *The Record of Federal Investments*

It is perhaps no longer really news that federal water projects have been heavily subsidized, that repayment records are poor, and that the techniques of benefit-cost analysis have been abused. In 1953, for example, the House Committee on Interior and Insular Affairs found that the majority of reclamation projects with repayment histories of ten years or more have needed amended contracts or other relief from repayment obligations.[16] In 1955, after a comprehensive study of federal water-resource programs, the Hoover Commission task force concluded that the federal government has paid too much of the costs of the programs and has required insufficient payment from the beneficiaries:

> Water users in irrigation projects are required to pay back a portion of the irrigation capital costs which is judged to be within their capacity, but they pay no interest. The portion they are judged capable of repaying rarely is the full cost per acre of the project. Recently the general range has been between one-quarter and one-third of the capital costs, and a few are as low as 10 per cent. Thus, even in projects classed as reimbursable, there is a considerable element of subsidy. Over and above the portion of the construction costs that water users do not pay, the foregoing of interest alone usually provides an additional subsidy equal to the total costs of construction. Thus in some cases, the Federal subsidy amounts to some 95 per cent of capital costs plus interest.[17]

Since the Hoover Commission report was completed, a number of studies have appeared which have reviewed the record of federal-water resource participation and which question the efficacy of techniques of project evaluation by federal agencies.[18]

[13] *The Report of the President's Water Resources Policy Commission*, Vol. I: *A Water Policy for the American People* (Washington, D.C.: Government Printing Office, 1950), p. 151.

[14] Alfred R. Golzé, *Reclamation in the United States* (New York: McGraw-Hill Book Co., 1952), pp. 247–48.

[15] *The Report of the President's Water Resources Policy Commission,* I, 69.

[16] Subcommittee on Irrigation and Reclamation of the House Committee on Interior and Insular Affairs, *Construction Costs and Repayment on Federal Reclamation Projects* (82d Cong., 2d sess. [Washington, D.C.: Government Printing Office, 1952]).

[17] Task Force on Water Resources and Power, *op. cit.*, p. 15.

[18] For extensive reviews of federal water-resource programs and federal evaluation techniques see Roland N. McKean, *Efficiency in Government through Systems Analysis* (New York: John Wiley & Sons, 1958); Edward F. Renshaw, *Toward Responsible Government* (Chicago: Idyia Press, 1957); Otto Eckstein, *Water Resource Development* (Cambridge, Mass.: Harvard University Press, 1958); Krutilla and Eckstein, *op. cit.*; Ben Moreell, *Our Nation's Water Resources—Policies and Politics* (Chicago: The Law School, University of Chicago, 1956); Raymond Moley, *What Price Federal Reclamation?* (New York: American Enterprise Association, Inc., 1955).

It is apparent that policies and techniques of project planning and valuation are seriously lax from the point of view of economic efficiency. Renshaw, for example, scrutinized the benefits and costs of forty-three existing federal irrigation projects and found that "only about one-fourth of these projects now appear to have been justified on the basis of realized benefits in fact exceeding costs."[19] It should be noted that Renshaw used assumptions favorable to the estimation of benefits and that he did not include in his survey some five projects entirely abondoned and written off as complete failures.

Federal water programs have been referred to in the less scholarly analyses as the "federal water scandal"—with justice, we believe. Both Moley and Moreell have pointed out that the pay-out records of reclamation projects even in terms of the costs charged to irrigators have been poor. Only two projects have repaid 90 per cent of the costs assessed against them, and in most cases costs have been renegotiated downward (based upon "ability to pay") and pay-off periods have been extended beyond forty years.[20] The poor pay-off records of reclamation projects are only part of the story, because the project costs allocated to irrigation are heavily subsidized to begin with. Repayment without interest involves a subsidy of 50 per cent for a pay-out period of fifty years even at a low interest rate of 2.5 per cent; at 6 per cent interest the subsidy is almost 70 per cent. (An appropriate rate of interest would be one that reflected the risk to the government in financing such projects and not simply the interest paid upon riskless federal government bonds, which is what the rates like 2.5 per cent are supposed to reflect. The poor repayment record of existing projects would seem to demonstrate that the risk assumed by the government is substantial, so that a higher discount rate is justified.)[21] And, finally, only a small fraction of irrigation costs (e.g., 12 per cent in the Upper Colorado Project)[22] may even be scheduled for repayment by irrigators.

The consideration of all these factors has resulted in estimates of the total subsidy to irrigation of over 90 per cent on several recent projects. For example, Green has calculated that the total subsidy to irrigation in the Columbia River Basin Project has amounted to 94 per cent of the cost of irrigation; that is, 6 per cent of the cost is to be repaid by irrigators.[23] It is interesting to point out that, astounding as Green's figures are, he did not take into consideration the fact that in recent years approximately 80 per cent of the wheat grown in the Columbia River Basin has been purchased by the United States Department of Agriculture under the farm price-support program.

The economic record of the flood-control and navigation projects is apparently no better than that of irrigation projects, though the results have not received as much publicity. This lack of attention stems in part from the fact that irrigation projects are assessed with certain repayment requirements which make it easier to evaluate project performance. Navigation and flood-control projects, in contrast, require almost no local contributions and produce no federal revenues. For example, the chief of the Corps of Engineers reported in 1952 that "non-federal contribution to the first cost of the entire authorized flood control program, including reservoirs, is expected to be about 7.4 per cent."[24]

[19] *Op. cit.*, p. 5 and also chap. ix.

[20] See Moley, *op. cit.*, chap. v; Moreell, *op. cit.*, p. 126.

[21] See chap. vi.

[22] Moreell, *op. cit.*, p. 128.

[23] Donald S. Green, "Federal Irrigation Subsidy" (unpublished University of Chicago Agricultural Economics Research Paper No. 5601, January 11, 1956), p. 7. Green used an interest rate of 6 per cent in his calculations.

[24] Task Force on Water Resources and Power, *op. cit.*, p. 15.

The benefits of reclamation, flood-control, and navigation projects accrue primarily to regional and local interests. And there is no denying that the benefits to these local groups are substantial. Indeed, it would be an unusual project where the expenditure of money did not provide benefits to someone somewhere. The basic questions to ask, however, are: Do the benefits exceed the costs? Can society justify expenditure of federal moneys in water projects at the expense of other worthwhile investments in the economy (e.g., in roads, schools, industrial plants, defense, and hospitals)? Should federal taxpayers be required to subsidize local and regional benefits?

It is also of importance to note that federal planning for water-use projects has consistently underestimated project costs and overestimated the probable benefits. Moreell reports that the Bureau of Reclamation had estimated the original cost of all its 90 projects authorized up to 1953 (excluding the Missouri River Basin Project) to be $1.5 billion but that by June 30, 1952, the estimated cost of completion had risen to $3.3 billion.[25] In 1951 the Committee on Appropriations of the House of Representatives found in 182 projects then under construction by the Corps of Engineers that construction costs had been increased by $3.27 billion, or 124 per cent, over the original estimates. Only 57 per cent of the increase in cost could be ascribed to changes in the price level.[26]

In regard to the overestimation of benefits the Hoover Commission task force stated:

> Overestimation of irrigation benefits has reached a point where the Bureau of Reclamation has claimed justification for the expenditure of $1000 to $2000 an acre for the development of irrigated land which, on the basis of information available to the task force, would not be worth more than $200 an acre under present prices of mature reclamation projects.[27]

Study of benefits from flood-control projects has shown similar inflation of project values. To illustrate, the task force cited the case of the Barnitz Creek watershed in Oklahoma, where flood-control benefits were calculated to be $180,342 annually. Local authorities pointed out that equivalent flood-free land would provide net returns of only $59,000 a year, or about one-third of the benefits claimed by federal officials.[28]

It is quite probable that the economic record of the newer projects will be no better, perhaps even worse, than the record of the older projects. Renshaw has examined the Missouri River Basin Project and the Upper Colorado River Project, two of the largest and most important reclamation projects to be authorized in recent years. He concludes that "contemporary public investment in both the Missouri and Colorado River Basin cannot be justified in terms of expected increases in land and water values exceeding expected costs."[29] Under assumptions favorable to probable irrigation benefits, Renshaw found that benefits exceeded costs in only one of a total of thirty subprojects authorized for the two basins.[30] The significance of these findings is more striking when it is realized that the historical costs of all federal reclamation projects (ninety) total $1.9 billion, while the Missouri River Basin Project will cost more than $2.2 billion, and the Upper Colorado River Basin Project will cost almost $1 billion (counting only the allocations to irrigation).

The increasing federal participation in the development of water resources raises a number of interesting questions. On the one hand, there sometimes are important legal and administrative factors that make federal control or action desirable. For ex-

[25] Moreell, *op. cit.*, pp. 120–21.

[26] Task Force on Water Resources and Power, *op. cit.*, p. 18.

[27] *Ibid.*, pp. 18–19.

[28] *Ibid.*, p. 20.

[29] *Op. cit.*, p. 113.

[30] *Ibid.*

ample, economic efficiency may call for integrated development of a river-basin or a watershed system and, because interstate problems may be involved, federal co-ordination and action may be required. Our feeling is that the number of cases where federal action is required is probably exaggerated but, that, if it is required, there is certainly no reason for failure to follow economic principles of efficient resource use. It seems that much of the pressure for federal participation stems not from sound legal or economic reasons but rather from special-interest groups who hope to benefit from federal provision of subsidized benefits. With navigation and flood-control costs borne almost entirely by federal taxpayers and with large-scale subsidies to irrigation, prospective beneficiaries have extremely strong incentives to push for more federal development.

From the standpoint of rational decision-making, improvement in the record of public investment in water-resource development is urgently needed. If the projects engaged in are, as is almost always claimed, efficient ones, then the benefits will exceed the costs and subsidy should not be required. It is possible, of course, to subsidize a project that is economically efficient. In this case the question of subsidy relates to the desirability of redistributing income from the taxpayers to the project beneficiaries.[31] The more typical situation currently is one where subsidies are required to finance projects that cannot be justified on economic grounds. In such cases the subsidy leads not merely to a changed distribution of income but to a lower level of over-all economic production.

Apart from the general propriety of subsidy, it may be questioned whether a project can be developed and operated efficiently if the beneficiaries pay only a small share of the costs. Without the restraining and rationing influence of prices, there may be little or no incentive for either the government decision-maker or the project-user to be efficient.

It might be argued that the public expresses its willingness to accept any losses of national income involved in adoption ot inefficient projects by (indirectly) voting the projects into existence. But the question remains as to whether the electorate is informed at the time the decision is made.[32] The fact is that projects can seldom, if ever, be evaluated by the public, because accurate information as to what the costs and benefits are and who will bear and receive them is not made available.

4. *State Activities*

In contrast with federal development in the field of water resources, the scope of *direct* participation on the part of state governments has been relatively small. For the most part state governments have not in the past engaged in the business of constructing and operating water projects for flood-control, navigation, or irrigation purposes (although a number of states have provided water recreation facilities in connection with state parks). State governments have influenced decision-making primarily through the structure and operation of state laws that govern the acquisition and transfer of water rights on the part of individuals, firms, and local governmental bodies.

[31] It should be noted that the collection of taxes may have effects upon efficiency of production and that ideally these effects should be considered as a cost of changing the distribution of income.

[32] Compare the observation by Eckstein (*op. cit.*, p. 222) in connection with his analysis of the Chief Joseph Dam Project in the state of Washington: "It might also be noted that the federal subsidy which is granted through the absence of interest charges and through other devices discussed in section 12 below, is about $22,000 per farm. This is an extremely large amount of money to be spent for the benefit of one family. While the justice or propriety of such a subsidy is beyond the scope of the present discussion, the simple fact should be made known to all who participate in the decision-process and to the general public."

It is evident that state activity in the field of water resources will increase substantially in the future. One visible line of development is the creation of state water boards with the specific role of determining the allocation of water supplies among competing users. This trend is discussed in a later section of this chapter. It is also likely that some states may actually engage in project construction, though this may be determined in large part by the scope of federal participation in water-resource development.

California will apparently be the first state to engage in water-project construction and operation on a really large scale. Currently, California's Department of Water Resources is actively planning to build (and operate) the Feather River Project. The Feather River Project is expected to cost perhaps $3 billion and thus may be the most costly water project in the history of the world. Moreover, the Feather River Project is only the first stage of a grandiose plan, costing upward of $13 billion, for the "full development" of water resources in California. The California Water Plan, as it is called, is declared to be "a master plan to guide and coordinate the planning and construction by all agencies of works required for the control, protection, conservation, and distribution of California's water resources for the benefit of all areas in the State and for all beneficial purposes."[33] This quotation possibly suggests the future scope of state intervention in water-resource development.

C. Water Law and Property Rights

As we mentioned earlier, each state has been permitted to adopt its own system of water law insofar as is consistent with certain paramount federal powers. It is primarily through these state laws that the rights of individuals, firms, and local government bodies to develop and use water have been established. In both eastern and western states the increasing use of water is forcing reconsideration and modification of state water law. It is desirable, therefore, to review state water doctrine from the standpoint of its effects upon the allocation process, particularly in regard to the relative roles of centralized and private decision-making.

1. The Basic Doctrines

The subject of water rights in the United States is extremely complex because water law varies a great deal from state to state. As a result it is difficult to summarize or generalize without finding exceptions or contradictions in special circumstances. At least part of this difficulty stems from the fact that the hydrologic cycle is not completely understood. In addition, many features of water law were developed before hydrologists were able to supply reasonably correct classifications. This means that legal distinctions often do not correspond with physical and hydrologic relationships. Many questions in water law arise from the fugitive and fleeting nature of water resources which creates problems of commonality or "spillover effects" of use and consequent difficulties in appropriate definition of water rights.

A major source of confusion is the existence of two contrasting doctrines of water law. In the western states the primary basis of water law is the *doctrine of appropriation.* On the other hand, eastern states have traditionally used the *riparian doctrine* of water law. Both of these doctrines are subject to a number of variations, compromises, and exceptions.

A water right is generally treated as real property. It is usually considered to be a usufructuary right, that is, a right to make use of the water but not a right to the corpus or physical possession of the water, as

[33] California State Department of Water Resources, *The California Water Plan* (Bull. 3 [Sacramento, May, 1957]), p. vi.

long as the water is flowing in a natural watercourse. Once the water is diverted from the watercourse, it may be reduced to physical possession by artificial means and may be considered to be the personal property of the owner, particularly under the doctrine of appropriation. Rights to use waters in navigable streams are commonly usufructuary because of federal powers to control navigation and use of rivers as public highways. It is difficult, however, to maintain a precise distinction between usufructuary use and consumptive use. Virtually any use that involves the handling of water will either reduce its quantity or impair its quality and so is essentially consumptive to some degree.

The riparian doctrine is based upon the premise that the owner of land bordering a stream or lake has the right to take water for use on his land. The right to use the water exists solely because of the relation of the land to the water and resides in the ownership of the land. The first riparian user acquires no priority over those who may make use of the stream at a later date; the rights of upstream and downstream riparian users are viewed as being coequal.[34]

In its original formulation the riparian doctrine held that upstream riparians could divert water only for "natural" purposes, (e.g., domestic uses and watering of livestock) but that any substantial withdrawal from the stream or reduction of the "natural flow" was a violation of rights of other riparians. Since this provision or interpretation has proved unduly restrictive, the doctrine has been modified in most states to permit the use of riparian waters for "artificial" purposes (e.g., irrigation and other commercial uses). The withdrawal, in each case, however, must be "reasonable" with respect to the requirements of the other riparians.

The task of determining what constitutes reasonable use is usually left to the courts and depends primarily upon the judge and on the situation. It is important to note that determination of reasonableness is always subject to re-evaluation at a later date with a change in circumstances. The uncertainty of the matter is increased by the fact that riparian rights are not generally considered to be lost by non-use. This means that existing riparian users may be required at any time to make way for a newly asserted right as long as the new use is "reasonable."

Within the framework of an economy operating under the institutions of private property and the market system, the riparian system of property rights in water is somewhat incongruous—even aside from the peculiarity that the rights are attached to particular tracts of land. A riparian right subject to the doctrine of "reasonable" use provides no guaranty to a definite quantity of water and thus loses much of its meaning as real property. This lack of quantification creates uncertainty for the individual holder and for all property owners along a given watercourse. The exchange or transfer of water rights between competing uses and users by the market process is severely hampered. It appears that the allocation of water among alternative users is accomplished in the main by judicial discretion. Although the courts may be well qualified to decide matters of equity, it does not follow that they are equally qualified to determine questions of the relative economic productivity of competing uses for a given supply of water. Probably the major reason why the riparian doctrine of "reasonable" use has not had obviously harmful effects is that its application has been confined mainly to areas and situations where the supply of water has been large in relation to the demands. As the demands for water increase in future years, however, the

34 The same riparian principles that relate to surface waters are usually applied to the ownership of land overlying an underground stream or the underflow of a surface stream. In these cases the riparian right arises out of the ownership of land overlying the watercourse.

question of efficient allocation of water resources will become crucial, and the inefficiency of judicial decision-making governing uncertain riparian rights may become acute.

In contrast, the doctrine of appropriation gives no preference to the use of water by riparian landowners. Under this doctrine the water right is acquired by use. The earliest water right on a given watercourse has preference over later users—"first in time means first in right." This means that in times of shortage senior or older rights have precedence over junior or newer rights. Appropriative rights attach to specific quantities of water and very often to specific times, places, and methods of diversion. The right may be kept in good standing as long as use continues, but it may be lost in various ways discussed below for non-use over a period of time. Both riparian and appropriative rights may be lost by prescription (adverse possession) or taken by condemnation.

It is common for state law to stipulate that the highest use is "domestic and municipal"; second priority is usually accorded to irrigation; and commercial and industrial use is given third priority. In most states the priorities come into play in the original granting of the appropriations. If there are several competing applications, the one with the higher ranking on the priority list will be given the appropriative grant. Once the appropriation is granted, it becomes a right senior to subsequent appropriations regardless of its statutory priority ranking. The only exception to this is in periods of extreme drought when the water is sometimes rationed according to priority ranking regardless of the seniority of rights, subject to payment of compensation to senior users deprived of water.

Since appropriative rights are clearly defined with respect to quantity and priority, enough certainty and security would seem to exist to permit their efficient economic allocation through the price system. In most states, however, important restrictions are placed upon the transfer of appropriative rights, so that the market mechanism is hampered in its allocative function.

The riparian doctrine is generally followed in the eastern states, although it is being subjected to question, and some states are moving closer to appropriation doctrine.[35] Most western states follow the doctrine of appropriation, but the riparian doctrine has been explicitly repudiated in only eight of the seventeen western states.[36] This means that in some states the doctrines are concurrent, so that confusion is not difficult to find.

In general, the differences between appropriative and riparian water rights with regard to surface and underground watercourses are also applied to so-called percolating waters—ground waters that are not part of a definite underground watercourse. Hydrologists have argued that the distinction between underground waters in definite channels and diffused or percolating waters is highly tenuous because nearly all ground water is percolating, that is, moving by laminar flow as contrasted with the turbulent flow of most surface waters.[37] In the eight states where the riparian doctrine has been explicitly repudiated, use of percolating water is governed by the doctrine of appropriation. For states where the riparian doctrine holds, even in part, the right to

[35] The state of Mississippi adopted the Water Rights Act on April 6, 1956, and became the first of thirty-one humid-area states to adopt the doctrine of appropriation. For further discussion of changes in eastern water law see Harold H. Ellis, "Some Current and Proposed Water-Rights Legislation in the Eastern States," *Iowa Law Review,* XLI (Winter, 1956), 237–63.

[36] The eight states which have abrogated the riparian doctrine are Idaho, Montana, Wyoming, Colorado, Nevada, Utah, New Mexico, and Arizona. The remaining nine western states are California, Washington, Oregon, North Dakota, South Dakota, Nebraska, Kansas, Oklahoma, and Texas.

[37] Thad G. McLaughlin, "Hydrologic Aspects of Ground Water Law," *Journal American Water Works Association,* XLVII (May, 1955), 449.

percolating water is subject to considerable variation in that three subdoctrines or versions may apply.

Some states apply the English rule of absolute ownership, which gives the overlying landowner an absolute right to pump and use the percolating water without regard to quantity and without regard to the effects of the pumping upon the water table in adjacent lands. The consequent divergence between private and social costs, in cases where the underground percolating waters are interdependent and common to adjacent lands, has been discussed by us previously, especially in Appendix B to chapter iii. Another source of conflict arises when percolating waters, governed by the rule of absolute ownership, are sources of supply for surface or ground waters that are controlled by the law of appropriation. Apparently, there is no legal basis for reconciliation in such cases.[38]

In many riparian jurisdictions the doctrine of absolute ownership has been replaced by the view that the rights of the overlying landowner to percolating water must be held to "reasonable" use. The determination of reasonableness is primarily a judicial one and is always related to the demands of adjacent landowners to the common supply.

A third version of riparian law for determining rights to percolating waters is the doctrine of "correlative rights." It is often difficult to distinguish this doctrine from that of "reasonable" use. All overlying owners are held to reasonable use, and their rights are viewed as being coequal. The law of correlative rights, which originated in California, provides that in cases of shortage or overdraft each taker shall be limited to his proportionate share. Assuming that the uses are reasonable, those pumpers with a larger historical record of use would receive a larger proportionate share or quota.

[38] Wells A. Hutchins and Harry A. Steele, "Basic Water Rights Doctrines and Their Implications for River Basin Development," *Law and Contemporary Problems* (School of Law, Duke University), XXII (Spring, 1957), 290.

2. Evaluation of Water Law

It is evident that current laws do not effectively establish water rights as property capable of the economic treatment accorded to other types of property like land or mineral rights. If water rights were allowed to become secure and certain without limitation on transferability, individual decision-making and the market process would tend to allocate water resources to their most productive use; high-valued uses would bid the water away from low-valued uses. The arguments for establishing water rights in this fashion are the same ones generally justifying the market process and individual decision-making—this process is believed to achieve high efficiency with minimal impairment of individual freedom of choice.

It is important to emphasize that the general logic of market exchange of water rights between competing uses and users does not mean that public needs for water rights and water supplies are to be denied. If water supplies are desired by a public body, they can be obtained by market purchase of water rights. What would be objectionable from the standpoint of promoting efficiency in water use would be the use of public prerogative to pre-empt private property rights in water without compensation, as can be done under water law in some states. If a market in water rights is operative, public uses of water may be subjected to better scrutiny because the value of the water in alternative private or public uses will be more apparent.

Under the market principle the only restrictions that need be placed upon individual decision-making in the use of water resources are the same ones that govern the use of all other property. Just as certain limitations are imposed on the use of one's own land when private use has important spillover effects on other parties (e.g., residential zoning or smoke-prevention laws), it may be desirable to place some restrictions on the exercise of property rights in water. Spillover effects in the use of water might justify legislation restricting stream pollution or limiting pumping upstream that causes salt-water intrusion at the coast downstream. It may turn out that in many cases (see Appendix B, chap. iii) the spillover effects actually result from an incomplete definition of the water rights, so that the problem may be viewed as one of vesting rights rather than of passing legal prohibitions (e.g., assignment of quotas in a common pool as property rights may be an alternative to government regulation of output). Furthermore, it may well be convenient to handle the problem of spillover damages through court action on claims for compensation. In general, judicial procedures are better suited for evaluating the facts of damages than for determining efficient economic use of resources. Still another device which could be used to deal with a divergence between private and social costs is the imposition of use taxes. What this actually amounts to is the payment of compensation to the general public for losses imposed upon outside parties.

In other words, there are a number of solutions or techniques available for dealing with the problem of spillover effects in the use of water rights. Such effects can be prevented or compensated without destroying the important advantages of private property in water rights. This point is significant because the existence of spillover effects constitutes the strongest argument for the assertions of many writers that private property is undesirable in this field and that public ownership of water resources is to be preferred.

To operate effectively as private property in the market system, the water right must be clearly defined and have legal certainty, and it must be capable of being transferred by purchase and other voluntary means between competing uses and users. Riparian and appropriative water law both possess serious deficiencies in regard to these qualities. With some modifications, however, the doctrine of appropriation could be used as a basis for a system of water rights designed to facilitate private decision-making. We might add that, although a number of writers have expressed a preference for appropriation doctrine as opposed to riparian doctrine, they commonly do so for the very reasons and qualities we believe to be deficiencies of appropriative water law.[39]

a) *Certainty aspects.*—Certainty is perhaps the most important quality of real property law. If property rights are uncertain, the incentive to develop and invest in water resources will be seriously reduced. Uncertain property rights greatly hamper the transfer or sale of property to competing uses and users. For example, a riparian water right, which is always subject to a future determination of "reasonable" use, provides no guaranty to a prospective buyer that he can purchase an established quantity of water.

The concept of certainty in water rights may itself be subject to some confusion. What is important for use of the market mechanism is legal certainty or certainty of *tenure;*[40] that is, buyers and sellers

[39] An exception is Frank J. Trelease, who argues that the doctrine of appropriation can be the basis of an improved system of law on grounds essentially similar to ours. For an unusually good discussion of water law see his "A Model State Water Code for River Basin Development," *Law and Contemporary Problems* (School of Law, Duke University), XXII, No. 2 (Spring, 1957), 301–22.

[40] One commentator has distinguished between *legal* certainty and *tenure* certainty, the former supposedly representing protection from unlawful acts of others and the latter representing protection from lawful acts. Both are distinguished from *physical* certainty (see S. V. Ciriacy-Wantrup, "Concepts Used as Economic Criteria for a System of Water Rights," *Land Economics,* XXXII [November, 1956], 297). We will not make use of the first distinction but will say that a right is legally

should be able to determine without question who owns specifically defined rights to the water supply. It may often be necessary to define the timing of diversion (a dry-season right is more valuable than a wet-season right) and priority standing in case of short supplies in addition to mere quantity of water. Under the appropriation doctrine, legal certainty means that prior appropriators are protected against junior users and juniors are protected against increases in use by senior users.

In contrast, physical uncertainty is a fact of nature which law cannot be expected to remedy. Rainfall will vary, wells will go dry, and rivers may change their courses—and, while each of these may create substantial problems for individuals, there is no reason for any difficulties to arise for the structure of water law. In particular, both riparians and appropriators are subject to the changeability of weather, so that periods of drought are likely to cause hardship no matter which doctrine of water law is in effect. Under the system of appropriation, however, water rights are typically set up so that the physical uncertainty is reduced a great deal for senior appropriators but increased at the same time for junior appropriators. That is, rights are specified as to priority, so that in dry weather junior appropriators may have their supply cut off entirely while senior users may get their full quotas.

Following strict priorities in time of drought is sometimes criticized as being "unfair" to junior users or as uneconomic in that (it is asserted) higher benefits may be achieved if part of the stream flow in drought years is devoted to saving the crops of the junior appropriator instead of the reduced flow going entirely to the senior user. In our opinion the latter problem is really one that is capable of an economic solution, no legislative action being required. If the gain to the junior user does in fact exceed the loss to the senior appropriator, it is clearly possible for the junior user to buy the water from the senior user, to the benefit of both. Furthermore, in the market for water rights, the relative market prices of senior and junior water rights will reflect the relative priorities in times of scanty rainfall. This means that senior rights will tend to command higher prices and that the price system will tend to allocate these rights to their most economic uses. The physical uncertainty associated with a junior right will presumably be reflected by the price differential prevailing between senior and junior rights. This answers the question of "fairness"; the junior appropriator has paid less for his right than the senior user did, the latter's price incorporating a kind of drought insurance premium. Or we can simply say that the senior appropriator is the owner of a more valuable commodity than is the junior appropriator —a commodity that the latter can acquire by paying the market price.

To deal with the case of drought, the states of Colorado, Idaho, and Nebraska provide a special system of priorities which supersedes existing priorities. Domestic uses are given first preference, agricultural uses are placed second, and third preference is allotted to commercial and industrial uses. Exercise of the preference is made subject to the payment of compensation to holders of existing water rights. Although the enforcement of such preferences in emergency situations may conflict with the efficient use of resources (e.g., an industrial user may create more economic value with the water than an agricultural user), the payment of compensation mitigates some of the undesirable features of a preference system. Actually, there is no reason in principle why the allocation of the scarce water should not take place by the market process in drought periods as well as in

---

certain when so defined and delimited that no serious question arises as to its application as circumstances vary. Physical certainty is discussed by us below.

periods of normal rainfall. If water is really needed for domestic use, the cities will be able to purchase water from agricultural or industrial users.[41]

In periods of drought, riparian water rights are usually subject to judicial allocation of the scarce water supplies. The court may prorate supplies among existing uses coequally or may make a redetermination of "reasonable" use. Legal uncertainty arises because of the difficulty of predicting judicial decision in the absence of some clear guiding line and from the fact that a reasonable use in a period of adequate rainfall may become unreasonable in time of drought. In addition, the judicial allocation may bear little or no relation to the most economic allocation.

The doctrine of appropriation facilitates the making of investments to improve stream characteristics, for example, the development of upstream storage. Under riparian law the rights to stored water or to the increased firm supply of the river due to upstream regulation are all coequal, with perhaps little or no advantage to the constructor of the works. In contrast, the rights to stored water in appropriation doctrine are clearly established, and junior users always have the incentive to construct storage facilities to "firm" up their rights, though of course they cannot use the facilities to impair the rights of others.

Although appropriative rights are perpetual in nature, they may be lost through abandonment, forfeiture, and prescription. Abandonment is loss through voluntary relinquishment, while forfeiture is a deprivation of right for failure to meet some legal requirement. Prescription is loss of right through adverse possession, the legal owner having failed to take steps to protect his right within the period specified by the statute of limitations. The most serious question here concerns the principle of *forfeiture for non-use*,[42] where the owner does not wish to abandon his right but simply does not choose to make current use of the water under that right. We do not see the force of the argument for depriving such an owner. If someone else can make productive use of the water, the solution to the problem is economic rather than legislative or judicial. That is, the potential user can purchase the right from the owner, either in full or in part, perpetually or for a term of years, as mutually agreed. If the owner chooses not to sell, that can only mean that he foresees the possibility of greater revenue—that is, of turning the water to a still more productive use—in the future, in which case current non-use has a useful function of preventing premature commitment of the water supply of the community.

Logically, there is no essential difference between non-use of a water right and holding idle an undeveloped piece of property in an urban area. The avoidance of premature commitment in the latter case is more obvious, but in both situations the costs incurred (interest and tax charges) serve to prevent excessive reservations for the future.[43] A real problem does arise where state law prohibits or limits transfers of water rights because in such cases non-use may not reflect economically efficient reservation for the future but only inability of the owner to sell his right to a more

[41] This is subject to a qualification in that strategically located owners of water rights might refuse to sell except at extremely high prices. That is, acquisition of water supply may involve sequential locational problems like those in constructing a new highway, so that eminent domain powers may be a practical necessity.

[42] This principle was strongly defended by Frank J. Trelease, "Desirable Revisions of Western Water Law" (address delivered at the Western Resources Conference, Boulder, Colorado, July 15, 1959).

[43] One technical point is that water rights probably escape taxation to a greater degree than does landed real property. (Pointed out to the authors by Mr. Charles E. Corker in a personal communication.) If true, this is a matter for correction by tax legislation rather than by the drastic rule of forfeiture.

productive current user. In this case the problem is obviously due to the unwise restrictions on market transfer of property in the form of water rights rather than to the fact of non-use as such.

Water rights may also be taken through the process of condemnation under the power of eminent domain. If compensation is paid, the impairment of property rights is not too significant. The doctrine of appropriation seems better suited to condemnation procedures than is riparian law; the appropriative right is more clearly defined so that the question of adequate compensation is less subject to controversy.

In some states condemnation is not limited to eminent domain proceedings for municipal water supply but is instead broadly permitted under statutory preferences, so that a "higher" use of water can condemn a "lower" use. Thus industrial water supply may be condemned for use in irrigation. The requirement of compensation limits the potentially great evil of this practice (only rarely will an irrigation project be able to compensate any other user deprived of water supply). With the proper transferability of water rights no statutory preferences would be necessary; it would be possible to rely upon market forces to put water to its "highest" use.

On this question of statutory preferences, some writers seem to prefer judicial decision-making as an alternative.[44] While judicial judgment may be more flexible than legislative judgment, it does not follow that the courts possess more economic wisdom than legislative bodies. From the standpoint of promoting economic efficiency in the use of water resources, neither has any strong claim to superiority over the economic forces of the market.

The most striking example of reliance upon statutory wisdom is found in Texas water law. Since 1931 all water appropriations, except those on the Rio Grande River, are subject to future appropriations for municipal purposes *without* the necessity of condemnation and compensation.[45] It is difficult to see how such a statute can be justified either on grounds of economic efficiency or on those of equity and protection of investment.

In connection with tenure or legal certainty it is interesting to examine the question of "waste" of water by the owner of the water right. Currently, almost every state prohibits the "waste" of water: "At present, a riparian owner has no more license to waste water than has an appropriator; and the appropriator never has had the right to do that, although in practice, he may, in many cases, actually have diverted more than he put to beneficial use."[46] Many writers seem to view the statutory and judicial prohibition of "waste" with approval and argue that water should be put to "beneficial" use. It is somewhat difficult to understand this position. The logic of the situation is the same as in the case of statutory preferences or the loss of water rights through non-use. It is not clear why a person should not be free to use his own property as he sees fit, so long as losses are not imposed upon others. If water rights are salable, and if protection is provided to third parties, it is difficult to see why owners of water rights should be so irrational as to waste water rather than use it efficiently or sell it to someone else who can do so. To deny rationality in the use of one's own water right is to question the basis of private decisions in the use of all resources.

The California case of *Chow* v. *Santa Barbara* may serve to illustrate judicial judgments on "waste" of water.[47] Chow, as a riparian water-user, had for many years used the flood waters of a stream for leach-

[44] S. V. Ciriacy-Wantrup, "Some Economic Issues in Water Rights," *Journal of Farm Economics*, XXXVII (December, 1955), 881.

[45] Texas Civil Statutes, Acts 7471, 7472.

[46] Hutchins and Steele, *op. cit.*, p. 288.

[47] *Gin S. Chow* v. *Santa Barbara*, 217 Calif. 673, 22 Pac. (2d) 6 (1933).

ing purposes on his riparian lands. In 1933 the California Supreme Court declared this use of water to be unreasonable and also wasteful.

> It is the established law of the state that as between riparian proprietors the right of each as against each other is confined to the amount of water reasonably necessary for useful and beneficial riparian purposes.
>
> The duty not to commit waste is enjoined on all users of water.

As a result the city of Santa Barbara was allowed to appropriate the "waste" waters formerly used by Chow *without* any compensation.

There is probably little doubt that the economic worth of the water to the city exceeded the value of the water for leaching purposes. What is important here is that the court took the responsibility of saying that the well-established practice of leaching was wasteful and unreasonable and that the court deprived Chow of his use of water without compensation, thus shaking the security of all water rights in California. If Chow's property right had been certain and clearly defined, the city of Santa Barbara could have purchased that right in the ordinary manner of transfer of property. Alternatively, condemnation with payment of compensation could have been undertaken.

We should perhaps make clear here that we are not criticizing the decision of the California Supreme Court as being *legally* incorrect; presumably, the California Supreme Court is the ultimate authority on what is law in California. In this case the decision was quite in accord with a 1928 constitutional amendment (California Constitution, Art. XIV, sec. 3) which held riparians to the same standards of beneficial and reasonable use of water that had long been applied to appropriators. On this ground a lawyer might therefore be inclined to argue that no property was taken from Chow because the water right in question was authoritatively, in the circumstances, determined to be not his property. We are saying not that the court's interpretation of the law was incorrect but rather that any law or judicial decision that makes tenure of water rights or of any other form of wealth uncertain is going to have deleterious economic effects.

b) *Transferability of appropriative and riparian rights.*—Although a great deal of law has been developed regarding the ownership and use of water, relatively little legal attention has been given to the question of the transfer of property rights in water from one use to another and from place to place. Since even the best pattern of use for any form of property or resource will become inefficient as population grows, some industries expand and others contract, etc., and since the market process is an exceptionally convenient device for shifting resources from less to more highly valued uses, transferability of rights through purcase and sale is crucial to securing continuous readaptation of the structure of use.

Although suited in principle to permit transfer of rights, the doctrine of appropriation as presently interpreted or adopted is ordinarily associated with a number of limitations that interfere with sale or exchange and thus introduce undesirable rigidity of water use. A few states even prohibit the transfer of water from the land and the use for which it was originally appropriated.[48] The water law of Arizona requires special approval from the state water commissioner for a change of use. Wyoming law provides that water rights to a stream cannot be transferred from the land, place, or purpose of use without loss of priority. In such cases the water right may become frozen to a particular piece of land and to a particular use (except when it becomes impractical to continue the use for one reason

[48] Wells A. Hutchins, *Selected Problems in the Law of Water Rights in the West* (U.S. Department of Agriculture, Miscellaneous Pub. 418 [Washington, D.C., 1942]), pp. 378 ff.

or another) even though the value of the water on alternative lands or in alternative uses might be considerably greater. Fortunately, such complete restrictions are not the rule, but most states do have limitations on transfer of appropriative rights that serve to hinder market allocation and thereby reduce economic efficiency.

Trelease believes that the purpose or origin of these restrictive provisions was a desire to prevent abuses in the transfer of water rights: "Many early adjudications gave the irrigators far more water than they really needed, so that the appropriator not infrequently sold his unused water to which he really had no right."[49] The abuse, if any exists here, lies not in the transfer of the right but in its initial grant. It may well have been the case that the original irrigator applied for more water than he really "needed" or should have received, but that is a past mistake—the result of the means adopted to encourage development of resources in the past. (Had the government at the time wished to avoid this accrual of gain to private parties, instead of making free grants it could have auctioned off the water rights to the highest bidders, thus retaining or capturing the discounted value of the future gain from holding "excessive" water rights.) However arbitrary the method of initially establishing property rights, once they have been vested, efficiency can be achieved only if the recognized owners of the rights are permitted to put the water to its most productive use in terms of economic values. Note that an attempt to correct a past mistake in vesting property rights by simple deprivation or confiscation may have only distributional effects (except insofar as insecurity of rights affects incentives of others) but freezing the right to the original use of water has an adverse efficiency effect from which the community as a whole loses.

The question of reserving a water right for future needs is somewhat more complicated. As we have seen, there is nothing objectionable in a process by which any individual, firm, or city anticipating future needs provides for them by a reservation of sites, facilities, or water rights, providing that in this reservation a comparison is made between the present value of the returns from the reservation and its cost (primarily, the cost of depriving other users). This comparison is, of course, automatically made by market processes when prospective present or future users bid competitively for the resource. But it is a different matter in the case of California, for example, where state law allows municipalities to appropriate water in excess of present needs and at the same time gives municipalities first preference in being granted appropriations. Provision is made for the use of these reserved "excess" waters by temporary permit to interim users. In such cases the municipalities may recapture the excess waters upon payment of compensation for the loss of investment incurred by the temporary user. Despite the allowance for temporary use, it is clear that municipalities do not have to compete against alternative users for the water rights involved. In fact, because they do not have to bid for the rights, they have every incentive to reserve as much water as possible for "future" needs without the balancing offset of increases in cost. Under such conditions one can hardly argue that "blanket" reservations serve to promote efficient use of water resources.[50]

Another type of "blanket" reservation

[49] Trelease, "A Model State Water Code for River Basin Development," *op. cit.*, p. 315.

[50] It is doubtful if these blanket reservations for municipalities constitute water rights that are (legally) capable of being permanently transferred to non-municipal users. If reservations were actual rights, the municipality would be in a position similar to anyone holding a water right that is not currently being exercised. There is nothing to be deplored per se in the existence of unused water rights as long as the decision-maker rationally considers the economic advantage of selling the right as opposed to holding it.

is found in the California "county of origin" and "watershed of origin" statutes. Under these statutes sufficient waters are reserved to particular regions in order "adequately [to] supply the future beneficial needs of the area." The important thing to notice here is that the reservation is completely open-ended, so that the effect is to tie the water supply to a particular area. The determination of what constitutes the future beneficial needs of entire areas is an awesome task, indeed.

If one wished to preserve the "county of origin" concept and yet promote efficient use of water resources, it might be possible to provide for some adjudication or quantification of these vague open-ended rights to convert them into secure property. Once the rights were made certain, provision for the transfer of these rights through the market process would then allow an efficient allocation to develop. The county would always have the option of reserving these water rights for its future needs, but the real cost of doing this, of course, would be the income foregone from not selling part of its water rights.

The "county of origin" concept gave rise to one of the major sources of controversy between northern California and southern California concerning the Feather River Project—under which the State Department of Water Resources proposes to transport "surplus" waters from northern California to the more arid southern California areas. It is easy to understand why the northern California counties were reluctant to have some of their waters declared "surplus" by an administrative agency and transported for use outside the region without payment of compensation. If these water rights were certain and transferable, the acceptance of a formula like "county of origin" for vesting of rights would not freeze the water itself; the actual allocation of waters to various areas would be amenable to market influences and to economic bargaining. Apparently, the lack of certainty or transferability of water rights means that the allocation of water will be determined not by economic forces but rather by the political pressures present in the legislatures.

A third type of reservation exists in some western states where unappropriated waters are sometimes withdrawn from appropriation to preserve recreational or scenic values. Idaho and Oregon have followed such policies.[51] Although it may be desirable in many instances to preserve recreational and scenic values, it should be made clear to all concerned that the economic cost of the reservation is the foregoing of the economic worth of the water in its alternative uses. Because public scenic and recreational facilities are usually provided without cost to those who use them (and because market exchange of water rights is limited), there is no direct way of knowing whether the benefits to the users equal the cost of providing the service.

Restrictions upon the transfer of water rights, like those upon the transfer of any type of property, should be viewed with suspicion. As a general rule, all voluntary transfers of water rights should be permitted except in those cases where damage to third parties can be demonstrated. Normally, such damages could be dealt with by court action or by an administrative agency set up for this quasi-judicial function. Judicial procedures are more suitable for assessing damages and determining rights as established under relevant legislation than they are for stipulating the most economic pattern of water use.

The states of California and Colorado apparently provide for a great deal of flexibilty in the transfer of appropriative rights. In Colorado "the use of water is not limited to the land to which it was first applied and a water right may be alienated apart from the land, its use transferred from one

[51] Trelease, "A Model State Water Code for River Basin Development," *op. cit.*, p. 317.

place to another, or even the character of its use changed, so long as change does not result in the use of a larger quantity of water than the right calls for."[52] In California the appropriator is allowed to change the point of diversion, place of use, or character of use, provided the rights of other appropriators are not impaired.[53]

The requirement that the transfer of the right not injure third parties is correct and important. For example, a transfer of right might deprive downstream users of return flow. If the new use is actually more productive, it will be possible for the new user to pay compensation to the downstream users or provide alternative supplies of water to them. Presumably, under the laws of these states, adversely affected interests can insist on such arrangements being made.

Among the common restrictions upon the exercise of appropriative rights are those upon the place of use. Nebraska, New Mexico, and Texas place limitations upon taking water out of its "natural" watershed. Colorado, whose laws are so reasonable in many respects, has imposed restrictions upon the transportation of Colorado River water across the Continental Divide to eastern Colorado.

In early appropriations the right to transport waters across state lines was common and universally upheld.[54] Recently the tendency has been to restrict the use of water to intrastate locations, presumably in the interest of "local development." Colorado offers an extreme example in this regard because its statutes expressly prohibit the transportation of water found in Colorado outside its boundaries. Evidently, Colorado does not believe that its citizens are shrewd enough bargainers to receive sufficient value in return for the sale of water across the state line. One may wonder whether Colorado brewing interests (e.g., Adolph Coors Company of Golden, Colorado) may not actually violate state law by selling beer brewed in Colorado outside the state. Following this Colorado reasoning, the state of Texas should reconsider its policy of permitting the export of petroleum or natural gas outside state boundaries.

The states of Wyoming and Utah are somewhat more rational on this matter. In these states diversion and use of water outside the state is permitted if the state in which use is made grants reciprocal privileges or if the state legislature gives special and specific approval for each diversion.

Turning now to transfer under the riparian doctrine of water law, we have seen that, since the contiguity of the land and the water is the basis of the riparian right, use of water is normally restricted to riparian land. The general rule seems to be that a riparian has no right to use water on non-riparian land, nor can he sell such a right. The water right is tied to the ownership of land; the right is really part of a general property right in land and is not property itself. In some states, however, a riparian may sell land without the riparian right and thus reserve the water for use on the remaining lands retained by the riparian owner.

Fortunately, the laws of several states do introduce a small amount of flexibility in the use of water by non-riparians. In California, for example, a riparian may grant his right to another person who proposes to use the water on non-riparian land. The grant is not actually a transfer of the right:

> The riparian owner himself is not entitled to take water away to non-riparian land; and he cannot authorize another person to do what he himself has no right to do. But he can lawfully contract with another party that he will

[52] *Ibid.*, p. 314.

[53] Wells A. Hutchins, *The California Law of Water Rights* (Sacramento: Printing Division, State of California, 1956), p. 175.

[54] Trelease, "A Model State Water Code for River Basin Development," *op. cit.*, p. 305.

make no objection to the acts of that party in diverting water from the stream to non-riparian land.[55]

While such a contract is binding upon the agreeing parties, it is not binding upon other riparians on the stream. This qualification means that the non-riparian grantee will not be permitted to divert water to non-riparian lands if other riparians object to the transfer. A few states, however, do give full effect to the grant of riparian rights to non-riparians even against other riparians.[56] In all cases the grant is still subject to the interpretation of "reasonableness" as compared to the reasonable demands of other riparians.

3. *Fallacious Views of Water Law*

Many discussions of water law commonly end with a summary of the advantages and disadvantages of each of the major doctrines in an attempt to strike some sort of a balance. In our opinion the actual advantages and disadvantages of the riparian and appropriation doctrines are often just the reverse of the ones usually given. Perhaps it will be helpful to discuss some of these mistaken views.

Almost without exception the doctrine of appropriation is charged with inflexibility toward new uses, while riparian law is credited with promoting flexibility of use. The standard argument is that rights established by prior appropriation tend to favor the historical pattern of water use at the expense of new uses for water. On the other hand, it is stated that the riparian doctrine provides for flexibility toward new uses under the concept of "reasonable" use which allows the courts to modify use patterns. The alleged inferiority of appropriation law is based upon the implicit assumption that exchange of these rights between competing users is not permitted. It is true that many states place restrictions upon transfer of appropriative rights; nevertheless, they probably can be more easily transferred to new uses than can riparian rights. The alleged advantage of riparian doctrine in promoting flexibility of use is achieved by a judicial determination of "reasonableness" which in some cases involves taking water from existing users without compensation. Aside from the question of equity to existing users, neither judicial procedures nor the professional training of judges are particularly suited to the task of directing water resources to their most productive uses. The fact that under appropriation doctrine "new" users must purchase rights from "old" users is actually an advantage of the latter system. If the "new" user is not able to do so, then his prospective use is presumably not more productive than the old, however "reasonable" it might appear to a judge. Under judge-made allocation of water supplies there is no guaranty that water may not be shifted from more productive to less productive uses.

Another alleged disadvantage of the law of appropriation is that it may encourage waste. This charge makes sense only to the extent that water rights are non-transferable. Only then would a person with a fixed quota not have incentive to consider the value of water to alternative users. But, if the right can be transferred, wasting water will be less advantageous to the owner of the right than selling the water to a productive user.

One of the most plausible of the arguments used against the doctrine of appropriation is that it may lead to "waste" in a somewhat different sense. It is argued that strict obedience to priorities may sometimes lead to the need to maintain large upstream flows in order to protect a small, but senior, right located downstream. In the French-

[55] Wells A. Hutchins, *Irrigation Water Rights in California* (California Experiment Station, University of California, Circular 452, April, 1956), p. 22.

[56] Trelease, "A Model State Water Code for River Basin Development," *op. cit.*, p. 310.

man's Creek area of Colorado, for example, it is necessary to reduce upstream pumping by 100,000 acre-feet of water per year to protect downstream uses of 15,000 acre-feet; or at Beaver Creek an increase of pumping upstream by 20,000 acre-feet would reduce downstream flow by only 1,000 acre-feet.[57] The common reaction to such cases is that the doctrine of appropriation is unreasonable and that it is clearly against the public welfare.

Here again the solution could be provided by a functioning market in water rights. If the situation is really as described, the potential upstream user could follow several courses of action in order to make use of the water "lost" to maintain the senior downstream rights. One solution would be simply to purchase the downstream water rights. Or it might be possible to provide the downstream user with an alternative source of supply.[58] In some cases the major stumbling block may be the problem of organizing a number of upstream users to act as a group in achieving the desired action.

On the other hand, the doctrine of appropriation is often credited with an "advantage" that appears dubious to us. Consider the following excerpt taken from a discussion of the advantages of appropriation water law:

> Appropriation statutes can, and many of them do, provide restrictions on the right to appropriate water in the interest of the public welfare. Such restrictions have not yet included criteria based upon the character of the land; but there is no reason why the state could not provide that an application to appropriate water shall be rejected where the land proposed to be irrigated is poor, thus withholding the water in favor of later applicants for use on better land. The state grants the right to appropriate water, and it can certainly regulate the method of appropriation. This would be a proper exercise of its police power.[59]

What is implied here is that the doctrine of appropriation is desirable because it can provide a convenient instrument for state regulation of water rights and use of water. The basic economic question here is, of course, whether administrative officials are better qualified to achieve an efficient allocation of water resources than is the market process. In the case just cited, we would ask why the potential irrigators of better land are not making the application for water rights themselves? Or, if it is an oversight on their part, the opportunity always remains to buy out the right of the irrigator of poorer land.

4. Possible Problems

In our view, water law should treat water rights as private property with no restrictions upon the place or kind of use except for methods of dealing with damages inflicted upon outside parties. In the evaluation of current thinking in regard to water law we did not touch upon a number of problems with which water law must deal. Most of these problems are ones that are currently on the scene and may be somewhat more amenable to solution under a private property system of water law.

Because of the complex interdependence of water flows, it would be desirable to have a unified or master list of property rights for a common source of supply regardless of state lines. Interrelated supplies should not be treated as separate entities. This means that it would be preferable for the various states to have a common type of water law to avoid duplication in the defi-

[57] *Ibid.*, p. 311.

[58] Trelease takes a position similar to the one we have expressed: "The solution to the problem may be economic, in that if the benefits that would accrue from upstream use are, in fact, much greater than those realized by the senior appropriator, it would seem feasible for the upstream user to buy out the lower priority rights and transfer the use upstream" (*ibid.*, p. 306).

[59] Hutchins and Steele, *op. cit.*, p. 292

nition of water rights. The fugitive character of water resources discussed earlier creates important but not insurmountable problems for the development of property rights in water.

Another class of problems arises from failure to define the property right in terms of the full conditions of diversion. For example, a subsequent appropriator may reduce the level of ground water (or, in some cases, reduce stream flow) so as to increase the pumping lift to a senior appropriator downstream. Should the second appropriation be prohibited? The same problem arises in the pumping of ground water from a common basin when increased pumping on the part of one well-owner may increase the pumping lift to all. It is likely that no system of water law can deal with these types of spillover cost completely, but they can be handled in large part through the payment of compensation to damaged parties if property rights are clearly defined in the first place. Ideally, the water right should specify the conditions of diversion within proximate limits. This means that new appropriators should be required to pay compensation when the spillover costs upon senior users are substantial.

Most of the preceding discussion applies to the quality of the water as well as to the method of diversion. In some cases the quality of the water may be just as important as the quantity. If upstream users pollute or substantially reduce water quality to senior users downstream, measures should be taken either to reduce the spillover effects or to compensate senior users. Here, again, the solution is to specify the property right and to require the payment of damages when rights are violated.

A great deal of concern has been expressed for the problem of unused riparian water rights. These unused riparian rights represent property and, in most states, the owner is entitled to exercise them at his discretion. Such rights are not lost by nonuse. The presence of unused rights, each with an open-ended limitation governed by "reasonable" use, would constitute a serious obstacle to the development of the certainty necessary for an improved system of water law. Yet any attempt to abolish these rights might be an unconstitutional deprivation of property without due process of law.

What is needed here is a vesting or a definition of these rights by a process of adjudication so that the right becomes certain and clearly defined instead of being subject to shifting interpretation of "reasonable" use. Admittedly, the standard used in the adjudication process for defining the unused rights may be arbitrary in some respects—that is a question of distributive equity. From the efficiency point of view, the need is to create certainty in property rights, whatever their distribution may be, so that market forces can then allocate the resources to their most productive uses.

The price system, in itself, cannot provide the perfect answer to all questions or solve all problems in water use. It will not always be possible to develop private property rights and to use the market mechanism for the allocation of water supplies. Public action will be required not only to "establish the ground rules"—to define property rights and to facilitate market exchange—but also to deal with cases where the commonality of the situation makes collective action necessary. The difficulty of establishing rights and providing a market in terms of quality of water flow along a stream, for example, was pointed out earlier. On the other hand, the institutions of private property and the market system can be utilized to facilitate efficient use of water resources to a much greater extent than is usually recognized. Also, as we believe our historical and case studies show, the administrative or bureaucratic alternative to market processes is one which can scarcely be expected to function ideally either.

D. Current Trends in Water Law

1. The Eastern States

The growing use of water in recent years has resulted in increased attention to water law. It is not surprising that much of the discussion has taken place in the eastern states, where increasing dissatisfaction with the previously dominant riparian law is creating a movement for "modernization" of state water laws. Most of the discussion has dealt with the advisablilty of substituting for riparian law some form of appropriation law with "adequate protection of vested property rights."

If the changes being contemplated were mainly concerned with the problems of definition of property rights, of permitting transfers between uses by market transactions, and of handling spillover effects, we would be highly enthusiastic. However, the proposed changes are largely in the opposite direction. In other words, the trend is toward centralized control of water resources through use of priorities and administrative determination of what constitutes "reasonable and beneficial use."

Perhaps the outstanding example of the trend toward administrative control of water resources is found in the new law of water rights for the state of Iowa. The Water Rights Act of Iowa, which was established in 1957 with a unanimous vote by the legislature, declares:

> Water occurring in any basin or in any watercourse, or other natural body of water of the state, is hereby declared to be public waters and public wealth of the people of the State of Iowa and subject to use in accordance with the provisions of this Act, and the control and development and use of water for all beneficial purposes shall be in the state, which, in the exercise of its police powers, shall take such measures as shall effectuate full utilization and protection of the water resources of the State of Iowa.[60]

Essentially, the Iowa law decrees that the waters of the state belong to the people of the state and are therefore "public" in nature. The use of water is subject to regulation by an administrative tribunal known as the Iowa Natural Resources Council. Prospective users must apply to the council for a permit to use water. Certain uses are exempt from regulation, for example, municipal use as of May, 1957, and uses of less than 5,000 gallons a day. It is the responsibility of the tribunal to allocate water to its "greatest beneficial use."

Under this law the permits cannot be granted for a period of more than ten years. Apparently the ten-year limitation was established

> to make it possible to resolve the problems that will arise in this pioneer effort, and point clearly to the fact that *Iowa does not believe in granting water rights in perpetuity.* This periodic review will permit intelligent use of additional, much-needed data as they become available to meet changing conditions which inevitably must come.[61]

Although it is comforting to note that the law recognizes that change does occur and that flexibility is desirable, it would appear that the legislators (unanimously) possess a complete distrust or perhaps only lack of understanding of the ability of the market to adjust to changing conditions. A grant of perpetual rights under a property system does not perpetually freeze the uses of property, if a market in rights is permitted to operate. In the Iowa law the short-term duration of the permits and their seeming non-transferability weaken private property rights to the vanishing point. These two aspects will systematically reduce economic incentives for private investment in water development and, by preventing a market from functioning, will make the reliance on

[60] Quoted by Richard G. Ballard (water commissioner, Iowa Natural Resources Council), "The New Water Rights Law in Iowa," in "Ninety-eighth Meeting of Missouri Basin Inter-Agency Committee, Des Moines, Iowa, January 23, 1958," p. 2. (Mimeographed.)

[61] *Ibid.*, p. 5. (Italics ours.)

bureaucratic control and development of water resources virtually complete.

It should be emphasized that the type of thinking embodied in the new Iowa law of water rights has an excellent chance of being duplicated in a number of eastern states. In Massachusetts, for example, a state board has been created to prepare a "master plan" for the development and conservation of water resources.[62] Temporary permits for the use of water, issued by administrative boards, are already being used in Wisconsin, Minnesota, North Carolina, and Ohio.[63] These short-term permits are such weak and uncertain private property rights as to provide little incentive to the holder to make substantial investments in the development of water-supply facilities.

The states of Michigan, Wisconsin, Arkansas, North Carolina, and South Carolina are actively considering legistation involving comprehensive reconsideration of water law. In each case there is a strong possibility of a shift toward administrative control of water resources "to promote the fullest beneficial use of water and to prevent waste."[64]

Another illustration of the current trend of thinking on water law is provided by the "Model Water Use Act" recently approved by the National Conference of Commissioners on Uniform State Laws. The purpose of the act is to provide

> for a practicable new and modern system of water law. The administration is placed in a Commission instead of the courts. The two-party system of determining water use rights is eliminated. All due process safeguards have been preserved. The agency is given broad powers to provide for comprehensive development of the state's water resources within the framework of beneficial use. Domestic uses are exempted because the quantity of water consumed thereby is not sufficient to justify control.[65]

As one of the general statements of policy the Model Act declares: "The water resources of the State can best be utilized, conserved and protected if the utilization thereof is restricted to beneficial uses controlled by a state agency responsible for proper development and utilization of the water resources of the State."[66]

This policy statement is obviously written in general terms, so that it may be subject to a number of interpretations. It is evident, however, that one possible interpretation is that the state agency would (or could) substantially control by administrative decree all rights to develop and use water supplies. What the scope for the market process and for private decision-making in the allocation of water resources might be is not clear, but it can be noted that the act gives no positive assurances in this regard.

The wording of the act recognizes all existing diversions and uses as property rights. But, apparently, an "owner" cannot transfer his water right without securing a permit from the administrative commission—a very serious weakening of the right. New uses of water may be initiated *only* by obtaining permission from the commission in the form of a permit of limited duration. The commission is given the great responsibility of guaranteeing the "maximum beneficial use" of all the waters of the state.

The act provides that the commission shall have the power to require compulsory relinquishment of a water-use permit if "there exist one or more applicants for per-

[62] "Water Law in Eastern United States: A Symposium," *Journal American Water Works Association,* XLIX No. 6 (June, 1957), 722.

[63] Ellis, *op. cit.,* pp. 237–56.

[64] *Ibid.*

[65] National Conference of Commissioners on Uniform State Laws, *Model Water Use Act (Approved at Annual Conference, Los Angeles, California, August 18–23, 1958)* (Chicago, 1958), pp. 5–6.

[66] *Ibid.,* p. 8.

mits to make water uses which would be more beneficial" than the existing permit-holder is making.[67] The new applicant is required to furnish "reasonable" compensation to the old permit-holder. No guides are given as to what constitutes "more beneficial" use. The requirement of payment of compensation to the old water-user appears to be a desirable procedure. It might be pointed out, however, that "reasonable compensation" tends to take place automatically under contractual market exchange of private property rights.

It is of some importance here to distinguish between the proposed procedure under the Model Water Use Act and the principle of compulsory taking, with compensation, under eminent domain. The latter principle concerns condemnation *for a public use.* We regard it as a necessary power of government, though a dangerous one which should be carefully limited. Its necessity is obvious from the example of the problem of routing highways, where each property-owner along the route is in a powerful semimonopolistic position to demand an extremely high price (once the route has been selected, other properties purchased, etc.) far in excess of the value in use of the property to him. Here it is reasonable on distributive grounds to base compensation upon a judicial estimate of the value of the property to the user before the highway location decision was made. In the case of water supply, a large irrigation user may in some cases be in a monopolistic position in regard to a city wishing to purchase his supply for municipal use, so that compulsory taking with compensation at nonmonopolistic value is justifiable. But note that, in contrast, the Model Act proposes to universalize the dangerous principle of compulsory taking of property *for private uses* as well as public, the commission to decide who gives up the water supply and who gets it and what the "reasonable" compensation required may be. Aside from the substantial impairment of freedom involved, it is difficult to see why a commission would be expected to be superior to the market in assigning water resources to their "most beneficial" uses.

[67] *Ibid.,* Sec. 410, p. 38.

The rather arbitrary discretion proposed for the commission should certainly be a matter of some concern. By failing to set forth basic criteria, other than vague generalities, for the decisions of the commission, the Model Act is an invitation to corruption and might become an instrument of dictatorial control. In any event, it is clear that a commission like that envisaged would reduce the exercise of local and private initiative in the development of water resources.

2. *The Western Position*

Actually, state ownership and control of water resources is not uncommon in the West. Although it appears that the trend in the eastern states may be in that direction, it is probably just as important to emphasize the extent to which the philosophy of government control of water resources is already accepted (apparently) in almost all western states:

> In Wyoming, Montana, Idaho, North Dakota, and Texas the water is declared to be the property of the state; in California the property of the people of the state. In Arizona, Colorado, Nebraska, Nevada, New Mexico, South Dakota, Oregon, Utah, and Washington, the waters are the property of the public. Kansas, with the newest declaration, seems to have the weakest of all, merely dedicating all waters to the use of the people of the state. In Nebraska the constitution dedicates the use of the water to the people of the state, though the statutes declare the water to be the property of the public. In most of these states the declaration relates to all waters (at least those in watercourses), but in Colorado and New Mexico (and formerly Oklahoma) the declaration was limited to unappropriated water.[68]

[68] Frank J. Trelease, "Government Ownership and Trusteeship of Water," in Committee on Re-

Perhaps the major question raised by such declarations of public ownership of water resources in state constitutions or statutes is whether the language is an innocuous form of words to indicate that the state has an interest in water-resource development, or whether the language actually means what (in extreme cases) it says, that is, that the state "owns" the water. The latter interpretation not only is at variance with existing laws of the same states permitting private property rights in water but may also violate (if enforced against existing owners of water rights) the due-process clause of the federal Constitution. [69] The primary effect of such declarations will probably be not to abolish all private water rights but to transform them into uncertain tenure arrangements subject to administrative or judicial determination of "reasonableness."

The current trend, in sum, runs strongly against the development of a system of water law based upon individual choice and the market mechanism. However, we do not regard this trend as representing a deliberate social decision beyond the scope of criticism on our part. Rather, we think the evidence is fairly clear that the tenor of the legislative and judicial edicts we have reviewed is a product of the ignorance of even importantly placed and generally well-informed individuals today about the functioning of economic systems—and, in particular, it is a product of the common though incorrect opinion that the public interest can be served only by political as opposed to market allocation processes (see chap. iv). That there are defects in present systems of private water rights is very clear; but to abolish property rights rather than cure the defects is a drastic and, we believe, unwise remedy.

3. *Recent Federal Cases*

Relations between federal powers and state laws regarding water rights have become a source of uneasiness in recent years. Several important Supreme Court decisions have served to strengthen the position of the federal government and to create uncertainty with respect to state water law and individual rights to water.

The Pelton Dam decision is probably the best-known example of the trend.[70] In this case the Supreme Court held that the Federal Power Commission could license a hydroelectric power project on a non-navigable stream despite the objections of the state of Oregon that this action was contrary to state law. The Court observed that the dam was to be constructed on reserved federal lands. The basis of the decision was that the power of the federal government to administer its own property is not subject to state control. Students of constitutional law believe that the Pelton Dam case raises serious questions with regard to state law and private property rights in areas where federal lands are involved.[71]

Less than three weeks after the Pelton Dam decision, the fears of those who viewed the case with alarm were partially realized. At the time the Pelton Dam case was being presented the Naval Ammunition Depot at Hawthorne, Nevada, secured permits from the state engineer of Nevada to dig six wells at the depot in compliance with Nevada law.[72] In order to secure final approval of the permits, the Navy was re-

search in Water Resources, University of California, *Legal Problems in Water Resources* (1957), p. 89. Footnote citations and references by Trelease are omitted.

69 This criticism does not apply to those states (Colorado and New Mexico) asserting state ownership only of unappropriated water—a much more reasonable position.

70 *Federal Power Commission* v. *Oregon,* 349 U.S. 435 (1955).

71 Charles E. Corker, "The Western Water Rights Settlement Bill of 1957," in Committee on Research in Water Resources, University of California, *Legal Problems in Water Resources* (1957), pp. 41–46.

72 *Ibid.,* pp. 52–54.

quired to pay a fee of $1.00 and to fill out a statement giving intention of beneficial use of the water, no problems or complications being evident. The Pelton Dam decision was given, and suddenly (in three weeks' time) the Navy withdrew its application and forfeited the permits for the six wells. It is likely that the commandant of the depot had received instructions to withdraw the application on the grounds that the wells were to be located on reserved federal lands and that the Pelton Dam decision made federal powers paramount in regard to its own property.

The issue here appears to be clear cut. The state of Nevada was willing to grant permission for the construction of the wells. The question is whether the federal government has to comply with Nevada law by securing a permit to dig and operate the wells. If the federal government does not have to comply with state law in such cases, the whole structure of water law in many western states may be in need of re-examination. The issues become quite serious when it is realized that the reserved land of the federal government constitutes many millions of acres in the West. Reserved lands of the federal government include public land devoted to military reservations, Indian reservations, national parks and forests, power-site withdrawals, wilderness areas, and wildlife refuges.

In what is commonly known as the Hawthorne case, the state of Nevada brought suit in the federal courts in an attempt to require the Navy to comply with Nevada's water laws.[73] Six western states supported Nevada in the case.[74] In August, 1958, the United States district judge dismissed the action, however, and ruled that the federal government did not have to comply with Nevada water laws. The tenor of the opinion is indicated by the following statement taken from the case:

> Both on reason and, as we shall see in a moment, on authority, this Court is forced to the conclusion that there is no mandate in Constitutional, statutory, or decisional law that compels the Federal Government to bend its knee to this type of state law and regulation, whether it be arbitrary or benign.[75]

It is quite probable that Nevada authorities will appeal the case, so that the final outcome is still in doubt.

An equally well-known (and interesting) action involving the question of whether the federal government is required to comply with state water law is the Fallbrook case, currently being considered by a federal district court in southern California.[76] The Fallbrook action deals with a dispute between the Fallbrook Public Utility District (and several thousand individual landowners) and the federal government over the rights to the Santa Margarita River. The federal government wishes to use the water on the United States Marine Training Base at Camp Pendleton. In an extension of the Pelton Dam doctrine, federal authorities have made sweeping claims to the waters of the river that conflict with long-established water rights developed under California water laws.

In sharp contrast with the ruling in the Hawthorne case, the district court has held in the Fallbrook case in a comprehensive pretrial opinion that "the rights of the United States to the waters of the Santa Margarita River for use on Camp Pendleton will be determined by the same rules that apply to any private individual, and that the extent of the rights of the United

[73] *Nevada ex rel. Shamberger, State Engineer* v. *United States.*

[74] California, Nebraska, North Dakota, South Dakota, Washington, and Wyoming.

[75] Quoted by Porter A. Towner, chief counsel, California Department of Water Resources, in *Western Water News,* X, No. 10 (October, 1958), 4.

[76] *United States* v. *Fallbrook Public Utility District,* 165 F. Supp. 806 (S.D. Calif., 1958).

States will be determined by State law."[77] Because of the importance of the issues involved, it seems obvious that the Fallbrook case will eventually be appealed to higher courts.

From several cases relating to federal control over navigable waters has come another source of strain in regard to federal-state relations. One student of the problem believes that an elastic definition of what constitutes "navigation" has been used to increase federal control over water resources:

> The difficulty arising in the cases is that both the Congress and the courts have been content to treat the word "navigation" as an open sesame to constitutionality. So long as Congress uses the word in a statute and the case relates to something moist, the court takes at face value the declaration that the legislation is in furtherance of navigation. Moreover, the test of what constitutes a navigable stream has been stretched to embrace most of the water in the United States.[78]

Two cases are important in this area. In the Washington Department of Game decision,[79] the Supreme Court used the concept of a fictitious navigable purpose to permit the federal government to override state law designed to protect salmon spawning. Two years later, in the Twin City Power Company case,[80] the government took private property rights without compensation under the doctrine of a fictitious declaration of a navigable purpose.

A third area of federal-state conflict may be found in the administration of Indian water rights. The federal government takes the position that, when the Indian reservations were established, there was an implied water right granted to the reservations sufficient to irrigate the Indian lands to their "ultimate" development.[81]

The claim that the reservations are guaranteed sufficient water for their ultimate usage is clearly open-ended. Who can say what "ultimate" needs are without consideration of cost-price relationships, and when all we can be sure of is that the future is uncertain? Because the Indian claims for water are undefined and uncertain, the water rights of an entire area or watershed may be similarly uncertain. The fact is that the historical use of water by the Indian tribes has never been large, with the result that most western waters have already been put to use by other persons under appropriative rights granted by state laws.

Until a few years ago the legality of non-Indian water use on streams adjacent to Indian reservations was not in question, as open-ended Indian water rights had never been claimed. The whole issue came to light, however, in the *Arizona* v. *California* suit over Colorado River water tried before a special master in San Francisco. In this case the federal government intervened to advance claims to Colorado River water for the purpose of irrigating Indian lands in Arizona, California, Nevada, Utah, and New Mexico.

These claims are based upon the "ultimate" needs of the lands and are many times the amount of water ever actually used on the lands. Several of the reservations in question do not now have any Indians in residence, and the Indian population on the other lands has declined sharply in recent years.[82] If the claims for

77 "Pre-trial Opinion Blasts United States' Claims," *Western Water News,* X, No. 9 (September, 1958), 1.

78 Corker, *op. cit.,* p. 48.

79 *Washington Department of Game* v. *Federal Power Commission,* 347 U.S. 936 (1954). See also *City of Tacoma* v. *Taxpayers of Tacoma,* 357 U.S. 320 (1958).

80 *United States* v. *Twin City Power Company,* 350 U.S. 22 (1956).

81 The basic case in this area is *Winters* v. *United States,* 207 U.S. 564 (1908).

82 As one interesting sidelight, the federal government claims a water right for the Fort Mohave Indian Reservation with priority date of 1870. The justification for the priority is that in 1870 President Grant signed an executive order reserving

Indian lands advanced by the federal government are sustained, Colorado River water rights of long standing will be placed in jeopardy, and the problem of allocating the waters in an already "overappropriated" river will be intensified. Of equal importance is the fear that the same open-ended principle of Indian water rights may soon create problems of water rights where other Indian reservations are involved.

Attempts are being made currently to deal with the problem of federal-state relations in regard to water rights. Several bills have been introduced in the United States Congress by western congressmen with the principal aim of safeguarding state water rights and subjecting federal agencies to state water laws.[83] However, previous efforts to enact federal legislation on this matter have not been successful. In this connection it should be emphasized that there is no federal water law as such. Existing water law as it applies to the development of property rights is state law. The issue is whether the federal government must submit its claims to water to the same rules that apply to other users or is to be free from all local regulation, however ill or well advised.

E. Concluding Remarks and Suggestions for Improvement

This chapter has been concerned with a survey and evaluation of decision processes in the use and development of water resources. We have stressed two alternatives: (1) government decision-making through the use of centralized administrative or judicial action or (2) decentralized decision-making through the use of the institutions of the market and private property. Each process has its special advantages and disadvantages, and each has a role to play in the efficient development of water resources. We do feel, however, that insufficient attention has been given to the role the price system can play in determining the efficient use of water resources. Our analysis of state water law, for example, has shown that it would be desirable to increase the scope of individual decision-making and to permit greater development of the market process.

Our survey of federal water-resource expenditures confirmed the views of critics who have maintained that water-resource projects frequently or even typically do not yield enough benefits to pay the costs. For example, the Corps of Engineers and the Bureau of Reclamation construct and operate projects on a subsidized basis, and apparently the trend is toward continuation of this record on an increasing scale. It is quite possible that huge reclamation projects, large dams and canals, and massive river-basin planning may be taking on many of the characteristics of national "pyramids" or "monuments."

Our study examined the appropriation and riparian doctrines of water law. While the law of appropriation as presently interpreted is subject to a number of defects, it can be modified to provide the basis of an improved system of water law based upon clearly defined property rights, transferable by market processes so that the water can find its most productive use. The riparian doctrine is ill suited to the development of transferable property rights in water resources, the rights being so ill defined and uncertain that major reliance must be placed upon judicial judgment for the allocation of water supplies to efficient uses as circumstances change. Recently proposed or even enacted changes in eastern water law in some cases approach abolition of the property system in favor of centralized decision-making processes for allocat-

---

the real estate for a military fort designed to defend the country *against* the Indians. There are no Indians on this reservation (personal communication from Mr. Charles E. Corker, July 9, 1959).

[83] See "States' Rights Recognized," *Western Water News,* XI, No. 4 (April, 1959), 1.

ing water, the new Iowa law of water rights being the leading example. In general, recent years have seen a strong trend toward increased bureaucratic control of water resources, and, in our opinion, the pendulum has swung much too far in this direction.

The best that can be said here, about either the recent or the long-standing enactments of the various states, is that their bark has probably been worse than their bite. Despite the sweeping "socialist" language of some of the constitutional amendments and water codes, theory has not yet been (and very likely never will be) matched by practice. In some states, for example, commissions with very broad discretionary powers in theory have adopted the procedure, which we strongly approve, of not exercising this discretion and instead automatically granting all requests for transfer of rights in the absence of objections from injured third parties.

Many writers seem to agree that there is a great deal of room for improvement in the decision-making process at the public level, not only in water-resource development, but in all types of government expenditure.[84] All we can do here is to sketch out in brief fashion some suggestions which we believe will secure more efficiency in public water development. Our firm belief is that careful economic evaluation can make a significant contribution to rational decision-making by forcing the persons concerned to give systematic attention to the alternatives involved. We believe that the failure to achieve efficiency in the use of water resources stems in large part from a widespread feeling on the part of public officials and laymen alike that "water is different," that is, that water is different from other resources in the sense that economic principles of resource allocation do not apply in the case of water. Until and unless it is appreciated that water resources do not in themselves lead to magical growth of wealth, that water is not something "holy" or "sacred," and that water resources are subject to the same economic forces that govern the use of all other economic resources, there may be little progress in the direction of efficiency in the use of water.

With the foregoing in mind we believe that the following general suggestions have some promise for improving government water-resource investment decisions, now primarily undertaken at the federal level but also by state governments to some extent (California being the leading example).

1. Steps should be taken to increase the amount of local and regional responsibility for water-resource development. These efforts should include not only increased local planning and operation but also increased local financial participation. The level of government involved in project development should more closely approximate the scope of the operation involved. Federal payment for and operation of water projects that are purely local in character seems to us not only dubious in terms of redistribution of wealth from taxpayers to beneficiaries but also dangerous because of the temptation for prospective beneficiaries of inefficient projects to band together at the expense of the taxpayer.

2. One of the strongest safeguards against uneconomic projects would be to have the costs of development repaid with interest by the direct beneficiaries of the project. Such a requirement would undoubtedly have a cooling influence upon the ardor of those advocating uneconomic projects. If subsidies are to be granted by a public agency, they should be made explicit and open, so that who will be subsidized and who will pay the bill are known to the decision-makers and to the electorate.

3. Provision should be made for the reimbursement of cost to private firms (and

[84] For a generalized analysis see Arthur Smithies, *The Budgetary Process in the United States* (New York: McGraw-Hill Book Co., 1955).

to other agencies) when these firms provide benefits that may be deemed public in nature (e.g., wildlife preservation or navigation improvements). Developers of upstream facilities should also be compensated for benefits produced downstream. If such reimbursement is provided, it will be possible to co-ordinate activities of groups overlying a common ground basin or operating within a given watershed without total government control or operation of the interrelated resource system.

4. In federal or state water-investment decisions, account should be taken of the principles and recommendations outlined in chapters vi and vii. Most importantly, projects or portions of projects should not be built unless the benefits promise to exceed the costs; for separable extensions or additions to projects, cost and benefits should be evaluated according to the incremental principle; and efficiency calculations in terms of present worths or annual net benefits should use an interest rate allowing for project risk and taxes burdening comparable projects in the private sphere, a figure in the neighborhood of 10 per cent being a reasonable estimate under recent (1959) capital market conditions.

With regard to the improvement of state water law, we suggest the following:

1. The recent line of "reform" of state water law in the direction of providing for total administrative control of private water uses, as in the Iowa Water Rights Act or the Model Water Use Act, should be abandoned. The all-powerful water commission envisaged under such legislation will be tempted to exercise its discretion arbitrarily or dictatorially; it will constitute a natural target of pressure by corrupt influences seeking the gifts only the commission can grant; and, most importantly of all, the commission in its function of allocating water resources to efficient uses cannot have the detailed knowledge or capacity to integrate that knowledge possessed by the alternative allocation process —decentralized decision-making co-ordinated through the market.

2. To facilitate the functioning of a market in water, there should be established a system of water law, based upon the appropriation doctrine, which provides for clearly defined and certain property rights in water (including, where relevant, such attributes as water quality, timing of withdrawals, mode of discharge, etc.). It should be possible for individuals, firms, or public agencies to hold property rights in water that are unambiguous in scope and certain in tenure.

3. Water law should provide a clear basis for the firm transfer of secure water rights between individuals, firms, and public agencies under voluntary agreements of purchase and sale. Compulsory transfer of water rights to public agencies should be carried out only by condemnation proceedings that involve the payment of fair compensation.

4. Water law should regulate otherwise free market transactions by recognizing, where it exists, commonality or interdependency of use which involves divergence between private and social costs. Devices to protect third parties from the spillover actions of water-right owners in such situations may include the establishment of zoning restrictions, assignment of quota rights to common pools, the imposition of "use" taxes, and the payment of compensation for damages inflicted.

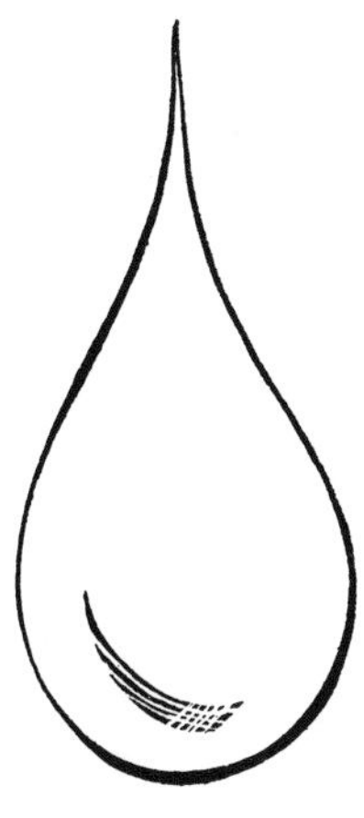

CHAPTER X

NEW YORK'S "WATER CRISIS": CASE STUDY OF A CRUCIAL DECISION

The basic purpose of this chapter is to illustrate the relevance of the principles of choice discussed earlier for one important recent municipal water-supply decision: that of the city of New York in 1955 to build the Cannonsville dam and reservoir project as the third stage of the city's Delaware water system (Fig. 20). Most municipal water-supply decisions are made with relatively little informed public discussion of the pros and cons, though often dissenting outsiders may come forward with alternative schemes. Proponents of alternatives to "official" plans almost never justify them by detailed analyses of costs and returns, but for that matter even the official proposals ordinarily lack such justification. In the particular case under discussion, however, there happened to be in existence a temporary committee of independent experts—convened for a different purpose—which, when consulted on the immediate issue of augmentation of New York's water supplies, produced a report making public an unusual amount of information about both the official proposal and the alternatives to it. Our analysis here will attempt primarily to discover what was the economically correct choice for the city to make in the circumstances—that is, which alternative made the best use of the resources available to the city. We will not concern ourselves with the social, political, and administrative pressures that may have influenced, for good or bad, the process of actual decision.

A. New York's Water Problem in the Postwar Period

In 1949 and 1950 New York City went through a water crisis. Everyone knew of the water shortage, though scarcely any could tell unambiguously what, if anything, a water shortage might be.[1] Historically, what had happened was that rising population, and an upward trend in average use rate reaching 150 gallons per capita per day (gpcd) in 1948, had made consumption exceed the safe or dependable water-system yield (see Table 25).

This was not in itself catastrophic; "safe yield" is a conservative measure of availability ordinarily defined as a level of system output so low as to be attained only once in a hundred years of normal weather

[1] See the discussion of "shortages" in chap. i.

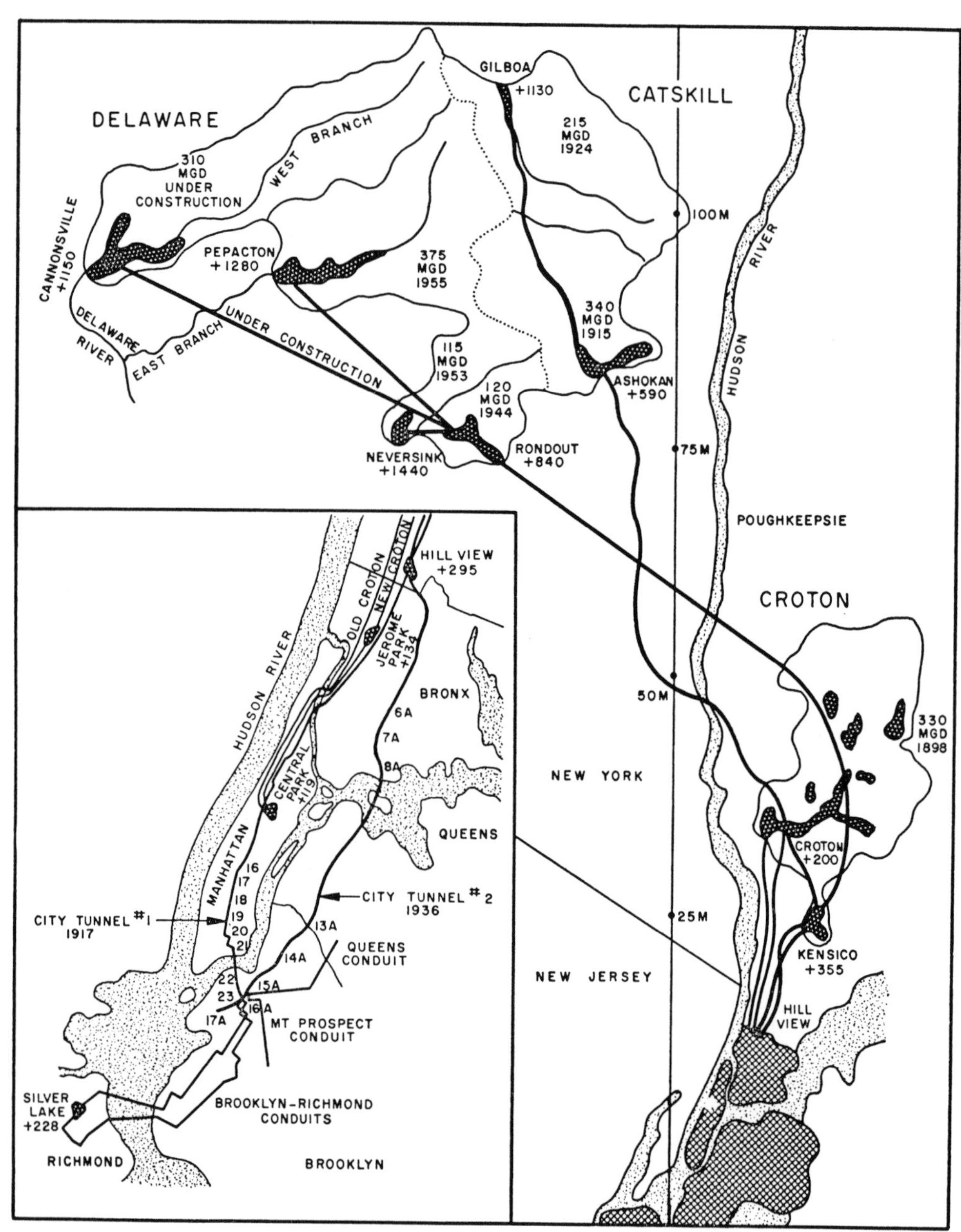

Fig. 20.—New York water-supply system, 1955 (major elements). (From Board of Water Supply, *1,820,000,000 Gallons per Day* [New York, 1955], pp. 6–7.)

variation. But poor rainfall in 1949 reduced the available yield below current withdrawals, with a consequent drop in reservoir levels and a near prospect of actual dry faucets. Water-conservation measures were introduced in October, 1949, involving both voluntary and compulsory restrictions on use. The restrictions were not removed until September, 1950; they appear to have reduced total water consumption by perhaps as much as 300 million gallons per day (mgd),[2] close to 25 per cent of the pre-conservation total. Another measure taken was the rapid construction of a plant for withdrawing 100 mgd from the Hudson River below Poughkeepsie; because of the poor quality of the river water, this facility was not to be used except in emergencies. In addition, the prospective completion of the Rondout-Neversink first stage of New York's Delaware Project in 1951–52 promised to help solve the immediate crisis by supplying about 200 mgd safe yield of additional water. Furthermore, completion of the East Branch second stage of the project, scheduled for 1956, was expected to provide a comfortable margin of 375 mgd more.

The agency charged with securing new water sources for the city, the Board of Water Supply (BWS), began at this time to press for approval of a West Branch third stage to the Delaware Project—the Cannonsville Dam and Reservoir and associated aqueduct—although this construction could not help in the current crisis. The Cannonsville Project was to provide about 310 mgd additional of safe yield, at a capital cost of $140 million. During 1950 two other proposals were made for securing additional long-term water for the city. One was the Beck proposal for construction of a dam with navigation locks on the lower Hudson, with use of the water above the dam for municipal supply. The other was an Incodel (Interstate Commission on the Delaware) plan which would have employed the Cannonsville site as part of an integrated scheme for use of the Delaware River system.

In view of the serious questions raised

TABLE 25*

CONSUMPTION AND AVAILABILITY OF WATER, NEW YORK CITY, 1946–53

Year	City Population	City Consumption (mgd)†	Per Capita Consumption (gpcd)	City Plus Non-City Consumption (mgd)‡	System Safe Yield (mgd)§	Surplus of Safe Yield over Consumption (mgd)
1946	7,664,000	1,117.1	145.8	1,143.6	1,055	− 88.6
1947	7,772,000	1,159.0	149.1	1,191.4	1,055	−136.4
1948	7,815,000	1,172.3	150.0	1,203.9	1,055	−148.9
1949	7,859,000	1,166.9	148.5	1,203.8	1,055	−148.8
1950	7,906,000	953.3	120.6	982.8	1,055	72.2
1951	7,963,000	1,041.9	130.8	1,070.6	1,120‖	49.4
1952	8,021,000	1,087.0	135.5	1,120.3	1,120‖	− 0.3
1953	8,078,000	1,093.9	135.4	1,139.3	1,250‖	110.7

* Source: New York City Department of Water Supply, Gas, and Electricity (DWSGE) table provided authors in 1958, except for last two columns.

† Includes around 50 mgd from private companies.

‡ Total city consumption plus amounts supplied by city system to non-city areas.

§ Source: New York City Board of Water Supply (BWS), *1,820,000,000 Gallons per Day* (New York, 1955), pp. 10–11. Includes 40 mgd from private companies.

‖ Excludes 100 mgd from the emergency pumping plant on the Hudson River.

[2] 1 mgd = 1,121 acre-feet per year. In this chapter only, the standard measure of deliveries will be million gallons per day rather than acre-feet per year.

by these alternatives to the BWS proposal, the mayor asked his Committee on Management Survey to examine the question of water-supply policy. This committee, popularly known as the "Little Hoover Commission," was a temporary group of distinguished citizens who had been asked to investigate the administrative efficiency of the various operations being carried on by the city. For this particular assignment the committee was able to secure the services of four nationally known water-supply experts, constituting the Committee's Engineering Panel on Water Supply.[3] The report of this panel, dated July, 1951, represents undoubtedly the most impressive and informative study of a municipal water-supply problem ever made public.[4]

The recommendations of the panel were highly controversial. Stated briefly, they opposed all the existing proposals, including the officially supported Cannonsville Project of the BWS. The major conclusions of the panel were: (1) that there was no immediate need for further construction; (2) that elimination of leakage and waste from street mains could perhaps save 150 mgd at nominal cost and should be vigorously pursued; (3) that the question of metering should be given prompt study, in the hope of achieving a substantial further saving of water at reasonable cost—a result which had been achieved in a number of other cities; (4) that, when it became necessary to begin developing new sources, the city would find the most economical source to be water from the Hudson River, secured by pumping from a point upstream of Poughkeepsie; (5) and that all city water including the Delaware supply should be subjected to filtration.[5]

The report of the Engineering Panel on Water Supply was met by heated official opposition, although no documented answers to its recommendations were ever made public. In the unusual administrative organization of New York City for water supply, the Board of Water Supply is exclusively charged with procuring water. An entirely separate organization, the Department of Water Supply, Gas, and Electricity (DWSGE), is responsible for distributing the water to users within the city. Consequently, the panel's recommendations concerning waste detection and metering fell into the province of DWSGE, while those involving need for new construction, future sources, and the question of filtration primarily affected BWS.

The BWS, in its reply,[6] did not address itself to the question of the need for new construction. Instead, it maintained the superiority of the proposed upland source to Hudson water, primarily on grounds of quality but also in terms of financial calculations. The board also argued that filtration of the city supply would not be necessary in the absence of the low-quality Hudson water. The DWSGE strongly concurred with BWS on the undesirability of the Hudson proposal in view of poor water quality and on the lack of necessity for filtration if the Hudson water were not used.[7] The department agreed with the

[3] The panel consisted of Dean Thorndike Saville, chairman, and Messrs. W. W. Horner, L. R. Howson, and Abel Wolman.

[4] *Future Water Sources of the City of New York: Report of Engineering Panel on Water Supply to Mayor's Committee on Management Survey of the City of New York* (New York, July, 1951) (hereinafter cited as "*Panel Report*").

[5] *Panel Report,* pp. 77–81.

[6] This was in the form of a letter from the board dated October 30, 1951, addressed to Mr. Bernard F. Gimbel, chairman, Subcommittee for Water Supply, Mayor's Committee on Management Survey. The letter was supported by a document entitled "Cost Estimates of Proposed Water Supply Projects," prepared by the Engineering Bureau, New Sources Division of the BWS, and dated October 29, 1951 (hereinafter cited as "BWS, 'Cost Estimates' [1951]"). These documents were not published, but we were permitted to examine them at the offices of the BWS.

[7] The views of DWSGE were expressed in a document entitled "Analysis of 'Report of Engineering Panel on Water Supply,'" dated May

panel's views on the desirability of expanded efforts to control leakage from street mains and also on extension of metering—both of which were in line with previous recommendations of DWSGE. On the matter of urgency of new construction, the department's analysis indicated that, even failing adoption of the proposals to control waste and extend metering, consumption would not reach the safe yield until 1970. The DWSGE consumption forecast was in fact lower than the panel's, in effect supporting the view that there was no urgent indication for new construction.

The final outcome in terms of actual decisions was in opposition to every recommendation of the panel's report, even those concurred in by DWSGE. Whereas the panel assumed that the new source, whichever was adopted, would become available in 1968 (an assumption consistent with the Board of Water Supply's own estimates of consumption growth), construction on Cannonsville was actually begun in 1955, with completion planned for 1961 or 1962. And this was true despite the fact that later data becoming available indicated that actual consumption was falling short of both the BWS and the panel forecasts. No further efforts have been made to detect and eliminate waste, aside from those procedures already in effect before the panel's study. Metering has not been extended, nor has there been any apparent further consideration of filtering the upland supplies.

The sections that follow will attempt to present a detailed analysis of the economic issues involved in the history we have just reviewed. First, conforming with our approach throughout, we will study the economics of possible improvements in the use of existing supplies, and afterward we will turn to an examination of the alternative proposals for developing additional supplies for the city.

12, 1952 (hereinafter cited as "DWSGE, 'Analysis,' [1952]"). This document was not published, but a copy is in the New York Public Library.

B. On Improving Use of Existing Supplies

One of the reasons, perhaps, why the rationalization of existing uses has not seemed urgent to New York City's water planners is that the rate of per capita use has not seemed high in comparison with other cities. The 1949 New York figure of 146 gpcd was equal to the 1955 mean water production reported in Table 7 (chap. ii) for cities of over 500,000 population. In comparison with eight other large cities, New York's per capita consumption is lower than any with the exception of Boston (see Table 26).

TABLE 26*

WATER CONSUMPTION IN LEADING AMERICAN CITIES, 1949

City	Consumption (gpcd)
Boston	116
New York	146
Los Angeles	149
Detroit	155
Baltimore	161
Philadelphia	164
St. Louis	175
Cleveland	181
Chicago	234

* Source: *Panel Report*, p. 13.

These figures are rather misleading, however, as there are a number of reasons why water use in New York City should be unusually low. First, New York is not a very heavily industrialized city, relatively speaking (see Table 27), and such industry as is contained within the city limits is not of the heavily water-using type.[8] Industrial use typically accounts for large fractions

[8] Aside from steam-electric power, major water-using industries (both in terms of total water used and intensity of use per dollar of value added) are steel, oil-refining, and paper and pulp. Except for steam-electric power, New York City does not figure importantly in any of these industries. New York's manufacturing is concentrated in the apparel trade and light assembly work, neither of which uses water heavily. As for steam power, New York's standing here is roughly proportionate to its importance in population and industry.

of over-all water consumption in cities (irrigation is important in Los Angeles). Furthermore, watering of lawns and gardens is characteristically responsible for a significant share of residential use, and New York is, of course, predominantly a city of apartment dwellers. On the other side of the scale, it should be mentioned that New York has at any given time a large commuting and tourist population using water, but such consumption is limited almost entirely to the small amounts associated with strictly personal needs.[9] In their discussion of this question, the Engineering Panel indicated that the per capita consumption figure for New York City should not exceed, on a well-managed basis, 100 gpcd.[10]

The Engineering Panel pointed to three main areas for improving the use of existing supplies. The first was leakage from street mains; a historical survey of use data in comparison with figures available from other cities suggested that a saving of from 100 to 200 mgd—10–20 per cent of total apparent consumption—was possible with an expanded detection and correction program. The second area was the tendency toward underregistration of meters, which would be relevant for the fraction of over-all water service transmitted through meters. In 1950 this was roughly 25 per cent of the total, comprising essentially all service to commercial and industrial users plus some fraction of service to residential users. Correction of this underregistration would not directly save water, but it was expected to lead to an increased recording and payment for about 40 mgd, with a likely consequence of more economical use by metered consumers. A still larger area for improvement, in the opinion of the panel, was waste on the premises of unmetered consumers. The panel here estimated an apparent purely domestic use

TABLE 27*

IMPORTANCE OF MANUFACTURING ACTIVITY IN LARGEST UNITED STATES CITIES

City	U.S. Rank in Population	Population, 1950 (000's)	All Employees, Manufactures 1947 (000's)	Per Cent of City Population Engaged in Manufactures
New York	1	7,892	933	11.8
Chicago	2	3,621	668	18.4
Philadelphia	3	2,072	328	15.8
Los Angeles	4	1,970	167	8.5
Detroit	5	1,850	340	18.4
Baltimore	6	950	121	12.7
Cleveland	7	915	211	23.1
St. Louis	8	857	173	20.2
Washington	9	802	18	2.2
Boston	10	801	101	12.6

* Source: U.S. Bureau of the Census, *County and City Data Book, 1956*.

9 Unfortunately, New York City is extremely backward in collection of water-use statistics, and the typical analyses by type of use which other cities make are unavailable for New York—even as to the crudest distinction among residential, industrial, and commercial uses. We cannot, therefore, determine statistically which categories of use might be out of line with use rates observed in other cities.

10 *Panel Report*, p. 21.

of 80 gpcd or even more, of which perhaps 50 per cent was highly wasteful, there being no incentive for unmetered consumers to maintain, repair, or even turn off water fixtures. A purely residential consumption figure of 40 gpcd[11] was believed by the panel to be adequate on the basis of comparable figures of 67 gpcd for Los Angeles (high because of lawn-sprinkling in an arid area), 40 for Detroit, and 35 for Louisville. The remedy proposed by the panel, though further study of the subject was recommended before making a decision, was extension of metering, which, like correction of meters, would not save water directly but would be expected to lead to more economical use and, in particular, to consumers' elimination of wastes from leakage on their premises. The panel anticipated a further saving of from 100 to 200 mgd here, but, as we will show below, there is reason to believe that this figure may be quite conservative.

Waste elimination is not costless, and it is necessary therefore to consider in some detail the economics of the proposed alternatives. In our comparisons of these water-saving proposals, the most relevant bench mark would seem to be the cost of additional water from the official Cannonsville Project, which we find to be (see Table 31 below, Standard Case) $459 per million gallons delivered, at an interest rate of 6 per cent, or $1,023 per million gallons at an interest rate of 10 per cent. It should be borne in mind that in a number of respects these Cannonsville figures are too low for proper comparisons with the water-saving alternatives. Water saved by correction of leakages or in other ways is water that has been fully treated, transported to the city, and perhaps partially or wholly distributed to the consumers' taps. In addition, there will be the advantage as compared with a new supply of not adding to the load on the sewage-disposal system.

11 *Ibid.*, p. 22.

1. Wastage from Mains

The panel conjectured, on the basis of experience of other cities, that an expenditure of between $500,000 and $750,000 annually should save from 100 to 200 mgd by reducing wastage from mains. There is some question as to how to interpret these figures. If we assume that, say, an initial year's expenditure of $750,000 would correct a leakage of 150 mgd which would otherwise have run on indefinitely, then the $750,000 could be regarded as a once-and-for-all capital expenditure which provides a recurrent flow of 150 mgd, subject only to the eventual failure of the repair after the passage of time. A present-worth average-cost calculation can be made, using the short-cut formula (7) of chapter vii with operating costs o equal to 0, life of investment n equal to twenty years, and unit capital cost of $5,000 per million gallons per day. The result is a cost figure of only $1.19 per million gallons at 6 per cent, or $1.61 at 10 per cent!

If we interpret the panel's meaning more conservatively as indicating that over the years an annual average expenditure of, say, $600,000 a year would involve an annual saving of 150 mgd, then the corresponding cost is $11 per million gallons. The more extreme estimate, a saving of 150 mgd for a once-for-all expenditure of $750,000, is probably the one intended by the panel. We believe this is the case because the inadequate detection program already being carried on by the city had been stopping leaks at the rate of 20–30 mgd each year, at extremely low cost. Of course, the first years of any such expanded detection program would be by far the most productive. We may conclude, therefore, that, if the panel is correct, augmentation of supply through elimination of leakage in mains promised to make available an amount of perhaps 50 per cent of the Cannonsville yield at a cost, per million gallons, of far under one one-hundredth of Cannonsville costs. As far as we have been able to determine, these conclusions have been nowhere challenged,[12] and yet the recommended program of waste detection and elimination was never adopted by the city.

2. *Waste and Use on Consumers' Premises*

While the panel's report asserted that universal metering would save between 100 and 200 mgd of water now wasted on domestic consumers' premises, its discussion[13] seems to justify a higher estimate of the saving. The panel apparently believed that domestic consumption was close to 80 gpcd, while the amount actually used was probably less than 40 gpcd—the difference representing leakage. Metering would induce consumers to repair a large fraction of the leaks and, at any rate, to turn off fixtures when not actually used. If the full 40 gpcd could be saved, with a population of around 8,000,000, this would amount to 320 mgd for the city as a whole. Since there are costs of locating and repairing leaks, the actual saving would presumably be somewhat less —but we are inclined to think that the panel was excessively conservative here, since there would be some purposive reduction of *use* as well as of *leakage*. Our assumption will be that 200 mgd, the upper limit of the panel's range, is the water saving to be anticipated.

As against this saving, a number of cost elements must be considered. The panel quoted an estimate of $40 million for the capital cost of introducing metering, to which should be added in a fuller analysis the continuing costs of reading meters and billing customers. There are also the costs to the consumers of repairing leaks and loss to them of value in use to the extent that actual use is restricted. Unfortunately, we can only conjecture about these magnitudes; but it is necessary to do so, since they aggregate to substantial sums.

If we assume that consumers are rational, once metering is introduced and billing for water takes place at the current rate of 15 cents per 100 cubic feet, consumers will restrict water use until their marginal value in use rises to 15 cents per 100 cubic feet—and, correspondingly, they will carry on leak-repair activities until the marginal cost of another unit of water thus saved rises to the same level. However, it is the aggregate cost of leak repair and the loss in aggregate value in use which interest us. The only other item of information we can bring to bear is that, since, in effect, the price was zero before introduction of metering, the first marginal water savings can be assumed to take place at zero marginal cost for leak repair and at zero loss in marginal value in use for restriction of use—if consumers had previously been rational. In the absence of any other data, we will strike a simple arithmetic average and assume that the average cost to consumers for either form of saving is 7.5 cents per 100 cubic feet. This comes to around 10 cents per thousand gallons saved, or $100 per million gallons.

Again, using our short-cut formula (7) of chapter vii, and assuming a twenty-year life for the meters, the capital cost of $40 million or $200,000 per million gallons per day becomes $48 per million gallons at 6 per cent, or $64 per million gallons at 10 per cent. The total of capital costs and losses imposed on consumers is then only $148 per million gallons at 6 per cent, or $164 per million gallons at 10 per cent,

[12] The reply of DWSGE to the panel's report indicated that inspection could be expected to save 60 mgd at an aggregate cost of $316,000 (DWSGE, "Analysis" [1952], p. 12). This is about the same cost per million gallons per day saved as estimated by the panel, though, of course, the quantity is much smaller. The DWSGE reply does not specifically indicate disagreement with the panel's figures, nor does it explain why 60 mgd was used as the estimate of the saving. Increments to the amount saved could still be purchased advantageously, actually, at unit costs up to ten times or even fifty times that indicated by the panel or by DWSGE.

[13] *Panel Report,* pp. 21–23.

as compared with the corresponding Cannonsville figures of $459 and $1,023. (As we shall see later, however, the Hudson supply comparison is less extreme.) This is not the full picture, of course, because of the considerations raised earlier—that the water saved has been fully transported and treated, that sewering costs will be less (as compared with the alternative of introducing a new, additional supply), and the like. A full analysis would have to consider such details carefully, together with those cutting in the other direction, like the recurrent cost of reading and testing meters. It appears, however, that a prima facie case for extending metering has been made as against the alternative of Cannonsville construction, although further study to develop better data seems called for. It is possible that a program of selective expansion of metering might prove to be unquestionably economic, but we do not have enough information to come to a conclusive judgment on this either. One unusual feature of the New York situation is that under current regulations all meters are owned by consumers. The city might therefore conceivably introduce metering and place almost all the costs thereof—the costs of the meters together with the costs of correcting wastes and foregoing submarginal uses—upon the consumers. We will not emphasize this distributive consideration, which does not affect the efficiency comparison.

3. *Meter Rates*

One recommendation of the panel urged correction of meter underregistration, but no estimate of the cost of this program was indicated. In some respects correction of underregistration can be looked at as simply an increase in price—a possible source of water saving not explicitly considered by the panel. Here, again, some reduction in consumption could be anticipated as a result of consumer decisions to eliminate wastes or to forego uses not justified at the higher per unit billing rate for water used.

Actually, the correction of underregistration is quantitatively unimportant (though involving questions of both equity and efficiency as between different consumers) in comparison with the more fundamental question of an increase in rates. A strong water-conservation program in 1949–50 might have involved both an extension of metering and an increase in meter rates,

TABLE 28*

METERED RATE SCHEDULE COMPARISON BY VOLUME TAKEN

(1950 Monthly Rate, in Dollars per 1,000 Cubic Feet)

Volume Taken (Cubic Feet)	New York City	Mean of Eight Largest Cities in Volume of Water Production
1,000	$1.50	$1.25
10,000	1.50	1.02
100,000	1.50	0.84
1,000,000	1.50	0.70

* Source: H. F. Seidel, A. S. Johnson, and D. O. Dencker, "A Statistical Analysis of Water Works Data for 1950," *Journal American Water Works Association*, XLV (December, 1953), 1309–33 (at p. 1331).

even though New York's rates are, in comparison with typical large-city figures, already higher than the average of large water systems and especially high for very large consumers (see Table 28). New York charges on a fixed per-unit basis, as opposed to the more typical declining block rates. It is remarkable that neither the panel nor the city's water-supply agencies seem to have given any consideration at all to the possibility that price adjustments might be an alternative to Cannonsville or other construction projects. As an aside, it may be remarked that New York's present meter rate has remained unchanged since 1934, and the rate effective before that date had remained constant since 1870. Evidently, those concerned with New York's water problems had come to think of water rates as almost a constant of nature. A price increase would have helped to restrain consumption (of metered consumers) in the immediate 1949–50 crisis, even if on a longer-run basis new construction was also justifiable.

From a longer-run point of view, we can rather briefly consider the question of increasing rates (to metered consumers) as an alternative to Cannonsville construction. Assuming consumer rationality as before, 15 per cents per 100 cubic feet (the current billing rate) must be the marginal value in use to consumers. Consequently, however much water may be saved as consumers restrict use (or eliminate waste through leakage) in response to the price increase, the loss in aggregate value in use to consumers is, at a minimum, 15 cents per 100 cubic feet—or $200 per million gallons independent of the interest rate. A price rise to 25 cents per 100 cubic feet would, under our previous assumption, involve an average value loss to consumers of 20 cents per 100 cubic feet or $267 per million gallons. This is still well under the cost of the Cannonsville alternative, except at very low interest rates.

4. *Conclusion on Use of Existing Supplies*

It appears from the present analysis that the possibilities considered for eliminating wasteful current uses as an alternative to major new construction differed substantially in cost. Our rough results, subject to the qualifications and assumptions discussed in the text, are summarized in Table 29. Such crude figures cannot, of course, pretend to do more than give the broadest sort of indications of the economic desirability of the suggestions made. Still, some of the results are so striking as to leave room for substantial error without affecting the outcome. We may say, in general, that the case for an expanded program of detection and correction of leakage from street mains seems overwhelming; the case for extension of metering to domestic consumers is impressive; only the case for a substantial increase in rates remains arguable—measuring each against the alternative of constructing the Cannonsville Project.

TABLE 29

COST TO COMMUNITY OF IMPROVEMENT IN USE OF EXISTING SUPPLIES—CRUDE COMPARISON

Source of Saving	Possible Amount Saved (mgd)	Cost per Million Gallons Saved	
		At 6 Per Cent	At 10 Per Cent
Elimination of leakage from street mains....	60–150	$1.19	$ 1.61
Extension of metering..	200	148	164
Price increase for metered consumers (to 25 cents/100 cubic feet)..	?	$ 267	$ 267
	Capacity	Cost per Million Gallons	
Cannonsville........	310	$ 459	$1,023

C. Alternative New Supplies—Cannonsville versus Hudson

Despite the significance of the proposals for improvement of utilization of existing supplies discussed above, the most controversial recommendation of the Engineering Panel was that concerning the economic desirability of a Hudson River source of new water supply in preference to the Cannonsville Project of the BWS. The panel's conclusion was based on a detailed comparison of all the major possible water sources available and included the then current Beck and Incodel proposals as well as Cannonsville. We shall only be able to devote space, however, to the choice between the Hudson and the Cannonsville alternatives.

1. Need for New Water Supply

First, it is of the greatest importance to examine the question of whether a new major water source was needed at all, and, if so, how soon. Such questions were psychologically awkward to raise in the crisis period of 1949–51, but, as we have shown earlier, the time lag in construction was such that the Cannonsville Project could have been of no assistance in the immediate crisis. To review the supply-demand picture briefly (see Table 30), it was not until 1970 that consumption was expected (under any of the estimates in the table) to rise to the level of the safe yield available as of 1956. Moreover, the 1956 safe yield of 1,510 mgd excludes 100 mgd available from the emergency pumping plant on the Hudson and also excludes 120 mgd from Long Island and private sources previously included in the total safe yield. Furthermore, there was the possibility of a substantial reduction in consumption (perhaps 350 mgd) by an expanded program of detection and correction of leakage on street mains and by introduction of metering for domestic consumers.

The conclusion of the panel about the absence of urgent need for initiating consideration of new supplies in 1951 seems

TABLE 30

FORECASTS OF FUTURE NEW YORK CITY WATER CONSUMPTION AND SCHEDULED AVAILABILITY, INCLUDING CANNONSVILLE

(In Million Gallons per Day)

Year	Consumption* Forecasts†			Actual Consumption‡	Available Safe Yield§
	Panel, 1950	BWS, 1950	DWSGE, 1951		
1950	....	....	....	983	1,055
1951	....	....	....	1,071	1,120
1952	....	....	....	1,120	1,120
1953	....	....	....	1,139	1,250
1954	....	....	....	1,110	1,250
1955	....	....	....	1,156	1,250
1956	....	....	1,230	1,160	1,510
1957	....	....	....	1,226	1,510
1958	....	....	....	....	1,510
1959	....	....	....	....	1,510
1960	1,365	1,320	1,315	....	1,510
1970	1,495	1,500	1,445	....	1,820‖
1980	1,600	1,680	1,530	....	1,820
1990	1,680	1,860	1,590	....	1,820
2000	1,755	2,020	1,640	....	1,820

* Consumption figures include all city consumption, from city or private sources, plus deliveries from city system to non-city areas. No savings allowed for waste detection or extension of metering.

† Source: DWSGE, "Analysis" (New York, 1952), p. 11.

‡ Source: DWSGE table provided to authors in 1958.

§ Source: Board of Water Supply, *1,820,000,000 Gallons per Day* (New York, 1955), pp. 10–11. Excludes 100 mgd from emergency pumping plant and, after 1955, 120 mgd from Long Island and private sources.

‖ Includes Cannonsville supply.

certainly to have been justified.[14] Nevertheless, construction on the Cannonsville Project was begun in 1955, with completion anticipated in six years. In general, then, it appears that, even if Cannonsville was the better alternative source of new supply, it will have been started a decade or more too early—with a consequent unnecessary burden on the taxpayers of the city. Furthermore, the benefit of hindsight does not enter into this conclusion in any important way, since the most generous assumptions about growth in population and in per capita use current in 1950–55 all indicated that construction could be safely deferred until better information became available.

2. *Cannonsville Project*

The Cannonsville Project of the BWS is to be the third and final stage of New York's Rondout-Delaware system. Aside from miscellaneous minor sources with an aggregate safe yield of some 15 mgd and Long Island sources maintained in stand-by condition (80 mgd), the city's two other major systems are Croton (safe yield 330 mgd) and Catskill (safe yield 555 mgd).

Construction on the Delaware system was begun in 1937; a Supreme Court decree of 1931 then prohibited the city from taking more than 440 mgd from the Delaware River and prescribed in addition certain water releases to augment low flows of the river. The first stage involved construction of two major reservoirs on Rondout Creek and the Neversink River, a tunnel connecting these, and the 85-mile Delaware Aqueduct from Rondout Reservoir to the city. The adopted safe yields, net of required state and interstate releases, were 120 mgd from Rondout and 105 mgd from Neversink. The Rondout yield, however, is not charged against the Delaware limitations, as Rondout Creek is a tributary of the Hudson rather than the Delaware. The second stage of the Delaware system involved impounding the waters of the East Branch of the Delaware and constructing a tunnel to Rondout Reservoir—the adopted safe yield being 335 mgd, which, together with Neversink, makes up the 440 mgd permitted under the Supreme Court decree. As it happened, World War II prevented completion of these stages as originally scheduled, though an emergency connection completed during the war brought in 35 mgd from Rondout.

As originally planned, the third stage of the Delaware system was to tap the Little Delaware, Willowemoc, and Beaver Kill, all Delaware tributaries, with a designed safe yield of 160 mgd. Before going to the Supreme Court for revision of the 1931 decree, the original third stage was dropped by the BWS in favor of the Cannonsville Project on the West Branch of the Delaware, for which a safe yield of 310 mgd is usually cited. But a point of some significance for the economics of the latter project is the fact that the change in plan enlarging the third stage was made after completion of the Rondout-Delaware Aqueduct, which in consequence represents a bottleneck of the Delaware system (see Fig. 21). In fact, the panel calculates the safe available yield of the Rondout-Delaware system with Cannonsville, after all required releases, as being 35 mgd *in excess of* the aqueduct capacity in dry years.[15] In any case, there is little if any capacity for carrying surplus waters of normal or wet years to the city. If these figures are accepted, the net increment of safe yield to the city is not 310 mgd but 275 mgd—the difference of 35 mgd, being undeliverable in the dry years, should not be counted in dry-year safe yield. As there seems to be some question as to the effective capacity of the aqueduct, however, we shall use 310 mgd as the safe-yield basis, this latter

[14] *Ibid.*, p. 7.

[15] In a very dry year, the panel maintains, aqueduct deliveries under gravity flow conditions will be limited by the low head at Rondout Reservoir (*ibid.*, pp. 42–44).

being the figure quoted by the BWS in 1955.

The project involves construction of a dam and reservoir near Cannonsville, New York, about 125 miles northwest of New York City. The dam is to be of earth embankment, about 1,500 feet long and 175 feet above the bed of the river. The reservoir will impound about 91,000,000,000 gallons. The water collected there will move by gravity through a West Branch tunnel to be constructed to connect with the Delaware Aqueduct at the existing Rondout Reservoir.

The cost assigned by the BWS to the Cannonsville Project was $140 million—the dam and reservoir cost being $59.3 million, and the tunnel $80.7 million. Costs of operation and maintenance are cited in the panel's report at $422,000 per annum,[16] this figure being that used by BWS in its own analyses at that time. In a BWS working chart dated September, 1954, the annual cost of operation was revised upward to $478,000.[17]

[16] *Ibid.*, p. 73.

3. Engineering Panel's Hudson River Proposal

The Engineering Panel proposed, as an alternative to the Cannonsville Project, that a supply ultimately reaching the level of 325 mgd be obtained by pumping from the Hudson River. It will be remembered that, in the crisis of 1950, New York had constructed a Hudson River pumping plant with a capacity of 100 mgd. Because of the poor quality of this water, the plant was not to be used except in emergency, and, in fact, it was never used. The emergency plant was located at Chelsea, New York, below the city of Poughkeepsie (see Fig. 22), whose sewage the river carries, and where the river is still tidal. Furthermore, the emergency plant was to use the raw river water for the municipal supply system, subject only to heavy chlorination

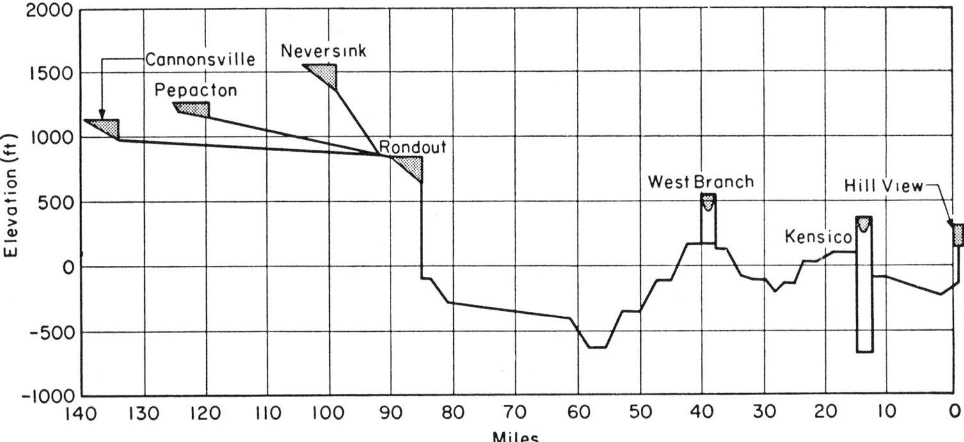

FIG. 21.—Major elements of Delaware system, with Cannonsville. (From Board of Water Supply, *op. cit.*, pp. 8–9.)

[17] *Investigations of the Hudson River as a Source of Water Supply for the City of New York, 1948–1954: Report of Engineering Bureau, Department of Research and Development, Board of Water Supply* (New York, 1955) (hereinafter cited as "BWS, *Hudson River Investigations* [1955]"), Chart I, Acc NS 487.

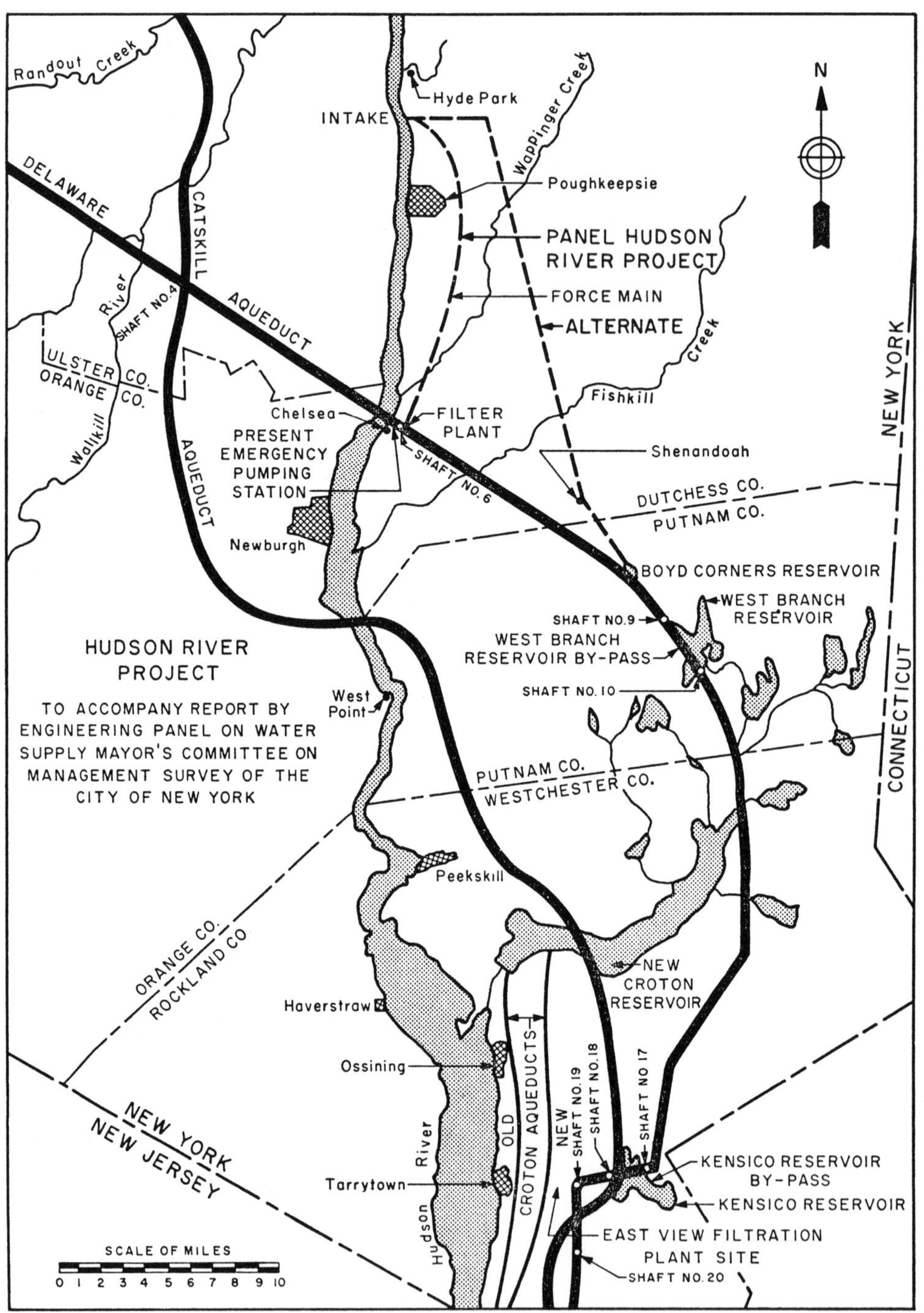

Fig. 22.—The Hudson River Project of the Engineering Panel on Water Supply. (From *Panel*, p. 65.)

and ordinary detention and mixing with the other city waters. The panel's proposed intake was near Hyde Park, north of Poughkeepsie, and the plan included provision for conventional filtration which would suffice, in the panel's opinion, to provide water of standard quality for municipal supply, aside from the expected mixing with other city waters.

In somewhat more detail the panel's plan called for an initial capacity of 200 mgd, it being anticipated that the remaining 125 mgd could be deferred for twenty-five years or more. The major facilities required were intakes and low-lift pumping station near Hyde Park, force main to Chelsea, filter plant, high-lift pumping plant, and connection to Delaware Aqueduct at Chelsea. It was proposed to make use of the 120 mgd high-lift pumping equipment and connection to the aqueduct already constructed for the city's emergency pumping plant at Shaft 6 near Chelsea. This plan and an alternate scheme are mapped in Figure 22.

On the assumption that construction would start in 1960, the panel estimated initial capital costs for this project at $31 million, a further capital expenditure of $8,185,000 being required for the increment of capacity assumed to be provided in 1985. These costs are much lower than the comparable capital costs for Cannonsville. The operating costs of a pumping plant, however, are much higher per unit of water delivered than those of a gravity-aqueduct system. As as result, the question of just how much water delivery will be required enters importantly into the over-all cost calculation.

The amount of delivery required from the pumping plant would depend upon the demand for water and the supply from the existing alternative sources which, being cheaper in terms of operating cost, would be used to their practical capacity before turning to the pumping plant. A qualification here is the fact that the panel assumed a minimum plant output of 30 mgd to maintain efficiency of equipment and personnel. The demand was assumed by the panel to grow at a rate that seems conservatively high, although for years beginning around 1980 the BWS estimates become substantially higher.[18] This very uncertainty is a good argument for deferring construction, and an advantage of the panel's plan is the fact that it is divisible into two stages. The difference between the panel and the BWS estimates is due entirely to the divergence between their population forecasts, and more recent evidence indicates that in this respect both are too high.[19]

On the supply side, the panel envisaged a pattern of maximum use of other sources (except for the aforementioned 30 mgd of pumping) until the upland reservoirs were depleted to 80 per cent of capacity, after which time the excess demands would be met from pumping. This appears to be highly or even excessively conservative, as eight months' supply of the safe yield would still remain stored. The panel estimated that allowing reservoir depletion to 60–70 per cent of capacity would reduce pumping required by 10–20 per cent. One other consideration was the possibility of reduction in pumping load as a result of drawing 33 mgd more safe yield from the Delaware than was permitted under the 1931 Supreme Court decree. The original 440-mgd limitation was based on safe-yield estimates that had proved to be too conservative, so that additional net withdrawals of

[18] *Panel Report,* p. 14, Table 7, col. (C). The BWS consumption estimates in *Hudson River Investigations* (1955), Appendix Table Acc NS 540, were similar to but somewhat lower than the BWS estimates cited by the panel.

[19] The panel and the BWS both expected population growth from around 8,000,000 in 1950 to around 8,500,000 in 1960, but the special 1957 Census showed an actual decline in population to around 7,800,000. Preliminary 1960 Census figures put the total for 1960 below 7,700,000 (*New York Times,* June 7, 1960, p. 1).

33 mgd would not impair the low flows of the Delaware River. In view of the fact that the Supreme Court eventually granted New York City the right to increase withdrawals from 440 mgd to 800 mgd from the Delaware, we assume that there would have been no difficulty about the proposed request for an additional 33 mgd.

On the basis of these supply-demand estimates, the panel computed a schedule of operating costs for the Hudson plant rising rather slowly from a minimum of \$615,000 per annum in the early years to \$1,269,000 per annum in 1980 and \$2,709,000 per annum in 2000.[20] On this basis, even in 2000 the pumping capacity would cover the deficiency of upland safe yield relative to predicted demand with a comfortable margin, and on the average pumping would take place only at about 50 per cent of the 325-mgd capacity. If the growth estimates proved to be correct, therefore, a new source might be considered for about the year 2000.

One important separate consideration is the question of filtration. The panel recommended the filtering of *all* of the city's surface-water supplies, and, if this recommendation were adopted, no separate Hudson filter plant would be needed. Instead, a combined plant could be built on a site already reserved by the BWS for that purpose. The net effect would have been to make the increment of cost assignable to the provision of filtered Hudson water somewhat smaller. We have not adopted this plan in our standard calculations, however; the matter will be discussed below in our comparison of the projects.

4. Comparison of the Projects

A quick overview of the comparative economics of the Cannonsville and Hudson River proposals reveals that the Hudson River Project is much cheaper as to initial or capital costs, while Cannonsville is much cheaper as to operating or continuing costs. Before turning to the economic calculations, however, it is necessary to consider certain matters that precede the economic comparison by touching upon the basic feasibility of the one project or the other, economics aside, or upon the detailed engineering cost estimates provided.

a) *The question of quality.*—The BWS argued against the Hudson River proposal on the ground that it would result in a *quality* of water that would be unacceptable to the people of New York.[21] The board cited the pollution of the Hudson River, the danger of water-borne disease, and the likelihood of occasional failures of the filtering procedure. In reply, the panel maintained that the Hudson water at Hyde Park, in contrast with that at Chelsea, was eminently satisfactory for simple orthodox filtering. They pointed to the willingness of BWS to accept, as a source of emergency supply, the much inferior waters at Chelsea without filtration. Furthermore, the panel maintained that, from a health and sanitation viewpoint, it is the unfiltered upland water which presents a more serious danger than the Hudson water after filtration.

We cannot entirely resolve this conflict of views, as some uncertainties necessarily remain: What are the relative risks of failure of the filtration process, on the one hand, or the inspection process for unfiltered upland water, on the other? It is clear, however, that the water from both sources under normal conditions would meet ordinary quality standards. Ultimately, an element of sheer taste or preference may be necessarily involved in the decision. For our present purposes we will simply have to suspend judgment on these issues, conducting our analysis on the assumption that the water from either source is of satis-

[20] *Panel Report,* p. 64, Table 28, Project B.

[21] BWS letter dated October 30, 1951, addressed to Mr. Bernard F. Gimbel, chairman, Subcommittee for Water Supply, Mayor's Committee on Management Survey.

factory quality. We will turn once again to the question of quality later on.

b) *Legal considerations.*—A second extra-economic consideration was the legal situation. Writing in 1951, the panel viewed the necessity of seeking Supreme Court permission to increase withdrawals from 440 mgd to 800 mgd from the Delaware as a substantial disadvantage of the Cannonsville Project. In contrast, the panel's plan envisaged seeking an increase in net withdrawals of only 33 mgd (48 mgd gross less 15 mgd of required releases), such an increase being feasible while still meeting the low-water requirements of the 1931 decree. Nor would denial of this small increase have crucially affected the panel's proposal. The increase to 800 mgd has now been granted, resolving that particular issue. New York City's success here was surprisingly easy. The states of New Jersey and Pennyslvania, which had refused to give their consent to withdrawals of 440 mgd in the proceedings leading to the 1931 decree,[22] did consent to withdrawals of 800 mgd in the 1954 proceedings. It should also be remarked that the Supreme Court retained jurisdiction of the case should any party desire relief at a later date, and the 1954 decision[23] emphasized that the proceedings conferred no prior or special rights on New York City and were in no sense an appropriation of the waters of the Delaware. There remains, therefore, a possibility that the permission to withdraw 800 mgd may at some later date be revoked or scaled down.

The panel's plan was not entirely free of possible legal difficulties either, aside from the relatively minor matter of the recommended 33-mgd increase in net Delaware diversion. The major adversely affected interest here would be that of the city of Poughkeepsie, whose present water intake on the Hudson is below that proposed by the panel. The 1955 BWS report, in fact, claimed that the combination of maximum pumping-plant withdrawals and the worst recorded low-river flows, experienced in 1941, would have led to unacceptable chloride concentrations (over 250 ppm) at Poughkeepsie.[24] This seems to be in conflict, however, with evidence of relatively low chloride content (maximum of 40 ppm) at Poughkeepsie in that year.[25] It seems reasonable to suppose that the interests of Poughkeepsie could be protected by prohibition of pumping under certain low-flow conditions, the probability of which could be minimized by scheduled releases from Sacandaga Reservoir in the Adirondacks. Even if some provision of storage facilities for Poughkeepsie at New York's expense were to be made to eliminate the residual risk to the former city, or if New York undertook to supply Poughkeepsie's needs directly, it appears that the additional cost which must then be assessed against the panel's plan would be relatively minor (the total 1950 water consumption of Poughkeepsie is believed to have been around 6 mgd, about 2 per cent of the capacity of the proposed Hudson supply for New York).

c) *Some technical questions.*—We now turn to a number of more or less technical questions which must be settled before we can have usable cost figures for either project. Several of these, such as the required Hudson pumping load over time or the net incremental yield of Cannonsville, have been discussed under the descriptions of the separate proposals, but we have by no means resolved all the important debatable points yet.

The first such point relates to the design and capital costs of the panel's project. The BWS maintained in its 1951 report that a Hudson River pumping plant, if

22 283 U.S. 336–48.

23 347 U.S. 995.

24 BWS, *Hudson River Investigations* (1955), p. 4.

25 *Panel Report,* p. 36.

constructed, should be located on the *west* side of the river opposite Hyde Park. Reasons given included the assertion that the panel's proposed connection with the Delaware Aqueduct at Shaft 6 near Chelsea rather than at Shaft 4 on the west bank would require the complete dewatering of the aqueduct, a process which would prevent use of the aqueduct for over a year; that legal difficulties on the west bank would be less; that a higher degree of safety would be attained; and that real estate costs would be less. The indicated delay for connection and dewatering of at least a year, certainly the most serious of these objections, seems dubious. Inquiries on our part have elicited no explanation why the connection should require more than a month's shutdown at the outside. However that may be, the 1951 BWS report indicated that plant costs would be an initial $48 million (in place of the panel's $31 million), the deferred cost of the future increment of supply remaining about the same ($8 million).[26]

The 1955 BWS report contains a rather detailed investigation of three Hudson River supply possibilities. The dewatering objection to a connection at Shaft 6 is repeated, but apparently the other objections were dropped, for two of the possibilities considered involve intakes and plants on the east bank. Proposal No. 3, the most desirable of the three according to the 1955 report, would lie entirely on the east bank but would involve construction of an aqueduct longer than that proposed by the panel, connecting with Shaft 8 rather than Shaft 6 of the Delaware Aqueduct. The first stage of this proposal was assigned a construction cost of $66.9 million, and the deferred second stage $16.1 million.[27] This is a very substantial increase over the figures quoted in 1951, and, in fact, for the Proposal No. 1 corresponding most closely to that considered in the 1951 report, the cost is even greater. These costs are more than twice the level estimated by the panel.

One minor source of difference between the panel and the BWS 1955 figures is that the former is based upon an ultimate plant capacity of 325 mgd; the latter, on 360 mgd. The 360-mgd figure involves an exaggerated concept of the pumping capacity necessary to equal the incremental safe yield from Cannonsville. It is based upon the difference between the permitted withdrawals of 440 mgd before the 1954 Supreme Court decision and 800 mgd afterward.[28] The correct figure must be taken net of required interstate and intrastate releases and must allow for the fact that 48 mgd of the increased withdrawals on a gross basis, or 33 mgd on a net basis, are in no way due to Cannonsville construction but rather constitute an increase in permitted yields of the first two stages of the Delaware system. Another document of the BWS gives 310 mgd as the safe increment of yield on this correct basis.[29]

A further relatively minor adjustment is for increase in the price level between 1950 and 1954, which we assume to be the dates of the analyses underlying the BWS reports of 1951 and 1955. The construction-cost index of *Engineering News-Record* indicates that an increase in dollar costs of about 25 per cent took place between these dates.[30] Despite this fact, cost estimates in the 1955 report for Cannonsville were unchanged from the 1951 report. One suspects that the figure quoted in 1951 must have been too high, or else the 1955 figure was too low.

Despite adjustments indicated by the considerations just raised, it is clear that

26 BWS, "Cost Estimates" (1951), pp. 5–6.

27 BWS, *Hudson River Investigations* (1955), Appendix Table Acc NS 520.

28 Letter of January 20, 1955, to BWS from Karl R. Kennison, chief engineer, pp. 2–3.

29 Board of Water Supply, *1,820,000,000 Gallons per Day* (New York, 1955), p. 6.

30 "1957 Construction Costs and Price Trends," *Engineering News-Record,* October 17, 1957, p. 88.

a rather enormous cost difference persists between the panel's estimates and the 1955 BWS estimates for Hudson River sources. The Engineering Panel, having gone out of existence, could not reply to the arguments of the 1955 BWS analysis, but an informal communication to one of the authors from Dean Thorndike Saville, chairman of the panel, stated in explanation of the cost difference that in his opinion the projects analyzed in the 1955 report were simply not the same as those recommended by the panel. In our own analysis, we will make separate calculations under the panel cost assumptions and the 1955 BWS assumptions, revising the latter to a comparable capacity and price-level basis.

A second major discrepancy between the panel and the BWS analyses relates to the level of operating costs. In part, this is due to the question of pumping requirements discussed earlier, since BWS assumes for later years much larger consumption figures than those used by the panel. We regard even the lower consumption estimates of the panel as on the high side. The BWS 1955 report also uses 1,500 mgd as the average available from non-Hudson sources throughout; the panel lists these sources as having an average yield starting with 1,425 mgd in 1967 and rising to 1,590 mgd in 2000. In view of the substantial excesses over safe yield obtainable from these other sources when surplus aqueduct capacity is left available by not constructing the Cannonsville Project, the panel's figures seem reasonable. Consequently, we will use the panel's pumping requirements as our standard, and we regard them as erring on the high side, if at all. A separate calculation will show the results under BWS delivery assumptions.

A rather technical, though still important, question concerns the operating cost of the pumping plant per unit of flow. The panel's cost figures were based on a detailed analysis of personnel and materials requirements; in the range considered these were broadly around $20,000 per mgd delivered on an annual average basis. The corresponding figures in the BWS 1955 report are of about the same magnitude. In the 1951 report, by way of contrast, substantially higher operating costs were assumed, to which the panel took strong exception. We will use the panel's figures in our standard calculations.

d) *Economics—capital charges.*—We are finally in a position to turn to the issues of economic logic involved in the comparison. We will take up three major topics here: (*a*) how to handle the problem of capital charges; (*b*) whether the comparison should be on the basis of actual delivered yield or safe yield available for delivery; and (*c*) how to discount the anticipated costs and returns in present-value analysis, our recommended method of comparing alternatives involving choices between the present and future.

Both the panel and the BWS were considerably in error in their methods of comparing the projects: in each analysis costs were simply cumulated without discounting (except for one comparison in the BWS 1955 report). With regard to capital costs, interest and amortization charges were included in both analyses until retirement of the assumed debt, and excluded thereafter, the comparison being taken to an arbitrary cutoff point in the distant future. The differences between the two analyses lay in variation in the cost and delivery assumptions and, to some extent, in differences of cutoff date.

In all but one of the panel and BWS analyses, capital charges were handled by simple aggregation of annual amounts expended for interest and amortization (repayment of amounts borrowed).[31] This is conceptually incorrect on a number of grounds, as explained in our theoretical chapters, though it may provide a rough approximation of the annual equivalent

[31] See, especially, *Panel Report,* p. 73; BWS, "Cost Estimates" (1951), pp. 12–15.

cost. In the first place, expenditures in different years cannot be compared without discounting or compounding to a common time dimension; we recommend always discounting to the present or time zero by the process of finding present values as of the starting point of the projects under consideration. In the second place, repayment of a loan is a purely financial arrangement not necessarily tied to the length of life of the investment, the latter being the datum of economic significance. But, most important, in order to relate costs to deliveries, the timing of the latter must be taken into account as well as the timing of the costs (see formula [5] of chap. vii).

The procedure of the reports under consideration was to charge amortization expenses over forty years and interest at 2½ per cent, presumably because the projects were to be financed by bonds of that term. But, as a dam and reservoir are ordinarily of longer life than a pumping plant, this procedure overestimated the relative cost of the Cannonsville Project. As discussed in our earlier chapters, estimation of length of economic life is highly uncertain. Actually, while forty years is not an unreasonable period to use for a pumping plant, it seems that a hundred years may be more appropriate for a dam and reservoir project. The physical lives of dams and aqueducts are, in fact, ordinarily well in excess of even the hundred-year figure, but there is the matter of obsolescence or loss in value for a variety of other economic reasons to allow for.

We will make use of different discount rates in our presentation of results, to show the sensitivity to this element in the calculation. As explained in chapter vi, if there were no project risks, and ignoring tax considerations, for presently considered projects we would favor discounting at a rate around 4 per cent, representing (currently) the riskless rate on long-term investments. If, however, the risks (of underestimation of costs and overestimation of benefits) are comparable to those of privately owned utilities (and allowing as explained in chap. vi for the tax factor), a rate of around 9–10 per cent would be appropriate. This implies that the cost and benefit data used in the calculation have not themselves been sufficiently conservatively estimated as to be effectively equivalent to figures known with certainty. If the estimates under consideration were regarded as unusually conservative ones, then a rate somewhere between 5 per cent (incorporating a property tax adjustment) and 10 per cent would be indicated.

In the case at hand, however, we must take note of the fact that we are dealing with a historical rather than a current question. The proposals here studied were made and debated at various dates between 1950 and 1955—a period that saw a considerable variation in capital market conditions. The long-term rate on government debt in 1950 was around 2.3 per cent, and in 1951–55 it fluctuated between 2.5 and 2.9 per cent—as compared with 1959 rates generally in excess of 4 per cent. Public utility bond yields are also higher today. On the other hand, stock yields currently are rather lower than those prevalent in the earlier period. Making use of our method of analysis in chapter vi and the general formula in Table 11, marginal opportunity rates (before adjustment for property and minor taxes) were calculated for selected years as follows: 12.15 per cent (1950), 9.29 per cent (1952), and 8.40 per cent (1955).[32] After incorporating a small adjustment for minor taxes,[33] it seems to be

[32] U.S. Department of Commerce, *Business Statistics, 1957,* p. 100. Equity earnings yields calculated from Moody's data on public utility prices and earnings, and bond yields are Moody's series for public utilities.

[33] While we ordinarily recommend an adjustment of between 1 and 2 per cent for these taxes, as will be seen below only a partial adjustment is indicated here because these New York City projects were liable to property taxes in the jurisdictions where the physical works were located, and the taxes were included in the calculations.

the case that the appropriate discount rate for the 1950–55 period remains comparable to (or even slightly higher than) the 9–10 per cent range currently recommended by us—the higher earnings yield on equity required at that time just about offsetting the lower bond yield.

The discount rate used makes a considerable difference in the calculation, the Cannonsville Project looking relatively (but not absolutely) better at lower rates of interest, and the Hudson Project looking better at higher rates.

e) Actual delivery or available yield?—One of the important issues in the economic calculation is whether to measure the cost on the basis of *available safe yield,* on the one hand, or *actual delivered yield,* on the other. The panel used the available safe supply as the basis for comparison. The BWS declared that the only fair basis of comparison was actual delivery of water. Since the pumping source has relatively high operating cost, it will be used to meet demand only after a capacity limit is reached on water from upland sources. Consequently, safe deliverable yield of the Hudson Project will substantially exceed actual yield on the average, making the unit pumping costs lower when computed on the former basis.

It certainly seems wrong to calculate, as the panel does, the cost of making *actual* deliveries and then to divide through by the capacity or *potential* deliveries. And the BWS is at least partially correct in implying that the economic commodity being purchased is the actual delivery, not the available delivery. The existence of unused capacity, however, has a certain insurance value in view of the annual fluctuations in supply and demand for water. Thus the emergency pumping plant at Chelsea will, as it turns out, never supply any water to the city; consequently, it was a sheer waste of money in the light of hindsight. That does not prove that in 1950 the decision to build it was a mistake, in view of the substantial possibility of low-supply or high-demand conditions coming into being before completion of the expected increase in permanent supplies. The BWS itself, by its insistence upon building supplies far ahead of demand, has implicitly placed a high insurance value on capacity in excess of that probably needed. The most rigorous method of calculation of the value of an additional supply would credit, over and above the expected deliveries, the value of preventing a "shortage" multiplied by the probability of conditions developing that would otherwise create a shortage.

The difficult calculations required with such a probabilistic model are not really necessary here, however. It is true that, until its second stage is completed, the Hudson plant will not provide the full safe-yield equivalent of Cannonsville; but we regard that as a very minor consideration. If developments over time seem to indicate an earlier need for the second stage, it could be built a bit earlier, while, on the other hand, if (as we think more likely) it were not needed until later than planned, it could be further deferred. Therefore, we do not think that there is any significant difference between the two proposals in terms of their insurance value.

Nor, properly analyzed, is there any important difference between them on the basis of actual expected deliveries. It is true that the Hudson plant would be necessarily a residual source and so would directly supply less than Cannonsville. However, in the absence of the Cannonsville Project, there would be surplus capacity in the Delaware Aqueduct for carrying the greater-than-safe-yield flows of the first two stages of the Delaware system. These excess flows, which would be precluded by Cannonsville, together with the pumped supplies, total to the same deliveries as are anticipated from Cannonsville. Consequently, minor adjustments aside, there is no difference between the actual deliveries to be credited to the two projects.[34] In its analysis of the panel's project, the BWS seems to have neglected this factor, thus confusing the actual flow *through* the Cannonsville Project with the really relevant incremental flow *due to* the project.

Properly interpreted, then, there is no significant difference in either of the dimensions of output associated with the proposals—actual water deliveries to meet expected requirements or safe yield[35] to insure against extreme needs. We can simply compare the projects on the basis of their costs or else calculate the costs per unit of actual incremental delivery.

f) *Present-value cost comparison—standard case.*—Our "standard-case" comparison of the two projects is based upon calculating the unknown cost of water with the following formulas:

$$\text{Cannonsville: } \sum_{t=0}^{47} \frac{q_t x}{(1+i)^t} = \sum_{t=0}^{47} \frac{K_t + O_t + P_t + S_t}{(1+i)^t}, \quad (1)$$

$$\text{Hudson: } \sum_{t=0}^{47} \frac{q_t x}{(1+i)^t} = \sum_{t=0}^{47} \frac{K_t + T_t + O_t + S_t}{(1+i)^t}. \quad (2)$$

These formulas are based on equation (5) of chapter vii. In each case, x is the unknown average cost of water delivered, i the discount rate, and q_t the delivery in year t. The formulas find the present-worth average cost of water for each alternative by setting the discounted present value of the water delivered (the left-hand side of the equations) equal to the discounted present value of the cost stream.

It is assumed in each case that construction begins in 1960, which is time zero for each project. For Cannonsville, project life extends to 2066 (seven-year construction period and one-hundred-year useful life), while for the Hudson Project it extends to 2024 (seven-year construction period and a conservative forty-year life after completion of the project increment in 1985). For Cannonsville, the elements of the cost summation are K_t (construction cost), O_t (operating cost), P_t (a cost offset due to reduced pumping cost for Croton water), and S_t (salvage value due to unexpired life at year 47). For Hudson, the terms are similarly defined, except that there is no P_t cost offset but rather an additional cost T_t (property taxes).[36] Details of the cost estimates are provided in the appendix to this chapter. Costs are in 1950 dollars.

In Table 31 the results labeled "Standard Case" show that the present value of the cost per million gallons actually delivered, using the panel's cost and delivery schedule accepted by us, is substantially

[34] The excess flows from the upland sources involve some incremental cost, which should properly be added to the costs of the actual flows through the Hudson Project components. We have not made any adjustment here, however, in the belief that these incremental costs are negligible in magnitude.

[35] A minor difference is that the Cannonsville safe yield is 310 mgd, as assumed here, while the Hudson Project is designed for 325 mgd in the panel's plan (when completed), or 360 mgd in the BWS 1955 analysis. The extra Hudson capacity may be regarded as an additional amount of insurance, which tends to compensate for the possible need to shut off pumping under unfavorable input water conditions. (See discussion of quality below.)

[36] While the projects of public agencies escape income taxes and also a wide variety of the minor taxes burdening private enterprise, New York City in this case would have been required to pay property taxes on that portion of the project lying outside the city and within other taxing jurisdictions. Taxes were calculated at about 0.5 per cent of cost for the first stage, and 1 per cent for the second stage. Taxes for Cannonsville (about $100,000 per year) are included in the operating-cost figure, O_t (see BWS, "Cost Estimates" [1951], pp. 3, 9). But note that the taxes on Cannonsville facilities (costing $140,000,000) seem to be assessed at a much lower rate than 0.5 per cent. The reason for this disparity is unknown.

lower at all interest rates for the Hudson than for the Cannonsville alternative. Figure 23 shows how the estimated costs vary as a function of the discount rate assumed. As indicated above, and following the argument of our theoretical chapters, we recommend in this efficiency comparison the use of a rate in the neighborhood of 10 per cent—representing the opportunity cost of capital for public projects (the anticipated return from investment, before deducting corporate and property tax liability, for projects of comparable risk in the private utility sphere). On this basis the cost comparison is $307 per million gallons for Hudson and $1,023 for Cannonsville. We have also shown the results at other discount rates. The 6 per cent

TABLE 31

COST COMPARISONS—CANNONSVILLE VERSUS HUDSON

(Costs in 1950 Dollars)

Discount Rate (Per Cent)	Cost per Million Gallons Delivered		Total Net Costs ($000,000's)	
	Cannonsville	Hudson	Cannonsville	Hudson
	Standard Case (Comparison 1)			
2.5	$165.88	$110.40	$105.6	$ 70.3
3.5	233.08	125.73	111.3	60.0
6	458.58	177.31	113.5	43.9
10	1,023.48	306.63	105.8	31.7
	No Filtration Charges* (Comparison 2)			
2.5	$165.88	$ 70.63	$105.6	$ 45.0
3.5	233.08	77.84	111.3	37.2
6	458.58	101.32	113.5	25.1
10	1,023.48	129.34	105.8	13.4
	Using BWS Cost Estimates (Adjusted) for Hudson (Comparison 3)			
2.5	$165.88	$144.57	$105.6	$ 92.1
3.5	233.08	168.02	111.3	80.2
6	458.58	247.60	113.5	61.3
10	1,023.48	448.96	105.8	46.4
	Using BWS Cost and Delivery Estimates (Comparison 4)			
2.5	$ 76.52	$ 90.62	$109.2	$129.3
3.5	106.12	101.13	113.8	108.5
6	207.50	137.72	114.7	76.1
10	482.63	237.90	106.2	52.3

* On this basis costs from both sources are equally underestimated, the assumption being that in either case the water would be subjected to identical filtering at a central plant (see text).

figure represents the minimum discount rate we regard as conceivably acceptable. The 3.5 per cent figure would be appropriate for riskless investments under capital market conditions as of 1956, 2.5 per cent being more representative of 1950 capital market conditions. Both the panel and the BWS actually used in their calculations a rate of 2.5 per cent, that figure being an estimate of the city's borrowing costs in the capital markets around 1950. At 2.5 per cent, Cannonsville improves relative to Hudson but is still the more costly, the figures being $166 per million gallons against $110.

Table 31 also shows the total net costs (i.e., total costs less offsets indicated in eqs. [1] and [2] above) of the two projects. While the cost per million gallons delivered rises as the discount rate goes up, total net cost generally declines with an increasing discount rate. The reason is that the total net cost is a present sum of a future stream of predominantly positive costs, and such sums decline with greater time discount of the future. The contrasting rise in the cost per million gallons delivered as the discount rate increases is due to the fact that the increasing discount rate has a still greater effect on the coefficient of x on the left-hand side of equations (1) and (2)—the time-weighted sum of the deliveries. This is due to the fact that the deliveries have a higher degree of futurity than the costs; the costs are, on the whole, incurred relatively early, but

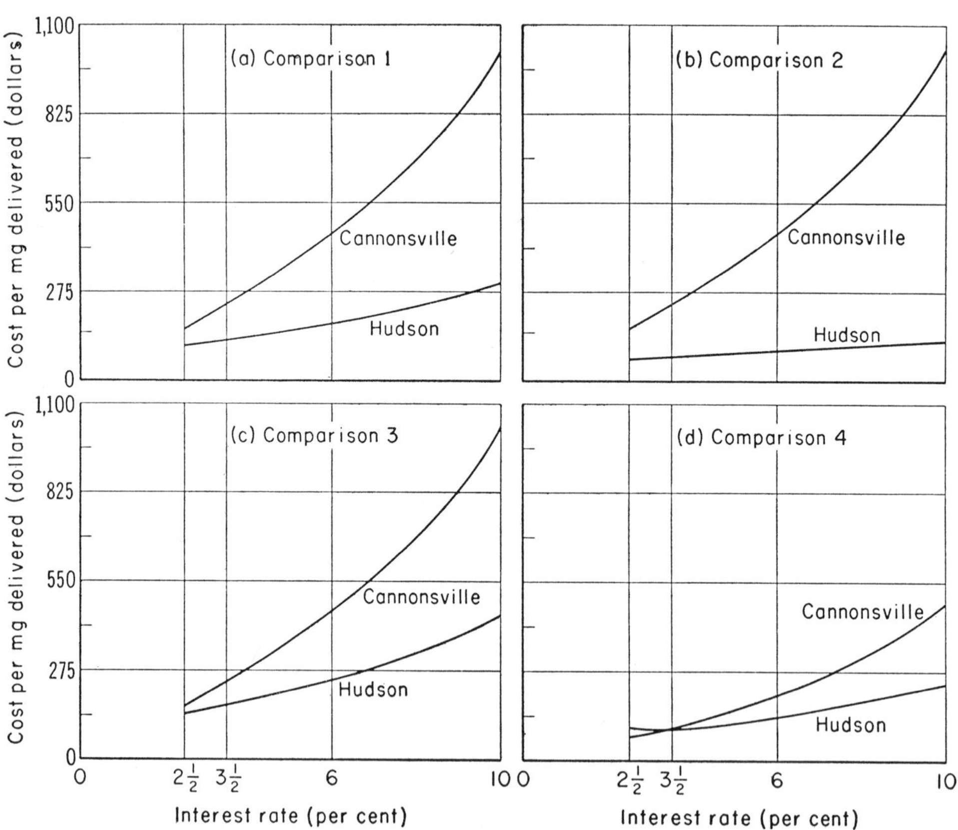

FIG. 23.—Hudson versus Cannonsville

the deliveries are small at first and greatest in the later periods.

Failure to use a discounting technique to allow properly for the timing of deliveries—in a situation with exceptionally slow load-building—is one major explanation for the enormous underestimation of costs by both the panel and the BWS.[37] The second crucial factor is, of course, the use of 2.5 per cent interest.

g) Sensitivity tests.—In the previous section the standard-case comparison between the alternative projects was made at a number of interest rates. Sensitivity of result to variations in the discount rate was shown for information purposes, although we did not mean to imply that anyone could equally reasonably choose any discount rate he pleased for project comparison; rather, we believe on economic grounds that a figure near 10 per cent is approximately correct for project efficiency calculations of this type. In this section we will consider sensitivity to uncertainties about matters of fact or of policy that cannot be entirely resolved by us, although we do believe that the "standard" assumption is in each case the most reasonable one to make.

Three divergencies of assumptions from the standard ones will be given explicit attention here: (1) filtration requirement for upland water; (2) use of BWS construction-cost estimates for the Hudson Project; and (3) use of BWS delivery-requirement estimates for both projects.

As indicated above, the panel had recommended that all the municipal water supply from upland sources (Croton, Catskill, and Delaware systems) be subjected to a conventional filtration procedure like that proposed for the Hudson water. The BWS and DWSGE both strongly disagreed with this recommendation, arguing that existing safeguards of rigid inspection, long storage, and chlorination without filtration sufficed to achieve a quality of water from upland sources far superior to the Hudson water with filtration. We do not intend to evaluate these arguments here, our purpose being merely to show the consequences for the Cannonsville-Hudson comparison if the need to filter all waters were conceded.

If all water from either Hudson or Cannonsville were to be filtered, the cost of filtration would no longer be an element of difference between the two proposals. This is especially the case under the panel's proposal, since the filtration would take place at the same site at Eastview, downstream of the Kensico Reservoir, where the Catskill, Delaware, and Hudson waters would all mix. Consequently, we could either increase the Cannonsville costs by an allowance for filtration or eliminate the filtration component from the Hudson estimates. The latter is the simpler and suffices for providing an acceptable basis of comparison for the projects under the assumption here considered.

The panel's report provides sufficient information for separating out filtration elements from both the construction and the operating costs for the Hudson Project.[38] The early construction costs of around $31 million would be reduced to some $13.6 million, the deferred capacity payment of about $8 million remaining the same in either case. The annual operating costs would be reduced by the elimination of filtering charges to the extent of about 20 per cent. Details of the cost calculation are provided in the appendix.

The result, as expected, is a substantial relative improvement for Hudson, whose cost at 10 per cent falls to $129 per million gallons delivered as compared with $1,023 for Cannonsville. Note that in this comparison both costs are underestimated by omission of filtering charges, and so, while

[37] Figures of $48 and $24 per million gallons, for Cannonsville and Hudson, respectively, are cited in *Panel Report*, p. 73. (An additional source of divergence here is the panel's use of *safe supply* instead of *deliveries* as the measure of yield.) The BWS cites $42 for Cannonsville in "Cost Estimates" (1951), p. 15.

[38] *Panel Report*, pp. 64, 70.

the comparison is valid, the absolute levels are not.

We have just seen the result of a variation from our standard-case assumptions favorable to the Hudson Project. The other two variations we will consider are favorable to the Cannonsville Project. The first of these involves the use of BWS cost estimates (as adjusted by us for price-level changes and capacity of the Hudson plant) instead of the panel's estimates for the Hudson Project (see the appendix for details).

As shown in Table 31, while using BWS estimates of costs for the Hudson Project raises the relative cost of the latter, it still appears that the Hudson water is the cheaper. At 10 per cent the costs per million gallons delivered are $449 for Hudson against the same $1,023 for Cannonsville, and even at 2.5 per cent the Hudson remains cheaper.

The most extreme case favorable to the Cannonsville Project occurs if we accept not only the BWS cost estimates but also the BWS delivery estimates described above for the two projects. The much higher deliveries assumed by BWS tend to lower the present-value average costs of each of the alternatives by spreading the fixed costs over a larger number (weighted by time discount) of units delivered. Partially offsetting this for the Hudson Project is the increase in pumping and filtering costs made necessary by the increased throughput of the system. Thus, Table 31 shows that at 10 per cent the total net Hudson cost rises from $31.7 million in the standard case to $52.3 million under the present assumptions. While in principle there should also be a small increase in Cannonsville operating costs with increased deliveries (e.g., increased cost of chlorination), we have accepted the BWS assumption that the Cannonsville operating costs are not in any part proportional to output. The result is a net decrease in costs per million gallons delivered for both projects. While the relative and absolute decrease for Cannonsville is greater (see Table 31), the latter remains the more expensive at 10 per cent —the figure for Hudson being $238 and for Cannonsville $483. When low discount rates like 2.5 or 3.5 per cent are used, the costs for the alternatives considered approach equality, and at 2.5 per cent Cannonsville actually becomes the cheaper in this extreme case. We interpret this not as an argument for Cannonsville but rather as a strong indication of the danger of an inappropriately low discount rate.

h) *Which is the better project—cost, quality, and intangibles?*—So far as the cost comparisons are concerned, then, the result indicates strongly that the Hudson alternative was superior to the Cannonsville Project now actually under construction, and by quite a large margin. The major qualification we must attach to this result relates to the question of water quality. The raw Hudson water is certainly inferior to raw Cannonsville water, but the question is whether Hudson water after filtration is inferior to Cannonsville water which is unfiltered, though subject to rigid inspection and chlorination. This is a point on which the BWS and the panel disagree. The former maintained that filtering can at best only mitigate the dangers of an initially polluted source of water, especially in view of the likelihood of human or mechanical failure, while the panel replied that filtration is such an important protection that unfiltered upland water is a greater menace to public health than the processed Hudson water would be. Of course, many important municipalities today are drawing their water supplies from sources which before processing are no better than the Hudson, and the Hudson itself is being used by the city of Poughkeepsie, so that there is no question that the latter source can meet conventional standards of public health and safety. An interesting sidelight on these latter standards is the fact that permitted levels of bacteriological contamination for milk are hundreds, or even thousands, of times higher than for public water supply, despite the fact that milk is a product particularly consumed by infants, sick people, and other especially vulnerable groups. A point to consider in the opposite direction is that there may be unidentified diseases transmitted by viruses or related organisms which are less fully removed by orthodox filtration treatment than are the bacteria responsible for the known water-borne diseases.

There are dimensions of water quality aside from bacteriological content. The BWS has pointed to the possibility of salt-water intrusion from the river mouth as well as of industrial spills of dangerous chemicals. The former seems only likely under extreme and unusual conditions, and the venting of noxious chemicals to the river is also being increasingly controlled by a state agency established for this purpose. In either case, arrangements would be made to bypass the water for the period of the contamination, but all such arrangements are subject to some risk of failure.

Other considerations, particularly emphasized by the DWSGE (which would actually distribute the water to users within the city), include the following: (*a*) increased hardness of the Hudson supply (but it is less corrosive), which would decrease the efficiency of home and commercial laundries; (*b*) increased organic and mineral content, which would raise costs of controlling biological growths in the water transmission and distribution system; (*c*) chemical tastes and odors; and (*d*) substantially higher temperature (about 12° in summer), which would impair palatability, promote biological growth, and reduce efficiency of water used for cooling purposes.[39] Actually, all these considerations (including even the matter of palatability) are in principle subject to economic analysis; at least a rough measure of these "intangible" costs of the Hudson Project should have been provided to guide the final decision. Unfortunately, we cannot here go so far afield as to make these detailed estimates ourselves, but some brief comments based on our quality discussion in chapter viii may be appropriate.

First, we found increased hardness to be generally quite costly in terms of cleaning efficiency—a rough figure being $2.00 cost per capita per annum for each 100 ppm of hardness. The Hudson source was estimated by DWSGE as adding "at least 10 ppm" of hardness, so that for a population of 8,000,000 a very substantial Cannonsville advantage of $1.6 million per year would be indicated. To this might be added other advantages of softness in terms of reduced scaling, etc. But the hardness of the present New York supply was extraordinarily low to begin with, certainly under 50 ppm[40] (100 ppm is the conventional level dividing "hard" water from "soft"). Within this range it seems very likely that, as claimed by the Engineering Panel,[41] the added hardness would have a *beneficial* net effect in reducing the corrosiveness of existing supplies. It may be noted that the DWSGE maintained that corrosiveness was not a serious problem,[42] but this appears to be at variance with other published information.[43]

39 DWSGE, "Analysis" (1952), pp. 21–24.

40 See *Panel Report,* pp. 29, 31, 34–35.

41 *Ibid.,* p. 34.

42 DWSGE, "Analysis" (1952), pp. 26–27.

43 Sussman states, for example: "Scale formation is often the most serious problem in recirculating cooling water systems, and corrosion is of secondary importance. In the New York metropolitan area, however, the combination of soft, low alkalinity make-up water and heavy atmospheric contamination reduces scaling to a negligible problem and creates unusually severe corrosion problems." He goes on to cite many illustrations of the heavy cost of corrosive water in New York (see S. Sussman, "Cooling Water Problems in the New York Metropolitan Area," *Industrial and Engineering Chemistry,* XLIV [August, 1952], 1740–44).

With the higher Hudson temperature, there will certainly be loss of cooling efficiency, most importantly for water-cooled but non-conserved air-conditioning equipment (initial water temperature is relatively unimportant for units recirculating cooling water). Since the Hudson is about 12° higher in summer than present sources, after dilution the over-all increased temperature would be about 3°. In contrast, it is claimed that the Cannonsville supply would permit a lowering of summer temperatures by about 5°.[44] Our calculations indicate, on the basis of the 8° difference and a cost of $1.50 per 1,000 cubic feet of water, a saving of some $2.13 per year per ton of cooling capacity for Cannonsville. Unfortunately, we have not been able to locate data on the extent of water-cooled but non-conserved equipment in New York (the larger installations are practically always water cooled but conserved, while the common room units are not water cooled). As a crude guess, currently there might be around 300,000 tons of air conditioning of this type in the city,[45] implying a total city-wide excess cost of Hudson over Cannonsville in the amount of $640,000 annually.[46] To this total, which will undoubtedly rise steadily in the future, should be added an allowance for industrial cooling as well. However, the higher Hudson temperature does have some advantages—most importantly, in fuel savings for processes requiring heated water. Assuming that 10 per cent of the water supply is heated, that the system-wide average annual temperature difference would be 3°,[47] that 10 BTU per degree per gallon are used in heating, and that 1,000,000 BTU cost $1.00, the indicated cost advantage for the Hudson source is in excess of $1 million per year.

On balance, our rough attempts above to quantify corrosion versus hardness and temperature factors, in terms of dollar costs or productive values of the dimensions of quality involved, favor the Hudson supply. One consideration, extremely difficult to quantify, is the value to consumers of the superior palatability (largely, but not entirely, due to lower temperature) of the Delaware supply. It might appear at first that this consideration cannot be too important, because of the low cost of home cooling of water (bottle in the refrigerator). However, if avoiding this slight inconvenience is worth only 10 cents per capita per year to consumers in New York City, the annual value of the better water is $800,000—not a trifling sum. If this gain of $800,000 per year or about $2,200 per day is attributed to the Cannonsville production of 310 mgd at full capacity, the value superiority of Cannonsville is around 2,200/310, or close to $7.00 per million gallons. If consumers were willing to pay as much as $1.00 per capita per year for the cooler water, the value superiority would be $70 per million gallons. This latter disparity is sufficiently great to make Cannonsville look considerably more interesting, though in all but the most extreme Comparison 4 in Table 31 even an adjustment of this magnitude will not suffice to make Cannonsville competitive at either 6 per cent or 10 per cent interest. Also, it should be remembered that even with the Hudson supply the system temperature after mixture may not exceed 70° F. While we can easily believe that people might be willing to pay $1.00 per year per capita to have

44 DWSGE, "Analysis" (1952), pp. 23–24.

45 A figure of 275,000 tons of all air conditioning other than window (air-cooled) types has been given for Manhattan only as of 1955 (Committee Report, "Trends in Air-Conditioning Use and Regulation," *Journal American Water Works Association,* L [January, 1958], 77).

46 The correct current figure must be far above that for 1951, when the proposals reviewed here were first made. On the other hand, the trend of growth of air conditioning was foreseeable at that time.

47 The temperature difference of 8° refers to the summer only, at which season heating demand is at a minimum.

cool summer water rather than thoroughly warm summer water, in this case the alternative is still sufficiently cool as not to justify any very large penalty on this score.

To sum up, therefore, on the basis of our very rough calculations, no very clear advantage for Cannonsville is shown in terms of temperature and hardness-corrosion considerations. Beyond the immediate question at hand, the most significant point brought out by this analysis, we feel, is that what are often thought to be "intangibles" are quite amenable to economic analysis and may often be quantitatively very important. Analyses of water supply generally can easily go much farther in the direction of bringing quality considerations into economic calculations, as opposed to the present practice of leaving the evaluation of quality (in its several dimensions) against cost solely in the realm of "judgment." The comparative crudity of our quick calculations, using only data conveniently at hand, by no means indicates that a careful study, generating the required data if necessary, could not have been performed to guide this decision.

All in all, however, we cannot clearly resolve the question of quality, especially in view of major uncertainties like the probability of water-borne virus disease. On the whole, there does seem to be an increased degree of safety attached to the upland water, the question remaining being whether the price being paid to achieve this safety is out of line. The over-all present cost excess of the Cannonsville Project is approximately $75 million (standard case at 10 per cent), and this amount of money could perhaps purchase much more public health if invested in other directions (like construction of hospitals, scholarships for medical students, rodent control, etc.) than in the increased water-supply safety represented by the difference between the Cannonsville and the Hudson sources.

We may mention in passing that other elements of comparison also not immediately quantifiable in the cost estimates should not be entirely neglected. Of these, perhaps the most striking is the fact that for neither project would the city secure safe title to the water being used. This is the more crucial as against the Cannonsville Project, as the Supreme Court in its decree of 1954 strongly emphasized that its grant of permission to use the Delaware water in no way constituted a title or right and might at any time be reconsidered or revoked upon application of any of the other states interested in the Delaware. The disadvantages of such uncertain tenure of water rights were strongly emphasized in chapter ix above.

In our own weighing of the uncertainties with the economic calculations performed, we believe that the Hudson alternative was the better project for the city to adopt, if it had to adopt either. Actually, however, as will be summarized below, there was no need to push for early construction, and wise delay (masterly inaction) would not only have saved unnecessary interest costs but might have led to the gathering of further information about the remaining uncertainties involved in the decision.

D. New York Water Policy: Conclusion

Substantively, our analysis has indicated: (1) New York's water crisis of 1949–50 provided no sound justification for early construction of a large further augmentation of water supplies, inasmuch as projects already under way created a large overcapacity beginning in 1953. (2) There was no current need to begin new construction (even in the absence of measures to promote more efficient use of existing supplies) either in 1951, when approval of the Cannonsville source was first sought, or in 1955, when construction began. In fact, even using the high consumption estimates of BWS, the new source should have been deferred until 1970 (completion date). (In confirmation of these arguments it now appears that a decision was made some time after initiation of construction on Cannonsville to defer completion to 1966 or 1967 instead of the originally scheduled 1961 or 1962).[48] (3) Before initiation of expensive new construction, it would have been wise to consider the possibilities for economizing on existing uses: the panel's proposal for elimination of wastage from street mains was highly economic. The panel's suggestion about extension of metering seemed convincing on efficiency grounds, though undoubtedly warranting the more detailed study called for by the panel. (Our tentative calculations suggest that water saved by metering is cheaper per unit than new Cannonsville water and even cheaper than Hudson water.) The possibility considered by us of saving water through an increase in meter rates may be in the doubtful range as a long-term proposition, though temporarily raising prices would have helped ration water to its most productive uses in the crisis of 1949–50. (4) As between the alternative new sources, the Hudson was substantially cheaper although possibly inferior quality-wise (even after processing). While an element of taste or preference, as well as certain factual uncertainties, may enter into the willingness to pay a higher price for better water (in terms of biological, chemical, and physical quality characteristics), in our judgment the Hudson was on balance the better choice.

Our conclusions, in short, almost entirely parallel those of the Engineering Panel in 1951. One rather strong argument for the BWS decision might be made, however. As we bring out elsewhere, premature or uneconomic construction of water facilities is often undertaken in order to secure legal or practical title to desired supplies—and it may well have been the case that at this time a favorable conjunction of circumstances was seized to secure Supreme Court approval of an increase in the city's Delaware withdrawals from 440 to 800 mgd. On the other hand, New York gained only temporary permission rather than firm title, so that the entire $140-million investment stands on legally insecure ground.

Methodologically, our analysis revealed that neither the BWS nor its critics had a satisfactory basis for project efficiency calculations. The panel's intuition that thought be given first to suggestions for improving the economy of utilization of existing supplies was sound, but these can only properly be evaluated by a comparison of their costs with those of new construction. All in all, the results support the judgment that water-supply decisions are typically made without proper economic analysis, this being true not only of small or backward municipalities but of our greatest cities; that, in the absence of the discipline of a competitive market in water supply, the scale of error possible in such decisions is very large; and that, consequently, the dissemination of knowledge about methods of efficiency calculations and other techniques of economic analysis would be likely to yield very high returns to agencies now using incorrect methods of analysis (or none at all). We will remark finally on how curious it is that political authorities usually insist on a high level of engineering or technological analysis in project design or justification, while the equally vital economic aspect, where considered at all, usually represents the offhand ideas of personnel untrained in the appropriate techniques of analysis.

[48] The later dates are quoted in the *New York Times,* March 6, 1960, p. 65.

APPENDIX

HUDSON VERSUS CANNONSVILLE—DETAILS OF COST CALCULATIONS

This appendix is designed to present information about our techniques and numerical assumptions in sufficient detail so as to permit independent check upon our results. It goes almost without saying that such information should always be provided in efficiency analyses; even aside from conceptual errors which might thus be revealed, mere arithmetical mistakes are never an insignificant possibility, especially where the computations are of substantial magnitude.

Table 32 summarizes the data used to derive estimates of the cost of water to be provided through the different Hudson or Cannonsville projects considered. Table 32 is not quite in the same form as Table 31, but Table 33, which shows the present-value calculations, indicates how the text results are derived from the underlying data.

In Table 32, figures of costs and of water deliveries are indicated for each year of project life, 1960 being taken as year zero when construction begins. (Actual construction of Cannonsville began in 1955, but the actual starting date used for the computation does not affect the project comparison; we use 1960 because that was the date assumed in the conflicting analyses presented by the panel and BWS.) The dollar figures are generally in terms of a 1950 price level, 1950 being the approximate date when the basic figures underlying the panel's analysis were estimated. Again, differences in price level would not affect the comparison, except for a proportionate change in the dollar-cost magnitudes for each project.

TABLE 33

PRESENT-VALUE CALCULATIONS WITH COLUMNS OF TABLE 32*

(Cost per Million Gallons Delivered)

Comparison	Cannonsville	Hudson
1.	$\frac{(2)+(3)+(4)+(5)}{(1)}$	$\frac{(6)+(7)+(8)+(9)}{(1)}$
2.	$\frac{(2)+(3)+(4)+(5)}{(1)}$	$\frac{(10)+(11)+(12)+(9)}{(1)}$
3.	$\frac{(2)+(3)+(4)+(5)}{(1)}$	$\frac{(13)+(14)+(15)+(16)}{(1)}$
4.	$\frac{(2)+(3)+(18)+(5)}{(17)}$	$\frac{(19)+(20)+(21)+(22)}{(17)}$

* In denominators, multiply figures from Table 32 by 365. For total net costs use numerators only.

We now turn to the details of the data in Table 32.

Comparison 1, Cannonsville:

This is our standard case described at length in the text.

Column (1): "Deliveries," q_t.—For each year *t* Cannonsville deliveries are based on those given for the Hudson Project (i.e., deliveries for both projects are assumed by us to be identical, for reasons explained in the text) in *Panel Report,* page 63 (Table 26). Intermediate years have been interpolated by us, and after the year 2000 an increase of 8 mgd per year is assumed.

Column (2): "Construction costs," K_t. —The sum of $140 million is spread over the seven-year construction period in project years 0–6 according to the schedule in BWS, "Cost Estimates" (1951), page 23.

Column (3): "Operation and maintenance," O_t.—These costs are assumed to be $422,000 per annum, independent of output, beginning in project year 7 (*Panel Report,* p. 73). This is consistent with BWS, "Cost Estimates" (1951), page 15. The figure of $478,000 per annum is used in BWS, *Hudson River Investigations* (1955), Appendix Table Acc NS 491, but we assume that this increase represents only a price-level change between the dates of the two documents (our analysis is based on the earlier price level). The figures include tax expenses.

Column (4): "Pumping offset," P_t.—Negative terms here indicate how use of Cannonsville water reduces cost of pumping from Croton, based on BWS, "Cost Estimates" (1951), page 24. The saving shown in this source is based on BWS consumption estimates and is used therefore in our Comparison 4 below (col. [18]). Using the panel's consumption estimates, the saving is larger—the full reduction in pumping would be possible through about the year 2006, as shown in this column. Note that this substitution of Cannonsville water for pumped Croton water will make the physical water flow through Cannonsville greater than through the Hudson Project; but, since a corresponding amount of Croton water is displaced, the incremental flows due to each project remain equal.

Column (5): "Salvage value," S_t.—Our detailed analysis of deliveries and costs ends in project year 46 (calendar year 2006). But at this time there will still be substantial project life remaining, and it is necessary to make some allowance for this factor. Obviously, with information about the distant future necessarily limited and uncertain, only a very rough estimate can be made. Our assumption was that the Cannonsville Project life was a hundred years and, consequently, that there were sixty years of life remaining after project year 46. It is obviously inappropriate to charge the entire capital investment, designed to yield benefits over the full one hundred years, against the benefits of the earlier project years alone. The simplest way to correct for this is to credit a crude rebate of the capital cost, in proportion to the unexpired life of the project, in project year 47. The actual amount so credited is $84 million.

Comparison 1, Hudson:

"Deliveries," q_t, are same as for Cannonsville shown in column (1) above.

Column (6): "Construction costs," K_t. —The initial construction cost of $31 million is distributed evenly over a seven-year construction period in project years 0–6. The second construction stage cost of $8,185,000 is assigned in its entirety to project year 25.

Column (7): "Tax expense," T_t.—Based on *Panel Report,* page 64, Table 29, Project B. Figures between 1960 and 1967 were interpolated by us.

Column (8): "Operation and maintenance," O_t.—Also based on *Panel Report,* page 64, Table 29, Project B. Figures for intermediate years were interpolated by us, and the factor for the year 2000 (the ratio of O_t to q_t) was used for years 2001–2007.

Column (9): "Salvage value," S_t.—On the same principle as for Cannonsville, but assuming a forty-year life for project elements, there is an undepreciated balance after the year 2006 of 18/40 of the investment of $8,185,000 made in 1985. This amount, $3,683,000, is credited in the year 2007 (project year 47). Strictly speaking, we should have charged for replacing the first-stage capacity in the years from 2000 to 2006 and then again credited a salvage value against that charge. However, the effects would be almost fully offsetting (they would be exactly offsetting except for the time lag between construction expenses and project benefits), and accordingly they are omitted.

Comparison 2, Hudson (Cannonsville unchanged):

Column (10): "Construction costs," K_t. —The figures shown are based upon a first-stage construction cost of $13,583,000 omitting filtration items, as indicated in *Panel Report,* page 70. This cost is spread over the seven-year construction period. The second-stage costs is unchanged ($8,185,000 in 1985).

Column (11): "Tax expense," T_t.—These figures are our estimates, calculated as $\frac{1}{2}$ per cent of previous year's accumulation of capital invested in early stages, and 1 per cent for the second stage of construction. This is roughly similar to the relative order of magnitudes in column (7) above.

Column (12): "Operation and maintenance," O_t.—Based on *Panel Report,* page 64, Table 28, Project B. Interpolations as in column (8) above.

Deliveries unchanged from Comparison 1. Salvage value also unchanged, since second-stage construction cost is the same.

Comparison 3, Hudson (Cannonsville unchanged):

Column (13): "Construction cost," K_t. —The cost assigned to the first stage is $48,300,000, spread evenly over the seven-year construction period. This figure is adjusted from the first-stage cost of $66,939,000 shown for "3rd Proposal" in BWS, *Hudson River Investigations* (1955), Appendix Table Acc NS 520. The BWS cost was adjusted downward for excess capacity assumed by BWS by multiplying by the factor

$$0.902\left(=\frac{325\text{ mgd of Panel Plan}}{360\text{ mgd of BWS Plan}}\right)$$

and for change in price level by multiplying by the factor 0.8 (= 1/1.25), the *Engineering News-Record* construction-cost index cited in the text having risen by about 25 per cent between 1950 and 1954. Corresponding adjustment of the BWS second-stage figure of $16,129,000 brought it down to the $11,650,000 used in the table.

Column (14): "Tax expense," T_t.—The same method as in column (11) was used, based on the figures of column (13).

Column (15): "Operation and maintenance," O_t.—The basic figures used are those shown in BWS, *Hudson River Investigations,* Appendix Table Acc NS 540, for deliveries of 30, 87, and 161 mgd. The three categories of cost were adjusted for price level by dividing through by the following price indexes: chemicals, 161.4; electric power, 101.7; and personnel, 126.1. The price indexes used were based upon the most comparable categories for the years 1950 and 1954.[49] Intermediate figures representing delivery assumptions of the panel were interpolated by us.

Column (16): "Salvage value," S_t.—Method of column (9) used for construction cost of column (13).

Deliveries unchanged from Comparison 1.

Comparison 4, Cannonsville:

Column (17): "Deliveries," q_t.—Based on BWS, *Hudson River Investigations,* Appendix Table Acc NS 540, except that we

[49] Data from U.S. Department of Commerce, *Business Statistics, 1957.* For chemicals, category "Chemicals, industrial" was used (p. 28); for electric power, category "Electricity" (p. 29); for personnel, category "Average hourly earnings, gas-electric utilities" (p. 77).

fixed the upper limit on deliveries at 310 rather than 360 mgd (see text).

Column (18): "Pumping offset," P_t.—See explanation for column (4) above.

Comparison 4, Hudson:

"Deliveries," q_t, are same as for Cannonsville shown in column (17) above.

Column (19): "Construction cost," K_t.—Identical with column (13) except that second-stage cost moved to 1980 because of earlier need indicated by BWS delivery schedule.

Column (20): "Tax expense," T_t.—Same as for column (14) except for adjustment because of earlier construction of second stage.

Column (21): "Operation and maintenance," O_t.—Method of column (15) above used, but timing changed to correspond to BWS delivery schedule.

Column (22): "Salvage value," S_t.—Same as that in column (16) except that because of earlier construction only thirteen years of life of second stage remain to be credited.

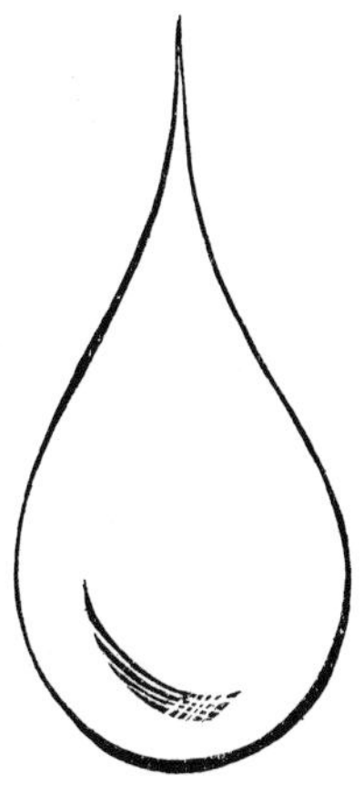

CHAPTER XI

WATER FOR SOUTHERN CALIFORNIA

CASE STUDY OF AN ARID REGION

In our chapter on the New York City water situation we examined the problems of an area that is fully urbanized, located in a humid region, and unified by a common local government. The southern California area to be discussed here presents an interesting contrast. First of all, it is an arid region which is experiencing a rapid increase in growth, so that water problems take on a special urgency. Second, southern California is of course much less fully urbanized than New York, and in fact use of water for irrigation still comprises almost 40 per cent of total water consumption in the area. Third, responsibility for water supply is divided among a bewildering variety of municipalities and water districts often arrayed in a multitier fashion. Much of the area adheres to a water superagency—the Metropolitan Water District—which imports water to southern California from the Colorado River. And, finally, there is the state government, whose Department of Water Resources is seeking to play a major role in water-supply activities of this region and other regions of California.

Is southern California running out of water? Should new water supplies be developed? We hope that the analysis in this chapter may be of particular importance not only for illustrating principles of economic choice in regard to water supply but also for providing a basis for answering these and similar questions.

A. The Area and Its Problems

1. Definition of the Area

Interpretations of the term "southern California" vary considerably. Most broadly defined, the term denotes the lower half of California comprising the fourteen southernmost counties. For purposes of this case study we sometimes speak of the broader southern California area, but we shall be primarily concerned with the region technically known as the South Coastal Area (see Fig. 24). This area is one of the major hydrographic regions of the state; it extends some 200 miles along the Pacific Ocean from northern Ventura County southward to the Mexican border, and from the ocean inland to a distance of approximately 75 miles. The land area covered is some 10,930 square miles—about 7 per cent of the area of the state of California. Included are the coastal plains of six southern California counties—Ventura, Los Angeles,

Orange, San Bernardino, Riverside, and San Diego—and the large metropolitan areas of Los Angeles and San Diego. As of January, 1960, the South Coastal Area had an estimated population of some 8,600,000 people, over 50 per cent of the estimated 15,300,000 population of California.

2. Background of Growth

The South Coastal Area is characterized today by rapid urban and industrial development superimposed upon an intensely irrigated agricultural base. The 1960 population of 8,600,000 may be compared with a figure of about 3,700,000 for 1940 and

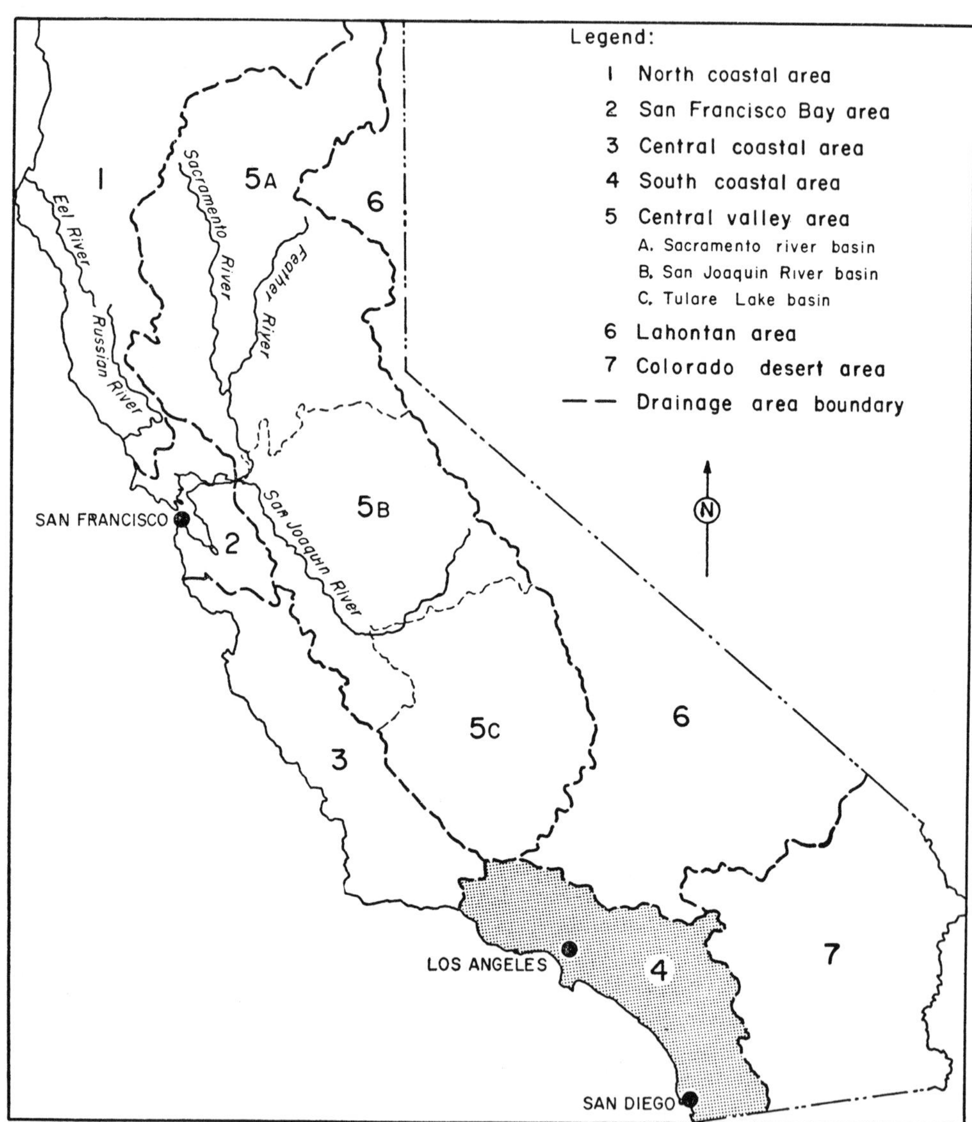

FIG. 24.—Major hydrographic areas of California. (Adapted from *Bulletin No. 78* [*Preliminary*], Pl. III.)

5,400,000 for 1950. The Los Angeles–Orange Counties Metropolitan Area at present ranks third among the industrial areas of the nation, behind the metropolitan areas of New York and of Chicago. Among the major industries are petroleum production and refining, aircraft and missile production, automobile assembly, clothing manufacture, and tire production.

From 1930 to 1950 the acreage devoted to irrigation remained fairly stable—approximately 650,000 acres, or about 10 per cent of all irrigated land in California. As urban development pre-empted land devoted to agriculture, new lands on the edges of the basin were put into cultivation. Since 1950, however, a decline in the number of acres irrigated has been observed; 1957 estimates of irrigated acres total only 580,000, with most of the decline taking place in Los Angeles and Orange counties. Urban encroachment upon agricultural lands, together with the prospect of rising costs of water supplies, will very likely result in sharp declines in irrigation within the coming decades.

3. *Local Water Supplies*

In direct contrast with the relatively large portion of the state's population and economic activity concentrated in the South Coastal Area is the relative poverty of its natural water supply. The area receives about 5.7 per cent of the state's precipitation; the annual average is approximately 18 inches, in comparison with the national average of 30 inches. Almost every year the rainfall over the entire area occurs largely during the winter months; the principal growing season from April to October receives less than 16 per cent of the average amount. In many portions of the area the naturally occurring rainfall is too small to contribute to the local water supply; it either evaporates directly from the soil or passes through beneficial or non-beneficial plant life and is transpired without recharging the underground water table. The result is that the local runoff is only 1.7 per cent of the state total.

The amount of water entering the South Coastal Area, whether by direct precipitation or by inflow from mountain runoff water, is not only highly seasonal but is and always has been highly variable over the years. Very few years are "normal" or "average," and the amount of rainfall may vary by a factor of 5 between a typical "wet" year and a typical "dry" year. A record high was established in 1883–84 when the fall measured 38.18 inches; the recent 1958–59 year brought a record low of 5.59 inches (measurements at Los Angeles). Furthermore, dry years tend to be followed by dry, and wet by wet years, the periodicity of the cycle being about eleven years. As can be imagined, this cyclical variability of rainfall has been associated with overoptimistic development during wet periods followed by cries of alarm (as at present) during dry phases of the cycle.

The purely local supplies are of two types: surface diversions from streams and pumping of ground water from underground basins or aquifers. It is estimated that safe yield of local supplies is about 1,098,000 acre-feet annually. Approximately three-quarters of this amount is secured by pumping from a network of underground basins. It is only with the extensive underground storage of heavy flows (from precipitation and mountain runoff) in wet years which recharge the basins that it is possible to provide a supply in dry years.[1] The usable storage capacity of these aquifers exceeds 8,000,000 acre-feet.[2]

[1] Cesspools formerly were an important source of recharge. The construction of extensive sewer lines to the ocean has resulted in a decrease in this form of ground-water recharge.

[2] California Department of Water Resources, *The California Water Plan* (Bull. 3 [Sacramento, May, 1957]), pp. 82, 84 (hereinafter cited as "*Bulletin No. 3*"). It may be noted that this estimate is conservative because the storage was calculated

4. Overdraft and Salt-Water Intrusion

Rights to pump water in California are based upon riparian and appropriation doctrines of water law. Individual pumpers have little incentive to consider the effects of overpumping on other users. In part as a result of the divergence of private and social costs which is characteristic of fragmented production in the common-pool case, water-mining (or overdraft) is taking place. One consequence of excessive pumping is salt-water intrusion at several places in the area, particularly at San Diego and Long Beach and below Santa Monica. The costs of salt-water intrusion are usually not borne by those who have caused the condition; the bulk of the pumping takes place far upstream from the coast.[3] We estimate that the current *net* overdraft is some 130,000 acre-feet a year;[4] the accumulated overdraft is about 1,500,000 acre-feet.

The solution to the problem appears to lie in the adjudication of water rights throughout the region (or the imposition of restrictions on water-mining). Not only is this procedure expensive but it is exceedingly time-consuming; it will require years of tedious action by water engineers and water lawyers.[5] The paucity of pumping records in itself is a tremendous problem, though by recent state law the extraction of ground water in this region must be recorded and filed with the state, so that a basis is being established for eventual adjudication.

In the meantime certain public agencies are attempting to raise ground-water levels and to increase the supply of water in storage by purchasing Colorado River water from the Metropolitan Water District and spreading it for percolation underground. During the 1958–59 year approximately 170,000 acre-feet were delivered to the Orange County Water District and the Los Angeles County Flood Control District for spreading in the Santa Ana and San Gabriel river basins. (The Flood Control District derives its funds from a general property tax; the Orange County Water District, however, has imposed a unique use tax of $3.90 an acre-foot on all ground-water pumping in Orange County in an attempt to assess the costs of replenishment upon the pumpers directly.) Since 1949 the Orange County Water District has spread almost 500,000 acre-feet of water, and a recent report indicated that average well levels had risen over 10½ feet in the previous two years.[6] Plans are now

upon the basis of the "economic pumping lift," which may be expected to increase as the economic demand for water increases and technology improves.

[3] In a recent action the city of Long Beach and the Orange County Water District brought suit against four cities upstream on the Santa Ana River, charging that upstream pumping was contributing to sea-water intrusion on the coast. The court upheld the charge and ordered the cities of San Bernardino, Riverside, Colton, and Redlands to reduce their ground-water pumping by 30 per cent.

[4] Estimates of overdraft, pumping in excess of "safe yield," are currently subject to a wide margin of error and constitute a species of educated guessing for most of the region. In addition, the term "safe yield" itself is not always defined in a consistent fashion. In this chapter we accept the safe-yield estimates of state authorities, which generally are based upon the rate of long-run natural recharge. We estimate the current annual overdraft to be approximately 300,000 acre-feet. However, spreading of imported Colorado River water for recharge is taking place at the rate of 170,000 acre-feet per year, leaving a net overdraft of 130,000 acre-feet.

[5] Thus far pumping rights have been adjudicated in the Raymond Basin near Pasadena, and they are in the process of being determined in the West Basin Area south of Santa Monica. In both areas total pumping has been limited to the safe yield of the basins involved.

[6] Paul Bailey, *Engineer's Report upon Ground Water Conditions in the Orange County Water District* (Santa Ana, Calif., March 11, 1959). However, well levels dropped about 6 feet in the record dry year 1958–59.

in process for the formation of a giant replenishment district, covering a large portion of Los Angeles County, for the spreading of approximately 200,000 acre-feet annually, with the costs to be covered by a use tax imposed upon persons pumping from wells in the area to be benefited.[7] As outlined in our earlier theoretical discussion, the imposition of use taxes is an important method of correcting a divergence between private and social costs in such common-pool situations.

The spreading of water for percolation in underground aquifers may be desirable for several reasons. First, raising the water table in areas near the coast may prevent further encoachment of sea water in addition to reducing the salinity of wells already contaminated. Second, the underground basins may function as valuable storage reservoirs, particularly when the cost of surface storage in an urbanized area may be almost prohibitive. And, third, the network of underground basins may function as a distribution system transporting water to all parts of the area—in fact, carrying water directly to the pumps of existing well-owners. Because of these factors, it is usually economical to spread the water underground and then pump it out again when needed rather than to attempt construction of new surface storage and distribution facilities.

In addition to spreading activities, the Los Angeles County Flood Control District is experimenting with injection wells in the sand-dune area on the coast near Manhattan Beach. Here water is being forced underground to create a fresh-water barrier and prevent further intrusion of sea water. Use of reclaimed waste waters for this purpose has been tried, and the results appear to be very promising.

[7] A tax of $6.60 an acre-foot on *all* pumping within the district has been suggested. After an adjudication of water rights is accomplished, only water pumped in excess of such rights would be taxed.

5. Imported Water Supplies

To secure imported water supplies, it is necessary to go considerable distances, because the South Coastal Area is isolated hydrographically. There are no long rivers flowing into southern California from outside the basin; the lands immediately beyond the encircling mountains are arid and produce little water. The nearest areas of heavy precipitation are in the Sierra Nevada Mountains to the north. Presently, water is imported to the South Coastal Area from two sources: the Colorado River Aqueduct, operated by the Metropolitan Water District, and the Los Angeles Aqueduct, which comes from the Owens and Mono basins in the Sierra Nevada Mountains (see Fig. 25).

The Los Angeles Aqueduct is 240 miles in length and has a capacity of 320,000 acre-feet annually. This supply is available only to the city of Los Angeles. The water flows by gravity and generates hydroelectricity for the municipal power system. Currently, the aqueduct supply is fully utilized; it furnishes about 60 per cent of the city's water supply.

The Colorado River Aqueduct system is the largest and longest domestic water-supply line in the United States. It extends from an intake at Parker Dam 242 miles across mountains and desert to the terminal reservoir near the city of Riverside, from which point a distribution system 300 miles in length carries Colorado River water to over seventy cities in southern California. This aqueduct, constructed and operated by the Metropolitan Water District of Southern California, has an ultimate capacity of 1,200,000 acre-feet annually, or approximately a billion gallons of water a day. The district does not supply water to individual consumers but limits itself to wholesale delivery of water to district members. Composed of various cities and subsidiary water districts, the district covers 3,300 square miles and includes most of the South Coastal Area except for territory in Ventura County. The Colorado River Aqueduct first supplied water in 1941; it has recently been operating at about 50 per cent of its ultimate capacity, yielding about 600,000 acre-feet a year.[8]

6. Source-Use Balance

Table 34 shows source-use balances which we have constructed for 1950 and 1957, and forecast for 1960, after studying federal and state reports on water supply and water use for the region. On the use side, the most conspicuous change visible is the increase in urban uses, offset somewhat by the decline in agricultural uses, leading in total to a prospective rise in use from 1950 to 1960 of approximately 23 per cent. It can be seen that the population increase during the same period is anticipated to be approximately 60 per cent. The fact that the proportionate

[8] For a critical analysis of the history and policies of the Metropolitan Water District see Jerome W. Milliman, "The History, Organization, and Economic Problems of the Metropolitan Water District of Southern California" (unpublished Ph.D. dissertation, University of California, Los Angeles, 1956).

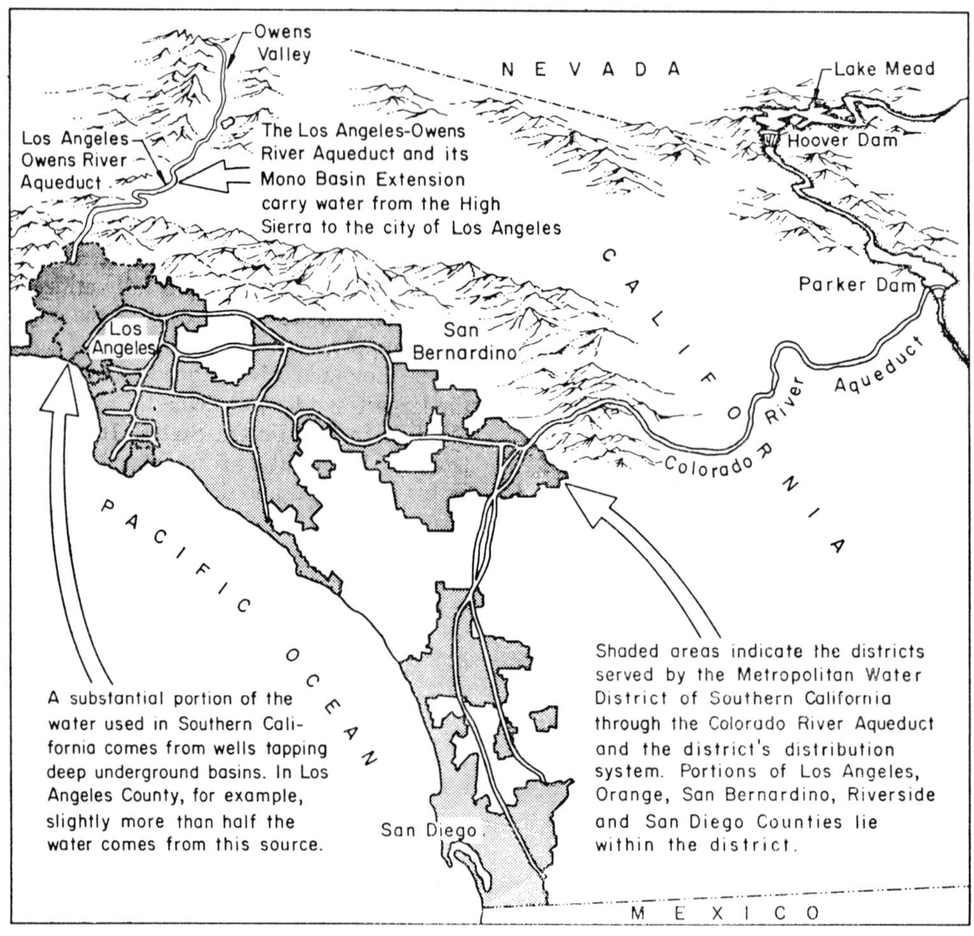

FIG. 25.—Major water systems serving the South Coastal Area. (From *Los Angeles Times,* January 24, 1960, Part II, p. 1.)

population increase far exceeds the increase in total water use is principally accounted for by the decline in agricultural use of water.[9] As we shall emphasize later, the decline of agricultural water use can provide the basis for a substantial further increase in domestic and industrial water consumption.

[9] On the basis of an urban consumption rate of 160 gallons per capita per day, the decline in agricultural water use of 250,000 acre-feet was sufficient to supply over 40 per cent of the population increase.

On the supply side we see that the Los Angeles Aqueduct and local water sources were fully utilized, so that the net increase in use was met almost entirely by imports from the Colorado River. The Colorado River Aqueduct may be operating at close to 60 per cent of capacity in 1960.

B. The California Water Plan

Southern California today, like New York City in 1951, stands on the brink of a major water-supply decision. The question is

TABLE 34

SOURCE-USE BALANCE FOR SOUTH COASTAL AREA

	WITHDRAWALS FOR USE (ACRE-FEET)		
	1950	1957	1960
Water source:			
Local surface and ground water:			
1. Developed safe yield	1,066,000	1,098,000	1,098,000
2. Gross overdraft*	(300,000)	(300,000)	(300,000)
3. Net overdraft*	275,000	150,000	120,000
Los Angeles Aqueduct	320,000	320,000	320,000
Colorado River Aqueduct (capacity 1,200,000 acre-feet):			
1. Agricultural and urban use	142,000	394,000	527,000
2. Water-spreading	25,000	150,000	180,000
Total	1,828,000	2,112,000	2,245,000
Water use:†			
Irrigation	954,000	790,000	700,000
Urban	874,000	1,322,000	1,545,000
Total	1,828,000	2,112,000	2,245,000
Water-use assumptions:			
1. Agricultural use:			
Irrigated acres	650,000	580,000	500,000
Water applied in feet	1.5	1.4	1.4
2. Urban use:			
Population	5,480,000	8,000,000	8,656,000
Use rate in gallons per capita per day‡	140	150	160

* "Gross overdraft" refers to total pumping in excess of long-run natural recharge. "Net overdraft" is gross overdraft minus the spreading of imported water. Most estimates of current overdraft do not make this distinction and report only gross figures.

† Our estimates of water use are generally consistent with those made by the California Department of Water Resources. For example, *Preliminary Summary Report on Investigation of Alternative Aqueduct Systems To Serve Southern California* (Bull. 78 [Sacramento, 1959]) places agricultural use for 1960 at 669,000 acre-feet and urban use at 1,564,000 acre-feet.

‡ A handy rule of thumb is: 1 acre-foot per year supplies $\left\{\begin{matrix}7.4\\6.4\\5.6\\5.0\end{matrix}\right\}$ people at $\left\{\begin{matrix}120\\140\\160\\180\end{matrix}\right\}$ gallons per capita per day (gpcd).

whether or not to participate—and the participation of southern California will be decisive—in the state's Feather River Project, which is to be submitted to the voters of the state in November, 1960, for a decision on a giant bond issue to initiate the undertaking. This project is the first and central component of the California State Water Plan—a grand scheme for geographically distributing the waters of California from the regions of "surplus" to the regions of "deficiency." With capital expenses alone of approximately $3 *billion*, the Feather River Project will dwarf the Cannonsville Project in New York, which was expected to cost the comparatively small sum of $140 million. This single project will about equal in magnitude the cost of the Tennessee Valley Authority. The cost of the California Water Plan as a whole has been estimated at upward of $13 billion.

The California Water Plan[10] is a result of a ten-year survey of the water resources of California in relation to present and prospective "ultimate requirements" for water for all consumption uses.[11] It is designed to serve as a master plan for the development of California's water resources by all agencies "for the benefit of all areas of the State and for all beneficial purposes." As we pointed out in chapter ix, many states are moving in the direction of centralized control over the development and use of water resources. Because the California Water Plan constitutes one of the most ambitious illustrations of planned water development, it may have some influence upon the course of action taken by other states in the formulation of their plans.

The legal foundation of state-wide water planning for water resources in California has been long established. For example, the State Water Code contains the following statements:

> It is hereby declared that because of the conditions prevailing in the State the general welfare requires that the water resources of the State be put to beneficial use to the fullest extent of which they are capable, and that the waste or unreasonable use or unreasonable method of use of water be prevented, and that the conservation of such water is to be exercised with a view to the reasonable and beneficial use thereof in the interest of the people and for the public welfare. . . .[12]

> It is hereby declared that the protection of the public interest in the development of the water resources of the State is of vital concern to the people of the State and that the State shall determine in what way the water of the State, both surface and underground, should be developed for the greatest public benefit.[13]

Although we are primarily concerned in this chapter with the economic aspects of water supply for southern California, we find it difficult not to comment upon the possible implications of the principles of state-wide planning set forth in the water code. We will only point out here that the growing cities and the large agricultural areas of California did secure their water supplies in the past without the advantage or disadvantage of a centralized state planning agency deciding which areas had a water "surplus" and which had a "deficiency," what works were to be constructed to remedy these calculated imbalances, and who was to pay how much. Although the legal bases of state-wide water planning and control of water use have been long established, it is also true that sweeping centralized powers have not been extensively exercised so far. Instead, those who have had an economic need for water (whether private individuals, mu-

[10] *Bulletin No. 3.*

[11] Two earlier bulletins were issued as preparation for the plan: (1) State Water Resources Board, *Water Resources of California* (Bull. 1 [Sacramento, 1951]) (hereinafter cited as *"Bulletin No. 1"*). This study presents an inventory of California's water resources. (2) State Water Resources Board, *Water Utilization and Requirements of California* (Bull. 2 [Sacramento, June, 1955]) (hereinafter cited as *"Bulletin No. 2"*). This bulletin estimates 1950 water use and presents forecasts of "ultimate" requirements based upon assumed land-use patterns under "full" development.

[12] Sec. 100.

[13] Sec. 105.

tual associations, or municipal corporations) have been able, by and large, despite difficulties due to imperfect property rights in water, to secure title to water through established market procedures and to arrange for its transport to points of service. We wish to emphasize here, though subject to qualifications discussed at length earlier, that water, like any other economic good, will tend—without deliberate centralized planning—toward its most economic and valuable use via the market process, if that process is permitted to operate.

Basically, the California Water Plan represents a mechanical or arithmetic approach to the water-supply problems of the various parts of California. It starts by examining the total water received in the state by precipitation and by imports, subtracts unavoidable losses such as those from evaporation, and arrives at a gross figure of some 70,000,000 acre-feet per year available for state-wide use. Since this is far in excess of the aggregate quantities likely to be demanded in the foreseeable future, it is concluded that there is enough water for all of California's needs. The "only" problem remaining is to construct facilities to transport water from where it is found to where it is needed.

The state planners examined each of the major hydrographic areas of the state to determine how much water will be available and how much will be "required" under conditions of "ultimate development."[14] The excess, if any, is the area's "surplus" which the state plan proposes to take for transport to regions of "deficiency."[15] The estimate of the "ultimate" requirements for water in each area was established on a purely physical basis. For urban areas, present population and industrial trends were crudely extrapolated to the future,[16] and estimated residential and industrial use factors were applied to determine future domestic and industrial water needs. For irrigation, certain topographic, climatic, and crop characteristics were used for each region to establish future agricultural expansion potential and thereby the water requirements. With the future ultimate requirements determined in this manner, works were designed to supply the deficit areas with the excess waters of the surplus areas.

Tables 35 and 36 are presented to show some of the specific estimates which the plan makes for the state as a whole. Table 35 shows the major types of land use; it is interesting to note that agriculture is shown as almost tripling its land use despite the general state-wide tendency for urban encroachment on irrigated lands. Much of the projected expansion in irrigation is to be found in areas presently classified as deserts; for example, the Lahontan and Colorado desert areas are assumed to expand irrigated acreage by approximately 8,700,000 acres.[17] We may incidentally note that the acres currently irrigated in California make up 25 per cent of the total irrigated acreage in the United States. From Table 36 it can be seen that the dominating use of water in California is for irrigation; in 1957 consumption of water by agriculture was almost 90 per cent of the total, and under "complete development" irrigation will still use almost five times as much water as will be consumed for urban and industrial purposes.

It thus appears that most of the official projected increase in water "requirements" is designed to satisfy an expanded irrigated agriculture so that, insofar as water "short-

14 Defined as representing "an unspecified but distant time in the future, when land and other resources of California have essentially reached a complete stage of development" (*Bulletin No. 3,* p. xxv).

15 The plan is not clear on matters of water rights in relation to the "surplus" supplies. Whether the transfer of water between regions can be imposed unilaterally by the state planners under present law is open to question.

16 For example, it was assumed that "ultimate" population in all urban areas would be approximately 300 per cent greater than in 1950 "under a saturated condition of development" (*Bulletin No. 2,* I, 48).

17 *Bulletin No. 3,* p. 14.

ages" develop in California, they may well be shortages of (cheap) water for agriculture rather than for urban, suburban, and industrial uses. On the other hand, because of the large proportion of water used in agriculture, it would be possible for relatively small *declines* in agricultural use to support large increases in urban and industrial use. For example, let us make a rather extreme assumption and suppose that no new water supplies are developed in California; does this mean that the projected urban development could not be supplied? Because of the typically greater value of water for urban purposes, it is to be expected that natural economic forces would cause the water to be transferred from irrigation to urban uses. The safe yield of presently developed supplies in California is approximately 18,000,000 acre-feet a year, and hence the "ulti-

TABLE 35

LAND USES IN CALIFORNIA

Type	Acres Occupied		
	1950*	1957†	Ultimate*
Urban, suburban, and industrial	1,050,000	1,200,000	3,600,000
Agricultural	7,000,000	7,000,000	20,000,000
Total	8,050,000	8,200,000	23,600,000‡

* California Department of Water Resources, *The California Water Plan* (Bull. 3 [Sacramento, May, 1957]).

† Our estimate.

‡ California has a total area of approximately 101,000,000 acres. At "ultimate" development approximately 77,000,000 acres will still be sparsely settled, constituting, for the most part, mountain and desert regions.

TABLE 36

PRESENT USE AND OFFICIAL USE PROJECTIONS FOR WATER IN CALIFORNIA

	1950*	1957†	Ultimate*
Use categories:			
Total population	10,600,000	14,600,000	40,000,000‡
Acres irrigated	7,000,000	7,000,000	20,000,000
Water use (in acre-feet):			
Urban, suburban, and industrial	1,700,000	2,600,000	8,500,000
Irrigation	19,000,000	19,000,000	42,000,000
Total	20,700,000	21,600,000§	50,500,000‖
Implied water-use assumptions:			
1. Per capita urban, suburban, and industrial water use in gallons per day	140	160	190
2. Per acre agricultural use in feet per year	2.7	2.7	2.1

* *Bulletin No. 3.*

† Our estimate.

‡ This figure has now been increased to 56,000,000 people by year 2020 in projections made two years later (see *Preliminary Summary Report on Investigation of Alternative Aqueduct Systems To Serve Southern California* [Bull. 78 (Sacramento, 1959)]).

§ In 1957 estimated annual overdraft in the state as a whole was approximately 4,000,000 acre-feet, most of which was taking place in the San Joaquin Valley.

‖ Gross water supply is estimated to be 70,000,000 acre-feet annually.

mate" urban demand seen in the plan of 8,500,000 acre-feet[18] could be satisfied and still leave over 9,000,000 acre-feet yearly for irrigation purposes. This amount would be sufficient to irrigate about 4,000,000 acres, a large number if one realizes that much of the urban growth would pre-empt agricultural lands anyway.[19] This bit of arithmetic is intended not to prove a case against new construction but only to illustrate that the failure to develop huge new water supplies does not necessarily mean that California's urban and industrial growth must come to a sudden halt.

Based upon 1955 prices, the costs of the engineering features of the California Water Plan amount to $11.9 billion. This sum does not include allowances for the acquisition of water rights or for any of the required local distribution facilities. The physical features projected by the plan include 376 reservoirs with a capacity of 77,000,000 acre-feet, approximately 600 miles of tunnels, 5,000 miles of canals, and seventy-five pumping plants with an installed capacity of 12,300,000 kilowatts. The total gross energy requirement to deliver water to all areas of the state is 49,000,000,000 kw-h. per year;[20] the net energy requirement, however, is around 15,000,000,000 kw-h. because of power generation of approximately 34,000,000,000 kw-h. per year from 122 power-generation plants.

As shown in Table 37, the California Water Plan envisages the development of approximately 29,000,000 acre-feet per year in new supplies; about 7,000,000 acre-feet of the new yield would be local supplies, while nearly 22,000,000 acre-feet would be transported to areas of deficiency by a gigantic California Aqueduct System. In addition to surface storage facilities, about 31,000,000 acre-feet of ground-water storage would be utilized in the San Joaquin Valley to produce the required degree of control and regulation of the irregular annual natural flows.

The ultimate development projected in Table 37 for the South Coastal Area involves an increase in annual use from 1,910,000 acre-feet in 1950 to 5,550,000 acre-feet. The new supplies are to be provided by additional local projects yielding 149,000 acre-feet, by an increase in imported water from the Colorado River, and by a new supply of 2,878,000 acre-feet to be transported by the state-controlled aqueduct system. According to earlier state plans, 1,800,000 acre-feet were to be delivered through works associated with the Feather River Project. The remainder was to be provided at some later date by another aqueduct (generally paralleling the Feather River Project Aqueduct but on a substantially larger scale) delivering some 6,200,000 acre-feet to the Colorado Desert and Lahontan areas in addition to the extra supply for the South Coastal Area. More recent official thinking, however, appears to have rejected the twin-aqueduct idea. Apparently "System B" (recommended in the preliminary version of *Bulletin No. 78*)[21] will have major features of sufficient scale to transport over 8,000,000 acre-feet per year to areas in the southern half of California, of which some 3,191,000 acre-feet are to be delivered (by the year 2020) to the South Coastal Area inclusive of Ventura County.[22]

18 At a consumption rate of 160 gallons per person per day, 8,500,000 acre-feet could support an urban population of 47,600,000 people, in contrast to the assumption of 190 gallons per day for 40,000,000 people used in the plan.

19 In this connection it is interesting to note that the state planners did not predict locations of urban encroachment upon agricultural lands, nor was irrigated area reduced to allow for such encroachment (*Bulletin No. 2,* I, 48).

20 About 30,000,000,000 kw-h. per year would be required to serve high desert areas with water largely destined for irrigation purposes (*Bulletin No. 3,* p. 213).

21 Department of Water Resources, *Preliminary Summary Report on Investigation of Alternative Aqueduct Systems To Serve Southern California* (Bull. 78 [Sacramento, February, 1959]).

22 *Ibid.,* p. VIII-15.

TABLE 37*

SUMMARY OF ULTIMATE DEVELOPMENT AND TRANSFER OF WATER UNDER THE CALIFORNIA WATER PLAN

(In Acre-Feet per Year)

Hydrographic Area	Water Requirements		Supplemental Water Requirements		Requirement Met by Existing Local Development Works	Potential Transfer under Existing or Claimed Rights†		Additional Yield from Prospective Local Development Works	Development and Transfer of Water by Facilities of California Aqueduct System		Total Ultimate Available Water Supplies
	Present, 1950	Probable Ultimate	Present, 1950	Probable Ultimate		Export	Import		Export	Import	
North Coastal	513,000	2,064,000	13,000	1,564,000	500,000	....	....	1,564,000	11,620,000	....	2,064,000
San Francisco Bay	710,000	3,512,000	42,000	2,257,000‡	420,000	....	835,000	103,000	....	2,154,000	3,512,000
Central Coastal	630,000	2,246,000	65,000	1,681,000	565,000	....	....	468,000	....	1,213,000	2,246,000
South Coastal	1,907,000	5,552,000	370,000	3,027,000	1,066,000	....	1,459,000§	149,000	....	2,878,000	5,552,000
Sacramento River Basin	3,819,000	7,427,000	124,000	3,732,000	3,668,000	34,000	27,000	3,732,000	10,274,000	....	7,427,000
San Joaquin–Tulare Lake Basin (excluding Delta)	8,539,000	15,549,000	1,661,000	8,671,000	6,878,000	830,000	....	877,000	....	7,794,000	15,549,000
Sacramento–San Joaquin Delta	834,000	756,000	....	756,000‖	....	....	....	....	....	756,000	756,000
Operation of Salinity Control Barrier	....	876,000	....	876,000	....	....	....	....	....	876,000	876,000
Lahontan	741,000	6,736,000	279,000	6,148,000	451,000	329,000	11,000	126,000	....	4,835,000	5,423,000
Colorado Desert	3,340,000	6,410,000	....	2,181,000	79,000	....	4,150,000#	....	....	1,388,000	5,617,000
Total	21,033,000	51,128,000	2,554,000	30,893,000	13,627,000	1,193,000	6,482,000**	7,019,000	21,894,000	21,894,000	49,022,000

* Source: *Bulletin No. 3*, p. 214.

† Does not include imports or exports of water by facilities considered as features of the California Aqueduct system.

‡ Includes delivery of 146,000 acre-feet per season through Contra Costa Canal, considered a feature of the California Aqueduct system.

§ Does not include conveyance and regulation loss of 73,000 acre-feet from Colorado River Aqueduct.

‖ Under ultimate conditions, the Delta would be served an imported water supply.

\# From Colorado River.

** Includes California's rights in and to the waters of the Colorado River, amounting to 5,362,000 acre-feet per year.

The reasoning underlying the California Water Plan ignores the economic fact that "requirements" are not fixed or absolute but are a function of the price and hence of the cost of water;[23] that it is extremely costly to transport water hundreds of miles and pump it over mountains thousands of feet high; and that, consequently, the costs incurred by the transport of water must be measured against the advantages of doing so. Even though the required cost comparison can perhaps be better made by the water-users in the various regions in their decisons to procure new supplies, it is clear that the State Department of Water Resources cannot ignore costs if the department is to take over all such decisions. The naturally occurring distribution of water resources, in fact, is not a mere obstacle to be overcome by magnificent feats of engineering but enters into the over-all economic advantage of one area relative to another. An alternative way of looking at the matter is to emphasize that water is a commodity whose utility is a sensitive function of locality, because its cost of transport is high relative to its productivity.

Some of the defects of the official approach were suggested by the brief report of the members of the Board of Engineering Consultants (Messrs. A. H. Ayres, R. A. Hill, W. L. Huber, S. B. Morris, and R. A. Tudor), who, in a letter to the director of the Department of Water Resources, stated, among other things, that the plan "includes projects of doubtful economic justification and works of unproven physical feasibility —the irrigation of desert areas involving net pumping lifts of several thousand feet is not now and may never be within the limits of economic justification and financial feasibility—this Board further recommends that no specific project be authorized for construction prior to detailed investigation of its engineering feasibility, economic justification, and financial feasibility."[24]

State water officials have become sensitive to this type of criticism and now point out that "economic and financial tests must be made for each project of the Plan as the projects are proposed for construction" and that the plan does not purport to do this.[25] While this reply is a sound one, it merely supports the viewpoint that the "requirements" set forth in the plan have little or no relation in themselves to present or future economic demands for water. It is difficult to see what valid purpose any such grand plan serves if its component parts are not now and may never be economically justified. Even if the plan were to serve only as a general directive and guide, it is likely that a number of sound projects would then be barred solely because they conflict with one or more of the uneconomic projects that do find a place in the plan.

Although the California legislature did not formally accept the California Water Plan as a guide for water development until 1959, the Feather River Project, the first component of the plan, was authorized for construction in 1951 *without* a showing of economic feasibility. Actual construction has been held up, primarily because of sectional conflict between nothern and southern California over water rights and because of the sheer difficulty of financing the project. In June, 1959, however, the legislature passed a compromise bill providing for a general bond issue of $1.75 billion for the Feather River Project to be submitted for approval to the voters of the state in the general election of November, 1960. In addition, the Department of Water Resources has issued a new bulletin which appears to

[23] It is stated, for example, that "inasmuch as the concept of ultimate development adopted for present studies presupposes maximum land use within physical limitations, *economic factors were not given consideration in determining the probable ultimate irrigated area*" (*Bulletin No. 2,* I, 47). (Italics ours.)

[24] *Bulletin No. 3,* p. xv.

[25] Harvey O. Banks and N. D. Sturm, "Some Economic Problems Confronting California Development of Water Resources" (paper presented before Conference on the Economics of California Water Development, Lake Arrowhead, August 13, 1957), p. 5.

make part of the required economic study of the project.[26] In a following section we shall subject this new study (or, rather, the preliminary version of it available to us at the time of writing) to critical analysis.

C. On Best Use of Existing Supplies

Our study of the New York area indicated that the water planners of that region tended to ignore the possibilities of making better use of existing supplies as an alternative to construction of expensive facilities for new supplies. We find in the South Coastal Area that possibilities also exist for improving the present use of water before provision of costly new supplies need be attempted. However, while in New York the important questions relating to present uses concerned losses in the distribution system and the provision of unmetered service, in the South Coastal Area of California a different kind of problem comes to the fore. In general, water in southern California has been made artificially cheap to users in comparison to the costs of providing increments of supplies. This underpricing is especially serious when measured against the cost of water that the state planners wish to transport to the area via the Feather River Project. The particular questions of interest in New York are not relevant for the South Coastal Area because metering is almost universal in municipal systems in southern California, and, partly as a consequence, distributive losses are generally kept within reasonable bounds.[27] In addition to general underpricing of water, discriminatory pricing in favor of agriculture apears to be responsible for some degree of misallocation in water use.

It is, unfortunately, very difficult to secure statistical breakdowns of water use in the area, because of the multiplicity of political units and private companies and the lack of any system of central reporting or even standardization of reporting methods. Generally, we will be forced to rely upon statistics for the Metropolitan Water District (MWD), the major wholesaler of the region, and for the city of Los Angeles representing the largest retail distributing system. In 1960 the MWD will supply about 20 per cent of the area's aggregate use; the city of Los Angeles will distribute about 20 per cent of the total water on the retail level.

As we pointed out earlier, local water-supply facilities are fully utilized,[28] and, for the most part, new water demands are being met by increased importation of Colorado River water via the MWD Aqueduct. While MWD water is not available to all the area (e.g., Ventura County is not in the district), about 85 per cent of the water use of the South Coastal Area takes place within the boundaries of the MWD. Because the Colorado water is the source of new supply and because it is also the most expensive supply now used by most agencies, it follows that the marginal cost of water in the area is the unit cost of the MWD water. It is somewhat questionable whether present water prices, at the wholesale and retail levels, properly reflect the true cost of the MWD water.

[26] Department of Water Resources, *Investigation of Alternative Aqueduct Systems To Serve Southern California* (Bull. 78 [Sacramento, December, 1959]). At the time of writing only a preliminary version of this document, also called Bulletin No. 78 but with the title *Preliminary Summary Report on Investigation of Alternative Aqueduct Systems To Serve Southern California,* was available to us (see n. 21 above). Our analysis is based on the preliminary report; to avoid confusion, we will hereinafter cite it as "*Bulletin No. 78 (Preliminary)*." We may remark that, although the final version bears the date December, 1959, it does not seem to have been publicly available until late April, 1960.

[27] Unaccounted-for water in the Los Angeles city system runs about 8 per cent of the total supplied. This is largely explained by underrecording of house meters and unmetered water use for street flushing and fire protection, as well as some leakage in the mains.

[28] We suggest below that some increases in local supplies are possible by additional local entrapment and reduction of reservoir evaporation. Also, reclamation of sewage and waste waters can provide substantial new supplies, possibly only for somewhat restricted use.

1. Municipal Water Rates and Pricing Practices

Although we shall not attempt a complete assessment of the water-pricing policies in existence throughout the area, we will indicate the general nature of the problem. First of all, what are water prices at the retail level in southern California? Table 38, for twenty cities in the South Coastal Area, shows data taken from a survey of 497 water utility systems in the United States serving populations of 10,000 or more.[29] All twenty cities are members of the MWD.

The data in Table 38 are not exhaustive or conclusive, but they indicate the general pattern of water pricing at the municipal level for retail consumers in the South Coastal Area. It is interesting to compare the rates for monthly use of 1,000 cubic feet of water, a use bracket covering much of residential water consumption, with the general level of water rates throughout the United States. In a study of the data contained in the 1955 survey of water works, Seidel and Baumann reported that the unweighted average charge for some 480 cities that reported water rates was $2.75 for the first 1,000 cubic feet used; the reported rates ranged from a

[29] *A Survey of Operating Data for Water Works in 1955* (New York: American Water Works Association, 1957). Only twenty southern California cities responded to the questionnaires sent out by the Association.

TABLE 38*

RETAIL WATER RATES IN DOLLARS PER 1,000 CUBIC FEET FOR TWENTY SOUTHERN CALIFORNIA CITIES, 1955

City	Monthly Water Use in Cubic Feet			
	1,000	10,000	100,000	1,000,000
Alhambra	$ 1.60	$ 1.600	$ 1.1800	$ 1.01800
Anaheim	2.05	1.285	1.1085	1.01085
Arcadia	1.41	0.911	0.8236	0.80736
Beverly Hills	1.80	1.800	1.2900	1.20900
Burbank	1.75	1.430	1.1730	0.84730
Fullerton	1.85	1.040	0.7020	0.70200
Glendale	1.70	1.700	1.3500	0.76000
Huntington Park	1.50	1.500	1.5000	1.50000
La Mesa	3.10	1.440	0.9540	0.90540
Long Beach	2.50	1.890	1.2650	0.89650
Los Angeles	1.70	1.347	1.0613	1.00347
Manhattan Beach	2.66	1.256	1.1156	1.09890
Monterey Park	1.80	1.670	1.5185	1.51850
Newport Beach	2.91	1.491	1.2387	1.23870
Oceanside	2.50	0.790	0.6190	0.60190
Orange	2.25	2.130	1.8330	1.80330
Pasadena	2.25	1.585	1.3500	1.04180
South Gate	1.30	1.020	0.7660	0.76600
Torrance	2.14	1.654	1.2454	0.83454
Whittier	2.00	2.000	1.1500	1.15000
Unweighted average	$ 2.04	$ 1.477	$ 1.1622	$ 1.03568
Equivalent rate in dollars per acre-foot	$88.86	$64.34	$50.63	$45.11
Los Angeles prices in dollars per acre-foot	$74.05	$58.68	$46.23	$43.71

* Source: *A Survey of Operating Data for Water Works in 1955* (New York: American Water Works Association, 1957). The acre-foot prices are our computations.

low of \$0.68 to a high of \$7.50. The median value for the same data was \$2.60; 50 per cent of all water systems had rates between \$2.01 and \$3.33.[30] The comparable unweighted average for the twenty California cities in Table 38 is \$2.04. It is evident that water rates at the retail level in southern California are lower than those found in many parts of the United States where natural water supplies are much more abundant. It seems fair to say that, in comparison to rates elsewhere, the price of municipal water in the area is not a very strong deterrent to low-valued water use.

Table 38 also shows that the rates for the twenty cities, with the exception of Huntington Park, decline as water use increases; most cities in southern California employ a system of declining or "promotional" rates.[31] In discussing this topic in chapter v, we pointed out that there was some justification in terms of cost for rate reductions to large users. Primarily, large users require less of a distribution network than do a group of small users taking the same quantity of water in the aggregate; billing and collection expenses are less; maintenance and wastage will presumably be less; and, finally, there may be less frictional pressure loss. A proper study of the question of whether these declining rates to large users are actually justified by cost differences, or whether they constitute special favors to large water-users, would involve a careful study of the factors mentioned above. We could not undertake this and can only state our impression that the block differentials are typically larger than would be justified on the basis of cost differences. In partial explanation of this statement, we should point out that some of the cost savings in serving larger users can be and already are reflected in reduced charges for initial connection to the system and in smaller recurrent fixed charges (per unit of connected capacity).

"Promotional" rates not based on cost differentials may be somewhat justifiable in situations where the system has idle capacity, so that the marginal cost of delivery is small; they would represent a form of price discrimination designed to augment revenues while keeping marginal prices low. But in this area, which is apparently approaching full use of its current water-supply facilities and which is considering the importation of expensive new supplies, the excess-capacity argument does not hold. It would seem logical at this point for responsible authorities to reconsider their structure of declining block rates. As water is made more costly to them, of course, large users will be induced to make more economical use of existing supplies.

An indication of the general underpricing of water in southern California is a comparison of the retail rates in terms of dollars per acre-foot with the costs of imported Colorado water from the MWD Aqueduct and with estimated costs of Feather River water. Most of the cities listed in Table 38 are currently purchasing some MWD water at a price of around \$25 an acre-foot. Even if the retail prices in Table 38 were consistent with the fact that the marginal cost of water procurement alone[32] is currently near \$25 an acre-foot, they are certainly not consistent with costs of Feather River water, officially estimated at \$60 an acre-foot delivered to the South Coastal Area,[33] under assumptions that we believe to be optimistic (see Sec. F below). (Furthermore, the figure \$60 is based upon the interest rates in the neighborhood of 3.5 per cent used in current offi-

[30] Harris F. Seidel and E. Robert Baumann, "A Statistical Analysis of Water Works Data," *Journal American Water Works Association,* XLIX (December, 1957), 1531–32.

[31] As we saw in chapter v, similar patterns of block rates are used in many important cities in the United States.

[32] In addition to procurement costs, the marginal cost of treatment and distribution must also be considered.

[33] *Bulletin No. 78 (Preliminary)*, p. VIII-13. The figure shown in the source is \$58 per acre-foot, but this has since been corrected to \$60 in a separate table provided to the authors.

cial analyses rather than on the much higher rates like 6 per cent or, better still, 10 per cent, which we believe to be relevant for cost estimates of this type.)

Most municipal water systems, including those in southern California, tend, as we have discussed earlier, to price water on the basis of the average cost of production and distribution. Such pricing is correct in situations where the average costs are relatively constant. But, where average and marginal costs diverge, average-cost pricing will lead to inefficient use. To illustrate the nature of the problem, we will assume that the incremental production costs of water supply for the city of Los Angeles are as follows:

Source	Amount in Acre-Feet	Production Cost per Acre-Foot
Los Angeles Aqueduct	320,000	$ 2.00
Local wells	105,000	10.00
MWD water	38,000	25.00
Total	463,000	

On the basis of these figures, which are roughly indicative, the average production cost of water for Los Angeles is $5.70 an acre-foot. Yet, because all increases of water use in Los Angeles are being satisfied by MWD water, it is clear that the marginal cost of water to the city is $25 an acre-foot. To the extent that the city bases its current water prices upon the average cost of water, increased water use is taking place at prices that are inadequate in terms of the unit costs of the extra water needed to supply the increased use. In the absence of data on the marginal costs of treatment and distribution, we cannot confidently state that the city, in charging prices descending to $44 per acre-foot, is failing to reflect the $25 marginal procurement cost in its price schedules—though this is our impression. If it is doubtful whether municipalities have adjusted their price schedules to reflect the marginal use of MWD water at $25 an acre-foot, it is quite certain that their retail rates fail utterly to reflect the cost of prospective Feather River water even at the officially estimated $60 an acre-foot.

2. *MWD Price Policy*

We indicated above that most of the cities using Colorado water are buying it from the MWD at $25 an acre-foot. While this is approximately correct, the actual pricing schedule used by the MWD is somewhat more complicated: softened Colorado water is sold at $25 and $22 an acre-foot west of the LaVerne softening plant, and the untreated or raw water is priced at $15 and $12 an acre-foot and delivered to district members east of LaVerne. The lower price in each instance is a favorable price quoted for water that is to be used for recharging underground aquifers or for agricultural purposes.[34] The $10 differential between softened and unsoftened water is supposed to reflect the cost of the softening treatment.[35] Most cities are served the softened water, the principal exception being San Diego.

MWD water is available only to district members, and they in turn retail the water to the final users. All members are subject to MWD taxes in addition to water prices; in 1960 this tax rate was 17 cents per $100 of assessed valuation. Agencies that have joined the district after its inception (1928) have been assessed "back" taxes—taxes

[34] After this chapter was written, the MWD announced in March, 1960, a new per acre-foot price schedule to begin to take effect in July of that year. The major changes were a reduction of the softening differential from $10.00 to $8.00; an increase in the basic rate for water before softening in the amount of $6.00, to take effect in three equal annual steps; and a widening of the differential (in the form of a smaller increase than that in the base rate) favoring agricultural and replenishment uses. The final rates will be (as of 1963) $21.00 and $14.25 for untreated water, and $29.00 and $22.25 for the treated, the latter figure in each pair representing the preferential rate. Because of the late date of the change, our text discussion is based on the old rate schedule.

[35] While $8.00 is now quoted as the cost of softening (see n. 34), the quality of the service appears also to have been reduced. Water has recently been softened only down to the still rather hard level of 167 ppm instead of to the 125-ppm level previously achieved.

which would have been paid if the agency had been an original member.

Most of the agricultural use of MWD water takes place east of LaVerne and is charged the $12 price. In 1959, agricultural water use was about 18 per cent of MWD sales, or approximately 100,000 acre-feet.[36] The rationale of the discriminatory price schedule favorable to agricultural use of water (and water for recharge) is not altogether clear. Presumably, the MWD is interested in increasing water sales as long as the extra sales more than cover marginal cost; a policy of low prices makes good economic sense as long as excess capacity exists (marginal cost is low). But the MWD has recently embarked upon a $200-million expansion program, to be completed in 1960, in order to bring its aqueduct facilities up to the ultimate capacity of 1,200,000 acre-feet a year, the previously effective capacity being only half this figure. This expenditure amounts to over $300 per acre-foot of capacity added. On the basis of a seventy-year life and full-capacity deliveries throughout, and using an interest rate of 3.5 per cent, these incremental capital costs would amount to $12.82 per acre-foot of water (note that we are correctly assessing no charge for the previous or sunk capital investment required to build the dam, secure rights-of-way, etc.). To this figure we must add the operating costs of transporting the water through a series of five pump lifts, totaling 1,600 feet and requiring 2,000 kw-h. of energy per acre-foot, and also the incremental operation and maintenance costs of the 300-mile aqueduct. The MWD also pays the federal government 25 cents for each acre-foot of water diverted from the river.

If incremental operating costs total to approximately $15 an acre-foot,[37] the full incremental cost of Colorado water would be in the neighborhood of $28 an acre-foot, before softening, and (accepting the $8.00 differential) $36 an acre-foot for the softened water. Furthermore, if we calculate the capital costs at more realistic rates representing the marginal opportunity cost of capital, these figures become substantially higher. Even at 6 per cent, a low estimate of the marginal opportunity rate, the incremental capital cost is $20.34 per acre-foot, and the full incremental cost becomes about $35 per acre-foot, unsoftened, and $43 softened. At our generally recommended rate of 10 per cent, the corresponding figures are $33 for the unit capital cost and $48 and $56 for the unsoftened and softened full incremental costs. It would seem that current prices for MWD water are lower than the cost of the increment of supply; the new construction should have been preceded by an increase in rates.[38] Furthermore, these results are based on use of our formula (7) of chapter vii, with full utilization of the increment of capacity assumed. Incorporating a reasonable load-building assumption would raise the present-worth average cost for the increment of supply.

It is also true that current MWD revenues from water sales, as has been true for every year in its history, are insufficient to cover current operating and capital outlays. In the 1958–59 water year, the most favorable to that date in the seventeen-year project history, operating cost and interest charges exceeded water revenues by $2.9 million—an average deficit of almost $5.00 per acre-foot

[36] In the 1958–59 year total water sales by the MWD were 601,000 acre-feet—284,000 acre-feet of softened water and 317,000 acre-feet of raw water.

[37] The MWD currently receives hydroenergy from Hoover and Parker dams on the Colorado River at a cost of approximately 2 mills per kilowatt-hour, so that power costs for pumping now average about $4.00 an acre-foot. The MWD, however, has an allotment of power from these sources sufficient to pump only about 800,000 acre-feet a year. It is expected that power to pump water in excess of that amount will cost at least 6 mills; in this case the incremental power costs alone may amount to $12 an acre-foot.

[38] The recently announced price increases mentioned above have certainly come too late; they appear to be a reflection of the costs already incurred for the new construction.

sold. (MWD cost calculations make inadequate provision for depreciation, assessed only at the rate of $2.00 per acre-foot.) Funds to cover interest charges (and also bond repayments) are provided by taxes which the MWD levies on its members. In the 1958–59 year, tax collections were $27.5 million and water revenues only $11.1 million. These deficits are mainly a consequence of a low-price policy designed to promote the use of idle capacity and, as such, do not particularly disturb us. Actually, when the new construction is complete in 1960, the MWD system will be overbuilt again, and the current level of rates will be approximately representative of marginal cost until the next new construction seems required. The main point is that new construction should not have taken place until the price for rationing existing supplies exceeded the unit cost of the increment of supply.

The extent to which the MWD has relied on its taxing power to carry the capital and operating costs of the Colorado River Aqueduct is enlightening because it may serve as an example of how water planners can overestimate future demands by ignoring important economic factors. Over its entire history through the year 1958–59, MWD tax collections totaled $334 million in comparison to total water revenues of only $55 million. The total operating loss for the 1941–59 period was $121.5 million, or an average deficit of $31 for every acre-foot of Colorado River water delivered. All this occurred in the face of factors favorable to the sale of water, particularly when one considers that almost one-third of all water sales have been made to the San Diego County Water Authority, an area not even included or considered in original district planning.[39] Even more important as a factor favorable to water sales has been the drought conditions recently predominant in the area. Since 1944, in fact, the southern California area has had only three years of above-normal rainfall. Despite the fact that the population projections upon which district planning was based have turned out to be surprisingly accurate, the estimates of water demand have proved far too high.

One result of the reliance upon taxation has been that cities with relatively large assessed valuations, but using relatively small amounts of MWD water, have tended to carry the project. The most important example is the city of Los Angeles, which by the 1958–59 year had paid a total of $167 million in taxes—about 50 per cent of all taxes collected by the MWD—yet had purchased only some 8 per cent of the total water sold by the district. On the other hand, the San Diego County Water Authority purchased about 30 per cent of all water sold yet paid only around 7 per cent of the taxes. In the 1958–59 year alone Los Angeles paid $7.5 million in taxes—at a time when the city purchased some 83,000 acre-feet at a cost of $2,070,000. When tax collections are considered, the MWD water is proving to be an extremely expensive source of supply to the city of Los Angeles.[40]

With the exception of a few cities (e.g., Burbank, Pasadena, Glendale, and San Diego), the common municipal practice is to add the MWD tax levies directly to property tax bills and not to show these tax levies in water-department accounts or pay them out of water-department revenues. The result is that costs for the provision of an expensive water supply do not show up as water costs and are not paid directly by water-users. Water taxes should at least appear in water-department accounts, so that they can more readily be seen for what they are—

[39] See Jerome W. Milliman, "Economic Problems of the Metropolitan Water District of Southern California," *Proceedings of 32nd Annual Conference of Western Economic Association, 1957* (Salt Lake City, 1958), pp. 42–45.

[40] We should point out that the tax payments are presumably buying the city a future water right; entitlements to MWD water when the aqueduct is operating at full capacity will be based upon the proportion of taxes paid by each member in relation to total taxes collected.

costs of water supply. If this is done, the electorate can better decide how these costs should be borne—by property-owners or by water-users.[41]

3. *Water Prices and Use of Water*

We do not have the data required to assess in detail the effect of current underpricing of water in southern California (relative to the cost of prospective Feather River supply, if not current MWD supply) upon the total amount of water consumed and upon the composition of uses. We can predict with confidence, however, that retail prices reflecting the marginal cost of water supply would change the pattern of use as well as the total amount of water consumed. Most of our evidence on this score is only qualitative, but it is very persuasive.

Agricultural use of water is probably more sensitive to changes in water prices than most other kinds of use. We think that it is not unreasonable to estimate that at least one-half of the 800,000 acre-feet per annum currently used for irrigation in the South Coastal Area would be uneconomic if water costs at the wholesale level, not counting the costs of delivery to the farmer's headgate, were on the order of $20–$30 an acre-foot. At this price range only citrus, avocados, and some truck crops would be economically feasible. The growing of alfalfa, pasture, hay and grain, and some orchard crops would definitely appear to be submarginal.[42] A diversion of 400,000 acre-feet per year would support an urban population (with concomitant industrial and commercial use) of approximately 2,500,000 people at a consumption rate of 160 gallons per person per day, the predicted consumption rate for 1960. Not only does the MWD give agricultural water use a favorable rate but this appears to be fairly standard practice throughout the area. It may be a surprise to some readers to learn that the city of Los Angeles still sells water for irrigation use within the city limits. In 1958–59 irrigation sales by Los Angeles were over 30,000 acre-feet, or about 6 per cent of the city's total water sales. Most of this irrigation service is provided at favorable rates which average about $11 an acre-foot. We may comment here that it is difficult to understand why Los Angeles purchased 83,000 acre-feet of water at $25 an acre-foot from the MWD at the same time that it was selling water for irrigation purposes at prices of approximately $11 an acre-foot. With the rapid rate of urbanization of the city it is likely that agricultural use of water within the city will decline, even at the $11 rate, but, as recently as 1951, irrigation sales were 55,000 acre-feet, or about 15 per cent of total water use.[43]

In regard to other types of water use, our evidence is less definitive and only of a suggestive nature, but there are a number of signs that indicate that a sharp increase in water rates would lead to increased conservation of water. For example, it is common throughout southern California for gardeners to "rake" leaves and grass clippings by squirting a stream of water from a hose. In addition, most apartment dwellers in southern California are not charged directly for the water they use. The almost universal practice is for the landlord to provide "free"

[41] In the city of Los Angeles the total cost of operating the water department for the 1958–59 year was $27.7 million (including interest and bond expenses). The presence of an item of $7.5 million for MWD taxes in the accounts of the department would show that the costs of this supply to the city are substantially higher than they now appear to be. The annual department reports simply ignore MWD taxes in stating, for example, that "the Department of Water and Power continued to be fully self-supporting, with no burdens imposed on the taxpayers" (see *58th Annual Report of Board of Water and Power Commissioners, City of Los Angeles* [*1958–59*] [Los Angeles, 1959], p. 5).

[42] In 1950, in the South Coastal Area, there were 42,000 acres planted in alfalfa, 41,200 in pasture, and 19,800 acres in hay and grain. The applied water requirement for these types of plantings is between 2 and 2.5 feet (*Bulletin No. 2*, I, 129, 135).

[43] In 1950–51 Los Angeles purchased 15,852 acre-feet of water from the MWD at a price then of $20 an acre-foot.

water to the tenant, with the result that the marginal cost of water to the user is zero. We have not studied what the cost of individual metering would be for apartments, but it is evident that increases in retail water prices and an abandonment of "promotional" rate schedules would increase the advantage to owners of installing apartment meters.

Many industrial and commercial firms in the southern California region use large amounts of water for cooling purposes on a once-through basis without recirculation. Only in some newer plants (e.g., Kaiser Steel at Fontana and Lever Brothers in Los Angeles)[44] is a great deal of attention paid to the recirculation and reuse of water. We do not condemn the industrial and commercial firms for their failure to recirculate and reuse water; at prices that are currently being charged for water supplies in southern California, particularly to large users, it just does not pay to make the investment in facilities for reuse of water.[45]

We have estimated that the average use of water in the South Coastal Area, excluding agricultural use, will soon be 160 gallons per person per day. Although one might expect per capita water use in southern California to be somewhat high because of the warmer temperatures and the lower rainfall, there is strong indication that water use is uneconomically great. Of the 160 gallons, approximately 80 gallons per person per day represent domestic or residential use; the remaining amount goes for commercial, industrial, and public purposes. Pasadena and Beverly Hills, areas with large estates and lawns, have per capita totals of 190 and 250 gallons daily; in Los Angeles per capita use is about 168 gallons; and in San Diego the figure is 116 gallons per person per day. In this connection it is interesting to note that the San Diego area has higher average annual temperatures and lower yearly rainfall than Los Angeles! The principal difference between the two cities is that water rates at the retail level in San Diego are almost double those in effect in Los Angeles. (In northern California the city of San Francisco also has retail prices almost double those of Los Angeles, and consumption of only about 100 gpcd.)

An increase in water prices would ordinarily not reduce all classes of use in the same proportion. If Fourt's analysis of the residential demand for water is applicable to the South Coastal Area, a doubling of residential retail water rates may be expected to reduce water use by about 40 per cent.[46] The effect of price increases upon industrial and commercial users will depend upon a variety of factors, but it seems reasonable to assume that their demand for water would be rather sensitive to water rates. Certainly, the recirculation of water for cooling would be increased.

In short, then, we conclude that the South Coastal Area is a region where water rates

44 The Kaiser Steel plant has reduced its net water requirements to 1,600 gallons per ton of steel as compared to typical use of 40,000 gallons per ton. The Lever Brothers' soap plant in Los Angeles, by careful design and extensive use of recirculatory cooling towers, reduced its water requirements from an estimated 6,000,000 gallons per day to a net of about 400,000 gallons per day (see *Proceedings* [*of the*] *Conference on Industrial Uses of Water in California, Los Angeles, California, December 10–11, 1956* [Committee on Research in Water Resources, University of California], pp. 85, 89–90).

45 Mr. Herbert C. Davis, of the California Fish Canneries Association, in speaking about the use of water for cannery operations on Terminal Island near San Pedro, noted that, "under present costs for water, we have not attempted to reclaim or reuse it" (*ibid.*, p. 59). Mr. Ernest Tonges, chief engineer, Pioneer Division of the Flintkote Company, Los Angeles, commented that the degree of reuse of water in a paper mill depends entirely upon economic conditions, and he further asserted that "water pumped from the ground costs us about $13.00 or $15.00 per acre-foot, and it can be purchased at most of our plant sites from between $25.00 to $33.00 an acre-foot. As these costs go up, it will then pay us to install equipment to clean the effluent further" (*ibid.*, p. 62).

46 Louis Fourt, "Forecasting the Urban Residential Demand for Water" (unpublished Agricultural Economics Seminar Paper, University of Chicago, February 14, 1958).

that understate marginal water costs have led to profligate use of water, thus creating an apparent "need" for new supplies when what is more urgently required is economical use of existing supplies.

D. The Timing of New Supplies

The question of when to bring new supplies into southern California is related to the question of how far the area goes in rationalizing the use of existing supplies as discussed above. Supplies already in hand or available from fuller use of the Colorado River Aqueduct are sufficient to support at least a 60 per cent increase in population and industry beyond the expected level of 1960.[47] This increase involves primarily physical displacement of irrigated cropland by urban and industrial development; economic displacement of irrigation water use as municipal and industrial users purchase or bid away rural water supplies; elimination of favorable water rates to agriculture and promotional rates to industry; and the use of the full Colorado River entitlement. We say that the existing supplies will support *at least* a 60 per cent increase in growth because that figure is based only on a partial displacement of agriculture and the maintenance of a per capita consumption rate for urban users of 160 gallons per day. Further rationalization of use would not only reduce agricultural acreage but would undoubtedly involve a reduction in industrial and residential consumption as well, as the rising cost of water served as an incentive to curb excessive low-valued water use. If per capita consumption were to fall to 140 gallons per day (the average consumption in 1950 in this area) or to 116 gallons per day (the 1958 consumption in the city of San Diego), a much larger increase in population could be supported by existing supplies. Just how long the process of rationalization will permit economic postponement of new construction depends, of course, upon the pattern of growth of population and industry and the relative costs of providing new supplies.

Forecasts of population growth are in almost every case called upon by "practical" planners to justify large water-supply projects in excess of currently visible needs. The most crucial point to appreciate in reference to population predictions is that there is no such thing as a "scientific" forecast. However eminent the demographer responsible may be, all techniques currently in use represent crude extrapolations of existing trends, and the startling unreliability of such projections in the past[48] should make us wary of placing excessive reliance upon them now. By "excessive reliance" we mean commitments to expensive building programs designed to meet needs supposed to arise in the relatively far-off future, and we certainly would consider anything beyond twenty years as "far off."

There is, as well, some interdependence between water availability and cost, on the one hand, and population growth, on the other, though the actual relationship is often misunderstood. If true water costs in an area are high—that is to say, if water is simply

[47] In Table 34 above we estimated that the 1960 population in the South Coastal Area would be about 8,650,000. At that time the MWD Aqueduct will have an unused capacity of at least 500,000 acre-feet annually. Total agricultural use will be at least 700,000 acre-feet. If we estimate that approximately 400,000 acre-feet is in low-valued agricultural uses compared to the value of water for urban uses, a total of 900,000 acre-feet would be available to support new urban growth. This amount could support an urban growth of over 5,000,000 people at a consumption rate of 160 gallons per person per day.

[48] Thus the Bureau of the Census in 1947 forecast a 1950 United States population of 145,500,000, representing a decennial increase from 1940 of 13,800,000. The enumerated 1950 population was 150,700,000, the decennial increase being 19,000,000. This represents a 27 per cent underestimate of the increase for the decade, the estimate being made at a date two-thirds of the way through the decade in question. In New York City, on the other hand, water planners were embarrassed by the apparent fact that the city declined in population from 1950 to 1957 instead of increasing as was forecast (see chap. x above).

hard to come by—that will be one of the intrinsic disadvantages of a region which will limit its growth, unless outside agencies (e.g., the Bureau of Reclamation) can be induced to subsidize artificial local development by paying for the local water supply with funds collected elsewhere. In the absence of such an external subsidy, the region cannot escape the limitational scarcity of water. A common confusion is to believe that a domestic water subsidy paid with local funds—that is, a low water price with deficits made up by local taxpayers—will have the same effect as an external subsidy. This is incorrect; a purely domestic subsidy merely twists the direction of local development toward water-intensive, low-tax-base industries which represent quite inappropriate forms of expansion for a water-scarce area. In the circumstances of southern California, water subsidies typically favor irrigation agriculture and possibly large industrial users as against small residential users. In addition, urban water use, in most cities of southern California, is subsidized by property taxes.

With these warnings in mind, we may turn now to the population projections being used in the official calculations of the state water planners (Table 39). About all that can be said concerning such forecasts is that responsible authorities should think twice before staking large funds on these prospects.[49]

The next step in conventional "water-requirements" calculations is to estimate the future course of per capita water use. The

TABLE 39*

POPULATION PROJECTIONS FOR STATE WATER PLANNING

(In Millions)

Year	United States	California	Nine Southern California Counties†	South Coastal Area
1950‡..........	150.7	10.864	5.869	5.4
1958...........	173.4	14.6	8.7	8.0
1960...........	180.4	15.8	9.38	8.658
1970...........	210.0	21.7	13.1	11.978
1980...........	247.0	28.2	16.838	15.048
1990...........	288.0	35.0	19.92	17.255
2000...........	330.0	42.0	23.08	19.387
2010...........	375.0	49.0	25.955	21.176
2020...........	420.0	56.0	28.550	22.730

* Source: *Bulletin No. 78 (Preliminary)*, pp. II-17, II-21. These are the "median" projections.

† The nine counties are San Luis Obispo, Santa Barbara, Kern, Ventura, Los Angeles, Orange, San Bernardino, Riverside, and San Diego. The South Coastal Area, in contrast, includes only the coastal plains of the last six counties named.

‡ 1950 figures were taken from United States Census data.

[49] This is in contrast to assertions of the state planners that the "median projections were most probable of attainment" in comparison with the "high" and "low" projections and that "during the ensuing 20 years, there is a high probability that the projected median populations will be realized. This is readily seen as the high and low Southern California region population forecasts show only a 4% variation from the 'median' population in 1980. Over the full study period, the possible deviation from the 'median' projection increases with the probable variation, indicated by the 'high' and 'low' projections, being about 12% in 2020" (*Bulletin No. 78 [Preliminary]*, pp. II-17, II-19). Of course, the small variation among the projections should not automatically justify strong confidence in the median estimate, as all three projections may be widely off the mark.

most recent (1959) official "requirements" projections, of *Bulletin No. 78 (Preliminary)*, are summarized in Table 40. For the most part, these projections also represent crude extrapolations. Before we comment upon the nature of the assumptions used in deriving these projected requirements, we wish to point out that they differ quite strikingly from projected requirements for the same area by the same state agency in a study made only two years earlier. As Table 41 shows, irrigation "requirements" were reduced from 1,901,000 acre-feet per year under "ultimate" conditions of development (as given in the California Water Plan, 1957) to 514,800 acre-feet for the year 2020 in the 1959 study—this revision, representing a 70 per cent reduction in projected use, being made only two years after the original estimate. At the same time urban "requirements" were increased about 40 per cent from 3,635,000 acre-feet under "ultimate" conditions to 5,289,000 acre-feet by the year 2020. This rather drastic change within a two-year period illustrates some of the risks of freezing water-supply development patterns through a master plan, dependent for its justification upon ability to make reasonably correct forecasts perhaps sixty years in advance. It is to be noticed that the changes are compensating; total requirements in the 1959 study are not very different from those reached earlier, so, as it happened, construction plans based upon the 1957 study did not have to be altered to any great extent.

The primary analytical difference between the two studies of projected water requirements is that the 1959 report purportedly uses the concept of "economic demands" (i.e., water use as a funtion of cost-price relationships), while the 1957 study was based solely upon physical "needs" apart from costs and prices under "ultimate" conditions.[50] This conceptual improvement is the primary reason for the belated recognition that agricultural use of water in the South Coastal Area must decline (as has already been experienced in the 1950–60 period) as population grows and as water costs rise.

The 1959 study uses what appears to be a rigorous, and generally correct, planning assumption:

> The full cost of water at the main aqueduct involved in delivering water to each service area, including full recovery of capital cost with interest, is the proper basis for estimating economic demands for supplemental water for purposes of aqueduct system selection and preliminary design. The term growth in economic demand for water connotes a relationship between demand and price of water.[51]

However, upon a careful look at the procedures actually followed by the state planners (insofar as it is possible to do so, many crucial assumptions being unspecified in the bulletin), we find that the actual "requirements" or economic demands derived do not represent quite the rigorous standard implied by the quotation above. This judgment is apart from the question of reliability of the estimated costs of the imported water—which we accept for purposes of analysis here but subject to analysis in a following section.

The first sort of error which appears in the derivation of economic demands is one that does not affect the South Coastal Area but does concern some areas, particularly Santa Barbara and San Luis Obispo. The costs used for the estimation of demands are the least costs of serving each particular area by one of the variations of three major alternative aqueduct systems considered.[52] The costs of serving each area under the system that is recommended ("System B") are

[50] Incidentally, it is not clear why all current planning is based on a target date of the year 2020. The only statement we can find in support of that year is "development trends and water demands were estimated for a period sufficiently far in the future that proper aqueduct sizing will be assured" (*Bulletin No. 78* [*Preliminary*], p. II-1).

[51] *Ibid.*, p. II-4.

[52] *Ibid.*

TABLE 40*

WATER "REQUIREMENTS" IN SOUTH COASTAL AREA

Year	Urban Requirements (Acre-Feet per Year)	Per Capita Use per Day† (Gallons)	Irrigation Requirements (Acre-Feet per Year)	Total Requirement‡ (Acre-Feet per Year)
1950§	874,000	140	954,000	1,828,000
1957§	1,322,000	150	790,000	2,112,000
1960	1,564,000	160	699,200	2,263,200
1970	2,282,000	170	676,200	2,958,700
1980	2,978,000	176	599,400	3,577,400
1990	3,601,000	186	594,900	4,195,900
2000	4,312,000	199	587,000	4,899,000
2010	4,876,000	207	547,100	5,423,100
2020	5,289,000	210	514,800	5,803,800

* Source: *Bulletin No. 78 (Preliminary)*, pp. II-31, II-33.

† This is an average representing "urban requirements" in terms of the projected population. Actually the state planners use different consumption rates for various parts of the South Coastal Area; for example, in 2020 the San Fernando Valley rate is 240 gpcd, the Upper Santa Ana Valley rate is 260 gpcd, while the rate for San Diego County is 200 gpcd (*ibid.*, p. II-28).

‡ Some minor miscellaneous uses are omitted.

§ 1950 and 1957 figures are our estimates taken from Table 34.

TABLE 41

COMPARISON OF WATER "REQUIREMENT" PROJECTIONS FOR THE SOUTH COASTAL AREA BY STATE DEPARTMENT OF WATER RESOURCES

	"Ultimate Requirements" (Computed, 1957)*	Requirements for Year 2020 (Computed, 1959)†
Use categories:		
Total population	18,000,000	22,730,000
Irrigated acres	1,159,000	275,000
Water use (in acre-feet):		
Urban	3,635,000	5,289,000
Irrigation	1,901,000	514,800
Miscellaneous	16,000	....
Total	5,552,000	5,803,800
Implied water-use assumptions:		
Urban use in gallons per person per day	180	210
Per acre agricultural use in feet per year	1.8	1.87

* *Bulletin No. 3*, pp. 76–90.

† *Bulletin No. 78 (Preliminary)*, pp. II-28–II-33.

not the same in each case as the costs used in computing the "economic demands."[53] For example, in the Santa Barbara area a cost of $27 an acre-foot is used as a basis for estimating the growth in demand for imported water, but "System B" shows scheduled costs of $46 an acre-foot at the main aqueduct for Santa Barbara (and $81 an acre-foot delivered in the Santa Barbara area). Fortunately, System B is the lowest-cost system for the South Coastal Area, so this error is avoided for the area we are examining.

The most important source of error in the derivation of economic demands for the South Coastal Area is the following planning assumption in the state report:

> Individual consideration was given to the present service area of the Metropolitan Water District of Southern California with recognition of present pricing policies of the District under the assumption that these policies would prevail in the future. A direct charge to the user of $30 per acre-foot was assumed in projecting development in the District area. *By this $30 estimate, it is assumed that the District would recover the difference between this charge and the cost of water at the main aqueduct of $43, under its present procedure of taxation or otherwise.* This value represents an estimated average charge that might be assessed in the future for both Colorado River water and northern California water.[54]

This assumption may be true to fact, but the result can hardly be called an economic demand for water at prices that cover all costs. For the purpose of assessing the economic demand for Feather River water, it should be assumed that the MWD would recover the full cost, about $60 an acre-foot, rather than half the cost, or $30 an acre-foot, from sales to water-users. A $30 price to users would be less than the incremental cost of the water; the remaining costs would have to be borne by taxpayers in much the same fashion as are the costs of the present MWD water. It follows that (in line with our earlier discussion of MWD pricing policies) areas with large assessed valuations and little need for extra water would support areas with small assessed values but with large water use. And, if the cities continued to exclude MWD taxes from municipal water-department accounts, the high costs of water supplies would tend to be hidden from water-users. We are strongly concerned with this assumption about economic demand for water because by far the greatest increase in water requirements in the entire South Coastal Area is projected to take place within the present MWD service area; in the year 2020 the state planners estimate that 17,400,000 people, of 22,700,000 for the area as a whole, will reside within MWD boundaries.[55]

As Table 40 shows, the bulk of the projected future requirements for water in the South Coastal Area represents urban demands estimated at 5,289,000 acre-feet, while irrigation use of 514,800 acre-feet is projected. The state planners have not given many clues on how these demands were computed, so that it is not possible to determine whether careful economic study was actually given to the problem. We are told that "total future water requirements were estimated by applying appropriate values of unit water use to the projection of population"[56] and that "estimates of future unit values of urban water use were prepared from analyses of historical trends in these values relating the factors of climate, levels of industrial development, personal income and price of water."[57] We are not given any information about the crucial working assumptions; for example, it would be important to know the degree and composition of industrial development and the assumptions about personal income and about the price of water to retail consumers. The study of urban demands concludes with the state-

[53] Compare p. II-5 with p. VIII-13 (*ibid.*).

[54] *Ibid.*, p. II-5. (Italics ours.)

[55] *Ibid.*, pp. II-20–II-21.

[56] *Ibid.*, p. II-27.

[57] *Ibid.*

ment that, "within the range of costs estimated for delivery of surplus northern California water by the alternative aqueduct systems, it does not appear that there would be any appreciable variation in the magnitude of the demand for water by urban entities."[58] It appears to us that this conclusion is quite unwarranted. Urban water use is depicted as rising from 1,500,000 acre-feet in 1960 to 5,300,000 acre-feet in 2020—with per capita use rising from 160 gallons a day in 1960 to 210 gallons a day in 2020, in the face of rising water costs. All this would seem to call for a careful discussion of the crucial economic assumptions involved. The experience elsewhere, particularly with the MWD, has shown that urban use is highly sensitive to the price of water.

In regard to the projected agricultural use of water, *Bulletin No. 78* (*Preliminary*) found that the demand "would be significantly affected by variations in the price of water charged to the irrigators," particularly in San Diego, Ventura, and Riverside counties.[59] As it happens, these are the parts of the South Coastal Area that are expected (by the state planners) to expand irrigation acreage in the 1960–70 period and to reduce acreage only slowly thereafter.[60] Apparently, detailed farm-budget studies were made of the various amounts of water needed by farmers under a number of alternative assumptions. None of these studies, or the primary assumptions used in deriving the future demand for irrigation water, is shown in the latest official state report, although we are given the demand schedules (i.e., the functional relationships between price at the main aqueduct and the amount of irrigation water used) which apparently are the end results of these budget studies and which are said to have governed the irrigation projections. As Figure 26 shows, the irrigation demand schedule is expected to increase (shift to the right) with the passage of time, but its basic shape is expected to remain the same. The 2020 curve, for example, shows that at a price of $40 an acre-foot at the main aqueduct the demand for irrigation water would be approximately 300,000 acre-feet and that at $25 demand would increase to about 335,000 acre-feet.[61]

In addition to the demand schedules presented in Figure 26, we are given one other set of clues as to the result of the farm-budget studies; the state report gives the "average primary benefits" in dollars per acre-foot of water for irrigation agriculture. The measure of primary benefits is defined as "the difference between net returns from farming operations with and without the availability of this water. The net return from farming operations, as used herein, is defined as the difference between the gross income and all farm expenses, except water costs, including either land rental or interest on capital invested in land."[62] For the South Coastal Area the primary benefits due to an acre-foot of water (for "System B") appear to be quite handsome (Table 42).[63] It is not clear how these values relate to those given in Figure 26, which does not show water prices above $50 an acre-foot. We have strong doubts that these "primary benefits," as computed, show the prices that farmers can pay for water in a sustained profitable farming operation, even with relatively high-valued crops.

58 *Ibid.*, p. II-40.

59 *Ibid.*

60 In fact, coastal San Diego County and southwestern Riverside County are expected to increase irrigation from 61,000 acres in 1957 to 178,000 acres in 2020. This amount is the major portion of the 275,000 acres expected to be irrigated in the entire South Coastal Area in year 2020 (*ibid.*, p. II-25).

61 The 335,000 acre-feet figure just mentioned is the highest shown in the demand diagram. Nevertheless, the "irrigation requirements" specified in Table 40 are supposed to be 514,800 acre-feet for the South Coastal Area (the projected acreage for the three counties in the diagram represents all the projected irrigation acreage in the area). The source of this discrepancy is unknown.

62 *Bulletin No. 78* (*Preliminary*), p. VII-11.

63 *Ibid.*, p. VII-14.

But here again, as with the urban demands for water, no final answer can be given because the basic assumptions used in the computations of the various demands are not given in the state reports. Our analysis of these demand projections indicates that some skepticism can be expressed, but we cannot categorically say that the projections are invalid until more complete study is given to the matter. It is clear, however, that a rigorous and detailed study of prospective future de-

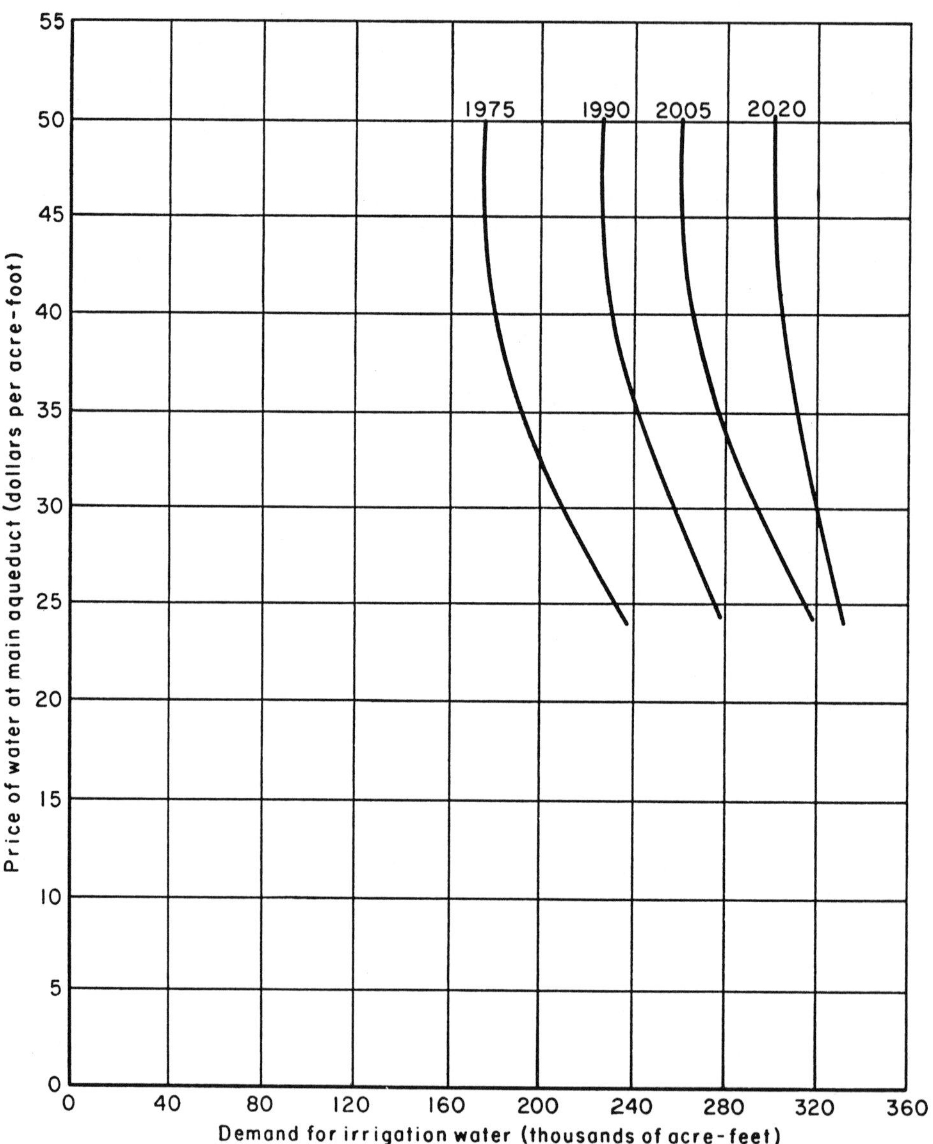

FIG. 26.—The demand for irrigation water in Ventura, coastal Riverside, and San Diego counties (computed by Department of Water Resources). (From *Bulletin No. 78* [*Preliminary*], Fig. 6.)

mands needs to be made, with all crucial assumptions explicit and open, before one can accept the projections in the state reports and before the state can prudently invest several billion dollars in project construction—the stakes appear to be too high for anything less than a most careful study.

from northern California, we believe that elimination of one-half of the projected irrigation requirement of 676,700 acre-feet for 1970 and of low-valued urban uses as well would permit the postponement of new supplies for about another decade until after 1980.

TABLE 42

PRIMARY IRRIGATION BENEFITS

(Dollars per Acre-Foot)

Area	Year					
	1970	1980	1990	2000	2010	2020–65
Ventura County	103	103	103	109	110	0
Southern California Coastal Plain and Coastal San Diego	147	147	150	150	150	144

Table 43 shows the total "need" or demand for additional water supplies for the South Coastal Area as projected by the state planners; all the "deficiency" is to be met by imports from northern California, the most immediate and urgent proposal being the Feather River Project.

In contrast, we will summarize our own view here. Although the Colorado River Aqueduct is operating today at only half-capacity, the official forecast shows that in 1970 this supply will be fully used. As emphasized earlier, this forecast accepts the pricing practices of the MWD without even raising the question of future changes in those practices. But the MWD prices have been highly "promotional" in nature. While their failure in the past to cover total cost may be defended in view of the desirability of setting prices low enough to induce some use of the capacity that would otherwise have been idle (the marginal-cost pricing principle as applied to overbuilt supply situations), this argument fails once aqueduct capacity becomes scarce. When this occurs, marginal cost will be rising steeply, and higher prices will be indicated. At prices substantially higher than those now in effect, but still well under the true cost of water

TABLE 43

"NEED" FOR IMPORTED NORTHERN CALIFORNIA WATER IN SOUTH COASTAL AREA

(In Acre-Feet per Year)

Year	Total "Requirements"*	Safe Yield of Existing Supplies†	Additional Imports Required‡
1950	1,828,000	2,618,000	....
1955	2,112,000	2,618,000	....
1960	2,263,000	2,618,000	....
1970	2,958,700	2,618,000	340,700
1980	3,577,400	2,618,000	969,400
1990	4,195,900	2,618,000	1,577,900
2000	4,899,000	2,618,000	2,281,000
2010	5,423,100	2,618,000	2,805,100
2020	5,803,800	2,618,000	3,285,800

* See Table 40 above.

† The safe yield of existing supplies is given as follows:

	Acre-Feet
Local surface and ground water	1,098,000
Los Angeles Aqueduct	320,000
Colorado River Aqueduct	1,200,000
Acre-feet per year	2,618,000

Bulletin No. 78 (Preliminary) lists the Colorado River Aqueduct supply as 1,150,000 acre-feet after deducting evaporation losses but indicates that local supplies can be increased about 56,000 acre-feet, so that the total net yield is approximately 2,618,000 acre-feet per year.

‡ These figures are in general agreement with those given in *Bulletin No. 78 (Preliminary)*, Fig. 4.

Allowing 300,000 acre-feet to be used for irrigation, the remaining water supply of 2,300,000 acre-feet per year could support industrial, commercial, and domestic use of 130 gallons per person per day for a population of about 16,000,000 people. The estimated 1958 population was 8,000,000, and official 1959 state population projections do not anticipate a population of 16,000,000 in the area until about 1985 (see Table 39). And we should point out that 130 gallons a day per person is not an unreasonably small amount of water. Seidel and Baumann show that one-half of the 477 cities reporting in the 1955 waterworks survey had consumption rates of *less* than 123 gallons per person per day.[64] For New York City the report of the Engineering Panel on Water Supply indicated that the per capita consumption should not exceed, on a well-managed basis, 100 gallons per day (as opposed to *unmetered* consumption of 146 gallons per day).[65] One important factor tending to reduce future per capita water consumption in southern California is that the enormous population growth predicted will require a large increase in the proportion of multiple-dwelling units. These have a much lower per capita use rate (primarily because of reduced lawn-sprinkling) than the single-family dwelling units now dominating the region. Wolff reports that areas with small lots or apartment dwelling units tend to consume only 65 gallons per person per day.[66] Actually, even daily consumption rates on the order of 100 gallons per person are relatively high compared to rates in other parts of the Western world. For example, Sleeman found British municipal water consumption in 1951 to range from 27.3 gallons per capita per day in Durham to a high of 69.6 gallons per capita per day in Glasgow.[67]

All this indicates, even accepting official population projections, that it does not follow that a new supply must be provided as of 1970. The most obvious alternative is to raise the price to water-users as the capacity limit is approached, so that efficient use tends to be insured. Only when the price necessary to ration existing supplies, after elimination of promotional and discriminatory rates favoring preferred users, comes to equal the incremental cost of the new supply is that new supply economically justified. It seems clear that a period of rising water prices should intervene before incremental supplies costing at least $60 an acre-foot (raw water at wholesale) are introduced to this area—if, indeed, importation of Feather River water is the best new source, and accepting the official cost estimate. Of course, if cheaper alternatives to the Feather River source are available, it would pay to introduce them somewhat earlier. In the next section we survey a number of major supply alternatives for the South Coastal Area to provide a rough indication of their relative costs.

E. Alternative Sources of New Supply

We will present here brief sketches and tentative evaluations of a number of possible sources of increased water supplies for the South Coastal Area before turning our attention to an analysis of the Feather River Project. Some of these are old proposals; some are new. Limitations of time and knowledge have forced us to confine our study to a few of the most promising candidates. Also because of these limita-

[64] Seidel and Baumann, *op. cit.*, p. 1535.

[65] See chap. x.

[66] Jerome B. Wolff, "Forecasting Residential Requirements," *Journal American Water Works Association,* XLIX, No. 3 (March, 1957), 227.

[67] J. F. Sleeman, "The Economics of Water Supply," *Scottish Journal of Political Economy,* II (1955), 241. These figures include the use of water for all purposes. Sleeman was careful to point out that Glasgow possessed a relatively cheap water supply, in addition to the fact that 43 per cent of its use was unmetered. The industrial city of Liverpool had a daily rate of 43.6 gallons per capita.

tions, our evaluations represent only relatively crude indications of the relative desirability and cost of these alternative sources. With these qualifications, Table 44 summarizes our findings, which are discussed in more detail below.

The major conclusion drawn from this survey is that, aside from the special case of reclamation of sewage and waste waters, there are several sources of substantial additional water supplies for the South Coastal Area which, while expensive, seem to be less costly than water imported from northern California, even accepting the official estimates for the latter calculated at 3.5 per cent interest. At 10 per cent interest the superiority of the alternatives becomes very large. In addition to the general qualifications relating to inadequacy of data and the like, we must point out that there is one element of systematic bias in Table 44: the estimates for Feather River water were based on our general formula (5) of chapter vii and so allow for load-building, while all the other estimates have been calculated by us on the basis of full-capacity deliveries using the short-cut formula (7) of chapter vii. It should be realized, however, that load-building will be much more powerful in raising costs for a huge increment of supply like Feather River than for the smaller alternatives considered, which can be con-

TABLE 44

POSSIBLE ADDITIONAL SOURCES OF SUPPLY FOR THE SOUTH COASTAL AREA*

SOURCE	ANNUAL AMOUNT (ACRE-FEET)	ESTIMATED COSTS PER ACRE-FOOT (DOLLARS)		
		Interest at 3.5 Per Cent	Interest at 6 Per Cent	Interest at 10 Per Cent
Colorado River Aqueduct (additional deliveries):				
Before expansion of capacity	500,000–600,000	28, 36†	35, 43†	48, 56†
After expansion of capacity		15, 20‡	15, 20‡	15, 20‡
Additional local entrapment	100,000	20–45	34–76	56–126
Reduction in local evaporation	50,000	10	10	10
Reclamation of sewage	First 350,000	15	20	25
	Additional 150,000	30	40	50
Purchase and transport from adjoining regions:				
Owens-Mono	200,000	28	45	74
Kern River	100,000–400,000	32§	42§	59§
Colorado River	1,000,000	50§‖	60§‖	80§‖
Feather River Project (official estimates)#	3,000,000**	60, 67††‡‡	...	...
Feather River Project (our estimates)#	...	63, 70‡‡	105, 112+‡‡	221, 228+‡‡

* Not all the possible sources of supply (e.g., Eel River, Wiley Plan, etc.) are shown in this table but only those for which enough data were available to make at least a rough estimate of costs. Except for the Feather River Project, all estimates are based on full-capacity deliveries.

† These estimates are for expansion of MWD deliveries to full capacity; the first figure is for the raw Colorado River water and the second for the treated water.

‡ These figures represent a crude calculation of the incremental cost of additional MWD deliveries on the assumption that the recent expansion of capacity represents a sunk investment. As before, the two figures represent costs for raw and treated water, respectively.

§ These figures include an allowance of up to $15 an acre-foot per year for the purchase of water rights.

‖ These estimates are based on extensions of the Coachella Canal. Alternative transport possibilities may be cheaper.

\# Based on recommended System B of *Bulletin No. 78 (Preliminary)*.

** See Table 50 below.

†† $60 is the official corrected estimate where *Bulletin No. 78 (Preliminary)* shows $58 (p. VII-20).

‡‡ The $7.00 differential reflects the additional cost of filtered urban deliveries. These figures allow for load-building

structed seriatim as demand develops. On this ground we consider the element of bias to be minor, given the general inaccuracy and unreliability of the data.

Our final judgment on alternative new supplies will be given in the concluding section of this chapter, but we will say again that *better use of existing supplies* can offer a considerable amount of leeway before the development of large-scale new supplies should be attempted.[68] In addition, the delay will permit accumulation of better information as to demands and costs than is presently available as a basis for decision.

1. Unused Capacity of the Colorado River Aqueduct

In 1960 the Colorado River Aqueduct is expected to deliver around 700,000 acre-feet of water; about 500,000 acre-feet will be put to use directly, and approximately 200,000 acre-feet will go to recharge the underground aquifers. This means that the unused capacity of the aqueduct will be about 500,000 acre-feet a year. If consumption rates are maintained at the current level of 160 gallons per capita per day, this unused supply could support an increase of population (and industry) of some 2,800,000 people. At the 1950 consumption rate of 140 gallons per capita per day it would be sufficient to support an extra 3,000,000 people, almost a 40 per cent population increase for the entire South Coastal Area.[69]

There are several uncertainties concerning the MWD supply from the Colorado River which should be mentioned here. First is the suit now being considered by the United States Supreme Court involving a thirty-seven-year-old dispute between Arizona and California over the waters of the Colorado River. The current suit was brought by Arizona in 1952 against California and seven California public agencies[70] in an attempt to gain water for the proposed Central Arizona Project.[71] If the suit is decided in favor of Arizona, California's current claims for Colorado River water, which total about 5,378,000 acre-feet a year, may be reduced to 4,400,000 acre-feet a year (the amount specified in the California Limitation Act).[72] In 1931 the various California agencies using Colorado River water executed the Seven-Party Water Agreement (see Table 45) to resolve the priority of their various claims for the water.[73] One result of this agreement was

[68] Perhaps we should stress that a "small" increment of 100,000 acre-feet, for example, is actually a rather large quantity of water—about 32,500,000,000 gallons a year. It would be sufficient to supply the urban activities of over 560,000 people at a consumption rate of 160 gallons per person per day.

[69] With an allowance of 300,000 acre-feet for agriculture, the total supplies of the South Coastal Area (including the Colorado River Aqueduct) would provide about 2,300,000 acre-feet a year for urban use. This amount could supply the needs of 13,800,000 people at 140 gallons per capita per day —almost a 70 per cent population increase over the 1960 figure.

[70] Palo Verde Irrigation District, Imperial Irrigation District, Coachella Valley County Water District, City of Los Angeles, City of San Diego, County of San Diego, and the Metropolitan Water District of Southern California.

[71] The Central Arizona Project is a billion-dollar proposal to divert 1,200,000 acre-feet of water annually from the Colorado River, raise it nearly 1,000 feet, and carry it more than 200 miles by aqueduct to the Phoenix area of Arizona.

[72] In 1929, California agreed to a limitation of its annual use of Colorado River water, in the event that Arizona failed to ratify the Colorado River Compact, to 4,400,000 acre-feet for water apportioned by paragraph 3-A of the compact plus "not more than one-half of any excess or surplus waters unapportioned by said compact." The meaning of the compact and the Limitation Act are at issue in the trial. There is also some question as to whether the Limitation Act is binding, since Arizona purportedly ratified the compact in 1944. For a recent discussion of these and other issues see Charles E. Corker, "The Issues in Arizona versus California" (paper presented to the Western Resources Conference, University of Colorado, Boulder, Colorado, July 17, 1959).

[73] See "Seven-Party Water Agreement, August 18, 1931," in Ray Lyman Wilbur and Northcutt Ely, *The Hoover Dam Doc ments* (2d ed.; Wash-

the placing of only 550,000 acre-feet of the MWD entitlement to Colorado River water within the limitation of 4,400,000 acre-feet; the remaining 662,000 acre-feet fell outside the limitation, to be satisfied by "excess or surplus waters unapportioned by the Colorado River Compact." The upshot of all of this is that over one-half of the Colorado River claims of the MWD are in jeopardy.[74]

Although the Colorado River entitlement held by the MWD is subject to legal jeopardy, we do not feel that the presently developed water supply to the South Coastal Area is threatened even if there is a decision adverse to California in the Supreme Court.[75] One reason is that there is general agreement that the Upper Basin states on the Colorado River will not make full use of their entitlement for many years to come. This unused water is part of what California calls "provisional supply," which can be used to satisfy claims in excess of the safe yield of the river in the Lower Basin.[76] On this point, the Bureau of Reclamation estimates that all presently authorized Upper Basin development will not take place until the year 2062.[77] If the MWD were to suffer loss of any of its Colorado River entitlement, it would still be able to deliver a full-capacity supply from this "provisional supply" for many years to come, so there is no cause for immediate alarm as is sometimes implied. Second, evaporation control (see below) promises to augment supplies somewhat. In addition, there always remains the possibility that the MWD can purchase (or, perhaps, the municipalities involved can condemn) a part of the 3,850,000 acre-feet of Colorado River first-priority entitlements held by the Palo Verde, Imperial, Yuma, and Coachella irrigation districts—all of which are senior to the MWD entitlement and within the 4,400,000 acre-feet limitation.[78] (In this connection we might mention what may be an unworthy suspicion on our part: that California interests were in part motivated to put the major fraction of the MWD allocation outside the secure supply of 4,400,000 acre-feet in order to place psychological pressure on Congress and the courts, the suggestion being that city dwellers would be in danger of dying of thirst if Arizona's claims were upheld! We have little doubt, in any case, that an unfavorable decision would lead to a readjustment of priorities within California, possibly with some form of compensation.) Finally, it should not seem to be a ridiculous idea that, in the event of Arizona's ownership of the disputed water being established,

ington, D.C.: Government Printing Office, 1948), Appendix 1003.

[74] Actually, if California estimates concerning the dependable supply of the main stream of the Colorado River are correct, claims in excess of 4,400,000 by California agencies may be in some jeopardy no matter who wins the suit (see "Excerpts from Findings of Fact and Conclusions of Law, Filed by California Defendants, April 1, 1959," in *Arizona* v. *California et al.,* p. viii).

[75] On May 8, 1960, as our manuscript went to press, the draft report of findings of the Special Master appointed by the Supreme Court to hear the Arizona-California suit were announced. These findings were favorable to Arizona; if made final and approved by the Court, they would limit California's use to 4,400,000 acre-feet annually in years of normal flow (sufficient to provide 7,500,000 acre-feet to the Lower Basin states in the aggregate). In addition, California may use 50 per cent of surplus flows available but must bear 44/75 of any deficiency in flow (*New York Times,* May 9, 1960, p. 1). As our analysis takes full account of the possibility of such an adverse decision, we have not attempted to change the text to accord with the latest legal situation. The Master's findings are not binding upon the Court itself, which still must make the final decision on the basis of these findings and the appeals to be filed by California and other states.

[76] "Excerpts from Findings of Fact and Conclusions of Law," *op. cit.,* pp. ii, viii.

[77] "Financial and Economic Analysis of Colorado River Storage Project and Participating Projects," in *Report of the Secretary of the Interior* (Senate Doc. 101 [85th Cong., 2d sess.] [Washington, D.C., February, 1958]), p. 13.

[78] See our discussion of regional water reallocations below.

the MWD would then proceed to buy the water back from her.[79]

The second question in regard to the Colorado River supply is that the quality of the water is likely to be reduced in future years because of increased return flow of irrigation waters in the Upper Basin of the river. The major source of difficulty stems from the Upper Colorado River Project, authorized in 1955, which provides for some twelve new irrigation projects to be constructed at a cost of a billion dollars by the Bureau of Reclamation. In the current suit with Arizona, California has submitted evidence to show that the total dissolved solids in the water may rise to a total of 1,100 ppm with full upstream development.[80] In 1958 the river had total dissolved solids of approximately 738 ppm.[81]

Although it will be many decades before the water in the Lower Basin of the Colorado River suffers such a reduction in quality, we must regard the quality of Colorado water as a matter of some concern. At mineral concentrations approaching 1,100 ppm of dissolved solids, it will be necessary to apply larger quantities of water for irrigation purposes in order to maintain soil moisture and to obtain greater leaching action. Also, the suitability of Colorado water for urban purposes will be reduced; though still usable for household use and for drinking, the costs of treatment for certain industrial and commercial uses will be increased. We cannot here comment at length on the wisdom of a federal policy that subsidizes irrigation projects without consideration of such spillover costs on downstream users. California interests may ultimately be forced to buy out these inefficient upstream irrigators in order to stop them from utilizing the facilities constructed for them at enormous expense by the federal taxpayers.

2. *Additional Local Entrapment*

Most authorities agree that it is possible to provide for small increases of locally developed water supplies by additional storage and entrapment of local runoff and flood waters. We have not attempted a special study of the matter on our own but instead have relied upon materials published in the various federal and state reports. Our survey indicates that a new supply of about 100,000 acre-feet a year may be developed from this source. It is not clear, however, just what the costs of providing this new supply will be. Because presently developed supplies (1,098,000 acre-feet) already constitute a high percentage of the estimated mean seasonal runoff (1,227,000 acre-feet)[82] for the South Coastal Area, there exist only limited opportunities for further conservation of flows to the ocean (exclusive of sewage and waste waters).[83]

[79] Arizona, in fact, would have very little use for the water in question, were it not for the Central Arizona Project mentioned earlier. Preliminary indications are that this would be an unusually uneconomic project, even in terms of the record established by previous federal investment in reclamation discussed in our chapter ix. If, for this reason or others, Congress refused to initiate the Central Arizona Project, Arizona might be well advised to sell or perhaps lease the water right.

[80] Memorandum dated August 15, 1958, from Raymond A. Hill to Northcutt Ely *re:* Future Salt Burden of Colorado River, Exhibit No. 5585, Admitted: August 22, 1958 (*Arizona* v. *California et al.*).

[81] Metropolitan Water District of Southern California, *Twentieth Annual Report* (Los Angeles, 1958), p. 53.

[82] *Bulletin No. 1,* p. 240. This figure was estimated for the fifty-three-year period from 1894 to 1947 and is based upon "natural" conditions. There is reason to believe that the available water under present conditions may be somewhat in excess of this amount.

[83] In *Bulletin No. 3* (pp. 83–92) estimates are presented showing that it would be possible to increase the safe yield of local supplies in the South Coastal Area to a total of 1,215,000 acre-feet a year; this is 117,000 acre-feet more than the present annual yield of 1,098,000 acre-feet. Additional reservoir and surface storage is shown to be possible at various sites in San Diego and Ventura counties. The total capital cost (1955) for nine reservoirs in these areas to yield a total annual safe delivery of 93,500 acre-feet is estimated to be $93,386,000.

If the additional entrapment is to be provided solely by means of surface storage, it will be relatively expensive. The major difficulty is that very large storage reservoir capacities must be constructed in order to conserve relatively small amounts of runoff. The reason for this is that rainfall and, consequently, runoff are highly variable over time, so that the costly storage capacity would stand empty much of the time. Based on the data in *Bulletin No. 3,* and assuming a useful life of a hundred years, we calculate that the average capital costs of water produced by the reservoir storage of flood flows will be $36.12 per acre-foot at 3.5 per cent interest, $60.37 at 6 per cent, and $99.90 at 10 per cent. The cheapest increment, 9,000 acre-feet per year (from Jamul Creek), will cost $20.20 per acre-foot at 3.5 per cent interest, $33.62 at 6 per cent, and $55.87 at 10 per cent. The most expensive increment, 17,000 acre-feet per year (from the San Dieguito River), will cost $45.50 per acre-foot at 3.5 interest, $75.70 at 6 per cent, and $125.80 at 10 per cent.

On the other hand, if some of the additional entrapment were accomplished by the sand-dune storage method pioneered by Dutch hydrologists and engineers (see chap. viii), the cost of the water produced might be appreciably lower. Inexpensive land could be used, and, with some assistance through dredging, the storage capacity is provided free by nature on alluvial soil at river mouths. A meaningful estimate of the costs of dune entrapment in comparison with the costs of conventional surface storage for this region is not possible without more data about the specific locations for the dunes, local ocean current characteristics, the need for protective sea walls or groins, the elevation of areas to be served, the recovery efficiency of the dunes, etc. It is our belief, however, that some combination of additional surface and sand-dune storage could provide approximately 100,000 acre-feet of new supply at costs ranging from $20 an acre-foot at 3.5 per cent interest to $126 an acre-foot at 10 per cent, particularly when the surface storage is integrated with the operation of groundwater basins.

3. Evaporation Control on Reservoirs

In chapter viii we described the very promising development of monomolecular oil films to reduce evaporation from reservoirs. As these techniques are applied on local reservoirs, saving water at high elevations close to the point of use, they will provide an extremely cheap new supply, probably at a cost under $10 an acre-foot. This cost is practically independent of the interest rate, because the capital investment is negligible. Unfortunately, the small surface area of local reservoirs limits the available saving to around 50,000 acre-feet per annum.[84]

Much more important quantitatively are the possible savings on the Lower Colorado River—especially at Lake Mead behind Boulder Dam—where an expenditure of about $10 an acre-foot might be expected to save something in excess of 500,000 acre-feet per year.[85] From the point of view

[84] This calculation is based upon the following assumptions and procedures: (*a*) From Nathan O. Thomas and G. Earl Harbeck, Jr., *Reservoirs in the United States* (Geological Survey Water Supply Paper 1360-A [Washington, D.C., 1956]), we computed the surface area of reservoirs in the South Coastal Area—not counting flood-control dams or reservoirs smaller than 5,000 acre-feet—to be 43,945 acres. (*b*) The average evaporation rate in the South Coastal Area is 48 inches (see chap. viii, Fig. 15). (*c*) Assuming that evaporation control might save 50 per cent of the annual evaporation, the potential savings amount to 87,890 acre-feet a year if the reservoirs are full. (*d*) This amount is reduced to about 50,000 acre-feet a year when it is assumed that the reservoirs contain an average surface area of about 60 per cent of capacity. This is a very conservative assumption.

[85] This calculation is based upon the following procedures: (*a*) From Thomas and Harbeck, *op. cit.*, the surface area of Lake Mead is given as

of the South Coastal Area, however, the major effect of these savings from evaporation control would be to increase the firm supply of the Lower Colorado River and serve as further protection of the MWD supply in the event of a decision unfavorable to California in the current litigation with Arizona. For this reason we do not credit these rather substantial savings as possible additional water supplies for the South Coastal Area.[86]

4. Reclamation of Sewage Waters

We now turn to a source which, despite its apparent unconventionality,[87] has long been discussed in southern California water circles[88] and which represents a truly major and inexpensive potential supply. In chapter viii we estimated the costs of water from large reclamation plants providing complete (primary and secondary) treatment at around $18 per acre-foot at 3.5 per cent interest, $22 at 6 per cent, or $29 at 10 per cent. In the special circumstances of the South Coastal Area some adjustments (which we discuss below) would have to be made in cost calculations, but the net figures remain about the same. We estimate that in 1960 it would be feasible to reclaim approximately 350,000 acre-feet per year at total costs not exceeding $25 an acre-foot, even at 10 per cent interest. Furthermore, the potentiality of this source will grow with the expansion of urbanization. As a rough rule of thumb, perhaps 25 per cent of urban use in the South Coastal Area can be reclaimed at these moderate costs, and a somewhat larger fraction, possibly up to 50 per cent, can be made available at costs under $50 an acre-foot.[89]

146,500 acres and the dams on the Colorado River below Lake Mead contain a total of 83,280 acres of surface area. (*b*) The average evaporation rate in the Lower Colorado River is approximately 96 inches per annum. (*c*) If evaporation control could save 50 per cent of the annual evaporation, the potential savings amount to 586,000 acre-feet on Lake Mead and 333,120 acre-feet on the Lower Colorado or a total of 919,120. (*d*) On the assumption that these reservoirs have surface area averaging 60 per cent of capacity, the annual savings may be on the order of 550,000 acre-feet a year for all the reservoirs, including Lake Mead.

[86] Actually, these savings would firm up the claims, not only of the MWD, but also of other Lower Basin claimants to supplies in excess of the safe yield of the river.

[87] The reclamation of sewage and waste waters is not as unconventional as it first appears because reclaimed waters have been used throughout the world for many years, primarily for irrigated agriculture. In 1953 reclaimed waste waters were used for irrigation at 106 places and for recharge of ground water at 112 places, all in California. There were also 118 places in the United States where such waters were used for industrial purposes (see A. F. Bush and S. F. Mulford, *Studies of Waste Water Reclamation and Utilization* [Department of Engineering, University of California, Los Angeles, Report 52-4 (January, 1954)], p. 10).

[88] For early discussion of use of reclaimed sewage for southern California see California Department of Public Works, Division of Water Resources, *Santa Ana River Basin* (Bull. 31 [Sacramento, 1930]), p. 4. The leading later studies are: (*a*) G. E. Arnold, H. E. Hedger, and A. M. Rawn, *Report upon the Reclamation of Water from Sewage and Industrial Wastes in Los Angeles County* (Los Angeles: County Sanitation Districts of Los Angeles, 1949); (*b*) H. E. Hedger and A. M. Rawn, *A Report upon the Potential Reclamation of Sewage Now Wasting to the Ocean in Los Angeles County* (Los Angeles, November, 1958). The authors of the last-cited work are, respectively, chief engineer of the Los Angeles County Flood Control District and chief engineer and general manager of the Los Angeles County Sanitation Districts. They urge an immediate start on a reclamation program.

[89] Our cost estimates are similar to ones reached elsewhere: (*a*) Arnold, Hedger, and Rawn (*op. cit.*, pp. 12–13) show total costs (including interest and amortization and the costs of spreading) ranging from $9.00 to $19 an acre-foot (at 4 per cent) for reclamation at five plant locations. However, these are low-cost locations. (*b*) Hedger and Rawn (*op. cit.*, pp. 1, 7) show costs of $12 an acre-foot for a demonstration plant at the Whittier Narrows (interest rate not specified but believed to be near 4 per cent). This report estimates that Los Angeles County 1958 sewage outflow was 523,000 acre-feet per year and that 60 per cent, or about 306,000 acre-feet a year, was

Reclamation of sewage and waste waters, however, does not offer a panacea as far as water supply is concerned. Even though it is a promising source of new water, its use should be restricted and controlled. Despite claims that a modern well-designed plant for the reclamation of sewage can produce "a well oxidized, sparkling and sterilized effluent which is of better quality, chemically and biologically, than many public raw water supplies,"[90] we feel that it is prudent to limit use of completely treated effluent to certain agricultural and industrial uses and to the recharge of ground-water basins. Some enthusiasts regard this restriction as an outright concession to public prejudice. In our opinion, however, uncertainty about the complete effectiveness of the reclamation process (at least until we have had more experience with it) makes these limitations not unreasonable.[91]

Of course, the restrictions upon use will have some influence on the economic feasibility of this supply. For one thing it is doubtful if agricultural use can be large because of the increased displacement of agriculture by urban growth and because of the distance of much of the remaining agricultural land from treatment plants. Similarly, although the reclaimed water would be suitable for lawn-sprinkling at parks and golf courses and for impounding in receational lakes,[92] its use would necessarily be limited to recreational areas in the vicinity of reclamation plants because of the high cost of separate water-distribution lines. Widespread industrial use of sewage effluent would also be controlled by the cost of distribution facilities. On this point, however, Hedger and Rawn estimate that suitable industrial uses (27,375 acre-feet per year) and recreational uses of 15,000,000 gallons per day (16,425 acre-feet per year) presently exist within close proximity to proposed treatment-plant sites in Los Angeles County.[93] It would seem reasonable that such uses might increase in the future as the availability of low-cost reclaimed water influenced the location of industrial plants, parks, and golf courses.

The most satisfactory way to employ large amounts of reclaimed water would be for recharging the underground aquifer system. In this manner the effluent could be made available for general unrestricted use; percolation through ground provides a strong safety factor because of the increased filtering and bacteriological action which takes place. In addition, the effluent would then be mixed with other ground waters. Recharge can be accomplished in two ways: through injection wells or by surface spreading.

---

suitable for reclamation and reuse. (*c*) *Bulletin No. 78* (*Preliminary*), pp. II-8–II-9, estimates that the present sewage outflow in southern California is about 600,000 acre-feet per year and that about 40 per cent of this can be reclaimed at costs ranging from $13 to $40 an acre-foot (calculated at 3.5 per cent interest). (*d*) Harris Zeitzew, Donal A. Meier, Jack C. Monroe, Edward H. Lynch, Melvin S. Mann, and Frederick J. Seufert, "An Economic Study of Water Supply for Southern California (unpublished Master's thesis, Department of Engineering, University of California at Los Angeles, 1958), p. IV-12. Here costs of reclamation are estimated to fall in the range of $27–$35 an acre-foot, with interest around 3 per cent, for a plant at the Whittier Narrows. These costs, however, include the extra costs of wells and pumps for reuse of the water after recharge. As we suggest below, existing wells and pumps probably have enough excess capacity to increase ground-water drafts considerably. Additional pumps and wells would not have to be constructed until the volume of recharge reached very high levels, and then the transmission capacity of the aquifers would be the limiting consideration.

[90] Arnold, Hedger, and Rawn, *op. cit.*, p. 11.

[91] See in particular the statement by the California Department of Public Health contained in Hedger and Rawn, *op. cit.*, pp. 11–14.

[92] Golf courses currently using sewage effluent are located in Las Vegas, Nevada, Santa Fe, Los Alamos, and Carlsbad, New Mexico, and at Camp Pendleton and El Cajon, California. Golden Gate Park in San Francisco has used reclaimed sewage to irrigate about 400 acres since 1932.

[93] Hedger and Rawn, *op. cit.*, p. 6.

Experimental injection wells have been in operation since 1955 near Manhattan Beach, where a fresh-water barrier has been established to halt the intrusion of sea water. Ultimate plans call for an 11-mile fresh-water barrier along the coast line from Santa Monica to Manhattan Beach. Tests have shown that sewage effluent taken from the Hyperion treatment plant is suitable for injection purposes.[94] Although imported Colorado River water has been the primary source of injection water to date, sewage effluent could very well be used for this purpose.

The surface spreading of sewage effluent would probably be its largest and most economical use. The South Coastal Area is fortunate in having many spreading grounds already functioning which would be suitable for this purpose. Currently, these recharge areas (located in river channels and dry washes) are used to spread flood waters and thus are idle much of the time. Also, some are located near existing trunk sewer lines.[95]

In addition to restrictions upon use, the reclamation of sewage water must be governed by the build-up of dissolved salts which generally accompanies the reuse of water.[96] The extent of reuse or recycle of water would depend upon the total amount of dissolved solids as well as upon the composition of the salts; waters that are of good quality to begin with can be reused more times than water initially high in mineral concentration. It has been estimated that domestic and commercial use may add an increment of 250 ppm of dissolved solids.[97] Waters from the Los Angeles Aqueduct and from most local wells are generally of good quality, containing about 200–300 ppm of dissolved solids, and could be recycled several times before a serious build-up occurred. Colorado River water, however, has an initial concentration in excess of 700 ppm; only one reuse would be desirable under ordinary circumstances. Fortunately, most of the surface-spreading grounds in the South Coastal Area are located in the forebay areas of the major ground-water basins. Water spread for recharge at these points would be available for reuse only in areas with elevations lower than the point of recharge, so that multiple recycle would not develop. However, the location of any new spreading grounds would have to consider the problem of salt build-up due to recycle, particularly where the sewage source used Colorado River water.

One final word of caution may be given in regard to large-scale sewage reclamation. We have suggested that the effluent be used primarily for recharge of ground-water basins; perhaps up to 400,000 or 500,000 acre-feet a year could be employed for this purpose, depending upon the recharge capacity of spreading grounds, the transmission capacity of the underground aquifers, and the pumping capacity of existing wells. Construction of additional spreading grounds or the installation of more pumps and wells, of course, would raise the cost of the reclaimed water. We doubt, however, that much could be done to increase the transmission capacity of the aquifers. All of this suggests that reclamation of sewage in excess of, say, 500,000 acre-feet a year (while possibly economically feasible otherwise) would seem to

[94] H. A. Van der Goot, "Water Reclamation Experiments at Hyperion," *Sewage and Industrial Wastes,* XXIX (October, 1957), 1144.

[95] Perhaps the most promising site is the Whittier Narrows on the San Gabriel River, where a plant to reclaim about 100,000,000 gallons a day (about 112,000 acre-feet annually) could be constructed.

[96] This is related, of course, to the necessary segregation of toxic industrial and chemical wastes from other types of sewage discharge. For this reason it would never become desirable to reclaim all sewage waters—probably about 50 per cent of sewage flows should be left in any case to perform the valuable function of disposing of toxic and inorganic waste products from urban development.

[97] Bush and Mulford, *op. cit.,* p. 7.

depend upon suitability of the effluent for surface consumption, which remains doubtful at this time. On the other hand, we must not forget that advancing urbanization will require increased sewage-disposal facilities whether the sewage is reclaimed for reuse or not. This means that the extra costs of reclamation (and recharge of the effluent) may be very low or even zero when the alternative is to construct expensive ocean outfall lines in addition to providing the standard sewage treatment.

5. Regional Reallocations

We have noted above that, as population and industry grow in the South Coastal Area, it is both natural and desirable that agricultural (and other low-valued) uses of water within the region come to be displaced by urban uses. To the extent that voluntary exchange by purchase and sale is allowed, water will tend to find its most valuable use through the market place—and, as irrigation agriculture generally requires a supply of cheap water,[98] it becomes an uneconomic use when rising residential, commercial, and industrial demands relative to limited supplies make water no longer cheap. There is no logical reason why this process of rational reallocation should be limited to transfers *within* a hydrographic region. As a matter of fact, one can hardly fail to note that substantial possibilities for such reallocations exist because of the tremendous irrigation usage now taking place in other nearby regions. It seems obvious that the purchase of water rights in nearby regions and transport of the acquired water should be considered as an alternative to importation of water over much longer distances from northern California.

We have given some tentative consideration to several regional reallocations (see Fig. 27). Generally, these appear to be fairly expensive sources as compared with supplies currently available. Still, for the few cases we have been able to estimate, the indicated cost figures are less than those of Feather River water. At low interest rates like 3.5 per cent we cannot be very confident about this conclusion, however, because of the aforementioned bias in the employment of the full-capacity cost equation (7) of chapter vii for the alternative sources and the actual-delivery equation (5) of chapter vii for the Feather River estimates. But at the higher interest rates like our recommended 10 per cent figure, the Feather River source becomes unquestionably much more costly.

a) Purchase of Colorado River rights.—California claims to the waters of the Colorado River total 5,378,000 acre-feet per year; contracts with the federal government call for 5,362,000 acre-feet, and the remaining amount (16,000 acre-feet) covers miscellaneous irrigation of long standing along the river and water for the city of Needles. The Seven-Party Water Agreement (1931) sets forth the relative priority of the claims covered by federal contracts (see Table 45). Most of the California claims for Colorado water are for irrigation purposes; MWD rights of 1,212,000 acre-feet are the exception. We pointed out earlier that all amounts or claims in excess of 4,400,000 acre-feet are subject to dispute in the litigation with Arizona now being considered by the United States Supreme Court.

In the event of a decision unfavorable to California, or as a source of additional supplies, the MWD might consider the purchase of rights held by other users of Colorado River water, especially by irriga-

[98] We suggested above that only about half of the current agricultural use of water in the South Coastal Area might compete on even terms for scarce water supplies at wholesale costs in excess of $30 an acre-foot (to which must be added delivery costs to the farmer's headgate) when used for producing avocados, citrus, and some high-valued truck and nursery crops. However, the value of the agricultural *land* in its alternative uses might well be even more crucial than water costs in determining the future feasibility of agriculture in the area.

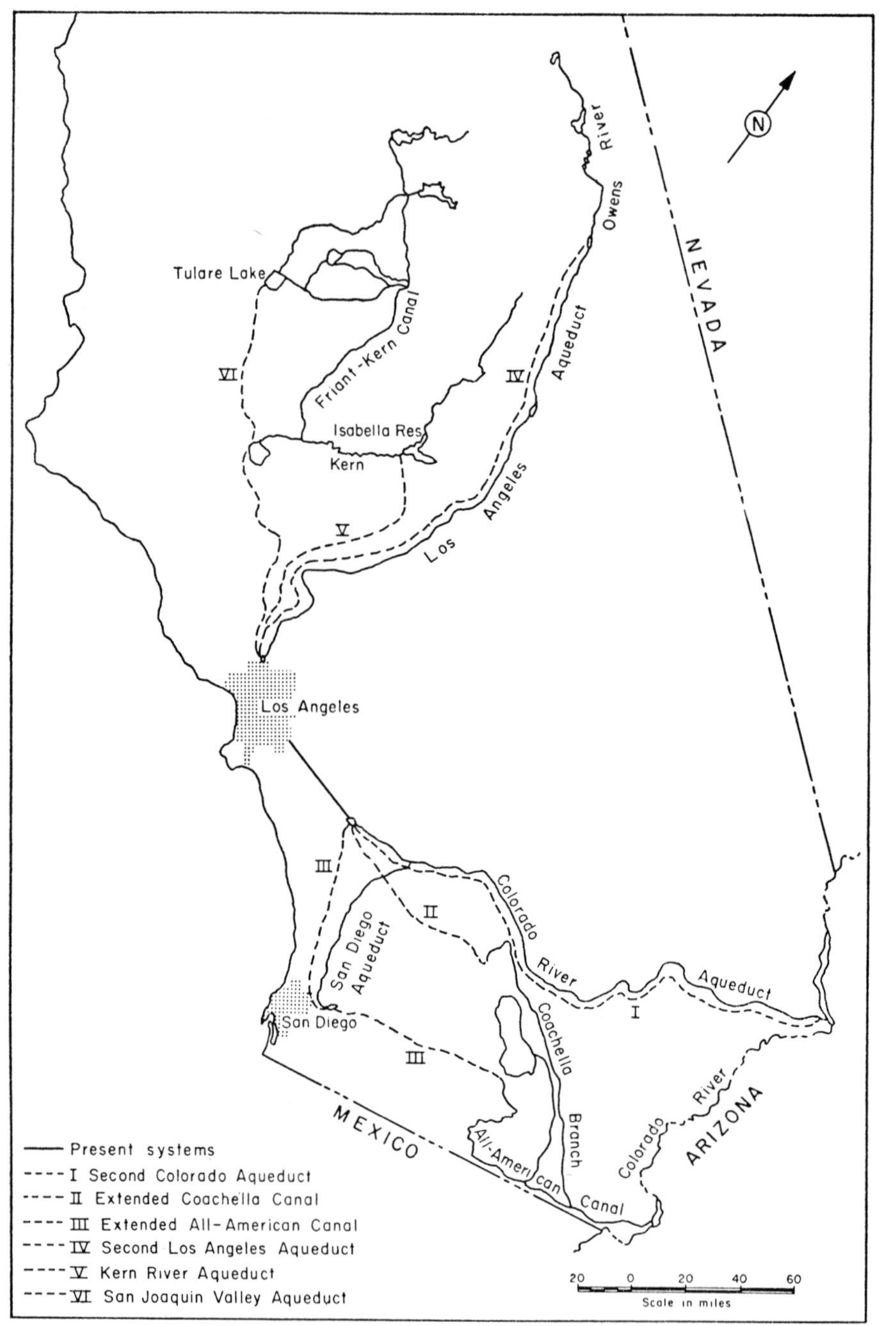

FIG. 27.—Some alternative interregional water-transport systems for southern California (approximate locations). (Redrawn, with changes, from Pl. IV of *Bulletin No. 3.*)

tion districts in the Imperial area. Our tentative conclusion is that a purchase of up to 1,000,000 acre-feet per year might be negotiated at a price favorable to all parties concerned—one which would provide a net income to the irrigation districts substantially in excess of the earnings foregone from irrigation and which (when added to the cost of transport) would still be competitive with water imported from northern California. The purchase of Colorado River rights in excess of 1,000,000 acre-feet, however, would be increasingly expensive and perhaps could be accomplished only at prices that would rule out its feasibility as a water supply for southern California. Of course, the mere availability of this water in the Colorado desert regions is but the first step of the analysis. In order to estimate the possible cost of this water to the South Coastal Area, it is necessary to estimate the price at which water rights might be acquired from present holders and then to add the cost of transport to points of possible use. Obviously, each estimate would require very considerable study if made in full rigor, and only broad indications of the costs can be given here.

First, with respect to acquisition of water rights, purchase of partial allocations would be much less costly per unit of water acquired than purchase of full rights. That this must be so is evident from the following consideration. Suppose that, for a given farm or irrigation district, 25 per cent of the attached water rights were purchased. The farmer would almost certainly remain in business. He could either reduce the application of water to his initial crop, shift to a crop demanding less moisture, or cut back on his acres irrigated. Alternatively, he could make investments designed to eliminate waste by seepage and evaporation (often reaching 50 per cent at canal-side) and thus indirectly recoup some of the water lost by sale. In any case, the net return to *farming* operations will have been somewhat reduced, in exchange for an in-

TABLE 45*

PRIORITIES AMONG CALIFORNIA CLAIMANTS FOR COLORADO RIVER WATER

Priority No.	Agency	Annual Amount (Acre-Feet)
1	Palo Verde Irrigation District	420,000
2	Yuma Project, California Division	70,500
3	Imperial Irrigation District, Coachella Irrigation District, Palo Verde Irrigation District (Lower Mesa)—served by All-American Canal	3,359,500
		3,850,000
4	Metropolitan Water District of Southern California	550,000
	First four priorities within California limitation	4,400,000
5	Metropolitan Water District of Southern California	662,000
6	All-American Canal (Imperial, Coachella, and Palo Verde)	300,000
		5,362,000
Miscellaneous claims		16,000
Total		5,378,000

* Source: "Seven-Party Water Agreement, August 18, 1931," in Ray Lyman Wilbur and Northcutt Ely, *The Hoover Dam Documents* (2d ed.; Washington, D.C.: Government Printing Office, 1948), Appendix 1003; "Findings of Fact and Conclusions of Law, Filed by California Defendants, April 1, 1959," in *Arizona* v. *California et al.*, Table 4-C.

crement in revenue from water sales. If the sale is voluntary, the gain to the farmer from water sales will exceed the loss in farming. In contrast, purchase of full water rights will require abandonment of farming or, alternatively, a radical shift to dry culture—and only a very handsome offering price for the water is likely to induce an agreement to sell. In somewhat more technical language, we may say that the value placed upon the last unit of water applied (the marginal value in use) is less than the average value in use.

Without having made the thorough study that the topic requires, it is our belief that something like the last 25 or 30 per cent of the Colorado Desert irrigation rights could be purchased for under $15 an acre-foot per year. The districts now charge such low prices for the Colorado River water (in the Imperial Irrigation District, $2.00 an acre-foot)[99] that the farmer has little incentive to take measures to avoid water waste or to concentrate on high-valued crops. In fact, it is quite conceivable that, say, 10 per cent of the water rights could be acquired extremely cheaply (perhaps under $5.00 an acre-foot per year). There should be some allowance for the element of bargaining that would be expected to drive up the price somewhat, on the assumption that the water is not to be acquired by methods involving compulsion.[100]

[99] Water prices in some irrigation districts are purely nominal, intended to cover only part of the expenses of the district (the rest being borne by taxes), the water being then rationed by administrative decree or by historical rights. For the Imperial Irrigation District, however, the $2.00 charged is a true price.

[100] It is possible in California for municipalities to condemn or acquire rural water rights through the process of eminent domain. The California Department of Water Resources has not been granted powers to condemn water rights, except in connection with the Central Valley Project (*Bulletin No. 3,* pp. 218–19). The MWD does not possess the power of eminent domain with regard to water rights. (Metropolitan Water District Act, Deerings General Laws, Act 9129, sec. 5, par. 5.)

The amount of irrigated land in the Palo Verde, Imperial, and Coachella irrigation districts varies from year to year; recently, it has ranged from 560,000 acres to about 600,000 acres. Correspondingly, the amount of Colorado River water used varies also, but it nearly approximates the full entitlement of 3,850,000 acre-feet per year. This means that the use of water (including canal losses, seepage, and evaporation) is in excess of 6 feet per acre—a relatively large amount even for desert conditions. It is instructive to see that over 75 per cent of these acres were planted in relatively low-valued crops (data from 1950): 203,000 acres in alfalfa, 8,200 acres in pasture, 100,000 acres in hay and grain, 34,000 acres in sugar beets, and 85,000 acres in miscellaneous field crops (e.g., milo, hemp, flax, safflower, field corn, and beans).[101] The high-valued crops—orchard, citrus, dates, grapes, cotton, and truck crops—occupied only a total of 134,100 acres. The annual consumptive use of water per acre by the low-valued crops is rather substantial: 4.2 feet for alfalfa, 5.0 feet for pasture, 1.8 feet for hay and grain, 2.5 feet for sugar beets, and 2.4 feet for miscellaneous field crops.[102] Of the high-valued crops, dates require the most water—about 6 feet per year. While this brief survey is not conclusive, it does indicate that a substantial amount of water in the Colorado Desert Area is devoted to the growing of relatively low-valued crops.

In 1954 the average value of all farm land and buildings in Imperial County was estimated to be $369.54 per acre.[103] Undoubtedly, land used for the production of specialty and high-valued crops was worth considerably more, possibly up to $2,000 an acre. On the other hand, land devoted to low-valued crops (e.g., alfalfa) was

[101] *Bulletin No. 2,* I, 209.

[102] *Ibid.,* p. 214.

[103] *United States Census of Agriculture,* Vol. I, Part 33 ("California") (Washington, D.C.: Government Printing Office, 1954), p. 51.

probably worth less than the average, particularly since the average figure included the value of buildings as well as high-valued lands. A purchase of about 25 per cent of the Colorado rights of the area would have its principal impact upon the use of water for low-valued crops. In this connection we note that even a low $5.00 price per acre-foot sold, where water is now being used in the amount of 5 feet per acre (e.g., alfalfa), and with land valued at $400 an acre (a generous figure), would yield a return of 6.25 per cent to the owner of the land (and water rights). In addition, the land might have some remaining value in dry farming or other uses. A price of $10 an acre-foot for 1,000,000 acre-feet per year would provide the irrigation districts with an income of $10 million a year and still leave them with enough water to plant more acreage of high-valued crops than were planted in 1950. Possible water revenues of $10 million compare significantly with the market value of all crops in Imperial County for 1954, which was $109 million.[104] The latter is a gross figure from which must be deducted all costs of production; in contrast, a water sale of $10 million would constitute a return net of all costs.

Turning now to the question of transportation, there are a number of possibilities. The water rights acquired through purchase could be drawn from the Colorado itself, perhaps most conveniently by adding capacity to the existing Colorado Aqueduct belonging to the MWD. If rights to 1,000,000 acre-feet were obtained, it would be necessary to almost double the capacity of the aqueduct. Although it may be expensive in comparison with current sources, there seems little reason to doubt that a new Colorado aqueduct would be cheaper than going to the Feather River. The distance is less, the pump lift required is smaller, and, in addition, there are already facilities like access roads and communications in place. Furthermore, in many locations existing real estate will permit the duplication of capacity without new land acquisition. While this seems likely to be the cheapest of the transport systems for additional Colorado River water, we have not made the calculations required to evaluate this plan.

Another possibility would be to acquire Imperial and Coachella rights and transport the water by extending the All-American and Coachella Canal system toward the Los Angeles area. It is interesting that this possibility was originally considered as an alternative to the Parker Route eventually adopted for the Colorado River Aqueduct; the official calculations actually indicated that it would be cheaper than the Parker Route. This route was nevertheless rejected because of fear of operating conflicts with irrigators, geological hazards, and poor quality of water at the end of a long irrigation line.[105] We regard the last of these considerations as being the most weighty; they all apply, however, with equal force to the Feather River Project as well. We believe that this transport possibility still justifies study. Our rough estimates of the present-day costs of water from the Coachella Branch of the All-American Canal are based upon the excellent study of this system by F. E. Weymouth and others in 1930.[106] Table 46 presents these estimates.[107] To these figures must be added the cost of the purchase of the water rights, which might run as high as $15 an acre-foot.

104 *Ibid.*, p. 69.

105 Metropolitan Water District of Southern California, *Summary of Preliminary Surveys, Designs and Estimates for the Metropolitan Water District Aqueduct and Terminal Storage Projects*, by F. E. Weymouth (chief engineer) (Los Angeles, November, 1930), pp. 63–65.

106 *Ibid.*, pp. 122–26.

107 For a comparison we note that *Bulletin No. 78 (Preliminary)* (p. II-11) estimates that the cost of facilities to transport water from the Salton Sea to the South Coastal Area would be approximately $45 an acre-foot.

Still a third possibility would be to extend the main branch of the All-American Canal from its western terminus approximately 110 miles toward San Diego, with one branch serving that city, while another turned north to the Los Angeles area. Here again it is historically interesting that San Diego originally intended to transport its Colorado River allocation (112,000 acre-feet) in just this way. That city is still paying for its share of the construction costs of the All-American Canal,[108] though this plan was abandoned in 1946 in favor of a connection to the MWD system. The difficulties alluded to in connection with the Coachella extension would also be encountered, though the geological hazard would be less severe. Because of the complexity of the problem, we have not attempted to make cost estimates for this route.

TABLE 46

ESTIMATED COSTS FOR DELIVERY OF COLORADO RIVER WATER TO SOUTH COASTAL AREA VIA COACHELLA CANAL EXTENSION

Interest Rate (Per Cent)	Cost per Acre-Foot
3.5	$33.49
6.0	45.15
10.0	65.31

ASSUMPTIONS

1. Delivery of 986,705 acre-feet per year.
2. Capital expenses were adjusted to current price levels by multiplying the Weymouth estimates by a factor of 3.61. This factor is the *Engineering News-Record* construction-cost index ratio for 1957 as compared with 1930, calculated from *Engineering News-Record,* October 17, 1957, pp. 83–84.
3. Capital costs do not include $20 million for lining of part of the All-American Canal, which does not appear necessary.
4. Electric-power rates for pumping were taken from *Bulletin No. 78* (*Preliminary*), p. V-26.
5. Operation and maintenance costs were estimated by using double the 1958 operation and maintenance costs of the MWD Aqueduct to allow for the larger number of pumps (7 versus 5) in the Coachella extension and for the possibility of greater maintenance (Metropolitan Water District of Southern California, *Twentieth Annual Report* [Los Angeles, 1958], p. 153).

b) *Other regional transfers.*—Before leaving the subject of regional reallocation, we should mention that there are several other possibilities that also warrant examination. One of the most promising is additional Owens-Mono water for the city of Los Angeles. We have studied two excellent reports prepared for the Los Angeles Department of Water and Power in 1924 and 1926, when the city was concerned about the safe yield of its water supply during the period of drought affecting its Sierra Nevada source of supply.[109] Both of these reports suggested that the city build a *second* aqueduct from the Owens-Mono region by ending all irrigation on lands already owned by the city and by pumping from ground-water supplies during dry years. The 1924 report gave the capacity of the second aqueduct as 350 cubic feet per second;[110] the 1926 report reduced the safe yield of the second aqueduct to 323 second-feet. (The yield on the first aqueduct was then 400 second-feet.)[111] If these figures are correct, the safe yield of the Owens-Mono region is 723 cubic feet per second (523,450 acre-feet per year). In 1931 the yield of the present Owens-Mono Aqueduct was increased from 400 second-feet to 440 second-feet (320,000 acre-feet per year) when the city built an extension up to Mono Basin. It appears that an additional 283 second-feet of flow (over 200,000 acre-feet per year) on a safe-yield basis may be available from that region. Unfortunately, we have no convenient means for estimating the cost of such a second aqueduct. As a crude guess, we can

[108] See Wilbur and Ely, *op. cit.*, Appendix 1111, pp. A671–A686.

[109] Louis C. Hill, J. B. Lippincott, and A. L. Sonderegger, *Report on Available Water Supply of the City of Los Angeles and Metropolitan Area* (Los Angeles, August, 1924); *Supplementary Report* (Los Angeles, March, 1926).

[110] Hill *et al.*, *Report on Available Water Supply,* p. 2.

[111] Hill *et al.*, *Supplementary Report,* p. 31.

take the original 1913 cost of $25 million for the first aqueduct's 400 second-feet of capacity and multiply this by 7.57 to get a comparable 1957 figure[112] and by 70.75 per cent to adjust proportionately for the smaller capacity. The result is probably on the high side, because no credit is taken for possible use of existing real estate and facilities already in place. The costs per acre-foot, calculated at seventy-year life, are $28.35 at 3.5 per cent interest, $44.99 at 6 per cent, and $73.80 at 10 per cent. No allowance is made in these figures for the possibility of generating hydroelectric power along the gravity-flow route.

Another interarea transfer that is intriguing is the diversion of the waters of the Kern River via a tunnel in the Tehachapi Mountains to the Mojave Desert, from which area an aqueduct could generally follow the route of the present Los Angeles Aqueduct to the metropolitan area. This proposal was made in 1920 by Robert B. Marshall, then chief geographer of the United States Geological Survey, as part of a state water plan.[113] Marshall estimated that, at a cost of $50 million, it would be possible to construct a 300-foot dam, approximately at the site of Lake Isabella (a dam at this location was completed in 1954) on the Kern River, and to tunnel through the mountains at an elevation of about 2,700 feet for a gravity-flow aqueduct to Los Angeles. To accomplish this transfer, it would be necessary to purchase the rights to the flow of the Kern River, about 400,000 acre-feet a year, or to provide other supplies in place of the Kern flow to irrigators north of the Tehachapi Mountains. An estimate of the costs this scheme would entail can be obtained by multiplying the $50-million Marshall figure by an *Engineering News-Record* construction-cost index of 3.476 (early 1920's to 1957) to get a comparable 1957 figure of $173,800,000. The costs per acre-foot (calculated at seventy-year life) are then $16.70 at 3.5 per cent interest, $26.50 at 6 per cent, and $43.50 at 10 per cent. Allowing $15 an acre-foot for purchase of water rights, the total costs become $31.70 at 3.5 per cent, $41.50 at 6 per cent, and $58.50 at 10 per cent. It would seem sensible to provide a substitute supply for the Kern River flow from the Feather River *north* of the Tehachapi Mountains rather than to pump the Feather River water over the mountains. Even though the water from the Kern River now generates a substantial amount of power from 66,000 kilowatts of installed capacity,[114] it is clear that the power generated by the Kern would be less than the power required to pump an equivalent flow over the mountains.[115] And if the Kern were diverted at an elevation of 2,700 feet, as Marshall suggested, it would offer possibilities for power generation on its way to the South Coastal Area.

Other regional reallocations can only be speculated about at this time. For example, in connection with the Colorado River there is at least the theoretical possibility of interstate or even international purchase of water rights—from Arizona or the Upper Basin states, in the one case, or the Republic of Mexico, in the other. Finally, it may be that economic rationality will dictate a reduction in the enormous irrigation usage in the southern end of the San Joaquin Valley for possible transfer to the South Coastal Area. In the Tulare Lake Basin alone (the section of the region closest to southern California), 4,280,000 acre-feet were used in 1950 (practically all

112 The *Engineering News-Record* construction-cost index for 1957 relative to 1913 is 7.37 (*Engineering News-Record,* October 17, 1957, p. 84).

113 See Clair Engle, *Central Valley Documents,* Part I (84th Cong., 2d sess. [House Doc. 416 (Washington, D.C., 1956)]), pp. 139–50, for pertinent portions of the Marshall Plan of 1920.

114 *Bulletin No. 2,* I, 181.

115 As a rough rule of thumb, a foot of fall can generate about about three-fifths of the energy required for a foot of pump lift.

for irrigation).[116] Transport of a fraction of this water to the South Coastal Area would involve a distance of about one-third to one-half as great as the transport of Feather River water.

6. Miscellaneous Sources

In this section we will make a number of brief comments on still other possibilities which, while they should perhaps be further investigated, do not appear on the basis of present knowledge to be major alternatives competitive with the importation of water from northern California via the Feather River Project.

a) *Rain-making.*—It has been maintained that a controlled plan of weather modification could increase the usable precipitation so as to reduce the need for supplemental water. In the present state of knowledge it would be impossible to rely on rain-making as an alternative to conventional water-supply techniques (see our discussion in chap. viii). Nevertheless, we should in our current decisions place some weight on the risk that future developments in weather modification might make obsolete a huge investment in development of a conventional source.

b) *Sea-water conversion.*—Everything in the above paragraph applies equally well to the possibility of securing fresh water by conversion of a saline source. In the South Coastal Area the proximity of the centers of demand to the ocean lends special promise to this possibility. However, as we discussed at length in chapter viii (see especially Table 24), all presently known methods appear to be very costly, even on the basis of extrapolations downward from present costs to take into account foreseeable improvements. On this basis the cheapest method from an ocean source appears to be the least unconventional—multiple-effect evaporation—for which figures not lower than about $200 an acre-foot at 4 per cent interest, or $240 at 10 per cent, can now be foreseen.

A special comment here should be made about the possibilities of a breakthrough in nuclear (or other unconventional) sources of power. No presently known method appears to provide cheaper power than conventional hydro- or fossil-fuel plants; current optimistic estimates merely assert that nuclear power may prevent the threshold of power costs from rising if and when fossil fuels become increasingly scarce. There is nothing to be gained in linking expensive atomic power to expensive sea-water conversion. Futhermore, any development that reduced the cost of power, atomic or other, would also reduce the cost of pumping in the provision of conventional water supply.[117] Once more, however, we can say only that there is some possibility of a major technological breakthrough which should not be ignored in assessing the risks associated with large capital commitments in conventional water systems.

c) *Tanker transport.*—One possible major source of supply, which may seem unconventional but really is not, is to transport surplus waters of northern California (or possibly of the Columbia River) via ocean-going tankers. Sea transport is generally a cheap method for moving bulk commodities, and certain circumstances favor it here. The points of most important demand (Los Angeles and San Diego) are on or close to the sea, while a truly enormous supply relative to present or foreseeable future demands is available in the North Coastal Area of California and in the ocean runoff of the Pacific Northwest. Nevertheless, our preliminary cost estimates appear to rule out conventional tanker transport, the figures being in the neighborhood of $1,000 an acre-foot.

Efficient adaptations or improvements in

116 *Bulletin No. 2,* I, 182–84.

117 The power requirements in conversion of sea water may run about 5,000 kilowatts per acre-foot, approximately the amount of power required to pump an acre-foot of water over the Tehachapi Mountains to southern California.

tanker technology are perhaps possible for vessels specializing in the carriage of water. As compared with typical oil tankers, expensive fire-control and safety measures can be dispensed with, and it may even be possible to tow trains of barges or plastic bags. However, it seems unlikely that costs could be reduced enough to make sea transport a cheap long-run or large-scale source of supply.

d) *Conventional alternatives.*—The statements above about the undetermined future promise of unconventional methods do not apply, of course, to proposals for facilities of conventional type that happen to be in conflict with the official plans of state authorities. Two such proposals have received some discussion.

The first of these is the use of the Eel River in northern California as the source of water to be conveyed by an aqueduct to the South Coastal Area. The MWD has, in fact, made a filing as required by state law for 2,200,000 acre-feet from the Eel now going unused. The Eel, however, is no closer than the Feather River at Oroville, and water from the Eel cannot be conveyed southward for 150 miles in river bed at negligible cost, as can the Feather River water. It is difficult to see how the Eel can be regarded as a reasonable source for conventional aqueduct transport to southern California. There are indications that the Eel filing is part of a power struggle between the MWD and the State Department of Water Resources over responsibility for water supply in southern California.

Another alternative is the so-called Wiley Plan or "Gravity Plan." This is essentially a proposal to build a number of smaller upstream dams to facilitate transfers of water with a minimum of pumping. We do not have information that would permit us to make any evaluation of this idea.

The leading candidate for consideration as a conventional source of new supply for the South Coastal Area is, of course, the Feather River Project. Since this is the officially approved proposal, we devote the following section to an economic evaluation of its advantages for the region. The cost figures summarized in Table 44 should be borne in mind for comparison with our Feather River results.

F. The Feather River Project

1. History and Description of the Project

The Feather River Project is intended to be the initial unit in the realization of the California Water Plan, the basic goal of the latter being the redistribution of water in California from the "surplus" areas of the north to the "deficiency" areas of the south. The major objectives of this project are flood control in the area north of Sacramento, along the Feather River and the Sacramento River after its junction with the Feather; water supply for irrigation purposes in the San Joaquin Valley; water supply primarily for urban purposes in southern California and especially in the South Coastal Area; and associated hydropower development in northern California (though the project is, on balance, a large net consumer of energy).

Critical analysis of the project has been made difficult by the fact that a multiplicity of aqueduct routes and associated delivery systems have been under continual consideration and modification, long after official authorization of the project. In consequence, the official reports include a vast amount of detail on ten to twenty variant schemes. The currently recommended plan[118] (see Fig. 28) begins with an enor-

[118] It is by no means easy to find adequate data on the currently recommended plan for which funds are being sought from the voters. Our description relies primarily upon *Bulletin No. 78* (*Preliminary*) (February, 1959). This bulletin says nothing, however, about facilities north of the Delta or about the South Bay Aqueduct, aside from indicating their continued existence as part of the project. We will at times have to employ data provided in older publications to fill in the information gaps.

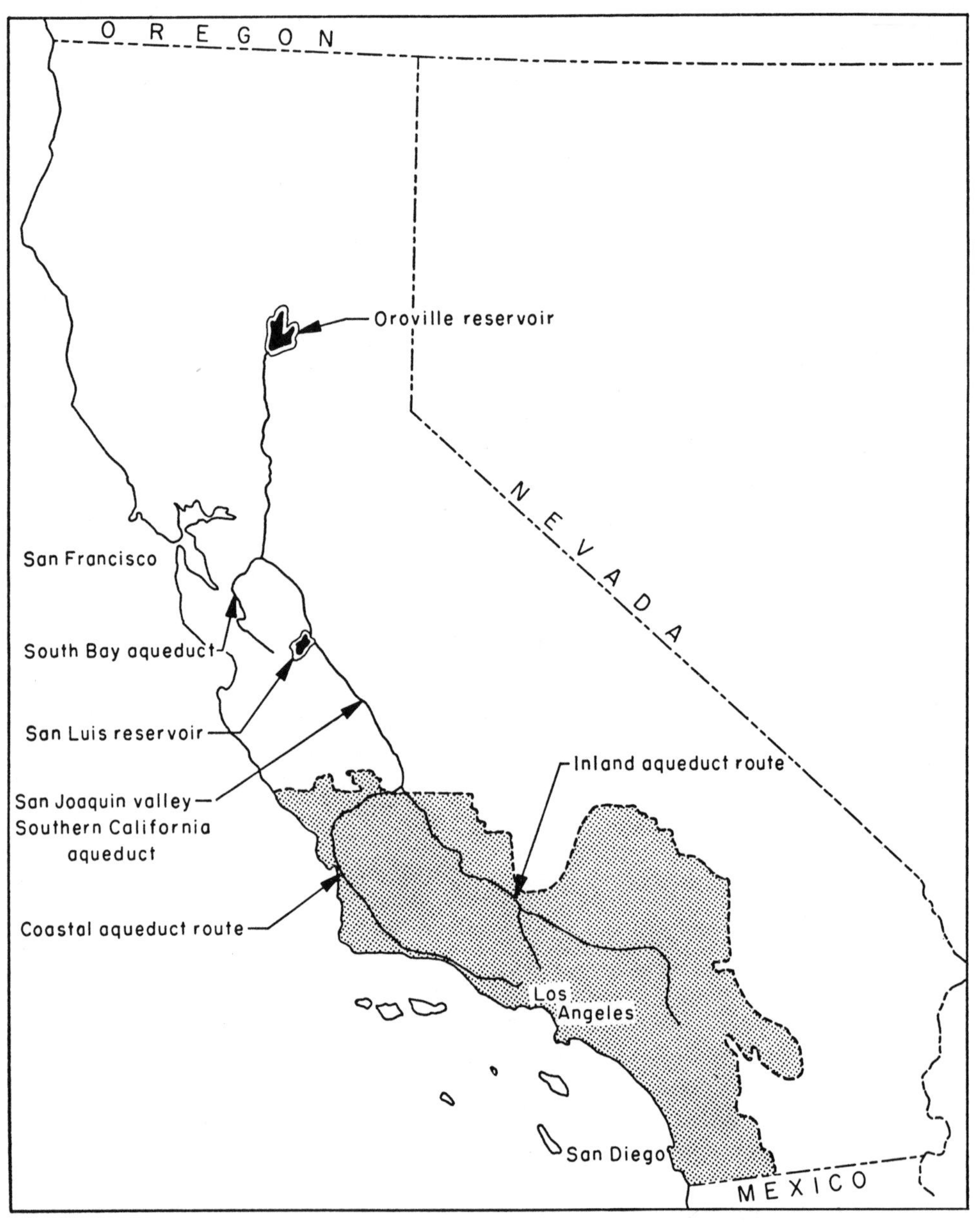

FIG. 28.—Proposed Feather River Project and southern California service area. (From *Bulletin No. 78* [*Preliminary*], Pl. I.)

mous dam and reservoir on the Feather River near the city of Oroville in north-central California. From the dam the water would proceed through an afterbay dam and power plant; thence in the natural channels of the Feather and the Sacramento to the Delta Cross Channel to be constructed near the confluence of the Sacramento and San Joaquin rivers east of San Francisco Bay (the so-called Delta Pool). From the Cross Channel the main aqueduct takes the water some 585 miles to southern California, with a side conduit for delivery to Alameda and Santa Clara counties southeast of San Francisco Bay (the South Bay Aqueduct). At the Avenal Gap (near the line dividing Kings and Kern counties), a coastal aqueduct branches off to serve San Luis Obispo and Santa Barbara counties. The main aqueduct crosses the Tehachapis and divides into two branches north of Los Angeles (see Fig. 29). The smaller West Branch serves the Los Angeles metropolitan area and Ventura County, while the larger East Branch serves San Bernardino and Riverside counties and connects with the Metropolitan Water District system and with the second San Diego aqueduct now under construction. As we shall see later, the water in the Delta from existing flows plus the regulation provided by Oroville Dam is insufficient to meet the ultimate delivery schedule projected, so that additional dam construction will presumably be required at some future date (though the official reports contain no hint of this).

The costs of this project are enormous, although even the official estimates are hard to determine for lack of an integrated current description (see n. 118). *Bulletin No. 78* (*Preliminary*) quotes a figure of $1.807 billion for undiscounted capital costs only, excluding an estimated federal contribution of $100 million and costs of $736 million for the construction of local conveyance and delivery facilities—but these figures still do not include any costs for north-of-Delta facilities (among them Oroville Dam itself) or for aqueduct facilities not serving southern California.[119] The older Bechtel study provided estimates for the two major elements omitted in *Bulletin No. 78* (*Preliminary*): $434 million for Oroville Dam and related facilities and $28 million for what is now known as the South Bay Aqueduct.[120] Accepting these as still roughly correct, the project total is thus about $3 billion, for capital costs only, and without regard to possible additional dam construction required. Among the reasons for the high costs are the enormous scale of the undertaking (Oroville Dam being larger than any dam now existing in the world); the unprecedented length of the delivery system (about 150 miles in river bed, 585 in aqueduct); and the need to pump water some 3,300 feet over the Tehachapis (this last appears most importantly in the operating cost rather than the capital cost).

The urgent pressures for the Feather River Project, aside from those due to the State Department of Water Resources itself, stem primarily from certain regions in California, especially those pumping water from underground basins with declining water levels. Most especially in the west side of the San Joaquin Valley, irrigation interests (and to some extent associated industrial and municipal developments) are threatened by decline as the cost of water from local or nearby sources steadily increases. (It is for this reason that some proponents of the project, and at times officials of the Department of Water Resources itself, have described it as a "rescue" operation for which strict standards of economic justification need not be applied.) In addition, the continuing growth of urban demand in the Los Angeles and

[119] *Ibid.*, p. VII-24.

[120] Bechtel Corporation, *Report on the Engineering, Economic, and Financial Aspects of the Feather River Project* (*San Francisco, December 31, 1955*) (Sacramento, 1956), p. 53 (hereinafter cited as "Bechtel *Report*").

San Diego regions has made the project of serious interest to these areas as well. Official projections now current indicate a necessity to begin construction soon in order to meet "requirements" expected to develop by 1970.[121]

The project was proposed in 1951 to the California legislature in a feasibility report prepared by a predecessor agency of the present Department of Water Resources,[122] and in that year the legislature authorized the project. Perhaps because there was no immediate intention to start construction, the inadequacy of the feasibility report was overlooked. In 1955 a more serious program[123] was submitted to the legislature, with a request for appropriation of funds to initiate construction. The Bechtel Corporation was retained by the legislature to prepare an independent review, which they provided in their *Report* of December, 1955.[124] Construction of the project has been delayed, primarily because of a dispute on water rights between northern and southern California interests: the southerners have not wanted construction begun unless a firm right to the water can be guaranteed, while the northerners do not wish the water taken away without a firm promise that they can have it or the equivalent back when and if they need it. In the meantime, the legislature appropriated some $9 million in 1956 and $25 million in 1957 for design studies and preliminary construction work. In May, 1959, the legislature authorized submission to the voters of a proposed bond issue in the amount of $1.75 billion to permit construction to go ahead.

It may be noted here that newspaper reports and statements by public officials in California repeatedly refer to the Feather River plan as a "$1,750,000,000 Project." This is a rather serious error, the sum named representing only the bond issue covering a first instalment of costs. In the official reports the bond-issue amount corresponds most closely to the $1.807-billion figure of *Bulletin No. 78 (Preliminary)*, but we have shown just above that this latter sum excludes the cost of many vital project features, including Oroville Dam itself. The correct figure, for capital costs only and accepting official estimates, is certainly in excess of $3 billion.

2. Previous Evaluations and Discussion

It is noteworthy that in the long period that the project has been under discussion, before and after its official authorization, there was neither an official attempt at a showing that the benefits would exceed the costs nor, alternatively, any real indication of the cost of water to be supplied through the project—until *Bulletin No. 78* was published, partially remedying these deficiencies. (The bulletin limits itself, however, solely to the aqueduct system serving southern California.) While the charge of the legislature to the Bechtel Corporation called for an assessment of "economic feasibility,"[125] the Bechtel *Report* stated only that the project had engineering and financial feasibility.[126] Engineering feasibility means only that it is physically possible to construct the project. As to financial feasibility, both the 1955 state *Program* and the Bechtel *Report* misinterpreted the meaning of this concept, the underlying idea of which is that the beneficiaries of a project will repay its cost (sometimes

121 *Bulletin No. 78 (Preliminary)*, p. II-34. See also Table 43 above.

122 State Water Resources Board, *Report on Feasibility of the Feather River Project and Sacramento–San Joaquin Delta Diversion Projects Proposed as Features of the California Water Plan* (Sacramento, May, 1951).

123 Division of Water Resources, *Program for Financing and Constructing the Feather River Project as the Initial Unit of the California Water Plan* (Sacramento, February, 1955) (hereinafter cited as *"Program"*).

124 Bechtel *Report*.

125 *Ibid.*, p. 7.

126 *Ibid.*, p. 6.

known as the "self-liquidating" character of a project). Both the state *Program* and the Bechtel *Report* envisaged that a substantial part of the costs would be explicitly met by contributions or subsidy from the state's general funds.[127] In the accepted sense of the term, then, the Bechtel *Report* really confirmed what could be inferred from the state *Program*—that the project was not financially feasible under the cost and revenue estimates made in each case. All that was really shown by either report, in fact, is that it would be *possible* to finance the project with a sufficient contribution from the general taxpayer—a statement which could also be made, perhaps, for a proposal to throw a billion silver dollars into San Francisco Bay. As for economic feasibility, this differs from financial feasibility in involving certain corrections of costs or revenues where market forces do not fully reflect all the relevant costs or benefits. No attempt to demonstrate economic feasibility appeared in either document.

The only information incorporated in the state *Program* that might be interpreted as representing some kind of economic summary was a schedule of prices for the different service areas (ranging from $8 per acre-foot in the San Joaquin Valley to $45 per acre-foot in the South Coastal Area, for the basic Route 1), and certain tabulations called "financial analyses." Essentially, the *Program* calculated an allocated (not an incremental) cost for each service area and then *assumed* that demand would be sufficient to absorb the contemplated deliveries at the supposed "cost" price. There was no calculation of the present value or over-all rate of return on the project, although the "financial analyses" revealed that over a period of seventy years the undiscounted revenues would exceed the undiscounted costs, interest and amortization being included among the costs.[128] Contributions from the state's general fund to cover deficits were included as "revenues"! On the other hand, these costs were overstated in failing to allow for any salvage value after termination of the calculations at seventy years, and no value was attached to certain anticipated flood-control benefits. An interest rate of 2.5 per cent was employed in these estimates.

The Bechtel *Report* improved on this performance in some respects. An appendix on water demand (prepared by economists of the Stanford Research Institute), while negative on the prospect of water sales in some areas, concluded that the two major service areas referred to above could conservatively be expected to take their allotted deliveries at allocated-cost prices as recalculated by Bechtel. In the Bechtel *Report* the prices ranged from $9 to $12 per acre-foot in the San Joaquin area and from $29 to $44 for the South Coastal Area (depending upon route and delivery point). The interest rate employed was 2.7 per cent.

The pioneer critical work by Neuner[129] pointed out that these supposed allocated-cost prices in the *Program* and the *Report* do not actually generate enough revenue to cover the aggregate cost of the project. His cost reconstruction of the Bechtel figures for Route 10A (a Bechtel alternate route) yielded $9 per acre-foot in the San Joaquin area and $36 in the South Coastal Area, as compared with corresponding figures of $9–$11 and $30 in the Bechtel *Report*. Neuner also maintained that the cost figure shown for southern California precluded the possibility of irrigation use of the water, assuming that prices charged were to equal cost. While a number of minor criticisms of Neuner's calculations might be made,[130] the really vital objection to his

[127] *Program*, p. 56; Bechtel *Report*, p. 12.

[128] *Program*, p. 56.

[129] E. Neuner, Jr., "Economics of the Proposed Feather River Project," *Proceedings of the 31st Annual Conference of the Western Economic Association, August, 1956* (Salt Lake City, 1957).

[130] Neuner (*ibid.*) calculated annual cost "at full development" instead of making a present-value calculation in proper form, which would al-

figures concerns his acceptance of the low 2.7 per cent interest rate in figuring cost over time. Neuner himself was fully aware of this objection, and his treatment suggests the social inefficiency of using the state's money cost of capital for public projects while private agencies building comparable projects must cover the private cost of capital (see our discussion in chap. vi above). Neuner went on to show, in a sarcastic vein, that the low interest factor could be used to reduce apparent cost even further by building excess steam-power facilities and merging their accounts with those of the project instead of relying only on sales of the hydropower physically associated with the project.

The second critical paper, by DeHaven and Hirshleifer,[131] was addressed primarily to estimating the over-all present worth of the project as a whole and to presenting a correctly calculated cost figure for southern California (again based on a reconstruction of official data). In Table 47 the present-worth calculations for Routes 1, 8A, and 10A take the official estimates of receipts as the benefits of the project (after proper discounting) and similarly for official cost estimates. The negative net present values show that at the assumed market prices for water the project is not "financially feasible," even at 2.7 per cent (i.e., the financial receipts do not cover the costs). As the cost and revenue estimates were both believed to be optimistic, no benefits of an extramarket nature were credited, although in principle these might be some consumers' surplus associated with the large increment of supply provided (see our discussion in chap. vi above). The figures incorporate an adjustment for the flood-control benefit and for salvage value. The 5 per cent calculation used a somewhat more appropriate discount rate, which has the effect of making the negative net present worths enormous. The authors now believe that a rate closer to 10 per cent should be employed in such

TABLE 47*

PRESENT VALUES OF THE FEATHER RIVER PROJECT

(Based on Data in 1955 *Program* and Bechtel *Report*)

Interest Rate	Costs	Receipts	Net Present Value	Net Present Value, Adjusted†
2.7 per cent:				
Route 1‡	$1,240,723,000	$1,079,086,000	$−161,637,000	$− 97,200,000
Route 8A§	1,122,918,000	1,012,301,000	−110,617,000	− 46,200,000
Route 10A‖	1,029,277,000	918,933,000	−110,344,000	− 45,900,000
5 per cent:				
Route 1	1,035,393,000	515,435,000	−519,958,000	−501,770,000
Route 8A	860,606,000	445,384,000	−415,222,000	−397,030,000
Route 10A	799,128,000	408,536,000	−390,592,000	−372,400,000

* Source: J. C. DeHaven and J. Hirshleifer, "Feather River Water for Southern California," *Land Economics*, XXXIII (August, 1957), 201.

† Adjustment credits flood-control benefit and salvage value.

‡ State High Line Route to Barrett Reservoir.

§ Bechtel High Line Route to Devils Den and Coastal Route to Terminal at Granada Hills Reservoir.

‖ Bechtel High Line Route to Quail Lake terminating in Granada Hills Reservoir.

low also for the load-building phase of the project; he accepted in part the erroneous "proportionate-use" allocation method of the state *Program* and Bechtel *Report;* and, while he did show a flood-control cost offset, he failed to credit a salvage value.

[131] J. C. DeHaven and J. Hirshleifer, "Feather River Water for Southern California," *Land Economics,* XXXIII (August, 1957), 198–209.

evaluations; the effect of doing so would be to make the cost-receipts balances for the project still more adverse.

The cost summary of Table 48, also based on the 1955 proposals, represents the unit costs of water for southern California specifically. For this analysis it was necessary to estimate on an incremental basis those project costs relating to southern California deliveries. On this basis the present-value average cost at 2.7 per cent for Route 1 is in the neighborhood of $48, the comparable Bechtel figure being $42 and the state *Program* figure $45. While these differences are small, a great change is introduced when we go toward more appropriate interest rates, the relevant figure at 5 per cent being around $83,[132] while the figure at 10 per cent (calculated by the present authors from the DeHaven-Hirshleifer data) is $287!

The third critical document of interest is an unpublished thesis prepared by a group of graduate students in the Department of Engineering at the University of California at Los Angeles.[133] This work, which centers around a comparison of the Feather River source with the possibility of securing water from reclamation of sewage, is especially interesting in providing sensitivity analyses for a number of the critical variables of the Feather River Project. The routes studied were 3 and 10A; while Neuner's method of cost allocation was followed, the calculations themselves were based on the present-worth formula used in DeHaven and Hirshleifer—essentially equation (5) of our chapter vii. The "standard" results (assuming seventy-year life, 3 per cent interest rate, state or Bechtel costs as allocated, and state or Bechtel delivery schedules) came to $36 for Route 3 and $46 for Route 10A. While there are certain minor errors in the analysis,[134] the most serious defect concerns the low interest rate of the standard case. The authors provide a sensitivity analysis for interest-rate variations, but the highest rate considered is 5 per cent, as in the DeHaven-Hirshleifer paper. At 5 per cent the Route 3 cost shown is $58, and the Route 10A cost is $72. Other interesting calculations showed sensitivity to changes in assumed project life, "capitalization" (construction costs, apparently), power rates, power revenues, and delivery schedule.

TABLE 48*

OUR COST ESTIMATES, FEATHER RIVER WATER TO SOUTHERN CALIFORNIA VIA ROUTE 1

(Based on Data in 1955 *Program* and Bechtel *Report*)

INTEREST RATE	DOLLARS PER ACRE-FOOT	
	State Schedule (Early Construction)	Bechtel Schedule (Late Construction)
2.7 per cent....	$ 47.76	$48.18
5 per cent......	83.32	75.65
10 per cent......	287.01	....

* Source: DeHaven and Hirshleifer, *op. cit.*, p. 202. Some corrections and additions have been incorporated.

At the risk of misleading somewhat through failure to provide qualifying detail, we present in Table 49 a summary of costs as estimated in the different sources discussed. The *Bulletin No. 78* (*Preliminary*) cost estimate for "Aqueduct System B," generally similar to Route 1 of the earlier studies, is provided for comparison (this estimate will be analyzed in detail below). In comparing these estimates, it must be remembered that, while Route 1 is a high-cost route, this is at least in part because it delivers water to San Diego, while the

[132] The DeHaven-Hirshleifer paper shows that at higher interest rates the Bechtel schedule (deferred construction of Oroville Dam) is cheaper —$76 against $83 as 5 per cent. However, we will continue to analyze the costs based on early dam construction, as the Bechtel recommendation for late construction seems to have been rejected.

[133] Zeitzew *et al., op. cit.*

[134] The study follows Neuner (*op. cit.*) in accepting in part the erroneous "proportionate-use" allocation principle of the official documents.

others terminate north of Los Angeles. Route 10A is very similar to Route 3, the major difference being that smaller deliveries to southern California are involved in the former, larger deliveries being made to the San Joaquin area instead. The sensitivity to the interest rate is of course apparent from this table, and it is evident that the costs must be very high if rates in the neighborhood of 10 per cent are used.

two alternative proposals, as in the New York case. We do have the additional complication, however, that it will be necessary somehow to separate out the costs associated with deliveries to the area we are interested in from the total of costs estimated for the entire project.

As indicated above, critical analysis of the Feather River Project has been made extremely difficult by the fact that, despite official authorization of the project, appropriation of $34 million for preliminary work, and the placing of a proposal for a $1.75-billion bond issue before the public, no single route has yet been definitely chosen. Our analysis will be based upon the recommended "Aqueduct System B" of *Bulletin No. 78* (*Preliminary*), the latest official document available at the time of writing. However, this bulletin concerns itself exclusively with the cost of transporting water from the Delta to southern California and intermediate points. Costs north of the Delta, including the cost of Oroville Dam itself, are not explicitly considered; instead, a charge of $1.00 per acre-foot is made for water at the Delta.[135] We will be forced,

TABLE 49

SUMMARY OF ESTIMATES, AT DIFFERING INTEREST RATES, OF FEATHER RIVER WATER COST TO SOUTHERN CALIFORNIA

(Dollars per Acre-Foot)

Source*	Route 1					Route 3				Route 10A			
	2.5%	2.7%	3.5%	5%	10%	2.5%	2.7%	3%	5%	2.5%	2.7%	3%	5%
Program†	$45					$25							
Bechtel *Report*‡		$42					$29				$30		
Neuner§											36		
DeHaven-Hirshleifer‖		48		$83	$287#								
Zeitzew *et al.***						32	33	$36	$58	$42	43	$46	$72
Bulletin No. 78 (*Preliminary*)††			$60										

* See text for complete citations.
† At p. 51.
‡ At p. 71.
§ Table 3 in source.
‖ At p. 202.
\# Recalculated from data in DeHaven-Hirshleifer.
** At p. VI-6.
†† At p. VII-20, as corrected.

3. *Projected Deliveries and Cost Allocations*

Some of the principles underlying the calculations to be presented here should by now be familiar after the theoretical discussions in earlier chapters and their application to the Cannonsville-Hudson alternatives of New York City. As in the latter case, we will be estimating a present-value average cost of actual deliveries contemplated under the project. We will show results for a number of discount rates, but, as before, our own preference is for a rate near 10 per cent as the closest approximation of the marginal alternative productivity of capital funds, in the private sector, for investments of comparable risk. We will here be considering one project rather than

[135] *Bulletin No. 78* (*Preliminary*), p. IV-29.

therefore, to take certain information from the DeHaven-Hirshleifer analysis of data in the state *Program* and Bechtel *Report* in order to estimate the relevant costs of the facilities north of the Delta.

Still another complication of *Bulletin No. 78 (Preliminary)* is that the total deliveries of 6,839,000 acre-feet there contemplated (see Table 50) far exceed those used as the basis for planning the Oroville works (maximum deliveries of 3,880,000 acre-feet).[136] It is apparently assumed that any additional facilities required to make available the further increments required at the Delta can still provide water at the same acre-foot price of $1.00.[137] Even if the Oroville facilities can be assumed to represent the equivalent of a $1.00 cost per acre-foot, however, it is reasonable to expect that additional facilities required would be relatively more expensive, on the principle that the least costly sites and facilities are being used first. Actually, according to Bechtel, enough water is available at the Delta without Oroville Dam to supply deliveries up to 2,900,000 acre-feet annually.[138] It is, nevertheless, far from clear that the dam will permit firm deliveries of some 7,080,000 acre-feet (the total in Table 50 for the year 2020, plus 240,000 for the South Bay Aqueduct).[139] The omission of the slightest suggestion that additional dam construction seems to be required to meet the projected deliveries is a striking gap in the official reports.

TABLE 50*

WATER DELIVERIES FROM RECOMMENDED AQUEDUCT SYSTEM
(In Thousands of Acre-Feet)

Service Area	1965	1970	1980	1990	2000	2010	2020
San Joaquin Valley (north of Kern County)†	1	6	24	701	1,272	1,371	1,344
San Joaquin Valley (Kern County)	13	146	823	1,409	1,606	1,700	1,785
Subtotal—San Joaquin Valley areas	14	152	847	2,110	2,878	3,071	3,129
Coastal Aqueduct areas (other than Kern County)‡	....	....	51	83	111	152	211
Antelope-Mojave	....	....	75	142	175	195	208
Whitewater-Coachella	....	....	....	35	55	90	100
Ventura County	....	....	41	55	115	168	236
South Coastal Area (other than Ventura County)§	....	....	864	1,513	2,160	2,635	2,955
Subtotal—southern California areas	....	....	1,031	1,828	2,616	3,240	3,710
Total	14	152	1,878	3,938	5,494	6,311	6,839

* Source: *Bulletin No. 78 (Preliminary)*, p. VIII-15, except for deliveries north of Kern County, for which separate data were obtained from the Department of Water Resources.

† Delta to Avenal Gap Service Area.

‡ San Luis Obispo and Santa Barbara service areas.

§ Southern California Coastal Plain and Coastal San Diego County Service Area.

136 *Program*, p. 37. This 3,880,000 included 240,000 acre-feet for the South Bay Aqueduct, the requirements for which are not covered in *Bulletin No. 78 (Preliminary)*.

137 *Bulletin No. 78 (Preliminary)*, p. IV-29.

138 Bechtel *Report*, p. 19. This assumes integrated operation with San Luis Reservoir.

139 At one point, *Bulletin No. 78 (Preliminary)* states that the aqueduct system will deliver in excess of 8,000,000 acre-feet annually to the San Joaquin and southern California areas (p. VIII-1). The discrepancy between this last figure and the largest total in our Table 50 is unexplained.

As a relatively minor point, *Bulletin No. 78* (*Preliminary*) still contains the error, repeatedly committed both by the state analysts and by independent critics, of allocating common costs among regions on the principle of "proportionate use" rather than calculating incremental cost of service. That is, "the ratio of the cost allocated to a given service area to the total cost of the system is the same as the ratio of the capacity provided in the system for that service area to the total capacity."[140] It should be noted, however, that this definition of the "proportionate-use" concept (it should, more properly, be denoted "proportionate capacity") is an improvement over that in previous studies. Assignment of capital costs in proportion to capacity may represent a fair approximation of what is really desired—the incremental cost of expanding capacity to handle demands of the region in question. By way of contrast, the previous method based cost assignment literally upon proportionate *use;*[141] under that concept, in any year in which a certain region received no water deliveries it escaped any allocation of cost, even though enormous capacity might have been in existence solely because of the need to provide deliveries to that region.

Our aim is to determine the cost incremental to South Coastal Area deliveries. That is, we are in effect estimating the cost appropriate for answering the question of whether the aqueduct system should be extended to the South Coastal Area (and other associated areas of southern California), on the hypothesis that it will be constructed to serve the more northerly areas anyway. Aside from the question of whether the entire project is justifiable, its extension to southern California is economic only if the incremental cost is sufficiently low.

There are two difficult questions about north-of-Delta costs: (1) how much to allow for possible additional dam construction required in future to maintain the specified delivery schedule and (2) how to allocate these together with the Oroville facility costs among the service areas. In view of the complete silence of state plans on the first of these topics, it is extremely difficult for us to come to any very acceptable conclusion about the incremental cost allocation to the South Coastal Area. We will be forced, therefore, to make some relatively crude approximation. It is convenient to follow the procedure of the DeHaven-Hirshleifer analysis cited above,[142] which assumed that Oroville Dam costs are all incremental to southern California deliveries. This assumption was highly reasonable in terms of the 1955 state *Program* then being analyzed, which projected maximum deliveries of only 2,080,000 acre-feet annually to areas other than southern California.[143] For the much larger program presently envisaged, deliveries to San Joaquin and the South Bay areas in 2020 come to around 3,370,000 acre-feet.[144] However, it is still not unreasonable to assume that, in the absence of southern California demands, the dam would not be constructed. Making the dam incremental to southern California tends to overestimate the cost of water to southern California, because the net benefits of the additional 470,000 acre-feet of deliveries made possible to other areas are not credited against the dam costs (we do credit power and flood-control benefits, however). On the other hand, since Oroville Dam will not firm up enough water supply for all the deliveries tabulated, we are omitting an important cost element at least partially assignable to southern California. Our belief is that this factor (the need to construct an additional dam or dams) is much the more significant, so that on balance our dam allocation to

[140] *Bulletin No. 78* (*Preliminary*), p. VII-3.

[141] Bechtel *Report,* pp. 71–72.

[142] DeHaven and Hirshleifer, *op. cit.,* p. 202.

[143] *Program,* p. 37.

[144] This is on the assumption that projected deliveries via the South Bay Aqueduct remain at 240,000 acre-feet as specified in the *Program*—the latest information available on this question.

southern California is too low. The source of our difficulty here, as already mentioned, is the failure of the state authorities to present data on an integrated system capable of actually providing the deliveries specified in *Bulletin No. 78* (*Preliminary*).

Next, we must pay some attention to the deliveries projected to southern California other than to the South Coastal Area. In 2020 these come to a total of 755,000 acre-feet (including Ventura County) as compared to 2,955,000 for the South Coastal Area (Southern California Coastal Plain).[145] We adopt a crude proportionate-capacity assumption here, thus assigning 80 per cent of the Oroville cost (less offsets) to the South Coastal Area specifically. This assumes that, in the absence of the other southern California demands, the net cost of Oroville Dam would be less in proportion to the reduced 2020 deliveries.

Bulletin No. 78 (*Preliminary*) does provide cost allocations for facilities south of the Delta serving the San Joaquin Valley and southern California areas, based on the proportionate-capacity assumption.[146]

TABLE 51*

OUR COST ESTIMATES, FEATHER RIVER WATER

(Based on Data in *Bulletin No. 78* [*Preliminary*])

	DISCOUNTED COSTS (THOUSANDS)†				DOLLARS PER ACRE-FOOT			
	0 Per Cent	3.5 Per Cent	6 Per Cent	10 Per Cent	0 Per Cent	3.5 Per Cent	6 Per Cent	10 Per Cent
System B (totals):								
Main aqueduct	$4,452,517	$1,817,534	$1,179,188	$732,827	$20.61	$32.67	$ 48.53	$ 91.51
South Coastal Area:								
Main aqueduct	2,928,557	1,149,693	717,173	419,664	33.23	51.17	73.58	132.45
Local conveyance	439,052	244,133	171,662	105,171	......	......	....	....
Total	$3,367,609	$1,393,826	$ 888,835	$524,835	$38.21	$62.03	$ 91.19	$165.64
Adjustments	$−664,678	$ 21,447	$ 130,659	$175,845	......	......	....	....
Adjusted total	$2,702,931	$1,415,273	$1,019,494	$700,680	$30.67	$62.99	$104.59	$221.14

* For further detail see Table 53.

† Includes construction, energy, and other expenses (operating costs, maintenance, replacements, etc.).

4. Cost Estimates

Table 51 shows our basic cost estimates for the recommended System B of the bulletin and for the allocated cost to the South Coastal Area (exclusive of Ventura County). The figures for main aqueduct costs and local conveyance and distribution costs, as well as delivery estimates, were provided to the authors by the Department of Water Resources as totals and broken down by

145 To permit convenient use of official cost breakdowns, we will use the term "South Coastal Area" henceforth as equivalent to the "Southern California Coastal Plain and Coastal San Diego County Service Area." The two are essentially the same, except that the latter excludes the Ventura County Service Area, which is usually considered a hydrographic subunit of the South Coastal Area. Our "South Coastal Area," then, excludes Ventura County for the purpose of the present analysis.

146 While *Bulletin No. 78* (*Preliminary*) is vague on this point, we assume that the allocation was calculated by service reaches. On this basis costs of the aqueduct from the Delta to Avenal Gap, for example, would be distributed among all downstream users in proportion to capacity—but users in this reach would not be allocated any fraction of the cost of facilities constructed to the south of them from which they derive no benefit.

service areas; they are reproduced in the appendix to this chapter, together with some details about our procedures.[147] Our adjustments represent allowance for Oroville Dam costs as discussed in the section above, less credit for power and flood-control benefits, and also a separate credit for dam and non-dam salvage value at the terminal date of the analysis (2020).

The most interesting figure, perhaps, is the final adjusted dollar per acre-foot cost for the South Coastal Area, at our recommended interest rate of 10 per cent—some $221 per acre-foot, a very high figure. Even at a rate of 6 per cent, corresponding generally to the rate we recommend for cost-benefit analyses after expected-value adjustment for risk (i.e., where there is no need to take into account either risk aversion or any systematic pattern of overoptimism in the cost or benefit estimates), the figure is about $105 an acre-foot.

The result most closely comparable to the official calculations of *Bulletin No. 78* (*Preliminary*) is the unadjusted total at 3.5 per cent discount, the rate used in the state calculations. Here our figure of $62 per acre-foot corresponds very closely to the state's $60 estimate.[148] It is also interesting to note that the state's estimates employ a $1.00 cost for water at the Delta, without providing any justification for this figure; our own incremental allocation of north-of-Delta facilities to the South Coastal Area, when calculated at 3.5 per cent, is in fact extremely close to $1.00 per acre-foot. The difference between our adjusted and unadjusted cost figures, entirely due to the north-of-Delta facilities (except for a part of salvage value), actually comes to $0.96 per acre-foot (at 3.5 per cent). This close correspondence reflects the fact that, at an interest rate of 3.5 per cent the net cost of Oroville Dam is relatively small—the annual flow of power and flood-control benefits comes close to recovering the capital cost of the dam. At higher interest rates this is no longer true (the far-future benefits are discounted more heavily than the near-future costs). At 10 per cent, in fact, the difference between the adjusted and the unadjusted figures is in the neighborhood of $55 per acre-foot.

Some other qualifications to or omissions from the calculations may be noted at this point. First, the expected federal contribution of $100 million is omitted from the main aqueduct costs. In addition, the estimated cost of the second San Diego aqueduct, now under construction by the MWD, is omitted from local conveyance and distribution expenses for the South Coastal Area—despite the fact that this aqueduct is being constructed to carry Feather River water. Finally, official sources indicate that for urban deliveries in the South Coastal Area a unit cost of $7.00 per acre-foot

147 We should note, however, that while the System B main aqueduct construction costs in the separate tables provided us checks with the total of $1.807 billion shown in *Bulletin No. 78* (*Preliminary*), p. VIII-12, excluding anticipated federal contribution of $100 million, the annual schedule does not conform in detail.

148 *Bulletin No. 78* (*Preliminary*), p. VII-20, actually shows a figure of $58, but a corrected table has been provided the authors by the Department of Water Resources showing the unit cost as $60. The causes of the discrepancy between $60 and $62 are unknown. As noted in n. 147, however, there are certain divergences in the details of the cost schedules among the several state sources. One possibly important inconsistency is that the state's present-worth calculations shown on p. VII-20 (and on the corrected table provided us) indicate results approximately 10–20 per cent higher than our results at 3.5 per cent in all cost categories tabulated—for System B as a whole and for the South Coastal Area. For one category, the state's result is over ten times as great as ours (local conveyance facilities, operating costs, South Coastal Area); we believe there may be a decimal-point error in the state document (and also the corrected table) at this point, in addition to the fairly stable 10–20 per cent discrepancy mentioned above. While the cause of this regular divergence is unknown, the puzzling thing is that, to be consistent with these higher totals (since the delivery figures check perfectly), the state should be getting cost-per-acre-foot results that are 10–20 per cent higher than ours for the same 3.5 per cent interest rate, instead of just slightly lower.

should be added to cover costs of filtration, while agricultural deliveries require additional unit costs of $15 per acre-foot.[149] These factors were presumably calculated at 3.5 per cent, so that larger upward corrections would be required at the interest rates we regard as more appropriate. Unfortunately, data have not been provided that would permit us to make this calculation.

In summary, then, even at 3.5 per cent the Feather River water cannot be estimated as costing less than $70 per acre-foot, wholesale, in the South Coastal Area (this allows for none of the qualifications or omissions noted above except for adding $7.00 for filtration of urban water to our adjusted unit cost of $63 in Table 51). At higher interest rates the upward correction indicated over the already high figures ($105 at 6 per cent, $221 at 10 per cent) must be quite substantial.

G. Conclusion

The water-supply planners of California, and of the South Coastal Area in particular, find themselves faced with a great conundrum. On the one hand, with rapidly expanding population and industry, it seems obvious that more water is "needed"; on the other hand, it is equally obvious that customers are going to be hard to find at prices based on the unit costs for the Feather River supply, so that subsidy in one form or another seems the only way out. And, indeed, planners who are aware only of the "requirements approach" to water demand—that each man, each factory, each irrigated acre "require" just so much water, based upon extrapolation of historic trends of use—will never find the solution to the dilemma. The answer, of course, is that these "requirements" and historic trends are largely based upon a low, heavily subsidized price for water. There is a shortage of water at $20 per acre-foot in just the same sense that there is a shortage of new Cadillacs at a price of $500, except that desires for Cadillacs are usually not dignified by the term "needs" or "requirements." What has been forgotten is that desires are not economic demands. Only if an economic demand exists at the level of present-worth unit costs for the water produced can the Feather River Project be called economically feasible. It should be demonstrated in addition, of course, that the project in question is cheaper than alternatives capable of satisfying the same demands.

The Feather River Project, if constructed as planned at the time of writing, will provide a very expensive increment of water to the South Coastal Area. Our cost estimate, discounting at 10 per cent, is at least $228 per acre-foot before certain indicated upward corrections. Even at 3.5 per cent the urban figure is $70 and rural $78. All these figures are at wholesale; that is, they represent procurement and treatment costs only. (The corresponding cost for the Cannonsville development of the city of New York was around $1,023 per million gallons, or $333 per acre-foot at 10 per cent—approximately $76 per acre-foot at 3.5 per cent.) While it is not hard to imagine circumstances justifying projects yielding such high-cost water, these circumstances simply do not exist in the area.

Aside from the prospects indicated in Table 44 of finding cheaper alternative sources of water—reclamation of sewage, subject to the qualifications noted, and purchase and transport from the Kern, Owens, and Imperial regions seem especially important to investigate with care—the wide divergence between Feather River costs and current water prices suggests strongly that a large fraction of current use is very low valued. In the area, *on the retail level,* practically nobody is paying prices comparable to the real *wholesale* cost

149 Communication dated June 30, 1959, from Mr. Max Bookman, district engineer, Southern California District, Department of Water Resources (signed by R. M. Edmonston, principal hydraulic engineer).

of Feather River water. It certainly seems almost fantastic to believe that farmers could pay even the $78 price for irrigation water based on the low 3.5 per cent discount rate. In the city of Los Angeles the highest-bracket domestic consumers are currently paying *at retail* only 17 cents per 100 cubic feet, in the neighborhood of $74 per acre-foot. As demands grow to exhaust existing supplies at current price levels, the rational response is to raise prices for the purpose of restricting market demand to the limit set by the available supply. While marginal value in use may, eventually, exceed the unit cost of Feather River water, we conjecture that it will be many a long day before the price necessary to restrict demand within available supplies comes to exceed the cost from the Feather River source.

As was the case in New York in 1951, according to our analysis, in southern California also the first order of business for the region is to make better use of existing suppies. Even the expansion of the Colorado River Aqueduct capacity, we have indicated, could scarcely have been justified at a unit incremental cost of even $28 (unsoftened basis, calculated at 3.5 per cent) or, better, $48 (unsoftened basis, at 10 per cent)—when the prices in effect at the time of the decision to undertake construction were $15 for regular and $12 for preference users (unsoftened basis). In addition, the MWD wholesale prices may be inadequately reflected in retail water rates. The immediate need throughout the area is for an increase in the over-all level of rates, thus permitting deferral of new construction until and as justified by rising marginal value in use reflecting increased demand. It seems fair to state that the current levels of rates at retail have generally not been established with any rational purpose in mind. Rather, water rates seem to be largely the accidental reflection of historical costs incurred when price levels were much lower, combined with the use of average-cost rather than marginal- or incremental-cost reasoning. In a few cases where special water-supply problems have existed (San Diego being the leading example), much higher rates have wisely been put into effect with the anticipated economic consequences in terms of restriction of use. (At the wholesale level the MWD has represented an opposite special case. Given a highly overbuilt situation, rates have historically been established at a very low level to achieve some use of idle capacity. As the capacity limit is approached, however, the rationale for such low prices will disappear.)

In addition to the matter of the general level of rates, it is especially urgent to eliminate certain discriminations that seem to be peculiarly designed to preserve low-valued use of scarce water: (1) The most extreme case is the preferential rates given to irrigation—not only by the MWD at wholesale but by many municipalities, including Los Angeles. (2) The MWD preferential rate for water-spreading seems also dubious from the point of view of the owners and ordinary customers of the MWD. While water-spreading is a cure for the divergence of social and private cost, the source of the evil is overpumping in a few basins. Why should all MWD customers and taxpayers be forced to contribute to the remedying of this evil which neither affects nor is caused by them? (3) Excessively "promotional" schedules of declining block rates at retail will become increasingly inappropriate as demand is approaching a steep cost barrier, though we concede that economies in distribution may justify some differential (primarily in the fixed charge rather than the unit price, we would argue).

Some attention to the peak-load problem as discussed by us in chapter v seems also urgent; flattening a peak that could never carry the full cost of an increment of supply, by assessing a penalty price, may prove highly useful. A summer premium price seems certainly called for (no special metering would be required); such a seasonal differential has at times been an element of the wholesale-price schedule of the MWD.

Turning back to the Feather River Project and to *Bulletin No. 78 (Preliminary)*, we will not attempt to provide a complete review of the places where we agree and where we disagree with that document in substance and in methodology. Instead, we will comment only on a few significant points: (1) The bulletin is praiseworthy in being one of the few official documents in the water-supply field making a present-value analysis in proper form. Furthermore, our independent calculations, generally speaking, yield confirming results given the assumptions. (2) On the other hand, we have seen that the document is defective in not presenting and costing an integrated dam-aqueduct system actually capable of generating the deliveries scheduled in the text. In particular, the cost of Oroville Dam itself, together with all north-of-Delta facilities (including an apparently required second dam), enters into the analysis only via the $1.00 per acre-foot of water charged at the Delta. This figure might or might not be adequate, depending upon the assumptions made, but in any case the capital investment required for the project is grossly understated. (3) We have shown that the demand assumptions are throughout, and in various complex ways, highly optimistic. (4) In addition, there is little or no consideration of technological or economic alternatives to construction—except for sea-water conversion. (5) Based on all previous experience in this field, we are confident that the cost estimates will prove optimistic as well.

We will conclude this discussion by commenting on a number of possible counter-arguments that might be used to oppose some of the positions we have indicated above.

The first of these is that the high costs arrived at by us are primarily due to the high discount rate used; if only we concurred with the use of the 3.5 per cent discount rate, representing the state's cost of borrowing,[150] our figures would not be too different from the official $60 per acre-foot cost (before adjustments). Our objection here is that the state's borrowing cost is far less than the productivity of equivalent private investments (or the value to consumers of an equivalent amount of consumption) that will have to be foregone because of the use of real resources for this project. The main reason why the borrowing rate is so low is that the bonds are to be general obligations of the state, so that few of the risks associated with the project are taken into account by investors. Aside from the obvious risks of general overoptimism in calculating costs and benefits, there are any number of possibilities that could make the project a total or partial failure; for example, population migration to California may slow or stop, or the flow may shift away from the presently favored arid areas, or new techniques like weather control or new sources of power for cheap conversion of sea water may make large-scale overland water transport unnecessary. Many other possibilities, more or less likely, can be cited; for example, a destructive war may prevent the facilities from ever being put to use.

The main point to remember is that all investments are subject to risk. The bondholders are willing to lend at 3.5 per cent because they are essentially protected from project risks, which must then be a contingent liability on the taxpayers. It should be obvious that a project that looks good

150 At the time of writing, the latest borrowings of the state were $50,000,000 of veterans' bonds and $25,000,000 of school-building-aid bonds, sold on June 28, 1960, at interest costs of 3.95 per cent and 3.92 per cent, respectively (see *New York Times*, June 29, 1960, p. 45). Actually, a number of financial experts have expressed serious doubts as to whether California can sell its enormous $1,750,000,000 water bond issue at interest costs anywhere near the 3.5 per cent assumed.

when nearly all risks are ignored need not be a good proposition when risks are considered. The justification for our use of the particular figure of 10 per cent will be found in our chapter vi; it is based essentially on the before-tax discount rate used in conservative private investments in the utility sphere. We may add that our figures indicate that, *even in terms of the 3.5 per cent rate,* current water prices are too low and that raising prices will permit deferral of the new construction. Also, the alternative sources of new water that look cheaper at 10 per cent still generally look cheaper at 3.5 per cent.

The second argument we will comment on is the possibility of providing water more cheaply to users than it actually costs, the taxpayers bearing the difference. This would indeed tend to make water from the expensive Feather River source used to a greater extent than it would otherwise be; and, in fact, exactly this procedure has been followed in the case of the Colorado River Aqueduct of the MWD. Logically, once the facilities are in existence, and if demand is sufficiently low, the relevant costs of additional units supplied (the marginal cost) may be so low as to justify a low price as the best way of living with the past mistake of overbuilding. However, when we are considering new construction, and assuming that there is no particular reason for redistributing wealth from taxpayers to water-users, all the costs should be weighed against all the benefits.

Finally, we may turn to an interesting argument brought out in *Bulletin No. 78* (*Preliminary*). It is there maintained that the benefit-cost ratio of the project is 2.38[151]—the average dollar of cost brings in $2.38 of benefits. It turns out that municipal and industrial benefits are evaluated at $150 per acre-foot on the basis of the projected cost of water from the least expensive alternative source—supposedly, conversion of sea water.[152] Such a method of estimating benefits permits justification of any project, so long as a still worse one can be found and declared to be the least costly alternative source. Conceivably, at some time in the future, the water in question might be worth $150 or even $250 per acre-foot—but, whatever the figure is, it must be estimated directly from determinations of marginal value in use rather than from an irrelevant supply alternative.

Summing up,[153] then, we find that the Feather River Project is a very expensive source of water for the South Coastal Area. Comparison of the Feather River costs with those of alternative new supplies in Table 44 suggests strongly that the Feather source is much more expensive than a number of alternatives. Reduction in local evaporation, a small amount of additional local entrapment, reclamation of sewage (subject to restricted use, however), additional Owens water, and purchase and

151 *Bulletin No. 78* (*Preliminary*), p. VII-24.

152 *Ibid.*, pp. VII-16–VII-17. This figure was "somewhat less than presently estimated minimum future cost of demineralizing ocean water."

153 We may add a note here on the bearing of the adverse preliminary finding announced on May 8, 1960, in the California-Arizona suit, upon the desirability of the various recommendations made by us. Public officials in California have made statements to the effect that the adverse final decision now in prospect makes construction of the Feather River Project especially urgent and essential. Actually, our analysis is unaffected in all important respects, since we considered throughout the possibility of such a court decision. Delay is still called for before going to so expensive a new source as the Feather River, so that low-valued uses which cannot bear the cost of Feather River water can gradually be eliminated by higher prices. During such a period of delay the less expensive though individually smaller sources we recommend can be constructed when and as justified by growth in demand. As a final remark, we need only mention that the "catastrophic" court decision means at most the loss of 662,000 acre-feet for the South Coastal Area (see Table 45); this hardly necessitates going ahead immediately upon a proposal to construct capacity for bringing 3,000,000 acre-feet annually into the area when there are relatively cheap smaller supply sources available.

transport of a fraction of other areas' Colorado River allocations (primarily Imperial Valley) all appear definitely cheaper. (However, since none of these seems to promise supplies of comparable magnitudes with those projected for delivery from the Feather, the latter may represent an economic source for the South Coastal Area at some date in the future—perhaps in thirty or forty years.) Furthermore, even excluding these other sources, aside from the fuller utilization of the Colorado River Aqueduct allowed for in the official plans, economic considerations indicate that the marginal value in use of water in the South Coastal Area does not currently justify jumping to such an enormously expensive new source. Only after the competition for water within the area has raised the marginal value in use to levels comparable with the average incremental cost of the Feather source will going to the latter be warranted. This consideration indicates, as the more immediate policy need in the area, raising prices as water begins to be scarce at the present low tariffs and introducing a summer peak-load premium price, together with the ending of discriminatory price discounts to preferred users—most particularly, to irrigators.

APPENDIX

SOME DETAILS OF FEATHER RIVER PROJECT CALCULATIONS

The basic data employed in the calculations reported in Section F of this chapter are set out in Table 52. These data were provided the authors, in response to a request for supplementary information underlying some of the reported tabulations in *Bulletin No. 78* (*Preliminary*), by the Glendale office of the Department of Water Resources.[154] As indicated in the chapter, the tables provided us do not entirely agree with the bulletin, but, because of the source and the later date, we have treated them as superior to those of the published document. The tables themselves are straightforward; they show deliveries and a classification of expenses, divided into main aqueduct and local conveyance and distribution expenses, for Aqueduct System B as a whole and as allocated to the South Coastal Area (in our terminology).[155]

Table 53 shows the results of our computations with these data as supplemented and adjusted by certain information derived from previous official studies. This table is a back-up for the summary Table 51. In each case, the discounting has been performed at 3.5 per cent (the rate used in the bulletin), 6 per cent, and 10 per cent; the figures at 0 per cent discount represent, of course, the simple numerical totals without regard to date.

The unadjusted sums for the dollar-cost components in Table 53 are derived directly from the corresponding state data reported in Table 52, each being discounted back to $t = 0$ as of the year before 1960, the supposed first year of the project. The discounted net sum of deliveries, as indicated in the footnote to the table, is the expression

$$\sum_{t=1}^{61} \frac{q_t}{(1+i)^t},$$

where q_t are the deliveries in year t (starting with $t = 1$ for 1960) and i is the interest rate assumed. This expression facilitates computation of the present-value unit cost of deliveries, which we denote by x. We find

[154] Letter dated June 30, 1959, from Max Bookman, district engineer (signed by R. M. Edmonston, principal hydraulic engineer).

[155] In the source the allocation is to the "Southern California Coastal Plain and Coastal San Diego County Service Area."

TABLE 52

State Cost and Delivery Schedule, Feather River Water

Year	System B Totals					South Coastal Area								
	Deliveries (Thousands of Acre-Feet)	Main Aqueduct Costs (Thousands of Dollars)				Deliveries (Thousands of Acre-Feet)	Allocated Main Aqueduct Costs (Thousands of Dollars)				Local Conveyance and Distribution (Thousands of Dollars)			Total (Thousands of Dollars)
		Construction	Energy	OMRGE*	Total		Construction	Energy	OMRGE*	Subtotal	Construction	Operation and Energy	Subtotal	
1960	...	$ 3,796	...	...	$ 3,796	...	$ 1,557	...	...	$ 1,557	...	...	...	$ 1,557
1961	...	16,410	...	...	16,410	...	4,937	...	...	4,937	...	...	...	4,937
1962	...	52,691	...	...	52,691	...	17,485	...	...	17,485	...	...	...	17,485
1963	...	93,314	...	$ 26	93,340	...	35,409	...	$ 6	35,415	...	...	...	35,415
1964	...	110,834	...	26	110,860	...	50,749	...	6	50,755	...	...	...	50,755
1965	13	87,825	$ 42	688	88,555	...	42,551	...	304	42,855	...	...	...	42,855
1966	40	74,797	139	2,646	77,582	...	45,248	...	1,468	46,716	...	...	...	46,716
1967	72	119,195	285	2,712	122,192	...	68,826	...	1,468	70,294	...	...	...	70,294
1968	98	131,055	393	2,740	134,188	...	76,593	...	1,468	78,061	$39,566	...	$39,566	117,627
1969	125	116,073	500	4,766	121,339	...	74,531	...	2,301	76,832	79,131	...	79,131	155,963
1970	152	72,081	456	7,113	79,650	...	50,698	...	3,679	54,377	39,566	...	39,566	93,943
1971	370	58,349	2,505	7,550	68,404	95	46,322	$ 1,218	3,950	51,490	...	$ 465	465	51,955
1972	537	25,575	3,849	8,277	37,701	181	19,828	2,218	4,570	26,616	8,385	465	8,850	35,466
1973	705	22,325	5,199	9,077	36,601	266	17,174	3,217	5,211	25,602	16,769	465	17,234	42,836
1974	872	19,569	6,557	9,316	35,442	351	16,152	4,216	5,343	25,711	8,385	465	8,850	34,561
1975	1,040	10,049	7,907	9,759	27,715	437	8,299	5,215	5,709	19,223	...	567	567	19,790
1976	1,208	2,675	9,257	9,796	21,728	522	1,279	6,214	5,741	13,234	...	567	567	13,801
1977	1,375	18,075	10,609	9,840	38,524	608	14,497	7,213	5,769	27,479	3,723	567	4,290	31,769
1978	1,544	49,107	11,962	9,840	70,909	693	40,529	8,213	5,769	54,511	7,445	567	8,012	62,523
1979	1,711	56,069	13,310	10,944	80,323	779	50,073	9,212	6,656	65,941	16,753	567	17,320	83,261
1980	1,878	69,459	14,661	11,064	95,184	864	64,875	10,211	6,725	81,811	26,060	603	26,663	108,474
1981	2,066	74,461	15,716	11,288	101,465	919	68,518	10,855	6,843	86,216	13,030	603	13,633	99,849
1982	2,330	38,991	18,343	12,767	70,101	1,018	33,981	12,457	8,126	54,564	13,604	883	14,487	69,051
1983	2,531	18,109	19,680	13,755	51,544	1,080	12,130	13,291	8,555	33,976	27,208	885	28,093	62,069
1984	2,732	16,725	21,061	14,252	52,038	1,142	8,174	14,145	8,973	31,292	13,604	889	14,493	45,785
1985	2,933	16,014	22,442	14,560	53,016	1,204	7,898	14,999	8,973	31,870	...	1,041	1,041	32,911
1986	3,134	18,664	23,824	14,681	57,169	1,266	11,638	15,852	9,024	36,514	...	1,044	1,044	37,558
1987	3,335	12,720	25,216	16,680	54,616	1,328	9,200	16,710	10,059	35,969	7,243	1,047	8,290	44,259
1988	3,536	10,419	26,598	16,680	53,697	1,390	8,223	17,564	10,059	35,846	14,486	1,050	15,536	51,382
1989	3,737	35,201	27,980	17,233	80,414	1,451	31,218	18,417	10,503	60,138	7,243	1,053	8,296	68,434
1990	3,938	66,749	29,362	17,602	113,713	1,513	57,496	19,271	10,796	87,563	...	1,143	1,143	88,706

TABLE 52—*Continued*

Year	System B Totals					South Coastal Area								
	Deliveries (Thousands of Acre-Feet)	Main Aqueduct Costs (Thousands of Dollars)				Deliveries (Thousands of Acre-Feet)	Allocated Main Aqueduct Costs (Thousands of Dollars)				Local Conveyance and Distribution (Thousands of Dollars)			Total (Thousands of Dollars)
		Construction	Energy	OMRGE*	Total		Construction	Energy	OMRGE*	Sub-total	Construction	Operation and Energy	Sub-total	
1991	4,110	$39,999	$30,671	$18,485	$ 89,155	1,578	$32,968	$20,166	$11,547	$64,681	....	$1,147	$1,147	$65,828
1992	4,283	13,920	31,981	18,485	64,386	1,643	8,772	21,060	11,547	41,379	$ 245	1,150	1,395	42,774
1993	4,455	12,379	33,159	19,708	65,246	1,707	9,060	21,905	12,214	43,179	488	1,153	1,641	44,820
1994	4,628	14,649	34,466	19,708	68,823	1,772	10,987	22,798	12,214	45,999	245	1,157	1,402	47,401
1995	4,801	15,248	35,770	20,862	71,880	1,837	6,966	23,691	12,872	43,529	....	1,261	1,261	44,790
1996	4,973	12,453	37,075	20,862	70,390	1,901	1,572	24,584	12,872	39,028	....	1,265	1,265	40,293
1997	5,146	9,943	38,379	21,037	69,359	1,966	4,018	25,476	12,937	42,431	1,542	1,269	2,811	45,242
1998	5,275	7,679	39,592	21,087	68,358	2,031	6,480	26,369	12,937	45,786	3,084	1,272	4,356	50,142
1999	5,384	7,168	40,758	21,477	69,403	2,095	4,679	27,262	13,268	45,209	1,542	1,276	2,818	48,027
2000	5,493	20,698	41,925	21,477	84,100	2,160	16,057	28,155	13,268	57,480	....	1,290	1,290	58,770
2001	5,575	41,565	42,828	21,477	105,870	2,208	32,325	28,812	13,268	74,405	....	1,292	1,292	75,697
2002	5,657	20,502	43,367	22,650	86,519	2,255	15,976	29,323	14,175	59,474	....	1,295	1,295	60,769
2003	5,739	7,249	44,266	23,395	74,910	2,303	4,762	29,978	14,499	49,239	....	1,296	1,296	50,535
2004	5,821	8,269	45,162	23,395	76,826	2,350	6,837	30,632	14,499	51,968	....	1,300	1,300	53,268
2005	5,903	7,248	46,060	23,794	77,102	2,398	4,764	31,287	14,828	50,879	....	1,302	1,302	52,181
2006	5,984	3,119	46,957	23,794	73,870	2,445	1,350	31,942	14,828	48,120	....	1,305	1,305	49,425
2007	6,066	9,912	47,855	24,548	82,315	2,493	6,997	32,596	15,153	54,746	690	1,306	1,996	56,742
2008	6,148	13,683	48,753	24,548	86,984	2,541	11,275	33,251	15,153	59,679	1,380	1,308	2,688	62,367
2009	6,230	7,040	49,650	25,022	81,712	2,588	5,662	33,905	15,549	55,116	690	1,311	2,001	57,117
2010	6,312	120	50,548	25,032	75,700	2,636	....	34,560	15,549	50,109	....	1,319	1,319	51,428
2011	6,364	....	51,109	25,032	76,141	2,668	....	35,000	15,549	50,549	....	1,320	1,320	51,869
2012	6,417	4,129	51,768	25,032	80,929	2,700	3,412	35,439	15,549	54,400	....	1,320	1,320	55,720
2013	6,470	8,269	52,379	25,032	85,680	2,731	6,837	35,879	15,549	58,265	....	1,322	1,322	59,587
2014	6,522	4,129	52,988	25,442	82,559	2,763	3,414	36,319	15,882	55,615	....	1,322	1,322	56,937
2015	6,575	....	53,598	25,442	79,040	2,795	....	36,759	15,882	52,641	....	1,323	1,323	53,964
2016	6,628	....	54,208	25,442	79,650	2,827	....	37,199	15,882	53,081	....	1,323	1,323	54,404
2017	6,680	....	54,819	25,442	80,261	2,859	....	37,638	15,882	53,520	....	1,324	1,324	54,844
2018	6,733	....	55,429	25,442	80,871	2,891	....	38,078	15,882	53,960	....	1,324	1,324	55,284
2019	6,786	....	56,038	25,442	81,480	2,923	....	38,518	15,882	54,400	....	1,325	1,325	55,725
2020	6,839	....	56,649	25,442	82,091	2,955	....	38,958	15,882	54,840	....	1,325	1,325	56,165

TABLE 53.—PRESENT WORTHS OF COST AND DELIVERY COMPONENTS*

	SYSTEM B (TOTALS)				SOUTH COASTAL AREA			
	0 Per Cent	3.5 Per Cent	6 Per Cent	10 Per Cent	0 Per Cent	3.5 Per Cent	6 Per Cent	10 Per Cent
Deliveries—discounted sum (thousands of acre-feet)†	216,009	55,628	24,296	8,008	88,126	22,470	9,747	3,169
Main aqueduct (thousands of dollars):								
Construction	$1,806,746	$1,109,116	$ 856,269	$616,549	$1,201,258	$ 693,177	$ 511,617	$347,374
Energy	1,686,060	428,188	185,241	60,159	1,138,247	286,882	123,283	39,499
OMRGE‡	959,711	280,230	137,678	56,119	589,052	169,634	82,273	32,791
Total	$4,452,517	$1,817,534	$1,179,188	$732,827	$2,928,557	$1,149,693	$ 717,173	$419,664
Local conveyance (thousands of dollars):								
Construction					$ 385,614	$ 228,746	$ 164,339	$102,428
Operation and energy					53,438	15,387	7,323	2,743
Total					$ 439,052	$ 244,133	$ 171,662	$105,171
Combined total, unadjusted (thousands of dollars)					$3,367,609	$1,393,826	$ 888,835	$524,835
Adjustments (thousands of dollars):§								
Oroville Dam					$ 315,260	$ 284,333	$ 264,692	$236,855
Power revenue					−537,230	−194,455	−110,451	−53,500
Flood-control benefit					− 68,688	− 24,120	− 13,494	− 6,490
Salvage value					−374,020	− 44,311	− 10,088	− 1,021
Net sum					$−664,678	$ 21,447	$ 130,659	$175,845
Main aqueduct total, adjusted (thousands of dollars)					$2,263,879	$1,171,140	$ 847,832	$595,509
Combined total, adjusted (thousands of dollars)					$2,702,931	$1,415,273	$1,019,494	$700,680
Unit costs (dollars per acre-foot):								
Main aqueduct, unadjusted	$ 20.613	$ 32.674	$ 48.535	$ 91.512	$ 33.231	$ 51.166	$ 73.576	$132.447
Combined, unadjusted					38.214	62.031	91.186	165.639
Main aqueduct, adjusted					25.689	52.121	86.980	187.944
Combined, adjusted					30.671	62.986	104.591	221.136

* Totals may not check perfectly with summands because of rounding.

† Discounted sum of deliveries is calculated from the formula

$$\sum^{61} q_t$$

where q_t is annual delivery in year t, i is the interest rate, and 1960 is year 1. Note that this mathematical expression is not a *dollar* value of deliveries.

‡ Operating, maintenance, replacement, and general expenses.

§ For details see text of appendix.

x from the following equation,[156] based on formula (5) of chapter vii, which sets the present worth of the revenues at the price x equal to the present worth of the costs:

$$\sum_{t=1}^{n} \frac{x q_t}{(1+i)^t} = \text{sum over all cost components of } \sum_{t=1}^{n} \frac{c_t}{(1+i)^t}.$$

Here, in the expression on the right, c_t is supposed to indicate the dollar amount of a particular component of cost incurred in year t. The total present worth of all costs requires, of course, summing each component from year 1 through year n (the terminal year of the calculation) and then taking the grand sum over all cost components (e.g., construction cost, energy cost, etc., as well as the negative components appearing as cost offsets).

The unadjusted dollar per acre-foot figures, finally, are derived by simply dividing the present-worth sum of all costs by the discounted sum of deliveries. In terms of the equation above, since x is a constant, it can be factored out of the summation; the right-hand side is then divided by

$$\sum_{t-1}^{61} \frac{q_t}{(1+i)^t},$$

which is what we have called the "discounted sum of deliveries."

The adjustments also shown in Table 53 (and in Table 51) are based upon a number of considerations, generally paralleling the earlier DeHaven-Hirshleifer paper.[157] As explained in the chapter, on the basis of projected delivery schedules but with the insufficient information provided on north-of-Delta facilities, it was determined that the best assumption possible to make was that Oroville Dam was incremental to southern California deliveries (and so the full cost should be assessed against the latter region). However, the South Coastal Area is scheduled for only 80 per cent of the southern California deliveries, so a crude proportionate-capacity assumption was used, the final result being that 80 per cent of the dam cost was assessed against the South Coastal Area. The Oroville Dam cost figure used was close to \$394 million.[158]

However, there are certain offsets against cost to be considered as well. We take account of an anticipated flood-control benefit as well as power revenues from Oroville Dam. In addition, there is a salvage value to consider at the end of the analysis period in the year 2020 ($t = 61$), because the facilities will have substantial useful lives remaining at that date. Generally speaking, these were calculated by adapting the DeHaven-Hirshleifer results.

Flood control was the simplest of all. The benefit was calculated as \$1,590,000 annually[159] from project years 8 through 61. The power revenue credit was also based on the DeHaven-Hirshleifer data.[160] A modification was required, however, to correct for the difference in the terminal year of analysis in the current study ($t = 61$) as compared with the DeHaven-Hirshleifer study ($t = 71$). Finally, the present worths were multiplied by 80 per cent to correspond with the 80 per cent of dam costs assessed against the South Coastal Area.

[156] See DeHaven and Hirshleifer, *op. cit.*, p. 202. The state apparently used the same formula in *Bulletin No. 78* (*Preliminary*), according to a letter dated April 2, 1959, from Max Bookman, district engineer (signed R. M. Edmonston, principal hydraulic engineer).

[157] *Op. cit.*, esp. pp. 201 ff., 209.

[158] Based on Bechtel *Report*, p. 37. The Bechtel figure was used, not counting interest during construction. To simplify computations, we applied all dam costs as a lump sum in project year 3.

[159] DeHaven and Hirshleifer, *op. cit.*, p. 209.

[160] *Ibid.*, pp. 207–8.

Salvage value was figured separately for the dam and the non-dam facilities. The dam exclusive of power plant was assigned a life of one hundred years from 1960. This left 39 per cent of the life remaining after $t = 61$ (2020), so that the salvage value was assessed as 39 per cent of $365,500,000, the latter figure being the cost of the dam aside from power facilities. However, again only 80 per cent of this result was allocated to the South Coastal Area. The power facilities at the dam (cost around $28 million) were assigned a useful life of sixty years, so that no salvage-value calculation was required. For the non-dam facilities, a crude assumption was necessary to hold the calculations within reasonable bounds. We assigned an over-all average life of fifty years and then went through the construction-cost schedules of the main aqueduct allocation to the South Coastal Area as well as of the corresponding local conveyance facilities to find the unexpired proportionate costs (e.g., 98 per cent of expenditure in 2020, 96 per cent of expenditure in 2019, etc.), which were then summed. The unexpired total came to $218,462,000 for the main aqueduct allocation and to $41,522,000 for the local conveyance facilities. These were added to the 80 per cent of the dam salvage value and credited as a lump sum as of the year $t = 62$.

The dollar-per-acre-foot figure for the adjusted total was computed as before.

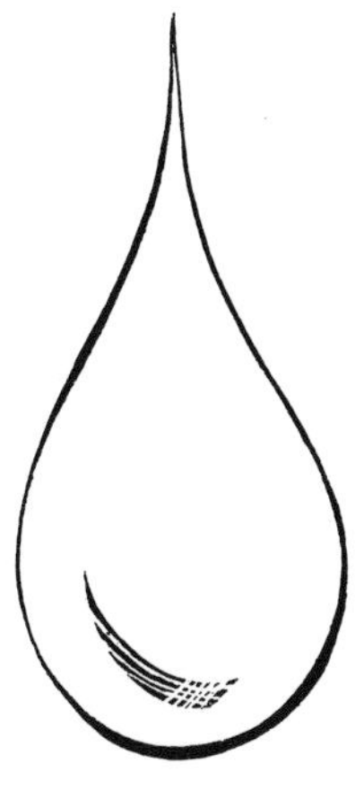

CHAPTER XII

SOME CONTROVERSIAL CONCLUSIONS AND THEIR IMPLICATIONS

To those who have followed with us from chapter i, it will indeed appear that a variety of economic, legal, and technological problems relating to water supply justify popular interest and concern. Many of these questions are grossly misunderstood today—for example, the problem of whether and how to establish property rights in water—so that the current trend of "reforms" may be exactly in the wrong direction. Some questions are quite complex, like the problem of achieving efficient utilization of the resource when there are a large number of users whose decisions interact with one another. Finally, still other questions need not be problems at all (e.g., the question of how the provision of uneconomic water supplies can be financed), for by our actions and misunderstandings we have created difficulties where none need exist or where the solutions should be simple and automatic.

Water-supply problems should and will receive increasing attention in the future because water is becoming relatively less abundant in comparison with other resources. It is in transition from an almost free good in the humid areas (or a very cheap good in the most arid) to a more expensive commodity. Consequently, competition among uses and users is becoming more intense. In addition, the costs are increasing in terms of other resources and services foregone to obtain additional supplies of water. The absolute magnitudes of the investments required to obtain these increased supplies are also of substantial importance in respect to the total wealth both of the nation and of local regions proposing these supply increments. Thus California alone talks of $3 billion for one water transport system, the first step in a $13-billion state plan.

In our previous chapters we have discussed a great variety of problems connected with water supply. Our purpose here is not to restate all the conclusions previously arrived at but rather to concentrate on those which are most significant and, especially, most controversial. We will not bother, therefore, with any elaborate argument or demonstration to support conclusions such as that more hydrological research is desirable, that conflicts and overlaps of government agencies in the water field should be resolved, or that project analyses should be checked and rechecked to avoid arithmetical errors, though all these recommendations are of some importance.

A. Economic Efficiency and Welfare

We have attempted throughout this work to show by argument and example that the correct application of economic principles will produce the greatest efficiency in water-supply procurement and utilization *in relation to, and in competition with, all the other desires of the community.* Perhaps we have not stressed strongly enough the implication of economically efficient decisions for the long-term welfare of the local areas involved and for the nation as a whole. Critics of economic analysis may have partially succeeded in creating the impression that economic criteria for decision-making are abstruse theoretical postulates invented and circulated only by academic professional economists or, at best, that economic analysis is suitable only for application to idealized situations that have little relation to the real world.

Some cynics plausibly argue, for example, that the United States is a wealthy nation and can well afford the luxury of overinvesting in waterworks. The construction of huge dams and lengthy aqueducts to make the desert bloom even as the rose might then be an example of a "monument syndrome." The people like to see these constructed as demonstrations of our engineering skills and national wealth. They vote for politicians who push the construction of these works, thereby demonstrating their tastes and preferences in this regard. These preferences may therefore be considered a mark of the citizen-voters' non-pecuniary valuation of these works.

There are several important things wrong with this argument. In the first place, such works are not presented to the voters for consideration as national or regional monuments. Rather, they are promoted as financially attractive and necessary investments to increase the wealth and development of the nation or of local regions. The voters are therefore misinformed about the issues on which they express their preference, so that their choices are no firm indications of non-pecuniary values. Second, as we have pointed out, the political decision process for allocation of resources is highly imperfect, so that even if voters were perfectly informed the actual choices made may, for example, be influenced by such factors as a coalition of minorities against the general interest ("logrolling").

The use of economic criteria of efficiency in resource investments will contribute to the wealth, living standards, and possibly even survival of the nation. Provision for national military security and military and economic aid to foreign countries constitute large demands on our collective income and wealth. Our allocation of resources to these ends does not create wealth; they are not productive investments. Rather, they are costs for insurance that we may survive as a nation. With so much of our wealth allocated to these non-productive ends, there is even more reason to invest our remaining wealth as productively as possible. There is no guaranty that further industrialization and improving technology can continue to increase our over-all productivity fast enough to compensate for profligate investment in relatively unproductive plant such as economically inefficient water-supply projects.

Unwise investments in water projects may particularly injure individual regions, states, and metropolitan areas. With wealth available for investment being limited, the choice of less rather than more productive investments by a region means that it will be poorer in the future than if wiser decisions had been made. Even if the funds invested come from outside, as from the federal government, residents of the region will be relatively less benefited than if more productive investments had been made with these funds. Of course, if a grant of funds to a region is conditioned upon adoption of an inefficient water project, it may be best from the region's point of view to make the investment. Unfortunately, the political decision process does work this way to some extent—Congressman A may have no efficient projects awaiting construction in his district, but he expects some return for casting his vote in favor of projects in the districts of Congressmen B, C, D, and E. These abuses are sufficiently obvious as not to require extended comment on our part.

B. Overinvestment and Pricing Decisions

Perhaps the most controversial substantive conclusion in this book, justified by a wide variety of evidence from our separate case studies and from our survey of federal and local experience in water-supply decisions, is that in this country major water investments are typically undertaken prematurely and on an overambitious scale. Consequently, at any given time there exists overinvestment in water supply.

Overinvestment for any particular area is indicated when facilities stand idle or else are put to makeshift uses, either to avoid the appearance of idleness or to minimize the losses due to past mistakes. Or uneconomic overinvestment may be indicated not by idle facilities but by relatively low return earned on capital invested in water supply. Here the water is actually being put to use, but the price charged is so low that the revenue to the water enterprise is small in relation to cost. There is overinvestment because the same capital investment could have been put to work producing goods and commodities valued more highly on the margin by consumers; consumers' marginal values in use for water are low in comparison with what could have been obtained had the dollars been spent elsewhere. Specifically, our two major area studies both revealed the highly premature nature of the decision to build the Cannonsville Project in the one case and the proposal for construction of the Feather River Project in the other. Or, looking at return to capital, we have seen that, for public water-supply systems in general, this is of the order of 2 per cent—an astonishingly low figure.

The reasons for the prevalence of overinvestment in water supply are complex and interrelated, and, to the extent that they are outside the sphere of economic analysis, we can only speculate about them. One possible explanation is that those responsible for the construction of "engineering wonders" become romantic figures, heroes not only to their own age but to later generations—and heroes whether their great projects were wise or unwise, timely or premature. In contrast, individuals credited only with sound stewardship of the resources of society are scarcely known in their own day and certainly never appear in history books. Regrettably, it must be added that certain strictly rational though sordid considerations may often reinforce the pressure of irrational romanticism—the gravy train runs in the same direction as the glory trail. Without overemphasizing the point, we cannot paint the full picture unless we mention the attractiveness to bureaucrats and politicians of the power inherent in being able to influence the award of contracts valued in the millions or hundreds of millions, the employment of thousands of workers, the enhancement of real estate values on contiguous or related lands, the creation of an enormous variety of business opportunities, etc. Such power cannot but be a temptation to merely human administrators and legislators.

Despite the possible importance of considerations like those adduced above, our own emphasis throughout has been upon errors of fact or of reasoning which have played a role in bringing about the pattern of overinvestment. Perhaps the most important of these might be simple oversight: that, when the total of water use begins to approach system capacity, administrators simply do not think of attempting to make better use of existing supplies as an alternative to initiating new construction. The possibility of adjusting prices does not often occur to those responsible, even though studies have shown that demand is responsive to price and that the widely divergent price levels and price structures existing in different cities suggest that a schedule presently in effect in a particular city is not necessarily the only one possible or even the best available in the circumstances. Of course, rationing water use by raising prices across the board, or by eliminating discrimination benefiting certain classes of use, has its cost, but it is a cost which should be properly analyzed against the alternative of new construction.

Equally ignored, at times, are possibilities for avoiding or deferring expensive new construction by taking better care of existing supplies or by seeking out possibly unconventional but cheaper sources. Thus we have seen in the New York case that the major construction decision ignored the promise of the extremely large saving that could be made simply by detecting and correcting leaks in the city's own distribution system. And, in California, the responsible authorities have shown little interest in such technological possibilities as evaporation control on reservoirs or in economic solutions involving reallocation of water from agricultural uses as urban demand rises.

The third major class of error leading to overinvestment in water supply is the systematic bias toward excessive construction inherent in conventional techniques of project analysis. The most obvious and well-known source of error in these practices consists of the inventing and counting of "secondary" or "intangible" benefits—a topic which we analyzed exhaustively to separate the kernel of validity in these conceptions from the gross errors committed in practice. Rather more interesting to us, because less fully or less successfully analyzed by others, is the history of overoptimism in estimates of project benefits and costs. In part connected with this is the fact that conventional project analyses for government investments discount future benefits and costs at interest rates that reflect the ability to borrow of the agency concerned—and that, consequently, represent little or no allowance for the risk of failure of the project in question. We have shown that these risks of failure in the most closely comparable private class of investments (privately owned regulated utilities) require companies to finance new projects at rates that preclude their undertaking investments that promise to yield less than around 10 per cent. Consequently, if our fundamental postulate of neutrality on the margin between publicly and privately owned enterprises is accepted, public agencies also should restrict themselves to investments of comparable apparent yield. (The true result of projects "apparently" promising to yield 10 per cent will be much less favorable, of course, after history exposes the overoptimism of the initial benefit-cost calculation.)

The adoption of such a strict standard would, correctly, indicate as uneconomic the great bulk of the investment programs of the major federal agencies in the field—Bureau of Reclamation, Corps of Engineers, and Department of Agriculture—as well as many of the more grandiose state and local projects. The same conclusion can be arrived at without the use of the high discount rates (10 per cent) which allow for risk; if costs and benefits were correctly rather than optimistically estimated, cost-benefit calculations employing a long-term riskless rate like 4 per cent (5 per cent with tax adjustment) would also reveal the inefficiency of these programs.

The most sophisticated of the arguments for adoption of inefficient water projects is the claim that the subsidy to water-users involved in construction of an inefficient project is justified because of certain "development" needs of the region in question. (Inefficient projects require subsidy because, by definition, the beneficiaries cannot repay the cost, and so the taxpayer must.) But such a subsidy will cause the development to occur in a manner ill suited to the natural advantages of the region. In particular, in an arid region where water is costly to provide, a subsidy making water cheap to users will encourage them to be wasteful—to be unconcerned with possible economies in water use. A likely and unfortunate result is the development of water-intensive, low-tax-base industries, for which the area's low water prices but high taxes present the best combination of comparative advantages. The interests of a region will in general be best served by the adoption of efficient projects —whether under government or private auspices, or whether directed to the provision of water supply, power, transport facilities, or consumers' goods and conveniences.

The typical pattern of overinvestment is related in various ways to our argument that water prices are too low. What we mean by this latter statement is that raising prices will in general be the major alternative to building new water supplies; in that sense we have clearly overbuilt and correspondingly underpriced, so as to receive inadequate return on capital invested in water-supply developments. On the other hand, once a water-supply system finds itself in an overbuilt situation, it *will* typically be justifiable to charge quite a low price rather than have the installation lie idle (i.e., marginal costs are quite low for dam-aqueduct systems operating well below capacity). Thus the Metropolitan Water District of Southern California—given the initial error of premature construction—was correct in charging prices far below average cost. And in New York City, once Cannonsville begins to operate, it will probably be justifiable to reduce water prices (to those consumers who are metered) rather than have that enormous capacity lie idle.

Our second important conclusion about prices concerns the importance of the peak-load problem in the case of water supply. The cost of special metering is such, however, that very elaborate schemes of differential peak and slack prices are not justified. Introduction of a peak-*season* price (in the summer, normally), on the other hand, will not require any special metering and seems clearly indicated as an alternative to expensive new construction when it is only the peak-season loads that press on system capacity.

C. Centralized or Decentralized Water-Supply Decisions?

The reader will have noted that the authors have a certain "old-fashioned" sympathy with the principle of decentralization of authority in respect to economic decisions in general and to water-supply decisions in particular. Other things being equal, we prefer local to state authority, state to federal—and private decision-making (the extreme of decentralization) to any of these. Our fundamental reason for this preference is the belief that the cause of human liberty is best served by a minimum of government complusion and that, if complusion is necessary, local and decentralized authority is more acceptable than dictation from a remote centralized source of power. This is an "extramarket value" for which we at least would be willing to make some sacrifices in terms of loss of economic efficiency. Despite all this, we have tried to leave this consideration out of our basic analysis, which assumes neutrality on the question of the proper locus of decision except insofar as questions of economic efficiency are involved. Even on grounds of efficiency, however, we have some faith that, the more nearly the costs and benefits of water projects are brought home to those who make the decisions, the more correct those decisions are likely to be—a consideration which argues for decentralization in practice.

We have seen, in previous chapters, that the interrelated nature of water-supply decisions ideally requires, on grounds of economic efficiency, some departure from complete laissez faire. There is in principle an argument for centralized regulation whenever private and social benefits or costs diverge ("technological spillover effects" of private decisions exist), and they do to an important extent in water-supply decisions; for example, pollution of a stream by its use for waste disposal may cause great loss to downstream users. In the common-pool situation we have shown that unregulated pumping will lead to excessive withdrawals in terms of the net social balance of benefits and costs, so that there is a prima facie case for government intervention to remedy this deficiency. We cannot leave the subject without noting, however, that the record of governmental intervention in the resource field does not demonstrate that it will actually improve matters over the admittedly inefficient unregulated result. To cite only one instance, the sound argument for intervention in the common-pool situation has been used, in the case of petroleum, as an excuse to form state-directed cartels designed to restrict output and raise prices to consumers. We do have hope, however, that, with a clearer understanding of the justifications for and the desirable limitations upon governmental intervention and control in the sphere of water supply, the record of regulation in the future may be better than in the past.

One reason often given why water projects must be planned and constructed by state or federal governments instead of by local private or public agencies is that the costs are now too great for the local or private agencies to bear. However, the private corporation has proved to be an efficient institution for the accumulation of large amounts of capital for investment in productive development of natural resources —witness the utility corporations, pipelines, television, and other instances too numerous to mention. The relative magnitude of the cost of the next increment of water supply is certainly no greater now in comparison with the total resources of local regions and cities than it was years ago when the then small city of Los Angeles built the aqueduct to Owens Valley, or when New York reached to the Catskills, or when the Metropolitan Water District of Southern California was organized on a regional basis to tap the distant Colorado River. The large investment barrier to local development is a bogy often raised by those who hope to secure taxpayers' contributions to defray at least some of the costs of providing water. Or, to put it another way, costs do seem high in relation to resources when what is under consideration is an uneconomic project.

It is, nevertheless, possible to plan for, construct, and operate water projects at the central state or federal level in an efficient manner—and, whatever the locus of decision, we think that it is desirable to achieve economic efficiency. Our extensive discussion of principles of project analysis is most applicable, in fact, to the decisions of centralized decision-making agencies, since the market will tend to regulate the projects of private agencies. The economic principles we have presented are generally independent of the agency by which they are to be applied—private individuals or local, regional, or national bodies. If properly evaluated, the same alternative water project would be chosen as best by local individuals (if the rules protect against spillover effects) or by a central decision-making group. The chief analytical problem for centralized decisions is the difficulty of securing the relevant information at a level remote from the actual effects of the project in question and where the costs are to be borne by others than those to whom the benefits accrue. The crucial defect of private and local decision-making—the spillover effects—we have shown to be at least partly remediable through a more appropriate definition of property rights to coincide with the span of the decisions involved.

D. Trends in Water Law and Their Effects

We have tried to demonstrate that much of the present misuse of water within the sphere governed by the market can be traced to imperfections in water law and its administration. These ills occur because in most jurisdictions water rights are not clearly defined, do not have the necessary legal certainty, and cannot be transferred with ease as are rights to other types of property—land, mineral rights, etc. As a consequence, the market processes that ordinarily direct resources to uses that maximize their productivity—chiefly, voluntary exchange through purchase and sale—are either severely limited or prevented entirely from operating in the case of water. Individuals and local private and public organizations do not have proper incentives to invest in improving or increasing water-supply resources when their tenure in these resources is uncertain. Economically desirable transfers of water between lower- and higher-valued uses and among regions, to the mutual advantage of all parties, are discouraged by these imperfections of rights and by the lack of a clear legal basis under which such transfers can be consummated.

The establishment of clear property rights to water does pose difficulties. Water is a fleeting resource. It exists partly as a store and partly as a flow. The development of water law occurred when very little was understood about the phases of the hydrologic cycle from which our supplies are obtained. Then, too, water, until fairly recently, has been in a position of surplus supply in relation to demand, so that it has been a free good or at least a very cheap one. Therefore, little consideration had to be given to its efficient allocation or to the laws governing its use and ownership. With increasing demand, however, even the humid regions have begun to recognize the inadequacy of their doctrines of water law. We believe the wrong direction is being taken in modifying present law, as represented by drafts of "model" state water codes and the recent actions of several states in this connection. These actions tend to attenuate the already weak fabric of property rights in water. The tendency is to arrange matters so that allocation of water can take place only through grants or permits to users by central administrative commissions or by cumbersome court procedures, based on fuzzy criteria of "reasonable" or "beneficial" use. In these circumstances, tenure of water rights becomes uncertain, dependent upon the changing wills of the commissions or courts. This line of legal development, it can be confidently predicted, will lead to serious misallocations of water among competing users; it will, unless revised, seriously weaken or stop altogether the exercise of local and private initiative in the development of water resources.

We believe it to be justifiable, however, for the state to assume ownership of *unappropriated* water. Rights to this water may then be distributed by auction among the competing claimants against the reservation price representing the value of the state's own public uses. This procedure allows the state, and ultimately the individual citizen-taxpayer of the state, to receive compensation from the fees paid for the rights to use these unappropriated but potentially valuable water resources.

We believe that the law of prior appropriation as developed in some western states has most of the elements required to make the system we suggest work. This type of water law needs to be strengthened primarily in its provisions for the transfer of rights. Under the system we propose the courts would function, as they do for other real property, to adjudicate disputes as to the ownership and extent of the property right and to hear pleas relating to breach of contract in transfers or from parties who consider themselves injured by the actions of the owners of the water rights. The judicial system would be freed of its present inappropriate administrative-economic function of issuing and revising rights to use water on the basis of criteria like reasonable beneficial use.

What, then, do we suggest is the place for government entities in a system of water law based on property rights in water? Briefly, we believe that they should perform the same functions for water as they do for other resources. These functions, paralleling those provided by governments for resources such as land, minerals, and petroleum, may be briefly listed as follows:

1. Establish a system of law that permits a clear definition of the extent of property rights in water, particularly adapted to eliminate commonality problems which may pertain with particular force in the case of water.

2. Provide certainty of tenure for these rights and establish a clear basis for their transfer between individuals and private or public agencies under voluntary contractual agreements of purchase and sale.

3. Provide a procedure whereby rights to yet-unowned water may be secured by individuals, private or public agencies, or political entities.

4. Establish rules and procedures for the protection of outside parties against the spillover effects caused by the actions of water-right owners. These rules would be similar to zoning in the case of land use and would protect against harmful effects such as pollution, flooding, and the creation of drainage problems by water-right owners. Alternatively, procedures could be set up whereby injured parties can obtain compensation for damages.

5. Develop and provide information regarding the extent and quality of water resources and the technical and economic factors relating to the various possible sources of supply.

The level of goverment intervention required depends upon the physical extent of the water resource in question. If only a local common pool (aquifer) is involved, then only the local government unit encompassing the pool need be concerned. This might be a municipality, a county, or a water district. If several political units are physically encompassed, then they may act co-operatively in one or more of the ways listed. In either event, it is important that the laws of the larger political entity allow advantageous actions by the smaller political jurisdictions, individuals, and other organizations. Thus a special enactment of legislation by California should not have been required to allow Orange County to solve its common-pool problems and provide for recharge by its own actions.

It is widely claimed that the large river basins encompass so many political units, including states, and that their optimum development entails so many different uses for water, ranging from power generation to navigation, that only the largest political entity, the federal government, is qualified to plan for and to operate interstate river-basin developments. It is maintained that, if smaller entities plan and construct the works, their calculations are not likely to include all the social benefits and costs. Therefore less than optimum investments will be made.

We maintain again that in these cases the federal government need only intervene in the ways we have listed. Federal law should provide incentives and mechanisms to encourage states, smaller political entities, private and public agencies, even individuals, to develop these water resources either separately or co-operatively when it is economic to do so. More specifically along this line, federal law should provide a basis for the specific and firm allocation of title to water resources traversing state boundaries among the several states and, through them, to the local agencies involved in water development. It should then also provide for the subsequent voluntary transfer of these allocations and for protection against harmful spillover effects of the actions of the several states and smaller agencies. Federal law, of course, must also recognize and protect the specific constitutional responsibilities of the federal government in water, primarily navigation. Even here, however, there is no requirement for the federal government to engage in the maintenance and operation of waterways. It need only establish rules such that water navigation will be protected against the actions of the other agencies. If deemed necessary, the federal government could contribute the costs of navigation improvements to the agencies developing all or part of a river basin. The same direct contribution could be made by the federal government to these other agencies for elements related to power generation, wildlife preservation, recreational areas, etc., if these are deemed to be federal responsibilities. Thus these presumed benefits would enter the calculations of the local agencies.

The responsibility of government in the system we are here discussing is to create rules under which the market system can operate, while protecting outside parties and the general public against any divergence of private and social costs and benefits that might otherwise influence the decisions of property-owners. The state can still tax water uses considered less desirable, on extra-economic or extramarket grounds, and subsidize those considered more desirable. There is no need to assume ownership of the water in the name of the state or to undertake responsibility for its distribution among regions and among uses.

We should say once again that, when there is centralized administration and control of water resources, economic efficiency remains a valid aim. Under such circumstances, indeed, efficiency will not automatically tend to be brought about by market competition among users bidding for scarce resources. Instead, under centralized administration, efficient use of resources must and should be consciously and deliberately sought. Existing procedures of project analysis for new water-resource projects (cost-benefit analysis) can be sympathetically interpreted as mechanisms for distinguishing between efficient and inefficient projects. However, two comments are appropriate here. First, as we have already seen, the existing procedures are far too lax—as may be inferred both from a theoretical analysis of the official reasoning and from the experience records of projects constructed. Second, the political decision process is such that even these standards are violated; for example, Congress has authorized adoption of projects when even official analyses show that the benefits do not exceed the costs. In short, it is a never ending battle to maintain standards of efficiency in development of water supplies through political or bureaucratic processes. Nevertheless, there is perhaps room for optimism here, since at least the basic principle of efficiency—that benefits should exceed costs—has been officially accepted and to some extent formalized into actual procedures.

In contrast, however, where reallocation of existing supplies among different claimants is involved, even the basic principle of efficiency—that each unit of the resource should go to that use for which marginal value in use is highest—is unknown to official procedures. This lack of understanding has not in any way deterred the line of legal "reform" we have observed above, tending to place all use of water resources under the discretionary authority of state water commissions. If this trend toward centralization continues, if commissions are really to have the authority to deprive certain users for the benefit of others, the need is urgent for establishing rules and procedures guiding commission decisions in the direction of economic efficiency.

E. Technological Prospects

We have stressed the importance of considering a wide range of technical and economic alternatives in planning for increased water supply, if maximum efficiency is to be realized. This is not the usual procedure, whether the plans are made at the local, state, or federal level. There is a great tendency to consider dam and aqueduct construction as the only solution for obtaining a net increase in supply. Perhaps this is because civil engineers are usually employed in planning water developments, and aqueduct and dam construction is one of their specialties. Perhaps this narrowness of outlook is a reflection of the "monument syndrome." Commemorative bronze plaques can be prominently displayed on a dam but not on repaired leaks or on an improved schedule of prices.

The relative costs of all the alternatives should be determined, too. We have attempted to present the most acceptable ways for determining these costs, both by describing the principles involved and by illustrating their use through specific practical examples. Often these costs are difficult to estimate because of uncertainty in the basic information required as inputs. Even so, the discipline of going through the appropriate cost determinations provides insights not otherwise possible. Although the costs so determined may be but rough first approximations, they can provide a better basis for decision-making than "hunches" or generalized rules of thumb. The increased use of meters may or may not be economic, increased price may or may not be a better alternative than a new imported supply, etc., depending upon each local situation and time.

Aside from the historical tendency to overemphasize long-distance importation as the source of increased water supply, we believe that among other technical alternatives the possibilities for sea-water conversion are overblown. There should be no objection to a modest research and development program exploring the potentialities of producing fresh water from the sea. However, nothing so far in the laboratory gives any indication of promising a source of supply by conversion for municipal, and certainly not for irrigation, use at costs that approach those of many other technical and economic alternatives. Sea-water conversion processes are handicapped by high capital costs or by high power costs, or both. None of the presently conceived processes is likely to be chosen as a source of water in any significant amount for any purpose within the United States for many years to come—if the users must pay the costs of the water produced. Of course, there is always the possibility that installations will be subsidized by the government.

In contrast, we feel more optimistic about the future costs and returns of some of the possibilities for water-conservation techniques. Monomolecular film control of evaporation is progressing rapidly and will probably be widely used to produce the next increments of supply, especially in the more arid regions. The elimination of non-beneficial vegetation growing in and surrounding reservoirs, along streams, and on watersheds also holds promise for reducing the large water losses attributable to transpiration. Seepage losses from reservoirs and transmission canals appear to be large. At present only expensive lining techniques are available to reduce these losses. Little research appears to be directed toward studying inexpensive soil treatments to reduce seepage, especially in reservoirs, but it seems possible that such treatments could be developed. The creation of artificial aquifers for storage purposes, as in the Netherlands, is an especially interesting development in additional entrapment and storage of runoff water for areas near the sea.

The most interesting technological possibility not now being utilized is purposeful reclamation of sewage water. We use the word "purposeful" because reclamation is effectively occurring today in many river supply systems where one city's water intake may be a little below another city's sewage outfall. And, in rural areas, there ordinarily is hydrologic connection between wells and septic tanks. Despite the prevalence of unintended reclamation, and despite the favorable costs of such supplies (a reclamation plant will cost little more than the sewage-treatment plants often required anyway), we are inclined to be conservative here. At least until the mechanism of propagation of virus disease is better understood, we believe it to be a wise precaution to prevent direct human consumption of such supplies unless arrangements can be made to pass the water some distance through the ground before being used. Nevertheless, we feel safe in asserting that sewage reclamation is an important source of supply for the future, as expanding population and industry compete more and more avidly for the limited supply of suitable natural water.

F. The "Water-Is-Different" Philosophy

We cannot close without mentioning once again that peculiar, metaphysical line of reasoning which seems to pervade public thinking about water: the "water-is-different" or the "magic-of-water" philosophy. Even businessmen, engineers, and lawyers who are familiar with water supply often demonstrate this quirk. We frequently hear or read of their saying things like "We must not allow the waste of a single drop of our precious water to the sea" or "It is proper that a wasting resource, petroleum, pay for the renewal of a renewable resource, water." In the context in which such statements are made they can sound convincing—as though the speaker were firmly against sin. The reader of this book will, of course, immediately recognize the implications of such statements. The first says that, on the margin, water is more valuable than any combination of other resources necessary to recover it. The second implies that it is proper for users of petroleum products, primarily motorists and electric-power consumers, to subsidize water-users, primarily irrigation agriculture.

This attitude might be only amusing if it did not lead to some political actions having very serious implications; in particular, it has led to the near-universal view that private ownership is unseemly or dangerous for a type of property so uniquely the common concern of all. In chapter ix we quoted a declaration from the Water Rights Act of Iowa. If we paraphrase the wording of this act, substituting the word "land" for "water" (the former representing another type of property, also unquestionably a source of public interest and concern), the following appears:

> *Land* occurring in any valley, or along any watercourse or around any other natural body of water in the state, is hereby declared to be public *land* and public wealth of the people of the State of Iowa and subject to use in accordance with the provisions of this act, and the control and development and use of *land* for all beneficial purposes shall be in the state, which, in the exercise of its police powers, shall take such measures as shall effectuate full utilization and protection of the *land* resources of the State of Iowa.

Many individuals who would be shocked and who would strenuously resist proposals to have land declared a common public property of the state apparently fail to see any similarity when this same action is taken in the case of water. (To allay excessive fears, however, we must repeat that it is difficult to believe that the Iowa legislation and the comparable statutes of other states really mean or can enforce what they seem to say—that all private property rights in water have been confiscated by the state.) In tracing the history of private property, Blackstone notes that water resources were established as the exclusive property of individuals even while land remained yet in common:

> The support of these their cattle made the article of *water* also a very important point. And therefore the book of Genesis (the most venerable monument of antiquity, considered merely with a view to history) will furnish us with frequent instances of violent contentions concerning wells; the exclusive property of which appears to have been established in the first digger or occupant, even in such places where the ground and herbage remained yet in common. Thus we find Abraham, who was but a sojourner, asserting his right to a well in the country of Abimelech and exacting an oath for his security, "because he had digged that well." And Isaac, about ninety years afterwards, reclaimed that his father's property; and after much contention with the Philistines, was suffered to enjoy it in peace.
>
> All this while the soil and pasture of the earth remained still in common as before, and open to every occupant.[1]

[1] *Commentaries,* Vol. I, Book II, chap. i.

A POSTSCRIPT ON NEW YORK AND SOUTHERN CALIFORNIA[1]

The initial studies upon which this volume has been based were completed in 1960. During 1966 the authors had an opportunity to take a second look at water developments in our two major case-study areas—New York and southern California. The interval was an eventful one in both areas and casts considerable light upon our earlier evaluations and recommendations.

I

Our original investigation discerned a consistent pattern of underpricing and over-building in water supply. Rational reallocation of *existing* supplies, such as would occur if prices were raised in response to scarcity, is almost never considered as an alternative to new construction. There are several reasons, aside from electoral attractiveness of water projects. (1) Politically determined prices are inflexible. New York, for example, has not modified its price schedule since 1933. (Conceivably, an attempt by the City to do something about prices in coping with the 1965 shortage would have run into conflict with a source of federal pressure toward price inflexibility—the anti-inflationary "guidelines" of the Council of Economic Advisers.) (2) A higher-order political rigidity makes it commonly impossible for one water jurisdiction to sell title or rights to another—hence an incentive to rush into construction to nail down the supplies involved. (3) Certain errors in economic reasoning have played a role: ignorance of the marginal principle, double-counting of benefits, the use of inappropriately low discount rates, etc. But these analytical errors have had much less practical significance than what might be called the *non*-analytical error. This is the belief, usually quite unconscious, that there are "needs" or "requirements" for water rather than economic demands. No matter how conclusively refuted by observed sensitivity to prices (e.g., the all-too-common experience of inability to sell high-priced water), the belief that demands are absolutely inelastic continues to dominate all planning in this field.

However, it must be conceded that the economist is not yet the possessor of abso-

[1] This addendum is based upon a paper presented by two of the authors at the 79th Annual Meeting of the American Economic Association in December, 1966, reprinted in the Papers and Proceedings of that meeting. See Jack Hirshleifer and Jerome W. Milliman, "Urban Water Supply—a Second Look," *American Economic Review,* LVII (May, 1967).

lute truth. Even where his received theories are adequate, he may still make bad use of them in the world of affairs. We will therefore use this occasion to review the record on two important practical situations —New York and southern California—for which we dared in 1960 to make predictions and recommendations.

II

Our analysis of New York centered on the decision in 1955, taken in consequence of a water crisis five years earlier, to build a large dam (large, that is, by the standard of ten years ago) at Cannonsville on the Delaware. In making this decision the New York authorities ignored proposals that would have limited use or the growth in use through extension of metering, raising prices, or reducing system leakage. Also, going to the Delaware at Cannonsville was chosen over a nearer connection to the Hudson. Our analysis of 1960 supported the contentions that metering and leakage-control were highly economical substitutes for new supplies. In addition, we confirmed that, between the alternative new supplies, the Hudson would have been cheaper—though a question about the relative qualities of the two sources remained. As another point of interest, we questioned the solidity of New York's claim to Delaware water—the operative Supreme Court decree having granted New York not a legal right, but only a permission subject to reconsideration at any time. Finally, we believed that use projections had been exaggerated even in the absence of the pricing and rationing reforms we thought desirable. We were pleased, therefore, to be able to report in 1960 that New York had decided, after all, to delay completion of Cannonsville to the period 1966–67. Thereby hangs a tale.

TABLE 54

New York Supply-Demand Water Balance, 1955–65

Year	Use* (mgd)	"Safe Yield"† (mgd)	End-of-Year Storage‡ (BG)	Actual Yield§ (mgd)
1955	1155			
1960	1258	1550		
1961	1285	1550	250.4	
1962	1276	1550	195.6	1126
1963	1295	1550	162.2	1204
1964	1262	1550	124.0	1157
1965	950–1000	1550	181.7	1133

* Source: Board of Water Supply, 59th *Annual Report* (1965), p. 100. (1965 figure estimated.)

† As officially computed. See Northwest Desalting Team, "Potentialities and Possibilities of Desalting for Northern New Jersey and New York City" (June, 1966), pp. 3–7.

‡ *New York Times*, various dates.

§ This is use plus end-of-year increment (or minus decrement) in storage.

Table 54 demonstrates the seemingly overwhelming case for such a "stretch-out" of Cannonsville's completion. By 1960 actual use, lagging well behind the forecasts on which the Cannonsville construction had been premised, had stabilized below 1300 million gallons per day (mgd). Even without Cannonsville, the aggregate "safe yield" of 1550 mgd provided a very healthy margin over actual and prospective use, reinforced further by a storage capacity of 500 BG—over a year's supply—available for trapping excess runoff of wetter years. In these circumstances, the addition of a supposed 310 mgd of "safe yield" from Cannonsville seemed highly postponable.

What went wrong is evident in Table 55. The last year of "normal" rainfall in the New York area was 1960. In the phenomenal drought that followed, actual yields fell not only below "safe yields" but below actual use—requiring draw-down of accumulated storage. Emergency restrictions on water use were imposed in April 1965 and succeeded in reducing the rate of utilization some 25 per cent to around 950 mgd. This reduction also reflected campaigns for voluntary conservation and efforts to stem leaks throughout the system. Nevertheless, by mid-1965 crisis was at hand; the near prospect was for empty reservoirs and dry faucets. In June, New York unilaterally stopped releasing water downstream as required under the Supreme Court decree entitling it to use of Delaware water. This action in turn threatened saline contamination of the supplies of Philadelphia and other cities tapping the Delaware downstream. A series of compromises was worked out by the Delaware River Basin Commission, in effect requiring just enough releases from New York to keep the saltwater front safely below the Philadelphia intake. Private power companies contributed substantially by releasing storages on tributaries of the Delaware. Nevertheless, the situation was rescued only by good rains in the last quarter of 1965.[2]

What would have been the effect in the 1965 crisis of earlier construction of Cannonsville, or alternatively of a Hudson supply? It has been maintained that Cannonsville would have saved the day. Cannonsville could at most have stored around 50 BG more than it already held in 1965—about 50 days' supply at the reduced rate. But, since much higher releases downstream to the Delaware would have been legally required of New York upon completion of Cannonsville, it seems highly doubtful that the additional accumulation could or would have occurred. In fact, the required releases are so great that Cannonsville can hardly be said to provide *any* increment of yield to the city in time of drought. On the other hand, water in the Hudson in adequate volume was flowing uncontrolled past New York during the entire period. (New York's actual use of the

TABLE 55

RAINFALL STATISTICS, NEW YORK, 1959–1965*

Year	Rainfall in Inches	Per Cent above or below Average (42″)	Per Cent Accumulated Deficiency
1959	38.77	− 7.6	
1960	46.39	+10.4	
1961	39.32	− 6.4	6.4
1962	37.15	−11.6	18.0
1963	34.28	−18.4	36.4
1964	32.99	−21.5	57.9
1965	26.09	−37.9	95.8

* Source: Raymond J. Faust, "Northeast Water Crisis and Its Solution," *Journal American Water Works Association*, January, 1966. (1965 figures from *New York Times*.)

[2] See Delaware River Basin Commission, *Annual Report*, 1965. "How to Run a River," *Federal Reserve Bank of Philadelphia Business Review*, September 1965. Water Resources Association of the Delaware River Basin, *Delaware Basin Bulletin*, Vol. 6 (September, 1965). James F. Wright, "Water Resources of the Delaware River Estuary," *Journal American Water Works Association*, LVIII (July, 1966).

Hudson has an unfortunate history. An emergency connection to yield 100 mgd was rushed to completion in 1950, but arrived too late to assist in the crisis of that year. Subsequently, it was completely dismantled, only to be reconstructed as an emergency project again for the 1965 crisis. Again too late, it was shut down after pumping only seven days.)

What can we learn from the experience briefly reviewed here? First of all, perhaps, would be a healthy skepticism toward meteorology and hydrology—here we have a case where predictions about the social phenomena of use, while off the mark, still proved far more reliable than predictions as to the natural phenomena of supply. Analytically, we must take better account of uncertainty and variability of supply. In particular, "safe yield" must not be treated as a certainty-equivalent. In inferring from the evidence of the low rates of return on water investment that systems were typically over-built, we failed to allow fully for the insurance aspect of extra supplies. On the other hand, variability makes all the stronger our argument about the necessity for making better use of *existing* supplies as an alternative to new construction yielding uncertain water increments. A related consideration is that the variability of alternative new sources should be considered in weighing investment options; in the case of New York, the Hudson would have been a less variable, hence more reliable, source than the Delaware.

The legal history of New York's use of Delaware water is also significant. New York, in return for temporary permission to withdraw some 490 mgd from the Delaware, committed itself to downstream releases adequate to maintain a flow of 1525 cfs at Montague, New Jersey. In the dire emergency New York was able to pressure the other states, despite the danger to such cities as Trenton and Philadelphia, to consent to a relaxation. Evidently, in times of crisis the agency in actual possession or control of the upstream source is in a strong position regardless of legal technicalities.

We may end this section with some comments on the present prospects for New York.[3] The immediate situation looks somewhat better because of more normal rainfall. The "safe yields" have been written down some 20 per cent, but still inspire little confidence. Rationalization of existing uses has made a little progress. Efforts during the crisis to detect and repair leaks seem to have tightened the system considerably, though controversy persists on this point. Recirculation devices and conservation equipment have been required on industrial cooling and on air-conditioning units. Reluctance to use the price mechanism is as strong as ever, however; an increase in the water price seems out of the question. And while the principle of extension of metering is widely accepted, actual progress in that direction seems stalled. Cannonsville will be in full operation shortly—and the Hudson emergency tap provides a small reserve. But overall, New York remains very vulnerable in the absence of a return to long-term "normal" rainfall patterns.

The 1965 crisis also brought forward the usual desalinization enthusiasts. In this case, on direct instructions from President Johnson an interagency Northeast Desalting Team was appointed. Reportedly, economists on the team played a creditable role in insisting upon comparison with alternatives to desalinization—a process which showed that a Hudson source would cost only half as much.[4]

[3] For an excellent review, see Citizens Budget Commission, Inc., "Action on Water" (November, 1965).

[4] Northeast Desalting Team, "Potentialities and Possibilities of Desalting for Northern New Jersey and New York City" (June, 1966).

III

The water experience of southern California[5] since 1960 provides an interesting contrast with New York, accentuated by the parallel histories of continuing drought in both areas.[6] In New York a seeming surplus in terms of "safe yields" was revealed by hard experience to be illusory, and the supply remains tight. While new construction has taken place, for hydrological and legal reasons the city has reaped little or no benefit. In California, on the other hand, a political "water coalition" has created what appears to be an already excessive and costly supply; the coalition continues to seek out vast new increments, although supplies now arranged for cover growth needs for 30 to 50 years. In neither area have the responsible authorities shown much interest in rationalizing existing uses by appropriate pricing and reallocation.

In 1960 the voters of California, by a narrow margin, endorsed an enormous bond issue ($1,750,000,000) covering a first installment on the Feather River Project—the central component of the state's "Water Plan." We argued (in Chapter XI) that the project was premature, that an increase in water rates should have come first, and that cheaper alternatives were available from reallocation of agricultural supplies and from reclamation of waste waters. Throughout southern California water has been priced below the marginal cost of existing supply, not to mention the higher-cost Feather River supply. Discriminatory pricing in favor of agriculture, and failure to reallocate water from agriculture to the growing urban sector, have led to wide discrepancies in marginal values in use—within the area and also between the South Coastal Area and nearby agricultural regions (especially Imperial Valley).

Developments since 1960 are summarized in the source-use balance of Table 56. Lack of space prevents detailed review, but in the half-decade water use rose 13 per cent, somewhat less than the remarkable population increase of 22 per cent. (Adjusting for spreading to replace underground withdrawals, water *consumption* rose just 9 per cent.) The divergence is explained by the decline in agricultural use, which nevertheless remains some 25 per cent of the total. Discriminatory pricing has encouraged bringing outlying acreage under irrigation as subdivisions have displaced existing agriculture. Even at current relatively lavish consumption rates (160 gallons per capita per day), this agricultural water would support a further urban development of some 3,500,000 people—probably a decade of growth. And more rational pricing to residential and industrial users would easily extend the urban supplies another half-decade.[7]

Setting aside the rationalization of existing uses, Table 57 summarizes the existing and prospective sources. The margin of present development over the current rate of use is relatively small, but the huge Feather River supply coming in 1971 or 1972 will assure that water will be physically available into the foreseeable future. But economic availability is another question.

The Metropolitan Water District, water wholesaler to the area, was pressured into a commitment to absorb the enormous quantities to be delivered by the state; the price is likely to be very steep, around $65 per acre-foot of raw water. MWD must also cover the large expense of treatment and distribution. To meet these heavy commitments the MWD established a policy in 1964 of setting rates high enough to bring

[5] More technically, the South Coastal Area. This includes the coastal plains of the populous southern counties, with some 10,600,000 inhabitants (1965)—over half the population of California.

[6] In only 4 of the past 20 years has rainfall in southern California been "average" or better.

[7] Urban demand elasticities are around .4; a 50 per cent price increase, certainly called for, would cut use around 20 per cent.

in revenues sufficient to cover all operations costs plus one-half of all capital costs. From 1960 through 1965 wholesale prices for municipal water were doubled while rates for agricultural and replenishment use were increased about 30 per cent. Planned increases through 1975 would raise prices for municipal use to $58 an acre-foot, up from $15 in 1960, and for agricultural use to $26 an acre-foot, up from $12 to 1960.[8]

[8] A surcharge of $9 per acre-foot should be added for filtered and softened water. For details on pricing plans, see Metropolitan Water District of Southern California, *27th Annual Report* (1965) and Metropolitan Water District of Southern California, *Report No. 821: 1965 Water Pricing Investigation* (April, 1965).

However, we believe that there is little hope of selling much water at these prices. The MWD, thus, may have to load much of the financial burden on the tax base just as it has done in the first 30 years of its existence. Paradoxically, the planned water rates for the 1970's will very likely be too high; once the facilities for the Feather River supply are in place the marginal costs of supply will be relatively low. If we are correct that the Feather River supply will remain largely unsalable for the next several decades (if planned pricing policies are followed), this will repeat the deplorable history of the long-unused Colorado River aqueduct—another monument to the view that there are absolute "requirements"

TABLE 56*

SOURCE-USE BALANCE FOR SOUTH COASTAL AREA

	Withdrawals for Use (Acre-Feet)		
	1950	1960	1965
Water source:			
Local surface and ground water			
1. Developed safe yield	1,066,000	1,098,000	1,098,000
2. Gross overdraft†	(300,000)	(300,000)	(300,000)
3. Net overdraft†	275,000	88,000	(20,000)
Los Angeles Aqueduct	320,000	320,000	320,000
Colorado River Aqueduct (capacity 1,200,000 acre-feet)			
1. Agricultural & urban use	142,000	523,000	796,000
2. Water spreading	25,000	212,000	320,000
Total	1,828,000	2,241,000	2,534,000
Water use:			
Irrigation	954,000	700,000	630,000
Urban	874,000	1,541,000	1,904,000
Total	1,828,000	2,241,000	2,534,000
Water-use assumptions:			
1. Agricultural use			
Irrigated acres	650,000	500,000	450,000
Water applied in feet	1.5	1.4	1.4
2. Urban use			
Population	5,480,000	8,656,000	10,600,000
Use rate in gallons per capita per day	140	160	160

* This table is an extension of Table 34 on p. 295.

† Gross overdraft refers to total pumping in excess of long-run recharge. Net overdraft is gross overdraft minus the spreading of imported waters. In 1965 the spreading exceeded gross overdraft, thereby overstating actual water consumption by 20,000 acre-feet.

for water rather than *demands* at a price.[9]

We may comment briefly on the remaining items of Table 57. The second barrel for the Los Angeles Aqueduct is an economical project, in the range of $24–30 per acre-foot at 1965 costs.[10] This is a City of Los Angeles undertaking; being cheaper than even the out-of-pocket costs of buying MWD water, its construction was rational for the City despite the incoming Feather supply. What is scarcely comprehensible, however, is why Los Angeles consistently pushes the MWD into commitments for tremendous costly supplies, after which the City builds and uses its own cheaper sources instead. Since one-third (formerly, one-half) the MWD tax burden

[9] J. W. Milliman, "The History, Organization, and Economic Problems of the Metropolitan Water District of Southern California," UCLA Ph.D. thesis (1956).

[10] Max K. Socha, "Construction of the Second Los Angeles Aqueduct," *Journal American Water Works Association,* June, 1965.

TABLE 57

SOURCES OF WATER SUPPLY FOR THE SOUTH COASTAL AREA

	Acre-feet
Present development:	
1. Local surface and ground waters	1,098,000
2. Los Angeles Aqueduct	320,000
3. MWD'S Colorado River Aqueduct	1,200,000
	2,618,000
Scheduled development:	
1. Second Barrel to Los Angeles Aqueduct (1968)	150,000
2. Feather River Water (1972)	2,000,000
3. Nuclear Desalting Plant (1972–1980)	150,000
	2,300,000
Scheduled loss:	
MWD rights to Colorado River Water expected to be reduced by 650,000 acre-feet per year on a gradual basis from 1975 to 1990. Rights in 1990 to total 550,000	−650,000
Subtotal (Developed or scheduled for 1990)	4,268,000
Potential sources of supply at low cost:	
1. Reclamation of sewage and waste waters	450,000
2. Purchase of Colorado River rights from Imperial Irrigation District to fill unused capacity in Colorado River Aqueduct	650,000
	1,100,000
Grand total (Developed, scheduled, and low-cost supplies)	5,368,000

Higher-cost water sources:

1. Purchase of additional Colorado River water for transfer to the area.
2. Additional reclamation of sewage and waste waters.
3. Purchase and transfer of water from the San Joaquin Valley to the area.
4. Additional transfer of water from northern California.
5. Additional desalting plants.
6. Conveyance from Columbia River, Canada, Alaska, and the moon.

falls on Los Angeles, the cost to its taxpayers has been enormous.[11]

The prospective loss of MWD entitlement to 650,000 acre-feet of Colorado water, as a result of the Supreme Court decision favoring Arizona's claims, constituted one of the stronger arguments for the Feather River Project. Even before this decision, however, we pointed out that purchase of a portion of the 3,850,000 acre-feet of prior agricultural entitlements within California to Colorado water (from Imperial Valley and certain other districts) for transport to the South Coastal Area would have been cheaper than the Feather supply. The Supreme Court decision will have the effect of leaving MWD's Colorado River aqueduct half-unused again (when Arizona fully exploits her established rights); hence 650,000 acre-feet of purchased agricultural entitlements could be transported via existing, otherwise-idle capacity. Finally, reclamation of waste waters would have been another cheap source, far cheaper than the Feather supply. Of course, in the absence of escape from the Feather River commitment, MWD's problem at this point is disposing of water rather than seeking out new supplies, however economical.

Astonishingly, however, the MWD has gone ahead and committed itself further to a new source—nuclear desalinization. This was justified in a Bechtel Corporation study[12] by the consideration that the water (at about $88 per acre-foot) was cheaper than conventional delivery from the Columbia. (Next, presumably, a Columbia project will be justified as cheaper than delivery from sources in Canada and Alaska; not entirely a joke, as such a project is indeed being promoted!) Since this desalinization is a tie-in deal with electric power (the water production, at about 150,000 acre-feet, being relatively modest), it may be hoped that the power economics are more attractive. The press-agentry values of the project, in terms of enthusiastic newspaper reports, were considerable—thus possibly reducing resistance to the tax increases MWD will have to impose for paying off its Feather commitment.

IV

It is difficult to avoid a critical tone in reviewing what appear to be instances of inefficient stewardship of water resources by political or bureaucratic authorities. Certainly they ought not go on committing the same errors, having been deluged by a river of advice from economists.[13] But is our critical tone justified? Decision makers are just people, and people will make mistakes. In the private sector, those who regularly commit mistakes lose control, in the long run, over the disposition of resources. In the government sector, this process operates weakly, if at all. It appears that the agenda for economists, at this point, should place lower priority upon the further refinement of advice for those efficient and selfless administrators who may exist in never-never land. Rather, it should center upon the devising of institutions where fallible and imperfect administrators may be forced to learn from error. In short, can we construct a "hidden hand" for the government sector?

[11] The City has paid some $250 in MWD taxes for every acre-foot used (in comparison, the actual water *price* charged by MWD has been negligible). San Diego has, on the other hand, paid only 8 per cent of the taxes while taking 25 per cent of the water—its tax burden has only been $20 per acre-foot.

[12] Bechtel Corporation, *Engineering and Economic Feasibility Study for a Combination Nuclear Power and Desalting Plant* (December, 1965).

[13] In addition to the present volume and the works such as those by McKean, Eckstein, Krutilla, and Renshaw already cited (see p. 114 above), we may mention a number of more recent contributions to this literature: Arthur Maass, *et al.*, *Design of Water Resource Systems* (Cambridge, Mass.; Harvard University Press, 1962); Robert H. Haveman, *Water Resource Investment in Ten Southern States* (Nashville: Vanderbilt University Press, 1965); and Joe S. Bain, Richard E. Caves, and Julius Margolis, *Northern California's Water Industry* (Resources for the Future, 1967).

INDEX